THE BOOK OF
THE SWORD

Richard F. Burton

Dover Publications, Inc.

NEW YORK

IMPORTANT NOTE

When originally published in 1884, this book was intended by the author to be only the first part of an exhaustive three-volume work on the sword. Unfortunately, Parts II and III, which are described in some detail in the Introduction and referred to at various points throughout the book, remained incomplete at the time of the author's death in 1890 and were therefore never published.

Published in Canada by General Publishing Company, Ltd., 30 Lesmill Road, Don Mills, Toronto, Ontario.
Published in the United Kingdom by Constable and Company, Ltd.

This Dover edition, first published in 1987, is an unabridged, slightly altered republication of the first edition of the work originally published by Chatto and Windus, London, in 1884. The first four pages of the original volume (all superfluous) have been omitted, and the front matter has been partially rearranged and entirely repaginated in the present edition. In addition, several minor corrections have been made in the text, and the note above has been prepared specially for this edition.

Manufactured in the United States of America
Dover Publications, Inc., 31 East 2nd Street, Mineola, N.Y. 11501

Library of Congress Cataloging-in-Publication Data

Burton, Richard Francis, Sir, 1821–1890.
The book of the sword.

Originally published: London : Chatto and Windus, 1884.
Bibliography: p.
Includes index.
1. Swords. I. Title.
U850.B8 1987   355.8'241   87-9194
ISBN 0-486-25434-8 (pbk.)

'He that hath no Sword (-knife = μάχαιρα), let him sell his garment and buy one.' *St. Luke* xxii. 36.

'*Solo la spada vuol magnificarsi.*'

(Nothing is high and awful save the Sword.)

Lod. della Vernaccia, A.D. 1200.

'But, above all, it is most conducive to the greatness of empire for a nation to profess the skill of arms as its principal glory and most honourable employ.'

BACON'S *Advancement of Learning*, viii. 3.

'The voice of every people is the Sword
That guards them, or the Sword that beats them down.'

TENNYSON'S *Harold.*

FOREWORD.

'I WANTED a book on the Sword, not a treatise on Carte and Tierce,' said the Publisher, when, some years ago, my earliest manuscript was sent to him.

It struck me then and there that the Publisher was right. Consequently the volume was re-written after a more general and less professional fashion.

I have only one wish that reader and reviewer can grant : namely, a fair field and no favour for certain 'advanced views' of Egyptology. It is my conviction that this study, still in its infancy, will greatly modify almost all our preconceived views of archæological history.

RICHARD F. BURTON.

TRIESTE: *November* 20, 1883.

CONTENTS.

LIST OF ILLUSTRATIONS.

INTRODUCTION.

THE HISTORY OF THE SWORD is the history of humanity. The 'White Arm' means something more than the 'oldest, the most universal, the most varied of weapons, the only one which has lived through all time.'

He, she, or it—for the gender of the Sword varies—has been worshipped with priestly sacrifices as a present god. Hebrew revelation represents the sharp and two-edged Sword going out of the mouth of the King of Kings, and Lord of Lords. We read of a 'Sword of God, a holy Sword,' the 'Sword of the Lord and of Gideon'; and 'I came not to send peace but a Sword,'meaning the warfare and martyrdom of man.

On a lower plane the Sword became the invention and the favourite arm of the gods and the demi-gods : a gift of magic, one of the treasures sent down from Heaven, which made Mulciber ('Malik Kabír,' the great king) divine, and Voelunder, Quida, Galant, or Wayland Smith a hero. It was consecrated to the deities, and was stored in the Temple and in the Church. It was the 'key of heaven and hell' : the saying is, 'If there were no Sword, there would be no law of Mohammed'; and the Moslem brave's highest title was 'Sayf Ullah'—Sword of Allah.

Uniformly and persistently personal, the Sword became no longer an abstraction but a Personage, endowed with human as well as superhuman qualities. He was a sentient being who spoke, and sang, and joyed, and grieved. Identified with his wearer he was an object of affection, and was pompously named as a well-beloved son and heir. To surrender the Sword was submission ; to break the Sword was degradation. To kiss the Sword was, and in places still is, the highest form of oath and homage.

> Lay on our royal Sword your banished hands

says King Richard II. So Walther of Aquitaine :—

> Contra Orientalem prostratus corpore partem
> Ac nudum retinens ensem hac cum voce precatur.

The Sword killed and cured ; the hero when hopeless fell upon his Sword ; and the heroine, like Lucretia and Calphurnia, used the blade standing. The Sword cut the Gordian knot of every difficulty. The Sword was the symbol of justice and of martyrdom, and accompanied the wearer to the tomb as well as to the feast and the fight. 'Lay on my coffin a Sword,' said dying Heinrich Heine, 'for I have warred doughtily to win freedom for mankind.'

From days immemorial the Queen of Weapons, a creator as well as a destroyer, 'carved out history, formed the nations, and shaped the world.' She decided the Alexandrine and the Cæsarian victories which opened new prospects to human ken. She diffused everywhere the bright lights and splendid benefits of war and conquest, whose functions are all important in the formative and progressive processes. It is no paradox to assert *La guerre a enfanté le droit* : without War there would be no Right. The cost of life, says Emerson, the dreary havoc of comfort and time, are overpaid by the vistas it opens of Eternal Law reconstructing and uplifting society ; it breaks up the old horizon, and we see through the rifts a wider view.

War, again, benefits society by raising its tone above the ineffable littleness and meanness which characterise the every-day life of the many. In the presence of the Great Destroyer, petty feuds and miserable envy, hatred, and malice stand hushed and awe-struck. Very hollow in these days sounds Voltaire's banter on War when he says that a king picks up a parcel of men who have nothing to do, dresses them in blue cloth at two shillings a yard, binds their hats with coarse white worsted, turns them to the right and left, and marches them away to glory.

The Sword and only the Sword raised the worthier race to power upon the ruins of impotent savagery ; and she carried in her train, from time immemorial, throughout the civilised world, Asiatic Africa, Asia, and Europe, the arts and the sciences which humanise mankind. In fact, whatever apparent evil the Sword may have done, she worked for the highest ultimate good. With the Arabs the Sword was a type of individuality. Thus Shanfara, the fleet-foot, sings in his *Lamiyyah*, (L-poem) :—

> Three friends : the Heart no fear shall know,
> The sharp white Sword, the yellow Bow.

Zayd bin Ali boasts, like El-Mutanabbi :—

> The wielded Sword-blade knows my hand,
> The Spear obeys my lusty arm.

And Ziyád El-Ajam thus writes the epitaph of El-Mughayrah : 'So died he, after having sought death between the spear-point and the Sword-edge.'

This ' Pundonor ' presently extended westward. During the knightly ages the ' good Sword ' of the Paladin and the Chevalier embodied a new faith—the Religion of Honour, the first step towards the religion of humanity. These men once more taught the sublime truth, the splendid doctrine known to the Stoics and the Pharisees, but unaccountably neglected in later creeds :—

Do good, for Good is good to do.

Their recklessness of all consequences soared worlds-high above the various egotistic systems which bribe man to do good for a personal and private consideration, to win the world, or to save his soul. Hence Aristotle blamed his contemporaries, the Spartans : 'They are indeed good men, but they have not the supreme consummate excellence of loving all things worthy, decent and laudable, purely as such and for their own sakes ; nor of practising virtue for no other motive but the sole love of her own innate beauty.' The 'everlasting Law of Honour binding on all and peculiar to each,' would have thoroughly satisfied the Stagirite's highest aspirations.

In knightly hands the Sword acknowledged no Fate but that of freedom and free-will ; and it bred the very spirit of chivalry, a keen personal sentiment of self-respect, of dignity, and of loyalty, with the noble desire to protect weakness against the abuse of strength. The knightly Sword was ever the representative idea, the present and eternal symbol of all that man most prized—courage and freedom. The names describe her quality : she is Joyeuse, and La Tisona ; he is Zú 'l-Fikár (sire of splitting) and Quersteinbeis, biter of the mill-stone. The weapon was everywhere held to be the best friend of bravery, and the worst foe of perfidy ; the companion of authority, and the token of commandment ; the outward and visible sign of force and fidelity, of conquest and dominion, of all that Humanity wants to have and wants to be.

The Sword was carried by and before kings ; and the brand, not the sceptre, noted their seals of state. As the firm friend of the crown and of the ermine robe, it became the second fountain of honour. Amongst the ancient Germans even the judges sat armed on the judgment-seat ; and at marriages it represented the bridegroom in his absence. Noble and ennobling, its touch upon the shoulder conferred the prize of knighthood. As 'bakhshísh' it was, and still is, the highest testimony to the soldier's character ; a proof that he is 'brave as his sword-blade.' Its presence was a moral lesson ; unlike the Greeks, the Romans, and the Hebrews, Western and Southern Europe, during its chivalrous ages, appeared nowhere and on no occasion without the Sword. It was ever ready to leap from its sheath in the cause of weakness and at the call of Honour. Hence, with its arrogant individuality, the Sword still remained the 'all-sufficient type and token of the higher sentiments and the higher tendencies of human nature.'

In society the position of the Sword was remarkable. 'Its aspect was brilliant ; its manners were courtly ; its habits were punctilious, and its connections were patrician.' Its very vices were glittering ; for most of them were the abuses which could not but accompany its uses. It bore itself haughtily as a victor, an arbitrator ; and necessarily there were times when its superlative qualities showed corresponding defects. Handled by the vile it too often became, in the 'syllogism of violence,' an incubus, a blusterer, a bully, a tyrant, a murderer, an assassin, in fact 'death's stamp' ; and under such conditions it was a 'corruption of the best.' But its lapses were individual and transient ; its benefits to Humanity were general and ever-enduring.

The highest period of the Sword was the early sixteenth century, that mighty landmark separating the dark Past from the brilliant Present of Europe. The sudden awaking and excitement of man's mind, produced by the revival of learning and the marriage-union of the West with the East ; by the discovering of a new hemisphere, the doubling of the world ; by the so-called Reformation, a northern protest against the slavery of the soul ; by the wide spread of the printing-press, which meant knowledge ; and, simultaneously, by the illumination of that electric spark generated from the contact of human thought, suddenly changed the status of the Sword. It was no longer an assailant, a slaughterer : it became a defender, a preserver. It learned to be shield as well as Sword. And now arose swordsmanship proper, when the 'Art of Arms' meant, amongst the old masters, the Art of Fence. The sixteenth century was its Golden Age.

At this time the Sword was not only the Queen of Weapons, but the weapon paramount between man and man. Then, advancing by slow, stealthy, and stumbling steps, the age of gunpowder, of 'villanous saltpetre,' appeared upon the scene of life. Gradually the bayonet, a modern modification of the pike, which again derives from the savage spear, one of the earliest forms of the *arme blanche*, ousted the Sword amongst infantry because the former could be combined with the fire-piece. A century afterwards cavalrymen learned, in the Federal-Confederate war, to prefer the revolver and repeater, the breech-loader and the reservoir-gun, to the sabre of past generations. It became an axiom that in a cavalry charge the spur, not the Sword, gains the day. By no means a unique, nor even a singular process of progress, is this return towards the past, this falling back upon the instincts of primitive invention, this recurrence to childhood : when the science of war reverted to ballistics it practically revived the practice of the first ages, and the characteristic attack of the savage and the barbarian who, as a rule, throw their weapons. The cannon is the ballista, and the arblast, the mangonel, and the trebuchet, worked not by muscular but by chemical forces. The torpedo is still the old, old petard ; the spur of the ironclad is the long-disused embolon, rostrum, or beak ; and steam-power is a rough, cheap substitute for man-power, for the banks of oarsmen, whose work had a delicacy of manipulation unknown to machinery, however ingenious. The armed nations, which in Europe are again becoming the substitutes for standing armies, represent the savage and barbarous stages of society, the proto-historic races, amongst which every man between the ages of fifteen and fifty is a man-at-arms. It is the same in moral matters ; the general spread of the revolutionary spirit, of republicanism, of democratic ideas, of communistic, socialistic, and nihilistic rights and claims now acting so powerfully upon society and upon the brotherhood of nations, is a re-dawning of that early day when the peoples ruled themselves, and were not yet governed by priestly and soldier kings. It is the same even in the 'immaterials.' The Swedenborgian school, popularly known by the trivial name *Spiritualism*, has revived magic, and this 'new motor force,' for such I call it, has resurrected the Ghost, which many a wise head supposed to have been laid for ever.

The death-song of the Sword has been sung, and we are told that ' Steel has ceased to be a gentleman.'[1] Not so! and by no means so. These are mere insular and insulated views, and England, though a grand figure, the mother of nations, the modern Rome, is yet but a fraction of the world. The Englishman and, for that matter, the German and the Scandinavian, adopted with a protest, and right unwillingly, swordsmanship proper—that is, rapier and point, the peculiar and especial weapon, offensive and defensive, of Southern Europe, Spain, Italy, and France. During the most flourishing age of the Sword it is rare to find a blade bearing the name of an English maker, and English inscriptions seldom date earlier than the eighteenth century. The reason is evident. The Northerners hacked with hangers, they hewed with hatchets, and they cut with cutlasses because the arm suited their bulk and stature, weight and strength. But such weapons are the brutality of the Sword. In England swordsmanship is, and ever was, an exotic ; like the sentiment, as opposed to the knowledge, of Art, it is the property of the few, not of the many ; and, being rare, it is somewhat 'un-English.'

But the case is different on the continent of Europe. Probably at no period during the last four centuries has the Sword been so ardently studied as it is now by the Latin race in France and Italy. At no time have the schools been so distinguished for intellectual as well as for moral proficiency. The use of the foil 'bated' and 'unbated' has once more become quasi-universal. A duello, in the most approved fashion of our ancestors, was lately proposed (September 1882) by ten journalists of a Parisian paper, to as many on the staff of a rival publication. Even the softer sex in France and Italy has become cunning of fence ; and women are among the most prosperous pupils of the *salles d'armes*. Witness, for instance, the ill-fated Mdlle. Feyghine of the Théâtre Français, so celebrated for her skill in ' the carte and the tierce and the reason demonstrative.'

Nor is the cause of this wider diffusion far to seek. In the presence of arms of

[1] I refer to a vivacious but one-sided article on ' The Sword,' in *Blackwood's Edinburgh Magazine*, May 1881.

precision, the Sword, as a means of offence and defence, may practically fall for a time into disuse. It may no longer be the arm paramount or represent an idea. It may have come down from its high estate as tutor to the noble and the great. Yet not the less it has, and will ever have, its work to do. The Ex-Queen now appears as instructress-general in the art of arms. As the mathematic is the basis of all exact science, so Sword-play teaches the soldier to handle every other weapon. This is well known to Continental armies, in which each regiment has its own fencing establishment and its *salle d'armes.*

Again, men of thought cannot ignore the intrinsic value of the Sword for stimulating physical qualities. *Ce n'est pas assez de roidir l'âme, il faut aussi roidir les muscles,* says Montaigne, who also remarks of fencing that it is the only exercise wherein *l'esprit s'en exerce.* The best of callisthenics, this energetic educator teaches the man to carry himself like a soldier. A compendium of gymnastics, it increases strength and activity, dexterity and rapidity of movement. Professors calculate that one hour of hard fencing wastes forty ounces by perspiration and respiration. The foil is still the best training tool for the consensus of eye and hand ; for the judgment of distance and opportunity ; and, in fact, for the practice of combat. And thus swordsmanship engenders moral confidence and self-reliance while it stimulates a habit of resource ; and it is not without suggesting, even in the schools, that 'curious, fantastic, very noble generosity proper to itself alone.'

And now when the vain glory of violence has passed away from the Sword with the customs of a past age, we can hardly ignore the fact that the manners of nations have changed, not for the best. As soon as the Sword ceased to be worn in France, a Frenchman said of his compatriots that the 'politest people in Europe had suddenly become the rudest.' That gallant and courteous bearing, which in England during the early nineteenth century so charmed the 'fiery and fastidious Alfieri,' lingers only amongst a few. True the swash-buckler, the professional duellist, has disappeared. But courtesy and punctiliousness, the politeness of man to man, and respect and deference of man to woman—that *Frauencultus,* the very conception of the knightly character—have to a great extent been 'improved off.' The latter condition of society, indeed, seems to survive only in the most cultivated classes of Europe ; and, popularly, amongst the citizens of the United States, a curious oasis of chivalry in a waste of bald utilitarianism—preserved not by the Sword but by the revolver. Our England has abolished the duello without substituting aught better for it : she has stopped the effect and left the cause.

So far I have written concerning the Sword simply to show that my work does not come out ' a day after the fair' ; and that there is still a powerful vitality in the heroic Weapon. The details of such general statements will be established and developed in the following pages. It is now advisable to introduce this volume to the reader.

During the 'seventies' I began, with a light heart, my Book of the Sword, expecting to finish it within a few months. It has occupied me as many years. Not only study and thought, but travel and inspection, were found indispensable; a monograph on the Sword and its literature involved visiting almost all the great armouries of continental Europe, and a journey to India in 1875-6. The short period of months served only to show that a memoir of the Sword embraces the annals of the world. The long term of years has convinced me that to treat the subject in its totality is impossible within reasonable limits.

It will hardly be said that a monograph of the Sword is not wanted. Students who would learn her origin, genealogy, and history, find no single publication ready to hand. They must ransack catalogues and books on 'arms and armour' that are numbered by the score. They must hunt up fugitive pamphlets; papers consigned to the literary store-rooms called magazines; and stray notices deep buried in the ponderous tomes of *Recueils* and general works on Hoplology. They must wade through volume after volume of histories and travels, to pick up a few stray sentences. And they will too often find that the index of an English book which gives copious references to glass or sugar utterly ignores the Sword. At times they must labour in the dark, for men who write seem wholly unconscious of the subject's importance. For instance, much has been said about art in Japan; but our knowledge of her metallurgy especially of her iron and steel works, is elementary, while that of her peculiar and admirable cutlery is strangely superficial. And travellers and collectors treat the Sword much as they do objects of natural history. They regard only the rare, the forms which they ignore, or which strike the eye, and the unique specimens which may have no comparative value. Thus they neglect articles of far more interest and of higher importance to the student, and they bring home, often at great expense, mere lumber for curiosity shops.

The difficulty of treating the Sword is enhanced by the peculiar individuality which characterises it, evidenced by an immense variety of physique, and resulting as much from unconscious selection as from deep design. One of the characteristics of indigenous art is that no two articles, especially no two weapons, are exactly alike; and yet they vary only within narrow and measurable limits. The minute differentiæ of the Sword are endless. Even in the present day, swordsmen will order some shape, size, or weight which they hold—often unwisely enough—to be improvements on the general. One man, wishing to strengthen his arm, devises a weapon fit for a Titan and finds it worse than useless. A tale is told of a Sheffield cutler who, having received from Maroccan Mogador a wooden model to be copied in steel, made several hundred blades on the same pattern and failed to find a single purchaser.   Their general resemblance to the prevailing type was marred by peculiarities which unsuited them for general use ; they were adapted only to individual requirement, each man priding himself upon his own pattern having some almost imperceptible difference.   Such variations are intelligible enough in the Sword, which must be modified for every personality, because it becomes to the swordsman a prolongation of his own person, a lengthening of the arm.   The natural results are the protean shapes of the weapon and the difficulty of reducing these shapes to orderly description.   I cannot, therefore, agree with a President of the Anthropological Institute ('Journal,' October 1876) when he states : 'Certainly the same forms of Sword might be found in different countries, but not of so peculiar a nature (as the Gaboon weapon) unless the form had been communicated.'   Shapes apparently identical start up spontaneously, because types are limited and man's preferences easily traverse the whole range of his invention.

Thus the stumbling-block which met me on the threshold was to introduce sequence, system, and lucid order into a chaos of details.   It was necessary to discover some unity, some starting-place for evolution and development, without which all treatment would be vague and inconsequent.   But where find the clue which makes straight the labyrinthine paths ; the *point de mire* which enables us to command the whole prospect ; the coign of vantage which displays the disposition of details, together with the *nexus*, the intercommunication, and the progress of the parts and the whole ?

Two different systems of that 'classification, which defines the margin of our ignorance,' are adopted by museums ; and, consequently, by the catalogues describing them.   I shall here quote only English collections, leaving to the Continental reader the task of applying the two main principles locally and generally.   These are, first, the Topical or Geographical (*e.g.* Christy collection), which, as the words denote, examines the article itself mainly with reference to its media, nature and culture, place and date ; and which considers man and his works as the expression of the soil that bears him.   The second is the Material and purely Formal (General A. Pitt-Rivers' collection), which regards only the objects or specimens themselves, without respect to their makers or their media ; and which, by investigating the rival laws of continuity and of incessant variation, aims at extending our knowledge of mankind.   Both plans have their merits and their demerits.   The Topical is the more strictly anthropologico-ethnological, because it makes the general racial culture its prominent feature ; but it fails to illustrate, by juxtaposition, the origin, the life, and the death of a special article.   The Formal proposes to itself the study of specific ideas ; it describes their transmissions and their migrations ; and it displays their connection and sequence, their development and degradation.   It exemplifies the law of unconscious selection, as opposed to premeditation and design. Thus it claims superior sociological interest, while it somewhat separates and isolates the article from its surroundings—mankind.

Again, it would be unadvisable to neglect the chronological and synchronological order (Demmin's). This assists us in tracing with a surer hand the origin and derivation ; the annals, the adventures, and the accidents of an almost universal weapon, whose marvellously chequered career excels in dignity, in poetry, and in romance, anything and everything the world has yet seen. And here I have not been unmindful of Dr. Arthur Mitchell's sensible warning that 'the rude form of an implement may follow as well as precede the more finished forms.'[1] Due regard to dates enables us to avoid the scandalous confusion of the vulgar museum. Demmin found a large number of swords catalogued as dating with the time of Charles the Bold, when the shapes proved that they belonged to the late sixteenth and even to the early seventeenth centuries. I was shown, in the museum of Aquileja, a 'Roman sword' which was a basket-hilted Venetian, hardly two hundred years old. It is only an exact chronology, made to frame the Geographical and the Formal pictures of the weapon, that can secure scientific distribution.

In dealing with a subject which, like the Sword, ranges through the world-history, and which concerns the human race in general, it would, I venture to opine, be unwise to adopt a single system. As clearness can be obtained only by methodical distribution of matter, all the several processes must be combined with what art the artificer may. The Formal, which includes the Material, as well as the shape of the weapon, affords one fair basis for classification. The substance, for instance, ranges from wood to steel, and the profile from the straight line to the segment of a circle. The Topical, beginning (as far as we know) in the Nile Valley, and thence in ancient days overspreading Africa, Asia, Europe, and America, determines the distribution and shows the general continuity of the noble arm. It also readily associates itself with the chronologico-historical order, which begins *ab initio*, furnishes a proof of general progress, interrupted only by fitful stages of retrogression, and, finally, dwells upon the epochs of the highest interest.

After not a little study I resolved to distribute the 'Book of the Sword' into three parts.

Part I. treats of the birth, parentage, and early career of the Sword. It begins with the very beginning, in pre-historic times and amongst proto-historic peoples ; and it ends with the full growth of the Sword at the epoch of the early Roman Empire.

Part II. treats of the Sword fully grown. It opens with the rising civilisation

---

[1] *The Past in the Present*, &c. (Edinburgh : Douglas, 1880).

of the Northern Barbarians and with the decline of Rome under Constantine (A.D. 313–324), who combined Christianity with Mithraism ; when the world-capital was transferred to Byzantium, and when an imitation of Orientalism, specially of ' Persic apparatus,' led to the art decay which we denote by the term ' Lower Empire.' It proceeds to the rise of El-Islam ; the origin of ordered chivalry and knighthood ; the succession of the Crusades and the wars of arms and armour before the gunpowder age, when the general use of ballistics by means of explosives became the marking feature of battle. This was the palmy period of the Sword. It became a beautiful work of art ; and the highest genius did not disdain to chase and gem the handle and sheath. And its career culminates with the early sixteenth century, when the weapon of offence assumed its defensive phase and rose to a height of splendour that prognosticated downfall, as surely as the bursting of a rocket precedes its extinction.

Part III. continues the memoirs of the Sword, which, after long declining, re-vives once more in our day. This portion embraces descriptions of the modern blade, notices of collections, public and private, notes on manufactures ; and, lastly, the bibliography and the literature connected with the Heroic Weapon.

Part I., contained in this volume, numbers thirteen chapters, of which a bird's-eye view is given by the List of Contents. The first seven are formally and chronologically arranged. Thus we have the Origin of Weapons (Chapter I.) showing that while the arm is common to man and beast, the weapon, as a rule, belongs to our kind. Chapter II. treats of the first weapon proper, the Stone, which gave rise to ballistics as well as to implements of percussion. Follows (Chapter III.) the blade of base materials, wood, stone and bone, materials still used by races which can procure nothing better. From this point a step leads to the metal blade, in its origin evidently a copy of preceding types. The first, (Chapter IV.) is of pure copper, in our translations generally rendered by ' brass ' or ' bronze.' The intermediate substances (Chapter V.) are represented by alloys, a variety of mixed metals ; and they naturally end with the so-called ' age ' of early iron, which prevailed throughout Europe at a time when the valleys of the Nile and the Tigris-Euphrates wrought blades of the finest steel. This division concludes with a formal and technical Chapter (VII.) on the shape of the Sword and a description of its several parts. Here the subject does not readily lend itself to lively description ; but, if I have been compelled to be dull, I have done my best to avoid being tedious.

The arrangement then becomes geographical and chronological. My next five chapters are devoted to the Sword in its topical distribution and connection. The first (No. VIII.) begins with the various blade-forms in ancient Egypt, which extended throughout the then civilised world ; it ends with showing that the Nile valley gave their present shapes to the 'white arm' of the Dark Continent even in its modern day, and applied to the Sword the name which it still bears in Europe. The second (No. IX.) passes to Palestine, Syria, and Asia Minor, lands which manifestly borrowed the weapon from the Egyptians, and handed it on to Assyria, Persia, and India. The arms and armour of the 'great Interamnian Plain' afford material for a third (Chapter X.). Thence, retracing our steps and passing further westwards, we find manifest derivation and immense improvement of the Egyptian weapon in Greece (Chapter XI.), from which Mycenæ has lately supplied bronze rapiers perfectly formed as the steels of Bilboa and Toledo. The fifth Chapter (No. XII.) continues the ancient history of the Sword by describing the various blades of progressive Rome, whose wise choice and change of arms enabled her to gain the greatest battles with the least amount of loss. To this I have appended, for geographical and chronological symmetry, in a sixth and last chapter (No. XIII.), a sketch of the Sword among the contemporary Barbarians of the Roman Empire, Dacians, Italians, Iberians, Gauls, Germans, and the British Islands. This portion of the Sword history, however, especially the Scandinavian and the Irish, will be treated at full length in Part II.

Here, then, ends the First Part, which Messrs. Chatto and Windus have kindly consented to publish, whilst my large collection of notes, the labour of years, is being ordered and digested for the other two. I may fairly hope, if all go well, to see both in print before the end of 1884.

In the following pages I have confined myself, as much as was possible, to the Sword ; a theme which, indeed, offers an *embarras de richesses*. But weapons cannot be wholly isolated, especially when discussing origins : one naturally derives from and connects with the other ; and these relations may hardly be passed over without notice. I have, therefore, indulged in an occasional divagation, especially concerning the axe and the spear ; but the main line has never been deserted.

Nor need I offer an excuse for the amount of philological discussion which the nomenclature of the Sword has rendered necessary. If I have opposed the Past Masters of the art, my opposition has been honest, and I am ever open to refutation. Travellers refuse to believe that 'Aryanism' was born on the bald, bleak highlands of Central Asia, or that 'Semitism' derives from the dreary, fiery deserts of Arabia. We do not believe India to be 'the country which even more than Greece or Rome was the cradle of grammar and philology.' I cannot but hold that England has, of late years, been greatly misled by the 'Aryan heresy' ; and I look forward to the study being set upon a sounder base.

The illustrations, numbering 293, have been entrusted to the artistic hands of Mr. Joseph Grego, who has taken a friendly interest in the work. But too much must not be expected from them in a book which intends to be popular, and which is, therefore, limited in the matter of expense.   Hence they are fewer than I should have desired.   The libraries of Europe contain many catalogues of weapons printed in folio with highly finished and coloured plates which here would be out of place.   That such a work upon the subject of the Sword will presently appear I have no doubt ; and my only hope is that this volume will prove an efficient introduction.

To conclude.   I return grateful thanks to the many *mitwerkers* who have assisted me in preparing this monograph ; no more need be said, as all names will be mentioned in the course of the work.   A journey to the Gold Coast and its results, in two volumes, which describe its wealth, must plead my excuse for the delay in bringing out the book.   The manuscript was sent home from Lisbon in December 1881, but the ' tyranny of circumstance' has withheld it for nearly two years.

RICHARD F. BURTON.

Postscript.   An afterthought suggests that it is only fair, both for readers and for myself, to own that sundry quotations have been borrowed at second-hand and that the work of verification, so rightly enjoined upon writers, has not always been possible.   These blemishes are hardly to be avoided in a first edition.   At Trieste, and other places distant from the great seats of civilisation, libraries of reference are unknown ; and it is vain to seek for the original source.   Indeed, Mr. James Fergusson once wrote to me that it was an overbold thing to undertake a History of the Sword under such circumstances.   However, I made the best use of sundry visits to London and Paris, Berlin, Vienna, and other capitals, and did what I could to remedy defects.   Lastly, the illustrations have not always, as they ought, been drawn to scale, they were borrowed from a number of volumes which paid scant attention to this requisite.

LIST OF AUTHORITIES.

Academy (The), a Weekly Review of Literature, Science, and Art.

Agricola, *De Re Metallicâ*, First published in 1551.

Akermann (J. Y.), *Remains of Pagan Saxondom*. London : Smith, MDCCCLV.

Amicis (Edoardo de), *Marocco*. Milan : Treves, 1876.

Ammianus Marcellinus, Historian of the Lower Empire. Fourth century.

Anderson (J. R.), *Saint Mark's Rest : the Place of Dragons*, edited by John Ruskin, LL.D. Allen : Sunnyside, Orpington, Kent, 1879.

Anderson (Joseph), *Scotland in Early Christian Times*. Rhind Lectures n Archæology for 1879. Edinburgh : Douglas, 1882.

Anthropologia (London Anthropological Society. Established Jan. 22, 1873 ; first number, Oct. 1873 ; died after fifth number, July 1875.)

Anthropological Institute (The Journal of). London : Trübner.

Anthropological Review, Vol. I.-III. London : Trübner, 1863-65.

Antiquaries of London (Society of), from the beginning in 1770 to 1883.

Antiquities of Orissa, by Rajendralala Mitra, 2 vols. fol. ; published by Government of India.

Apuleius (A.D. 130).

Archæologia, or Tracts relating to Antiquity, published by the Society of Antiquaries of London, from the commencement in 1749 to 1863.

Archæological Association, vol. iv., *Weapons, &c., of Horn.*

Archæology (Transactions of the Society of Biblical), London : Longmans ; beginning in 1872.

Aristophanes.

Aristotle, *Meteorologica, &c.*

Arrian (Flavius), A.D. 90, *Anabasis, &c.*

Athenæum (The), Journal of English and Foreign Literature, &c.

Athenæus (A.D. 230), *Deipnosophists*.

Baker (Sir Samuel White), *The Nile Tributaries*. London : Macmillan, 1866. *The Albert Nyanza.* London, 1868.

Balthazar Ribello de Aragão ; Viagens dos Portuguezes, Collecção de Documentos, por Luciano Cordeiro, Lisboa, Imprensa Nacional, 1881. The learned Editor is Secretary to the Royal Geographical Society of Lisbon.

Barbosa (Duarte), *A Description of the Coasts of East Africa and Malabar*, translated for the Hakluyt Society, London, by Honourable Henry E. (now Lord) Stanley, 1866. Written about A.D. 1512-14, and attributed by some to Magellan.

Barth (Henry), *Travels, &c., in Central Africa* 1849-1855 ; 5 vols., 8vo. London : Longmans, 1875.

Barthélemy (Abbé J. J.), *Voyage du Jeune Anacharsis en Grèce, &c.*, 5 vols. 4to. Paris, 1788.

Bataillard (Paul) *On Gypsies and other Matters* Société Anthropologique de Paris, 1874.

Beckmann (John), *A History of Inventions, Discoveries, and Origins*, translated by W. Johnston. London : Bell and Daldy, 1872 (fourth edition, revised). It is a useful book of reference and wants only a few additions.

Berosus (B.C. 261), *Fragments*, edit. Müller.

Bollaert (William), *Antiquarian, Ethnological, and other Researches.* London : Trübner, 1860.

Bologna, *Congrès d'Archéologie et d'Anthropologie Préhistoriques, Session de Bologna*, 1 vol. 8vo. Fava and Garagnani : Bologna, 1871.

Bonnycastle (Captain R. H., of the Royal Engineers), *Spanish America*, &c. Philadelphia : A. Small, 1817.

Borlase (William), *Observations on the Antiquities, &c, of the County of Cornwall*. Oxford, 1754.

Boscawen (W. St. Chad), Papers in Society of Biblical Archæology.

Boutell (Charles), *Arms and Armour*. London, 1867.

Brewster (Sir David), *Letters on Natural Magic*, 12mo. London, 1833.

Brugsch (Heinrich), *A History of Egypt under the Pharaohs, &c.*, by Henry Brugsch-Bey (now Pasha). Translated from the German by the late Henry Danby Seymour ; completed and edited by Philip Smith, 2 vols. 8vo. London : Murray, 1879. The first part has been published in French, Leipzig, 1859. The archaistic German style of *Geschichte Aegypten's* is very difficult.

Bulletin de l'Institut Égyptien. Cairo : Mourès, 1882.

Bunsen (Baron C. C. J.), *Egypt's Place in Universal History, &c.*, with additions by Samuel Birch, LL.D., 5 vols. 8vo. London : Longmans, 1867.

Burnouf (Émile), *Essai sur le Veda, ou Études sur les Religions, &c., de l'Inde*, 1 vol. 8vo., 1863. ' L'Age de Bronze,' *Revue des deux Mondes*, July 15, 1877.

Burton (R. F.), *A Complete System of Bayonet Exercise*. London : Clowes, 1853. The *Athenæum*, Nov. 24, 1880. *Camoens, his Life and his Lusiads*, 2 vols. 12mo., Quaritch, 1881. *To the Gold Coast for Gold*. London : Chatto and Windus, 1883.

Cæsar (Julius), *Opera Omnia*, Delphin edit., variorum notes, 4 vols. 8vo. Londini, 1819.

Calder (J. E.), *Some Account of the Wars of Extirpation and Habits of the Native Tribes of Tasmania*, Journ. Anthrop. Instit., vol. iii. 1873.

Cameron (Commander Verney Lovett, C.B., D.C.L., &c.), *Across Africa*. London : Daldy and Isbister, 1877.

Camoens, *Os Lusiadas*.

Catalogue du Bulak Muséum, by the late Mariette-Bey (afterwards Pasha). Cairo : A. Mourès, imprimeur-éditeur.

Catalog. Die Ethnographisch-Anthropologische Abtheilung des Museums Godefroy in Hamburg, vol. i. 8vo. L. Frederichsen u. Co. 1881.

Caylus (Comte de), *Recueil d'Antiquités Égyptiennes, &c.*, 8 vols. 4to. Paris, 1752-70.

Celsus (A. Cornelius), *De Medicinâ*, edit. princeps. Florentiæ, a Nicolao impressus, A D. 1478.

Chabas, *Études sur l'Antiquité Historique d'après les sources Egyptiennes*, 1872.

Chaillu (Paul B. du), *Explorations and Adventures in Equatorial Africa, &c.* London : Murray, 1861. The *Gorilla-book*.

Chapman (Captain George), *Foil Practice, with a Review of the Art of Fencing*. London : Clowes, 1861.

Clapperton (Captain H.), *Journal of a Second Expedition into Africa*, 1 vol. 4to. London, 1829.

Clermont-Ganneau (Charles), *Horus et Saint George, &c.* Extrait de la *Revue Archéologique*, Dec. 1877. Paris : Didier et Cⁱᵉ. The author is a prolific writer and a highly distinguished Orientalist.

Cochet (Jean Benoît Désiré, Abbé), *Le Tombeau de Childéric I., Roi des Francs*. Restitué à l'aide de l'archéologie et des découvertes récentes, 8vo. Paris : 1859.

Cole (Lieutenant H. H., of the Royal Engineers), *Catalogue of Indian Art in the South Kensington Museum*.

—— *Illustrations of Ancient Buildings in Kashmir*, prepared under the authority of the Secretary of State for India from photographs, plans, and drawings taken by order of the Government of India. London, 1869. 4to.

—— *The Architecture of Ancient Delhi, especially the buildings around the Kutb Minar*, fol. London, 1872.

Cooper (Rev. Basil H.), *The Antiquity and the Use of Metals and especially Iron, among the Egyptians*, Transac. Devonshire Assoc. for the Advancement of Science, 1868.

Cory (Isaac Preston), *Ancient Fragments of the Phœnician, Chaldæan, Egyptian, Tyrian, Carthaginian, and other writers*, 8vo. London, 1832. Very rare. New edit. Reeves and Turner : London, 1876.

Crawfurd (John), *On the Sources of the Supply of Tin for the Bronze Tools and Weapons of Antiquity*, Trans. Ethnol. Soc., N.S., vol. iii. 1865.

Cunningham (General A.), *The Bhilsa Topes, &c.*, 8vo. London, 1854. *Ládak, &c.*, royal 8vo. London, 1854. *Archæological Survey of India*, 6 vols. 8vo. Simla, 1871-78.

Czoernig (Baron Carl von), jun. *Ueber die vorhistorischen Funde im Laibacher Torfmoor*. Alpine Soc. of Trieste, Dec. 8, 1875.

Daniel (Père Gabriel), *Histoire de la Milice Françoise, et des Changemens qui s'y sont faits, depuis l'établissement de la Monarchie Françoise dans les Gaules, jusqu'à la fin du Régne de Louis le Grand,* 7 vols. 8vo. À Amsterdam ; au dépens de la Compagnie (de Jésus), MDCCXXIV. It is a standard work as far as it goes.

Davis (Sir John F.), *The Chinese: a general Description of the Empire of China and its Inhabitants,* 2 vols. 8vo. London : Knight, MDCCCVI.

Day (St. John Vincent), *The Prehistoric Use of Iron and Steel.* London : Trübner, 1877. When sending me a copy of his learned and original study, Mr. Day wrote to me that he is bringing out a second edition, in which his ' collection of additional matter will modify and correct certain of his former views.'

Demmin (Auguste), *Illustrated History of Arms and Armour,* translated by C. C. Black, M.A. London : Bell, 1877. The illustrations leave much to be desired ; the Oriental notices are deficient, and the translator has made them worse. Otherwise the book gives a fair general and superficial view.

Denham (Major Dixon), Clapperton and Oudney's *Travels in Northern and Central Africa,* in 1822-24, 2 vols. 8vo. London, 1826.

Deschmann und Hochstetter, *Prähistorische Ansiedlungen, &c., in Krain.* Laybach, 1879.

Desor (Edouard), *Les Palafittes, ou Constructions lacustres du lac de Neuchâtel.* Paris, 1865. *Die Pfahlbauten des Neuenberger Sees.* Frankfurt a. M., 1866. Desor et Favre, *Le Bel Age du Bronze lacustre en Suisse,* 1 vol. fol. Neufchâtel, 1874.

Diodorus Siculus (B.C. 44), *Bibliotheca Historica,* P. Wesselingius, 2 vols. fol. Amstelod., 1746.

Dion Cassius (nat. A.D. 155).

Dionysius of Halicarnassus (B.C. 29), *Opera Omnia,* J. J. Reiske, 6 vols. 8vo. Lipsiæ, 1774.

Dodwell (Edward), *A Classical and Topographical Tour through Greece,* 1801-6, 2 vols. 4to. London, 1819.

Douglas (Rev. James, F.A.S.), *Nænia Britannica,* 1793, folio.

Dümichen, *Geschichte des alten Aegyptens.* Berlin, 1879.

Ebers (Prof. George), *Aegypten und die Bücher Moses.* Leipzig, 1868. Followed by sundry Germano-Egyptian romances, *An Egyptian Princess, Uarda, &c.*

Edkins (Rev. Dr.) *China's Place in Philology: an Attempt to show that the Languages of Europe and Asia have a Common Origin.* London, 1 vol. 8vo., 1871.

Ellis (Rev. William), *Polynesian Researches.* London : Murray, 1858.

Elphinstone, *History of India,* 2 vols. 8vo. 1841.

Encyclopædia Britannica.
—— *Metropolitana.*
—— *Penny* (one of the best).
—— *Knight's.*

Engel (W. H.), *Kypros : eine Monographie.* 2 vols. 8vo. Berlin : Reimer, 1841.

Ethnological Society of London (Journal of) 7 vols. 8vo. 1848-65.

Eusebius (Bishop of Cæsarea, A.D. 264-340), *Historiæ Ecclesiasticæ Libri Decem ;* denuo edidit F. A. Heinichen, 3 vols. 8vo. Lipsiæ, 1868.

Evans (Dr. John), *The Ancient Stone Implements of Great Britain,* 1 vol. 8vo. London : Longmans, 1872. *The Ancient Implements of Great Britain and Ireland,* ibid. 1881. Both works are admirably well studied and exhaust the subjects as far as they are now known.

Ewbank (Thomas), *Life in Brazil,* 1 vol. 8vo. New York, 1856 ; London : Sampson Low and Co., 1856. The Appendix is anthropologically valuable.

Fairholt (F. W.), *A Dictionary of Terms of Art,* 1 vol. 12mo. Virtue and Hall, London, 1849.

Farrar (Canon), *Life, &c., of Saint Paul.* Cassell and Co. : London, Paris, and New York (undated).

Ferguson (Sir James), *Transactions of the Irish Association.*

Fergusson (James), *A History of Architecture,* 4 vols. 8vo. London, 1874-76.

Festus (Sextus Pompeius), *De Verborum Significatione,* K. O. Müller. Lipsiæ, 1839. The Grammarian lived between A.D. 100 (Martial's day) and A.D. 422 (under Theodosius II.).

Ficke, *Wörterbuch der Indo-germanischen Grundsprache, &c.* Göttingen, 1868.

Florus (Annæus : *temp.* Trajan), *Rerum Romanarum libri IV.,* Delphin edit., 2 vols., 8vo Londini, 1822.

Fox (A. Lane-, now Major-General A. Pitt-Rivers). This distinguished student of Anthropology, who ranks foremost in the knowledge of early weapons, happily applied the idea of evolution, development, and progress to his extensive collection, the work of some thirty years. To show the successive steps he grouped his objects according to their forms and uses, beginning with the simplest ; and to each class he appended an ideal type, towards which the primitive races were ever advancing, making innumerable mistakes, in some cases even retrograding, but on the whole attaining a higher plane. The papers from which I have quoted, often word for word, in my first chapters, are (1) 'Primitive Warfare,' sect. i., read on June 28, 1867 (pp. 1–35, with five plates), and Sect. ii., 'On the Resemblance of the Weapons of Early Races, their Variations, Continuity, and Development of Form,' read on June 5, 1868 (pp. 1–42, with eight diagrams) ; and (2) 'Catalogue of the Anthropological Collection lent for Exhibition in the Bethnal Green Branch of the South Kensington Museum, with (131) Illustrations ;' pt. I. and II. (III. and IV. to be published hereafter), 1874, &c., 8vo., pp. 1–184. The collection, then containing some 14,000 objects, left Bethnal Green for the Western Galleries of the Museum in South Kensington. After a long sojourn there it was offered to the public ; but England, unlike France, Germany, and Italy, has scant appreciation of anthropological study. At length it was presented to the University of Oxford, where a special building will be devoted to its worthy reception. I have taken the liberty of suggesting to General Pitt-Rivers that he owes the public not only the last two parts of his work, but also a folio edition with coloured illustrations of the humble ' Catalogue.'

Genthe (Dr. Hermann), a paper on ' Etruscan Commerce with the North,' *Archiv für Anthrop.*, vol. vi. (from his work *Ueber den etruskischen Tauschhandel nach Norden*). Frankfurt, 1874.

Gladstone (Right Hon. W. E.), *Juventus Mundi*, 1 vol. 8vo. London, 1869. ' Metals in Homer,' *Contemporary Review*, 1874.

Glas (George), ' The History of the Discovery and Conquest of the Canary Islands,' *Pinkerton, Voyages*, vol. xvi.

Goguet (Antoine Yves), *De l'Origine des Lois, des Arts, et des Sciences, et de leur progrès chez les anciens peuples* (par A. Y. G., aidé par Alex. Conr. Fugère), 3 vols., plates, 4to. Paris, 1758. Numerous editions and translations.

Goguet (M. de), *The Origin of Laws, Arts, and Sciences, and their progress among the most Ancient Nations.* English translation by Thompson, 3 vols., plates, 8vo. Edinburgh, 1761.

Gozzadini (Senator Count Giovanni), *Di un antico sepolcro a Ceretolo nel Bolognese.* Modena : Vincenzi, 1872. The author has taken a distinguished place in antiquarian anthropology by his various and valuable studies of Etruscan remains found in and around Felsina, now Bologna. I have ventured upon suggesting to him that these detached papers, mostly printed by Fava, Garagnani, and Co., of Bologna, should be collected and published in a handy form for the benefit of students.

Graah (Captain W. A.), *Narrative of an Expedition to the Eastern Coast of Greenland, &c.* Translated from the Danish (Copenhagen, 1832) by C. Gordon Macdougall, 8vo. London, 1837.

Grant (Captain, now Colonel, James A.), *A Walk across Africa, or Domestic Scenes from my Nile Journal.* Blackwoods : Edinburgh, MDCCCLXIV.

Grose (Captain Francis), *Military Antiquities respecting the History of the British Army. From the Conquest to the Present Time.* A new edition with material additions and improvements, 2 vols. 8vo. London, printed for T. Egerton, Whitehall ; and G. Kearsley, Fleet Street, 1801. The first edition appeared in 1786, and the learned author died (æt. 52) of apoplexy at Dublin, May 12, 1791.

Grote (George), *History of Greece*, 12 vols. 8vo. 1846–56.

Guthrie (Mrs.), *My Year in an Indian Fort.* Hurst and Blackett : London, 1877.

Hamilton (Will. J.), *Researches in Asia Minor, Pontus, and Armenia, &c.*, 2 vols. 8vo. London : Murray, 1842.

Hanbury (Daniel), *Science Papers, &c.*, edited with Memoir by Joseph Ince, 1 vol. 8vo. London, 1876.

Heath (Rev. Dunbar Isidore), *Exodus Papyri*, 8vo. London, 1855. *Phœnician Inscriptions.* London, Quaritch, 1873. ' Hittite Inscriptions,' *Journ. Anthrop. Institute*, May, 1880.

Herodotus, Rawlinson's, 4 vols. Murray, 1858. This valuable work wants a second edition revised.

Herrera (Antonio, chief chronicler of the Indies), *Historia Geral, &c.*, VIII. Decads, 4 vols. folio. Madrid, 1601.

Hesiod, *Opera et Dies ; Scutum, &c.* Poetæ Minores Græci, vol. i.

Holub (Dr. Emil), *Seven Years in South Africa*, 2 vols. 8vo. Sampson Low and Co. 1881.

Homer, *Opera Omnia*, by J. A. Ernesti. 5 vols. 8vo. Glasgow, 1814.

Horatius, *Opera Om.*, ex edit. Zeunii. Delphin edit., 4 vols. 8vo. Londini, 1825.

Howorth (H. H.), 'Archæology of Bronze.' *Trans. Ethno. Soc.*, vol. vi.

Humboldt (Baron Alexander von), *Personal Narrative of Travels to the Equinoctial Regions of America*, 3 vols. 8vo. Bohn's Scientific Library, London, 1852.

Iron, an Illustrated Weekly Journal of Science, Metals, and Manufactures in Iron and Steel, edited by Perry E. Nursey, C.E., to whom I have to express my thanks.

Isidorus Hispalensis (Bishop of Seville, A.D. 600–636), *Opera Omnia* (including the 'Origines' and 'Etymologies'), published by J. du Breul, fol. Parisiis, 1601.

Jacquemin (Raphael), *Histoire Générale du Costume, &c.* Du IVme au XIXme Siècle (A.D. 315–1815). Paris.

Jähns (Major Max), *Handbuch einer Geschichte des Kriegswesens von der Urzeit an zur Renaissance*. Technischer Theil : Bewaffnung, Kampfweise, Befestigung, Belagerung, Seewesen. Leipzig : Grunow, 1880. Major Jähns, an officer upon the General Staff of the German army, has produced in 1 vol. imp. 8vo. (pp. 640) a most laborious and useful work, accompanied by an atlas of one hundred carefully drawn plates. He quotes authorities literally by the hundred. The work amply deserves to be translated into English, but its public would, I fear, be very limited.

Josephus (Flavius).

Justinus (Frontinus). *History, Fourth and Fifth Century*, abridged from Trogus Pompeius.

Kama Sutra of Vatsyayana, part i., with a preface and introduction. Printed for the Hindu Kama Shastra Society of London, 1883 ; for private circulation only. The poet whose name was Mallinaga or Mrillana (of the Vatsyayana family) lived between the first and sixth century of the Christian Æra. This, too, is only known by his poetry. Hindu-land is rich in Kama literature.

Keller (Dr. Ferdinand), *Die Kältischen Pfahlbauten in den Schweizer Seen*. Zürich, 1854–66. There is an English translation *The Lake Dwellings of Switzerland*.

King (late Dr. Richard), *Trans. Ethnol. Soc.*, vols. i. and ii.

Klemm (Dr. Gustav Friedrich), *Werkzeuge und Waffen*. Leipzig, 1854. An edition of Klemm's (G. F.), *Die Werkzeuge und Waffen, ihre Entstehung und Ausbildung*, with 342 woodcuts in the text, 8vo. Published at Sondershausen, 1858. *Allgemeine Culturwissenschaft*, 2 vols. with woodcuts, 8vo. Leipzig, 18:4-5.

Kolben (Peter) *Present State of the Cape of Good Hope, &c.*, 2 vols. 8vo., 1738.

Kremer (Ritter Adolf von) *Ibn Chaldun und seine Culturgeschichte*. Wien, 1879.

Lacombe, *Les Armes et les Armures*. Paris, 1868.

Land and Water, weekly paper published by William Bates ; it contains many articles by the late lamented Mr. Frank Buckland, F.Z.S.

Latham (John): this 'Assistant-Commissioner for Exhibitions' (1862, 1867, and 1873), who succeeded in business Messrs. Wilkinson and Son of Pall Mall, and who lately died, gave me copies of his two excellent papers, (1) 'The Shape of Sword-blades,' and (2) 'A Few Notes on Swords in the International Exhibition of 1862' (*Journal of the R.U.S. Institution*, vols. vi. and vii.). With the author's permission I have freely used these two valuable professional studies, especially in Chapter VII. The late Mr. Latham was a practical Swordsman, and his long experience as a maker of the 'white arm' renders his information thoroughly trustworthy. I wish every success to his son, who now fills his place in an establishment famous for turning out good work.

Latham (Robert Gordon), *Ethnology of the British Islands*, 1 vol. 12mo. London, 1852. *Descriptive Ethnology*, 2 vols. 8vo. 1859.

Layard (Sir Henry Austen), *Nineveh and its Remains*, 2 vols. 8vo., 1849. *Monuments of Nineveh*, 1st and 2nd Series, 1849–53. *A Popular Account of Discoveries at Nineveh*. London: Murray, 1851. *Fresh Discoveries in the Ruins of Nineveh and Babylon*, 1 vol. 8vo. London : Murray, 1853.

Legge (Dr. James), *The Chinese Classics*, 3 vols. 8vo. London, 1861–76 ; vol. i., 'Confucius'; ii., 'Mencius' ; iii., 'She-King or Book of Poetry.'

Lenormant (François), *Manuel d'Histoire Ancienne de l'Orient*, 2 vols., 12mo. Paris, 1868. *Les Premières Civilisations*, 3 vols. 12mo. Paris, 1874. Germ. Trans., Jena, 1875.

Lepsius (Dr. Richard), *Denkmäler aus Aegypten und Aethiopien nach den Zeichnungen der Preussischen Expedition. Denkmäler aus Aegypten und Aethiopien* (1842–45). Berlin, 1849–59. *Discoveries in Egypt, &c.*, translated by Kenneth R. H. Mackenzie, 8vo. London, 1852. *Die Metalle in den Aegyptischen Inschriften* (Akad. der Wiss., A.D. 1871), the latter translated into French 1877.

Lindsey (Dr. W. Lauder), *Proceedings of Society of Arts of Scotland*, vol. v. 327.

Livy.

Lopez (Vicente Fidel), *Les Races Aryennes du Pérou, &c.* Paris : A. Franck, 1871. A copy was sent to me by my old friend John Coghlan, C.E., of Buenos Ayres.

Lubbock (Sir John W.), *Pre-historic Times*, 1 vol. 8vo., 1865. *Primitive Inhabitants of Scandinavia* (Nillson's), 3rd edit. London, 1868. *Origin of Civilisation, &c.*, 8vo. London, 1870.

Lucan.

Lucretius.

Luynes (Duc de), *Numismatique et Inscriptions Cypriotes.* Paris, 1852.

Lyell (Sir Charles), *Principles of Geology.* London : Murray, 1830–3. *The Antiquity of Man from Geological Evidences.* London : Murray, 1863.

Major (R. H.), *The Select Letters of Columbus, &c.* London : Hakluyt Soc., MDCCCLX.

Manava-Dharma-Shástra (Laws of Menu), translated by Houghton. London, 1825.

Manetho (B.C. 285).

Marchionni (Alberto), *Trattato di Scherma, &c.* Firenze : Bencini, 1847.

Markham (Clements R.), *Pedro de Cieza (Cieça) de Leon,* 1869. *Commentaries of the Yncas,* 1871. *Reports on the Discovery of Peru,* 1872. All printed by the Hakluyt Society.

Massart (Alfred), *Gisements Métallifères du district de Carthagène (Espagne).* Liège, 1875.

Massey (Gerald), *A Book of the Beginnings.* London : Williams and Norgate, 1881. Two volumes were first published, and the two concluding are lately issued. A learned friend writes to him : ' I find little to remark upon or criticise. You seem to have got down far below Tylor, and to be making good your ground in many matters. If people will only read your book, it will make them cry out in some way or other. But you require a populariser, and may have to wait a long time for one.'

Mela (Pomponius), *De Situ Orbis* (A.D. 41–54). This little work deserves a modern English translation ; but what can be said of geographers whose Royal Geographical Society has not yet translated Ptolemy ?

Meyrick (Sir Samuel Rush), *Critical Inquiry into Ancient Armour as it existed in Europe, particularly in Great Britain, from the Norman Conquest to Charles the Second, with a Glossary of Military Terms of the Middle Ages.* I quote from the Second Edition. 3 vols. atlas 4to. London : Bohn, 1844. The first edition was published in 1824 without the supervision of the author, who found fault with it, especially with the colouring. The next edition, in 1844, was enlarged by the author with the assistance of friends, Mr. Albert Way and others. It was followed by *Engraved Illustrations of Ancient Arms and Armour*, the artistic work of Mr. Joseph Skelton.

Milne (John), ' On the Stone Age of Japan,' *Journ. Anthrop. Instit.*, May 1881.

Mitchell (Dr. Arthur), ' The Past in the Present,' &c., *Rhind Lectures*, 1876–78, 1 vol. 8vo. Edinburgh : Douglas, 1880.

Montaigne (Michel de), *Essais*, translated by William Hazlitt. London : C. Templeman, MDCCCLIII (3rd edition).

Monteiro and Gamitto, *O Muata Cazembe*, 1 vol. 8vo. Imprensa Nacional, Lisboa, 1854.

Moore, *Ancient Mineralogy.*

Moorcroft (William) and Trebeck (George), *Travels in the Himalayan Provinces of Hindustan and Punjab, &c., from* 1819 *to* 1825, 8vo. London : Murray, 1841.

Morgan (Lewis), *The League of the Iroquois.*

Mortot, ' On the Swiss Lakes,' *Bulletin de la Société Vaudoise*, vol. vi., &c. ' Les Métaux dans l'Age du Bronze ' (*Mém. Soc. Ant. du Nord*, 1866–71).

Mortillet (Gabriel de), ' Les Gaulois de Marzabotto dans l'Apennin,' *Revue Archéologique*, 1870–71. This anthropologist has published largely, and did good work at the Congress of Bologna.

Movers, *Die Phönizier.* Berlin, 1840–56. The book is somewhat antiquated, but still valuable.

Much (Dr. M.), ' Ueber die Priorität des Eisens oder der Bronze in Ostasien,' *Trans. Anthrop. Soc. of Vienna*, vol. ix. Separat-Abdruck.

Müller (Prof. F. Max), *Chips from a German Workshop*, 2 vols. 8vo. London, 1867. *Lectures on the Science of Language*, 2 vols. 12mo. London, 1873 (7th edit.). *Introduction to the Science of Religion*, 12mo London, 1873.

Neuhoff, *Travels in Brazil.* Pinkerton, vol. xiv.

Nillson (Prof. Sven), *The Primitive Inhabitants of Scandinavia,* translated by Sir John Lubbock. He is illustrated by Colonel A. Lane-Fox (*Prim. Warf.*, p. 135) and by Wilde (*Catalogue, &c.*).

Oldfield, 'Aborigines of Australia,' *Trans. Ethnol. Soc.,* new series, vol. iii.

Oppert (Professor), *On the Weapons, &c., of the Ancient Hindus.* London : Trubner, 1880.

Opusculum Fidicularum, the Ancestry of the Violin, by Ed. Heron Allen. London : Mitchell and Hughes, 1882. The author kindly sent me a copy of his work.

Orosius (Presbyter Paulus), A.D. 413), *Historiarum Libri Septem.* The Anglo-Saxon version of Aelfred the Great ; translated, &c., by Daines Barrington, 1 vol. 8vo. London, 1773, and by Bosworth, 1859.

Osburn (William), *Monumental History of Egypt,* 2 vols. 8vo. London, 1854.

Owen (Prof. Richard), *On the Anatomy of Vertebrates,* 3 vols. 8vo. London, 1866–68.

Palestine Exploration Fund, founded 1865 ; publishes Quarterly Statement. The Society's office, 1 Adam Street, Adelphi, W.C.

Palma (General Luigi di Cesnola), *Cyprus, its Ancient Cities, Tombs, and Temples,* 8vo. London : Murray, 1877. *Cypern.* Gena : Leipzig, 1879.

Palma (Major di Cesnola), 'On Phœnician Art in Cyprus,' *Brit. Archæol. Assoc.,* Dec. 6, 1882.

Paterculus (C. Velleius, B.C. 19).

Pausanias (*temp.* Antonin. Pius), *Periegesis (or Itinerary) of Greece.* The work of a good traveller, translated by Thomas Taylor, 3 vols. 8vo. London, 1824.

Percy (Dr. John), *Fuel, Fireclays, Copper, Zinc, Brass, &c.* London : Murray, 1861. *Metallurgy : Iron and Steel,* ibid., 1864. *Lead,* 1870. *Silver and Gold,* part i., 1880. These works are too well known and too highly appreciated to be noticed except by name.

Petherick (John), *Egypt, the Soudan, and Central Africa,* 8vo. Blackwoods, Edinburgh, MDCCCLXI. The late author was a Cornish miner who had the honesty not to find coal for Mohammed Ali Pasha of Egypt.

Petronius Arbiter.

Phillips (Prof. John A.), *A Guide to Geology,* 12mo. London, 1864. 'A Manual of Metallurgy, or a Practical Treatise on the Chemistry of the Metals,' illustrated. London, 1864 : *Archæological Journal,* vol. xvi.

Philo Judæus (A.D. 40).

Pigafetta (Antonio, of Vicenza, who accompanied Magalhaens, the first circumnavigator, 1519–1522), *Primo Viaggio intorno al Globo,* 4to. Milan, 1800 ; published by Amoretti. He was best known before that date by Ramusio's work.

Polyænus the Macedonian dedicated his 8 books of 900 Στρατηγήματα to M. Aurelius and L. Verus (A.D. 163).

Polybius (nat. circ. B.C. 204), Πραγματεία, not *Historia. Historiarum quæ supersunt.* Lips.: Holtze, 1866 ; 5 books and fragments out of 40. The writer was a captain in the field besides being an authority on military art, a politician, and a philosopher, who composed for instruction, not for amusement.

Pollux (Julius, A.D. 183), *Onomasticon.*

Porter (Rev. J. L.), author of *A Handbook for Travellers in Syria and Palestine.* London : Murray, 1868 (1st edition).

Porter (Sir Robert Ker), *Travels in Georgia, Persia, Armenia, Ancient Babylonia, &c.* (1817–20), 2 vols. 4to. London : Longmans, 1821–22.

Procopius (nat. circ. A.D. 500), *Histories, &c.*

Ptolemy, *Geographia.*

Ramusio (Giambattista, of Treviso, nat. 1485), *Raccolta di Navigazioni e Viaggi,* 3 vols. fol., 1550–59 ; the first collection of the kind, which gave rise to many others.

Rawlinson (Canon George), *The Five Great Monarchies of the Ancient Eastern World, &c.,* 4 vols. 8vo. London : Murray, 1862–66.

Records of the Past, being English translations of the Assyrian and Egyptian monuments, published under the sanction of the Society of Biblical Archæology, vol. i. (of 12), 12mo. London, 1874.

Revue Archéologique (under the direction of J. Gailhabaud), année 1–16. Paris, 1844–59, 8vo. Nouvelle Série, année 1, vol. i. &c., 1860, 8vo. *Table Décennale,* nouvelle série, 1860–1869, dressée par M. F. Delaunay. Paris, 1874, 8vo. In progress.

Rhind (A. Henry), *Thebes, its Tombs and their Tenants, &c.* 1862.

Richtofen (Baron Ferdinand von), *China, Ergebnisse eigener Reisen und darauf gegründeter Studien.* Vol. i. published in 1877 ; vol. ii. (4to.), Remier : Berlin, 1882. It has not yet found a translator.

Rivero (Mariano y Eduardo de) y Tschudi (Juan Diego de), *Antiguedades Peruanas,* 1 vol. 4to., with Atlas. Vienna, 1851. *Travels in Peru,* by J. J. von Tschudi, in 1838–42 ; was translated from the German by T. Ross, 8vo. London, 1847.

Rossellini (Prof.) *I Monumenti dell' Egitto e della Nubia.* Pisa, 1832–41.

Rossignol (J. P.), *Les Métaux dans l'Antiquité.* Paris : Durand, 1863.

Roteiro (Ruttier) *da Viagem de Vasco da Gama,* corrected by the late Professor Herculano and Baron do Castello de Pavia. Imprensa Nacional, Lisboa, MDCCCLI (2nd edition).

Rougé (Vicomte E. de), *Rituel Funéraire des Anciens Egyptiens, &c.,* imp. folio. Paris, 1861–66.

Rougemont, *L'Age de Bronze,* 1866.

Rowbotham (J. F.), 'On the Art of Music in Prehistoric Times,' *Journ. Anthrop. Inst.,* May, 1881.

Sacken (Baron E. von Osten-), *Das Grabfeld von Hallstadt und dessen Alterthümer.* Vienna, 1868.

Sainte-Croix (Baron de), *Recherches Historiques et Critiques sur les Mystères du Paganisme,* revues et corrigées par Silvestre de Sacy, 2 vols. 8vo. Paris, 1817.

Sallust.

Sayce (Rev. A. H.), 'On the Hamathite Inscriptions,' *Trans. Soc. Bibl. Archæol.,* vol. iv. part 1. Mr. Sayce has read other papers containing notices of more modern 'Hittite' finds; but I have failed to procure copies.

Schliemann (Dr. Henry), *Troy and its Remains,* translated and edited by Philip Smith. London : Murray, 1875. *Mycenæ and Tiryns,* ibid. 1878. *Ilios,* ibid. 1880.

Scott (Sir Sibbald David), *The British Army, its Origin, Progress, and Development,* 2 vols. London and New York : Cassell, Petter, & Galpin, 1868.

Sévez, notice of Japanese Iron-works in *Les Mondes,* tome xxvi., Dec. 1871.

Silius Italicus (nat. A.D. 25).

Smith (Captain John), *General Historie of Virginia, New England, and the Summer Isles, &c.,* fol. London : Pinkerton, xiii. He made his first voyage in 1606, and his second in 1614, when he changed 'North Virginia' into 'New England.' On his third (1615), he was captured by a Frenchman and landed at La Rochelle.

Smith (George), *Assyrian Discoveries.* London : Sampson Low & Co., 6th edit., 1876. The learned author wore himself out by travel, and died young.

Smith (Rev. W. Robertson), *The Old Testament in the Jewish Church.* Edinburgh : Blacks, 1881.

Smith (Dr. William), *Dictionaries.* London : Taylor & Walton—
　1. *Greek and Roman Geography,* 2 vols. 8vo. 1856–57.
　2. *Greek and Roman Antiquities,* 1 vol. 8vo. 1859.
　3. *Greek and Roman Biography and Mythology,* 3 vols. 8vo. 1858–61.
　4. *Of the Bible,* 3 vols. 8vo. 1863.

Solinus (Ca. Jul. Polyhistor, *alias* 'Pliny's Ape'), *Geographical Compendium.*

Speke (Captain James Hanning), *Journal of the Discovery of the Source of the Nile.* Edinburgh : Blackwoods, 1863.

Spensley (Howard), *Cenni sugli Aborigeni di Australasia, &c.* Venezia : G. Fischer, 1881.

Stade (Hans), *The Captivity of Hans Stade,* translated for the Hakluyt Society by Mr. Albert Tootal of Rio de Janeiro. London, 1874.

Stanley (Henry M.), *Through the Dark Continent, &c.* London : Sampson Low, & Co., 1874.

Stephens (J. Lloyd), *Incidents of Travel in Central America, Chiapas, and Yucatan,* 2 vols. 8vo. London : Murray, 1842. Germ. trans., Leipzig, 1843.

Stevens (the late Edward T.), *Flint Chips, a Guide to Prehistoric Archæology, as illustrated in the Blackmore Museum, Salisbury,* 8vo. London : Bell and Daldy, 1870.

Strabo (B.C. 54?).

Suetonius (C. Tranquillus).

Tacitus (Cornelius).

Taylor (Rev. Isaac), *Etruscan Researches.* London : Macmillan, 1874.

Texier, *Description de l'Asie Mineure.* Paris, 1849–52.

Theophrastus (B.C. 305), *Opera Græca et Latina,* J. G. Schneider, 5 vols. 8vo. Lipsiæ, 1818–

Tylor (E. B.), *Anahuac.* London, 1861. *Primitive Culture.* London : Murray, 1871 (Germ. trans., 1873). *Researches into the Early History of Mankind and the Development of Civilisation,* plates. London : Murray, 1870.

Ure (Andrew), *Dictionary of Arts, Manufactures, and Mines.* London, 1863.

Vallancey (General), *Collectanea de Rebus Hibernicis,* 6 vols. Dublin, 1770–1804.

Varnhagen (the late F. Adolpho de) : *Historia Geral do Brazil,* 2 vols. 8vo. Laemmert : Rio de Janeiro, 1854. Useful as 'documents pour servir.'

Varro (Terentius, nat. B.C. 116), *De Lingua Latina.*

Vegetius (Fl. Renatus, A.D. 375-92), *De Re Militari.*

Virgil.

Vitruvius (M. Pollio, B.C. 46), *Architecture,* 5 vols. 4to. Utini, 1829.

Volney (Const. F.), *Œuvres,* 8 vols. 8vo. Paris, 1826.

Waitz (Professor, Dr. Theodor), *Anthropologie der Naturvölker.* Leipzig, 1859-72. The first volume, *Introduction to Anthropology,* was translated by J. F. Collingwood and published by the Anthropological Society of London, 8vo., Longmans, 1863. The manuscript of the second volume of this valuable work, also by Mr. Collingwood, was long in my charge ; but the low state of anthropological study in England (and other pursuits unprofessional, and consequently non-paying) prevents its being printed.

Wilde (Sir William R.), *Descriptive Catalogue of the Antiquities in the Royal Irish Academy.* Dublin : Academy House, 1863. *A Descriptive Catalogue of Materials in the Royal Irish Academy,* 8vo., 1857-61. It is regretable that part I, vol. ii., of this admirable work, which has become a standard upon the subject, has not been printed ; nor has the public been informed of any arrangements for publishing. For permission to make use of the cuts, which were obligingly furnished to Mr. Grego, I am indebted to the courtesy of the Council, Royal Society of Antiquaries of Ireland.

Wilkinson (Sir J. Gardner), *The Manners and Customs of the Ancient Egyptians, their Private Life, Government, Laws, Arts, Religion, and History* (originally written in 1836), 6 vols. 8vo. London : Murray, 1837-41. The author abridged his life-labour with the usual unsuccess, and called it *A Popular Account of the Ancient Egyptians,* 2 vols. post 8vo. London : Murray, 1874.

Wilkinson (the late Henry, the eminent Sword-cutler in Pall Mall), *Observations on Swords*; *to which is added Information for Officers going to join their Regiments in India.* Pall Mall, London. No date.

Willemin, *Choix des Costumes Civiles et Militaires.* Paris, 1798.

Wilson (Daniel), *Archæology and Prehistoric Annals of Scotland.* Edinburgh : Sutherland and Knox, 8vo., MDCCCLI. *Prehistoric Man,* 2 vols. 8vo. London : Macmillan, 1862.

Wright (the late Thomas), 'On the True Assignation of the Bronze Weapons,' &c., *Trans. Ethno. Soc.,* new series, vol. iv.

Woldrich (Prof. A.), *Mittheilungen der Wien. Anthrop. Gesell.* Wien, 1874.

Wood (John George), *Natural History of Man, being an Account of the Manners and Customs of the Uncivilised Ways of Men,* 2 vols., 1868-70, 8vo.

Worsäae (J. J. A.), *Afbildninger fra det Kon. Mus. for Nordiske Oldsager i Kjöbnhavn.* Ordnede og forklarede af J. J. A. W. (aided by Magnus Petersen and Aagaard). Kjöbnhavn : Kittendorf, and Aagaard, 1859. The order is in careful accordance with the *Three Ages.* Worsäae's *Prehistoric Annals of Denmark* were translated by W. J. Knox, 8vo., London, 1849, and there is a *Leitfaden der Nordischen Alterthumerskunde* by Worsäae, Kopenhagen, 1837.

Wurmbrand (Count Gutaker), *Ergebnisse der Pfahlbauuntersuchungen.* Wien, 1875.

Yule (Colonel Henry), *The Book of Marco Polo the Venetian,* 2nd edit. London : Murray, 1875. The learned and exact writer favoured me with a copy of his admirable work, without which it is vain to read of 'The Kingdoms and the Marvels of the East.'

THE BOOK OF THE SWORD.

CHAPTER I.

PREAMBLE: ON THE ORIGIN OF WEAPONS.

MAN'S civilisation began with Fire—how to light it and how to keep it lit. Before he had taken this step, our primal ancestor (or ancestors) evidently led the life of the lower animals. The legend of 'Iapetus' bold son' Prometheus, like many others invented by the Greeks, or rather borrowed from Egypt, contained under the form of fable a deep Truth, a fact, a lesson valuable even in these days. 'Forethought,' the elder brother of 'Afterthought,' brought down the *semina flammæ* in a hollow tube from Heaven, or stole it from the chariot of the Sun. Here we have the personification of the Great Unknown, who, finding a cane-brake or a jungle tree fired by lightning or flamed by wind-friction, conceived the idea of feeding the σπέρμα πυρὸς with fuel. Thus Hermes or Mercury was 'Pteropédilos' or 'Alipes;' and his ankles were fitted with 'Pedila' or 'Talaria,' winged sandals, to show that the soldier fights with his legs as well as with his arms.[1]

I will not enlarge upon the imperious interest of Hoplology: the history of arms and armour, their connection and their transitions, plays the most important part in the annals of the world.

The first effort of human technology was probably weapon-making. History

---

[1] Frederick the Great declared that an army moves like a serpent, upon its belly. According to Plutarch, the snake was held sacred because it glides without limbs, like the stars. Fire, says Pliny (*Nat. Hist.* vii. 57, and xiii. 42), was first struck out of the stone by Pyrodes, son of Cilix—*silex*, or flint, the match of antiquity; and hence it was called πῦρ; and Vincent de Beauvais explains: 'Silex est lapis durus, sic dictus eo quod ex eo ignis exiliat.' It is the Sanskrit शिला (*shila*), a stone, both words evidently deriving from a common root, *shi* or *si*. The 'religiosa silex' of Claudian (*Rapt. Proserp.* i. 201) was probably a block of stone like those representing Zeus Kasios, the Paphian Venus, not to mention the host of stones worshipped in Egyptian and Arab litholatry, and the old Palladium of Troy transported to Rome. 'Prometheus,' who taught man to preserve fire in the ferule, or stalk, of the giant fennel, was borrowed by the Hindus and converted into Pramantha. 'Pramantha,' however, is the upright fire-stick, first made by Twastu, the Divine Carpenter, who seems to have been a brother of Ἑστία, the Hearth; and hence it has been held to be the male symbol. According to Plato, πῦρ (whence pyrites = sulphuret of iron), ὕδωρ, and κύων are Phrygian words; and evidently they date from the remotest antiquity. *Pir* (sun-heat) is found even in the Quichua of Peru, and enters into the royal name 'Pirhua.' The French and Belgian caverns prove that striking fire by means of pyrites was known to primitive man.

and travel tell us of no race so rude as to lack artificial means of offence and defence.[1] To these, indeed, man's ingenuity and artistic efforts must, in his simple youthtide, have been confined. I do not allude to the complete man, created full-grown in body and mind by the priestly castes of Egypt, Phœnicia, Judæa, Assyria, Persia, and India. The *Homo sapiens* whom we have to consider is the 'Adam Kadmon,'[2] not of the Cabbalist, but of the anthropologist, as soon as he raised himself above the beasts of the field by superiority of brains and hands.

The lower animals are born armed, but not weaponed. The arm, indeed, is rather bestial than human : the weapon is, speaking generally, human, not bestial. Naturalists have doubted, and still doubt, whether in the so-called natural state the lower animals use weapons properly so termed. Colonel A. Lane Fox, a diligent student of primitive warfare, and a distinguished anthropologist,[3] distinctly holds the hand-stone to be *the* prehistoric weapon. He quotes (Cat. pp. 156–59) the ape using the hand-stone to crack nutshells ; the gorillas defending themselves against the Carthaginians of Hanno ; and Pedro de Cieza (Cieça) de Leon [4] telling us that 'when the Spaniards [in Peru] pass under the trees where the monkeys are, these creatures break off branches and throw them down, making faces all the time.' Even in the days of Strabo (xv. 1) it was asserted that Indian monkeys climb precipices, and roll down stones upon their pursuers—a favourite tactic with savages. Nor, indeed, is it hard to believe that the Simiads, whose quasi-human hand has prehensile powers, bombard their assailants with cocoa-nuts and other missiles. Major Denham (1821–24), a trustworthy traveller, when exploring about Lake Chad, says of the quadrumans of the Yeou country : 'The monkeys, or, as the Arabs say, men enchanted (*Beny Adam meshood*),[5] were so numerous that I saw upwards of a hundred and fifty assembled at one place in the evening. They did not appear at all inclined to give up their ground, but, perched on the top of a bank some twenty feet high, made a terrible noise, and, rather gently than otherwise, pelted us as we approached within a certain distance.' Herr Holub,[6] also, was 'designedly aimed at by a herd of African

---

[1] There are still races which are unable to kindle fire. This is asserted of the modern Andamanese by an expert, Mr. H. Man, *Journ. Anthrop. Inst.* Feb. 1882, p. 272. The same was the case with the quondam aborigines of Tasmania.

[2] This Adam Primus was of both sexes, the biune parent of Genesis (v. 3)—'male and female created He them ;' hence the pre-Adamites of Moslem belief. The capital error of Biblical readers in our day is to assume all these myths and mysteries as mere historical details. Men had a better appreciation of the Hebrew *arcana* in the days of Philo Judæus.

[3] I have noted his labours in the list of 'Authorities.'

[4] Chap. iii. p. 43, translated for the Hakluyt Society by Clements R. Markham, C.B. (London, 1869). It is regretable that a senile Committee of exceeding 'properness' cut out so much of this

highly-interesting volume. The Spaniard travelled in A.D. 1532–50, published the first part of his work in 1553, and died about 1560. Readers who would study the most valuable anthropological parts of the book are driven to the French translation quoted by Vicente Fidel Lopez (*Les Races Aryennes du Pérou,* p. 199. Paris, Franck, 1873).

[5] We need not go to the classics, Greek and Roman, for the idea of metamorphosis. It is common to mankind, doubtless arising from the resemblance of beast to man in appearance, habits, or disposition ; and it may date from the days when the lower was all but equal to the higher animal.

[6] *Seven Years in South Africa,* 1872–79, vol. i. p. 245, and vol. ii. p. 199 (Sampson Low and Co., 1881). The Simiads were African baboons, which fear man less than those of other continents.

baboons perched among the trees;' and on another occasion he and his men had to beat an ignominious retreat from 'our cousins.' 'Hence,' suggests Colonel A. Lane Fox, 'our "poor relation" conserves, even when bred abroad and in captivity, the habit of violently shaking the branch by jumping upon it with all its weight, in order that the detached fruit may fall upon the assailant's head.' In Egypt, as we see from the tomb-pictures, monkeys (baboons or cynocephali) were taught to assist in gathering fruit, and in acting as torch-bearers. While doing this last duty, their innate petulance caused many a merry scene.[1]

I never witnessed this bombardment by monkeys. But when my regiment was stationed at Baroda in Gujarát, several of my brother officers and myself saw an elephant use a weapon. The intelligent animal, which the natives call Háthi ('the handed'[2]), was chained to a post during the dangerous season of the wet forehead, and was swaying itself in ill-temper from side to side. Probably offended by the sudden appearance of white faces, it seized with its trunk a heavy billet, and threw it at our heads with a force and a good will that proved the worst intention.

According to Captain Hall—who, however, derived the tale from the Eskimos,[3] the sole living representatives of the palæolithic age in Europe—the polar bear, traditionally reported to throw stones, rolls down, with its quasi-human forepaws, rocks and boulders upon the walrus when found sleeping at the foot of some overhanging cliff. 'Meister Petz' aims at the head, and finally brains the stunned prey with the same weapon. Perhaps the account belongs to the category of the ostrich throwing stones, told by many naturalists, including Pliny (x. I), when, as Father Lobo explained in his 'Abyssinia,' the bird only kicks them up during its scouring flight. Similar, too, is the exploded shooting-out of the porcupine's quills, whereby, according to mediæval 'Shoe-tyes'[4] men have been badly hurt

---

[1] Wilkinson, I. 1. Unruliness was punished by 'stick and no supper.' The old Nile-dwellers, like the Carthaginians and the mediæval Tartars, were famous for taming and training the wildest animals, the cat o' mountain, leopards, crocodiles, and gazelles. The 'war-lions of the king' (Ramses II.) are famed in history. They also taught domestic cats to retrieve waterfowl, and decoy-ducks to cater for the table.

[2] Thus Lucretius (v. 1301) calls the elephant 'anguimanus.' As is well known, there is a quasi-specific difference between the Indian and the African animal. The latter is shorter, stouter, and more compactly built than the former; the shape of the frontal bones differ, the tusks are larger and heavier, and the ears are notably longer. The latter trait appears even in old coins. Judging from the illustrated papers, I should not hesitate to pronounce the far-famed Jumbo to be an Asiatic, and not, as usually held, an African.

[3] The word wrongly written 'Esquimaux,' which suggests a French origin, is derived from the Ojibwa *Askimeg,* or the Abenakin *Eskimantsic,* meaning 'eaters of raw flesh.' Old usage applies it to the races of extreme North America, and of the Asiatic shore immediately opposite. *Innuit,* a more modern term, signifies only 'the people,' like *Khoi-khoi* ('men of men'), the Hottentots, and like 'Bantu' (Folk), applied, or rather misapplied, to the great South African race. *Innuit,* moreover, is by no means universal. The Eskimos supply a valuable study; amongst other primeval peculiarities, they have little reverence for the dead, and scant attachment to place.

[4] 'Brave Master Shoe-tye, the great traveller' (*Measure for Measure,* iv. 3). The tale of porcupines 'shooting their quills at the dogs, which get many a serious wound thereby,' is in M. Polo (i. 28). Colonel Yule quotes Pliny, Ælian, and the Chinese. The animal drops its loose quills when running, and when at bay attempts, hedgehog-like, to hide and shield its head. It is, as the Gypsies know, excellent eating, equal to the most delicate pork; only somewhat dry without the aid of lard.

and even killed. On the other hand, the Emu kicks like an Onager[1] and will drive a man from one side of a quarter-deck to the other.

But though Man's first work was to weapon himself, we must not believe with the Cynics and the Humanitarians that his late appearance in creation, or rather on the stage of life, initiated an unvarying and monotonous course of destructiveness. The great tertiary mammals which preceded him, the hoplotherium, the deinotherium, and other -theria, made earth a vast scene of bloodshed to which his feeble powers could add only a few poor horrors. And even in our day the predatory fishes, that have learned absolutely nothing from man's inhumanity to man, habitually display as much ferocity as ever disgraced savage human nature.

Primitive man—the post-tertiary animal—was doomed by the very conditions of his being and his media to a life of warfare ; a course of offence to obtain his food, and of defence to retain his life. Ulysses[2] says pathetically :

> No thing frailer of force than Man earth breedeth and feedeth;
> Man ever feeblest of all on th' Earth's face creeping and crawling.

The same sentiment occurs in the 'Iliad' ; and Pliny, the pessimist, writes—' the only tearful animal, Man.'

The career of these wretches, who had neither ' minds ' nor ' souls,' was one long campaign against ravenous beasts and their ' brother ' man-brutes. Peace was never anything to them but a fitful interval of repose. The golden age of the poets was a dream ; as Videlou remarked, ' Peace means death for all barbarian races.' The existence of our earliest ancestors was literally the Battle of Life. Then, as now, the Great Gaster was the first Master of Arts, and War was the natural condition of humanity upon which depends the greater part of its progress, its rising from the lower to the higher grade. Hobbism, after all, is partly right : ' Men were by nature equal, and their only social relation was a state of war.' Like the children of our modern day, helpless and speechless, primæval Homo possessed, in common with his fellow-creatures, only the instincts necessary for self-support under conditions the most facile. Uncultivated thought is not rich in the productive faculty ; the brain does not create ideas : it only combines them and evolves the novelty of deduction, and the development of what is found existing. Similarly in language, onomatopœia, the imitation of natural sounds, the speech of Man's babyhood, still endures ; and to it we owe our more picturesque and life-life expressions. But, despite their feeble powers, compulsory instruction, the Instructor being Need, was continually urging the Savage and the Barbarian to evolve safety out of danger, comfort out of its contrary.

For man, compelled by necessity of his nature to weapon himself, bears within

---

[1] Ammianus Marcellinus (xxiii. chap. 4), quoted in chap. 2.

[2] *Odyss.* xviii. 130, 131. 'Qui multum peregrinatur, rarò sanctificatur,' said the theologians. Hence the modern :—

> Whoso wanders like Ulysses
> Soon shall lose his prejudices.

him the two great principles of Imitation and Progress. Both are, after a fashion, his peculiar attributes, being rudimentary amongst the lower animals, though by no means wholly wanting. His capacity of language, together with secular development of letters and literature, enabled him to accumulate for himself, and to transmit to others, a store of experience acquired through the medium of the senses ; and this, once gained, was never wholly lost. By degrees immeasurably slower than among civilised societies, the Savage digested and applied to the Present and to the Future the hoarded wisdom of the Past. The imitative faculty, a preponderating advantage of the featherless biped over the quadruped, taught the former, even in his infancy, to borrow *ad libitum*, while he lent little or nothing. As a quasi-solitary Hunter[1] he was doomed to fray and foray, to destroying others in order to preserve himself and his family : a condition so constant and universal as to include all others. Become a Shepherd, he fought man and beast to preserve and increase his flocks and herds ; and rising to an Agriculturist, he was ever urged to break the peace by greed of gain, by ambition, and by the instinctive longing for excitement.[2]

But there was no absolute point of separation, as far as the material universe is concerned, to mark the dawn of a new ' creative period '; and the *Homo Darwiniensis* made by the Aristotle of our age, the greatest of English naturalists, is directly connected with the *Homo sapiens*. There are hosts of imitative animals, birds as well as beasts ; but the copying-power is essentially limited. Moreover, it is 'instinctive,' the work of the undeveloped, as opposed to 'reasoning,' the process of the highly-developed brain and nervous system. Whilst man has taught himself to articulate, to converse, the dog, which only howled and whined, has learned nothing except to bark. Man, again, is capable of a development whose bounds we are unable to determine ; whereas the beast, incapable of self-culture, progresses, under the most favourable circumstances, automatically and within comparatively narrow bounds.

Upon the imitative faculty and its exercise I must dwell at greater length. It is regretable that the delicious wisdom of Pope neglected to point out the great lesson of the animal-world in suggesting and supplying the arts of offence and defence :—

> Go, from the creatures thy instructions take . . .
> Thy arts of building from the bee receive ;
> Learn from the mole to plough, the worm to weave ;

[1] Sir John Lubbock has calculated that among the North American savages the proportion of man to the animals which feed him is 1 to 750 ; and, as the hunter is at least four times as long-lived as his prey, the ratio might be increased, 1 to 3000. If this were so, and all the bones were preserved, there would be 3,000 bestial skeletons to one human. Without assuming with Mr. Evans (p. 584) that ' respect for the dead may be regarded as almost instinctive in man,' and that human remains would be buried, we here find one cause of the present insufficiency of the geologic record.

[2] M. Eduard Pietri distributes Prehistoric Archeology proper into two ages, the Agreutic and the Georgic. Under the former he classifies the Barylithic (glacial Drift age) and the Leptolithic. Under the Georgic are included the Neolithic, the Chalcitic (copper and bronze), and the Proto-sideric.

> Learn from the little nautilus to sail,
> Spread the thin oar, and catch the driving gale.[1]

Man, especially in the tropical and sub-tropical zones—his early, if not his earliest, home, long ago whelmed beneath the ocean waves—would derive many a useful hint from the dreadful armoury of equinoctial vegetation ; the poison-trees the large strong spines of the Acacia and the Mimosa, *e.g.* the Wait-a-bit (*Acacia detinens*), the Gleditschia, the Socotrine Aloe, the American Agave, and the piercing thorns of the *Caryota urens,* and certain palms. The aboriginal races would be further instructed in offensive and defensive arts by the powerful and destructive *feræ* of the sunny river-plains, where the Savage was first induced to build permanent abodes.

Before noting the means of attack and protection which Nature suggested, we may distribute Hoplology, the science of arms and weapons of offence and defence, human and bestial, into two great orders, of which the latter can be subdivided into four species :—

1. *Missile.*
2. *Armes d'hast.—a.* Percussive or striking ; *b.* Thrusting, piercing, or ramming ; *c.* Cutting or ripping ; *d.* Notched or serrated.

Colonel A. Lane Fox ('Prim. Warfare,' p. 11) thus classifies the weapons of 'Animals and Savages' :—

Defensive.	*Offensive.*	*Stratagems.*
Hides	Piercing	Flight
Solid plates	Striking	Ambush
Jointed plates	Serrated	Tactics
Scales	Poisoned	Columns
	Missiles	Leaders
		Outposts
		Artificial defences
		War cries

My list is less comprehensive, and it bears only upon the origin of the *Arme blanche.*

I. As has been said, the missile, the βέλος, is probably the first form of weapon, and is still the favourite with savage Man. It favours the natural self-preservative instinct. *El-Khauf maksúm*—'fear is distributed,'—say the Arabs. 'The shorter the weapon the braver the wielder' has become a well-established fact. The savage Hunter, whose time is his own, would prefer the missile ; but the Agriculturist, compelled to be at home for seed-time and harvest, would choose the hand-to-hand

---

[1] *Essay on Man,* iii. 172–6.

weapon which shortens action. We may hold, without undue credulity, that the throwing-arm is common to beasts, after a fashion, and to man. Among the so-called 'missile fishes'[1] the Toxotes,[2] or Archer, unerringly brings down insects with a drop of water when three or four feet high in the air. The Chætodon, or archer fish of Japan, is kept in a glass vase, and fed by holding flies at the end of rod a few inches above the surface: it strikes them with an infallible aim. This process is repeated, among the mammalia, by the Llama, the Guanaco and their congeners, who propel their acrid and fetid saliva for some distance and with excellent aim.[3] And stone-throwing held its own for many an age, as we read in the fifteenth century :—

> Use eke the cast of stone with slynge or honde ;
> It falleth ofte, yf other shot there none is,
> Men harneysèd in steel may not withstonde
> The multitude and mighty cast of stonys.[4]

II. The stroke or blow which led to the cut would be seen exemplified in the felidæ, by the terrible buffet of the lion, by the clawing of the tiger and the bear, and by the swing of the trunk of the ' half-reasoner with the hand.' Man also would observe that the zebra and the quagga (so called from its cry, *wag-ga, wag-ga*[5]), the horse and the ass, the camel, the giraffe, and even the cow, defend themselves with the kick or hoof-blow ; while the ostrich, the swan, and the larger birds of prey assault with a flirt or stroke of the wing. The aries or sea-ram (*Delphinus orca*) charges with a butt. The common whale raises the head with such force that it has been held capable of sinking a whaler: moreover, this mammal uses the huge caudal fin or tail in battle with man and beast ; for instance, when engaged with the fox-shark or thresher (*Carcharias vulpes*).[6] These, combined with the force of man's doubled fist, would suggest the 'noble art' of boxing : it dates from remote antiquity ; witness the cestus or knuckle-duster of the classics, Greeks, Romans, and Lusitanians. So far from being confined to Great or Greater Britain, as some suppose, it is still a favourite not only with the Russian peasants, but also with the

---

[1] The sepia (squid, cuttle-fish, *Loligo vulgaris*) defends itself by discharging its ' ink-bag ' embedded in the liver, and escapes in the blackened water. This is as true a defence as a shield.

[2] From the Greek τὸ τόξον, the bow (and arrow, *Iliad*, viii. 296), which seems to be a congener of the Latin *taxus*, the yew-tree, a favourite material for the weapon. Hence *taxus*, like the Scandinavian *ír* or *ýr*, the Keltic *jubar*, and the Slavonian *tisu*, all meaning the yew-tree, denote the bow as well. The Skalds called the bow also *almr* (elm-tree), and *askr*, or mountain-ash, the μελία, which the Greeks applied to the spear. From τόξον came τοξικὸν, ' arrow-poison, the Latin *toxicum*, whose use survives in our exaggerated term ' intoxicating liquors.

[3] This I know to my cost, having offended a Guanaco at Cordova, in the Argentine Republic ; it straightway spat in my face with unpleasantly good aim.

[4] Strutt, *Sports and Pastimes*, ii. chap. 2.

[5] Not unlike the name of a certain Australian Wagga-Wagga which has been heard in the English law-courts.

[6] In *Land and Water* doubts have been thrown upon these single combats of the whale and thresher. See the late Mr. Buckland's papers (October 2, 1880) ; Lord Archibald Campbell's sketch ; and the same paper, February 26, 1881. Those on board the wrecked cruiser H.M.S. *Griffon*, myself included, witnessed a fight between whale and shark in the Bay of Biafra (1862 ?). The Carcharias family takes its name from the sharp and jagged teeth, ἀπὸ τῶν καρχαρῶν ὀδόντων.

Hausas, Moslem negroids who did such good service in the Ashanti war. A curious survival of the feline armature is the Hindu's Wágh-nakh. Following Demmin, Colonel A. Lane Fox [1] was in error when he described this 'tiger's-claw' as 'an Indian weapon of treachery belonging to a secret society, and invented about A.D. 1659.' Demmin [2] as erroneously attributes the Wágh-nakh to Sívají, the Prince of Marátha-land in Western India, who traitorously used it upon Afzal Khan, the Moslem General of Aurangzeb, sent (A.D. 1659) to put down his rebellion.[3] A meeting of the chiefs was agreed upon, and the Moslem, quitting his army, advanced with a single servant; he wore a thin robe, and carried only a straight sword. Sívají, descending from the fort, assumed a timid and hesitating air, and to all appearance was unarmed. But he wore mail under his flimsy white cotton coat, and besides a concealed dagger, he carried his 'tiger's-claw.' The Khan looked with contempt at the crouching and diminutive 'mountain rat,' whom the Moslems threatened to bring back in cages; but, at the moment of embracing, the Marátha

FIG. 1.—INDIAN WÁGH-NAKH.   FIG. 2.—WÁGH-NAKH, USED BY MARÁTHÁS (India Museum.)

struck his Wágh-nakh into his adversary's bowels and despatched him with his dagger. The Wágh-nakh in question is still kept as a relic, I am told, by the Bhonslá family.[4] Outside the hand you see nothing but two solid gold rings encircling the index and the minimus; these two are joined inside by a steel bar, which serves as a connecting base to three or four sharp claws, thin enough to fit between and to be hidden by the fingers of a half-closed hand. The attack is by

[1] *Anthrop. Collection*, p. 180. Demmin, however, is additionally incorrect by making the article 'two and a half feet in length' (*Arms and Armour*, p. 413, Bell's edition, London, 1877). In *Catalogue of Indian Art in the South Kensington Museum*, by Lieut. H. H. Cole, R.E. (p. 313), Sívají is made to murder the Moslem with the 'bíchwa,' or scorpion, a 'curved double blade.' This probably refers to the dagger which made 'sicker.'

[2] P. 402, where he calls 'Sívají' *Sevaja*.

[3] Elphinstone's *History*, ii. 468.

[4] It is, they say, adored at the old fortress and Marátha capital, Sattára (= Sát-istara, the seven stars or Pleiades). Here, too, is Sívají's Sword 'Bhawáni,' a Genoa blade of great length and fine temper. Mrs. Guthrie, who saw the latter, describes it (vol. i. p. 426) as a 'fine Ferrara (?) blade, four feet in length, with a spike upon the hilt to thrust with.' She also notices the smallness of the grip. The Indian

Museum of South Kensington contains a bracelet of seven tiger's-claws mounted in gold, with a claw clasp (No. 593, 1868). M. Rousselet, who visited Baroda in 1864, describes in his splendid volume one of the Gaekhwar or Baroda Rajah's favourite *spectacula*, the 'naki-ka-kausti' (kushti). The nude combatants were armed with 'tiger's-claws' of horn; formerly, when these were of steel, the death of one of the athletes was unavoidable. The weapons, fitted into a kind of handle, were fastened by thongs to the closed right hand. The men, drunk with Bhang or Indian hemp, rushed upon each other and tore like tigers at face and body; forehead-skins would hang in shreds; necks and ribs would be laid open, and not unfrequently one or both would bleed to death. The ruler's excitement on these occasions often grew to such a pitch that he could scarcely restrain himself from imitating the movements of the duellists.

ripping open the belly: and I have heard of a poisoned Wágh-nakh which may have been suggested by certain poison rings in ancient and mediæval Europe.[1] The date of invention is absolutely unknown, and a curious and instructive modification of it was made by those Indians-in-Europe, the Gypsies.

III. The thrust would be suggested by the combats of the goat, the stag, and black cattle, including the buffalo and the wild bull, all of which charge at speed with the head downwards, and drive the horns into the enemy's body. The gnu (*Catoblepas G.*) and other African antelopes, when pressed by the hunter, keep him at bay with the point. In Europe 'hurt of hart,' a ripping and tearing thrust, has brought many a man to the grave. The hippopotamus, a dangerous animal unduly despised, dives under the canoe, like the walrus, rises suddenly, and with its lower tusks, of the hardest ivory, drills two holes in the offending bottom. The black rhinoceros, fiercest and most irritable of African fauna, though graminivorous, has one or two horns of wood-like fibre-bundles resting upon the strongly-arched nasal bones, and attached by an extensive apparatus of muscles and tendons. This armature, loose when the beast is at peace, becomes erect and immovable in rage, thus proving in a special manner its only use—that of war. It is a formidable dagger that tears open the elephant and passes through the saddle and its padding into the ribs of a horse. The extinct sabre-toothed tiger (*Machairodus latidens*), with one incisor and five canines, also killed with a thrust. So, amongst birds, the bittern, the peacock, and the American white crane peck or stab at the eye ; the last-named has been known to drive its long sharp mandibles deep into the pursuer's bowels, and has been caught by presenting to it a gun-muzzle : the bird, mistaking the hole, strikes at it and is caught by the beak.[2] The hern defends herself during flight by presenting the sharp long beak to the falcon. The pheasant and partridge, the domestic cock and quail, to mention no others, use their spurs with a poniard's thrust ; the Argus-pheasant of India, the American Jacaná (*Parra*), the horned screamer (*Palamedea*), the wing-wader of Australia (Gregory), and the plover of Central Africa (Denham and Claperton), carry weapons upon their wings.

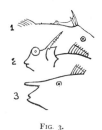

According to Pliny (viii. 38) the dolphins which enter the Nile are armed with a knife-edged spur on the back to protect themselves from the crocodiles. Cuvier refers this allusion to the *Squalus centrina* or *Spinax* of Linnæus. The European 'file-fish' (*Balistes capriscus*), found in a fossil state, and still existing, though rare in British waters, remarkably shows the efficiency, beauty, and variety of that order's armature. It pierces its enemy from beneath by a strong erectile and cirrated spine on the first anterior dorsal ; the base of the spear is expanded and perforated, and a bolt from the supporting plate passes freely through it.

FIG. 3.

1. BALISTES CAPRISCUS ;
2. COTTUS DICERAUS ;
3. NASEUS FRONTICORNIS.

---

[1] Pliny, xxxii. 6.   [2] Thompson's *Passions of Animals*, p. 225.

When the spine is raised, a hollow at the back receives a prominence from the next bony ray, which fixes the point in an erect position. Like the hammer of a fire-piece at full cock, the spear cannot be forced down till the prominence is withdrawn, as by pulling the trigger. This mechanism, says the learned and experienced Professor Owen,[1] may be compared with the fixing and unfixing of a bayonet: when the spine is bent down it is received into a groove in the supporting plate, and thus it offers no impediment to swimming.

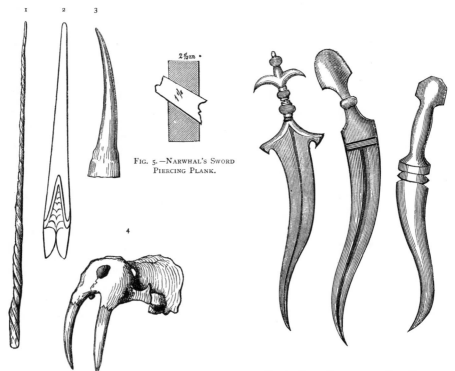

FIG. 5.—NARWHAL'S SWORD
PIERCING PLANK.

FIG. 6.—METAL DAGGERS WITH HORN CURVE.

FIG. 4.—1. SPEAR OF NARWHAL; 2. SWORD OF
XIPHIAS; 3. RHINOCEROS-HORN; 4. WALRUS
TUSKS.

The pugnacious and voracious little 'stickleback' (*Gasterosteus*) is similarly provided. The 'bull-head' (*Cottus diceraus*, Pallas [2]) bears a multibarbed horn on its dorsum, exactly resembling the spears of the Eskimos and the savages of South America and Australia. The yellow-bellied 'surgeon' or lancet-fish (*Acanthurus*) is armed, in either ocean, with a long spine on each side of the tail; with this lance it defends itself dexterously against its many enemies. The *Naseus fronticornis* (Lacépède) bears, besides the horn-muzzle, trenchant spear-formed blades in the

----

[1] *Comparative Anatomy and Physiology of Vertebrates*, i. 193.   [2] *Prim. Warfare*, i. p. 22.

pointed and serrated tail. The sting-fish or adder-pike (*Trachinus vipera*) has necessitated amputation of the wounded limb: the dorsals, as well as the opercular spines, have deep double grooves in which the venomous mucous secretion is lodged—a hint to dagger-makers. The sting-rays (*Raia trygon* and *R. histrix*[1]) twist the long slender tail round the object of attack and cut the surface with the strong notched and spiny edge, inflicting a wound not easily healed. The sting, besides being poisonous, has the especial merit of breaking off in the wound: it is extensively used by the savages of the Fiji, the Gambier, and the Pellew Islands, of Tahiti, Samoa, and many of the Low Islands.[2] These properties would suggest poisoned weapons which cannot be extracted. Such are the arrows of the Bushman, the Shoshoni, and the Macoinchi of Guiana, culminating in the highly-civilised stiletto of hollow glass.

The sword-fish (*Xiphias*), although a vegetable feeder, is men-tioned by Pliny (xxxii. 6) as able to sink a ship. It is recorded to have killed a man when bathing in the Severn near Worcester. It attacks the whale, and it has been known to transfix a vessel's side with its terrible weapon. The narwhal or sea-uni-corn (*Monodon mo-noceros*) carries a formidable tusk, a Sword-blade of the same kind similarly used.[3]

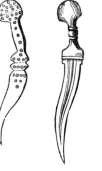

Fig. 7.—Mádu or Máru.

Here may be offered a single proof how Man, living among, and dependent for food upon, the lower animals, borrowed from their habits and experience his earliest practice of offence and defence. The illustration represents a 'Singhauta,'[4] 'Mádu' or 'Máru' (double dagger), made from the horns of the common Indian antelope, connected by crossbars. In its rude state, and also tipped with metal, it is still used as a weapon by

[1] *Prim. Warfare*, i. p. 21.

[2] *Ibid.* ii. p. 22.

[3] The spiral horn is shown by Colonel Yule (*Marco Polo*, ii. 273, second edition) in an illustra-tion as 'Monoceros and the Maiden.' The animal, however, appears from the short tail to be a tapir, not a rhinoceros. That learned and exact writer remarks that the unicorn supporter of the Royal

Arms retains the narwhal horn. The main use of the latter in commerce is to serve as a core for the huge wax-candles lighted during the ceremonies of the Roman Catholic Church.

[4] So it is called in the Catalogue of the India Museum at South Kensington ; the derivation is evidently from the Hindostani *singh*, a horn.

the wild Bhíls, and as a crutch and dagger by the Jogis (Hindús) and Fakirs (Hindís or Moslems), both orders of religious mendicants who are professionally forbidden to carry secular arms. It also served for defence, like the parrying-stick of Africa and Australia, till it was fitted with a hand-guard, and the latter presently expanded into a circular targe of metal. This ancient instrument, with its graceful curves, shows four distinct stages of development: first, the natural, and, secondly, the early artificial, with metal caps to make it a better thrusting weapon. The third process was to forge the whole of metal; and the fourth and final provided it with a straight, broad blade, springing at right angles from the central grip. This was the 'Adaga'[1] of mediæval writers.

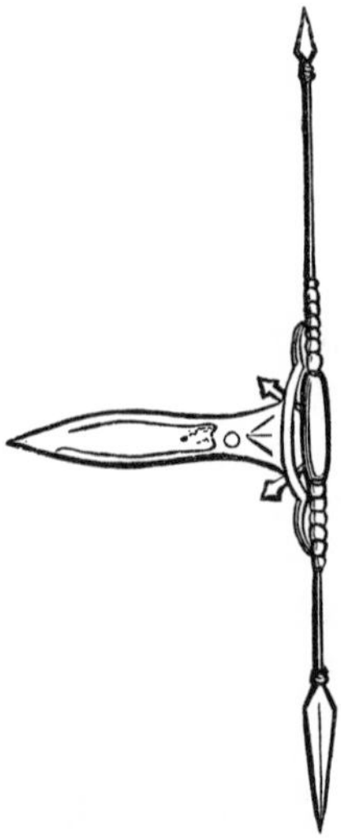

IV. The first idea of a trenchant or cutting instrument would be suggested by various reeds and grasses; their silicious leaves at certain angles cleave to the bone, as experience has taught most men who have passed through a jungle of wild sugar-cane. When full-grown the plants stand higher than a man's head, and the flint-edged leaves disposed in all directions suggest a labyrinth of sword-blades. Thus the Mawingo-wingo (*Pennisetum Benthami*), like the horse-tail or 'shave-grass' of Spain, was used as knives by the executioners of Kings Sunna and Mtesa of Uganda, when cutting the human victims to pieces.[2] Of the same kind are the 'sword-grass' and the 'bamboo-grass.' Many races, especially the Andamanese and the Polynesian Islanders, make useful blades of the split and sharpened bamboo: they are fashioned from the green plant, and are dried and charred to sharpen the edge. Turning to the animal world, the cassowary tears with a forward cut, and the wounded coot scratches like a cat. The 'old man kangaroo,' with the long nail of the powerful hind leg, has opened the stomach of many a staunch hound. The wild boar attacks with a thrust, followed by a rip, cutting scientifically from below upwards. This, as will appear, is precisely the plan adopted by certain ancient forms of sabre, Greek and barbarian, the cutting edges being inside, not outside, the curve. I may add that the old attack is one of our latest improvements in broadsword exercise.[3]

FIG. 8.—THE ADAGA.

---

[1] Boutell (*Arms and Armour*, fig. 61, p. 269) engraves a parrying weapon with a blade at right angles to the handle. He calls it a 'Moorish Adargue' (fifteenth century). The latter word (with the *r*) is simply the Arabic word *el-darakah*, a shield, the origin of our 'targe' and 'target.' The adaga (not *adarga*, cantos i. 87, viii. 29) with which Camoens in *The Lusiads* (ii. 95, &c.) arms the East Africans is a weapon of the Mádu kind. I have translated it 'dag-targe,' because in that part of the world it combines poniard and buckler. The savage and treacherous natives of the Solomon Islands (San Christoval, &c.) still use a nondescript weapon, half Sword and half shield, some six feet long.

[2] Captain Speke's *Discovery of the Source of the Nile*, p. 652 (Edinburgh : Blackwoods, 1863).

[3] In the form called *Manchette*, or cutting at hand, wrist, and forearm with the inner edge. It is copiously described in iv. 45–54 of my *New System of Sword Exercise*, &c. (London : Clowes, 1876).

The offensive weapon of the sting-ray, and of various insects, as well as the teeth of all animals, man included, furnish models for serrated or saw-edged instruments.   Hence Colonel A. Lane Fox observes : [1] 'It is not surprising that the first efforts of mankind in the construction of trenchant instruments should so universally consist of teeth, or flint-flakes, arranged along the edge of staves.'   But evidently the knife preceded the saw, which is nothing but a knife-blade jagged.

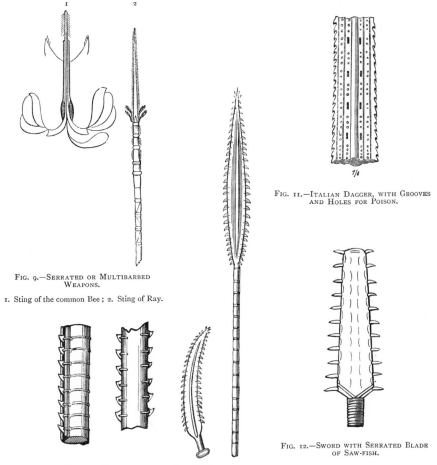

FIG. 9.—SERRATED OR MULTIBARBED WEAPONS.

1. Sting of the common Bee ; 2. Sting of Ray.

FIG. 11.—ITALIAN DAGGER, WITH GROOVES AND HOLES FOR POISON.

FIG. 10.—WEAPONS MADE OF SHARKS' TEETH.

FIG. 12.—SWORD WITH SERRATED BLADE OF SAW-FISH.

Other familiar instances would be the multibarb stings of insects, especially that of the common bee.   Again, we have the mantis, an orthopter of the Temperates and the Tropics, whose fights, enjoyed by the Chinese, are compared with the duels of sabrers.   For the rasping blow and parry they use the forearm, which carries rows of strong sharp spines ; and a happy stroke beheads or bisects the antagonist. To this category belongs the armature of the saw-fish (*Pristis*), a shark widely

[1] *Primitive Warfare*, p. 24.

distributed and haunting the arctic, temperate, and tropical seas. Its mode of offence is to spring high from the water and to fall upon the foe, not with the point, but with either edge of its formidable arm : the row of strong and trenchant barbs, set like teeth, cuts deeply into the whale's flesh. Hence, in New Guinea, the serrated blade becomes a favourite Sword, the base of the snout being cut and rounded so as to form a handle.

Thus man, essentially a tool-making animal, and compelled by the conditions of his being to one long battle with the brute creation, was furnished by his enemies, not only with models of implements and instruments, and with instructions to use them, from witnessing the combats of brutes, but actually with their arms, which he converted to his own purposes. Hence the weapon and the tool were, as a rule, identical in the hands of primeval man ; and this forms, perhaps, the chief test of a primitive invention. The earliest drift-flints ' were probably used as weapons both of war and the chase, to grub roots, to cut down trees, and to scoop out canoes.'[1] The Watúsi of Eastern Africa make their baskets with their sharpened spear-heads ; and the so-called Káfirs (Amazulu, &c.) still shave themselves with the assegai. Hence, too, as like conditions engender like results, the arms and implements of different races resemble one another so closely as to suggest a common origin and actual imitation, even where copying was, so to speak, impossible.

Let us take as an instance two of the most widespread of weapons. The blow-pipe's progressive form has been independently developed upon a similar plan, with distinctly marked steps, in places the most remote.[2] Another instance is the chevaux-de-frise, the spikes of metal familiar to the classics.[3] They survive in the caltrops or bamboo splints planted in the ground by the barefooted Mpangwe (Fans) of Gaboon-land and by the Rangos of Malacca.

---

[1] Sir Charles Lyell, *Geological Evidences of Antiquity of Man*, p. 13 (London : Murray, 1863). Dr. W. Lauder Lindsay (*Proc. Soc. Ant. Scot.* vol. v. p. 327) says of the Maori *tokis* or stone-hatchets, they were used chiefly for cutting down timber and for scooping canoes out of the trunks of forest trees ; for driving posts for huts ; for grubbing up roots, and killing animals for food ; for preparing firewood ; for scraping the flesh from the bones when eating, and for various other purposes in the domestic arts. But they were also employed in times of war as weapons of offence and defence, as a supplementary kind of tomahawk.

[2] The French *sarbacane*, the Italian and Spanish *cerbotana*, the Portuguese *gravatana*, and the German *Blasrohr* (blow-tube) is, according to Demmin (p. 468), *arbotana*, or rather *carpicanna*, derived from ' Carpi,' the place of manufacture, and the Assyrian (*Kane*), Greek and Latin κάννα (*canna*), whence ' cannon.' This tube, spread over three distinct racial areas in Southern Asia, Africa, and America, is used either for propelling clay balls or arrowlets, poisoned

and unpoisoned. It is the sumpitan of Borneo, where Pigafetta (1520) mentions reeds of this kind in Cayayan and Palavan Islands. The hollow bamboo is still used by the Laos of Siam, and is preserved among the Malagasy as a boyish way of killing birds. Père Bourieu notes it among the Malaccan negrito aborigines, whom the Moslem Malays call ' Oran-Banua' (men of the woods) ; the weapon they term *tomeang*. It is known in Ceylon, in Silhet, and on both sides of the Bay of Bengal. Condamine describes it among the Yameos (South American Indians) ; Waterlow and Klemm, in New Guinea, and Markham among the Uapes and other tribes on the Amazonas head-waters. In the New World it is of two varieties : the long heavy zarabatana, and the thinner, slighter pucuna. Finally, it has degraded to the ' pea-shooter ' of modern Europe. The principal feature of the weapon is the poisoned dart ; it is therefore unknown amongst tribes who, like the Andamanese, have not studied toxics (*Journ. Anthrop. Inst.* p. 270, February 1882).

[3] See the *hamus ferreus* pointed at both ends in

In the early days of anthropological study we read complaints that 'it is impossible to establish, amongst the implements of modern savages, a perfectly true sequence,' although truth may be arrived at in points of detail ; and that 'in regard to the primary order of development, much must still be left open to conjecture.' But longer labour and larger collections have lately added many a link to the broken chain of continuity. We can now trace with reasonable certainty the tardy progress of evolution which, during a long succession of ages, led to the systematised art of war. The conditions of the latter presently allowed society periods of rest, or rather of recovery ; and more leisure for the practice which, in weapons as in other things, 'maketh perfect.'[1] And man has no idea of finality : he will stop short of nothing less than the absolutely perfect. He will labour at the ironclad as he did the canoe ; at the fish-torpedo as he did the petard.[2]

From the use of arms, also, arose the rudimentary arts of savage man. Music began when he expressed his joy and his sorrow by cries of emotion—the voice being the earliest, as it is still the best, of music-makers. It was followed by its imitations, which pass through three several stages, and even now we know nothing more in the way of development.[3] When the savage clapped together two clubs he produced the first or drum-type ; when he hissed or whistled he originated the pipe-type (syrinx, organ, bagpipe, &c.) ; and the twanging of his bow suggested the lyre-type, which we still find—'tickling the dried guts of a mewing cat.'[4] Painting and sculpture were the few simple lines drawn and cut upon the tomahawk or other rude weapon-tool. 'As men think and live so they build,' said Herder ; and architecture, which presently came to embrace all the other arts, dawned when the Savage attempted to defend and to adorn his roost among the tree branches or the entrance to his cave-den.[5]

After this preamble, which has been longer than I expected, we pass to the first or rudest forms of the Weapons Proper used by Savage Man.

Demmin (p. 124) ; and the German *Fussängel* (p. 465). The larger caltrop was called *tribulus, stylus* or *stilus* (Veget. *De Re Mil.* iii. 24). The knights of mediæval Europe planted their spurs rowels upwards to serve the same purpose.

[1] 'Make your hand perfect by a third attempt,' said Timocrates in Athenæus, i. cap. 4.

[2] 'Hitherto,' remarks Colonel A. Lane Fox, 'Providence operates directly on the work to be performed by means of the living animated tool ; henceforth it operates indirectly on the progress and development of creation, first through the agency of the instinctively tool-using savage, and, by degrees, of the intelligent and reasoning man.'

[3] J. F. Rowbotham : 'Certain reasons for believing that the Art of Music, in prehistoric times, passed through three distinct stages of development, each characterised by the invention of a new form of instrument ; and that these stages succeeded one another in the same order in various parts of the world' (*Journ. Anthrop. Inst.* May 1881). The author states that the Veddahs (properly Vædiminissu, or 'sportsmen') of Ceylon, the Mincopis (Andamans), and the people of Tierra del Fuego 'have no musical instruments at all.'

[4] *Opuscula fidicularum,* &c. (London : Mitchell and Hughes).

[5] *Specus erant pro domibus.* Caverns appear to be divisible into three classes : dwelling-places—including refuges, where, as Prometheus says (i. 452), 'Men lived like little ants beneath the ground in the gloomy recesses of grots'—storehouses, and sepulchres. All were in Lyell's third phase. The first was when the rock began to form the channel by dissolution ; the second, when a regular river flowed ; and the third, when earth and air, instead of water, filled the bed.

CHAPTER II.

MAN'S FIRST WEAPONS—THE STONE AND THE STICK. THE EARLIEST AGES
OF WEAPONS. THE AGES OF WOOD, OF BONE, AND OF HORN.

WHAT, then, was Man's first weapon? He was born speechless and helpless, inferior to the beasts of the field. He grew up armed, but badly armed. His muscles may have been stronger than they are now; his poor uneducated fisti-cuff, however, could not have compared with the kick of an ass. As we see from the prognathous jaw, he could bite, and his teeth were doubtless excellent [1]; still, the size and shape of the maxilla rendered it an arm inferior to the hyæna's and even to the dog's. He scratched and tore, as women still do; but his nails could hardly have been more dangerous than the claws of the minor felines.

He had, however, the hand, the most perfect of all prehensile contrivances, and Necessity compelled him to use it. The stone, his first 'weapon,' properly so called, would serve him in two ways—as a missile, and as a percussive instrument. Our savage progenitor, who in days long before the dawn of history, contracted the extensor and relaxed the flexor muscles of his arm when flinging into air what he picked up from the ground, was unconsciously lengthening his reach and taking the first step in the art and science of ballistics. His descendants would acquire extraordinary skill in stone-throwing, and universal practice would again make perfect. Diodorus of Sicily (B.C. 44),[2] who so admirably copied Herodotus, says that the Libyans 'use neither Swords, spears, nor other weapons; but only three darts and stones in certain leather budgets, wherewith they fight in pursuing and retreating.' The Wánshi (Guanches) Libyan or Berber peoples of the Canarian Archipelago, according to Cà da Mosto (A.D. 1505), confirmed by many, including George Glas,[3] were expert stone-throwers. They fought their duels 'in the public

---

[1] Aristotle Darwin holds (sorrow! that we should say 'held'): 'Our male semi-human progenitors possessed great canine teeth,' as is still shown by a few exceptional individuals. Hence we derived the trick of uncovering the eye-tooth when sneering or snarling at 'Brother Man.'

[2] Quoted from Mr. Edward T. Stevens in *Flint Chips*; Col. A. Lane Fox (*Catal.* p. 158).

[3] *History of the Discovery and Conquest of the Canary Islands*, which dates from 1792. The unfortunate 'master-mariner' (see my *Wanderings in*

West Africa, i. 116) borrows from the Spanish of Abreu-Galindo. Mr. F. W. Newman (*Libyan Vocabulary*: Trübner, 1882) has illustrated the four Libyan languages—the Algerian Kabáil (ancient Numidian), the Moroccan Shilhá (Mauritanian), the Ghadamsi (of which we know little), and the Tuárik (guides), or Tarkiya (Gætulian). 'Guanche' is a corruption of *guan* (Berber *wan*), 'one person,' and *Chinet*, or Tenerife Island; *guan-chinet*, meaning 'a man of Tenerife.' I have returned to this subject in my last book on the Gold Coast (i. chap. 5).

place, where the combatants mounted upon two stones placed at the opposite sides of it, each stone being flat at top and about half a yard in diameter. On these they stood fast without moving their feet, till each had thrown three round stones at his antagonist. Though they were good marksmen, yet they generally avoided those missive weapons by the agile writhing of their bodies. Then arming themselves with sharp flints (obsidian?) in their left hands, and cudgels or clubs in their right, they fell on, beating and cutting each other till they were tired.' An instance is mentioned in which a Guanche brought down with a single throw a large palm-frond, whose mid-rib was capable of resisting the stroke of an axe. Kolben, who wrote about a century and a half ago, gives the following account of the ape-like gestures of the Khoi-Khoi or Hottentots [1]:—'The most surprising strokes of their dexterity are seen in their throwing of a stone. They hit a mark to a miracle of exactness, though it be a hundred paces distant and no bigger than a halfpenny. I have beheld them at this exercise with the highest pleasure and astonishment, and was never weary of the spectacle. I still expected after repeated successes, that the stone would err ; but I expected in vain. Still went the stone right to the mark, and my pleasure and astonishment were redoubled. You could imagine that the stone was not destined to err, or that you were not destined to see it. But a Hottentot's unerring hand in this exercise is not the only wonder of the scene ; you would be equally struck perhaps with the manner in which he takes his aim. He stands, not still with a lift-up arm and a steady staring eye upon the mark, as we do ; but is in constant motion, skipping from one side to another, suddenly stooping, suddenly rising ; now bending on this side, now on that ; his eyes, hands, and feet are in constant action, and you would think that he was playing the fool, and minding anything else than his aim ; when on a sudden, away goes the stone with a fury, right to the heart of the mark, as if some invisible power had directed it.'

Nearer home the modern Syrians still preserve their old dexterity : I have often heard the tale, and have no reason to doubt its truth, of a brown bear (*Ursus syriacus*) being killed in the Libanus by a blow between the eyes.[2] When the Arab Bedawin are on the raid and do not wish to use their matchlocks, they attack at night, and 'rain stones' upon the victim. The latter vainly discharges

[1] The word, also written 'Hüttentüt,' and originally Dutch, is supposed to be an uncomplimentary imitation of the cluck-like or smack-like 'sonant,' which characterises their complicated and difficult language, and which has infected the neighbouring sections of the great South African family of speech. The Hottentots had already reached the pastoral stage when first visited by Europeans ; whereas the Bushmans then, as now, were huntsmen. Some derive the Hottentot-Bushman 'click' from the Egyptian article T (á). But Klaproth found it in Circassia, Whitmee amongst the Melanesian Negritos, and Haldeman amongst certain North American tribes. Professor Mahaffy notices that 'old women among us express pity by a regular palatal click.' On the continent of Europe it expresses a kind of 'Don't-you-wish-you-may-get-it ?' Dr. Hahn, who has lately published a scientific work upon the Khoi-Khoi, favourably reviewed by Professor Max Müller in the *Nineteenth Century*, has treated the subject exhaustively.

[2] I can bear personal witness to the prowess of the ruffians of Nazareth, who call themselves, most falsely, Greeks. In 1871, when encamped near the village, three of my servants were so severely wounded with hand-stones that one was nearly killed.

his ammunition against the shadows flitting ghost-like among the rocks ; and, when his fire is drawn, the murderers rush in and finish their work. The use of the stone amongst the wild tribes of Asia, Africa, and America is almost universal. In Europe, the practice is confined to schoolboys ; but the wild Irish, by beginning early, become adepts in it when adults. As a rule, the shepherd is everywhere a skilful stone-thrower.

Turner makes the 'Kawas' of Tanna, New Hebrides, a stone as long as, and twice as thick as, an ordinary counting-house ruler : it is thrown with great precision for a distance of twenty yards. The same author mentions stones rounded like a cannon-ball, among the people of Savage Island and Eromanga. Commander Byron notices the stones made into missiles by the Disappointment Islanders. Beechey, whose party was attacked by the Easter Islanders, says that the weapons, cast with force and accuracy, knocked several of the seamen under the boat-thwarts. Crantz tells us that Eskimo children are taught stone-throwing

FIG. 13.—ANCIENT EGYPTIANS THROWING KNIVES.

at a mark as soon as they can use their hands. The late Sir R. Schomburg describes a singular custom amongst the Demarara Indians. When a child enters boyhood he is given a hard round stone which he is to hand-rub till it becomes smooth, and he often reaches manhood before the task is done. Observers have suggested that the only use of the practice is a 'lesson in perseverance, which quality, in the opinion of many people, is best inculcated by engaging the minds of youths in matters that are devoid of any other incentive in the way of practical utility or interest.'

In more civilised times the knife, as a missile, would take the place of the stone. We find that the ancient Egyptians [1] practised at a wooden block, and the German *Helden* (champions), seated on settles, duelled by casting three knives each, to be parried with the shield. The modern Spaniards begin to learn when children the art of throwing the *facon*,[2] *cuchillo* or clasp-knife. The reapers

[1] Prof. Maspero, of Bulak, told me that he had some doubts about the correctness of Wilkinson's illustration showing 'ancient Egyptians throwing knives.'

[2] The *facon* (faulchion) is about two feet long

Both weapons are thrown in two ways. The more common is to lay the blade flat on the palm, which is narrowed by contracting the thumb and the *musculus guinearum* at the root of the little finger. The

of the Roman Campagna, mere barbarians once civilised, also ' chuck' the sickle with a surprising precision.

The habit of stone-throwing would presently lead to the invention of the sling, which Meyrick considers,[1] strange to say, the 'earliest and simplest weapon of antiquity.' The rudest form of this pastoral weapon used only on open plains, a ball and cord, was followed by the various complications of string- or thong-sling, cup-sling, and stick-sling. The latter, a split stick which held the stone till the moment of discharge, may have been the primitive arm : Lepsius shows an Egyptian using such a sling and provided with a reserve heap of pebbles. Nilsson suggests that David was thus weaponed when Goliath addressed him, 'Am I a dog that thou comest to me with staves?'—that is, with the shepherd's staff turned into a sling. And this form survived longest in the Roman 'fustibulus,' which the moderns corrupted to 'fustibale'[2] : the latter, with its wooden handle, was used in Europe during the twelfth century, and was employed in delivering hand-grenades till the sixteenth. The primitive ball-and-cord, known to the ancient Egyptians, is still preserved in the Bolas of the South American Gaucho. A simultaneously invented missile would be the hurling or throwing-stick and its modification, the Boomerang, of which I have still to speak. The application of elasticity and resilience being now well known, would suggest the rudest form of the bow[3] and arrow. This invention, next in importance (though *longo intervallo*) to fire-making and fire-feeding, is the first crucial evidence of the distinction between the human weapon and the bestial arm. Nilsson and many others hold the invention to have been instinctive and common to all peoples ; and we cannot wonder that it was made the invention of demi-gods—Nimrod, Scythes[4] the son of Jupiter, or Perses son of Perseus.[5] The missile arm at once showed man and beast separated by an extensive difference of degree, if not of kind, and it has played the most notable part, perhaps, of all weapons in the annals of humanity or inhumanity. It led to the Greek *gastrapheta*, the Roman *arcubalista* (crossbow[6]) ; to the *palintonon* or *balista*, and the arblast (an enlarged species of the *arcus*, intended for throwing darts of giant size) ; to the *Belagerungs-balister*, a fixed form ; to the catapult, *enthytonon*, *tormentum*, scorpion or *onager*,[7]

---

other is by holding the handle and causing the dart to reverse, so as to strike point foremost. The best guard is a revolver.

[1] *Critical Enquiry into Antient Armour*, &c., by Sir Samuel Rush Meyrick, Kt., preface, p. viii. (4to, 1842).

[2] It is not, as usually supposed, a 'bastard French word,' from *fustis*, a staff, and βάλλειν, to throw.

[3] Our 'bow' is the Gothic *bogo* (a bender ?), Scand. *bogi*, Dan. *buc*, and Old Germ. *poko*. (Jähns, p. 18.) The ancients made fine distinctions in slings : thus the three-thonged weapon of Ægeum, Patræ, and Dymæ was held far superior to that of the Bale-

ares ('Slinging-Isles'), which had only one strap (Livy, xxxviii. 30).

[4] Pliny, vii. 57. The legend points to the excellent archery of the Scythians (Turanians) and the Persians.

[5] Even in modern days Dr. Woodward suggests that the first model of flint arrowheads was brought from Babel, and was preserved after the dispersion of mankind. This is admirably archaic.

[6] The crossbow is apparently indigenous amongst various tribes of Indo-China, but reintroduced into European warfare during the twelfth century (Yule's *Marco Polo*, ii. 143).

[7] The military engines of the ancients were chiefly

and to other formidable forms of classical artillery which preceded the 'cheap and nasty' invention of chemical explosives.

So much for the Hand-stone as the forefather of missiles and of ballistic science. Held in the fist it would give momentum, weight and velocity, force and bruising power, to the blow. Thus it was the forerunner of the club, straight and curved ; the flail, the *bâton ferré,* the 'morning star,' the 'holy-water sprinkler,' and a host of similar weapons [1] that added another and a harder joint to man's arm. Clubs —which in practice are aimed at the head, whereas the spear is mostly directed at the body [2]—would be easily made by pulling up a straight young tree, or by tearing down a branch from the parent trunk and stripping it of twigs and leaves. The club of Australia, a continent to which we look for original forms, has the branching rootlets trimmed to serve as spikes ; moreover, the terminal bulge has been developed in order to stop or parry the assailant's weapon. In fact the swell, ball, lozenge, or mushroom-head was the first germ of the Australasian shield. The next step would be to fashion the ragged staff with fire, with friction, and with flint knives, shells or other scrapers, into a cutting as well as a crushing instrument ; and here we have one of the many origins of the Sword and of its diminutives, the dagger and the knife. Pointed at the end, it would become the lance and spear, the spud, spade, and palstave, the *pilum,* the dart, the javelin, and the assagai.

Not a few authorities contend that the earliest weapons, the most constant in all ages and continuous in all countries, were the spear and the axe. The first would be a development of the pointed hand-celt [3]; the latter of the leaf-formed or almond-shaped tool. But firstly, these would be mostly confined to countries with a well-developed Stone Age [4]; and secondly, the conversion of the hand-stone

---

on the torsion principle ; those of the mediævals were of two types, the sling and the crossbow. The 'tormentum' was so called because all its parts were twisted ; the 'scorpion' (or catapult), because the bow was vertically placed, like the insect's raised tail ; and the 'onager,' because the 'wild asses, when hunted, throw the stones behind them by their kicks, so as to pierce the chests of those who pursue them, or to fracture them.' So at least says A. Marcellinus (*Hist.* xxiii. 4). I cannot but suspect that Anna Comnena's τϵάγρα is a corruption of *onager* (Yule's *Marco Polo,* ii. 144).

[1] The National Museum of Prague, Old Graben Street, now Kolowrat, contains a fine collection of war-flails, especially the huge 'morning star' of John Zsizka, generally called Ziska.

[2] Mostly, not always, as I learnt to my cost.

[3] In a subsequent work (*Bronzes,* &c., pp. 27–30) Dr. Evans discusses the suggestions of Beger and of Mr. Knight Watson (*Proc. Soc. Ant.* 2nd S. vii. 396) that *celte* in Job is a misreading for *certe.* He justly reprobates the fashion of writing 'Kelt,' and the newly-coined French plural *celtæ.* The truth is that not a few antiquaries have confounded the instrument with the Keltic or Celtic tribes. The word, meaning a stone axe, adze, or chisel, has been erroneously derived from the Celts, property Kelts, and by older philologists *a cælando,* which would convert it into a congener of *cælum.* It is the Latin *celtis* or *celtes,* a chisel, possibly a relative of the Welsh *cellt,* a flint. The word is found, according to Mr. Evans, only in the Vulgate translation of Job, in Saint Jerome, and in a forged inscription. He first met with its antiquarian use in Beger's *Thesaurus Brandenburgicus* (1696), where a metal *securis* (axe) is called *celtes.*

[4] In 1650 Sir William Dugdale (*Hist. of Warwickshire*) spoke of stone celts as the weapons of the Ancient Britons, and in 1766 he was followed by Bishop Lyttelton. In 1797 Mr. Frere drew the attention of the Society of Antiquaries to the Drift (palæolithic) instruments occurring at Hoxne, Suffolk, together with remains of the elephant and other extinct animals. He was one of several ; but, as usually happens, the wit of one man collected and systematised the scattered experience of many. The man was M. Boucher de Perthes, whose finds in the drift-gravels of St. Acheul, near Amiens (1858), appeared in the *Antiquités Celtiques et Anté-diluviennes,* and made an epoch, changing the accepted chronology of mankind.

into an *arme d'hast* would assuredly be later than the club and the sharpened stick or stake.

Herodotus, the father of ancient history in its modern form, a travelled student and a great genius, whose prose poem—for such it is—has proved incomparably more useful to us than any works of his successors, when describing a rock-sculpture of Sesostris-Ramses (ii. 106) makes him carry in his right hand a spear (Egyptian), and in his left a bow (Lybian or Ethiopian). Hence some writers on Hoplology have held that he considered these to be the oldest of weapons. But the ancients did not study prehistoric man beyond confounding human bones with those of extinct mammals. Augustus Cæsar was an early collector, according to Suetonius

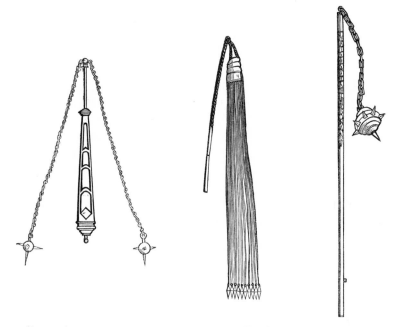

FIG. 14.—JAPANESE WAR-FLAIL.   FIG. 15.—TURKISH WAR-FLAIL.   FIG. 16.—MORNING STAR.

(in 'August.' c. xxii.). 'Sua vero . . . excoluit rebusque vetustate ac raritate notabilibus ; qualia sunt Capræis immanum belluarum ferarumque membra præ-grandia, quæ dicuntur gigantum ossa et arma heroum.'[1] The Emperor (whom the late Louis Napoleon so much resembled, even in the matter of wearing hidden armour[2]) preferred these curiosities to statues and pictures. The ancients also, like

[1] The stone-weapon was also called *betulus, belemnites,* and *ceraunius* (thunder-stone), *ceraunium* and *ceraunia.* So Claudian (*Laus Serenæ,* v. 77)—

Pyrenæisque sub antris
Ignea flumineæ legere ceraunia nymphæ.

'Fuerunt auctores' (says Aldovrandus) 'qui hunc lapi-

dem ceraunium, nempe fulminarem, indigitaverunt.' According to Skulius Thorlacius, the stone-axe typified the splitting ; the hammer, the shattering ; and the arrow, the piercing, action of the bolt (Om Thor og hans Hammer). People carried these belemnites about their persons, because lightning was supposed never to strike twice in the same place.

[2] According to Suetonius, the Roman Cæsar pre-

Marco Polo and too many of the moderns, spoke of the world generally after studying a very small part in particular. The Halicarnassian here evidently alludes to an epoch which had made notable advances upon the Quaternary Congener of the Simiads. We must return to a much earlier age. Lucretius, whose penetrating genius had a peculiar introvision, wrote like a modern scientist :—

> Arma antiqua manus, ungues dentesque fuerunt,
> Et lapides et item sylvarum fragmina rami ;
> Posterius ferri vis est, ærisque reperta,
> Sed prius æris erat, quam ferri cognitus usus. [1]

Gentleman Horace is almost equally correct :—

> Quum prorepserunt primis animalia terris,
> Mutum et turpe pecus, glandem atque cubilia propter
> Unguibus et pugnis, dein fustibus, atque ita porro
> Pugnabant armis quæ post fabricaverat usus. [2]

How refreshing is the excellent anthropology of these pagans after the marvel-myths of man's Creation propounded by the so-called ' revealed ' religions.

For the better distribution of the subject I shall here retain the obsolete and otherwise inadmissible, because misleading, terms—Age of Stone, Age of Bronze, Age of Iron. [3] From the earliest times all the metals were employed, without distinction, for weapons offensive and defensive : besides which, the three epochs intermingle in all countries, and overlap one another ; they are, in fact, mostly simultaneous rather than successive. As a modern writer says, like the three principal colours of the rainbow, these three stages of civilisation shade off the one

sided over the senate with a Sword by his side and a mail-coat under his tunic.

[1] *De Rer. Nat.* v. 1282. He speaks of Italy, where copper and bronze historically preceded iron.

[2] *Sat.* i. 3.

[3] Leading to the fourth, or Historic, and the fifth, or Gunpowder, age of weapons. In these ' ages ' we have a fine instance of hasty and indiscriminate generalisation. They originated in Scandinavia, where Stone was used almost exclusively from the beginning of man's occupation till B.C. 2000–1000. At that time the Bronze began, and ended with the Iron about the Christian era. Thomsen, who classified the Copenhagen Museum in 1836 ; Nilsson, the Swede, who founded comparative anthropology (1838 –43) ; Forchhammer and Worsaäee, the Dane, who illustrated the Bronze Age (1845), fairly established the local sequence. It was accepted by F. Keller, of the Zurich Lake (1853), by Count Gozzadini, of Bologna (1854), by Lyell (1863), and by Professor Max Müller (1863, 1868, and 1873), who seems to have followed the Swiss studies of M. Morlot (*Bulletin de la Soc. Vaudoise*, tome vi. etc.) Unhappily, the useful order was applied to the whole world, when its

deficiency became prominent and palpable. I note that Mr. Joseph Anderson (*Scotland in Early Christian Times*, p. 19) retains the ' three stages of progress '—stone, bronze, and iron. Brugsch (*History*, i. 25) petulantly rejects them, declaring that Egypt ' throws scorn upon these assumed periods,' the reverse being the case. Mr. John Evans (*The Ancient Stone Implements, &c., of Great Britain*, p. 2) adopts the succession-idea, warning us that the classification does not imply any exact chronology. He finds Biblical grounds ' in favour of such a view of gradual development of material civilisation.' Adam's personal equipment in the way of tools or weapons would have been but insufficient, if no artificer was instructed in brass and iron until the days of Tubal Cain, the sixth in descent when a generation covered a hundred years. Mr. Evans divides the Stone Age into four periods. First, the Palæolithic, River-gravel, or Drift, when only chipping was used ; second, the Reindeer, or Cavern-epoch of Central France, and an intermediate age, when surface-chipping is found ; third, the Neolithic, or surface stone-period of Western Europe, in which grinding was practised ; and, lastly, the Metallo-lithic age, which attained the highest degree of manual skill.

into the other; and yet their succession, as far as Western Europe [1] is concerned, appears to be equally well defined with that of the prismatic colours, though the proportion of the spectrum may vary in different countries. And, as a confusion of ideas would be created, especially when treating of the North European Sword, by neglecting this superficial method of classification, I shall retain it while proceeding to consider the development of the White Arm under their highly conventional limits.

I must, moreover, remark that the ternary division, besides having no absolute chronological signification, and refusing to furnish any but comparative dates, is insufficient. Concomitant with, and possibly anterior to, the so-called Stone Age, wood, bone, teeth, and horn were extensively used; and the use has continued deep into the metal ages. Throughout the lower valley of the River of the Amazons, where stone is totally wanting, primitive peoples must have armed themselves with another material. The hard and heavy trees, both of the Temperates and the Tropics, supplied a valuable material which could be treated simply by the use of fire, and without metal or even stone. Ramusio speaks of a sago-wood (*Nibong* or *Caryota urens*) made into short lances by the Sumatrans: 'One end is sharpened and charred in the fire, and when thus prepared it will pierce any armour much better than iron would do.' [2] The weapon would be fashioned by the patient labour of days and weeks, by burying in hot ashes, by steaming and smoking, by charring and friction, by scraping with shells and the teeth of rodents, and by polishing with a variety of materials: for instance, with the rasping and shagreen-like skin of many fishes, notably the ray; with rough-coated grasses, and with the leaves of the various 'sandpaper-trees' which are hispid as a cat's tongue. And the first step in advance would be dressing with silex, obsidian, and other cutting stones, and finishing with pumice or with the mushroom-shaped corallines. I shall reserve for the next chapter a description of the *sabre de bois*, unjustly associated in the popular saying with the *pistolet de paille*.

Bone, which includes teeth, presented to savage man a hard and durable material for improving his coarse wooden weapons. Teledamus or Telegonus, son of Circe and founder of Tusculum [3] and Præneste, according to tradition slew his father, Ulysses, with a lance-head of fish bone—*aculeum marinæ belluæ*. The teeth of the Squalus and other *gigantum ossa* or megatherian remains supplied points for the earliest projectiles, and added piercing power to the blow of the club. That a Bone Age may be traced throughout the world,[4] and that the phrase a ' bone- and stone-using people ' is correct, was proved by the Weltausstellung of Vienna (1873), whose

---

[1] In Denmark the division is marked even by the vegetation. The Stone Age lies buried under the fir-trees; the oak-stratum conceals the Bronzes, and the Iron Age is covered by birch and elders (Jähns, p. 2).

[2] Yule's *Marco Polo*, ii. 208.

[3] Servius, ad *Æneid*. ii. 44, ' Sic notus Ulysses.'

[4] Col. A. Lane Fox (*Prim. War.*, p. 24) notices the bone implements of the French caves and their resemblance, amounting almost to identity, with those found in Sweden, among the Eskimos, and the savages of Tierra del Fuego.

splendid collection found an able describer in Prof. A. Woldrich.[1]   The caves of
venerable Moustier (Département Dordogne), of Belgium, and of Lherm (Département Arrière) contributed many jawbones of the cave bear (*Ursus spelæus*) ; the
ascending ramus of the inferior maxilla had been cut away to make a convenient
grip, and the strong corner-teeth formed an implement or an instrument, a tool or
a weapon.   The caves of Peggau in Steiermark (Styria), of Palkau in Moravia, and
the Pfahlbauten [2] or Pile-villages of Olmütz, produced a number of bone articles
and remnants of the cave bear.   These rude implements remind us of the weapon
used to such good effect by the Biblical Samson, the Hebrew type of Hercules, the
strong man, the slayer of monsters, and the Sun-god (Shamsún).[3]

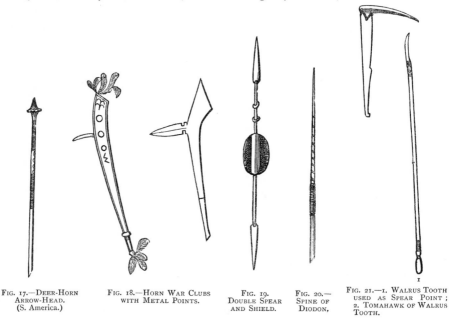

FIG. 17.—DEER-HORN
ARROW-HEAD.
(S. America.)

FIG. 18.—HORN WAR CLUBS
WITH METAL POINTS.

FIG. 19.
DOUBLE SPEAR
AND SHIELD.

FIG. 20.—
SPINE OF
DIODON,

FIG. 21.—1. WALRUS TOOTH
USED AS SPEAR POINT ;
2. TOMAHAWK OF WALRUS
TOOTH.

The wilder tribes of Cambodia convert the bony horn of the sword-fish into a
spear head, with which they confidently attack the rhinoceros.[4]   At Kotzebue
Sound Captain Beechey found lances made of a wooden staff ending in a walrus-
tooth ; and this defence was also adapted to a tomahawk-point.   The New Guinea
tribes tip their arrows with the teeth of the saw-fish and the spines of the globe-fish
(*Diodon* and *Triodon*).   The horny style of the Malaccan king-crab (*Limulus*), a

[1] *Mittheilungen der Wien. Anthrop. Gesellschaft.*
Vienna, 1874.

[2] *Pfahlbau* (*pfahl=palus*) was originally applied
to the pile-villages of the Swiss waters (*The Lake-
Dwellings of Switzerland*, by Dr. Ferdinand Keller).

[3] Wilkinson opines that the Egyptian Khons or
Khonsu, the new moon of the year which appeared

at the autumnal equinox when the ' world was made,'
becomes the Biblical Sem, and that ' Sampson' is
Sem-Kon, or Sun-fire. Jablonski (*Pantheon Egyp-
tiorum*) supported the theory that Son, Sem, Con,
Khons, or Djom was the god or genius of the summer
sun.

[4] *Travels into Indo-China*, &c. ii. 147, by Henri
Mouhot, 1858–59.

Crustacean sometimes reaching two feet in length, is also made into an arrow-pile.[1] The Australians of King George's Sound arm their spears with the acute barbules of fishes; and the natives of S. Salvador, when discovered by Columbus, pointed their lances with fish-teeth. The Greenlander's 'nuguit' (fig. 23) is mentioned by Crantz as armed with the narwhal's horn, and the wooden handle is carved in relief with two human figures. By its side is another spear (fig. 24) with a beam in narwhal-shape, the foreshaft being composed of a similar ivory, inserted into the snout so as to represent the natural defence. Here we see the association in the

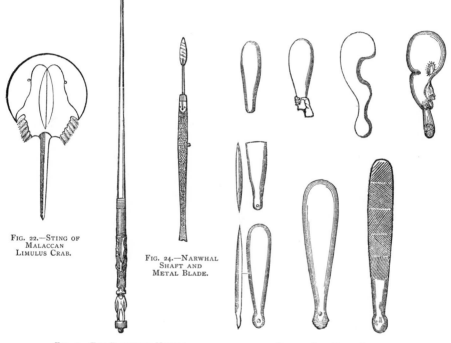

FIG. 22.—STING OF
MALACCAN
LIMULUS CRAB.

FIG. 24.—NARWHAL
SHAFT AND
METAL BLADE.

FIG. 23.—THE GREENLAND NUGUIT.

FIG. 25.—JADE PATTU-PATTUS.

maker's mind between the animal from which the weapon is derived and the purpose of destruction for which it is chiefly used. It also illustrates the well-nigh universal practice amongst savages of making their weapons to imitate animate forms. The reason may be a superstition which still remains to be explained.

Foreshafts and heads of bone are still applied to the arrows of the South African Bushmans. They alternate with wood, chert, and metal throughout the North American continent, from Eskimo-land to California. A notable resemblance has been traced between the bone-club of the Nootka Sound 'Indians,' and

[1] 'Pile,' applied to the arrow-head (as 'quarrel' to the bolt of the crossbow), is a congener of the German *pfeil*, an arrow. The Scandinavian is *pila*, the Anglo-Saxon *pil*, apparently a congener of the Latin *pilum*.

the jade Pattu-Pattu or Meri of New Zealand.   Hence it has been suspected that
this short, flat weapon, oval or leaf-shaped, and made to hold in the hand, as if it
were a stone celt, was originally an imitation of the os humeri.   Like the celt, also,
is the stone club found by Colonel A. Lane Fox in the bed of the Bawn river, north
Ireland.[1]

The long bones of animals, with the walls of marrow-holes obliquely cut and
exposing the hollow, were fastened upon sticks and poles, forming formidable darts
and spears.   The shape thus suggests the bamboo arrowheads of the North
Americans, whose cavity also served to carry poison.[2]   They would, moreover,
easily be fashioned by fracture, and by friction upon a hard and rough-grained
substance, into Swords and daggers.   The Fenni, or Finns, of Tacitus ('Germ.' c. 46),
having no iron, used bone-pointed arrows.   The Innuits, or Eskimos, of Greenland

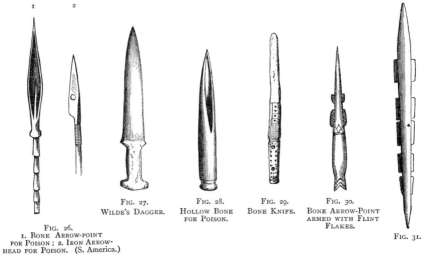

FIG. 27.
WILDE'S DAGGER.

FIG. 28.
HOLLOW BONE
FOR POISON.

FIG. 29.
BONE KNIFE.

FIG. 30.
BONE ARROW-POINT
ARMED WITH FLINT
FLAKES.

FIG. 26.
1. BONE ARROW-POINT
FOR POISON ; 2. IRON ARROW-
HEAD FOR POISON. (S. AMERICA.)

FIG. 31.

and other parts of the outer north, form with the ribs of whales their shuttles as
well as their Swords.   In 'Flint Chips' we find that the ancient Mexicans had
bone-daggers.   Wilde[3] gives a unique specimen of such a weapon found in the
bed of the River Boyne 'in hard blue clay, four feet under sand, along with some
stone spear-heads.'   Formed out of the leg-bone of one of the large ruminants, it
measures ten and a sixth inches long, the rough handle being only two and a half
inches[4] ; the blade is smooth, and wrought to a very fine point.   This skeyne (the

---

[1] *Ulster Journal of Archæology* for 1857.

[2] The Dacota tribe is said still to 'doctor' the
bullet by filling with venom four drilled holes, which
are covered by pressing down the projecting lips or
rims of the metal.   Unfortunately, travellers tell us
that the venom is the cuticle of the cactus, which is
quite harmless.   The Papuans tip their arrows with
a human bone, which is poisoned by being thrust

into a putrid corpse.   Hence, they say, Commodore
Goodenough met his death.

[3] P. 258, *Descriptive Catalogue of the Antiquities
in the Royal Irish Academy*, by the late (Sir) William
R. Wilde.   The Greeks, from the days of Homer,
followed by the Romans, considered the use of
poisoned arrows a characteristic of the barbarian.

[4] The learned author adds, 'thus confirming the

Irish ' scjan '¹) looks like a little model of a metal cut-and-thrust blade (fig. 27). Equally interesting is the knife-blade (fig. 29) found with many other specimens of manufactured bone in the Ballinderry ' Crannog '² (county Westmeath): the total length is eight inches, and the handle is highly decorated. Other bone knives are mentioned in the ' Catalogue ' (pp. 262–63). Bone prepared for making handles, and even ferules, for Swords and daggers is also referred to (p. 267): the material, being easily worked and tolerably durable, has, indeed, never fallen into disuse. In the shape of ivory,³ walrus-tusk, and hippopotamus-tooth it is an article of luxury extensively used in the present day for the hafts of weapons and domestic implements. Lastly, bone served as a base to carry mere trenchant substances. The museum of Professor Sven Nilsson⁴ shows (fig. 31) a smooth, sharp-pointed splinter, some six inches long, grooved in each side to about a quarter of an inch deep. In each of these grooves, fixed by means of cement, was a row of sharp-edged and slightly curved bits of flint. A similar implement (fig. 30) is represented in the illustrated catalogue of the Museum of Copenhagen. Of this contrivance I shall speak at length when treating of the wooden Sword.⁵

While bone was extensively used by primitive Man, horn was the succedaneum in places where it was plentiful. The Swiss lake-dwellings have yielded stag's horn and wooden hafts or helves, with bored holes and sockets ; borers, awls or drills ; mullers, rubbers, and various other instruments. The caverns of the Reindeer period in the south of France are not less rich. Stag-horn axes are common in Scandinavia, and one preserved by the Stockholm Museum bears the spirited outline of a deer. Beads, buttons, and other ornaments are found in England. This material, when taken from the old stag, is of greater density than osseous matter and of almost stony hardness, as the cancellated structure contains carbonate of lime ; moreover it was easily worked by fire and steam.

Diodorus (iii. cap. 15) describes the Ichthyophagi as using antelopes' horns in their fishing, ' for need teacheth all things.' The earliest mention of a horn-arm is by Homer (' Iliad,' ii. 827, and iv. 105), who describes Pandarus, the Lycian, son of Lycaon, using a bow made of the six-spans-long⁶ spoils of the ' nimble

---

opinion (deduced from the size of the hafts of our bronze Swords) that the hands of the race who used them were very small.' I can hardly agree with him, and will give reasons in a future page.

¹ Wilde writes : ' *Sceana*, which is the plural of *scjan*, a knife,' the Scotch *sgian-dhu*, or *skene* (Rev. Paul O'Brien's *Practical Grammar and Vocabulary of the Irish Language*, Dublin : Fitzpatrick, 1809).'

² It is better to write Crannog, lest the word be pronounced 'crannoje.' It derives from the Irish *crann* (a tree, e.g. *crann ola* = an olive-tree), and properly means a platform or plank-floor.

³ Pliny, the grumbler, complains (xxxiii. 54) : ' Our very soldiers, holding even ivory in contempt, have their *capuli* (sword-hilts) inlaid or chased (*cælentur*) with silver ; their *vaginæ* (scabbards) are heard

to jingle with their silver *catellæ* (chains), and their belts with the plates of silver (*baltea laminis crepitant*) that inlay them.' It will be seen that Divus Cæsar had juster and more soldier-like views. Scipio the younger, when shown a fine shield by a youth, said : ' It is really beautiful ; but a soldier should rely more on his right arm than on his left arm.'

⁴ Of Lund, Sweden. *The Primitive Inhabitants of Scandinavia*, &c., translated by Sir John Lubbock. Nilsson is quoted and illustrated by Col. A. Lane Fox (*Prim. War.* p. 135), and by Wilde (p. 254) from the *Scandinaviska Nordens Ur-Invanare*, 1843.

⁵ Chapter III.

⁶ A commentator volunteers the information that the bow was tipped with ram's-horn. Nor is there any need to translate ' goat ' by *ibex*.

mountain-goat.' The weapon may have retained the original form. The early Greek types were either simple or composite. The Persians [1] preferred, and till lately used, wood and horn, stained, varnished, and adorned as much as possible. Duarte Barbosa [2] describes the Turkish bow at Hormuz Island as 'made of buffalo-horn and stiff wood painted with gold and very pretty colours.' The 'Hornboge' occurs in the 'Nibelungenlied,' and the Hungarians appeared in Europe with horn-bows and poisoned arrows.

The bows of the Sioux and Yutahs are of horn, backed with a strip of raw hide to increase the spring. The Blackfoot bow is made from the horn of the mountain-sheep (Catlin), and the Shoshone of the Rocky Mountains shape it by heating and wetting the horn, which is combined with wood (Schoolcraft). The Eskimos of Polar America, where nothing but drift-timber is procurable, are com- pelled to build their weapons with several bits of wood, horn, and bone, bent into form by smoking or steaming.

Admirable bows of buffalo-horn—small, but throwing far, and strong—are still made in the Indus-valley about Multan. For this use the horns are cut, scraped, thinned to increase elasticity ; joined at the bases by wooden splints, pegs, or nails, and made to adhere by glue and sinews. Man would soon learn to sharpen his wooden shafts with horn-points, the spoils of his prey. Hence the ancient Egyptians applied horn to their light arrows of reed.[3] The Christy collection contains an arrow from South America (?) armed with a pile of deer-horn. The Melville Peninsula, being scant of materials, uses as arrow-piles the horns of a musk-ox (*ovibos*, more *ovis* than *bos*), and the thinned defences of the reindeer strengthened by sinews. Antelope-horns are still used as lance-points by the Nubians, the Shilluks, and the Denkas of the Upper Nile ; by the Jibbus of Central Africa, and by the tribes of the southern continent.[4] The 'Bantu' or Kafir races, Zulus and others, make their *kiri* (kerry) either of wood or of rhinoceros-horn. It varies from a foot to a yard long, and is capped by a knob as large as a hen's egg or a man's fist : hence it is called 'knob-stick' or 'throw- stick.' The Ga-ne-u-ga-o-dus-ha (deer-horn war-club) of the Iroquois ended in a point of about four inches long ; since the people had intercourse with Europeans they have learned to substitute metal. The form suggests that the *martel-de-fer* of Persia and India, used by Europe during the fifteenth and sixteenth centuries, was derived from a weapon of this kind : suitable points for arming it have been found in England and Ireland. The Dublin Museum (case 21, Petrie) contains an antler of the red deer converted into a thrusting weapon. The Jumbiyah (crooked

---

[1] Pemberton, *Travels*.

[2] Hakluyt's edit., p. 43. The index to this publication is very defective : one must look through the whole volume for a line of quotation. I shall again notice it in the next chapter.

[3] Wilkinson (Sir J. Gardner), *A Popular Account*

of the *Ancient Egyptians*, i. chap. 5, mentions only tips of hard wood, flint, and metals.

[4] The *Roteiro* or *Ruttier* of the *Voyage of Vasco da Gama* (p. 5, Lisboa, Imprensa Nacional) speaks of tribes about the Cape of Good Hope armed with horn-weapons 'worked by fire' (*huuns cornos tos- tados*). I should suggest that '*cornos*' is an error for *páos* (wooden staves).

dagger) of the Arabs, the Khanjar[1] of Persia and India, whence the Iberian Alfânge (El-Khanjar) and our silly 'hanger,' shows by form and point that it was originally the half of a buffalo-horn split longitudinally. The modern weapon, with metal blade and ivory handle, has one side of the latter flat, betraying its origin by retaining a peculiarity no longer required. The same is the case when the whole Jumbiyah is, as often happens, made of metal[2] (fig. 6, p. 10).

The sufficiency of horn for the slender wants of uncivilised communities was admirably illustrated by the discovery of a Pfahlbau, or crannog, some three miles south of Laibach, the capital of Carniola, and a little north of the Brunnsdorf village. The site is a low mountain-girt basin, formerly a lake or broad of the Lai-cum-Sava river, and still flooded after heavy rains. Surface-finds were picked up in 1854–55, and regular explorations began in July 1875.[3] During that year two hundred articles were dug up. The material was chiefly stag-horn, tines, and beams, the latter often cut at the burr or antler-crown. The chief objects—many of them artistic as those of the French 'Reindeer epoch'—were hatchets, hammers, needles, spindles, and punches of horn and split bone ; fish-hooks, pincers, and skin-scrapers of hog's tusks ; with ornaments set in bone, and teeth bored for stringing. Many of these articles showed signs of the saw-kerf or notch which had probably been cut with sanded fibre acting like a file. There were harpoon-heads of peculiar shape, supposed to be unpierced whistles, the hole not having been bored through[4] : evidently they were made to 'unship' when striking the Welsen (*Siluri*) of the old lake, some of which must have been

Fig. 32.
HARPOON HEAD.

---

[1] The khanjar proper is shaped like a yataghan, of which more presently.

[2] I avoid treating of armour in a book devoted to the Sword ; but the Horn Age compels me to show, in a few words, how that material, combined with hoofs, gave rise to scale armour. Pausanias, confirmed by Tacitus, informs us that the Sarmatians (Slavs) prepared the horse-hoofs of their large herds and sewed them with nerves and sinews to overlap like the surface of a fir-cone. He adds that this lorica was not inferior in strength or in elegance to the metal-work of the Greeks. The Emperor Domitian wore a corslet of boars'-hoofs stitched together ; and a fragment of such horn-armour was found at Pompeii. Ammianus Marcellinus describes the Sarmatians and the Quadi as protected by loricas of horn-flakes planed, polished, and fastened like feathers upon a linen sheet. A defence composed of the hoofs of some animal, made to hold together without the aid of an inner jerkin, and used in some parts of Asia, is represented in Meyrick (plate iii.). A stone figure of old type similarly defended, and bearing an inscription in a dialect cognate with Greek, appears in vol. iii. *Journ. Archæol. Assoc.* Herodotus (vii. 76) tells us of a people, whose name has disappeared, that, in addition to their brazen helmets, they wore the ears and horns of an ox in brass. This horn-helmet shows the savage practice of defending the head with the skins of beasts and their appendages.

[3] The *Pfahlbauten im Laibacher Moraste* were first noticed in the *Neue Freie Presse*, August 27, 1875 ; secondly, by the *Neue Deutsche Alpenzeitung*, of Vienna, Sept. 4, 1875 ; thirdly, by Herr Custos Deschmann (to whom the discovery is attributed) in his paper *Die Pfahlbauten auf dem Laibacher Moore* (Verhand. der Wiener K. K. Geolog. Reichsanstalt, Nov. 16, 1875) ; and, fourthly, by Carl Freiherr von Czoernig, whose study (*Ueber die Vorhistorischen Funde im Laibacher Torfmoor*) was read at the Alpine Society of Trieste on December 8, 1875. Between that time and 1880 the subject has been illustrated by many writers. The course of discovery also has been 'forwards ;' and the whole moor was about to be drained in 1881.

[4] Perhaps this may explain the 'pierced implements of unknown use' found with harpoon-heads of reindeer-horn in a cavern near Bruniguel, France. Two picks made of reindeer-antlers were produced by the 'Grimes Graves,' Westing Parish, Norfolk.

six feet long. The wooden foreshaft, joined by a string to its head, acted as float, and betrayed the position of the prey. This is the third stage of the harpoon: the first would be merely a heavy, pointed stick, and the second a spear with barbs. There were six horn *Dolche* (daggers), and one peculiar article, an edge of polished stone set in a horn-handle: the latter shows at once the abundance of game, and the value and rarity of the mineral, which probably belonged only to the rich. The eight stone implements were of palæolithic type ; the few metal articles—a leaf-shaped sword-blade, a rude knife, lance-heads, arrow-piles, needles, and bodkins—were chiefly copper, five only being bronze ; and the pottery corresponds with that of the neolithic period in the museums of Copenhagen and Stockholm. Thus the find, like several in Switzerland, showed a great preponderance of horns, bones, and teeth during a transitional age when the rest of Europe was using polished stone and metal.[1]

Prehistoric finds are still common in the Laibacher moorground (1882). Lauerza, a hamlet on the edge of the swamp, supplied (Nov. 7) a large stone-axe (*Steinbeil*), pierced and polished, of the quartzose conglomerate common in the adjacent highlands. This article was exceptional, most of the stone implements being palæolithic. At Aussergoritz appeared remnants of pottery and Roman tiles, a broken hairpin of bronze, a spear of Roman type, and a 'palstab,'[2] also of bronze : the latter is the normal chisel-shaped hatchet with the flanges turned over for fitting to the handle ; it measures 16·5 cent. long by 3·5 of diameter at the lower part. The sands of Grosscup also yielded sundry fine bronze armlets of Etruscan make found upon embedded skeletons. All the finds have been deposited in the Provincial Museum at Laibach.

The use of horn, like that of bone, has survived to the present day, and still appears in the handles of knives, daggers, and swords. It is of many varieties, and it fetches different prices according to the texture, the markings, and other minutiæ known to the trade.[3]

---

[1] The animal remains were of bears, wolves, lynxes, beavers, badgers (probably the cave-species), hogs, goats, sheep (differing in the jaw-bone from *ovis*), dogs (common, and not eaten), and cattle with small teeth like those of the aurochs. The bird-bones resembled those of the common duck. Man was rare, suggesting that the pile-villagers buried on the adjacent slopes ; the only human 'find' was an inferior maxilla with teeth much worn.

[2] The word *paalstab*, *palstab*, or *palstave* is usually translated 'labouring-staff,' from *at pula* or *pala*, to labour, *labourer*. Dr. John Evans (*Bronzes*, &c., p. 72) prefers 'spade-staff,' the verb being *at*

pæla, to dig, and the noun *pall*, a spade, spud, shovel ; the Latin *pala*, the French *pelle*, and our (baker's) *peel*, or wooden shovel. He confines the term 'palstave' to two forms ; the first is the winged celt with the lateral extensions hammered to make a socket ; the second is the spud-shaped form, with a thinner blade above than below the side-flanges.

[3] M. Kugelmann, of Hamburg—a wholesale merchant, who kindly showed me his warehouse—prefers the horns of the North American and Japanese stag, especially when buttons are to be made of the crown.

CHAPTER III.

THE WEAPONS OF THE AGE OF WOOD : THE BOOMERANG AND THE SWORD OF WOOD ; OF STONE, AND OF WOOD AND STONE COMBINED

The Sword of Wood.

THE ' Age of Wood ' began early, lasted long, and ended late. As the practice of savages shows, the spear was originally a pointed stick hardened in the fire ; and arrows, the diminutives of the spear, as daggers are of the Sword, were tipped with splinters of bamboo, whose Tabáshir or silicious bark acted like stone. The Peruvians, even after they could beat out plates of gold and silver, fought with pikes having no iron tips, but with the points hardened in the fire.[1] The same was the case with the Australians,[2] who, according to Mr. Howard Spensley,[3] also fashioned Swords of very hard wood : the Arabs of the Tihámat or Lowlands of Hazramaut (the Biblical Hazramaveth) are still compelled by poverty to use spears without metal. I pass over the general use of this world-wide material to the epoch when it afforded a true Sword.

The wooden Sword, as we see from its wide dispersion, must have arisen spontaneously among the peoples who had reached that stage of civilisation where it became necessary.[4] These weapons were found in the hands of the Indians of Virginia by the well-known Captain John Smith. Writing in 1606, Oldfield describes swords of heavy black wood in the Sandwich Islands, and Captain Owen Stansley in New Guinea. Mr. Consul Hutchinson notes the wooden swords used by the South American Itonanamas, a sub-tribe of the Maxos. Those preserved in Ireland and others brought from the Samoa Islands will be noticed in a future

---

[1] *Reports on the Discovery of Peru*, by Clements R. Markham, C.B., p. 53 (London : Hakluyt Soc. 1872).

[2] Oldfield's 'Aborigines of Australia ' (*Trans. Eth. Soc.*). The author was employed (1861) in collecting specimens of timber for the International Exhibition.

[3] Commissioner for Victoria at the Geographical Congress of Venice, September 1881.

[4] It is instructive to note the novel application of old inventions to general use when the necessities of the age demand them. The detonating and explosive force of gunpowder was known, in the form of squibs and fireworks, centuries before firearms were required.

The power of steam, as a whirling toy and a copper vessel prove, was familiar to the old Egyptians, and perhaps to the Greeks and Romans under the name of *æolipylæ* (αἰόλου πύλαι). But only at the end of the last century its motive force attracted general attention ; it became a necessary of civilised life, and at once superseded the sailer and the stage coach. And by aid of the Past we may project the Future. Man will bungle over the balloon, but he will never fly straight till railways and steamers become too slow for him : when ' levitation,' in fact, shall become a necessity. Now the mode of transit would be an unmitigated evil to humanity.

page. They may mostly be characterised as flat clubs sharpened at the edge, and used like our steel blades.

The shape of the wooden sword greatly varies, and so does its origin. Mr. Tylor fell into the mistake, so common in these classifying, generalising, and simplifying days, of deriving the sabre, because it is a cutting tool, from the axe, and the tuck or rapier from the spear because it thrusts. Wooden sword-blades alone have three prototypes, viz. :—

1. The club.
2. The throwstick.
3. The paddle.

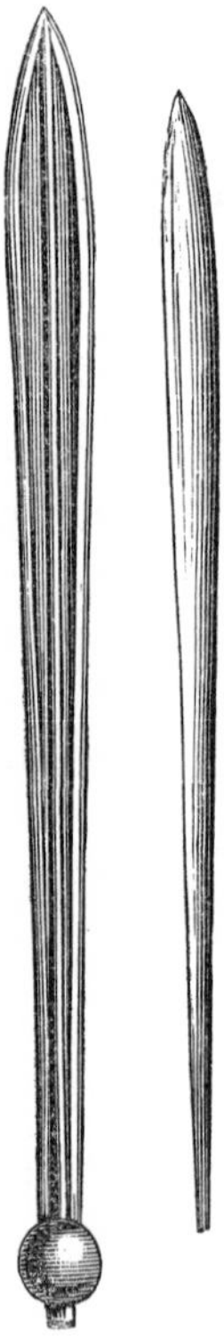

I. The Bulak Museum (Cairo)[1] shows two good specimens of the ancient 'Lisán' ('tongue'-weapon) club or curved stick. The first battles, says Pliny (vii. 57), were fought by the Africans against the Egyptians with clubs which they called *phalangæ*. The shorter club-sword (1 ft. 11 in.) has a handle ribbed with eighteen fine raised rings. The longer or falchion-shaped weapon (2 ft. 5 in.) is hatched at the grip with a cross pattern. Both are of hard wood blackened by age, and both have the distinct cutting edge. The ancient war-club was tipped with metal and whipped with thongs round the handle for firmer grasp, like the Roman fasces. The modern Lisán-club, made of tough mimosa-wood and about 2½ ft. long, is still used in close combat by the Negroid tribes of the Upper Nile. To the Bishárins and Amri the Lisán supplies, at dances and on festal occasions, the place of the sword. In Abyssinia there is a

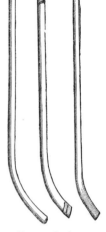

FIG. 33.—LISÁN IN EGYPT AND ABYSSINIA.

FIG. 34.—LISÁN OR TONGUE.

lighter variety (1 ft. 6 in.) banded alternately with red, blue, and green cloth, and protected by a network of brass wire. The Ababdeh (modern Æthiopians), content with this, the spear, and its pendant the shield, fear not to encounter tribes whose arms are the matchlock and a 'formidable looking, but really inoffensive sword with a wondrous huge straight blade.' These pastoral Nomads are of a peculiar and interesting type. The short stature and the well-curved and delicate limbs,

---

[1] In the Monuments Civils of the Salle de l'Est, Vitrine A. H., at the south side. I can give only the old arrangement, which was changed in 1879–80. During my last visit (November 1882) the new order had not been completed. These club-swords are accompanied by throw-sticks, hatchets, and knob-kerries. The old Lisáns from Thebes are illustrated by Wilkinson (*loc. cit.* i. 5). The name, however, is *not* 'lissan,' and they are *not* made of acacia, a soft wood that readily perishes. Why will writers confound acacia and mimosa?

whose action is quick, lithe, and graceful as the leopard's, connect them with the Bedawin of Arabia ; while the knotted and spiral locks standing on end, and resembling when tallowed a huge cauliflower, affiliate them to the African Somal. Their arms are more extensive than their dress, a mere waist cloth, the primitive attire of tropical man ; and they live by hiring their camels to caravans.

The Dublin Museum[1] also shows the transitional forms between the club and the Sword. The weapon (*a*) numbered 143 is some twenty-five inches long : the second (*b*) is labelled ' No. 144, wooden club-shaped implement, twenty-seven inches long.'

The club of the Savage developed itself in other directions to the shepherd's staff, the bishop's crozier, and the king's sceptre ; hence, too, the useless bâton of the field-marshal, and the maces of Mr. Speaker and My Lord Mayor. Here we may answer the question why the field-marshal should carry a stick instead of a Sword. The unwarlike little instrument is simply the symbol of high authority :[2] it is the rod, not of the Lictor, but of the Centurion, whose badge of office was a vine-sapling wherewith to enforce authority. Hence Lucan (vi. 146) says of gallant Captain Cassius Scæva who, after many wounds, beat off two swordsmen :—

Sanguine multo
Promotus Latiam longo gerit ordine vitem.

This use was continued by the drill-sergeant of Europe from England to Russia. The club again survives in the constable's staff and the policeman's truncheon.

The form of throwing-stick, which we have taught ourselves to call by an Australian name ' boomerang,'[3] thereby unduly localising an almost universal weapon from Eskimo-land to Australia, was evidently a precursor of the wooden Sword. It was well known to the ancient Egyptians. Wilkinson shows (vol. i. chap. 4) that it was of heavy wood, cut flat, and thus offering the least resistance, measuring 1 ft. 3 in. to 2 ft. long by $1\frac{1}{2}$ in. broad. The shape, however, is not the usual segment of a circle, but a shallow S-curve inverted (Ƨ), more bent at the upper end, and straighter in the handle. One weapon (p. 236) seems to bear the familiar asp-head.[4] The British Museum contains a boomerang brought from Thebes by the

---

[1] The arrangement of the Swords when I last visited the collection (August 1878) was temporary till classified. The wooden blades referred to were in the Petrie Section (Case 21) to the east.

[2] So the sovereign of England appointed his Lord High Treasurer by handing over to him a white rod, and the Lord Steward of the Household by presenting a white staff with the words : ' Seneschall, tenez le bâton de nostre hostiell.' Holding the staff was equivalent to the royal commission, and when not in the presence it was carried by a footman bareheaded. On the death of his liege lord the great functionary broke the staff over the corpse, and his duties were at an end. The Lord Marshall of England was expressly permitted to bear a gold truncheon with the royal arms at one end, and on the other his own

enamelled in black. The king solemnly gave the ' Marshall's rod ' into the hands of Maude, daughter of the Earl of Pembroke, who made it over to her son, Earl Roger.

[3] It derives from *booroomooroong* ; and the latter denotes, among the Maoris, a part of the ceremonies practised when the boys are being made men. The symbol, we are told (Collins, *New South Wales*, p. 346), is knocking out a tooth with the aid of a throwing-stick. Mr. Howard Spenseley (*loc. cit.*) makes the average boomerang 60 centimètres long by 0·6 broad and 0·15 thick : he gives it a flight of 100 mètres.

[4] Strangers in Egypt often suppose the true asp to be the *Cerastes*, or horned snake. As the hieroglyphics and the monuments prove, it is invariably

Rev. Greville Chester, and a facsimile was exhibited by General Pitt-Rivers.[1]   The end is much curved ; the blade has four parallel grooves, and it bears the cartouche of Ramses the Great.   In no instance have we found the round shape and the re-turning flight of its Australian congener.   Three illustrations [2] show a large sports-

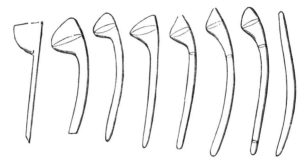

FIG. 35.—TRANSITION FROM THE BOOMERANG TO THE HATCHET (AUSTRALIA).

man (the master) bringing down birds which rise from a papyrus-swamp, while a smaller figure (the slave) in the same canoe holds another weapon at arm's length.

Strabo [3] describes the (Belgian) Gauls as hunting with a piece of wood resem-bling a pilum, which is hand-thrown, and which flies to a distance farther than an

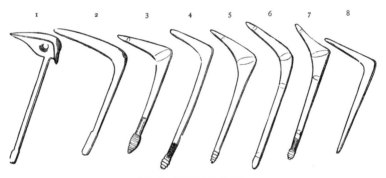

FIG. 36.—AUSTRALIAN PICKS.
1, 2. Pick of New Caledonia ; 3. Malga or Leowel Pick.

arrow.   He calls it the Γροσφὸs, which is also described as a pilum, dart, or javelin by Polybius ; [4] but evidently this Grosphus means the throw-stick, usually termed by the Greeks ἀγκύλη (Ancyle).   Silius Italicus arms in the ' Punica ' one of the

the cobra de capello (*Coluber Haja*), an inhabitant of Africa as well as of Asia.   The colour of this deadly thanatophid—which annually kills thousands in India —varies with its habitat from light yellow to dull green and dark brown.   The worst I ever saw are upon the Guinea Coast.

[1] Anthrop. Soc. July 11, 1882.   General Pitt-Rivers, I believe, would localise the boomerang to

the neighbourhood of the Indian Ocean, and deny it to Europe and America.

[2] *Loc. cit.* vol. i. chap. iv. pp. 235, 236, 237, in the abridged edition.

[3] Lib. iv. 4, § 3.

[4] *Pragmateia*, vi. 22, § 1; a fragmentaiy but ad-mirable account of the Roman army.

Libyan tribes which accompanied Hannibal with a bent or crossed *cateia* : the latter is identified with the throw-stick by Doctor (now Sir) Samuel Ferguson, poet and antiquary.[1] The encyclopædia of Bishop Isidore (A.D. 600–636) explicitly defines the *cateia* to be 'a species of bat which, when thrown, flies not far by reason

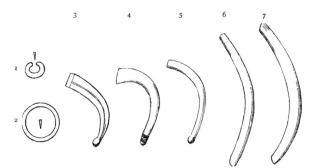

FIG. 37.—INDIAN BOOMERANGS.

1. War Hatchet, Jibba Negros ; 2. Steel Chakra, or Sikh Quoit ; 3. Steel Collery ; 4, 5. Collery of Madras, with knobbed handle.

of its weight ; but where it strikes it breaks through with extreme impetus, and if it be thrown with a skilful hand it returns to him who threw it :—rursum redit ad eum qui misit.' Virgil also notices it :—

> Et quos maliferæ despectant mœnia Abellæ
> Teutonico ritu soliti torquere cateias. (*Æn.* vii. 740).

Jähn (p. 410)[2] remembers the *Miölner*, or hammer of Thor, which flew back to the hand.

It has been noted that this peculiarity of reversion or back-flight is not generic, even in the true boomerang, but appertains only to specific forms. Doubtless it was produced by accident, and, when found useful for bringing down birds over rivers or marshes, it was retained by choosing branches with a suitable bend. The shapes greatly differ in weight and thickness, in curvature and section. Some are of the same breadth throughout ; others bulge in the centre ; while others are flat on one side and convex on the other. In most specimens the fore part of the lath is slightly 'dished' : hence the bias causes it to rise in the air on the principle of a screw-propeller. The thin edge of the weapon is always opposed to the wind, meeting the least resistance. The axis of rotation, when parallel to itself, makes the missile

---

[1] *Trans. Irish Assoc.* vol. xix. The Romans also called it *aclys* (*Æn.* vii. 730), which the dictionaries render as a 'kind of dart.' It was an archaic and barbarian weapon ; and Virgil (*Æn.* vii. 730) attributes it to the Osci :—

> Teretes sunt aclydes illis
> Tela : sed hæc lento mos est aptare flagello.

This would mean that after the weapon is thrown it might be drawn back again with a leather thong.

Possibly the *cateia* ot Isidore (*cateia*, to cut or mangle, and *catan*, to fight ; the Irish cać and the Welsh *kad*, a fight or a corps of fighters, Latin *caterva*), survives in the tip-*cat*. In the Keltic dialect of Wales *catai* is a weapon.

[2] See his learned note (p. 410) on the weapon and on Isidore (*Orig.* xviii. 7) : 'Hæc est cateia quam Horatius cajam dicit.' The disputed word probably derives from the Keltic *katten*, to cast, to throw.

ascend as long as the forward movement lasts, by the action of the atmosphere on the lower side. When the impulse ceases it falls by the line of least resistance,

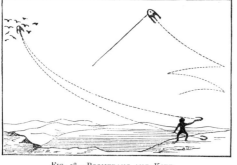

FIG. 38.—BOOMERANG AND KITE.

that is, in the direction of the edge which lies obliquely towards the thrower. In fact, it acts like a kite with a suddenly broken string, dropping for a short distance. But as long as the boomerang gyrates, which it does after the forward movement ends, it continues to revolve on the same inclined plane by which it ascended until it returns to whence it came. This action would also depend upon weight; the heavy weapons could not rise high in the air, and must drop by mere gravity before coming back to the thrower.

From Egypt the weapon spread into the heart of Africa. The Abyssinian

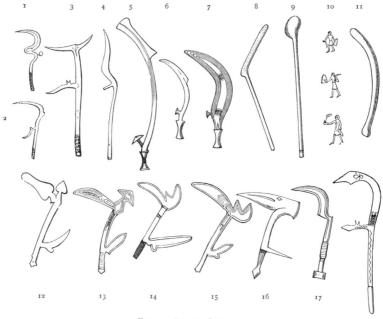

FIG. 39.—AFRICAN BOOMERANGS.

1, 2. Hunga-munga; 3. African Weapon; 4. Kordofan Weapon; 5. The same developed; 6. Faulchion of Mundo Tribe; 7. The same developed; 8. Jibba Negros; 9. Knob-stick; 10. Ancient Egyptians (Rosellini); 11. Old Egyptian; 12–15, Tomahawks of Nyam-Nyams; 16. Fan (Mpangwe) Tomahawk; 17. Dor Battle-axe; 18. Dinka and Shilluk Weapon.

'Trombash' is of hard wood, acute-edged, and about two feet long; the end turns sharply at an angle of 30°, but the weapon does not whirl back.[1] The boomerang

[1] *Nile Tributaries*, by Sir Samuel W. Baker, p. 51. The word has a curious likeness to the 'tombat,' a similar weapon in Australia (Col. A Lane-Fox, *Anthrop. Coll.* p. 31).

of the Nyam-Nyams is called *kulbeda*. Direct derivation is also shown by the curved iron projectile of the Mundo tribe on the Upper Nile, a weapon of the same form being represented on the old Egyptian monuments. The 'hunga-munga' of the negros south of Lake Chad, and the adjoining peoples, shows a further development of spikes or teeth disposed at different angles, enabling the missile to cut on both sides. The varieties of this form, with a profusion of quaint ornaments, including lateral blades which answer the purpose of wings, and which deal a severer wound, are infinite. Denham and Clapperton give an illustration of a Central African weapon forming the head and neck of a stork. So the

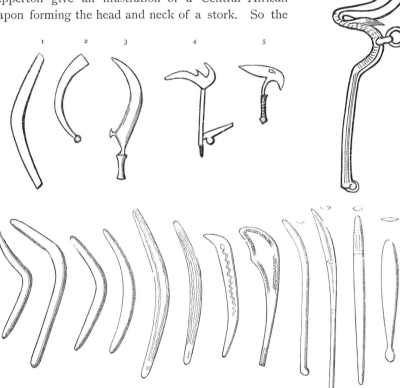

FIG. 40.—TRANSITION FROM THE MALGA, LEOWEL OR PICK TO THE BOOMERANG (AUSTRALIA).

Mpangwe negros[1] of the Gaboon River, West Africa, shape their missiles in the form of a bird's head, the triangular aperture (fig. 40, No. 5) representing the eye.

[1] The 'Fans' of M. du Chaillu, a corruption unfortunately adopted by popular works. In *Gorilla-Land* (i. 207) I have noticed the Náyin, or Mpangwe crossbow (with poisoned *ebe*, or dwarf bolt), which probably travelled up-Nile like the throw-stick. The *détente* and method of releasing the string from its notch are those of the toy forms of the European weapon. The Museum at Scarborough contains a crossbow from the Bight of Benin. The people of Bornu (North-West Africa) also use a crossbow rat-trap.

The throwing-stick has been found in Assyrian monuments: Nemrúd stran-
gling the lion holds a boomerang in his right hand.   Thence the weapon travelled
East; and the Sanskrit Ástara, or Scatterer, was extensively used by the pre-
Aryan tribes of India.   The Kolis, oldest known inhabitants of Gujarát, call
it 'Katuriyeh,' a term probably derived from 'Cateia'; the Dravidians of the
Madras Presidency know it as 'Collery,' and the Tamulian Kallar and Marawar (of

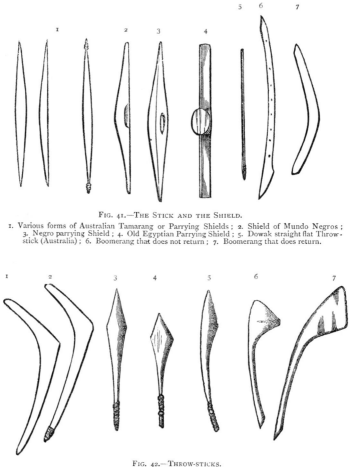

FIG. 41.—THE STICK AND THE SHIELD.
1. Various forms of Australian Tamarang or Parrying Shields; 2. Shield of Mundo Negros;
3. Negro parrying Shield; 4. Old Egyptian Parrying Shield; 5. Dowak straight flat Throw-
stick (Australia); 6. Boomerang that does not return; 7. Boomerang that does return.

FIG. 42.—THROW-STICKS.
1 Australian Tombat; 2. Malga War-pick; 3-6. Australian Waddy Clubs; 7. Hatchet Boomerang.

Madura), who use it in deer-hunting, term it 'Valai Tadi' (bent stick).   The
Pudukota Rajah always kept a stock in arsenal.   The length greatly varies, the
difference amounting to a cubit or more; and three feet by a hand-breadth may be the
average.   The middle is bent to the extent of a cubit; the flat surface with a sharp
edge is one hand broad.   'Its three actions are whirling, pulling, and breaking, and

it is a good weapon for charioteers and foot soldiers.' Prof. Oppert, writing 'On the Weapons, &c. of the ancient Hindus' (1880), tells us that the Museum of the Madras Government has two ivory throw-sticks from Tanjore and a common wooden one from Pudukota ; his own collection contains four of black wood and one of iron. All these instruments return, as do the true boomerangs, to the thrower. The specimens in the old India-House Museum conform with the natural curvature of the wood, like the Australian ; but, being thicker and heavier, they fall without back-flight. Not a few of the boomerangs cut with the inner edge, the shapes of the blade and of the grip making them unhandy in the extreme.

From the throw-stick would naturally arise the Chakrá, the steel wheel or war-quoit, which the Akális —a stricter order of Sikhs—carried in their long hair, and launched after twirling round the forefinger.[1] The boomerang-shape is also perpetuated in the dreaded Kukkri or Gurkha Sword-knife, now used, however, only for hand-to-hand fighting. I have mentioned the Cuchillo or Spanish clasp-knife- and the Italian sickle-throwing. The Australian weapon was unknown, like the shield, to Tasmania, whose only missile was the Waddy or throw-stick.

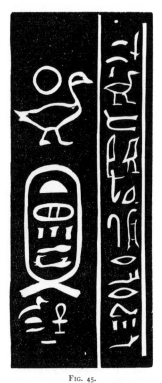

As the Australian club, swelling at the end, developed itself in one direction, to the Malga (war-pick) and hatchet, so on the other line it became, by being narrowed, flattened, and curved, the boomerang and the boomerang-sword.

FIG. 43.
OLD EGYPTIAN
BOOMERANG.

FIG. 44.
BULAK SWORD.

FIG. 45.
HIEROGLYPHIC INSCRIPTION ON
WOODEN SWORD, OF BULAK.

Finally, the immense variety of curves—some of them bending at a right angle—were straightened and made somewhat long-oval and leaf-shaped for momentum and impetus.

The direct descent of the curved wooden Sword of Egypt from the boomerang is shown in many specimens. The blade becomes narrow, flat, and more curved ;

---

[1] It is called *chakarani* in the *Coasts of East Africa and Malabar Coast*, by Duarte Barbosa or Magellan (?). The Jibba negroes of Central Africa wear a similar weapon as a bracelet, sheathed in a strip of hide.

the handle proves that it is no longer a mere missile, and the grip is scored with scratches to secure a firmer grasp.[1] The best specimen known to me is in the Bulak Museum.[2] It is a light weapon of sycomore wood, measuring in length 1 mètre 30 cent. (4 ft. 3 in.), in breadth nearly 15 cent. (6 in.), and in thickness 0.2 cent. (0.78 in.), while the depth of the perpendicular connecting the arc with the chord is 10 cent. But what makes it remarkable is that the Sword bears at one side the so-called 'Cartouche'[3] of King Ta-a-a (17th dynasty), and at the other end of the same side in a parallelogram the name and titles of Prince 'Touaou, the servant of his master in his expeditions.' This fine specimen was found with the mummy and other articles at the Drah Abu'l-Neggah, the Theban cemetery.

The paddle or original oar, mostly used by savages with the face to the bow,[4] is of two kinds. The long, pointed spear-like implement serves, as a rule, for deeper, and the broad-headed for shallower, waters. Both show clearly the transitional state beginning with the club and ending with the Sword

Mr. J. E. Calder,[5] describing the Catamaran of the swamp tea-tree (*Melaleuca*, sp.) on the southern and western coasts of Tasmania, says (p. 23): 'The mode of its propulsion would shock the professional or amateur waterman. Common sticks, with points instead of blades, are all that were used to urge it with its living freight through the water, and yet I am assured that its progress is not so very slow.' Spears were employed in parts of Australia to paddle the light bark canoes,[6] and the Nicobar Islanders have an implement combining spear and paddle: it is of iron-wood, and of pointed-lozenge shape, about five feet in length.[7]

The African paddles, usually employed upon lagoons and inland waters, are broad-headed, either rounded off or furnished with one or more short points at the

[1] Col. A. Lane-Fox, *Anthrop. Coll.*, p. 33. For a comparative anatomy of the boomerang the reader will consult that volume, pp. 28-61. I have here noticed only the most remarkable points.

[2] The Sword stood in Case 2 of the Salle du Centre, numbered 695; and was described in p. 225 of the late Mariette Pasha's catalogue. I cannot quite free myself from a suspicion that it was also a boomerang of unusual size. Some of the South African tribes still use throw-sticks a yard to a yard and a half long. 'They are double as thick at one end as they are at the other,' says Herr Holub (ii. 340), 'the lighter extremity being in the usual way about as thick as one's finger.'

[3] This meaningless word (*cartuccia*, a scrap of paper) was applied by Champollion to the elliptical oval containing a group of hieroglyphics. It is simply an Egyptian shield (Wilkinson, *loc. cit.* i. chap. 5), and the horizontal line below shows the ground upon which it rested. The old Nile-dwellers, like the classics of Europe and the modern Chinese, use the shield for their characteristics, their heraldic badges, &c. The same was the case with our formal heraldry, which

originated about the time of the Crusades, personal symbolism being its base. As Mr. Hardwick shows, the horse, raven, and dragon were old familiar badges; many of our sheep-marks are identical with 'ordinaries,' and the tribes of Australia used signs to serve as *kobongs*, or crests. Thus, too, in fortification the shield became the crenelle and the battlement, and it served to 'iron-clad' the war-galleys of the piratical Norsemen.

[4] So there are two ways of swimming. The civilised man imitates the action of the frog, the savage the dog, throwing out the arms and drawing the hands towards his chest.

[5] *Journ. Anthrop. Inst.* vol. iii. pp. 7-29, April 1873.

[6] An illustration is given in Mr. J. G. Wood's *Natural History of Man*. He also quotes Mr. F. Baines, who describes the paddles of the North Australians with barbed and pointed looms.

[7] Capt. James Mackenzie, in a paper read before the Ethno. Soc. by Mr. G. M. Atkinson (*Journal*, vol. ii. No. 2, of July 18, 1870. The paddle is figured pl. xiv. 2).

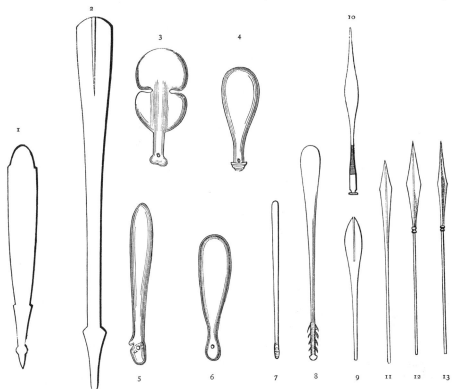

FIG. 46.—TRANSITION FROM CELT TO PADDLE SPEAR AND SWORD FORMS.

1. Wooden Club Sword from New Guinea ; 2. Paddle from New Guinea ; 3. New Zealand Pattu-Pattu, or Meri ; 4. Pattu-Pattu from the Brazil ; 5. Analogous forms ; 6. Ditto, ditto ; 7–10. Club Paddles from Polynesia ; 11–13. Wooden Spears from Friendly Islands.

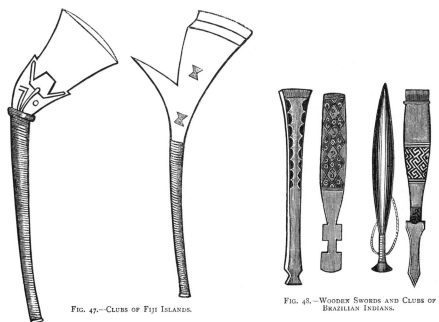

FIG. 47.—CLUBS OF FIJI ISLANDS.

FIG. 48.—WOODEN SWORDS AND CLUBS OF BRAZILIAN INDIANS.

end. Every tribe has its own peculiarities, and a practised eye easily knows the people by their paddles. A broad blade, almost rounded and very slightly pointed, is also made in the Austral Isles, in the Kingsmill Islands, and in the Marquesas.

The passage of the paddle into the Sword is well shown amongst the wilder 'Indians' of the Brazil. The Tupis still employ the Tacapé, Tangapé, or Ivera-

pema, which is written 'Iwarapema' by Hans Stade, of Hesse, in the charmingly naïve account of his travels and captivity.[1] It was a single piece of the hard, heavy, and gummy wood which characterises these hot-damp regions,[2] and of different shapes with and without handles.[3] The most characteristic implement is a long and rounded shaft with a tabular, oval, and slightly-pointed blade : it was slung by a lanyard round the neck and hung on either side. With a weapon of this kind the cannibal natives slaughtered Pero Fernandes Sardinha, first Bishop of Bahia, and all his suite ; the 'martyrs' had been wrecked on the shoals of Dom Rodrigo off the mouth of the Coruripe River. The scene is illustrated in the 'History' of the late M. de Varnhagen (p. 321).

A similar Brazilian instrument was the Macaná, still used on the Rio das Amazonas, and there called Tamarana. It retains the form of the original paddle, while for offensive purposes the pointed oval head is sharpened all round. In parts of the Brazil the Macaná was a rounded club ; and the sharpened paddle used as a Sword was called Pagaye.[4]

FIG. 49.—PAGAYA, SHARPENED PADDLE. The Peruvian Macaná and the Callua—the latter compared with a short Turkish blade—were made of chonta-wood (*Guilielma speciosa* and *Martinezia ciliata*) which was hard enough to turn copper tools.[5] Mr. W. Bollaert [6] tells us that the 'Macaná was said by some to be shaped

[1] Translated for the Hakluyt Society (1874) by Mr. Albert Tootal, of Rio de Janeiro, who wisely preserved the plain and simple style of the unlettered and superstition-haunted gunner.

[2] In Bacon's day (*Aphorisms*, book ii.) gummy woods were supposed to be rather a Northern growth, 'more pitchy and resinous than in warm climates, as the fir, pine, and the like.' They are as abundant near the Equator, where the viscidity preserves them from the alternate action of burning suns and torrential rains ; moreover, they are harder and heavier than the pines and firs of the Temperates.

[3] *Historia Geral do Brazil*, by F. Adolpho de Varnhagen, vol. i. p. 112 (Laemmert, Rio de Janeiro, 1854).

[4] M. Paul Bataillard (p. 409, *Sur le Mot Pagaie*, Soc. Anthrop. de Paris, 1874) is in error, both when

he calls the people of Paraguay 'Pagayas,' or 'carriers of lances,' and when he identifies Pagaya (not a spear, but a paddle-sword) with the 'sagaia or assagai.' The latter word is of disputed origin, and it is meaningless in the tongues of South Africa. Space forbids me to touch its history, except superficially. 'Azagay,' a lance, or rather javelin, appears in Spanish history as far back as the days of Ojeda (1509) ; and in 1497 the Portuguese of Vasco da Gama's expedition use the term 'azagayas' (p. 12, Roteiro or Ruttier, before alluded to). I believe both to be derived from the Arabic *el-khazúk*, a spit—in fact, the Italian *spiedo*, lance.

[5] Markham (p. 203, Cieça de Leon) makes 'Macaná' a Quichua word ; it also belongs to the great Tupi-Guarani family.

[6] *Antiquarian Researches*, quoted by Markham, *loc. cit.* p. 181.

like a long Sword, by others like a club.' It was both. The Tapuyas set these broad-headed weapons with teeth and pointed bones.

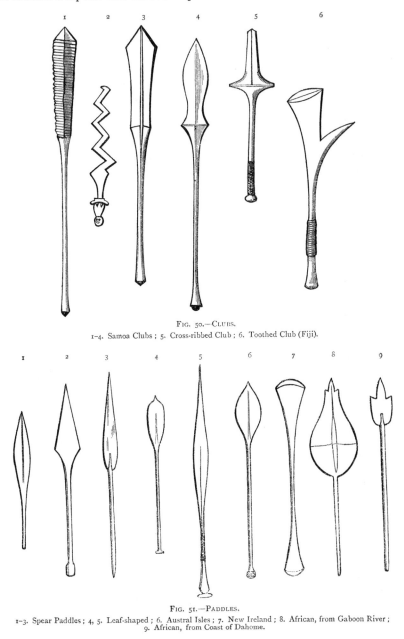

FIG. 50.—CLUBS.
1-4. Samoa Clubs ; 5. Cross-ribbed Club ; 6. Toothed Club (Fiji).

FIG. 51.—PADDLES.
1-3. Spear Paddles ; 4, 5. Leaf-shaped ; 6. Austral Isles ; 7. New Ireland ; 8. African, from Gaboon River ;
9. African, from Coast of Dahome.

Ojeda, during his famous voyage to Carthagena, found the warlike Caribs wielding great Swords of palm wood, and the women 'throwing a species of lance called *Azagay*.' General Pitt-Rivers' collection has a fine flat Club-Sword, five feet two inches long, straight and oval pointed, from Endeavour River, Queensland, and a smaller article, about three feet, with a longer handle, from Australia. Barrow River, Queensland, has supplied him with a half-curved wooden blade five feet long.

The fine Ethnological Museum of Herr Cesar Godeffroy[1] of Hamburg and Samoa, illustrating the ethnology of the Pacific Islands, contains many specimens of the knob-stick bevelled on one side of the head to an edge and gradually passing into the Sword. On the right-hand entrance-wall are, or were, two fine sabres (fig. 53) of Eucalyptus-wood, labelled 'Schwert von Bowen (Queensland).' The Sandwich Islanders, we see, still wield the Sword-club with sharp-cutting edges,

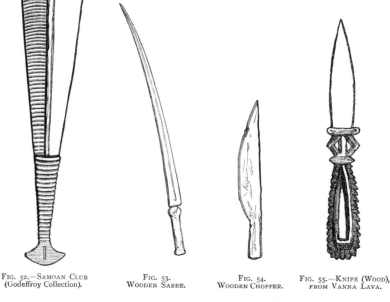

FIG. 52.—SAMOAN CLUB
(Godeffroy Collection).

FIG. 53.
WOODEN SABRE.

FIG. 54.
WOODEN CHOPPER.

FIG. 55.—KNIFE (WOOD),
FROM VANNA LAVA.

like their neighbours of New Ireland. The savage Solomon Archipelago has supplied a two-handed sabre of light and bright-yellow wood ; its longitudinal midrib shows direct derivation from the paddle-club. There is also a lozenge-shaped hand-club, which may readily have given a model to metal-workers. It is of hard, dark, and polished wood, and the handle is whipped round with coir (Tafel xx. p. 97) : the length is seventy cent. by four of maximum breadth. The Swords are unfortunately not figured in the catalogue ; but there is a fine wooden knife

---

[1] The Godeffroy Collection has produced a huge Catalogue of 687 pages (*Die ethnographisch-en-thropologische Abtheilung des Museum Godeffroy in Hamburg*, vol. i. 8vo (L. Friederichsen u. Co. 1881). It was shown to me by Dr. Graeffe, the naturalist often mentioned in ' *South Sea Bubbles*, by the Earl and the Doctor.' As a rule the Samoans had clubs and spears, but few Swords.

forty-nine cent. long by six cent. broad, with open handle and highly-worked grip (Tafel xxi. p. 135). It comes from Vanna Lava, Banks Group, New Hebrides, Polynesia (fig. 55).[1]

The wooden Sword extended deep into the Age of Metal. Articles of the kind have been brought from New Zealand, which are evident copies of modern European weapons. Wilde (p. 452) gives the wooden Sword, found five feet deep in Ballykilmunary near High Park, county Wicklow, with some bog-butter, but he finds no indications of its age. The length is twenty inches (fig. 56). Upon the side of the blade, and of a piece with it, stands a projection whose purpose is unknown : it is evidently inconvenient for a toy ; but if the relic be a model for a sand-mould, the excrescence would have left an aperture by which to pour in the metal. This view is supported by the shape of the handle, which resembles the grips of the single-piece bronze Swords found in different parts of Europe. The Dublin Museum also contains[2] a blade apparently intended for thrusting, and labelled 'Wooden Sword-shaped Object.' The material is oak, blackened by burial in bog-earth : it has a mid-rib, a bevelled point, and no appearance of being a model (fig. 57).

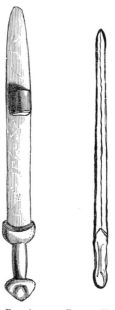

Fig. 56.
IRISH SWORD.

FIG. 57.—WOODEN
RAPIER-BLADE
(Dublin Museum).

Whilst wood was extensively used for Swords, the Age of Stone supplied few. The broad and leaf-shaped silex-flakes, dignified by the name of Swords, are only daggers and long knives. The fracture of flint is uncertain, even when freshly quarried.[3] The workmen would easily chip and flake it to form scrapers,

---

[1] This part of Melanesia has been familiar to the home reader by the life, labours, and death of Bishop Patterson.

[2] Case 21, Petrie, No. 142.

[3] The village of Abu Rawásh, north of the Pyramids of Jízah, still works this material in large quantities ; and its *caillouteurs,* or flint-knappers, have produced excellent imitations of the so-called prehistoric weapons. I have described the flint finds of Egypt in the *Journ. Anthrop. Instit.* (Feb. 1879), and shall have something more to say about them. A Mr. R. P. Greg, who writes in the same Journal (May 1881) on the 'Flint Implements of the Nile Valley,' is not aware of the fact that I found worked flints near the larger petrified forest (Cairo). Since that time General Pitt-Rivers made his grand discovery of 'Chert Implements in stratified Gravel in the Nile Valley' (*Journ. Anthrop. Inst.* May 1882). In March 1881, when visiting the Wady,

near Elwat El-Díbán (Hill of Flies) amongst the cliffs of Thebes, he came upon palæolithic flints, flakes worked with bulbs and facets embedded in the hardened grit, six and a half to ten feet below the surface. In the same strata tombs had been cut, flat-topped chambers with quadrangular pillars. The fragments of pottery enabled Dr. Birch to pronounce these excavations 'not later than the eighteenth dynasty, and perhaps earlier.' The New Empire in question was founded by Amosis (*Mah-mes,* or Moonchild) *circ.* B.C. 1700 ; it included the three great Tothmes, and lasted about three hundred years, ending with the heretic Amun-hotep IV., slave of Amun, *circ.* B.C. 1400, and Horemhib, the Horus of Manetho. The worked flints may evidently date thousands of years before that period. This is a discovery of the highest importance, and we may expect, with Mr. Campbell, that the 'works of men's hands will be found abundantly underlying the oldest history in the

axes, spear-heads, and arrow-piles ; but after a certain length, from eight to nine inches, the splinters would be heavy, brittle, and unwieldy. Obsidian, like silex, would make daggers rather than swords. Such are the stone dirk and cutlass in the Kensington Museum. Several European museums preserve these flat, leaf-shaped knives of the dark cherty flint found in Egypt. The British Museum contains a polished stone knife broken at the handle, which bears upon it in hieroglyphics the name of 'Ptahmes (Ptah-son), an officer.' There is also an Egyptian dagger, of flint from the Hay Collection, still mounted in its original wooden handle apparently by a central tang, and with remains of its skin sheath.[1] The Jews,

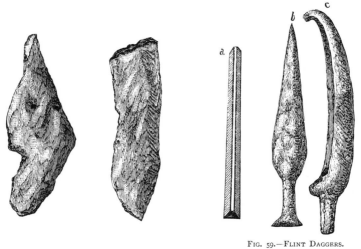

FIG. 58.—FRAGMENTS OF STONE KNIVES FROM SHETLAND.

FIG. 59.—FLINT DAGGERS.
a. Iberian or Spanish Blade (Christy Collection) ; *b.* Danish Flint Dagger ; *c.* Danish Flint Hatchet Sabre.

who borrowed circumcision from the Egyptians, used stone knives ($τὰς μαχαίρας τὰς πετρίνας$). Atys, says Ovid, mutilated himself with a sharp stone,—

Ille etiam saxo corpus laniavit acuto ;

and the Romans sacrificed pigs with flints. Several undated poniards in our collections are remarkable : for instance, the English daggers of black and white flint, rare in Scotland and unknown in Ireland ; (*a*) the Iberian or Spanish blade in the Christy Collection, five and a half inches long, and found at Gibraltar; the Tizcuco blade of chalcedony, eight inches long (*ibid.*); (*b*) the Danish dagger in the Copenhagen Museum, thirteen and a half inches long (the rounded handle makes it a ' marvel of workmanship') ; and (*c*) the flint hatchet-sabre of the same

world, in the hard gravel which underlies the mud of the Nile-hollow from Cairo to Assouan.' At any rate, this find disposes of the scientific paradox that Art has no infancy in Nile-land. The strange fancy has been made popular by the Egyptologist, who threatens to become as troublesome as the Sanskritist.

[1] It is figured (p. 8) by Dr. John Evans (*Ancient Stone Implements*, &c.), who offers another 'poniard' (perhaps a scraper) on p. 292. On p. 308 he notes the large thin flat heads called 'Pechs'' (Picts'?) knives.'

collection, fifteen and a half inches in length. It is a mystery how the minute and delicate ornamentation, the even fluting like ripple marks, on these Danish flint-daggers was produced.

A better substance than flint was found in the compact sandstone and in granitic serpentine, so called because that rock resembles a snake's skin. It is easily worked, while it is harder than the common serpentine. A dagger or knife found beside a stone cist in Perthshire is described as a natural formation of mica-schiste.

The Stone Age produced nothing more remarkable than the Pattu-Pattu or Meri of New Zealand, which an arrested development prevented becoming a Sword. Its shape, that of an animal's blade-bone, suggests its primitive material ; and New Guinea has an almost similar form, with corresponding ornamentation in wood. What assimilates it to the Sword is that it is sharp-edged at the top as well as at the side. It is used for 'prodding' as well as for striking, and the place usually chosen for the blow is the head, above the ear, where the skull is weakest. Some specimens are of the finest green jade or nephrite,[1] a refractory stone which must have been most troublesome to fashion.

Wood, however hard and heavy, made a sorry cutting weapon, and stone a sorrier Sword ; but the union of the two improved both. Hence we may divide wooden Swords into the plain and the toothed blades, the latter—

> Armed with those little hook-teeth in the edge,
> To open in the flesh and shut again.

An obvious advance would be to furnish the cutting part with the incisors of animals and stone-splinters. In Europe these would be agate, chalcedony, and rock-crystal ; quartz and quartzite ; flint, chert, Lydian stone, horn-stone, basalt, lava, and greenstone (or diorite) ; hæmatite, chlorite, gabbro (a tough bluish-green stone), true jade (nephrite), jadite, and fibrolite, found in Auvergne. Pinna and other shells have been extensively used—for instance, by the Andamanese—as arrow-heads and adze-blades.[2]

Tenerife, and the so-called New World, preferred the easily-cleft green-black obsidian,[3] of which the Ynkas also made their knives. The Polynesian Islands show two distinct systems of attachment. In the first the fragments, inserted into the grooved side, are either tied or made fast by gum or cement. In the second they are set in a row between two small slats or strips of wood, which, lastly, are lashed to the weapon with fibres. The points are ingeniously arranged in the

---

[1] Nephrite is so called because once held a sovereign cure for kidney disease. Jade is found in various parts of Europe (Page) ; in the Hartz (or Resin) Mountains ; in Corsica (Bristowe), and about Schweinsal and Potsdam (Rudler). Saussurite, the 'Jade of the Alps,' appears about the Lake of Geneva and on Monte Rosa. Mr. Dawkins limits Jade proper in the Old World to Turkestan and China.

Jade, the Chinese *you,* is popularly derived from the Persian *jádú* = (the) magic (stone).

[2] I need hardly notice that the mussel-shell was the original spoon, still a favourite with savages.

[3] Humboldt (*Pers. Narr.* vol. i. p. 100) makes the Guanches call obsidian 'tabona'; most authors apply the word to the Guanche knife of obsidian.

opposite direction, so as to give severe cuts both in drawing and withdrawing. The Eskimos secure the teeth by pegs of wood and bone. The Pacho of the South Sea Islanders is a club studded on the inner side with shark's teeth made fast in the same manner. The Brazilian Tapuyas armed a broad-headed club with teeth and bones sharpened at the point.[1] In 'Flint Chips' we find that a North American tribe used for thrusting a wooden Sword, three feet long, tipped with mussel-shell. Throughout Australia the natives provide their spears with sharp pieces

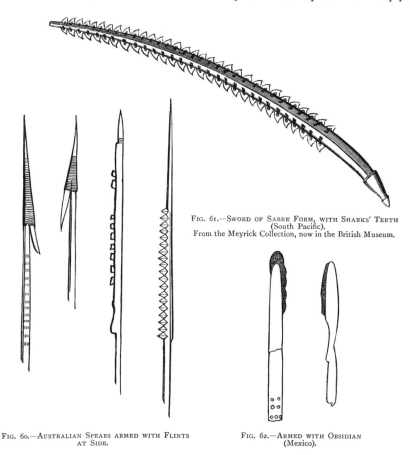

FIG. 61.—SWORD OF SABRE FORM, WITH SHARKS' TEETH
(South Pacific).
From the Meyrick Collection, now in the British Museum.

FIG. 60.—AUSTRALIAN SPEARS ARMED WITH FLINTS
AT SIDE.

FIG. 62.—ARMED WITH OBSIDIAN
(Mexico).

of obsidian or crystal : of late years they have applied common glass,[2] a new use for waste and broken bottles (fig. 70). The fragments are arranged in a row along one side near the point, and are firmly cemented. There is no evidence of this flint-setting in Ireland ; but the frequent recurrence of silex implements adapted for such purpose has suggested, as in the Iroquois graves, that the wood which held

[1] Neuhoff, *Travels*, &c. xiv. 874.
[2] Our word 'glass' derives from *glese* (*gless, gles-saria*), applied by the old Germans to amber (Tacit. *De Mor. Germ.* cap. 45). Pliny (xxxvii.chap.11) also notices *glæsum* (amber) and Glæsaria Island, by the natives called Austeravia.

them together may have perished. We read in 'Flint Chips' that the Selden Manuscript shows a flake of obsidian mounted in a cleft wooden handle, the latter serving as a central support, with a mid-rib running nearly the whole length. The sole use of the weapon was for thrusting.[1]

The people of Copan (Yucatan) opposed Hernandez de Chaves with slings, bows, and 'wooden Swords having stone edges.'[2] In the account of the expedition sent out (1584) by Raleigh to relieve the colony of Virginia, we read of ' flat, edged truncheons of wood,' about a yard long. In these were inserted points of stag-horn, much in the same manner as is now practised, except that European lance-heads have taken their place. Knives, Swords, and glaives, edged with sharks' teeth,[3] are found in the Marquesas ; in Tahiti, Depeyster's Island, Byron's Isles, the Kingsmill Group, Redact Island,[4] the Sandwich Islands, and New Guinea. Captain Graah notices a staff edged with shark's teeth on the east coast of Green-land, and the same is mentioned amongst the Eskimos by the late Dr. King.[5]

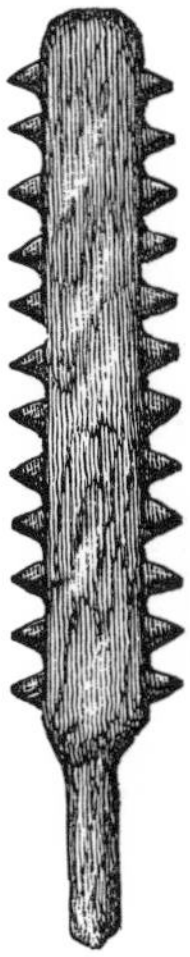

FIG. 63.—WOOD- AND HORN-POINTS.

In the tumuli of Western North America, Mr. Lewis Morgan, the 'historian of the Iroquois,' mentions that, when opening the ' burial mounds ' of the Far West, rows of flint-flakes occurred lying side by side in regular order ; they had probably been fastened into sticks or swords like the Mexican. Hernandez[6] describes the 'Mahquahuitl' or Aztec war-club as armed on both sides with razor-like teeth of 'Itzli' (obsidian), stuck into holes along the edge, and fastened with a kind of gum. Mr. P. T. Stevens ('Flint Chips,' p. 297) says that this Mexican broadsword had six or more teeth on either side of the blade. Herrera, the historian, mentions, in his 'Decads,' 'Swords made of wood having a gutter in the fore part, in which the sharp-edged flints were strongly fixed with a sort of bitumen and thread.'[7] In 1530, according to contemporary Spanish

FIG. 64.—MEXICAN SWORD OF THE FIFTEENTH CENTURY, OF IRON WOOD, WITH TEN BLADES OF BLACK OBSIDIAN FIXED INTO THE WOOD. (This weapon is twenty-five inches long.)

---

[1] Stephens, *Yucatan*, i. 100.

[2] The curious and artistic rock inscriptions and engravings of the South African Bushmen were traced in outline by triangular flint-flakes mounted on sticks to act as chisels. The subjects were either simple figures ; cows, gnus, and antelopes, a man's bust and a woman carrying a load ; or compositions, as ostrich and rider, a jackal chasing a gazelle, or a rhinoceros hunting an ostrich.

[3] See Chap. I.

[4] *Voyage Pittoresque autour du Monde*, par M. Louis Choris, Peintre, 1822.

[5] *Trans. Ethno. Soc.* vols. i. and ii. p. 290.

[6] Quoted by Col. Lane Fox, *Prim. War.* i. 25.

[7] *Prehistoric Man*, by Daniel Wilson (vol. i. pp. 216-17).

historians, Copan was defended by 30,000 warmen, armed with these and other weapons,[1] especially with fire-hardened spears. The same have been represented in the sculptures of Yucatan, which imitated the Aztecs. Lord Kingsborough's ruinous work on Mexican antiquities, mostly borrowed from Dupaix, shows a similar contrivance (*b* and *c*). A Sword having six pieces of obsidian in each side of the blade, is to be seen in a museum in Mexico.[2] A Mexican Sword of

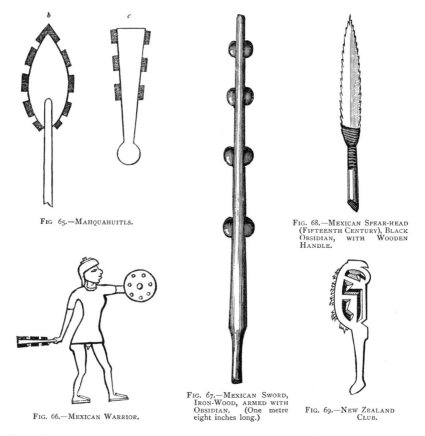

b   *c*

FIG 65.—MAHQUAHUITLS.

FIG. 68.—MEXICAN SPEAR-HEAD (FIFTEENTH CENTURY), BLACK OBSIDIAN, WITH WOODEN HANDLE.

FIG. 67.—MEXICAN SWORD, IRON-WOOD, ARMED WITH OBSIDIAN. (One metre eight inches long.)

FIG. 66.—MEXICAN WARRIOR.

FIG. 69.—NEW ZEALAND CLUB.

the fifteenth century is of iron-wood, twenty-five inches long, and armed with ten flakes of black obsidian ; and the same is the make of another Mexican Sword nearly four feet long.[3]

The next step would be to use metal for bone and stone. So the Eskimos of

[1] *Incidents of Travel in Central America*, &c., p. 51 ; by J. Lloyd Stephens. The work is highly interesting, because it shows Egypt in Central America. Compare the Copan Pyramid with that of Sakkarah ; the Cynocephalus head (i. 135) with those of Thebes ; the beard, a tuft on the chin ; the statue and its headdress (ii. 349); the geese-breeding at the palace (ii. 316) ; the central cross (ii. 346) which denotes the position of the solstices and the equinoxes and the winged globe at Ocosingo (ii. 259). In Yucatan the *Agave Americana* took the place of the papyrus for paper-making. Indo-China also appears in the elephant-trunk ornaments (i. 156).

[2] *Prim. War.* ii. p. 25.

[3] The two latter are in Demmin, p. 84.

Davis Strait and some of the Greenlanders show an advance in art by jagging the edge with a row of chips of meteoric iron.[1] This would lead to providing the whole wooden blade with an edge of metal, when the latter was still too rare and too expensive for the whole weapon. This economy might easily have overlapped not only the Bronze, but the Iron Epoch.

The tooth-shaped edge was perpetuated in the Middle Ages, as we see by serrated and pierced blades of Italian daggers. That it is not yet extinct the absurd saw-bayonet of later years proves.

We now reach the time when Man, no longer contented with the baser materials—bone and teeth, horn and wood— learned the use of metals, possibly from an accidental fire, when

> . . . a scrap of stone cast on the flame that lit his den
> Gave out the shining ore, and made the Lord of beasts a Lord of men.

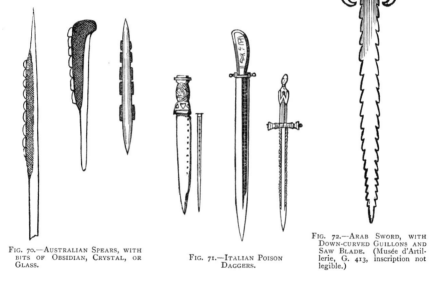

FIG. 70.—AUSTRALIAN SPEARS, WITH BITS OF OBSIDIAN, CRYSTAL, OR GLASS.

FIG. 71.—ITALIAN POISON DAGGERS.

FIG. 72.—ARAB SWORD, WITH DOWN-CURVED GUILLONS AND SAW BLADE. (Musée d'Artillerie, G. 413, inscription not legible.)

The discovery of ore-smelting and metal-working, following that of fire-feeding, would enable Man to apply himself, with notably increased success, to the improvement of his weapons. But many races here stopped short. The Australian, who never invented a bow, contenting himself with the boomerang, could not advance beyond the curved and ensiform club before he was visited by the sailors of the West. His simplicity in the arts has constituted him, with some anthropologists, the living example of the primitive and prehistoric *genus homo*.[2] The native of

---

[1] A specimen is in the British Museum, Department of Meteorolites. (*Prim. War.* p. 25.)

[2] The distinguished physicist, Prof. Huxley, extends, on purely anthropological grounds, the name 'Australioids' to the Dravidians of India, the Egyptians, ancient and modern, and the dark-coloured races of Southern Europe. I have ventured to oppose this theory in Chap. VIII. Mr. Thomas, curious to say, would make letters (alphabet, &c.) arise amongst the Dravidian quasi-savages.

New Guinea, another focus of arrested civilisation, was found equally ignorant of the metal blade. The American aborigines never taught themselves to forge either cutting or thrusting Swords ; and they entertained a quasi-superstitious horror of the 'long knife' in the hands of the pale-faced conqueror. This is apparently the case with all the lower families of mankind, to whom the metal Sword is clean unknown. If the history of arms be the history of our kind, and if the missile be the favourite weapon of the Savage and the Barbarian, the metal Sword eminently characterises the semi-civilised, and the use of gunpowder civi- lised, man.

A chief named Shongo, of Nemuro, in Japan, assured Mr. John Milne [1] that, 'in old times, when there were no cutting tools of metal, the people made them of Aji, a kind of black stone, or of a hard material called iron-stone. Even now imple- ments of this material are employed by men who dwell far in the interior.' Here, then, is another instance of the stone and the metal 'Ages' overlapping, even where the latter has produced the perfection of steel-work.

[1] *Trans. Anthrop. Inst.* May 1881. Mr. Milne brought home some fine specimens of worked stones, one of which (No. 17, pl. xviii.) is a chopper in the shape of the Egyptian flint-knives.

CHAPTER IV.

THE PROTO-CHALCITIC OR COPPER AGE OF WEAPONS.

I WILL begin by noticing that the present age has settled a question which caused much debate, and which puzzled Grote (ii. 142) and a host of others half a century ago, before phosphor-bronze was invented. This was the art of hardening (not tempering) copper and its alloys. All knew that these metals had been used, in cutting the most refractory substances,[1] granite, syenite, porphyry, basalt, and perhaps diorite,[2] by the ancient Egyptians, Assyrians, Trojans, and Peruvians. But none knew the process, and some cut the knot by questioning its reality. When you cannot explain, deny—is a rule with many scientists. The difficulty was removed by the Uchatius-gun,[3] long reported to be of 'steel-bronze,'[4] but simply of common bronze hardened by compression. At the Anthropological Congress of Laibach[5] (July 27–29, 1878), Gundaker Graf Wurmbrandt, of Pettau, exhibited sundry castings, two spear-heads and a leaf-shaped blade of bright bronze (Dowris copper) adorned with spirals to imitate the old weapons. They were so indurated by compression that they cut the common metal.

Again, at the Anthropological Congress of Salzburg (August 8, 1881), Dr. Otto Tischler, of Prussian Königsberg, repeated the old experiment, showing how soft copper and bronze could be hardened by the *opus mallei* (simple hammering). Moreover his metal thus compressed could cut and work the common soft

---

[1] Mr. Heath (who directed the Indian Iron and Steel Company) opined that the tools with which the Egyptians engraved hieroglyphics on syenite and porphyry were made of Indian steel. The theory is, as we shall see, quite uncalled for.

[2] For instance, the magnificent life-sized statue of Khafra (Cephren or Khabryes) in the Bulak Museum, dated B.C. 3700-3300 (Brugsch, *History*, vol. i. p. 78). Scarabæi of diorite can be safely bought in Egypt, the substance being too hard for cheap imitation work. Dr. Henry Schliemann constantly mentions diorite in his *Troy and its Remains* (1875); for instance, 'wedges' (i.e. axes) large and small, (pp. 21, 28, 154) : he speaks of an immense quantity of diorite implements (p. 75); of a Priapus of diorite twelve inches high (p. 169) ; of 'curious little sling bullets' (p. 236), and of hammers (p. 285). At Mycenæ he found 'two well-polished axes of diorite.'

But as he also calls it 'hard black stone,' I suspect it to be basalt, as his 'green stone' (*Troy*, p. 21) may be jade or jadeite.

[3] Casting the cannon called after the late General Uchatius is still kept a secret ; and I have been unable to see the process at the I. R. Arsenal, Vienna.

[4] *Stahl-bronce* = steel (i.e. hardened) bronze. The misunderstanding caused some ludicrous errors to the English press.

[5] I reported to the *Athenæum* (August 16, 1879) this 'recovery' of the lost Egyptian (and Peruvian) secret for tempering copper and bronze, which had long been denied by metallurgists. Copper hardened by alloy is described in the *Archæologia*, by Governor Pownall. Mr. Assay-Master Alchorn found in it particles of iron, which may, however, have been in the ore, and some admixture of zinc, but neither silver nor gold.

kinds without the aid of iron or steel. He exhibited two bronze plates in which various patterns had been punched by bronze dies. The hammering, rolling, beating, and pressing of copper for the purpose of hardening are well known to modern, and doubtless were to ancient workmen. The degree of compression applied is the feature of the discovery, or rather re-discovery.[1]

It may be doubted whether old Egypt and Peru knew our actual process of hydraulic pressure, whose simplest form is the waterfall. But they applied the force in its most efficient form. The hardest stones were grooved to make obelisks ; the cuts were filled with wedges of kiln-dried wood, generally sycomore ; and the latter, when saturated with water, split the stone by their expansion. And we can hardly deny that a people who could transport masses weighing 887 tons[2] over a broken country, from El-Suwan (Assouan) to Thebes, a distance of 130 miles, would also be capable of effecting mechanical compression to a high degree.

Buffon ('Hist. Nat.' article 'Cuivre') believed in the 'lost art.' Rossignol[3] (pp. 237–242) has treated of the *trempe* (διά τινος βαφῆς) *que les anciens donnèrent au cuivre* ; and relates that the chemist Geoffrey, employed by the Comte de Caylus, succeeded in hardening copper and in giving it the finest edge ; but the secret was not divulged. Mongez, the Academician, held that copper was indurated by immersion and by gradual air-cooling, but that *la trempe* would soften it.[4] In 1862 David Wilson, following Proclus and Tzetzes, declares the process of hardening and tempering copper so as to give it the edge of iron or steel, a 'lost art.' Markham[5] supposes that the old Peruvians hardened their copper with tin or silica ; and he erroneously believes that tin is scarcely found in that section of South America.

Modern archæological discovery has suggested that in many parts of the world we must intercalate an age of virgin Copper between the so-called Stone and Bronze Periods. The first metal, as far as we know, was the stream-gold, washed by the Egyptians ; and, as Champollion proved, the hieroglyphic sign for Núb (gold) is a bowl with a straining-cloth dripping water.[6] The fable of glass-discovery by the Sidonians on the sands of the Belus,[7] a tale which has *le charme*

---

[1] Of this I shall have more to say in Chap. V.

[2] This was the weight of the statue of 'Sesostris,' Ramses II., and his father Pharaoh Seti I.; see Chap. IX. The overseer standing upon its knee appears about two-thirds the length of the lower leg (Wilkinson, Frontisp. vol. ii.). Pliny treats of colossal statues, xxxiv. 18.

[3] *Les Métaux dans l'Antiquité*, par J. P. Rossignol. Paris : Durand, 1863.

[4] So Professor F. Max Müller, *Lectures on the Science of Language*, asserted, with a carelessness rare in so learned a writer (vol. ii. p. 255. London: Longmans, 1873), that 'the ancients knew a process of hardening that pliant metal (copper), most likely by repeated smelting (heating ?) and immersion in water.'

This latter is the common process for *softening* the metal.

[5] Cieza de Leon (Introd. p. xxviii.) : 'Humboldt mentions a cutting instrument found near Cuzco ('*the* City') which was composed of 0·94 parts of copper and 0·06 of tin. The latter metal is scarcely ever found in South America, but I believe there are traces of it in parts of Bolivia. In some of the instruments silica was substituted for tin.' The South American tin is mostly impure ; still it was and can be used.

[6] Apparently there are two forms of 'Núb' (gold), the necklace and the washing-bowl. See Chapter VIII.

[7] Pliny, xxxvi. 65.

des origines, explains, I have said, how a bit of metalliferous stone, accidentally thrown upon the fire in a savage hut, would suggest one of the most progressive of the arts. And soon the 'featherless biped,' like the Mulciber and the Mammon of Milton—

> Ransack'd the centre, and with impious hands
> Rifled the bowels of their mother earth
> For treasures better hid.

The greater antiquity of copper in Southern Europe was distinctly affirmed, as has been seen, by the Ancients. The use of sheeting, or plating, on wood or stone was known as long ago as the days of Hesiod (B.C. 880–850 ?) :

> Τοῖς δ' ἦν χάλκεα μὲν τεύχεα, χάλκεοι δέ τε οἶκοι,
> Χαλκῷ δ' εἰργάζοντο, μέλας δ' οὐκ ἔσκε σίδηρος.—*Erga*, 149.

Copper for armour and arms had they, eke Copper their houses,
Copper they wrought their works when naught was known of black iron.[1]

Copper sheets[2] were also used for flooring, as we learn from the χάλκεος οὐδός (Copper threshold) of Sophocles ('Œdip. Col.') ; and the treasury-room of Delphi, as opposed to the λάϊνος οὐδός (stone threshold). So in the Palace of Alcinous ('Odys.' vii. 75) the walls and threshold were copper, the pillars and lintels were silver, and the doors and dogs of gold.

The same practice was continued in the Bronze Period, as Dr. Schliemann proved when exploring the Thalamos attached to the Treasury of Minyas at Orchomenus. Nebuchadnezzar, in the 'Standard Inscription,' declares that he plated with copper the folding-doors and the pillars of the Babylon rampart, and it is suspected that gold and silver sheeted the fourth and seventh stages of the Temple of Belus, *vulgò* the Tower of Babel.

Lucretius[3] is explicit upon the priority of copper— [4]

> Posterius ferri vis est ærisque reperta,
> Sed prior æris erat quam ferri cognitus usus.
> Ære solum terræ tractabant, æreque belli
> Miscebant fluctus et volnera vasta ferebant.—V. 1286.

---

[1] Here Elton, like others of his age, mistranslates Chalcos by ' brass ' :

> Their mansions, implements, and armour shine
> In brass,—dark iron slept within the mine.

[2] Engraving on copper-plates is popularly attributed to Maso Finiguerra, of Florence, in 1460 ; but the Romans engraved maps and plans, and the ancient Hindus grants, deeds, &c. on copper-plates.

[3] I regret the necessity of troubling the learned reader with these stock quotations, but they are essential to the symmetry and uniformity of the subject.

[4] Sophocles and Ovid make Medea, and Virgil makes Elissa, use a sickle of chalcos. Homer, as will

be seen, uses the same material for his arms, axes, and adzes. Pausanias follows him, quoting his description of Pisander's axe and Meriones' arrow ; he also cites Achilles' spear in the temple of Athene at Phaselis, with its point and ferrule of chalcos, and the similar sword of Memnon in the temple of Æsculapius at Nicomedia. Plutarch tells us that the sword and spear-head of Theseus, disinterred by Cymon in Scyros, were of copper. Empedocles, who (B.C. 444)—

> ardentem frigidus Ætnam

> Insiluit—

was betrayed by his sandal shoon with chalcos soles.

He justly determines its relation to gold—

> Nam fuit in pretio magis æs, aurumque jacebat,
> Propter inutilitatem, hebeti mucrone retusum.—V. 1272.

And he ends with the normal sneer at his own age—

> Nunc jacet æs, aurum in summum successit honorem.—V. 1274.

Virgil, a learned archæologist, is equally explicit concerning the heroes of the Æneid and the old Italian tribes—

> Æratæ micant peltæ, micat æreus ensis.—Æn. vii. 743.

And similarly Ennius—

> Æratæ sonant galeæ : sed ne pote quisquam
> Undique nitendo corpus discerpere ferro.[1]

Even during her most luxurious days Rome, like Hetruria, retained in memoriam the use of copper (or bronze ?) for the sclepista or sacrificial knife. When founding a city they ploughed the pomœrium with a share of æs. The Pontifex Maximus and priests of Jupiter used hair-shears of the same material, even as the Sabine priests cut their locks with knives of æs. The Ancile or sacred shield was also of æs.

Pope, and other writers of his time, translated copper and bronze by 'brass' (copper and zinc) ; and in older English 'native brass' was opposed to 'yellow copper' (*cuivre jaune*). The same occurs in the A. V. Tubal Cain (the seventh in descent from Adam) is 'an instructor of every artificer in *brass* and iron'[2] (Gen. iv. 22). Moses is commanded to 'cast five sockets of *brass* for pillars'[3] (Exod. xxvi. 37). Bezaleel and Aholiab, 'artists of the tabernacle,' work in *brass* (Exod. xxxi. 4). We read of a 'land whose stones are iron, and out of whose hills thou mayest dig *brass*' (Deut. viii. 9). Job tells us, 'Surely there is a vein for the silver, and a place for gold where they fine it. Iron is taken out of the earth, and *brass* is molten out of the stone.'[4] Hiram of Tyre was 'cunning to work all works in *brass*' (casting and hammer-wrought), for Solomon's Temple, which dates from about two centuries after the time of the Trojan war (B.C. 1200). In Ezra (viii. 27) the text mentions 'two vessels of fine copper, precious as gold ;' and the margin reads 'yellow or shining *brass*.' Nor is the old word quite forgotten : we still speak of a ' *brass* gun.'

'In the *Brazen* Age,' unphilosophically says Schlegel ('Phil. of Hist.' sect. ii.), 'crime and disorder reached their height : violence was the characteristic of the rude and gigantic Titans. Their arms were of *copper*, and their implements and

---

[1] See Macrob. *Sat*. vi. 3.

[2] Or 'a furbisher (whetter, sharpener = *acuens*) of every cutting tool of copper and iron.' See Chap. IX.

[3] I can hardly understand why Dr. Evans (p. 5) insists upon these sockets being bronze, as they could 'hardly have been done from a metal so difficult to cast as unalloyed copper.' He greatly undervalues the metallurgy of the Exodist Hebrews, who would have borrowed their science from Egypt.

[4] Lead is also mentioned, but not tin.

utensils *brass* or bronze.' I should generally translate, with Dr. Schliemann and Mr. Gladstone, the Homeric χαλκός, 'copper,' not bronze, chiefly because the former is malleable and is bright, two qualities certainly not possessed by the alloy. There are alloys which are malleable,[1] and others (Dowris copper) which shine ; but this is not the case with common bronze, and no poet would note its brilliancy as a characteristic.

Pure copper, however, would generally be used only in lands where tin for bronze, and zinc for brass, were unprocurable : isolated specimens may point only to a temporary dearth. Thus, the Copper Age must have had distinct areas. M. de Pulsky and M. Cartenhac (' Matériaux,' &c.) held to a distinct Copper Age between the Neolithic and the Bronze. Dr. John Evans considers the fabrication due to want of tin or to preference of copper for especial purposes. But the types of copper tools, &c., are not transitional.

The native ore was used in many districts of North America. Celts of various shapes from Mhow, Central India, were analysed by Dr. Percy, who found no tin in them. Tel Sifr in Southern Babylonia and the island of Thermia in the Greek Archipelago supplied similar articles. They are also discovered exceptionally in Denmark, Sweden, Austria, and Hungary, France, Italy, and Switzerland. I have noticed the use of the unmixed metal in the Crannogs of Styria. It seems to have prevailed in Istria : at Reppen-Tabor near Trieste, the supposed field of battle with the Romans that decided the fate of the Peninsula (B.C. 178), was found a fine lance-head of pure copper eight and a half inches long : it is now in the Museo Civico. The same was the case with Dalmatia ; at Spalato and elsewhere I saw axe-heads of unmixed metal. And we have lately obtained evidence that old Lusitania, like Ireland,[2] was in similar conditions.

Thus the Age of Copper would be simply provisional in certain localities, separating the periods of horn and bone, teeth and wood, from that of alloys ; even as the latter led, in the due line of development, to the general adoption of iron and steel for Swords and other weapons. But we have no need for dividing the epochs with the perverse subtilties of certain naturalists, who use and abuse every pretext for creating new species. If there be any sequence, it would be copper, bronze, and brass. In most places, however, the ages were synchronous, and some races would retain the use of the pure metal, even when tin and zinc lay at their doors.

The Venus (♀) of alchemy was called in the Semitic tongues *nhs* or *nhsh*, in Arab *nahás*, and in Hebrew *nechosheth* (נחשת). The term is popularly derived from a triliteral root signifying a snake, the crooked reptile, the serpent that is in the sea (Job xvi. 13 ; Is. xxvii. 1 ; Amos ix. 3, &c.) ; either because the metal is poisonous, like the Ophidæ, or from its brightness of burnish. Similarly, *dhahab*

---

[1] A certain Herr Dromir patented in Germany a process for making malleable bronze. He added one per cent. of mercury to the tin, and then mixed it with the molten copper.

[2] For Irish copper swords see the *Archéologie*, vol. iii. p. 555. They will be exhaustively described in Part II.

(זהב), gold, was named from its splendour; and silver, also meaning money (*argentum*, argent), was *kasaf* (כסף), the pale metal, the 'white gold' of Egypt. Both *nechosheth* and *nahás* apply equally to copper, bronze, and brass; hence we must probably read 'copper Serpent' for '*brazen* Serpent,' and 'City of Copper' for 'City of *Brass*.'

There is the same ambiguity in the Greek and the Roman terms. The word χαλκός (*chalcus*) is popularly derived from χαλάειν, 'to loose,' because easily melted: I should prefer Khal or Khar, 'Phœnicia,' whose sons introduced it into Greece. The Hellenes dug it in Eubœa, where Chalcis-town[1] gave rise to the 'stone' χαλκῖτις (*chalcitis*, Pliny, xxxiv. 2). They also knew the ore as ἡ κύπρος; and when the Romans, who annexed Cyprus in B.C. 57, worked the mines, their produce, says Josephus, was called χαλκὸς κύπριος. *Chalcos* is essentially ambiguous unless qualified by some epithet, as ἔρυθρος (red), μέλας (black), αἴθιοψ (Ethiopian colour = ruddy brown), πόλιος (iron-grey), and so forth. In fact, like *æs*, it is a generic term for the so-called 'base metals' (iron,[2] copper, tin, lead, and zinc), as opposed to the 'noble metals'—gold and silver, to which we should add platinum.

Worse still, χαλκεύς (*khalkefs*), a copper-smith, was applied to the blacksmith,[3] and even to the *chrysochoös*, or gold-caster, at the court of Nestor ('Od.' iii. 420, 432); and to χαλκεῖα or χαλκήϊα, smithies in general. The Roman *æs*, opposed to the *cyprium* or *æs cyprium*[4] of Pliny (xxxiv. 2, 9), and *smaragdus cyprius* or malachite, is equally misleading unless we render it 'base metal.' We know not how to translate Varro[5] when he speaks of the cymbals at the feast of Rhea: 'Cymbalorum sonitus, ferramentorum jactandorum vi manuum, et ejus rei crepitus in colendo agro qui fit, significant quod ferramenta ea ideo erant ære' (copper, bronze, brass?), 'quod *antiqui* illum colebant ære antequam ferrum esset inventum.' Here he wisely limits the dictum to Greece and Rome.

According to S. P. Festus (*sub voce*), 'ærosam appellaverunt antiqui insulam Cuprum,[6] quod in eâ plurimum æris nascitur.' We now derive the Sacred Island

---

[1] So Chalcis in Mela (ii. 7), now Egripos (Negroponte).

[2] The confusion with iron appears in the Sanskrit (Pali?) *ayas*; Latin *æs* for *ahes* (as we find in *aheneus*); the Persian *áhan* (آهن); the Gothic *ais*, or *aiz*; the High German *er* (which is the Assyrian *eru* and the Akkadian *hurud*), and the English *iron*. J. Grimm (*Die Naturvölker*) connects Ἄρης with *æs*. That *æs* and *æris metalla* in Pliny mean copper, we learn from his tale of Telephus (xxv. 19), which, by the by, is told by Camoens (Sonnet lxix.) in a very different way.

[3] χαλκεύειν δὲ καὶ τὸ σιδηρεύειν ἔλεγον, καὶ χαλκέας τοὺς τὸν σίδηρον ἐργαζομένους. Jul. Pollux, *Onomasticon*, viii. c. 10.

[4] The full term was *æs cyprium*, which Pliny apparently applies to the finer kind; then it became *cyprium*, the adjective, which expressed only locality; and lastly *cuprum*. The third is first used by Spartianus in the biography of Caracalla (No. 5), *Cancelli ex ære vel cupro* (doors of *æs* or copper). Ælius Spartianus dates from the days of Diocletian and Constantine (Smith, *sub voc.*). When Pliny writes *in Cypro prima fuit æris inventio*, he leaves it doubtful if *æs* be copper or bronze; but we should prefer the former. So he makes the best 'Missy' (native yellow copperas) proceed from the Cyprus manufactories (xxxiii., iv.25, and xxxiv., xii. 31). The word *misi* or *missi* is still used in India for a vitriolic powder to stain the teeth. Cypros, the wife of Agrippa, was possibly named from Kafar = the henna plant: the Cyprus of Pliny (xii. 51) is also the *Lawsonia inermis*.

[5] *Frag.* tom. i. p. 226. Edit. Bipont.

[6] The island will be further noticed in Chap. VIII.

from 'Guib' (pine-tree), 'er' (great), and 'is' (island) ; 'Guiberis,' alluding to its staple growth. General Palma (di Cesnola[1]) prefers the Semitic 'kopher' (*Lawsonia inermis*), the henna-shrub, even as Rhodes took its name from the rose or malvacea ; and he finds in Stephanus Byzantinus[2] that the plant was then abundant. The diggings are alluded to by all the great geographers of antiquity, Aristotle ('de Anim.' v. 17[3]), Dioscorides (v. 89), Strabo (xvi. 6), and Pliny (xii. 60, xxxiv. 20). In Ezekiel (xxvii. 13) the trade in copper vessels is attributed to Javan (Ionia), Tubal, and Meshech ; the latter are the Moschi of Herodotus (vii. 78), a Caucasian people who may have originated the 'Moscows' or Russians. Agapenor and his Arcadians were credited with having introduced copper-mining into Neo-Paphos ; yet there is no doubt that the Phœnicians had worked metal there before the Greek colonisation. Menelaus ('Od.' iv. 83–4) visits Cyprus for copper ; and Athene-Mentor fetches it, as well as 'shining iron' (steel ?), from Temése (Τεμέση, 'Od.' i. 154).[4] These diggings, together with those of Hamath (Amathus, Palæo-Limassol), Soli, Curium, and Crommyon, are mentioned by Palma, who also alludes to an 'unlimited wealth of copper.' Yet, despite this and the general assertion that copper was the most important production of Cyprus, we have found only the poorest mines at Soli in the Mesaoria-plain, the counterslope of the Pedia. The island, it is true, has been wasted and spoiled by three centuries of the 'unspeakable Turk.' But the researches of late travellers and collectors—and these have been exhaustive since the British occupation—have hitherto failed to find extensive traces of mining. The rarity, together with the poverty of the matrix, would suggest the following explanation.

Cyprus was probably not so much a centre of production as a depôt of trade which collected the contributions of adjacent places—e.g. the isle of Siphanos (Sifanto), where copper has been found with iron and lead. Such was the general history of islands and archipelagos outlying barbarous and dangerous coasts on the direct lines of commerce, various sections of the world's great mercantile zone and highway of transit and traffic. The Cassiterides, also, served as storehouses for the stream-tin and the chalcopyrite (copper pyrites) of Cornwall and of Devonshire, whilst they enjoyed the fame of producing it. During the Middle Ages, Hormuz or Ormuz (Armuza), in the Persian Gulf, served, and Zanzibar still serves, as a centre of import, export, and exchange, as a magazine and as a shipping station for its mainland.

One of the ores which occurs in the greatest number of places[5] and in the

---

[1] *Cyprus*, &c., by General Louis Palma (di Cesnola). London : Murray, 1877. The author excavated from 1866 to 1876, and opened some 15,000 tombs, mostly Phœnician.

[2] Quoted in the *Kypros* of W. H. Engel (vol. i. p. 14). The two volumes are a mine of information ; much of it now antiquated, but useful to later students who have less leisure to accumulate learning.

[3] ' In Cyprus, where the manufacturers of the stone called chalcitis (copper-smelters) burn it for many days in fire, a winged creature, something larger than a great fly, is seen walking and leaping in the fire.' A brother of the salamander !

[4] Some commentators (Strabo, vi. 1) confound this place with Ausonian Temēsa, or Tempsa, in the land of the Brutii, with Temése of Cyprus.

[5] Herodotus (iii. 23) tells us that, copper being of all metals the most scarce and valuable in Æthiopia,

largest quantities; having a specific gravity ranging from 8·830 to 8·958; harder and more elastic than silver; the most tenacious of metals after iron and platinum; malleable when cold as well as when hot, so as not to require the furnace; melting at a temperature between the fusion points of silver and gold (1196° F.); and readily cast in sand-beds and moulds, Copper must have been used in the earliest ages, and has continued to our day, when the art of smelting it—at Swansea, for instance, in South Wales—is perhaps more advanced than that of any other ore. When the stone-and-bone weaponed peoples began their rude metallurgy, they would retain, with similar habits of thought, the same principles of design. The old Celtis, Celt, or chisel of serpentine or silex, would be copied in the newly-introduced and gradually-adopted weapon-tool of metal; and the transition would be so gradual that we trace without difficulty the process of development. The first metal blade was probably a dagger of copper, preserving the older shape of wood, horn, and stone: possibly it resembled the copper knife found at Memphis in 1851 by Hekekyan Bey; and this afterwards would grow to a Sword. Wood, stone, copper, and bronze, iron and steel, must long have been used simultaneously, slowly making way for one another, as the musket took the place of the matchlock, the rifle of the musket.

According to Pliny (vii. 57), 'Aristotle supposes that Scythes, the Lydian, was the first to fuse and temper copper; while Theophrastus,[1] in Aristotle's day, ascribes the art to Delas, the Phrygian. Some give the origin to the Chalybes, others to the Cyclopes.' Achilles, the pupil of Chiron (ibid. v. 20), is represented in pictures as scraping the *ærugo*[2] or verdigris off a spear into the wound of Telephus, the effect of which diacetate would soon be followed by the discovery of blue-stone (sulphate of copper, blue copperas) or blue vitriol, still a favourite in the East. Pausanias ('Æliaca') further informs us that Spanish copper, or copper from Tartessus, was the first used. The classics agree that Cadmus (not 'the foreigner,' but the 'old man,' *El-Kadim*, or the 'Eastern man,' *El-Kadmi*) introduced metallurgy into Greece.

We have ample evidence of extensive working and use of copper, called 'Khomet,' by the peoples of the Nile Valley. The ore occurs in the Wady Hammámát, the Egyptian Desert, and the so-called 'Sinaitic' Peninsula. As the Pyramids are the oldest of buildings, so the works in Wady Magharah (Valley of Caves) are perhaps the most ancient mines in the world.[3] They were first opened (circ. B.C. 3700—

---

prisoners were there bound with golden fetters. As will be seen, copper has lately been found in Abyssinia.

[1] An awful list of his works is given in Diogenes Laertius.

[2] This ærugo was artificially made by the Ancients with acetic acid, converting copper to a green salt (Beckmann, *sub v.* 'Verdigris or Spanish Green'). The green rust of the carbonate of copper is still erroneously termed verdigris (acetate of copper).

[3] Ample information is given by Brugsch (*Egypt under the Pharaohs*, vol. i. p. 64) of Senoferu; of the valiant Khufu or Suphis (Cheops); of the Pharaoh Sahura, or Sephris; of Menkauhor (Mencheres) and Tatkara (Fifth Dynasty); of the bas-reliefs at Wady Magharah dating from King Pepi (Sixth Dynasty); of Thutmes III. or the Great, and his sister Hashop (Eighteenth Dynasty before B.C. 1600), one of whose expeditions produced among other things ninety-seven Swords (Brugsch, i. 327), and who mentions 'gilt

3600) by the eighth king of the Third Dynasty, the Sephouris of Manetho, the Senoferu ('he that makes good ') of the inscriptions, who lies buried in the pyramid of Mi-tum (Maydúm).[1] A rock-tablet of this Pharaoh, the ' great god, the subduer,

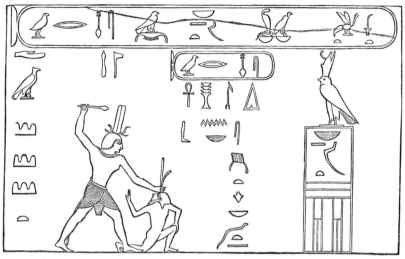

FIG. 73.—SEPHURIS AT WADY MAGHARAH (OLDEST ROCK TABLETS). THIRD DYNASTY.

FIG. 74.—SORIS AND THE CANAANITES AT WADY MAGHARAH (OLDEST ROCK TABLETS). FOURTH DYNASTY.

conqueror of countries,' shows him holding a foreigner by the hair and smiting the captive with a mace. Above his head are carved a graver (pick ?) and a mallet. Soris, first Pharaoh of the Fourth Dynasty, ' Lord of Upper and Lower Egypt, ever

copper '; of Amon-hotep III., also 'the Great' (Eighteenth Dynasty, about B.C. 1500) ; and of other Pharaohs who worked these diggings.

[1] Pottery has lately been found embedded in the bricks of the Maydúm Pyramid.

living,' also strikes down an enemy and shows the same symbols. They again appear in the tablet of Souphis, the Shufu or Khufu of the Tables of Abydos and Sakkara,[1] and the Cheops of the Great Pyramid, whilst they are wanting in that of his brother Nu-Shufu (Souphis II.) or Khafra (Cephren) of the Pyramid.

Fig. 75.—Tablet of Suphis and Nu-Suphis at Wady Magharah. (Fourth Dynasty.)

The diggings were not abandoned till the days of Amenemhat, of the Twelfth Dynasty, when the labourers were removed to Sarábit-el-Khádim, the 'Men-hirs' (not heights) of the Servant in the Wady Nasb or Valley of Sacrificial Stone. Here gangs of miners, guarded by a strong force, extracted (as the slag-heaps show) Mafka or Mefka[2] (copper? malachite?[3] turquoise?), 'black metal' (copper), 'green stones' (malachite?), manganese, and iron. Supt and Athor or Hathor (Venus), the Isis of pure light, who presided over the Mafka-land, and who was the 'goddess of copper,' are mentioned in a tablet. Other hieroglyphs contain the names and titles of the rulers, and fragments of vases bear the name of Mene-Pthah,[4] one of the supposed Pharaohs of the Exodus. The 'hands' left their marks by graffiti or scribblings, and there are extensive remains of slave-quarters, of deep cuts, and of rock-sunk moulds for running the metal

---

[1] The Souphis I. of Manetho is the second king of the Fourth Dynasty following Soris. Souphis II. is the Khafra of the Tables and the Cephren of the Greeks.

[2] The hieroglyphic is of several forms ;

may serve as a specimen.

[3] 'Malachite' is the Greek *molochotis*, from the mohokhe, or marsh-mallow ; whence the Arabic *mulukhīyeh*. In Poland, malachite and turquoise preside over the month of December.

[4] Meaning the Beloved of Ptah, the Opener, the Artificer God. The word is found in the Arabic *fath*. It is a better derivation for *Hephæstus* than 'Vaishravana' ; but Sanskrit is so copious that any given word can be derived from it.

into ingots. Sarábit-el-Khádim continued working until Ramses IV. (Twentieth Dynasty), the last royal name there found : his date in round numbers would be B.C. 1150. Agatharchides (B.C. 100) reports that chisels of chalcos ($\lambda\alpha\tau o\mu\acute{\iota}\delta\epsilon\varsigma\ \chi\alpha\lambda\kappa\alpha\hat{\iota}$) were found buried in the ancient gold mines of Egypt, and hence he, deduces that the use of iron was unknown.

From Kemi or Xημία, ' black-earth land,' *alias* Egypt, the art of metallurgy doubtless extended southwards into the heart of Africa. Hence travellers wonder when they see admirable and artistic blacksmiths amongst races whose sole idea of a house is a round hut of wattle and dab. The only coppers in South Africa with which I am familiar are those of Katanga in the Cazembe's country,[1] where the Portuguese have long traded. Captain Cameron [2] was shown a calabash full of nuggets found when clearing a water-hole. In Uguhha he procured a ' Handa' from Urua, a Saint Andrew's cross with central ribs to the arms, measuring diagonally fifteen to sixteen inches by two inches wide and half an inch thick : the weight was two and a half to three pounds. The people prefer this ' red copper ' to the ' white copper,' as they call gold. In the Pantheon of Yoruban Abeokuta, ' Ogun,' the local Vulcan and Wayland Smith, god of metal-workers and armourers, is symbolised by a dwarf spear of copper or iron, and human sacrifices are, or were, made to it. Barth (vol. iii.) notes the copper (ja-n-Karfi) in El-Hofrah ('the Diggings ') of Waday, south of Dar-For ; and in the Kano, the Runga, and the Bute countries. Copper wire is worn by the women of the hill-lands of Gurma, but it is supposed to be brought from Ashanti (?). Africa, however, is as yet unexplored as regards its mineral wealth, and we are only beginning to work our old-world California—the Gold Coast. Farther south the highly-important copper-mines of Pemba, now Bemba, and other parts of the inner Congo and Benguella regions, were discovered by the Capitão-Mór, Balthazar Rebello de Aragão, in 1621–23.[3] Still more to the south, Namaqua-land supplies chalcitic ores, a native carbonate, reduced with cow-chips.

In Asia mines were worked by the ancient Assyrians for copper as well as lead and iron, and the former was applied to their weapons, tools, and ornaments.[4] The Kurds and Chaldæans still extract from the Tiyari heights about Lizan and the valley of Berwari various minerals—copper, lead, and iron ; silver, and perhaps gold. Upon the Steppes of Tartary, and in the wildest parts of Siberia, the remains of old copper-furnaces, small and of rude construction, are met with. The Digaru Mishmís of Assam have copper-headed arrows.

The Chinese declare that in olden times men used the metal for arms, which in the days of the Thsin (B.C. 300) began to be made of iron. Sir John Davis (i. 230)

[1] *O Muata Cazembe*, by Monteiro and Gamitto, describes the copper works in South-East Africa long known to the natives. I am told by Mr. Hooker, C.E., that he has lately seen (*pace* Herodotus) ' magnificent specimens of native copper sent from Abyssinia.'

[2] R.N., C.B., &c., *Across Africa*, vol. i. pp. 134, 319 ; and vol. ii. pp. 149, 329.
[3] *Viagens dos Portuguezes, Colecção de Documentos*, &c.
[4] Layard's *Nineveh*, i. 224, ii. 415 ; 6th edit. 1854.

confirms the fact that the Chinese Sword and backsword, both wretched weapons, were originally of copper, long ago changed to iron. Dr. Pfizmaier tells us that about B.C. 475 the King of U sent a steel blade to his minister, U-tse-tsui, wherewith to behead himself. According to Pliny, the Seres exported iron to Europe together with their tissues and their skins. The Chinese distinguish between Thse-thung (purple copper) and Thing-sung (green copper) or bronze. They prefer the 'Tze-lae,' or natural ore, gathered in the torrent-beds of Kwei-chow and Yun-nan, and the latter exclusively produces the famous Pe-tung,[1] or white copper, which takes a fine polish like silver. They made copper the base of their coinage as well as their weapons. Amongst their many charms and talismans are the 'money-swords,' a number of ancient copper coins pierced with a square central hole, and connected by a metal bar shaped like a cross-hilted Sword. These are suspended over the testerns of beds and sleeping-couches, that the guardianship of the kings in whose reigns the money was issued may keep away ghosts and spirits.

The Japanese copper[2] is of the finest quality, and is used as a standard of comparison. The superiority of the metal, which contains a percentage of gold, enabled the self-taught native workmen to produce those castings which are the admiration and the despair of the European artist. The copper delivered at Nagasaki and Kwashi is from Beshki, Akita, and Nambu ; other places produce the more ordinary kinds. The rich red surface is due to a thin and tenaciously adhering film of dioxide : this has been imitated in England. The famous Satzuma copper, held to be the best in the world, was prepared under Government officials, none being sold privately. The ore was roasted in kilns for ten to twenty days, smelted in large furnaces with charcoal, and cast in water to make the well-known Japanese ingots. These were bars measuring about half an inch on the side, by seven to nine inches in length, and weighing some ten taels, nearly equal to one pound. They were packed in boxes each weighing a picul ($=125$ to $133\frac{1}{3}$ lbs. avoir.), about the load of a man. The price of course greatly varied. The trade was at first wholly in the hands of the Hollanders, who made a good thing of their monopoly. There was also an old traffic in Japanese copper on the eastern coast of India, especially Coromandel. The opening of the empire has caused revolutionary changes.

Copper was abundantly produced in Europe, and the pure metal was used throughout the continent with the exception of Scandinavia, where specimens are exceedingly rare. The iron age of Denmark begins with the Christian era, and was preceded only by bronze and stone. We know nothing of the discovery of copper in Ireland. It is supposed in legend to have been introduced by the Fir-bolgs (bag-men, Belgæ ?), or by the Tuatha (gens) de Danaan (the Danes ?).

[1] Hence our *packfong*, or German silver, of China, an alloy of copper (50 per cent.), nickel, and zinc (25 per cent. each).

[2] The *Chinese Repository* gives a hundred illustrations of the implements in use by the Chinese and the Japanese.

These oft-quoted races, known to us only by name, have been affiliated with a host of continentals, even with the Greeks.[1] It would be mere guess-work to consider the Irish style of treating the ores—by spalling or breaking the stone, by wasting, fluxing, or smelting. We have, however, many specimens which explain the casting. The metal was called by the natives Uma or Umha, a Keltic word ; also Dearg Umha, red copper, opposed to Ban [2] Umha (white copper) or tin ; and this term afterwards became ' stan,' evidently from stannum (Gall. Estain). There are still traditions of copper mines having existed at an early period ; and, among the wonders related by Nonnius (Archæol. Soc. Ireland), we find Loch Lein, now Killarney, surrounded by four circles of copper, tin, lead, and iron. Of late years ' miners' hammers,' the native name for stone pounders, have been dug up in the neighbourhood of that lake, in Northern Antrim, at an ancient mine in Ballycastle, and in sundry parts of Southern Ireland.[3] The metal occurs in small quantities at Bonmahon (Waterford) ; copper and cobalt at Mucross, and grey copper ore in Cork, Kerry, Tipperary, and Galway. In 1855 some 1157 tons were shipped to Swansea.

The Greenlanders and Eskimos cut and hammer their pure native copper, without smelting, into nails, arrow-piles, and other tools and weapons. Mackenzie (second voyage) tells us that pure copper was common among the tribes on the borders of the Arctic Sea, whose arrow-heads and spear-heads were cold-wrought with the hammer. Columbus (fourth voyage), before touching the mainland of Honduras, saw at Guanaga Island a canoe from Yucatan [4] laden with goods, amongst which he specifies ' copper hatchets, and other elaborate articles, cast and soldered ; forges, and crucibles.' [5] At Hayti the great Admiral (first expedition) had mentioned masses of native copper weighing six arrobas (quarters).[6] When the Spaniards first entered the province of Tupan they mistook the bright copper axes for gold of low touch, and bought with beads some six hundred in two days : [7] Bernal Dias describes these articles as being very highly polished, with the handle curiously carved, as if to serve equally for an ornament and for the field of battle.

In North America there are two great copper regions which supplied the whole continent [8]—Lake Superior and the lower Rio Grande. The former shows the

---

[1] *Fir* or *fear* (*vir*, a man), and *bolg* (*Bolgi, Belgæ*), a belly, bag, budget, or quiver. They occupied Southern Britain, and formed the third immigrant colony preceding the ' Milesians,' sons of Milidh or Miledh (Senchus Mor), evidently *Miles*, the soldier. He had two sons, Emer and Airem, from whom the Irish race is descended. Emer, says Prof. Rhys, may represent the Ivernii or pre-Celtic population mentioned by Ptolemy ; and Airem, which means ' a farmer,' the Iranian race which introduced agriculture amongst a horde of hunters. The fourth colony was the Tuatha (people, e.g. Tuatha-Eireann = people of Erin), named from Danair, a stranger, foreigner, and properly a Dane. We have lately been shown how much true history may be obtained from these names, which had become bye-words, almost ridiculous to use.

[2] *Bán* (our corrupted ' bawn,' as in ' Molly Bawn'), white, is the Latin *canus*. It is also a noun substantive, meaning ' copper.'

[3] Wilde, *Catalogue*, pp. 58, 356.

[4] Meaning *Tectetan* = ' I don't know.' So the *M'adri* on an old English chart of the Euphrates.

[5] *Select Letters of Columbus*, &c. p. 201. Translated by R. H. Major, Hakluyt Society, 1870.

[6] Humboldt, *Travels*, iii. 194.

[7] *Commentaries of the Yncas.* Translated by Clements R. Markham, C.B. Hakluyt Society, 1871.

[8] Daniel Wilson's *Prehistoric Man*, vol. i. chap.

first transitional steps from stone to metal. The ore occurs in the igneous and trappean rocks that wall in the vast fresh-water sea, and is found in solid blocks : one, fifty feet long, six feet deep, and six feet in average thickness, was estimated to weigh eighty tons. At Copper Harbour, Kawunam Point, a single vein yielded forty thousand pounds. The largest mass in the Minnesota Mine (Feb. 1857) occupied Mr. Petherick and forty men for twelve months : it was forty-five feet long, thirty-two feet broad (max.), and eight feet thick ; containing over forty per cent. ore, and weighing four hundred and twenty to five hundred tons. Malleable and ductile, representing an average of 3·10 per cent. native silver, and with a specific gravity of 8·78 to 8·96, it required no crucible but Nature's ; it wanted only beating into shape, and it needed nothing of the skilled labour necessary for the ores of Cornwall and Devon, which contributed so largely to the wealth of Tyre. The workings are supposed to belong to the race conveniently called ' Mound-builders,' and to date from our second century, when the Damnonians of Cornwall were in a similar state of civilisation. ' Cliff Mine ' supplied fine specimens of weapons and tools, arrow-piles and spear-heads, knives and three-sided blades like the old bayonet. The socket was formed by hammering flat the lower end, and by turning it over partially (without overlapping) at each side, so as to make a flange. Professor James D. Butler (' Prehistoric Wisconsin ') facsimiles twenty-four copper implements. The ' Indians ' called the metal Miskopewalik (red iron), opposed to black iron. As is also proved by the Brockville relics, the people had the art of hardening copper.

The mines of the lower Rio Grande supplied Mexico with materials for arms and tools. According to Captain R. H. Bonnycastle,[1] the metal was found in New Mexico and in the volcanic rocks of Mechoacan (Valladolid, New Spain). Mexico, like Peru, used the crucible and added bronze to copper. The metals were under the god Quetzalcoatl, an Aztec Tubal Cain-ben-Lamech.

Another great centre of the Copper Age was the land ' where men got gold as they do iron out of Biscay.' The Peruvian army, a host of three hundred thousand levied from a total population of twenty millions, was armed with bows and arrows, clubs, pikes, javelins, war-axes (of stone and copper), and the paddle-sword ;[2] while

viii.; *The Metallurgic Arts, Copper* (pp. 231–79). Prof. Brush, of Yale College, calculated that 6,000 tons were yielded in 1858.

[1] R.E., *Spanish America*, &c. (Philadelphia : Abraham Small, 1819), p. 49.

[2] It was divided, like the Greek and Roman, into centuries (*pachacas*), chiliarchies (*hurangos*), and inspectorships (*tokrikrok*), generally under royalties. The organisation was due to the Ynka Inti-Kapak (the Great), B.C. 1500–1600. There was a large fleet (' magna colcharum classis ') of ships not smaller than the contemporary European, ' navigiis velificantur nihili vestris minoribus,' says P. Martyr (*Decad.* ii. lib. 3). Neither traveller nor historian

has explained how this mighty organisation crumbled to pieces at the touch of a few European adventurers.

I have read with interest the able work of M. Vicente F. Lopez, *Les Races Aryennes du Pérou* (Paris : Franck, 1871) : he derives the word from Pirhua, the first Ynka deified to a Creator. He adopts (p. 17) against Garcilasso de la Vega, who gave the Ynkarial Empire 400 years, the opinions of the learned Dr. Fernando Montésinos el Visitador, of the later sixteenth century, who is set aside by Markham, *Narratives of the Yncas* (Hakluyt, 1873). Montésinos derives the Peruvians from Armenia five centuries after ' the Flood,' and assigns 4,000 years with 101 emperors to the dynasty ; it begins with Manko Kapak, son of Pirhua Manko ; and Sinchi

the people of Anahuac (Mexico) had bows and spears, clubs and axes, knives and Swords one-handed and two-handed, the Mahquahuitl set with obsidian teeth. In the former country the pre-Ynkarial Aymaras, who dug for gold and silver, copper and tin, and who employed alloys, almost ignored for their ' Ayri ' (cutting implements) the use of iron and steel, which they called Quella (Khellay). The Andes range is popularly derived from the Quichua word Anta[1] (copper) : the native ore occurred in the parts above the cultivation-line, and it abounded in the cupriferous sandstones of Bolivian Corocoro. The Huaunanchuco country (Rivero and Tschudi, p. 203),[2] conquered by the ninth Ynka, produced a fine collection of stone and copper axes, chisels, pins, and tweezers. Blas Valera, one of the earliest writers, still often quoted, tells us that 'Anta' served in place of iron, and that the people worked it more than other ores, preferring it to gold (*Khori*) and silver.[3] Of it were made their knives, carpenters' tools, women's dress-pins (*Tupies*), polished mirrors, and ' all their rakes and hammers.' Garcilasso de la Vega adds : ' pikes, clubs, halberts, and pole-axes,[4] made of silver, copper, and some of gold, the " tears of the sun," having sharp points, and some hardened by the fire' ; also carpenters' axes ; adzes and hatchets ; bill-hooks of copper, and blow-pipes of the same metal about a yard long applied to earthen or clay pots which they carried from place to place. A nugget or loose pebble acted as bell-clapper, and copper statuettes were coated or plated with precious metals. The ' Royal Commentaries of the Yncas' tells us

Roka (No. xcv. of Montésinos) is Garcilasso's official founder (p. 25).

But I cannot follow M. Lopez in his theories of ' Aryanism' (Zend and Sanskrit) or 'Turanianism' (Chinese and Tartar). The Quichua wants the peculiar Hindu cerebrals (which linger in English), and lacks the 'l,' so common in ' Indo-European' speech ; ' Lima,' for instance, should be ' Rima.' It has no dual, and no distinction between masculine and feminine. But with the licence which M. Lopez allows himself, any language might be derived from any other. For instance, *chinka* from *sinha*, 'the lion' (p. 138); *hakchikis = hashish*, 'intoxicating herb'; *kekenti*, 'humming-bird,' from *kvan*, 'to hum'; *hua-hua*, 'son,' from *su*, 'to engender,' *sunus*, &c., (when in Egypt we have *su*); and *mama*, 'mother,' from *mata*, μήτηρ, *mater*, when we have *mut* and *mute* in Nile-land. For *mara*, 'to kill,' 'death,' the old Coptic preserves *mer*, *meran*, 'to die'; and for *mayu*, 'water,' *mu*.

I thus prefer the monosyllabic Egyptian for Quichua roots, noting the two forms of pronoun, isolated (*nyoka* = I = *anuk*) and affixed (*huahua-i*, 'my son;' *huahua-ki*, 'thy son;' *huahua-u*, 'his son'). The heliolatry of the Andes was that of the Nile Valley ; *Kon* is the Egyptian *Tum*, 'the setting sun.' The god Papacha wears on his head the scarabæus of Ptah, or Creative Might. The pyramids and mega-lithic buildings are also Nilotic. The pottery shows three several styles, Egyptian, Etruscan, and Pelasgic. The population was divided into the four Egyptian

castes (p. 396), priests (*mankos* and *amautas*), soldiers (*aucas*, *aukas*), peasants (*uyssus*), and shepherds or nomads (*chakis*). According to Cieza de Leon (p. 197) they thought more of the building and adorning of their tombs than of their houses ; their mummies were protected by little idols, and the corpse car-ried the ferryman's fee. The pyramid of Copan (Yucatan), 122 feet high, with its 6-feet steps, is that of Sakkarah. The Yucatan beard in statues is Pharaohic. The elephant-trunk ornaments (Stephens, ii. 156) are Indo-Chinese. The geese-breeding (ii. 179) is Egyptian. See also the Toltec legend of the House of Israel (ii. 172).

[1] The 'lovely valley, Andahualas,' is from Anta and Huaylla, pasture – i.e. 'copper-coloured meadow.' Anta in Cieza de Leon appears to be copper, whereas other writers make it bronze.

[2] *Peruvian Antiquities*, by Don M. E. de Rivero and J. J. von Tschudi.

[3] They abandoned the native silver mines when the ore became too hard, and they smelted it in small portable stoves. They knew also the chemical com-binations, sulphate, antimonial, and others ; and they worked quicksilver. They had mines of Quella (Khellay, or iron), but they found difficulty in ex-tracting it. Besides smelting, they could use the tacana (hammer), cast in moulds, inlay, and solder.

[4] Ewbank, of whom more presently, sketches a well-cast axe (p. 455). He translates *anta* by bronze (p. 455).

that copper served in place of iron for making weapons of war : the people valued it highly because more useful than gold and silver ; the demand was greater than for any other metal, and it paid tribute (vol. i. pp. 25, 43, 48). We find notices of copper hammers, bellows-nozzles, adzes, axes, and bill-hooks (i. p. 102). Cieza de Leon (chap. lxiii.) tells us that the Peruvians placed a piece of gold, silver, or copper in the corpse's mouth. He mentions vases of copper and of stone (chap. civ.), and small furnaces of clay where they laid the charcoal and blew the fire with thin canes instead of bellows (ibid.). The Introduction (p. lii) notes the Peruvian use of copper-trowels for smoothing and polishing walls, and a 'terrible weapon of copper in the shape of a star.' According to Rivero and Tschudi (chap. ix.) the Peruvians could not work copper as well as gold or silver ; yet they made idols, vases, solid staves a yard long with serpents inlaid, and sceptre-heads decorated with condor-like birds. The household *vaisselle* of the Ynkas consisted of gold and silver, copper and stone. Rivero, analysing Peruvian weapons and tools (hatchets and chisels), found from five to ten per cent. silica : he could not determine whether it was an artificial or an accidental impurity. Tschudi (1841) discovered copper arms in a tomb three leagues from Huaco, and established the fact that the Peruvians used the paddle-sword and the scymitar.[1] A copper axe, found in a Huaca (old grave) at the now well-known Arica, was associated with a thong-sling and with other primitive instruments.

The people of New Granada, according to the tale of Bollaert,[2] 'gilt' their copper by 'rubbing the juice of a plant on it and then putting it into the fire, when it took the gold colour'—a process which reminds us of Pliny's ox-gall varnish. Ecuador forged copper nippers for tweezers. The Chitchas, or Muiscas (i.e. men), of Bogota, who knew only gold and ignored copper, tin, lead, and iron, made their weapons and tools of hard wood and stone. Thomas Ewbank,[3] of New York, catalogues as breast-plates two laminæ of copper and one of bronze, the latter being notably the lighter. Out of sundry 'bronzes' from Peru he found four of pure copper. Chile had abundant mines of copper, and her metal is held to be the toughest : a bar three-eighths of an inch thick will bend backwards and forwards forty-eight times before breaking. Her chief centres are Copiapo (i.e. 'turquoise'), Huasco, Coquimbo, Aconcágua and Caléo. The Couche range at Guatacondo, in sight of the desert of Atacama, which gave a name to Atacamite (submuriate of copper), is said to supply from the same vein gold, silver, copper, and coquimbite or white copperas called Pampua (pack-fong ?).[4] Gillis (Plate viii. 12, 3) described, amongst the antiquities found near the great Ynkarial High-

---

[1] Doubtless copied from Old-World articles. On the west side of Palenque the Sword is distinctly Egyptian (Stephens, *Yucatan*). I have attempted to show how easily castaway mariners could be swept by currents from Europe, Asia, Africa, and America. See 'Ostreiras of the Brazil' in *Anthropologia*, No. 1, October 1873.

[2] *Antiquarian, Ethnological, and other Researches.*

By William Bollaert. London : Trübner, 1860. We must probably change 'brass' into 'bronze' when he says (p. 90) that 'the Peruvians used tools of brass.'

[3] Appendix to *Life in Brazil* (Sampson Low, 1856).

[4] This white copperas was detected by Scacchi on the fumaroles after the Vesuvian eruption of 1855.

road, a cast copper axe, weighing about three and a quarter pounds: he doubts, however, that the ancient Chilians worked in that metal. The wild Araucanians called gold 'copper' (Bollaert, p. 184). According to Molina, the Puelche tribe extracted from the mines of Payen a copper containing half its weight (?) in gold; and the same natural alloy was found in the Curico mines.

Returning to the Old World, we see copper tools denoted in Egyptian hieroglyphs by a reddish-brown tint;[1] iron and steel, as in Assyria, being coloured, not grey, but water-blue.[2] With these yellow tools the old workmen are seen cutting stone blocks and fashioning colossal statues. Dr. John Forbes, of Edinburgh,[3] had a large chisel of pure copper, showing marks of use, found with a wooden mallet in an Egyptian tomb. A flat piece of copper, apparently a knife-blade, was turned up when boring thirteen feet below the surface where stands the statue of Ramses II. (B.C. 1400).[4] The Abbé Barthélemy proved, to the satisfaction of P. J. Rossignol, that the arms of the Greeks were first of copper; that iron was introduced about the date of the Trojan war (circ. B.C. 1200),[5] and that after this time 'Athor-Venus' was no more in use. Ulysses ('Iliad,' i. 4, 279) offers Achilles all the gold and copper he can collect, and Achilles will carry off all the gold, the red copper ($\chi\alpha\lambda\kappa\grave{o}\nu$ $\grave{\epsilon}\rho\upsilon\theta\rho\acute{o}\nu$), women, and iron or steel ($\sigma\acute{\iota}\delta\eta\rho o\nu$), when Peleides returns that noble answer:

> Hostile to me is the man as the hatefullest gateway of Hades,
> Whoso in thought one thing dare hide and utter another.[6]

Numa ordered the priests to cut their hair with copper, not iron, scissors.[7] Copper vases and kettles as tomb-furniture were found by Dr. Schliemann at Mycenæ: the museum of the Warwakeion at Athens contains seven of these funeral urns. They have also been met with at Etruscan Corneto and Palestrina, and in Austrian Hallstatt,[8] a cemetery which dates from the days when iron was coming

---

[1] Gold was shown by yellow, and silver by white. Dr. Evans (*Bronze*, &c. p. 7) suggests that the round blue bar used by butchers (Wilkinson, iii. 247) was not of steel; but his reasons are peculiarly unsatisfactory. The file is a common implement amongst savages, doubtless derived from the practice of cross-hatching wooden grips and handles. Mr. A. H. Rhind (*Thebes*, &c.) attributes little weight to the diversity of colours employed by ancient Egyptians to depict metallic objects, and he finds red and green confused.

[2] Thus we have a blue war-helmet of ring-mail (Lepsius, *Denkmäler*, iii. 115 &c.), a blue war-hatchet with wooden handle, and spears pointed with brown-red and blue (copper and iron) in the tomb of Ramses III. The war-car of an Æthiopian king, in the days of Tutankamun, has blue wheels and a body of yellow (gold). Lepsius, however, adds: 'It is very remarkable that in all the representations of the old empire, blue-painted instruments can scarcely be traced.' This simply proves that iron and steel were rare.

[3] *Prehistoric Man*, chap. viii.

[4] It was analysed by Mr. E. Tookey, with the following results:

Copper .	.	.	.	97·12
Arsenic .	.	.	.	2·29
Iron	.	.	.	0·43
Tin, with traces of gold .		.		0·24
				100·08

The presence of the tin may have been accidental. The proportion of arsenic ($2\frac{1}{4}$ per cent.) might have been expected to harden the metal, yet it was so soft as to be almost useless.

[5] See chap. ix.

[6] It is equivalent to the Roman's 'Aliud clausum in pectore, aliud in lingua promptum habere.'

[7] So amongst the Jews the sharp knives for circumcision (*Josh.* v. 2–3) were of the silex which they learned from the Egyptians; and the custom continued long after the invention of metal blades.

[8] It was opened by Herr Ramsauer, and carefully described in *Das Grabfeld von Hallstatt*, by Baron

into use, and apparently belongs to a much later period than Mycenæ. The Hindús had a copper coinage, and that of the sub-Himalayan Gangetic provinces appears older than Greek art. There is a copper coin bearing on the reverse the rude figure of a horse, and on the obverse a man with legend in old Buddhist (Pali) letters Khatrapasa Pagámashasa.[1] The Jews, who, like the Etruscans, had a copper coinage, used the metal for offence and defence. As amongst the Philistines, Phœnicians, and Carthaginians, whose relics have been found in the Cannæ Plain, the metal was at first pure. The 'bow of steel' (Job xx. 24, Ps. xviii. 34) should be rendered 'bow of copper,' either copper-plated or (more probably) so tempered as to be elastic. Goliah of Gath (B.C. 1063), who measured nine feet six inches, carried a target, greaves, a spear with an iron head, and a scale-coat[2] of copper : the spear-head weighed six hundred and the armour five thousand shekels (each 320 grains Troy), or 33·33 and 277·77 lbs.[3] David was armed (1 Sam. xvii. 38) with a helmet of copper. Ishi-benob (B.C. 1018), who was 'of the sons of the giant,' carried a spear weighing three hundred shekels (about sixteen and a half pounds) of copper. Finally, Buffon believes that the arms of the ancient Asiatics were cuprine.

Mr. John Latham declares :[4] 'Copper is a metal of which, in its unalloyed state, no relics have been found throughout England. Stone and bone first, then bronze or copper and tin combined, but no copper alone. I cannot get over this hiatus, cannot imagine a metallurgic industry beginning with the use of alloys.' But this is a negative argument. The simple mineral would soon disappear to make bronze, and we have some pure specimens. Sir David Brewster[5] describes a large battle-axe of pure copper found on the blue clay, twenty feet deep below the Ratho Bog. Philips[6] gives the analysis of eight so-called 'bronzes,' including three Swords, one from the Thames and two from Ireland : the spear-head was of impure but unalloyed copper, 99·71 to 0·28 sulphur. Dr. Daniel Wilson[7] analysed

---

E. von Sacken. I shall have more to say of it in chap. xiii.

[1] Prinseps' *Essays* (London, 1858), vol. i. p. 222, pl. xliv. fig. 12, and *Journ. R. As. Soc. Bengal*, vol. vii. pl. xxxii. fig. 12. Long descriptions of copper smelting in India are found in *Science Gleanings*, pp. 380 *et seq.*, No. 36, Dec. 1831, Calcutta, and in Percy (*Metall.* p. 387) ; the latter by Mr. H. F. Blanford, of the Geol. Survey, who made especial studies in Himalayan Sikkim and the Nepaulese Tirhai. The workmen, who are of low caste, win the stone in small blast-furnaces about three feet high, burning charcoal and cow-chips. They work not only the easily reducible carbonates, but sulphuretted ores, copper pyrites, with a mixture of mundic (iron pyrites).

[2] Scales are apparently implied by *kaskassin* (1 *Sam.* xvii.), which in Leviticus and Ezekiel applies to fish-scales.

[3] The shekel is usually estimated at 220 grs.

(Troy), which would reduce the weights to 22·91 and 190·97 lbs. respectively ; but Maimonides makes it = 320 grains of barley = as many grains Troy. See Parkhurst (*Lex., s.v.* 'Amat'). Either figure would form a fair burden for a horse ; and the spear would have been a most unhandy article, unless used by a man ten feet tall. I shall notice the Gathite's Sword in chap. ix.

[4] *Ethnology of the British Islands.* We also read: 'Copper Swords have been found in Ireland ; iron among the Britons and Gauls ; bronze was used by the Romans, and probably by the Egyptians ; and steel of varying degrees of hardness is now the only weapon employed.' (J. Latham : see chap. vii.)

[5] *Trans. Edinb. Philos. Soc.* Feb. 1822.

[6] J. A. Phillips, F.C.S. *Memoirs of the Chemical Soc.* vol. iv.

[7] *Archæology and Prehistoric Annals of Scotland*, p. 246.

in 1850 seven British 'bronzes,' and found one Scottish axe-head, rudely sand-cast, of almost pure copper, the natural alloy of gold and silver not reaching to one per cent. Moreover, the Romans certainly smelted copper in England, where lumps of pure metal, more or less rounded, have been found, but always in association with bronze articles. Pennant describes a relic discovered at Caerhun (or Caerhen), the old Conovium, near Conway and Llandudno, which still works copper : it was shaped like a cake of beeswax, measuring eleven inches by three and three-quarter inches in thickness ; it weighed forty-two pounds, and the upper surface bore in deep impression, 'Socio Romæ' (to the partner at Rome). Obliquely across the legend ran in smaller letters, 'Natsoc.' It had evidently been smelted upon the spot. In later days our country imported her copper from Sweden and Hungary : this appears in the specification of patent to George Danby, Jan. 21, 1636. Calamine was shipped as ballast. Our great works began during the last century and culminated in Swansea.

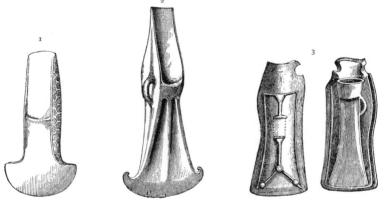

FIG. 76.—THE WINGED CELTS, OR PALSTAVE.

1. Semilunar blade ; the rounded side edges are ornamented in the casting with a raised hexagon pattern ; they project somewhat above the level of the flat surface of the implement. The curved stops, which are rudimentary, have their concavities facing the handle. 2. In the Palstave celt the loop is usually placed beneath the stock, and in the socketed ones it is always close to the top. The cut, drawn one-third of the actual size, represents the usual position of the loop. The lunette cutting edge, with marked recurved points, presents the appearance of having been ground.[1] These implements were cast in moulds of bronze, examples of which have been brought to light at various times. The third illustration represents the upper part of one of these celt moulds and the method of casting : they were for a long time a source of confusion to the discoverers, although Colonel Vallancy assigns them to their true use.

Wilde (p. 490) expresses the general opinion when he asserts that 'the use of copper invariably preceded that of bronze.' He well explains by two reasons why so few antique implements of pure copper have been found in Ireland : either a very short period elapsed between the discovery of treating the pure ores and the introduction of bronze ; or the articles, once common, were recast and converted into the more valuable mixed metal. The latter cause is made probable by the early intercourse with Cornwall, one of the great tin emporia. 'Tin-stone' (native peroxide of tin or stannic acid) is produced in small quantities by Ireland, and Dr. Charles Smith[2] declares that he collected it.

[1] See Sir W. Wilde's *Cat. Metallic Materials—Celts*, Museum of Royal Irish Academy.
[2] *History of Kerry*, p. 125.

Wilde also notices, in the Royal Irish Academy, weapons, tools, and ornaments of red metal or pure copper. These are thirty celts of the greatest simplicity and the earliest pattern, rudely formed tools, a few fibulæ, a trumpet, two battle-axes, and several Sword-blades of the short, broad, and curved shape usually called scythes.

The pure copper celts, formed upon two or three types, are the oldest in the

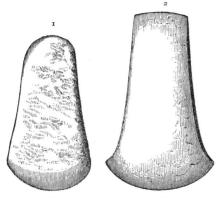

FIG. 77.—COPPER CELTS IN THE DUBLIN COLLECTION.

Dublin collection, and were probably the immediate successors of the stone implement. As a rule they have one side smoother than the other, as if they had been run into simple stone moulds ; they are also thicker and of rougher surface than the bronze article. For the most part they are rude and unornamented wedges of cast metal : a few are lunette-shaped and semilunar blades. The cleansed specimens show a great variety of colour. When first found, the brown crust, peculiar to the oxidised metal, readily distinguishes them from the bronze patina, the beautiful varnish of æruginous or verdigris hue, artificial malachite resembling in colour the true native carbonate of copper.

The broad scythe-shaped Swords, numbering forty-one, are supposed to be ' specially and peculiarly Irish.' The straight blades are shown by their large burrs, holes, and rivets either to end in massive handles of metal, or to be attached to wooden staves, long or short. Of this kind some are curved. As many are of ' red bronze ' (pure copper), darkened by oxidation, it is probable that they are of great antiquity, like the celts of that period. Although in some cases the points have been broken off, yet the edges are neither hacked, indented, nor worn ; hence the conclusion that they were true stabbing Swords. Yet Mr. John Evans declares that he knows no such thing as a copper Sword. In this matter he partially follows Lévesque de la Ravalière, who declared copper arms unknown to the Greeks [1] and Romans, Gauls and Franks : this savant was refuted and charged with unfairly treating his authorities by the Comte de Caylus in a description of seven copper Swords dug up (1751) at Gensal in the Bourbonnais. The Abbé Barthélemy attributed seven copper blades to the Franks in the reign of Childeric.

We have ample evidence that ' copper ' is ambiguously used by modern travellers. The modern discoverer of Troy [2] gives us, in his last and revised volume, a full account of exploring fifty-three feet deep of débris and laying bare the stratified ruins of seven cities, including that of the 'ground floor' and the Macedonian ruins. The two lowest bear witness to a copper age anterior to bronze, whilst they

[1] Yet Æschylus (*Agamem.*) uses both *chalcos* and *sideros* generically for a weapon.
[2] *Ilios*, &c. (London, Murray, 1880).

yielded the only gilded object, a copper knife, and the most advanced art in specimens of hand-made pottery.[1] The second from below was walled, and the third, the most important, was the Burnt City, the city of the golden treasures, identified with Ilios. The explorer claims to have reduced the Homeric Ilium to its true proportions. The grand characteristic in his finds is the paucity of iron, which appeared only in the shape of oxidised 'sling-bullets': tin is also absent. Both these metals, it is true, oxidise most readily ; yet, had the objects been numerous, they would have left signs, in rust and stains. From 'Troy' we learn (p. 22) that 'all the copper articles met with are of pure copper, without the

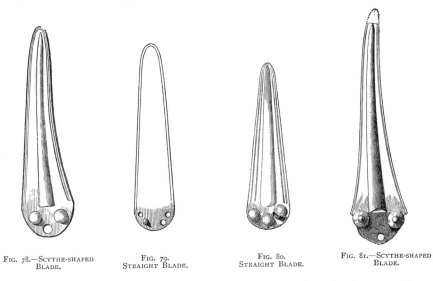

| FIG. 78.—SCYTHE-SHAPED BLADE. | FIG. 79. STRAIGHT BLADE. | FIG. 80. STRAIGHT BLADE. | FIG. 81.—SCYTHE-SHAPED BLADE. |

admixture of any other metal': the author also finds that 'implements of pure copper were employed contemporaneously with enormous quantities of stone weapons and implements.' He will not admit ('Troy,' p. 82) that he has reached the bronze period when he discovers in the 'Trojan stratum,' at a depth of thirty-three to forty-six and fifty-two feet, nails, knives, lances, and 'elegantly-worked battle-axes of pure copper.'[2] And we can accept the copper, for much of it was analysed by Professor Landerer, of Athens, 'a chemist well known through his discoveries and writings.' He examined the fragments found in the 'Treasury of Priam,' and made all of them to consist of pure copper, without any admixture of tin or zinc ('Troy,' p. 340). When treating of the Bronze Age, I shall show that alloys were not wanting.

[1] Some small objects are reported as wheel-made; but this requires confirmation, according to a writer in the *Athenæum* (Dec. 18, 1880).

[2] The copper bracelet (*Troy*, p. 150, No. 88) with its terminal knobs is the modern trade 'manilla' of the West African coast. This survival will again be noticed in chap. ix.

CHAPTER V.

THE SECOND CHALCITIC AGE OF ALLOYS [1]—BRONZE, BRASS, ETC.: THE AXE AND THE SWORD.

THE use of copper, I have said, would be essentially transitional; and the discovery of smelting one kind of metal would lead immediately to that of others and to their commixture. Moreover, when casting and moulding began to be a general practice, unalloyed copper difficult to smelt, and when melted thick, sluggish, and pasty, would not readily run without some mixture into all the sinuosities of the mould. In this chapter I propose to notice the second chalcitic age—that of the earliest combinations of metals, their workers, and their application to weapons.

J. P. Rossignol, following the opinion of the symbolists and mysticists, as the Baron de Saint Croix,[2] Creuzer, Freret, and Lobechs,[3] assigns a Divine origin—after the fashion of the day—to metallurgy, making it resemble in this point Creation, articulate language,[4] and the discovery of corn and wine. So he understands the θεολογούμενα (subjects of a theological nature) alluded to by Strabo (x. 3, § 7). It is the old hypothesis of supernatural agency in purely natural matters, a kind of luxus-wonder, as the Germans call useless miracles, which had waxed stale, even in the days of Horace—'parcus Deorum cultor et infrequens.' He considers the Curetes and Corybantes, the Cabiri (Kabeiroi) of Lemnos and Imbros, and the Idæi Dactyli of Crete, the Telchines of Rhodes, and the Sinties, Sinti, or Saii of Thrace (Strabo, xii. 3, § 20) as metallurgic δαίμονες, or genii prisoned in human form, and typifying the successive steps of the art. In these days we hardly admit the *intersit* of a deity when human nature suffices to loose the knot ; nor do we believe that our kind began by worshipping types. Man has always worshipped one thing,

---

[1] The word in its older form was written 'allay.' Johnson derives it from *à la loi, allier, allocare*: it appears to me the Spanish *el ley*, the legal quality of coinable metal. We have now naturalised in English *ley*, meaning a standard of metals. (Sub voc. *Dict. of Obsolete and Provincial English*, by Thomas Wright; London, Bell and Daldy, 1869.)

[2] *Recherches sur les Mystères*; and *Mémoire pour servir à la religion secrète*, &c. &c.

[3] The 'Aglaophemus,' so called from the initiator of Pythagoras. I see symptoms of a revival in assertions concerning a 'highly cultivated beginning, with the arts well known and practised to an extent which,

in subsequent ages, has never been approached; and from which there has not anywhere been discovered a gradual advancement ; but, on the contrary, an immediate and decidedly progressive declension.' This, however, is a mere question of dates. Man's civilisation began long before the Mosaic Creation ; and science has agreed to believe that savage life generally is not a decadence from higher types, not a degeneracy, but a gradual development.

[4] We now divide language into three periods: 1st, intonative, like the cries of children and lower animals ; 2nd, imitative, or onomatopoetic ; and 3rd, conventional, the civilised form.

himself, and himself only, either in the flesh or in the ghost—that is, in the non-flesh or the objective nothing—till he arrived at the transcendental Man, the superlative, the ideal of Himself.

How little of fact is known about the mysterious tribes above mentioned becomes evident by a glance at the classics. All six are supposed to be Asiatics, worshippers of Rhea (the earth), the great mother of the gods and queen of the metal workers. Yet Strabo explains Curetes from Greek terms κόροι (boys), κόραι (girls), κουρά (tonsure), and κουροτροφεῖν (to bring up the Boy, i.e. Jupiter). Similarly their brethren, the nine Corybantes, were termed from their dancing gait and negro-like butting with the head, κορύπτοντας. They inhabited Samothrace (Samothracia alta): this venerable and holy island, in hoar antiquity a general rendezvous of freemasonry, or rather of free-smithery, forms a triangle with metallic Thasos and with volcanic Lemnos.

The three or four Cabiri [1] bear a Semitic name, Kabir = the great or the old. They seem at first to have represented Ptah-Sokar-Osiris,[2] and Herodotus (iii. 37) mentions their temple at Memphis. They became in Phœnicia the earliest boatmen or primordial shipbuilders, identified by some with the Sesennu or Egyptian Octonary; by others with the seven planets or the stars of Typho, our Great Bear;[3] and by others, again, with the seven Khnemu (gnomes) or pygmy-sons who waited upon their father Ptah-Vulcan. They inhabited Lemnos, where Hephæstus, when expelled, like Adam, from the lowest heaven, took refuge among the Pelasgi (Diod. Sic. lib. v.): hence the latter preserved their worship. Damascius ('Life of Isidorus') says: 'The Asclepius of Berytus is neither Greek nor Egyptian, but of Phœnician origin; for (seven) sons were born to Sadyk, called Dioscuri and Cabiri, and the eighth of them was Esman (i.e. Octavius, No. 8), who is interpreted Asclepius.'[4]

The Idæan Dactyli (fingers or toes) who occupied 'fountful Ide'[5] consisted of five brothers, representing the *dextra* or lucky hand (science, art), and five sisters for the *sinistra* or unlucky (witchcraft, ill omens). The names of these 'hands' (iron-workers) were Kelmis (fire or heat = the smelter), Damnameneus (the hammer, or who governs by strength, Thor), Hercules (force, animal or mental), and Akmon (the anvil or passive principle). Hence Pyracmon the Cyclop, one of the seven architect brothers who, according to Strabo (viii. 6), came from Lycia

---

[1] *Axieros* (the earth-goddess), *Axiokersa* (Proserpine of the Greeks), *Axiokersos* (Hades), and *Casmilos* (Hermes or Mercury). Ennemoser may be right in making the Kabeiroi pygmies (i.e. gnomes), but not in rendering Dactyloi by 'finger-size.'

[2] The lame and deformed 'artificer of the universe,' who became Hephæstos (Vulcan) in Greece, and Vishvakarma in India. Sokar has left his name in the modern 'Sakkárah.'

[3] The Assyrian cuneiforms allude to 'the (Great) Bear making its crownship,' that is, circling round the North Pole.

[4] The temples of the Cabiri have lately been explored by Prof. Conze for the Austrian Government at Samothrace, and we may expect to learn something less vague concerning these mysterious ancients.

[5] The Rev. Basil H. Cooper believes that the Phrygian was the original Ida, which gradually passed to Crete; and here the Idæi were priests of Cybele. He is disposed to connect with it the Greek Σίδ(ηρο); the German *Eisen* (and our iron), and the *Ida feldt* and *Asi* of the Norse myths (Day, p. 133).

and built the 'Cyclopean Wall' in the Argolid. These Cyclopes[1] (monocular giants) worked metal, and under their magic hands,

> Fluit æs rivis aurique metallum ;
> Vulnificusque chalybs vasta fornice liquescit.

By later writers, the Cyclopes, who

> . . . Stridentia tingunt
> Æra lacu (*Æn.* viii. 445, *Georg.* iv. 172),

were held to be Sicilians.

The Telchines (fascinators, from θέλγειν, to charm) are mentioned as metallurgists by Stesichorus the Sicilian (nat. B.C. 632): they were the sons of Thalassa, i.e. they came from beyond the sea ; they colonised Telchinis, and they made arms and statues of the gods like the Dædalides or artist families of later Athens. The Sinties (plunderers) from τὸ σίνεσθαι (to pill), who, according to Hellenicus of Lesbos (nat. B.C. 496), were pirates besides being coppersmiths (χαλκυές), and who were eventually murdered by their wives, represented the ancient Lemnians. So Homer ('Od.' viii. 290) speaks of the 'barbarous Sintian men' who received Vulcan when kicked out of Paradise. A modern school of Tsiganologues would identify them with prehistoric Gypsies, who have still a tribe called Sindi ; but this theory would bring the arts from India westwards, whereas the current flowed the clean contrary way. Finally, Herodotus (i. 28), initiated in the mysteries, makes the Chalybes[2] or iron-workers, neighbours (and congeners ?) of the Phrygians.

It is not difficult to see the general gist of such legends. All these tribes probably came (like Pelops, Tantalus, and Niobe) from the same place, Phrygia, the fertile plateau of Asia Minor, and its Katakekaumene or volcanic tract. It was, as far as we know, the first western centre which developed the 'Aryan' or non-Semitic element of the old Egyptian tongue. It also formed the *point de départ* of the European[3] (miscalled 'Indo-European') branch of the family that owned the Aryaland (Airyanem-vaejo), whose ethnic centre was the barbarous region about Ray, Heri, or Herat.[4] Hence, says Herodotus (iii. 2), the Egyptians owned the Phrygians

---

[1] The name is derived by Bochart from Heb. *Lub* or *Lelub*, חיקלוב, chiefs of the Libu or Ribu, as the old Egyptians called the Libyans. Hence the Prom. Lilybæum (*Li-Lúb*) and the Sinus ad Libyam or Lilybatanus.

[2] We have satisfactory details concerning the Chalybes, who border on Armenia, in the *Anabasis* (iv. 5, &c.). They dwell two days from Cotyora, the colony planted by Sinope ; they are subject to the Mossynœci, and they subsist by iron-working (v. 5). Though few, they are a most warlike people, full of fight. Their armour consists of helmets, greaves, and cuirasses of twisted linen-cords, reaching to the groin. They carry spears about fifteen cubits long, 'having one spike' (i.e. without ferule); and at their girdles a short faulchion, as large as a Spartan crooked

dagger, with which they cut the throats of all whom they can master; and then, lopping off their heads, bear them away (iv. 7). Strabo makes the Chalybes the same as their neighbours the Chaldæi.

[3] The well-known inscription on the tomb of Midas, and another given by Texier (*Asie Mineure*, ii. 57) show the Phrygian tongue to have been a congener of Greek. Even the *Békos* of Herodotus (ii. 2) is allied to our 'bake,' and *Bédu* to our 'water.' We are greatly in want of further information about Phrygia, and it is to be hoped that Colonel Wilson and Mr. W. M. Ramsay will complete the labours of Texier and Hamilton.

[4] The Aryans of Herodotus, about the Arius river (*Heri-rúd*), are an undistinguished tribe, a mere

to surpass them in antiquity.   The emigrants would pass to the islands Samothrace, Lemnos, Thera,[1] the Cyclades and Crete ; to Greece, Thessaly and Epirus, Attica, Argos, and the farthest south, where ' Pelops the Phrygian,' son of King Tantalus, colonised the Morea and founded the Pelopid race.   Then they would find a home in Italy, Hetruria, and Iapygia (or Messapia), Peucetia and Daunia, and finally they would settle in Iberia, Spain, and Portugal, where the Briges or Brygi (Phrygians) have left their names in the Braganza of the present day.

These Proto-Phrygians and Phrygo-Europeans, of whom several tribes returned to Asia, were the prehistoric metal-workers.   The smith (from *smitan*, to strike) was sacred in the dawn of history ; and the Sword-maker was not inferior to him. Those who have witnessed the awe and reverence with which savages and barbarians regard a European mechanic at his forge will see exemplified the emotional feeling which led to the human becoming the superhuman.[2]

The first step in κρατέρωμα (hardening of metals) was, according to Hesychius, Μίξις χαλκοῦ καὶ κασσιτέρου (the mingling of copper and tin).   The alloy was known generically as chalcos (base metal), specifically as χαλκὸς μέλαινος (black chalcos).   The Latins persisted in terming it simply *æs* ; e.g. *æs inauratum* (gilt bronze).   Our word bronze derives from *brunus* (fuscous, sombre, brown) ; *brunum æs.*   Hence the Low Latin (A.D. 805) *brunea, brunia*, or *bronia*, a lorica or thorax ; and the Low Greek πόρτας μπρούτξινες (pronounce broutzines), ' portals of bronze.' The word is also derived from the Basque or Iberian *bronsea.*

Tin, one of the least durable of metals, at the same time readily fused and one of the easiest to treat metallurgically, was called by the Greeks κασσίτερος, and by the Latins *cassiteron*,[3] whence probably the Arab. قَصْدِير, and the Sanskrit कष्तिरा.

The Hebrew name is בְּדִיל (Badíl=a substitute, a separation, an alloy).   Hut (white metal) in Egyptian includes silver and tin : in Coptic it is Thram, Thran, or Basensh.   Kalaí (Linschoten's ' Calaem ') is the popular term for tin in India : the word is Arabic rather than Turkish.   Tenekeh (tin-plate) in Arabic is an evident congener of the Assyrian 𒀭𒈾𒃼 ' Anaker,' and it remarkably resembles the Scandinavian Din, German Zinn, and our Tin.   As we find ' Teyne ' in Chaucer

---

satrapy.   Strabo's Aria (xi. 9) is a tract about 250 by 40 miles.   In Pliny (vi. 23) Ariana includes only the lands of the Gedrosi (Mekran), the Arachoti (Kandahár), the Arii proper (Herat), and the Paraponisadæ (Kabul).   It has been truly said that even if Aryan and Turanian man (first) centred in and emerged from these areas (the table-lands of Asia), the so-called history is entirely based on the philological discoveries of the Sanskritist school.

[1] Therasia and Therassia, now Santorin.   Here have been found ruins of prehistoric cities buried by the great central volcano.   According to most geologists the latter was exhausted in B.C. 1800–1700.

[2] I have personally noticed this, and described it in *Midian Revisited*, vol. i. p. 143.

[3] Beckmann (*s.v.* 'Tin') tells us that the metal 'never occurs in a native state.'   He forgets stream-tin. He also denies that the oldest ' cassiteron ' and ' stannum' were tin ; and considers them to mean the German *Werk*, a regulus of silver and lead.   His *vasa stannea* are vessels covered with tin in the inside.   In the fourth century ' plumbum candidum ' or ' album ' was superseded by ' stannum.'   Speaking of electrum, Beckmann asserts that ' the ancients were not acquainted with the art of separating gold and silver.' ' Britain,' Ynis Prydhain Island, where the god Prydhain was worshipped, or rather ' Isle of the

and old writers, 'tin' may come from its easy 'thinning' or beating out. The later Latins changed the *plumbum album* or white lead of Pliny (iv. 30) to *stannum*: whence our word derived through the neo-Latin. The origin of Kassiteron, Kasdír, Kastira, is disputed, and philologists remark that Cassi is a British (Keltic) prefix, as in Cassi-belanus. Tin was found in the Caucasus, in India, in Southern Persia (Drangæ Country); in Tuscany, in Iberia (Spain and Portugal),[1] in Sweden, Saxony, Bohemia, Hungary, and notably in England. There are still deposits near the modern Temeswar (Pannonia), and the granite hills of Gallicia and Zamora are not exhausted. It is now produced in Russia, Greenland, the Brazil, and the United States. Wilkinson would fetch the alloy of ancient Egypt from Spain, India, Malacca, or even from Banca,[2] between Sumatra and Borneo; the Banca tin-mines, long worked by the Chinese were first visited by the Portuguese in 1506. But compounds of tin and copper were common in Egypt at the time of the Sixth Dynasty (B.C. 3000). Tin is mentioned as early as B.C. 1452 in the Book of Numbers (xxxii. 22), with gold and silver, 'brass' (copper, especially pyrites), iron, and lead[3] ('oferet'). In B.C. 760 the prophetic books, called from Isaiah (i. 25) and from Ezekiel (xxii. 18, 20), make tin an alloy of silver.

The Egyptians would derive their metals in the first place from Upper Egypt; and their first Kheft or mines of gold (*khetem*) and copper lay in the Thebaid. Secondly, they would resort to the land of Midian on the eastern flank, and running south of the long narrow gulf, El-Akabah: this grand range of Ghats or Coast Mountains was in those days a noted mining centre, and it has still a great industrial future. Thirdly, by means of the Phœnicians, who apparently taught the Greeks metallurgy which they learned in Egypt, they would import their tin from Southern France, Spain, and England.[4]

It is a disputed question whether the Phœnicians discovered the tin-stones and the stream-tin of the Cassiterides,[5] or whether the ore was worked by the 'Welsh of the Horn'—the barbarians of Cornwall and Devonshire, who in those days were

---

Brythons,' has been fancifully derived by the energetic Semitiser from Barrat-et-Tanuk = Land of Tin.

[1] Ezekiel tells us that the Tyrians received tin, as well as other metals, from Tarshish, or Western Tartessus, in the Bay of Gibraltar.

[2] M. Emile Burnouf, 'L'Age de Bronze,' *Revue des Deux Mondes*, July 15, 1877, also brings tin from Banca. The island is about 150 miles long by 36 broad; it has no mountain backbone, but the peak of Goonong Maras rises some 3,000 feet above the sealevel. Chinese coolies still work the mines of Mintok, and in 1852 the yearly yield was some 50,000 piculs (each = 133⅓ lbs.) at the cost of nine rupees per picul.

[3] Beckmann (*loc. cit.*), like Michaelis, is surprised at the Midianites possessing tin in the days of Moses. These were the views of the last century. I have suggested (*Athenæum*, Nov. 24, 1880) that the old

Nile-dwellers extended through Midian to El-Hejáz and El-Yemen, where they worked the mines which became known to the Hebrews.

[4] In 1866 De Rougemont made Phœnicia supply bronze to Europe, the copper being brought from Cyprus. Besides the Mediterranean, we find a Uralian and a Danubian branch of the industry. Before 1877 France had supplied 650 bronze Swords and daggers, Sweden 480, and Switzerland 86.

[5] *Alias* the Œstrymnides. Borlase was of opinion that the group formed one block, with several headlands, of which 'Scilly' was the highest, outermost, and most conspicuous. He conjectures the original name to be *Syllé*, *Sulla*, or *Sulleh*, a flat rock dedicated to the sun; hence the Lat. *Siliæ*, *Silures*, and *Sigdeles*; the Engl. *Sylley*, *Scilley*, and lately *Scilly*; the Fr. *Sorlingues*; and the Span. *Sorlingas*. The Keltic name of the chief feature was Inis Caer.

probably confined to small coast-clearings.[1] Herodotus, indeed, knows nothing (iii. 115) of 'any islands called the Cassiterides (tin islands) whence the tin comes.' These Silures or Scilly Islands were evidently mere depôts, not sites of production. The Phœnicians kept their secret well, and lost their ships rather than betray it ; so says Strabo (iii. 5, § 11), whose Cassiterides appear to be the Azores.[2] The age when the trade was first opened is disputed ; some place it B.C. 1500, others[3] reduce it to B.C. 400. Diodorus Siculus (v. 21–2) tells us that tin was found and run into pigs near the Belerium Promontory (Land's End) ; thence it was carted to Ictis (Vectis, not the Isle of Wight, but Saint Michael's Mount and Love Island) ;[4] and lastly horsed across Gaul to the Rhone. There is in the Truro Museum[5] a pig of tin, flat above and reniform below (the shape of the mould), two feet eleven inches by eleven inches broad, with a particular mark ; it has been suggested that this is Phœnician. 'Cassiter Street' in Bodmin is supposed to retain the classical name. The second Thursday before Christmas Day is called in Cornwall (Kern-Walli, Cornu Galliæ) 'Picrous Day,' from the man who discovered the 'streaming' (or washing) of 'stean' or tin. Strabo gives a bad account of the people of the twelve Cassiterides and their Cornishmen, the latter 'resembling the Furies we see in tragic representations.' These pleasant persons would find stream-tin, almost fit for use, lying upon the surface by the side of copper pyrites—the latter harder than tin, but still comparatively soft and ductile. Both ores were easily fused, while iron was comparatively difficult and tedious to smelt ; and the two (copper and tin) combined were not only more fusible, but they also continued longer in the fluid state, facilitating casting and moulding. Hence Worsäaee believes that England was an ancient centre of bronze, whence the alloy was diffused throughout Europe. It is usually stated that the bronze-using period in England began between B.C. 1400 and 1200, and lasted eight to ten centuries, the invasion of Cæsar taking place during the early 'Iron Age.'

The great bronze manufacture which we have first to consider is Egypt. The exact average proportion of the alloy is hard to ascertain,[6] the tin varying from ten to twenty per cent., and the copper from eighty to ninety per cent. A dagger analysed by Vauquelin gave copper eighty-five, tin fourteen, and iron one per cent. Wilkinson's bronze chisel, nine and a quarter inches long, and weighing one pound twelve ounces, found in a quarry at Thebes, contained in one hundred parts 94·0 copper, 5·9 tin, 0·1 iron ; consequently its edge is at once turned by hard stone. He repeatedly mentions bronze chisels (ii. ch. vii. &c.), and he seems to

---

[1] *Archæology and Prehistoric Annals of Scotland,* Part II. 'The Archaic or Bronze Period.' Daniel Wilson.

[2] Pliny represents the Cassiterides as fronting Celtiberia. He considers it a 'fabulous story' that the Greeks fetched 'white lead' from the islands of the Adriatic.

[3] *Prehistoric Times,* by Sir John Lubbock, 4th edit. (London : Williams and Norgate, 1878.)

[4] The identification is not settled ; some propose the Isle of Thanet.

[5] Beckmann, *sub voce* 'Tin.'

[6] According to Messrs. Wibel, Fellemberg, and Damour, who investigated even $\frac{10}{1000}$ parts, the average proportions were $\frac{1}{10}$ tin to 9 copper ; and $\frac{1}{4}$ tin for hard metal, as chisels, &c. M. E. Chauntre, *Age de Bronze.* 3 vols. (Paris : Baudry.)

suspect that they were sheathed and pointed with steel. Of course, he was puzzled to explain how the 'bronze or brass blades were given a certain degree of elasticity.'[1]

The result of Egyptian metallurgy is admirable, both in material and finish. At what period bronze was introduced we ignore ; a cast cylinder, however, bearing the name of Pepi, dates from B.C. 3000 in the Sixth Dynasty of Middle Egypt, which includes Nitaker (Nitocris). Knives appear in the sculptures dating from before that time. A bronze dagger in the Berlin Museum, found by Sig. Passalacqua in a tomb at Thebes, retains a spring which might be of steel. My friend, Mr. W. P. Hayns, of the Alexandrian Harbour Works, showed me a specimen brought from Thebes by the late Mr. Harris, made of bronze still slightly elastic. The total length measures one foot, of which the blade is half ; the latter, slightly leaf-shaped, has a minimum breadth of one inch and three-twelfths, and one inch at the shoulder. The tang, which is prolonged to the handle-end (four inches), has a minimum width of five-twelfths. The grip of two plates, hippopotamus hide (?), probably boiled, and not unlike wood, has twenty-six ridges for firmer hold, and there are bronze rivets at the sixth and the twenty-third ridges : it is without pommel, the end being simply rounded off.

FIG. 82. — FINE SPECIMEN OF EGYPTIAN DAGGER IN POSSESSION OF MR. HAYNS, BROUGHT BY MR. HARRIS FROM THEBES.

The material is bronze, and still is slightly elastic. There is a mid-rib, but not strongly marked. The tang, which is continued to the pommel, measures 4 inches long by a minimum of 5/12. The handle, of two slices of hippopotamus hide, has 26 ridges for firmer grasp, and there are rivets of bronze at the 6th and the 23rd ridges. There is no pommel, but here the handle is rounded off between two slices of hide, and the tang goes right through.

It is held that mummies of the Eleventh Dynasty were buried with bronze sabres ; and there is a bronze dagger of Thut-mes[2] III. (Eighteenth Dynasty), circa B.C. 1600. As late as Mene-ptah II. of the Nineteenth Dynasty (B.C. 1300–1266), we read in the list of his loot, after the Prosopis battle, of bronze-armour, Swords, and daggers. Among the Etruscans, before the foundation of Rome, bronze statues were known ; and Romulus is said to have placed a statue of himself, crowned by Victory, in a bronze quadriga taken at Comertium. According to Pausanias (iii. 12, § 8), Theodorus of Samos invented casting in bronze (B.C. 800–700): this author discredits the Arcadian legend that Neptune dedicated a bronze statue to Poseidon (the Sidonian ?) Hippios (Wilkinson, ii. chap. vii.). But the Samians cast a bronze vase in B.C. 630.

[1] The late General Uchatius, who 'trusted in princes,' and whose tragical death was greatly lamented by his friends, always declared that he had rediscovered (not discovered) the hardening of copper and bronze ; and that he hoped to arrive at other secrets. His career was cut short before he learned to make the metal and the alloy resilient.

[2] *Thut, Tuth, Toth, Thoth,* &c., the moon-god who became Hermes Trismegistus.

The importance of the Uchatius re-discovery, that is, of hardening bronze as well as copper by hydraulic pressure, not by phosphorus,[1] becomes evident by Wilkinson's reflections. 'We know of no means of tempering copper, under any form, or united with any alloys for such a purpose' (as hollowing out hieroglyphics). He suggests that the old Egyptian letters, sometimes exceeding two inches in depth, and the alt-reliefs nine inches high, on granite coffins, may have been worked with wheel-drill and emery powder.[2] The Egyptians had also the secret of gilding bronze, as many of their remains prove ; moreover, they produced by acids a rich patina of dark and light greens.

The Assyrians rivalled in metallurgy their ancient instructors the Egyptians : and the art passed eastwards to Persia, which inherited Assyrian and Babylonian civilisation. Diodorus Siculus, following Ctesias the oft-quoted contemporary of Xenophon, describes immense works of bronze decorating the gardens of Semiramis. In Assyria, again, the proportion of the alloy greatly varied. Layard[3] quotes the following assays of Assyrian bronze :

	No. 1	No. 2	No. 3	No. 4
Copper	89·51	89·85	88·37	84·79
Tin	0·63	9·78	11·33	14·10
	90·14	99·63	99·70	98·89

No. 1 shows the proportions found in a bronze dish from 'Nimroud' ; No. 4 in a bell ; and the fore-leg of a bull[4] yielded 11·33 tin to 99·70 copper. The Mesopotamians were able to cast their bronze extremely thin, which is no small difficulty ; they fashioned it into weapons, temple utensils, and domestic articles, and they skilfully 'elaborated it by chasing and by curious ornamental tracery.' They used it in their most sumptuous decorations, as the thrones prove ; and the beautiful workmanship of their vases shows abnormal skill in the toreumatic treatment of bronze. Gilt specimens of bronze from Nineveh are in the British Museum.

Dr. Schliemann questions the popular assertion that the age of Hesiod and of Homer ignored alloys and fusion, knowing only plating, the plates being hammer-

[1] Phosphor-bronze, for whose manufacture companies are now established in London and elsewhere, has the ordinary composition with the addition of red or amorphous phosphorus dropped upon the melted metal in the crucible. Berthier (*Traité des Essais*, ii. 410) states that a very small quantity of phosphorus renders copper extremely hard and suitable for cutting instruments. Percy (*Metallurgy*) found that copper will take up 11 per cent. of phosphorus ; the metal, which assumes a grey tint, is quite homogeneous, and so hard that it can scarcely be touched by the file. The addition of phosphorus promotes the reduction of the oxides, and enables an exceedingly sound and durable casting to be made ; but if it exceed ½ per cent. the metal becomes very brittle. Dr. Percy has described phosphor-silver, phosphor-lead, and phosphor-iron. The phosphorus is, according to some authorities, apt to volatilise with time. At present a new form of bronze, the antimonial, in proportions of 1–2 per cent., is coming into fashion : it is said to be malleable and ductile, and to resist torsion in a high degree. Another new bronze is the aluminium, whose price has been reduced from 1,000*l.* to 100*l.* per ton by Mr. Webster, of Hollywood, near Birmingham.

[2] So called from Cape Emeri in Naxos.

[3] Appendix to Layard's *Nineveh and Babylon* (London : Murray). The proportions are nearly those of our day. We may assume our common bronze at 11 : 100 for large, and 10 : 100 for small objects. Cymbals and sounding instruments, however, contain tin 22 : copper 78.

[4] Analysed by Mr. Robinson of Pimlico (Day, p. 110).

wrought (' Od.' iii. 425). This explorer found the strata of copper and lead scoriæ at the so-called Troy from twenty-eight to twenty-nine and a half feet deep. He notes also small crucibles and a mould of mica-schist (twenty-six feet deep), which was probably intended for bronze casting. He finds no iron ; but copper and its alloy, bronze, are abundant. M. Damour of Lyon[1] analysed the drillings of two ' copper' battle-axes from ' Ilium,' in fact, from 'Priam's Treasury' ; they contained 0·0864 and 0·0384 parts tin to 0·9067 and 0·9580 copper. Nearly the same proportion of alloy was found in a common two-edged axe dug at a depth of three and a quarter feet, and therefore in the remains attributed to a Greek colony. Dr. Percy analysed, with the following results, the handle of a bronze vase and a Sword :

$$
\begin{array}{lr}
\text{Copper (mean)} \ . \quad . \quad . & 86\text{·}36 \\
\text{Tin (mean)} \quad . \quad . \quad . & 13\text{·}06 \\
\hline
& 99\text{·}42
\end{array}
$$

The specific gravity (at 60° F.) was 8·858. The extreme proportions of the alloy in other articles were 10·28 tin to 89·69 copper (a usual ratio in ancient bronzes[2]), and 0·09 tin to 98·47 copper, the latter being almost pure.

Mongez, of the Institut, describing a bronze Sword found in France, gives the proportions as 87·47 per cent. of copper to 12·53 of tin. Analyses of Greek bronzes in the British Museum yielded 87·8 per cent. copper to 12·13 tin. A bronze knife has been found in the Palafittes (Pile-villages) of Neuchâtel, Switzerland.[3] Worsaäee (' Primæval Antiquities ') makes the Bronze Period in Denmark and Northern Europe begin about B.C. 500 to 600, and last some

FIG. 83.—BRONZE KNIFE, FROM THE PILE-VILLAGES OF NEUCHÂTEL. (Half-size.)

FIG. 84.—PERUVIAN KNIFE. METAL BLADE, SECURED IN A SLIT IN THE HAFT BY STRONG COTTON TWINE.

1,100 years. It is not found among the Normans. But it was developed in Ireland and Scotland, in China and Japan, in Mexico and in Peru : Cieza de Leon notes the admirable bronze work of the Ynkarial empire.

A Peruvian chisel, analysed by M. Vauquelin, contained 0·94 copper to 0·06 tin. In other tools the proportion of the latter metal varied from two to four, six and even seven per cent. As a rule the people used only half the proper proportion of

[1] Schliemann's *Troy*, p. 361 (London : Murray, 1875).

[2] Sir W. Gell found the bronze nails in the ' Treasury of Atreus ' composed of 12 tin to 88 copper.

The Trojan battle-axes, according to Dr. Schliemann, yielded only 4, 8, and 9 per cent. of the former metal.

[3] According to Helbig, the Palafittes and Terramare villagers had spears but not Swords.

tin, which they called Chayantanka—a name suggesting the Old-World 'Tanuk.' Humboldt mentions a cutting tool found near Cuzco with ninety-four per cent. of copper and six of tin. Rivero (i. 201) notices in Peru brass (?) hammers and bellows-nozzles, axes, adzes, bill-hooks, and other tools, of bronze as well as copper. The Mexicans cast their tin ingots in T-shape. The Peruvians hardened copper also with silver for quarrying-tools and crow-bars. Velasco (ii. 70) tells us that when the Ynka Huasca was being led to prison by order of his brother, a woman secretly gave him a bar of metal, 'silver with bronze, brass, or an alloy of silver, copper, and tin' (Bollaert, p. 90); by means of this he cut through the jail wall during the night. Hutchison (ii. 330) mentions a buckler from Ipijapa in Ecuador, and Ewbank (p. 454) notices an old Peruvian bronze knife.[1]

The admirable bronzes of China and Japan are well known in the English market, and Raphael Pumpelly,[2] who studied direct from the native workmen, has printed interesting notes on the ornamental alloys, or Mokume, applied to Swords and other articles. Damask-work is produced by soldering alternately thirty to forty sheets of rose-copper, silver, *shakdo* (copper one to gold ten per cent.), and *gui shi bu ichi* (silver and copper). The mass is then cut into deep patterns with the reamer. An alloy of silver (thirty to fifty per cent. of copper) produces the favourite tint, a rich grey colour, and this becomes a bluish black like niello by being boiled after polishing in a solution of sulphate of copper, alum, and verdigris. Dr. Percy (p. 340) describes the liquation of argentiferous copper in Japan.[3]

We owe to Dr. George Pearson[4] sundry experiments in alloys, which first determined that the norm of the Old World and the best proportion for weapons and tools are one tin to nine copper.

Fusing the metals, he found :

1 tin : 20 copper (5 per cent.) produces a dark-coloured bronze with the red fracture of the pure metal.

1 tin : 15 ($6\frac{1}{2}$ per cent.) gives a stronger alloy and obliterates the colour.

1 tin : 12, 9, 8, 7, 6, 5, 4, 3 gradually increases hardness and brittleness.

1 tin : 2 makes a mixture almost as brittle as glass.

The following table[5] shows the alloys now in common use, and the purposes to which they are applied :

Tin	Copper		Per cent. Copper		
11	108	=	90·76	. .	Cannon, statues, machine brasses.
11	99	=	90	. .	'Gun-metal' proper (cannon).
11	84	=	84·44	. .	'Gun-metal,' machinery bearings.

[1] For the tin-ore of Peru see *Ethnolog. Journal*, vol. lxx. pp. 258–261. Rivero, p. 230, and Garcilasso, vol. i. p. 202.

[2] *Amer. Journ. of Science, &c.* v. 42 ; July 1866.

[3] From descriptions and drawings by Mr. J. H. Godfrey, Mining Engineer-in-Chief to the Imperial Government of Japan.

[4] M.D., F.R.S., 'Observations on some Metallic Arms and Utensils, with Experiments to determine their Composition.' Royal Soc. London, June 9, 1796. *Philosophical Transactions.*

[5] Taken from Dr. Evans (*Bronze Impl. &c.* chap. xxi.). He compiled it from Martineau & Smith's *Hardware Trade Journal* (April 30, 1879).

Tin	Copper		Per cent. Copper.			
11	72	=	86·75	.	.	Harder composition.
11	60	=	84·50	.	.	Not malleable.
11	44	=	80	.	.	Cymbals, Chinese gongs.
11	48	=	81·35	.	.	Very hard, culinary vessels.
11 / 12	36 } 36 }	=	{ 76·69 } { 75 00 }	.	.	'Bell-metal.'
11	24	=	68·57	.	.	Yellowish, very hard, sonorous.
11	4	=	26·66	.	.	Very white,[1] specula.[2]

The most popular alloy of copper, next to bronze, is brass, which is harder and wears better than the pure metal. Originally, as now, it was a mixture of copper and zinc, popularly called spelter (old *speautre, speauter, spiauter, spialter*).[3] The proportions greatly varied, one part of the latter to two of the former being the older ratio, and the density increasing with the amount of copper from 8·39 to 8·56.

Beckmann tells us, in his valuable ' History of Inventions,'[4] ' in the course of time an ore which must have been calamine (carbonate of zinc) or blende [5] (sulphuret of zinc), was added to copper, and gave it a yellow colour. The addition made it harder, more fusible and sonorous, easily subject to the lathe, more economical to work, and a worse conductor of heat than the pure metal.' We have few specimens of old art-works in ' brass ' proper, although zinc was discovered by analysis in an ancient Sword, chiefly copper.[6] Gibel assures us that zinc occurs only in Roman alloys, the bronze of the Greeks containing nothing beyond copper, tin, and lead. The Romans also could varnish or lacquer brass, but it is not known whence they derived the art. Percy notes (p. 521) that brass was produced ' early in the Christian era, if not before its commencement.' He quotes in proof a large coin of the Cassia Gens (B.C. 20) which contained copper 82·26 and zinc 17·31; a Vespasian (Rome, A.D. 71), an imperial Trajan (Caria, circ. A.D. 110), a Geta (Carian Mylasa, A.D. 189–212), a Greek Caracalla (A.D. 199), and many others. In modern times zinciferous ore was imported by the Portuguese from the East a century before it was common throughout Europe.[7] In the early seventeenth century the Dutch captured one of their craft laden with spelter, and the secret became known. Bishop Richard Watson says (1783) the cargo was *calaem*, ' which he connects with ' calamine ': the latter, like the German *Galmei*, derives from *cadmia*.

Amongst the moderns *æs* gave rise to *airain*. The French *leton, laton, latton*,

---

[1] Wilkinson remarked that the Egyptian proportions of half tin and half copper were whitish.

[2] Lord Rosse, in casting specula, preferred using copper and tin in their atomic proportions, or 68·21 per cent. copper to 31·79 per cent. tin.

[3] *Speltrum* was introduced by Boyle. During the last century much zinc was imported from India (possibly supplied by China), and was called tutenag.

[4] Bohn's *Trans.* ii. 32–45. The learned German begins by stating that zinc was not known to the Greeks, Romans, and Arabs, and then proceeds to prove that it was. The word ' zinc ' (from *zenken* or *zacken*, nails, spikes?) first occurs in the works of the Iatro-chemist, Paracelsus, who died in A.D. 1541.

[5] *Blende* is a generic word, from *blenden*, to dazzle.

[6] Mongez, *Mém. de l'Institut.*

[7] At Goslar, however, according to Lohnriss, brass was made in A.D. 1617.

or *laiton* (*cuivre jaune*); the Italian *lattone, lottone,* and lastly *ottone,* and the Spanish *lata* and *laton,* German *Latun,* and English *latten* (thin sheet brass), the *latoun* of Chaucer ('Pardoner's Prologue,' 64), are either from *luteum,* yellow (metal), or from the plant *luteum* (*Reseda luteola*), used to stain chrysocolla.[1] Our *brass* is probably the Scandinavian *bras,* cement; and the German *Mosch, Meish,* and *Messing,* from *mischen=miscere.*[2]

It may be advisable to notice the ὀρειχάλκον[3] of the Homerids and Hesiod, which Strabo also calls ψευδάργυρος (false silver), and *aurichalcum,* and which the perverse ingenuity of commentaries has made so mysterious.[4] In the poetic phase, which loves the vague, this 'mountain-copper' was a mythic natural metal, ranking between gold and silver, and chimerical as was the *chalcolibanon*[5] of the Apocalypse (i. 15, ii. 18). The name does not occur in Pindar or the Dramatists. Plato (the 'Critias,' § ix., treating of Atlantis,[6] America) makes *oreichalc,* 'now known only by name,' the most precious metal after gold. Pliny (xxxiv. 2) tells us truly enough that *aurichalcum* no longer exists.

The next application of the word was to ruby copper (?), a suboxide whose beautiful crystals are formed in the natural state. Pollux and Hesychius the grammarian (A.D. 380) define it as copper (χαλκός) resembling gold; and Cicero puts the question whether, if a person should offer a piece of gold for sale, thinking he was disposing of only a piece of orichalcum, an honest man ought to inform him

[1] Pliny, xxxiii. 27. The solder (χρυσός and κόλλα, glue, or κόλλησις) is attributed by Herod. (i. 25) to Glaucus of Chios, a contemporary of Alyattes. The word *köllesis* is variously rendered 'soldering,' 'brazing,' 'welding,' and 'inlaying.' Köllesis was used to agglutinate metals, and treated with a peculiar alkali (Pliny, xxxiii. 24). The 'gold glue' (*chrysocolla*) is usually understood to be a hydrosilicate of copper; not to be confounded with the χρυσόκολλα or borax. The Mycenian goldsmiths soldered with the help of borax (borate of soda): Professor Landerer, of Athens, found this salt on an old medal from Ægina. It was called in the Middle Ages, Borax Venetus, because imported by the Venetians from Persia; and it is the Tinkal of modern India. According to Pliny, lead cannot be soldered without tin, or tin without lead, and oil invariably must be used. Later usage substituted for the latter colophonium and other resins : we now solder by means of electricity. The same writer makes Nero use chrysocolla-powder (a siliceous carbonate of copper, a kind of blue-stone which would turn green by exposure to damp) for strewing the circus, to give the course the colour of his favourite faction, the *Prasine* (green).

[2] The Germans, who delight in German derivatives for European words, would find *leiton,* &c., not in *luteum,* but in *löthen*=to unite. There is little doubt, however, that the first English manufactory of calamine brass at Esher, in Surrey, was set up in the seventeenth century by Demetrius, a German. In Grimm's *Dictionary,* as noticed by Demmin (chap. i.), bronze is erroneously called *messing* (brass),

[3] Derived from ὄρος, οὖρος (mountain), or from Ὀρεῖος, the discoverer. Metallic names in Greek are mostly masculine ; in Latin and modern usage, neutral. *Oreichalcum* or *aurichalcum,* a hybrid word, became *aurochalcum* in the ninth century : the last corruption (middle of the sixteenth century) was *archal.*

[4] *De l'Orichalque.* J. P. Rossignol (*loc. cit.*).

[5] Some translate this word 'yellow frankincense' (λίβανος) colour ; others derive it from Λίβανος, the Lebanon, and make it male, *argurolibanus,* while *leucolibanus* (white) was female. Finally, the word was explained by the old interpreters to be=ὀρείχαλκος=brass of Mount (Lebanon).

[6] The tradition of Atlantis, a middle-land in the Atlantic, has strong claims to our acceptance. The identity of the site with the 'Dolphin's Ridge,' a volcanic formation, and the shallows noted by H.M.S. 'Challenger,' have been ably pleaded in *Atlantis* (Ignatius Donnelly; London : Sampson Low, 1882). Perhaps we may trace the vestiges in Saint Paul's Rocks, the remarkable group of rocky islets situate in the equatorial mid-Atlantic. Mr. Darwin supposed the group to be an isolated example of non-volcanic oceanic insularity; but Prof. Renard finds the 'balance of proof decidedly in favour of the volcanic origin of the rock.' It will be remembered that Atlantis was dismembered by earthquakes, eruptions, and subsidence.

that it was really gold, or might fairly buy for a penny what is *worth a thousand times as much.*[1] Buffon compares it with tombac, or Chinese copper containing gold.[2] Beckmann (*s. v.* 'Tin') notes *aurichalcum* or Corinthian brass in Plautus, 'Auro contra carum.' Festus speaks of 'orichalcum (copper), stannum (zinc or pewter ?), cassiterum (tin), and aurichalcum (brass).' The same signification occurs in Ambrose, Bishop of Milan (fourth century); in Primasius, Bishop of African Adrumetum (sixth century), and in Isidore, Bishop of Seville (seventh century). Albertus Magnus (thirteenth century), the Dominican monk, in treating 'De Natura et Commixtione Æris,' describes how *cuprum* became *aurichalcum.*

Strabo is mysterious. In one place he tells us that the Cyprian copper alone produces the Cadmian stone, copperas-water, and oxide of copper. In another (lib. xiii.) he says, 'There is a stone near Andeira which, being burnt, becomes iron. It is then put into a furnace, together with some kind of earth,[3] when it (the stone ? the earth ? or both ?) drops or distils a ψευδάργυρος (mock silver, zinc ?), which, with the addition of copper, produces what is called *the mixture*, and which some term *oreichalcum*.' Pseudargyros, also found in the neighbourhood of Tmolus, would here seem to mean zinc or *Cadmia fossilis* (natural calamine or carbonate of zinc). Pliny (xxxiv. 22) confuses with cadmia, furnace calamine, and a particular ore of copper opposed to calchitis. When Dioscorides (v. cap. 84) seems to allude to artificial or furnace-calamine, an impure oxide of zinc, he may mean the more modern *tutiya* (Avicenna), *toutia*, *thouthia*,[4] *cadmie des fourneaux*, or tutty. Reduced to powder, and mixed with an equal quantity of wetted charcoal by way of fondant or flux, it is melted with copper to form brass. The Avocat de Launey (1780) and Bishop Watson both agree that Strabo's orichalcum is brass.

Lastly, aurichalcum was made synonymous with *electrum*, natural or artificial. The word Ἤλεκτρος[5] is popularly derived from Helios, as rivalling the sun in

---

[1] Quoted by Percy from Watson's *Chemical Essays* (iv. p. 85, 1786).

[2] The artificial mixture of copper (four fifths) and gold (one-fifth) was called *pyropus* (Pliny, xxxiv. 2), from its fiery red tint; it was also made of gold and bronze, and termed *chrysochalcos*, 'the king of metals.' *Æs corinthiacum* (Pliny, xxxiv. 3), or Corinthian brass, used for mirrors, composed of copper, silver (steel? zinc?), and gold, was more valuable than gold. According to Pausanias (ii. 3, § 3), this malleable and ductile metal was tempered in the Fountain of Pyrene. The vulgar legend, refuted by Pliny, who tells the tale (xxxiv. 6), dates it from the days of Mummius (B.C. 146). A medal of Corinthian brass was analysed by the Duc de Luynes. Pliny (xxxiv. 3) mentions three kinds, *candidum*, *luteum*, and *hepatizon* (liver-colour), of equal quantities of metal: this probably resembled our own alloys. Beckmann (*sub voc.* 'Zinc' and 'Tin') gives a list of these and other compositions, Mannheim gold, Dutch gold, Prince's metal, Bristol brass, &c.

[3] Possibly the Armenian bole (Bol-i-Armani), used

in the East as a flux from time immemorial. The 'dropping' or 'distilling' (*per descensum*) must allude to a distillatory or condensing apparatus, and the 'false silver' cannot be mercury, lead, or tin.

[4] Hence *tutaneg* and *tuṭanego*, which sometimes meant an alloy of tin and bismuth. M. Polo (i. 21) describes 'tutia' as very good for the eyes; and his notice of it, and of spodium, reads, according to Colonel Yule, almost like a condensed translation of Galen's pompholyx, produced from cadmia or carbonate of zinc; and spodos, the residue of the former, which falls on the hearth (*De Simp. Med.* p. ix). Matthioli makes pompholyx commonly known in the laboratories by the Arabic name 'tutia.' The 'tutia' imported into Bombay from the Gulf is made from an argillaceous ore of zinc, moulded into tubular cakes, and baked to a moderate hardness.

[5] Masc. and fem.; the neut. ἤλεκτρον is the purest form. Dr. Schliemann, noticing that it also means 'amber' (*Mycenæ*, p. 204), derives it from '*elek*, signifying resin in Arabic (?), and probably also in Phœnician (?).' He found earrings of electrum

sheen. According to Lepsius it is the 'usem'-metal of Thutmes III.; Brugsch (i. 345) understands by 'usem' brass, and thinks Asmara or Asmala equivalent to the Hebrew *hasmal* or *hashmal=electrum*. In Bunsen (v. 757) Kasabet and Kakhi are brass (*aurichalcum*), and Khesbet is a metal connected with Kassiteros =tin. The alloy was known to Hesiod ('Scut.' 142) and to the 'Odyssey'[1] (iv. 73), not to the 'Iliad.' Sophocles ('Antig.' 1037) applied 'Sardian electrum' to gold, not to silver. Herodotus (iii. 115), in the historic age (B.C. 480-30), gives the name of the mythical metal to the 'tears of the Heliades,' which the Latins called *succinum* (*succum*), the Low-Latins *ambrum*, the Arabs *anbar*, and we Amber. Pliny (xxxiii. 23), repeated by Pausanias (v. 12, § 6), notes two kinds, natural ('in all gold ore there is some silver'[2]) and artificial; in the latter the proportion of silver must not exceed one-fifth. The staters of Lydian Croesus, held by the Greeks to be the most ancient of coins, were, according to Böckh, of electrum, three parts gold and one part silver. Lucian applies the term to glass ($\upsilon\alpha\lambda o\varsigma$); and, lastly, it was taken for brass and confounded with aurichalcum.[3]

I would suggest that this aurichalcum might also be the 'Dowris bronze' of Ireland, so called because first observed at Dowris, near Parsonstown, King's County. Wilde (p. 360) supposes with others that the gold-coloured alloy depended upon the admixture of a certain proportion of lead, and compares it with the Cyprus copper termed by the Romans *Coronarium* (used for theatrical crowns), which was coated with ox-gall.[4] Of this *or molu* there are many articles in the Dublin Museum, preserving their fine golden-yellow lustre: they had probably been lacquered or varnished like modern brasses; and the patina might be some gum-resin. When much tarnished, they were cleaned by holding over the fire, and then by dipping in a weak solution of acid, as is done with modern castings. Two specimens, a Sword and a dagger-blade, were analysed (pp. 470, 483), and proved to contain copper 87·67 to 90·72, tin 8·52 to 8·25, lead 3·87 to 0·87, with a trace of sulphur in the Sword.[5] The specific gravities were 8·819 to 8·675. In a spear-head (p. 512), besides copper, tin, and lead, iron 0·31 and cobalt 0·09 were found.

There were other alloys of which we read but know little; such were the *æs ægineticum, demonnesium,* and *nigrum*; the *æs deliacum,* whose secret was

in the so-called 'Trojan Stratum,' 30½ feet below the surface (*Troy*, p. 164). The *guanin* or *gianin* of the Chiriquis was an aururet (electrum) of 19·3 per cent. of pure gold, with specific gravity 11·55. The *tombac* or *tombag* of New Granada, used for statuettes, was also a gold of low standard : 63 gold, 24 silver, 9 copper. Usually 'tombac' applies to an alloy like Mannheim gold; the manufacture was introduced into Birmingham, still its chief seat, by the Turner family, A.D. 1740.

[1] 'Elektron,' however, is generally translated 'amber'; and it may be the *harpax*, or drawer, for it occurs in the same verse with ivory. Amber beads and weapon-handles were amongst Dr. Schliemann's finds. Rossignol (p. 347) supposes that electrum, the

pale-yellow or amber-coloured alloy of gold and silver, gave a name to the gum amber.

[2] This text, stating a truth concerning native gold, suggests amongst many that the ancients knew the *départ*, or separation, of metals. It has been vehemently doubted whether they could mineralise the white metal; that is, convert it to sulphide and allow the gold to subside.

[3] Rossignol quotes Zonaras, Suidas, and John Pediasimus to prove this position.

[4] We now lacquer with shell-lac dissolved in proof-spirit and coloured with 'dragon's blood.'

[5] The lead was found in even larger proportions. See chap. xiii.

lost in Plutarch's day, and the Ταρτήσσιος χαλκὸς[1] from Southern Spain, probably shipped at Gibraltar Bay. *Ollaria* or pot-copper (brass) contained three pounds of *plumbum argentarium* (equal parts of tin and lead) to one hundred pounds of copper. *Æs caldarium* could only be fused. Finally, *græcanicum* (Greek-colour) was mould or second-hand copper (*formalis seu collectaneus*) with ten per cent. of *plumbum nigrum* (lead) and five per cent. of silver lead (argentiferous galena ?).

Metal, when first introduced, must have been rare and dear; the large modern Sword, axe, or mall would hardly have been imitated in copper, bronze, or iron. The earliest attempts at developing the celt[2] would have produced nothing more artful

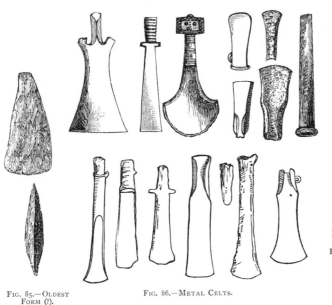

Fig. 85.—Oldest Form (?).

Fig. 86.—Metal Celts.

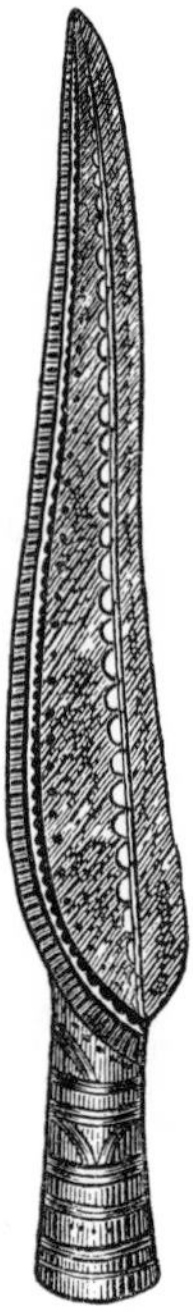

Fig. 87.—Knife Found at Réalon (Hautes Alpes).

Half-size. It greatly resembles the bronze knife from the Palafittes of Neuchâtel, figured by Desor. The Swiss knife, however, has a tooth at the edge, near the hollow.

than a cutting and piercing wedge of the precious substance (fig. 85). As smelting and moulding improved, the pointed end would develop into the knife, the dagger, and the Sword; and the broad end would expand to the axe. This composite weapon, uniting the club with the celt or hand-hatchet, and appearing in Europe with the beginning of the Neolithic period, plays a remarkable part in history,

[1] In my commentary on Camoens (*Camoens: his Life and his Lusiads*), and again in *To the Gold Coast for Gold* (i. 17), I have attempted to identify Western Tarshish or Tartessus with Carteia in the Bay of Gibraltar. Newton makes Melcarth 'King of Carteia'; but the word may mean either 'city-king' (*Malik-el-Karyat*), or 'earth-king' (*Malik-el-Arz*).

[2] The well-known anthropologist, M. G. de Mortillet, holds that the oldest type of bronze celt in France, Switzerland, and Belgium, is that with straight flanges at the sides. This was followed by the celt with transverse stop-ridge, by the true winged tool, by the socketed adaptation, and, lastly, by the simple flat tool wanting rib or flange, wing or socket, and formed of pure copper as well as of bronze. Archæologists usually determine the last form to be the earliest; but M. de Mortillet judges otherwise from the conditions under which the finds occur.

ancient, mediæval, and even modern ; whilst its connection with the Sword is made evident by the ' glaive.' [1] The expansion of the edge and of the flanges developed two principal forms. For cutting wood the long-narrow was found most service-able : where brute force was less required, the weapon became a broad blade with a long crescent-shaped edge.

The Akhu or war-axe was, as we might expect, known to ancient Egypt in early days, and became an *objet de luxe.* A gold hatchet and several of bronze were found buried as amulets in the coffin of Queen Askhept, the ancestress of the Eighteenth Dynasty. Again, a bronze weapon occurred with a mummied queen of the Seventeenth Dynasty (B.C. 1750). Useful in war, the implement, probably when

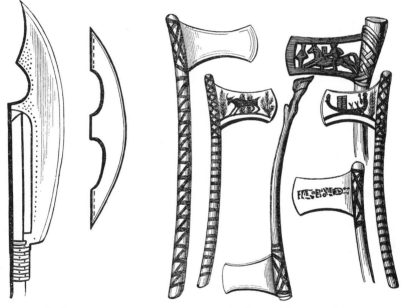

FIG. 88.—THE GLAIVE.   FIG. 89.—EGYPTIAN AXES OF BRONZE.

in the stone period, rose to be a symbol of the Deity : hence, doubtless, the *hâches votives* of the later Bronze Age without edge to serve for work or weapons, and intended only for religious use. The two-headed weapon was that outward and visible sign of Labrandian Jove, so called from the λάβρα, which in the Lydian tongue was synonymous with πέλεκυς. The emblem appears on the medals of three Carian kings, the most notable being Mausolus (or Mausollus), dating from B.C. 353. According to Plutarch (*De Pythiæ Oraculis*) the Tenedians 'took the axe from their crabs, . . . because it appears that the crabs alone have the figure of the axe in their shells.' Hence the double-headed weapon on the coins of Tenedos is

---

[1] This weapon (*gladius*) is a Sword-blade, double-edged or single-edged, straight or curved, and 4–9 inches long, much used in the fourteenth and fifteenth centuries. It originated from the old practice of binding the sickle, scythe, axe, hatchet, or Sword to the end of a pole and thus forming a pike.

a votive or sacrificial, rather than a warlike, symbol.   The Tenedian Apollo also held the axe, which some regarded as the symbol of Tennes.   Aristotle and others maintained that a certain King of Tenedos decreed that adulterers should be slain with the axe, and his carrying out the law upon his own son gave rise to the proverb, Τενέδιος πέλεκυς, denoting a rough-and-ready way of doing business.

Although the πέλεκυς is mentioned by Homer ('Il.' and 'Od.') as a weapon as well as a tool, the Greeks, like the Assyrians, did not much affect it.   The Romans, who worshipped Quirinus in spear-shape, bound the securis in a bundle of rods (*fasces*), bore it as a badge of office, and placed it on consular coins.   The weapon was lowered in the salute, and thus, perhaps, arose our practice of dropping the Sword-point, which is unknown to the East.   The axe with expanded blade upon Trajan's column is in the hands of a workman.   Possibly the classics of Europe despised the weapon because it was proper to the *securigerœ catervœ* of the effeminate East.   As early as the days of Herodotus (I. chap. i. 215) the σάγαρις, the Armenian *sacr*, and the Latin *securis*, made either of gold or chalcos, was the favourite weapon of the Amazon [1] and the Massagetæ [2] horseman.   In Ireland the axe plays a part in the tales of Gobawn Saer : this goblin-builder completed the dangerous task of finishing off a royal roof of cutting wooden pegs, throwing them one by one into their places, and driving them in by flinging the magic weapon at each peg in due succession.

From Egypt the axe passed into the heart of Africa.   Here it still serves, before and after use, as a medium of exchange ; and this circulation from tribe to tribe explains the various forms that have overspread the Dark Continent.   The Nile Valley again sent it eastward through Hittite-land and Assyria to Persia and India, where the crescent-shaped battle-axe has long been a favourite.   The varieties of form and colour are noticed by Duarte Barbosa [3] when describing the 'Moors' of Hormuz Island.   It was adopted by the Turkish horseman, who carried it at his saddle-bow.   Klemm ('Werkzeuge und Waffen') notices that it was a favourite Scandinavian weapon slung by a strap to the back ; and most of the deaths recounted in 'Burnt Njal' are the result of it.   The Norman long-hefted axe is common on the Bayeux tapestries.   A Scandinavian war-axe of the early seventeenth century was found on the battle-field of Norwegian Kringelen ; the handle is recurved so as to fit the back socket.   In Germany it was generally used during the fifteenth century ; in England during the sixteenth ; and in the seventeenth it became obsolete throughout Europe, except among the Slavs and the Magyars.

---

[1] The Amazons of the Mausoleum (Newton, *Halicarnassus*, p. 235) are armed with axe, bow, and Sword ; the Greeks with javelins and Swords.

[2] The Massagetæ (greater Jats or Goths) are opposed to the Thyssa (or lesser) Getæ, and both used the *sagaris*. But while some authors translate the word *securis*, others call it a 'kind of Sword,' and others confuse it with the ἀκινάκης, the *acinaces* which the Greek mentions separately (iv. 62, viii. 67).

Strabo (xi. 8) connects the Massagetæ (Goths) with the *Sacœ* (Saxons), and Major Jähn derives *Sacœ* (the *Shaka* of the Hindus) from *Saighead=Sagitta*.   The term '*Saxones*' was later than the age of Tacitus, and we first find it in the days of Antoninus Pius. 'Brevis gladius apud illos (*Saxones*) *Saxo* vocatur' suggests that the *Seax* was connected with the race of old (*Trans. Anthrop. Instit.* May 1880).

[3] *Loc. cit.* p. 43.

The German processional axe shows its latest survival ; blade and handle are of one piece of wood, ornamented with the guild-devices, and so modified that the original weapon can hardly be recognised. Similarly the Bergbarthe (mine-picks) of the German Bergmänner (miners) were used, according to Klemm, for the defence of cities, notably of Freiberg in 1643 ; and, made of brass as well as iron, they are still carried in State processions. The axe, like the spear, demarked boundaries. The charter given by Cnut (Canute) to Christ Church, Canterbury, grants the harbour and dues thereof on either side as far as a man standing on deck at flood-

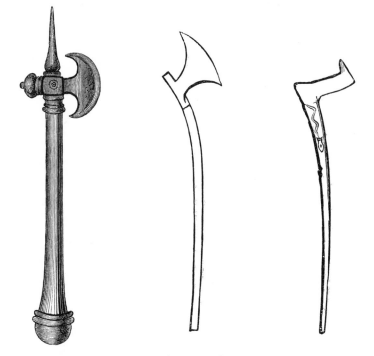

FIG. 90.—IRISH BATTLE-AXE.   FIG. 91.—AXE USED BY BRUCE.   FIG. 92.—GERMAN PROCESSIONAL AXE.

tide could cast a taper-axe, and the custom of throwing the tool to mark boundaries has been retained in some parts of the country to our day. It was with a battle-axe that the Bruce of Bannockburn clove the skull of an English champion to the chin. Monstrelet tells us that during the wars of Jeanne d'Arc (Patay fought in A.D. 1429) the English carried hatchets in their girdles.

The Axe [1] was adopted by the Franks, as well as by the Scandinavians and the Germans, especially the Saxons. Hence the two-edged axe when affixed to long staves, forming a spear, became the Icelandic Hall-bard [2] (hall-axe ?), the Teutonic

[1] Egypt. *akhu*, Lat. *ascia*, Germ. *Axt.* The oldest form is ' *aks* ' (*securis*), the bipennis, ' *dversahs*,' and the dolabrum ' *barte.*' In Lower Saxon *axt* is ' *exe*,' a congener of our ' axe.'

[2] The word is variously written and explained.

Alle-barde ('all-cleaver'), and the 'Pole-axe,' called from Poland (=Polje, the plain-country). This modification was universal in Northern Europe during the first ages of Christianity. The earliest shape (middle fourteenth to early sixteenth centuries) was a broad and massive axe, mounted on a thick and solid spear; in the sixteenth and seventeenth centuries the blade became more slender and hollow-

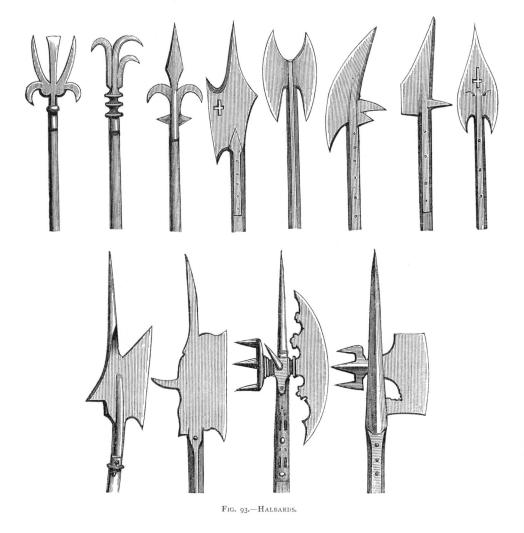

FIG. 93.—HALBARDS.

edged, and the head longer and more taper. The Swiss introduced the Halbert to France in the middle fifteenth century: in the seventeenth century it was conventionalised, the axe resumed its original aspect, and the spear grew to leaf-shape. In this form it was retained by the subalterns and sergeants of the British army till abolished with the pig-tails of 'Shaven England.' It is not wholly forgotten on ceremonious occasions in certain European Courts, and during all its changes it has ever retained its cousinly likeness to the broadsword.

I have shown how the stone celt might become a metal knife, and thence develop

FIG. 94.—HALBARDS.

into the straight Sword. By noting the modifications it is as easy to see that the axe. might have produced the scymitar. The earliest form would be a broad lance-head inserted into a common club (*a*), as is still practised in many parts of Africa. The

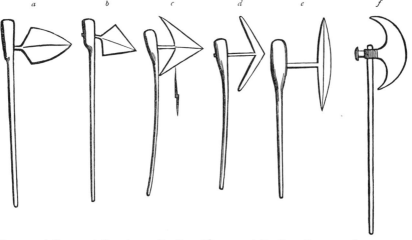

FIG. 95.—*a, b.* BECHWANA'S CLUB AXE ; *c.* THE SAME, EXPANDED; *d.* THE SAME, BARBED ; *e.* SILEPE OF THE BASUTOS; *f.* HORSEMAN'S AXE OF THE SIXTEENTH CENTURY.

next improvement (*c*) would convert the tool into an arm by increasing the cutting surface ; and another step (*d*) would make it lighter by reducing the blade to a triangle of mere barbs, ⊣. Then (*e*) we have the Khond or Circar battle-axe, and the Silepe of the South African Basutos who, virtually discovered by Dr. Livingstone, have become so troublesome of late years.[1] This T-shaped blade, perpetuated in the 'Baïonette Gras,' was used in Switzerland and in Venice till the sixteenth century, according to Meyrick and Demmin. Afterwards the straight back next to the staff would be formed into two small and graceful crescents (*f*); and the weapon became far better fitted for the requirements of cavalry. This shape is world-wide, and was used in England *temp*. Elizabeth. A congener of the glaive was the *Francisque à lance ouverte*, the broad-bladed 'taper-axe,' used for throwing as well as for striking. According to the Abbé Cochet, this

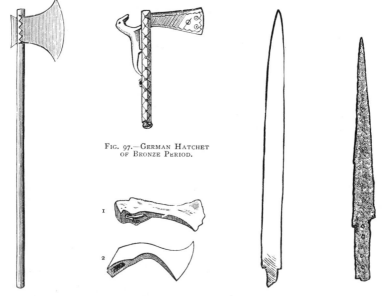

FIG. 97.—GERMAN HATCHET
OF BRONZE PERIOD.

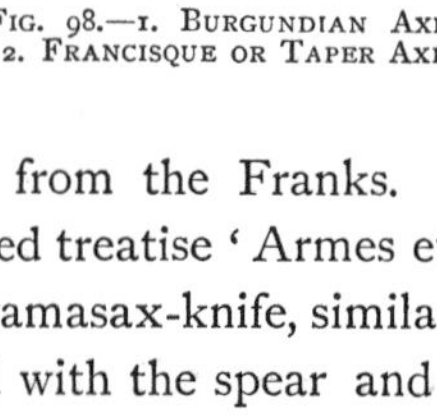

FIG. 96.—HINDÚ HATCHET
FROM RAJPUTANA.

FIG. 98.—1. BURGUNDIAN AXE;
2. FRANCISQUE OR TAPER AXE.

FIG. 99.—IRON SCRAMASAX
(16 inches long).

FIG. 100.—SCRAMASAX
(18 inches long).

weapon took its name from the Franks. The Francisque is termed a 'defensive weapon' in the illustrated treatise 'Armes et Armures.'[2] The Saxons preferred to it the Sahs, Seax or Scramasax-knife, similarly used. The Francisque is rare in the Saxon graves compared with the spear and knife, but it is more common than the Sword.[3]

The Bill[4] (A.-S. *byll*, Irish *biail*, *securis*) was introduced into England *temp*.

[1] A *silepe* from the armoury of King Mosesh was shown at the National Exhibition amongst objects from Natal (Col. A. Lane Fox, *Cat.* p. 145).

[2] Par Lacombe (Paris, Hachette, 1868).

[3] I have again noticed the *sahs, seax, sax,* and *scramasax* in chap. xiii.

[4] Our 'bill' is the German *Beil*, the *securis*, or axe.

Both words appear to me congeners of the Greek βέλος, Sword or dart, showing a missile-age, from βάλλειν, to throw; not, as Jähn thinks, from the Sanskrit *bhil*. Robert Barret (1598) preferred the pike, although owning that the bill had done good service. Even of late years Messrs. John Mitchel and Meagher ('of the Sword') advised the wretched Irish peasants to make pikes out of reaping-hooks.

Henry VI. about the fifteenth century, when it was allied in form to the Halbard. Skinner considers it a *securis rostrata* (beaked axe). It was long a favourite in Scandinavia, and the illustration represents the weapon of Gunnar, the Icelandic champion, which sang before battle, as also did the Sword of Sigurd.

The glaive of the fifteenth and sixteenth centuries was followed by the Guisarme, Gisarme, or Bisarme. This long blade, with a slender spear-point projecting from the back, is still used by the Chinese ; and the Despots of Dahome borrowed it, like other quaint arms and customs, from Europe. The *Voulge*, an intermediate form of

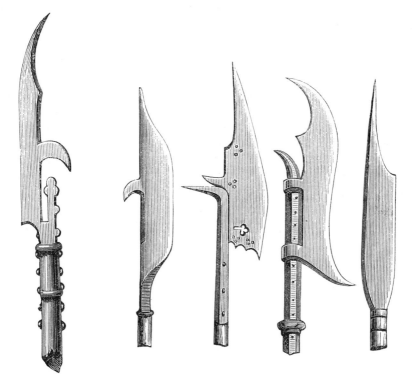

FIG. 101.—GUNNAR'S BILL.   FIG. 102.—VOULGES.

the halbert and the glaive, and probably a descendant of the former, was a battle-axe much used by the Swiss in the fourteenth century. The war-scythe of the same period figured by Demmin, and the scythe-Sword—a formidable-looking, but unhandy weapon—were adopted by the Hungarian rebels as lately as in 1848. Allied with these mediæval forms is a vast variety of shapes known as the Spetum (Spiedo or Spit), the Ronçeur or Ranseur, and the military fork. They were probably known to the Ancients, and reintroduced into Europe by the peasantry who, compelled hastily to arm themselves, would use the handy flails, sickles, and scythes. A well-arranged and complete collection is still wanted to show the links connecting them with a common prototype.

The interest of these weapons is chiefly connected with the various forms of curved broadsword. The leaf-shaped metal-blade for thrusting, which appears to be one of the earliest forms, and which is preserved by the Somal and other bar-barians, is, I have said, evidently a spear-head fixed in a wooden handle.

Briefly to describe the Sword of the Early Bronze Age, during which, by the by, cremation became almost universal in Europe. The weapon is to a certain extent North European, and seems to have travelled up the valleys of great rivers : Den-mark has yielded two hundred and fifty to six Italian bronze blades.[1] They are as a rule of fair length, averaging about seventy-five centimetres : the profile is either leaf-shaped, sub-leaf-shaped, or straight, ending in a bevelled point. The hilt is of two kinds : either tanged or untanged : the tang is broad, long, and pierced, with one or more holes for riveting ; in this case the handle was of wood, bone, or horn. Many hefts, however, as will afterwards appear, are cast in a single piece with or without guard ; and the latter often disappears in a hollow triangular base, a crescent or horse-shoe containing the shoulders with the concavity of the arch towards the point ; this also served in many weapons to receive the rivets. The pommel is of various patterns, frequently a cone, oval, globe, or dome with steps or with melon-like ridges.[2] In others, especially amongst the old Kelts and Germans, it ended with a crutch or crescent whose cusps were, in the richer kinds, adorned with spirals.

[1] *Prehistoric Times*, p. 20. The Dublin Museum contains 1,283 articles of the Bronze Age.
[2] I assume as a type, the bronze Sword (Tafel iv.) in *Die Alterthümer von Hallstätten, Salzburg, &c.* by Friedrich Simony (Wien, 1851).

CHAPTER VI.

THE PROTO-SIDERIC OR EARLY IRON AGE OF WEAPONS.

'Of all metallurgical processes, the extraction of malleable iron may be regarded as amongst the most simple.'—Percy, *Iron, &c.* p. 573.

WE now come to the King of Metals that 'breaketh in pieces and subdueth all things'; the only ore friendly as well as fatal to the human form; the most useful and the most deadly in the hand of man [1]—Iron.[2]

According to the Parian Chronicle (Arundelian Marbles), followed by Thrasyllus (Clemens Alex. in 'Strom.'), and by a host of writers, iron-working was discovered in B.C. 1432 or 248 years before the Trojan war. The latter, a crucial date, is, as will appear, wholly undetermined; the various authorities have made it range through nearly seven hundred years. But the life of Hellas is one great 'appropriation clause': the Greeks were doughty claimants, childish in their *naïveté* of conceit; they were burglars of others' wits (convey, the wise it call), and they made themselves do all things. Their legends, for instance, accredit 'Glaucus the Chian' with having invented the art and mystery of steel-inlaying. De Goguet (A.D. 1761) tells us that the Phœnicians ranked amongst their oldest heroes two brothers who discovered iron-working; the Cretans referred it to the oldest period of their history,[3] and the Idæan Daktyls learnt it from the 'mother of the gods.' Prometheus (in Æschylus) boasts of having taught mankind to fabricate all metals: he also wears an iron ring supposed to be a chain not an ornament; and it possibly symbolises the union of fire and ore. The art of iron-working is referred, now to the Cyclopes, of Sicily, then to the Chalybes,[4] who extended from

---

[1] Pliny, xxxiv. 39.

[2] The word comes from the root which gave the Persian *dhan*; the Irish *iaran* or *yarann*; the Welsh *hiarn*; the Armorican *uarn*; the Gothic *eisarn*; the Danish *iern*; the Swedish *iarn*; the Cimbric *jara*; the German *Eisen*, and the Latin *ferrum*, with the neo-Latin *ferro, hierro* (Span.), &c. From *iaran* also we derive *Harnisch*, harness.

[3] The unfortunate Cretans gained the name of 'ever liars' (ἀεὶ ψεῦσται) for telling what was probably the truth. They showed in their island the grave of Jupiter, who must have been originally some hero or chief deified after his death—evidently one of the origins of worship. The evil report began with Callimachus (*Hymn. in Jov.* 8); and was continued in the proverbial τρία κάππα κάκιστα (Krete, Kappadocia, and Kilikia). Hence the syllogistic puzzle of Eubulides: 'Epimenides said that the Cretans are liars: Epimenides is a Cretan: *ergo*, Epimenides is a liar: *ergo*, the Cretans are not liars: *ergo*, Epimenides is not a liar.'

[4] Chap. iv. The Chalybs of Justin (xliv. 3) is a river between the Ana (Guadiana) and the Tagus; called by Ptolemy and Martianus, Κάλιπους or Κάλιπος. Æschylus alludes to the original Chalybes when he personifies the Sword as the 'Chalybian stranger,' and in the same tragedy (*Seven against Thebes*) he entitles it 'the hammer-wrought Scythian steel.'

Colchis to Spain : Clemens (Alex.) refers the discovery of making malleable iron to the Noropes of Danubian Pannonia, who dwelt between Noricum (Styria) and Mæsia ; and finally, to quote no more, Mr. J. Fergusson, a careful writer, tells us that 'the Aryans (?) were those who introduced the use of iron, and with it dominated over and expelled (?) the older races.'

Modern discovery has proved that the invention, and indeed the general adoption, of 'Mars' (♂) dates from the very dawn of history ; and that it is a mere theory to assume everywhere preceding millennia of bone and stone, copper and bronze. It is clear, for instance, in Central Africa, where copper and tin were unprocurable, that man must first have used iron.[1] A good authority, Mr. St. John V. Day[2] (C.E.), who was in charge of iron works in Southern India, claims for iron—cast as well as wrought, and even for its carburet, steel—the credit of being 'unquestionably the earliest of substances with which man was acquainted.' This writer, however, denies, contrary to all tradition, a 'progressive rise in the quality of materials used by man ' : that is, from the soft and yielding to the hard and refractory. He holds that Man, once master of metallurgy, 'would be better able to deal with the much more easily manipulated bones, stones, or wood.' He supposes all the metals, noble and ignoble, as well as gems and precious stones, to have become familiar amongst Eastern races, ' whether they be Semitic, Aryan, Hamitic, Sporadic, or Allophyllian, by virtue of a civilisation due to a natural innate insight.' Hence he declares Egypt an enigma to those who accept the dictum of ' man's gradual evolution from the condition of a savage, an ignoramus,' and he opines that this grim being is simply a retrograde.[3]

These ideas trench upon old metallurgic superstitions and seem to run into extremes. We *know* nothing concerning the home of Proto-man, which is perhaps deep under the waters. Anthropologists, who locate him in Mesopotamia, 'Aryaland ' (Central Asia), or Ethiopia, look only to the origin of the present species, and the historic cycle. Our studies, as far as they go, suggest that Man began in the Polar regions, and that in hoar antiquity each racial centre had its own material—wood and horn, bone and stone, copper, bronze, and iron.[4]

[1] 'To the abundance of iron we may attribute the fact that the Africans appear to have passed direct from the stone implements, that are now found in the soil, to those of iron, without passing through the intermediate bronze period which, in Egypt and other countries, intervened between the ages of stone and iron.'—*Anthropol. Coll.* pp. 128–134.

[2] 'The High Antiquity of Iron and Steel,' a valuable paper read before the Philos. Soc. Glasgow, printed in *Iron* (1875–76), and kindly sent to me by the editor, Mr. Nursey ; also *The Prehistoric Use of Iron and Steel* (Trübner, London, 1877), from which Mr. Day has allowed me to make extracts.

[3] The question is to be determined by facts, not theories. Hitherto we are justified in believing, from the skeletons dug up at great depths, or found in caves associated with the mammals which they destroyed, that Man in prehistoric times was of a low physical, and therefore mental type. We shall believe the opposite view when we are shown ancient crania equal, if not superior, to those of the present day—relics that will revive the faded glories of ' Father Adam ' and ' Mother Eve.' But, meanwhile, we cannot be expected to believe in *ipse dixits*, inspired or uninspired.

[4] For instance, in North-Western Europe, the early iron age began about A.D. 250, according to Konrad Englehardt (*Denmark in the early Iron Age*, p. 4, London, 1866), quoted by Mr. Day.

For our first lesson in iron we must go back as usual to Kahi-Ptah (the Ptah-region), that Nile Valley which is the motherland of all science, of all art. Here Bunsen [1] provides us with the following table:

HIEROGLYPHS	PHONETIC VALUE	TRANSLATION
	Ba.	Earth, Metal, Soul, Circle, Seed, Corn.
	Ba.	Iron.
	Ba'a.	Iron, Earth.
	Ba'aenpe (Benipe or Penipe).	Iron.
	Bet.	Iron.

Mr. Day (who has drawn it up) observes that 'BA' is a constant in the phonetic values assigned to the uncertain hieroglyphs for iron, and feels disposed to believe it synonymous with χαλκός, base metal in general. He would translate the Saidic 'BENIΠE' and the Coptic 'ΠENIΠE' by 'stone (BE) of (NI) sky or heaven (ΠE)'; in fact, 'sky-stone,' alluding to meteoric iron, probably the first utilised. Dr. Birch holds 'BA' to be a general term for metal made particular, as in Greece, by prefixed adjectives (white, black, yellow) denoting the quality of the ore. And hence the determinative of 'BA' (metal, stone, or hard wood) is the cube or parallelogrammic block which denotes building and building materials.

Native iron may be distributed into two great divisions, extra-terrestrial and terrestrial. The former is known as meteoric or nickeliferous. Mr. Day (pp. 22–23) gives analyses of this form, and takes, from Chladni [2] and others, a list of masses that fell in Siberia, Thuringia, and Dauphiné; in West African Liberia, and in American Sta. Fé de Bogotá, and Canaan, Connecticut. Though many trials have been made in working extra-terrestrial metal, all have hitherto failed; the phosphorus, nickel and its *alter ego*, cobalt, render the forgings, in our present state of technology, too brittle for use. Terrestrial or telluric iron is again divided into two classes—the nearly pure ore and the native steel. According to the schedule of Rosset:

---

[1] *Egypt's Place in Universal History*, vol. v.; London, Longmans, 1867, with additions by Samuel Birch, LL.D.

[2] When Laplace made meteorolites ejections from lunar volcanoes, Chladni suggested that they were masses of metallic matter, moving in irregular orbits through interplanetary, and possibly interstellar, space.

Iron is a metal not cast and malleable.
Steel   „   cast and malleable.
Pig-iron   „   cast and not malleable.

That iron was common amongst the ancient Egyptians we may assume as proved. Mr. A. Henry Rhind, when opening the tomb of Sebau (nat. B.C. 68), noted on the massive doors 'iron hasps and nails,' as lustrous and as pliant as on the day they left the forge.' Belzoni, who died in 1823, found an iron sickle under the feet of one of the Karnak Sphinxes dating from B.C. 600. In June 1837, Mr. J. R. Hill, employed by Colonel Howard Vyse, when blasting and excavating the Jízeh[1] Pyramid, came upon a piece of iron, apparently a cramp, near the channel-mouth of one of the air-passages: it had thus been preserved from rust, and its authenticity cannot be doubted. Some suggested that it was used for scraping and finishing; others for finally levelling the faces of dressed stone, but it tapers off from the middle to an edge on either side and it narrows at one end.[2] This relic can hardly be of later date than B.C. 4000–3600, when Khufu (Cheops) built his burial-place and inscribed in it his hieroglyphic shield[3] or cartouche ⟨ hieroglyph ⟩. Stowed away in the British Museum, it excited scant attention till Dr. Lepsius at the Congress of Orientalists (London, 1874), suggested that it was of steel. A trial was made (Sept. 18); it yielded readily to a few turns of the drill, and the surfaces of the hole showed the whiteness and the brightness of newly-cut malleable iron. Since that discovery, sacrificial iron knives have been found in the Nile Valley, despite the ready oxidation of the metal in a climate of the hot-damp category. In the Bulák Museum (Salle de l'Est), with the wooden Swords, was a straight and double-edged iron blade that had two ribs running along its length. Another room showed a straight, double-edged, and round-pointed dagger of gilt iron. Of the latter weapon there are three fine specimens (Salle du Centre).

The literature of Egypt abounds in allusions to the use of iron.[4] The Rev. Basil H. Cooper[5] believes that Mibampes the 'Iron King,' sixth successor of

[1] This word is tortured by non-Orientalists into various ill-forms. The Arabs write it جِيزَه (*Jízeh*), and the Egyptians pronounce it *Gízeh*, not *Ghizeh*.

[2] A full-sized drawing appeared in vol. vii. of *Proceedings of the Phil. Soc. Glasgow*; and was repeated by Mr. Day in his book, Pl. II. He also gives Belzoni's sickle, Pl. I.

[3] When visiting the 'Tombs of the Soldans,' Cairo, I found a slab of blue basalt bearing the cartouche of Khufu, used as a threshold for one of the buildings. The characters had been partly erased; but the material was too hard for the barbarians who had misused it.

[4] I have elsewhere noticed (chap. iv.) the colours of metals in the painted tombs of Thebes, and the blue (cyanus-colour) of the butcher's steel. The history of this homely article is instructive. For hundreds of years it retained, in England and elsewhere, its original shape, an elongated cone. At last some 'cute citizen had the idea of breaking the surface into four edges, and of hardening it with nickel. The simple improvement now fits it for sharpening everything from a needle to a razor: it thus frees us from the 'needy knife-grinder,' who right well deserved to be needy, as he disadorned everything he touched.

[5] *Antiquity of the Use of Metals, especially Iron, among the Egyptians*, p. 18 (London, 1868). Also *Ueber die Priorität des Eisens oder der Bronze in Ostasien*, by Dr. M. Müller (*Trans. Vienna Anthrop. Soc.* vol. ix.).

primæval Mena (circ. B.C. 4560),[1] bore on his cartouche the word 'Benipe'; and that no less than three records[2] entitle him 'Lover of Iron' (i.e. the Sword); 'thus attesting, not only the extreme antiquity of the use of iron, but unfortunately (?) of that most dreadful evil of all which are the scourges of humanity—war (?).' And so we see the nineteenth century repeating the Herodotian half-truth, 'Iron has been discovered to the hurt of Man'; and looking only at one side of the question, the evils of War, without which, I repeat, strong races could not supplant the weaker to the general benefit of mankind. The Epos of Pentaur, the jovial temple scribe[3] (circ. B.C. 1350), mentions 'iron' thrice; and Pharaoh Mene-Ptah II., whose 'Sword gave no quarter,' had vessels of iron. In later hieroglyphic literature the notices become too numerous to justify quotation.

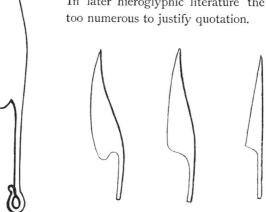

FIG. 103.—EGYPTIAN SACRIFICIAL KNIVES (IRON).

The old Egyptians, according to Plutarch,[4] held iron to be the ὀστέον Τυφῶνος, or bone of Set; whereas the σιδηρίτις λίθος, or magnet, was that of his foe-god Horus, degraded to Charon in Greece and Rome. This siderite was known to the Hellenes in its religious aspect as Ἡράκλεια λίθος or Ἡράκλειον, either from Heraclea-town or from Hercules (Pliny, xxxvi. 25). Siderite or load-

[1] I assume this date because it marks when the spring equinox (vernal colure) occurred in the Taurus-sign. The earliest of the six epochs proposed by Egyptologists is B.C. 5702 (Böckh), and the latest is B.C. 3623 (Bunsen); the mean being B.C. 4573, and the difference a matter of 2079 years (Brugsch, i. 30).

[2] The Table of Sakkarah (Memphis), found about the end of 1864 by the late Mariette Pasha, dates from Ramses the Great (thirteenth century B.C.), and makes Mibampes the first of his fifty-six ancestors. No. 2 is the new tablet of Abydos, discovered, also in 1864, by Herr Dümmichen; it enabled scholars to supply the illegible name in No. 3, the priceless Turin Papyrus, the hieratic Canon of the Ptolemies. Mir-

bampes, Mirbapen, or Mi-ba of the monuments is called in Manetho 'Miebides, son of Usarphædus' (*Cory's Fragments*, p. 112).

[3] Of Ramses II., who, with his father Seti, represents the Greek Sesostris, the Sesesu-Ra of the monuments. (Brugsch, *Hist.* ii. 53–62: see my chap. viii.) Prof. G. Ebers has made this Egyptian proto-Homerid the hero of his romance, *Uarda* (i.e. War-dah, 'the Rose').

[4] *De Iside et Osiride.* He quotes Manetho the Priest, who wrote during the reign of the first Ptolemy, and who told unpleasant truths concerning Moses, the Hebrews, and the Exodus.

stone, termed 'Magnet' from its supposed discoverer, was also entitled 'live iron,' and its wounds were supposed to be more deadly than those of the common ore.

The Nile-dwellers had not far to go for iron, which abounds in the well-known Wady Hammámát, one of the earliest centres of Egyptian mining ; and, as Mr. Piazzi Smyth showed, it accumulates everywhere in the fissures of the flaky limestone : [1] it is produced in Ethiopia (the Sudan and Abyssinia) ; and in Midian, where the old Kemites opened the copper mines, it appears in the shape of black sand and large masses of titaniferous [2] and other ores. The monuments (Karnak Table, &c.) specify, amongst objects of tribute, iron from the lands of the Thuhi [3] ('the fair people'), the Rutennu (Syrians and Assyrians), and the Asi (or rebels gene-rally ?) ; from these countries it was exported in the ore and in bricks and pigs. The tribute-tables of Thut-mes III. (B.C. 1600) mention :—

> One beautiful iron armour of the hostile king.
> One beautiful iron armour of the King of Megiddo.
> ? lbs. weight, two suits of iron armour from Naharayn.
> Iron suits of armour (taken by the warriors), and
> Five iron storm-caps (?).

Mr. Francis Galton [4] first discovered in the ancient copper-diggings of the so-called 'Sinaitic' peninsula, a blackish mass, not unlike iron-slag, which he con-jectured to date before Moses' days. A score of years afterwards (early 1873), Mr. Hartland [5] examined the junction of the Wadys Kemeh, Mukattab, and Maghárah, and found the iron-ore imperfectly extracted : assays and analyses of the slags that lay in heaps about the ruined works produced fifty-three per cent. of metal. He determined that the mines at Serábit El-Khádim had been con-structed on the principle of the Catalan (or rather the Corsican) forge ; [6] and he discovered near them a temple and barracks for the soldier-guards. [7]

---

[1] The limestones of Carniola produce heaps of pisoliths, which require only smelting ; and hence, probably, the early Iron Age of Noricum and its neighbourhood.

[2] They suggest the magnetic and titaniferous iron sands of Wicklow, of New Zealand, of Australia, and of a variety of sites mentioned in *To the Gold Coast for Gold*, ii. 111.

[3] The Naphtuhim of Scripture.

[4] *Percy's Metallurgy*, p. 874, first edit.

[5] *Proc. Soc. Antiq.* second series, vol. v., June 1873. Mr. Hartland added rubbings of various Pharaohnic stones, hoping to 'show how little the mind of civilised man has developed during 3,000 years.' A pleasant lesson to humanity ! But after all thirty centuries are a mere section of the civilisa-tion which began in Egypt.

[6] The Corsican is simply a blacksmith's forge. The Catalan has a heavy hammer and blowing-machine ; if the *trompe* be used, a fall of water is re-quired for draught. The Stückofen is a Catalan ex-tended upwards in the form of a quadrangular or cir-cular shaft, 10–16 feet high.

[7] It is to be noted that flint implements were found all about these works : Mr. Hartland brought home from them silex arrow-heads. The late lamented Professor Palmer observed them in other parts of the Pharan peninsula, and I made a small collection in Midian. In the *Journ. of the Anthrop. Soc.* 1879, I showed, following Mr. Ouvry, Sir John Lubbock, and others, that Cairo is surrounded by ancient flint-ateliers. M. Lartet explored them in Southern Palestine ; I picked them up near Bethle-hem (*Unexplored Syria*, ii. 289). The Abbé Richard and others traced them at Elbireh (in the Tiberiad) ; between Tabor and the Lake ; and, lastly, at Galgal, where Joshua circumcised. Lastly, my late friend Charles F. Tyrwhitt-Drake, when travelling with me, came upon an atelier east of Damascus. I have noticed General Pitt-Rivers' great Egyptian discovery in chap. ii.

It is hard to believe with Mr. Proctor that Abraham, a wandering Chaldæan Shaykh, taught the Egyptians astronomy, astrology, and arithmetic; or with Mr. Piazzi Smyth, that Melchisedek, the petty chief of a village in Palestine, built *the* Pyramid. Yet it is only reasonable to suppose that the Israelites set out upon their exodus or exodi, for there were probably many, provided with some of the technological wisdom of the Egyptians. Joseph, according to Brugsch ('Hist.' I. chap. xii.), rose to the honour of Zaphnatpaneakh (Governor of the Sethroitic home), and Ro-hir or Procurator, under the Shepherd-kings or 'Hyksos,' a word which he renders Hek-Shasu,[1] lord of the Shasu (Arabs); he makes the Pharaoh of the Oppression, Ramses II. (B.C. 1333–1300), and Mene-Ptah II. the Pharaoh of the Exodus (B.C. 1300–1266). The Pentateuch, whatever be its date, well knew the use of Barzil (ברזל), the Chaldæan Parzil or Parzillu. According to Sir John Lubbock ('Prehistoric Man'), 'iron' is four times mentioned, and 'brass' (copper, bronze?) thirty-eight times in 'the Law.'[2] From other sources we gather that the metal was either עשות (*ashúth*, that is, 'the worked,' from the rad. *ashah*), or מוצק (*muzak*, 'the melted,' fused, cast; from the root *zak*). The Lord threatens that He will make 'the skies as iron and the earth as copper' (Levit. xxvi. 19). In Deuteronomy (iv. 20), Egypt is compared with an iron furnace; and mention is made of iron shoes (xxxiii. 25). Job includes among riches, cattle, silver, gold, brass (copper?), and iron; he tells us (xxviii. 2) that 'iron is taken out of the earth and copper is molten out of the stone,' and he speaks of lithic writing (xix. 24), 'graven with an iron style and lead in the rock for ever.' But commentators are not agreed about the age of this author, and in the hands of the Rabbis he seems gradually to be growing younger—more modern —with every generation.

The Hebrews found the Iron-age wherever they went. 'Barzil' was among the metals taken from the Midianites by Moses (Numb. xxxi. 22). The 'bed-stead,' or rather divan, of Og, the King of Bashan, measuring nine cubits of man (each=sixteen inches) in length by four broad, was of iron (Deut. iii. 11). Joshua shows that the Canaanites owned 'chariots of iron' (xvii. 16). These tribes, displaced by the Jews, seem to have been accomplished workers in metal.[3] Traces of iron-smelting occur on the Libanus,[4] where I found copper-stone,[5] and where, during the present century, coal and asphalte have been mined. Many parts of the country, as Argob in ancient Bashan, produce an abundance of iron-stone.[6] The old Phœnician Sanconiathon, a name which may denote a history or its historian, tells us through the Greek translator Philo of Byblus, that the

---

[1] *Hek* or *hak* (chief) has a suspicious resemblance to *Shaykh*, and *sos* to *sús*, the mare, characteristically ridden by the Bedawin. In old Egyptian *sos* is a buffalo.

[2] Movers (*Phönicier*, ii. 3), quoted by Dr. Evans (*Bronze, &c.* 5), finds bronze (copper?) 44 and iron 13 times in the Pentateuch, and he theorises upon the later introduction of the latter. But when was the Pentateuch written in its present form?

[3] Rougemont, *L'Age du Bronze*, pp. 188 *et seq.*

[4] Volney, *Travels*, ii. 438.

[5] Much of it, however, was the amygdaloid greenstone, called in English 'toadstone,' a corruption of the Germ. *Todstein.*

[6] *Speaker's Commentary*, i. 831.

people were famous for their Technites, artisans and blacksmiths. The warlike Hittites, as will appear, were also iron-workers.

From Egypt the use of iron would spread through Asia Minor[1] eastward to Naharayn,[2] the two-river-land, Mesopotamia. But the date is disputed. The excavations of the late Mr. George Smith yielded no iron articles older than B.C. 1000–800. Mr. Day remarks that 'whilst Mesopotamia has not, up to the present time, produced any solid evidence in the form of material iron relics belonging to the oldest monarchies ; nevertheless, the monuments of those earliest times are numerous, and they yield abundance of testimony to the acquaintance of the contemporary people with iron.' In later ages he alludes to the rings and bangles of iron in the British Museum, which were possibly chain-links ; and particularly to the 'ombos of a shield,' as the most exquisite piece of their hammered iron-work he has met with : he doubts if it can in some respects be surpassed by the productions of to-day. The cuneiforms speak of iron fetters, and the people of the great Interamnian plain knew the art of casting bronze over iron,[3] only lately introduced into our metallurgy.

According to Mr. G. Smith there is no pure Assyrian word for 'iron.'[4] Its cuneiform symbol is ►✝ ✝, but the phonetic value or pronunciation has not yet been determined. 'It must have been in use 2000 B.C.,' and it is found in inscriptions of all ages. The word is supposed to belong to the ancient Turanian or Proto-Babylonian race (Akkadian[5] or Sumirian) that held the river-plains, and it has been grafted into the more recent Assyrian language. In the inscriptions, each god has his sign, and the symbol above given, accompanies, as his attribute, one of the deities of war and hunting : thus it is a parallel to that found in the cartouche of the Egyptian ' Iron King.'

Canon Rawlinson,[6] on the other hand, assigns to the symbol the phonetic value of *Hurud*, which thus became the Chaldæan equivalent for 'iron.' In concert with his distinguished brother, he came to the conclusion : ' There are two signs for metals in Assyria, with respect to which there is a doubt which is iron and which is brass (or bronze rather). These are ►✝ ✝ and ⊬⟨Ɣ. Sir Henry Rawlinson, on the whole, inclines to regard the first as bronze and the second

[1] This term seems first to have been used by Orosius (i. 2) in our fourth century.

[2] In chap. ix. I shall attempt to show that Naharayn (the dual of Nahr, a river) is also applied to Palestine in such phrases as ' Tunipe (Daphne-town) of Naharayn.'

[3] Dr. Percy found that certain Assyrian bronzes had been cast round a support of the more tenacious metal, thus combining strength with lightness.

[4] M. F. Lenormant (' Les Noms d'Airain et du Cuivre dans les deux Langues . . . de la Chaldée et de l'Assyrie, *Trans. Soc. Bibl. Archæology*, vi. part 2) renders *parzillu*, iron ; *abar*, lead ; *shiparru*

(Arab. نُحاس, brass), bronze ; *anaku*, tin ; *eru* or *erudu*, copper or bronze (Arab. اِبلُ, copper or brass) ; *kashpu*, silver ; and *kurashu*, gold. The learned author discovers in the cuneiforms repeated mention of the 'ships of Mákan' and the Kur Makannata (mountain of Makná), which he translates ' Pays de Mákan ' : finding it a great centre of copper, he is inclined to confound it with the so-called Sinaitic Peninsula. I have only to refer readers to ' Makná ' in my three volumes on the Land of Midian.

[5] Akkad is upper, Sumir lower Babylonia.

[6] *The Five Great Monarchies of the Ancient Eastern World*, vol. i. p. 62. London, 1871.

as iron, although the former is nowhere rendered phonetically. The latter is rendered in a syllabary as equivalent to *Hurud* in Akkadian and *Eru* in Assyrian. Mr. George Smith reverses the meanings of the two signs. The point is a very doubtful one.'

After the decay of the Proto-Babylonian or Chaldæan empire (B.C. 2300–1500), when the seat of Interamnian rule moved to the Tigris-Euphrates basin, and the three Assyrian periods flourished (B.C. 1500–555),[1] iron was largely used. It was produced, according to Layard (*loc. cit.*) in the Tiyari mountains, and it is still found in quantities on the slopes, three or four days' journey from Mosul. The north-western palace of Nimrúd (Kalah) showed, amongst the rubbish-heaps, much rusty iron and a perfect helmet like that represented in the bas-reliefs. There were Swords and daggers, shields and shield-handles, rods, and the points of spears and arrows, which fell to pieces on exposure. Amongst the few specimens preserved were the head of a trident-like weapon, some Sword-handles, a large blunt spear-pile, the point of a pick, several objects resembling the heads of sledge-hammers, and a double-handed saw of iron or steel (?), about three feet eight inches long by four inches and five-eighths broad, for cross-cutting timber. The British Museum owns a fine collection of Assyrian sheet or plate iron-work; pieces of unfinished forgings; a rude triangular lump through which a round hole has been driven (by a heated punch?); several cylindrical bars, straight and curved; wall-cramps, nails, and door-hinges; a ladle; rings of sizes (one being three inches in diameter); a signet-ring containing a silver bezel or seal; and, lastly, a portion of what seems to have been a double-sided comb. In much later days the Assyrians of Xerxes' army carried, according to Herodotus, shields, spears, daggers, and wooden clubs spiked with iron.

The Greeks learned their metallurgy, as they did all their arts, from Egypt; and, following in the footsteps of the Phœnicians, diffused them throughout the Western World. In Theseus' time, according to Wilkinson—that is, B.C. 1235—'iron is conjectured not to have been known, as he was found buried with a brass (copper, bronze?) Sword and spear.' They did not use iron weapons, and probably had no iron during their first foreign campaign—the Trojan war. The Parian (Arundelian) Chronicle (dating its notices from Cecrops, B.C. 1582) and the Rhodian myths refer to a conflagration in the Cretan mountains which taught

[1] The first period extended from B.C. 1500 to 909. The second from B.C. 909 to 745: the most marking names being Assurnazirpal = 'Ashur (arbiter of the gods) protects his son,' who built the north-west palace of Nimrúd, B.C. 884; and his son Shalmanezer II. of the Black Obelisk (Brit. Museum), B.C. 850. The third period (B.C. 745-555) numbered Tiglath-Pileser II., B.C. 745–727 (a single generation before the first Olympic, B.C. 776, when the mythic age of Greece emerges into the historical); Sennacherib (705–681); Esarhaddon (680–668), Assur-banipal (668–640); Nebuchadnezzar in 604–561, a contemporary of Solon (B.C. 594); Nergalsharuzur (B.C. 557); and the last Nabonidus (B.C. 555). Herodotus (A.D. 450) wrote about a century after the end of the third period, Ctesias in B.C. 395, and Berosus in B.C. 280. We have, it is clear, absolutely no historic proof that 'the patriarchal system of communities first locally developed itself at the mouth of the Euphrates Valley,' or began in any part of the great Mesopotamian plain.

metallurgy to the Idæan Daktyls (Δάκτυλοι Ἰδαῖοι):[1] this would, however, be a comparatively late date when we regard Egypt.[2]

With respect to the metal in the Hissarlik remains, Dr. Schliemann remarks (i. 31): 'The only objects of iron which I found were a key of curious shape and a few arrows and nails close to the surface.' It is no proof that it was used because Homer some centuries afterwards spoke of the κύανος (cyanus), steel tempered blue, a word which even in antiquity was translated by χάλυψ (chalybs, steel). The explorer remarks: 'Articles of steel may have existed: I believe positively that they did exist; but they have vanished without leaving a trace of their existence; for, as we know, iron and steel become decomposed much more readily than copper.' Yet, so contradictory is the whole book, and so uncertain are its conclusions, we find,[3] 'No. 4. Drillings of one of the Trojan sling-bullets, externally covered with verdigris, and internally the colour of iron'; while the assay shows that it consisted chiefly of copper and sulphur. Among the contemporary (?) finds of Mycenæ, which not a few authorities have pronounced to be Byzantine, and another observer Keltic,[4] Dr. Schliemann met with iron in the shape of knives and keys; but he holds these articles to be of comparatively late date, not older than the fifth century B.C.[5] At that time iron must have been general throughout Greece. In the fourth century, Aristotle ('Meteorologica') treats at length upon iron and its modifications. One passage runs: 'Wrought iron may be so cast as to be made liquid and to reharden; and thus it is they are wont to make steel (τὸ στόμωμα); for the scoria of iron subsides and is purged off by the bottom, and when it is often defæcated and cleansed, this is steel. But this they do not often, because of the great waste, and because it loses much weight in refining; but iron is so much the more excellent the more recrement it has.' Daimachus, Aristotle's contemporary, says of steels (τῶν στομωμάτων), 'There is the Chalybdic,[6] the Synopic, the Lydian, and the Lacedæmonian. The Chalybdic is best for carpenters' tools; the Lacedæmonian for files, drills, gravers, and stone-chisels; the Lydian also is suited for files, and for knives, razors, and rasps.' Avicenna (Abu Ali Sinâ), in his fifth book, 'De Anima,' according to Roger Bacon, has three species of the metal: (1) Iron, good for hammers and anvils, but not for cutting tools; (2) Steel,[7] which is purer and has more heat

---

[1] Rev. B. H. Cooper (loc. cit.) would derive 'Ida' from the Semitic יד (yad, hand), and make the Daktyls, or fingers, its peaks.

[2] I shall reserve for chap. xi. notices of iron by the classic and sacred poets of Greece.

[3] Troy and its Remains, p. 362; the analysis by M. Damour of Lyons.

[4] The theory of Stephani, Schulze, and others concerning the Byzantine date and Herulian origin of the Mycenæan graves, has been treated in England with some respect by Mr. A. S. Murray and Mr. Perry.

[5] According to Pausanias, Alyattes, the Lydian king (ob. B.C. 570), dedicated to his god, amongst other offerings, an inlaid iron saucer.

[6] Neither from this nor from any other passage can we ascertain whether the Chalybes tribe gave its name to chalybs (steel), or whether the material worked named the workmen.

[7] Colonel Yule (M. Polo, ii. 96) remarks that in the Middle Ages steel was regarded as a distinct natural species made of another ore, and relates how a native to whom an English officer had explained the process of tempering replied, 'What, would you have me believe that if I put an ass into the furnace it will come out a horse?'

in it ; it is therefore less malleable, but better able to take an edge ; and (3) Andena, ductile and malleable under a low degree of heat, and intermediate between iron and steel. Apparently the latter is the Hindiah or Hindiyáneh, the Ferrum Indicum and the Ondanique of Marco Polo (i. 17).

The Romans, a more cosmopolitan people than the Greeks, paid great attention to the mineral wealth of their conquests, and were careful to choose the best *acies*[1] for their weapons. Diodorus Siculus[2] describes the process by which the Celtiberians prepared their iron for Swords. Pliny, who was Procurator of Spain under Vespasian, may have studied iron-mining and ore-working in the country which still produces the Toledo blade. He characterises the metal generally as being universally used and occurring in every part of the world—especially in Ilva, now Elba, where there are mines of oligiste, specular iron or iron glance. His process of steel-making is that of the Greeks. ' Fornacum maxima differentia est ; in eis equidem nucleus ferri ' (the σίδηρος ἐργασμένος or worked iron of Aristotle) ' excoquitur ad indurandum ; aliter alioque modo ad densandas incudes, malleorumve rostra ' (xxxiv. 41). Hence it appears that the Romans had one way to make steel, and another to harden and temper tools, picks, and anvils. ' Possibly,' says Dr. Martin Lister, ' the latter were boiled in " sow-metal," as the term *densare* seems to suggest.'

Roman mining-operations were often conducted on a large scale. The Forest of Dean and the Wealds of Kent and Sussex, not to mention other parts of England, show heaps of old slag containing classical pottery and coins of Nero, Vespasian, and Diocletian. They obtained the regulus[3] by the direct process, and used charcoal in rude Catalan furnaces ; the work was imperfect, and the scoriæ contain a large percentage of metal. Ancient adits and shafts in Shropshire[4] and elsewhere have preserved the rude implements with which they made the natives labour in *corvée*. The hill-sides of Carthagena on the seaboard of Murcia (South-Eastern Spain) had been explored for lead and silver by the earliest Carthaginian colonists ; and the industry was at its height when Nova Carthago, under Roman rule, became (B.C. 200) a flourishing municipium, the centre of a large population. At this time as many as forty thousand hands were regularly employed. In our seventh century the Arab invasion ruined the mines, not only of this district, but of every province occupied by the ' Moors.' About the mid-fifteenth century a revival was attempted ; but this was checked at the beginning of the sixteenth, when the mines of Spanish America were opened : the Emperor

---

[1] *Acies* is properly the edge, that is, the steeled or cutting part of an instrument, which may be case-hardened. Hence the later words *aciare*, to steel, and *aciarium*, sharpening steel ; hence, too, the neo-Latin *acier*, *acciaio*, &c.

[2] See chap. xiii. Dr. Evans (*Bronze*, 275) says, ' How far their process of burying iron until part of it had rusted away would, in the case of charcoal iron, leave the remaining portion more of the nature of steel, I am unable to say.' It will appear that this

burying is often spoken of ; I have never seen it practised.

[3] Regulus (the ' little king ') is the residue of pure metal purged of its dross ; the old alchemists so entitled it because they ever expected to find the great king—Gold.

[4] At the Anthropological Congress of Austrian Salzburg (Aug. 1881) the tools attributed to the ' Keltic ' miners were almost the same as those which I had seen near the Wrekin.

Charles V. also would not see the soil of his European dominions disturbed by digging. The miners emigrated in mass, and New Carthage was forgotten till within the last half-century. According to M. Alfred Massart,[1] the ancient masses of plumbiferous scoriæ were large enough to pay for re-working. A superficial area of eight square leagues yielded some eight hundred thousand tons of iron-ore, of which two-thirds were ferro-manganese, and twenty thousand to twenty-five thousand tons of lead containing thirty thousand kilogrammes of silver. As regards the use of iron for many purposes by the ancient Britons before the Roman conquest, we may fairly, without attaching importance to the legend of 'Milesius,' believe that the industry may also have migrated northwards from a Spanish centre. Hence, Mr. Hutton, the local historian of Birmingham, believes that Sword-blades were made there before the landing of Julius Cæsar.

From Assyria the use of iron would extend through Persia to India, to Indo-China, and to China and Japan. Professor Max Müller, as Mr. Day justly observes, differs with himself when he states in one place[2] that 'iron was not known previously to the breaking up of the Aryan family'; and in another passage,[3] where we are told, 'Before the separation of the Aryan race . . . there can be no doubt that iron was known and its value appreciated.' Here, evidently, the Sanskritist had changed his first opinion, because he had noticed that 'Ayas' may also mean copper or bronze. The Rig Veda mentions mail-coats, hatchets, and weapons of iron; but so far from assigning to this work the age of B.C. 1300, we may fairly hold that its present shape was assumed in the early centuries following Christianity. We have trustworthy notices of the metal in India only at the beginning of authentic history, when the acumen of the Greeks was applied to the gross absurdities of Hindu fable.[4] The Malli and Oxydracæ presented to Alexander a hundred talents' weight of Indian steel (*ferrum candidum*) in wrought bars, just as Homer's Achilles ('Il.' xxiii. 826), nearly a thousand years before, offered at the funeral games of Patroclus, 'a rudely-molten mass of iron' (σόλον αὐτοχόωνον, self-melted?), which had been used for hurling at the foe by Eëtion, and which would supply the farm with metal for five years. The 'bright iron' of Ezekiel, named amongst the wares of Tyre (xxvii. 19) with cassia and calamus, was probably the same material. The Periplus mentions sideros indikos and

---

[1] Ingénieur des Mines: 'Gisements métallifères du District de Carthagène (Espagne),' Liège, 1875; a contribution to the *Proc. Geolog. Soc. Belgium*; and the result of extensive geological and mineralogical observation. The coloured map shows the strata-sequence (actual and in ideal order) to be tertiary limestone, iron-ore (carbonated, manganiferous, or plumbiferous); schistes; blende; schistes; silicated iron and schistes.

[2] *Lectures on the Science of Language*, pp. 254–55, vol. ii., edit. 1873.

[3] *Chips from a German Workshop* (set up in England), p. 47, vol. ii., edit. 1868.

[4] Mr. Day (*General Table of Terms*, given at end of this chapter) quotes as 'oldest Sanskrit' two names of iron, आर (*ár* or *ára*), meaning the planet Mars (*Ares*) or Saturn; iron (oxide of iron, iron-stone?), brass (copper?); and अयस, *áyas* (whence *ayas-kant*, a loadstone, and *ayaskár*, a smith), a word already noticed in connection with *æs*. But Mr. Day adds to his 'oldest Sanskrit' 'probably B.C. 1500'; and here again we recognise the master-touch of the subtle race—

'for profound
And solid lying much renowned.'

stómoma (steel) as imports to the Abyssinian harbours. Daimachus and Pliny specify, amongst the dearest kinds of steel, the ferrum Indicum and the ferrum Sericum ; and Salmasius refers to a Greek chemical treatise 'On the Tempering ($\pi\epsilon\rho\grave{\iota}$ $\beta\alpha\phi\hat{\eta}s$) of Indian Steel.'

The great iron-working age of India seems to have been in the fourth and fifth centuries of our era, when the blacksmiths must have been skilful and commanded an unlimited supply of the best metal. The Lát or iron-pillar of Delhi, to mention no other, is a solid shaft, showing that the people were unable to make a core. This simple piece of wrought metal, calculated to weigh seventeen tons and to contain eighty cubic feet of metal, measures in diameter 16·4 inches tapering to 12·05. The height above ground is twenty-two feet, and excavations of twenty-six feet did not reach the base : the known length therefore is upwards of forty-eight feet.[1] The sundry inscriptions punched upon it are of very various dates : Prinsep[2] assigns our third or fourth century to the Nagari character in which Rajah Dhava thus 'renowned it ' :—

' By him who, learning the warlike preparations and entrenchments of his enemies with their good soldiers and allies, a monument of fame engraved by his Sword on their limbs, who as master of the seven advantages,[3] crossing over (the Indus?), so subdued the Vahlikas of Sindhu [N.B. : they can hardly be the 'people of Balkh '] that even at this day his disciplined force and defences on the south (of the river) are sacredly respected by them,' &c. &c.

Metallurgists dispute as to the way in which this huge iron rod was wrought. One writer,[4] however, seems to have hit upon the solution of the problem : ' The column may have been forged standing, by welding on, one over another, thin iron plates or dires, the fire being built round the column as it grew ; and the ground raised in a mound to keep the top of the column on a level with the work-place.' Pyramid-building has been explained in the same way—a causeway.

But the Lát is not the only marvel of Hindu metallurgy. Mr. James Fergusson found in the Temple of Kanaruc, or Black Pagoda of the Madras Presidency, beams of wrought iron about twenty-one feet in length and eight inches section, to strengthen the roof, which the Hindus, in their distrust of the arch, formed after their usual bracket-fashion. In the fane of Mahavellipore he discovered sockets for similar supports. He assigns to the Black Pagoda a date between A.D. 1236 and 1241 ; and to Mahavellipore any time between our tenth and fourteenth centuries.[5] Colonel Pearse, R.A. presented to the trustees of the

[1] Report of Gen. A. Cunningham (Archæolog. Survey, 1861–62). It speaks highly for Anglo-Indian *vis inertiæ* and incuriousness when we are told that the 'whole length of the pillar is unknown,' and when every observer's account of it differs in essentials.

[2] The *savant* who first translated the inscription *Indian Antiquities*, vol. i. p. 319. The dates vary between the tenth century B.C. and A.D. 1052 (!).

[3] The Persian *haft-jilsh* (seven boilings), referred to by Ibn Batutah in Colonel Yule's letter, p. 145 (Day, p. 153).

[4] Quoted by Mr. Day (p. 24) from the *United States Railroad and Mining Register.*

[5] Mr. Day (quoting Fergusson's *Illustrations of Ancient Architecture in Hindostan*, London, 1848) cautions his readers that ' Mr. Fergusson's dates are

British Museum a unique collection of archaic tools, iron and steel, gouges, spatulæ, ladles, and similar articles, dug out of tumuli at Wari Gaon, near Kampti. But there are no grounds whatever for dating them 'about B.C. 1500, or the time of Moses.'

The *ferrum Indicum*[1] of the Classics may still be represented by the famous Wootz or Wutz,[2] the 'natural Indian steel,' still so much prized for Sword-blades in Persia and Afghanistan. The specimens first sent in 1795 to the Royal Society of London were analysed by Mr. Josiah M. Heath with the results given below.[3]

Colonel Yule remarks that the Wootz was, in part at least, the famous Indian steel, the σίδηρος Ἰνδικὸς καὶ στόμωμα of the 'Periplus,' the Hunduwání of the mediæval Persian traders; the Andanicum or Ondanique of Marco Polo and the Alkinde of the old Spanish. In the sixteenth century the exportation was chiefly from Baticala in Canara. The King of Portugal complains (in A.D. 1591) of the large quantities shipped from Chaul to be sold in the Red Sea to the Turks and on the African coast about Melinde.[4] And I would note that this industry by no means argues civilisation in India or elsewhere:[5] as Dr. Percy remarks, 'The primitive method of extracting good malleable iron direct from the ore, which is still practised in India and in Africa, requires a degree of skill very inferior to that which is implied in the manufacture of bronze.'

The system of Wootz-making, especially at Salem and in parts of Mysore, has

---

not to be relied on, however important his writings unquestionably are in other respects' (p. 168). Here again we see the misleading influence of the Sanskritists, who have allowed themselves to be cozened by the 'mild Hindu.' Mr. Day inclines (p. 151) to the tenth century B.C. (!), when the peoples of India were, we have reason to believe, the merest savages.

[1] The modern Hindus call steel *Paldah*, from the Persian *Fuláḍ*, the Arab. *Fuláḍ.* They apply to Spanish steel the terms *Ispát*, *Sukhela*, and *Tolad.* Their favourite trial of Sword-metal is with a bar of soft gold, which should leave a streak.

[2] Colonel Yule does not consider the word genuine, and with reason, as the Indo-Phœnician ('Safá') alphabet has no *w* and no *z*. The word first appears in 'Experiments and Observations to investigate the Nature of a Kind of Steel manufactured at Bombay, and there called *Wootz*,' . . . by G. Pearson, M.D. (paper read before the Royal Soc., June 11, 1795). He notes that 'Dr. Scott of Bombay, in a letter to the President, acquainted him that he had sent over "specimens of a substance known by the name of *wootz*, which is considered to be a kind of steel, and is in high esteem among the Indians"' (p. 322). In Wilkinson's *Engines of War* (1841) we read (pp. 203–206), 'The cakes of steel are called *wootz.*'

Dr. E. Balfour states that *uchhá* and *níchhá* (in Hindustani 'high' and 'low') are used in the Canarese provinces to denote superior and inferior

descriptions of articles, and that *Wootz* may be a corruption of the former. Colonel Yule and his coadjutor in the *Glossary of Indian Terms*, the late lamented Dr. Burnell, hold that it originated in some clerical error or misreading, perhaps from *wook*, representing the Canarese *ukku* = steel.

[3]

C.	{ combined	.	.	.	1·333
	{ uncombined	.	.	.	0·312
Si.	.	.	.	.	0·045
S.	.	.	.	.	0·181
As.	.	.	.	.	0·037
Fe (by difference)		.	.	.	98·092
					100·000

Phillips, *Metallurgy*, p. 317. Faraday found in Wootz 0·0128—0·0695 per cent. of aluminium, and attributed the 'damask' of the blades to its presence. Karsten, after three experiments, and Mr. T. H. Henry, failed to detect it, and suggested that it may have been derived from intermingled slag containing silicate of alumina (Percy, *Iron, &c.* pp. 183–84).

[4] *Archiv. Port. Oriental.* fascic. iii. p. 318.

[5] M. Keller (*Pres. Soc. Ant. Switz.*) notes that crudely formed lumps and quadrangular blocks of malleable iron, double pyramids weighing 10–16 lbs., have been found in prehistoric sites. They were probably produced in primitive Catalans. Pieces of iron slag worked by the Kelts were discovered in 1862 on the Cheviot Hills.

been described by many writers. About a pound weight of malleable iron, made from magnetic ore, is placed, minutely broken and moistened, in a crucible of refractory clay, together with finely chopped pieces of wood (*Cassia auriculata*). It is packed without flux. The open pots are then covered with the green leaves of the *Asclepias gigantea* or the *Convolvulus lanifolius*, and the tops are coated over with wet clay, which is sun-dried to hardness. 'Charcoal will not do as a substitute for the green twigs.' Some two dozen of these cupels [1] or crucibles are disposed archways at the bottom of a furnace, whose blast is managed with bellows of bullock's hide. The fuel is composed mostly of charcoal and of sun-dried *brattis* or cow-chips. After two or three hours' smelting the cooled crucibles are broken up, when the regulus appears in the shape and size of half an egg. According to Tavernier, the best buttons from about Golconda were as large as a halfpenny roll, and sufficed to make two Sword-blades (?). These 'cops' are converted into bars by exposure for several hours to a charcoal fire not hot enough to melt them : they are then turned over before the blast, and thus the too highly carburised steel is oxidised.[2]

According to Professor Oldham,[3] 'Wootz' is also worked in the Damudah Valley, at Birbhúm, Dyucha, Narayanpúr, Damrah, and Goanpúr. In 1852 some thirty furnaces at Dyucha reduced the ore to *kachhá* or pig-iron, small blooms from Catalan forges ; as many more converted it to *pakká* (crude steel), prepared in furnaces of different kind. The work was done by different castes ; the Hindís (Moslems) laboured at the rude metal, and the Hindús preferred the refining work. I have read that anciently a large quantity of Wootz found its way westward *viâ* Pesháwar.

When last visiting (April 19, 1876) the Mahabaleshwar Hills near Bombay, I had the pleasure to meet Mr. Joyner, C.E., and with his assistance made personal inquiries into the process. The whole of the Sayhádri range (Western Ghats), and especially the 'great-Might-of-Shiva' mountains, had for many ages supplied Persia with the best steel. Our Government, since 1866, forbade the industry, as it threatened the highlands with disforesting. The ore was worked by the Hill-tribes, of whom the principal are the Dhánwars, Dravidians now speaking Hin-dustani.[4] Only the brickwork of their many raised furnaces remained. For fuel

[1] The cupel (of old copel) is the French *coupelle*, little coupe. The muffle is a metal cupel.

[2] This is the process of working Wootz given by Mr. Heath; others pack the metal with finely-chopped stalks of asclepias as well as cassia. Mr. Mallet has described the Indian manufacture of large iron masses in *The Engineer*, vol. xxxiii. pp. 19, 20. Beckmann (*loc. cit. sub v.* 'Steel') notices the bloomeries or furnaces. The *Penny Cyclopædia* and Ure's *Dict. of Chemistry* (the latter the best), London, Longmans, 1839, may also be consulted. Dr. Percy gives a long account (pp. 254–66) of iron-smelting in India from Mr. Howard Blackwell. He notes three kinds of furnaces :—

1. Rude, like chimney-pots ; used by the hill-tribes of Western India, the Deccan, and the Carnatic.

2. Simple Catalan forge ⎱ Central India and the
3. Early form of Stückofen ⎰ N.W. Provinces.

The anvil is a square iron without beak. Three kinds of Indian bellows are noticed (pp. 255–56). The people, who love *stare super antiquas vias*, ignore the hot blast : this contrivance causes a more active combustion, an 'ultimate fact' as yet unexplained.

[3] Report of 1852.

[4] The dialect is much more ancient than we usually suppose : it existed long before Akbar the

they preferred the Jumbul-wood, and the Anjan or iron-wood. They packed the iron and fourteen pounds of charcoal in layers ; and, after two hours of bellows-working, the metal flowed into the forms. The 'Kurs' (bloom), five inches in diameter by two and a half deep, was then beaten into Táwás or plates. The matrix resembled the Brazilian, a poor yellow-brown limonite striping the mud-coloured clay ; and actual testing disproved the common idea that the 'watering' of the surface is found in the metal. The Jauhar ('jewel' or ribboning) of the so-called 'Damascus' blade was produced artificially, mostly by drawing out the steel into thin ribbons which were piled and welded by the hammer. My friend afterwards sent me from India an inkstand of Mahabaleshwar iron.[1]

I could not learn from Hindus that they bury iron in the earth till the 'core' is reached. But they are well acquainted with tempering by cold immersion, as noticed by Salmasius ('Exercit. Plin.' 763) : they still believe with Pliny, Justin, and a host of others, in 'a Sword, the icebrook's temper,' and all hold that the hardening of metal depends much upon the quality of the water. They quench delicate articles in oil, a method also alluded to by Pliny, but they ignore his statement (xxviii. 41) that rust produced by goat's blood gives a better edge to iron than the file. I am not aware that they have ever used for quenching pur-poses quicksilver, the best conductor of heat.

In Burmah, as in India, the chief peculiarity of iron-smelting is the use of green-wood fuel.[2] Throughout the mighty 'Hollander' Archipelago of the Farther East, this metal, known in former days only by importation, is now everywhere common. Java received the Egyptian arts from India, which colonised her about the beginning of the Christian era : the now untravelled Hindú was then a voyager and an explorer. Dr. Percy describes the iron-smelting of Borneo,[3] which produces the Parangilang, a peculiar Sword-like weapon equally fit for felling trees and men.[4] At Tahiti (Otaheiti), on the other hand, Captain Cook was unable to make the natives appreciate the use of metal till his armourer wrought an iron adze in shape like the native.

The oldest, and indeed the only, Chinese word for iron is 鐵—*tie*, formerly pronounced *tit*. It is first mentioned among the tribute-articles of Yu in the Yu-Kung section of the Shoo-King,[5] and the latter has been estimated to date from B.C. 2200–2000. If this be fact, hieroglyphic tablet-writing flourished amongst the 'Bak' some five hundred years before the age popularly attributed to the Hebrew Scriptures, and when the Greeks had not begun to form a nation.[6]

Great and his 'Urdú zabán' (camp language), for we find that the poet Chand wrote in it during the twelfth century.

[1] As will appear in Part II. there are many pro-cesses for making the Damascus ; the exact markings, however, are best produced by that noticed above.

[2] Pp. 270–3, from the descriptions of Mr. W. T. Blanford, of the Geol. Survey of India.

[3] Pp. 273–5 ; borrowed from *Travels in Borneo*,

by Dr. C. A. L. M. Schauer during 1843–47, p. 109.

[4] The Swords of the Borneo Dyaks and the islanders of Timor and Rotti are photographed by the Curator of the Christy Collection.

[5] Mr. Day quotes, book i., the Tribute of Yu, Legge's *Chinese Classics*, vol. iii. part i. p. 121 (Trübner, London, 1865).

[6] The 'Celestial Empire,' according to her annals,

Either then the Sinologues, like the Sanskritists, have been deluded by the artful native into admitting the preposterous claims to antiquity of culture always advanced by semi-barbarous peoples ; or, what is hardly likely, China formed a centre of Turanian civilisation wholly independent of Egypt and Chaldæa. Indeed, there appears to have been some contact of ideas in the matter of writing. The Kemite denoted 'man' and 'eye' by copying nature ; and probably the Chinese did the same. But the Turanian symbols have lost, by the law of pictorial evanescence, the original forms: 'man' has become 人 = jin (No. 9),[1] a pair of legs ; and 'eye' 目 = mŭh (No. 109), looks as if copied from a cat. The picture-origin of the Assyrian syllabary has also been satisfactorily established by the Rev. W. Haughton, but the later forms are as degraded as in the hieratic and demotic Egyptian.[2]

The passage above alluded to enumerates the articles of tribute as 'musical gems-stones,' iron, silver, steel, stones for arrow-heads, and sounding stones, with the skins of bears, great bears, foxes, jackals, and articles woven with their hair.' Dr. Legge adds in a note : 'By 鐵 = *Tie*, we are to understand "soft iron," and by 鏤 = *Low* or *Lowe*, "hard iron" or "steel." At the time of the Han dynasty, "iron-masters" (鐵官) were appointed in the several districts of the old Leangchou, to superintend the iron-works. Tsa'e refers to two individuals mentioned in the "Historical Records" ; one of the surname Ch'o, (卓氏)., and the other of the surname Ch'ing (程), both of this part of the empire, who became so wealthy by their smelting that they were deemed equal to princes.' According to the Rev. Dr. Edkins, 'with the exception of this passage there is probably no distinct allusion to iron in writings older than B.C. 1000 ; ' and his statement seems to establish the date of Chinese technology and civilisation.

About B.C. 400 the celebrated author and philosopher Leih-Tze mentions steel, and describes the process of tempering it. In the 'K'ang-hi-tse-tien' (康熙字典), better known as 'Kanghi's Dictionary,' published about A.D. 1710, the author represents the Serican contemporary of Aristotle as saying that 'a red blade will cut Hu (jade or nephrite) as it would cut mud.' Mr. Day makes this to mean a 'reddish-coloured blade,' red being one of the many tints which a clean surface of steel acquires in the process of tempering. It certainly cannot refer to red-hot

began B.C. 100,000–80,000 ; the date being probably astronomical, or rather astrological, founded, like the four Hindu æras, upon retrograde calculations. The first cycle of 60 years is attributed to the Emperor Hwang-tí, and its initiation to the 61st year of his reign, in B.C. 2637 (the Twelfth Dynasty of Egypt ?). The first historical dates are given in B.C. 651, a century after the foundation of Rome : these figures afford a curious contrast between pretensions and proof. But as Englishmen after long residence 'grow black' in Africa, and have become semi-Hinduised in India, so in China they have allowed themselves to be imposed upon by the 'magna fabuositas,' the marvellous self-sufficiency of astute semi-barbarians. 'China is a sea that salts all the rivers which flow into it.' Yet I am curious to ascertain by actual travel if China ever possessed a centre of civilisation independent of what she received from the West ; in other words, non-Egyptian.

[1] Of the 214 keys or radicals. The first three arithmetical figures are lines disposed horizontally, while the Egyptians wrote them vertically. In his Terminal Table (affixed to this chapter) Mr. Day assigns Chinese to the 'Sporadic or Allophyllian family.' I believe it to be the oldest and, as far as we know, the original form of Turanian speech, a kind of *tertium quid* deduced from the so-called 'Aryan' and 'Semitic' elements of Egyptian.

[2] *Trans. Bib. Archæol.* 1879. Sayce's *Grammar* gives 522 Assyrian characters.

steel, which would make no impression upon pietra dura. The description of steel-making in B.C. 400 is so far complete that it names and describes the several kinds. The first treatment produces 'Twan-Kang' or ball-steel, so called from the rounded bloom,[1] or 'Kwan-Kang' (sprinkled steel), because treated with cold affusion. There is also 'Wei-Tie' or false steel. The writer says : 'When I was sent on official business to Tse-Chow and visited the foundries there, I understood this for the first time. Iron has steel within it, as meal contains vermicelli. Let it be subjected to fire a hundred times or more ; it becomes lighter each time. If the firing be continued until the weight does not diminish, it is pure steel.'[2]

About the beginning of the Christian era a tax was levied upon iron by the State exchequer, showing that the manufacture had become important. According to the Pi-tan or Pencil-Talk, written probably under the Ming dynasty[3] (A.D. 1366–1644), steel is thus made : 'Wrought iron is bent or twisted up ; unwrought iron (i.e. iron-ore or cast-iron) is thrown into it ; it is covered up with mud and subjected to the action of fire, and afterwards to the hammer.' This is the old and well-known process of steeling practised by the Greeks. Wrought iron was either immersed into molten cast-iron as into a bath, or it was heated with iron-ore and layers of charcoal-fuel covered with alternate strata of clay to exclude atmospheric influence, a treatment somewhat similar to what is still called 'cementation.'[4] The ore was thus deoxidised by contact with excess of carbon ; and a molten carburet was the result. It is not a little curious, as Mr. Day observes, to find Aristotle and Lieh-Tze describing the same process about the same time. But I hesitate to conclude with that able writer that the fact has any bearing upon 'the old doctrine of the original unity of the human race ; each section of mankind carrying off with them that common stock of knowledge which the entire family possessed before separation.' Mr. Day, I have said, systematic-ally opposes the 'High Antiquity Theory' (p. 208) ; and, though he holds to Revelation and to Biblical chronology, he has a curious tendency towards the mystical etymology of the Jacob Bryant school, and the obsolete Phallic theories revived by the learned and able work of the late Dr. Inman.[5]

---

[1] The lump of iron worked into a mass more or less rectangular is called a bloom, from the Saxon *bloma*, metal in mass (Bosworth) : *Bloma ferri* occurs in the Domesday Book. Hence ancient furnaces were called *bloomeries* ; the Elizabethan spelling is a *bloomary*. The blooms were beaten out to bars.

[2] In Persia I was told that this was one of the 'secrets' of making the finest Khorasáni blades.

[3] It followed the Mongols and preceded the Man-chow Tartars, who still reign.

[4] This process of converting iron to steel is first described in '*Alchemiæ Gebri* (El-Gabr), *Arabis philo-sophi solertissimi, Libri, &c.*, Joan. Petreius Nurem-bergeñ. denuo Bernæ excudi faciebat. anno 1545.' The Arab, known to Albertus Magnus, flourished in the

eighth to the ninth century. According to Beckmann, he noticed the ore *cineritii* (cupellation) *et ce-menti* (cementation) *tolerans*. The mixture is usually of sal ammoniac, borax, alum, and fine salt : the many varieties are described by Percy, Ure, and a host of others. Compare also Ure's account of cast-steel and of shear-steel, the latter so called because cloth-shears were forged of it.

[5] At least it would so appear from the following passage (p. 176): 'When we examine the etymology of 'pole,' or 'pillar,' thus—Saxon, *pol* or *pal*; German, *Pfahl*; Danish, *paal* or *pol*; Swedish, *pale*; Welsh *pawl*—we arrive at the Latin *palus*, which, besides signifying a pole or stake, is also the φαλλός of the Greeks, *Mahadeva* (?) or *Linga* (?) of the Hin-

The Pent Saow, also attributed to the days of the Mings, speaks of three kinds of steel used for knives and Swords, a division which again reminds us of Dai-machus. The first is made by adding unwrought to wrought iron, while the mass is subjected to the action of fire. The second is simply the result of repeated firings as practised in Africa. The third is native steel produced in the south-west at Hai-shan : 'In appearance it resembles the stone called "Tsze-shih-ying" (purple stone efflorescence).' It is understood that the process of manufacture is kept secret.' The 'Hankow-steel,' which comes to Tien-tsin from the upper Yang-tse, is most prized ; and commands much higher prices than the best imported English and Swedish ; the Chinese, like the 'Caffirs,' look upon these as 'rotten iron.'

China also had her 'literary blacksmith,' like Wieland Smith, the northern Dædalus. We read that Hoang-ta-tie of T'ancheu, who lived under the Sung, followed the craft of an ironsmith. Whenever he was at his work he used to call without intermission on the name of Amita Buddha. One day he handed to his neighbours the following verses of his own composing to be spread about :—

> Ding-dong ! the hammer-strokes fall long and fast,
> Until the iron turns to steel at last !
> Now shall the long long Day of Rest begin,
> The Land of Bliss Eternal calls me in.

Thereupon he died. But his verses spread all over Honan, and many learned to call upon Buddha.

The oldest Chinese iron-works were at Shansi and Chilili in the Ho districts, where there are inexhaustible deposits of ore and coal, and where the metal is worked to the present day. In 1875 Commissioner Li-hung-Chang, raised from the Government-General of Chilili to be Minister of the young King, sent Mr. James Henderson to England with orders to bring out the most modern appliances and apparatus for metal-working. It was proposed to build the new works at Tsze-Chow, a town two hundred miles south-west of Tien-tsin, the head-quarters of the Governor-General. Mr. Henderson had visited (1874) the establishment near Yang-Ching, Shansi, which had before been described by Baron von Richtofen and Dr. Williamson.[1] The iron ore bought at Ping-ding-Chow was found at the Royal School of Mines, London, to contain fifty per cent. of iron, loose hæmatite with little or no sulphur.

M. Sévoz, an engineer of mines long resident in Japan, studied iron-working in the province of Ykouno.[2] He found the people using an imperfect Catalan

doos, *Bel* or *Baal* (?) of the Chaldeans, *Yakhveh* (?) of the Canaanites, *Ti-mohr* of the ancient Irish, and *Teih-mo* of the Chinese,' &c.

[1] *Notes from Mr. Henderson's Diary during a Ramble through Shansi, in March* 1874, published by Mr. Day (Appendix D, p. 251). Colonel Yule (*Marco Polo*, ii. 429), alluding to these enormous deposits of coal and metal, says : 'Baron Richtofen,

in the paper which we quote from, indicates the revolution in the deposit of the world's wealth and power, to which such facts, combined with other characteristics of China, point as probable ; a revolution so vast that its contemplation seems like that of a planetary catastrophe.'

[2] *Les Mondes*, tome xxvi., Dec. 1871.

method, but able to treat at once sixteen thousand kilogrammes of ore, and to produce blooms weighing one thousand three hundred kilogrammes. These huge rods were broken up under a hammer constructed in the style of a pile-driving ram, to which motion was given by a walking-wheel 11·5 mètres in diameter, mounted by men. The description does not promise much ; but Japan, though holding to her ancient methods in districts unknown to Europeans, produces iron cheaper than the English. Of her marvellous Swords I shall treat in Part II.

The people of Madagascar worked iron,[1] but their name of the metal is Malayan ; hence Mr. Crawford traced the art back to Malacca. Yet the Malay did not extend it far eastwards : according to Mr. E. B. Tylor,[2] ' In New Zealand, where there is good iron-ore, there was no knowledge of iron previously to the arrival of Europeans.' Passing over to the American continent, we find an immense industry of copper, but so little iron that, till late years, the indigenes were supposed not to have worked it. Ynka mines, however, have been discovered near Lake Titicaca ; while excavations in the tumuli of the mysterious ' Mound-builders,' who may have attempted to reproduce the Egyptian Pyramid, yielded axes described to be of ' hæmatite iron-ore,' one of the easiest metals to smelt, and for that reason probably one of the first worked. Mr. Day, who figures one of these tool-weapons with the hammer-marks (p. 218), supposes it to have been ' metallic iron,' pronouncing hæmatite ' extremely brittle and absolutely unforgeable.'[3] He quotes Mr. Charles C. Abbott,[4] who procured other specimens of aboriginal manufacture from the mounds. One hatchet was four and a half inches long by two broad, and nearly uniform in thickness, three-sixteenths of an inch ; it had a well-defined edge, which from its slightly wavy outline and varied breadth, appeared to be hammered, not ground. According to Major Hotchkiss, who owned two other similar specimens, a series of four was found under an uprooted tree on an Indian trail in West Virginia.

Fragments of unworked hæmatite, small and irregular, were used instead of flint for arrow-heads.[5] Mr. Abbott also notices ' a curious form of " relic," known as a " plummet," occasionally occurring and made of iron ore : one specimen [6] " is made of iron ore ground down until it is almost as smooth as glass." As such " plummets " are found in the Western Mounds, as well as on the surface of the ground throughout the Atlantic coast States, and are always polished, it seems fair to presume that a cutting instrument of such hard material would undoubtedly be polished and ground, if at the time of its manufacture grinding was known or

---

[1] *Polynesian Researches* (Rev. William Ellis).

[2] *Researches into the Early History of Mankind*, p. 167.

[3] Unless greatly mistaken, I have seen iron tools made of hæmatite near the old Gongo Socco gold-mines of Minas Geraes, in the Brazil. Worked hæmatite is also mentioned in Cyprus by General Palma (di Cesnola). See chap. ix.

[4] From *Nature* (Sept. 30, 1875) ; quoted by Mr. Day (pp. 217–19).

[5] *Flint Chips*, by Edmund T. Stevens, p. 553 (London : Bell & Daldy, 1870).

[6] The ' plummet ' is figured (No. cxxxii.) in the *American Naturalist* (vol. vi. p. 643).

practised among the aborigines in fashioning their various weapons and instruments.'

But if the savages and barbarians of Oceania and the New World rarely
worked iron, the contrary was the case with the equally uncivilised African races,
negroid and negro, who, however, had the advantage of dwelling within importing
and imitating distance of Egypt. I have elsewhere noticed the excellent assegai-
blades of the Bantu (Kafirs); nor is this art confined to the southern regions.[1]
Dr. Percy justly makes wrought iron the original form, which we see retained in
the obscurer parts of Asia and Africa. The people always worked by the ' direct
process,' the oldest style; which, however, is not wholly extinct in Europe. The
art, quasi-stationary among wild men, treats small quantities at a time: the 'voracious iron-works' of which Evelyn first speaks, are beyond its wants. Moreover
it can utilise only rich ores, unlike the ' indirect process' of producing cast-iron by
the blast-furnace.[2] When the ore is nearly pure, a small addition of carbon would
convert it into steel;[3] and the latter is so easily made, that the wild Hill-peoples
of Africa and India produce, and have produced from time immemorial, an excellent
article in the most primitive way. The proportion of charcoal is considerably
increased, and the blast is applied more slowly than when wrought iron is required.
The only apparatus wanted for the manufacture is a small clay furnace, four feet
high by one to two broad, like that used by the South Africans; charcoal for fuel,
and a skin with a pipe or twyers of refractory clay for the blast.[4] For the anvil a
stone-slab suffices, and for the hammer a cube of stone with sides grooved for fibre-
cords.

The ' Dark Continent' is emphatically an iron-land, and all explorers have
noticed its abundance of ore. Mungo Park[5] mentions the surface ironstone of
dull red tint with greyish spots used by his ' Mandingos': Barth confirms his
assertion by describing magnetic metal about Kuka of the Mandengas, and at
Jinninau in the Kel-owi or Tawareh country: Durham and Clapperton, when
near Murzuk, found kidney-shaped lumps upon the surface; and about Bilma,

---

[1] The people of Camarones River, Bight of
Biafra, work up old cask and bale hoops into very
creditable edge-tools and weapons, hoes, knives, and
Swords (Rev. G. Grenfell, *Proc. Roy. Geolog. Soc.*
Oct. 1882).

[2] The origin of the modern process is still debated.
Agricola (*nat.* 1494, *ob.* 1555) notices both malleable
and cast iron. Dr. Percy (p. 578) quotes from Mr. M.
A. Lower (*Contributions to Literature, &c.* 1854)
that Burwash Church, Sussex, contains a cast-iron
slab of the fourteenth century with ornamental cross
and inscription in relief. The same authority declares that iron cannon were first cast at Buxted
(Buckstead in Sussex) by Philip Hoge or Hogge in
1543 (35 Henry VIII.); and that his successor,
Thomas Johnson, made ordnance pieces for the Duke
of Cumberland weighing 6,000 lbs.

[3] Dr. Percy (pp. 764 *et seq.*) notices the three
processes of making steel (iron containing carbon in
certain proportions) : 1. The addition of carbon to
malleable iron; 2. The partial decarburisation of
cast iron; and 3. The addition of malleable iron to
cast iron.

[4] I borrow from O Muata Cazembe (Kazembe,
the King) a rude sketch (p. 38) of one of the better
kinds of iron-smelting furnaces used by the extensive
Maráve race dwelling north of the Zambeze (River of
Fish), which Europeans persist in miswriting *Zam-
besi.* The bellows, it will be remarked, are almost of
European shape; but this peculiarity may be attributed to the artist.

[5] *Travels,* pp. 275-77 (London, 1749).

capital of the Tibbús, nodules of iron-ore puddinged in the red sandstones—could this have been laterite or volcanic mud? It was the only metal seen in the hills of Mandara; but the Bornuese prefer to import their supply from the neighbouring Sudan. Mr. Warren Edwards, who had temporary charge of a Niger expedition, observed the natives supporting their cooking-pots over the fire with fragments of

FIG. 104.—IRON SMELTING FURNACE AMONGST THE MARÁVE PEOPLE.

surface ironstone; and it often struck him (as it does most men) that by some such means the smelting-process suggested itself. The metal is abundant in the Gaboon country, where the Mpangwe or Fans,[1] the western outliers of the great race, mostly cannibal, holding the heart of Africa, are able workers. They have a kind of 'fleam-money,' small iron bars shaped somewhat like a large lancet. I

[1] Colonel A. Lane Fox (*Prim. Warfare*, i. 38) believes that the 'Fans and Kafirs (Caffres) are totally different races.' But both speak dialects of the same tongue, the great South African language. Modern African travellers have traced community of customs from north to south, and from east to west, suggesting extensive intercourse, in former days, throughout the length and breadth of the Dark Continent.

came upon the metal everywhere in Unyamwezi, the 'Mountains of the Moon,' and to this universal presence of ironstone—not to damp and heat—the Portuguese attribute the marvellous displays of electricity throughout Central Africa. A whole night will pass during which the thunder is never silent ; and the lightning enables one to read small print, like an electric light. Captain Grant, in his 'Walk across Africa,' tells us that the people pick up walnut-sized nuggets of iron covered with dusty rust, and in a short time produce a spear-head that glistens like steel. My fellow-traveller to the Gold Coast, Captain Cameron, when crossing Africa, in most places found iron and iron-smelting.[1] In Kordofan, Mr. Petherick saw a rich surface oxide containing from fifty-five to sixty per cent. of pure metal. Livingstone remarked iron in the eastern regions of Angola,[2] and traced it up the Zambeze-line from east to west. Mr. C. T. Anderson describes it as occurring in large quantities, either of ironstone or pure in a crystallised state. Finally, good old Kolben mentions large iron-flakes on the surface near The Cape.

But, as Colonel A. Lane Fox remarks :[3] 'Simple heating is not sufficient for working iron : a continuous air-blast is required to keep the temperature at a certain height.' It is interesting to see the means adopted by barbarians for procuring this necessary ; and, having carefully studied it in various parts of Africa, I devote to it the remainder of this chapter. As Pliny repeats from Aristotle, 'Libya always produces something new.'

According to Strabo, Anacharsis[4] the Scythian, who flourished in the days of Solon (B.C. 592), invented not only the anchor[5] and the potter's wheel, but also the bellows. In Egypt, however, we find that these discoveries were already a thousand years old at least. The earliest appearance of the latter is the forge and bellows (in Egyptian 'H'ati'), depicted on the walls of a tomb in the days of Thut-mes III., about B.C. 1500. The workman stands on two bags of skin, such as are still used to hold water, alternately weighing upon one and upon the other; he inflates them in turns by pulling up a cord which opens a valve, and then he closes the hole with his heel. The bellows have twyers, and the illustrations[6] show a crucible and a heap of ore : while the material of the H'ati is indicated by its determinative, a hide with a tail. This rude contrivance was adopted by the Greeks and Romans : hence the 'taurini folles' of Plautus : and Virgil's—

. . . Alii ventosis follibus auras
Accipiunt redduntque.—*Æn.* viii. 449.

[1] *Across Africa*, chap. xix., July 1874 (Daldy, Isbister & Co., London, 1877).

[2] *Missionary Travels*, p. 402 (London, 1857).

[3] *Anthrop. Coll.* pp. 128–134. 'Specimens illustrating the geographical distribution of corrugated iron blades, or blades with an ogee section, double skin bellows, and iron work.' As regards the ogee section, the author should have compared it with the arrow-heads whose plane sides are 'bellied on a twist' to cause rotation or rifling.

[4] Diogenes Laertius tells us of Anacharsis only that he 'wrote also about war.'

[5] As all savage races show, the original anchor was a stone first bound round like a celt, and then pierced for a rope : hence the 'fugitive stone' used by the Argonauts as an anchor (Pliny, xxxvii. 24). In the spring of 1880 eight stone anchors of modern shape were found in Piræus harbour, and were sent to the Nautical School at Athens.

[6] Wilkinson, i. 174. Mr. Day, pp. 86, 87.

The wind-bag [1] would be made of ox-hide, of goat-skin, or of the spoils of smaller animals, according to the volume of draught required. And thus, also, would originate the bagpipe, an instrument common to almost all original peoples.

But in the Dark Continent we find still in use an older form than that known to Thut-mes, and the earliest of the four several varieties. The late Mr. Petherick describes this rude contrivance in Kordofan : 'The blast is supplied by skin bags worked by hand ; these bags are made of skins, which are flayed by two incisions from the tail down to the hocks ; the skin, being drawn over the body, is cut off at the neck, which makes the mouth of the bag. After tanning, the hind legs are cut off, and each side of the skin sewn on to a straight piece of stick ; loops are placed on the outside for the fingers of the operator to pass through. It can be opened and closed at pleasure ; the neck is secured to a tube of baked clay, and four men or boys seated round the cupola, each with a bellows of this primitive description, produce a blast by opening the bags when drawing them towards them, and closing them quickly, push them forward ; by which means the compressed bags discharge the air through the tubes into the furnace, quick alternate movements of the arms of the operator producing a blast, which throws out a flame about a foot high from the top of the furnace ; and the slag with the metal is allowed to collect in a hole beneath it.' Casalis similarly describes the Basuto bellows, and Mungo Park that of Mandenga-land ; Browne saw it in Dár-For,[2] and Clapperton in Kuka and in the Highlands of Mandara, where the anvil was a coarse bloom of iron, and the hammers two lumps weighing about two pounds each. This is the bellows of Kathiawád [3] and of Kolapor in the Deccan, where Captain Graham notices that the *mís* or tubes for the blast are clay mixed with burnt and powdered flint. Mr. E. B. Tylor found it used by a travelling tinker at Pæstum.

The second and improved variety of African bellows was described by myself during a visit to Yoruban Abeokuta. It deserves attention because it is a notable step in progress, leading to a further development ; the troughs are a rudimentary cylinder, and the handles form an incipient piston.[4] 'The two bags of goatskin are made fast in a frame cut out of a single piece of wood ; the upper part of each *follis* has, by way of handle, a stick two feet long, so that it can be worked by one man either standing or sitting. The handles are raised alternately by the blower, so that when one receives the air, the other ejects it ; the form is like that used on the Gold Coast ; and there is a perpendicular screen of dried clay through which the nozzle of the bellows passes, supplying a regular blast.'

Evidently in this stage of the bellows, the lower halves of the leather bags are useless : the result would be the same if only the upper part of the wooden

---

[1] Hence, too, we see our 'bellows' = 'bellies.'

[2] This word is curiously corrupted in Europe. It is formed upon the model of Dár-Wadái, &c. ; and means the abode, region, home (*Dár*) of the For tribe. My lamented friend General Purdy (Pasha) formerly of the United States Army, admirably surveyed it, and died at Cairo in 1881.

[3] *Vulgo* Kattywár ; described in 1842 by Captain (the late Sir G. Le Grand) Jacob in his *Report on Guzerat* (Gujarát).

[4] The sticks correspond with the strings on the bellows of the Egyptian monuments.

troughs were covered with skin, air-tight but loose enough to make play. This third step has been taken by the Djour (Júr) tribes of the Upper Nile, in north latitude 20°, and it is thus described by Mr. Petherick: 'The blast-pipes are made as usual of burnt clay, and are attached to earthen vessels about eighteen inches in diameter and six inches in height, covered with a loose, dressed goat-skin, tied tightly round them and perforated with a few holes, in the centre of which is a loop to contain the fingers of the operator. A lad, sitting between two of these vessels, by a rapid alternate vertical motion drives a continuous current of air into the furnace.'

This brings us to the fourth and last stage of African blast-improvement (fig. 105). Here the rudely-hewn wooden tube becomes a double-barrelled forcing-pump. The two air-vessels with their loose skin-coverings are attached to each base of the two central pipes that join into one. Such is the shape used in Madagascar, the cylinders being of bamboo, five feet long by two inches in diameter, and the piston a stick ending in a bunch of feathers.

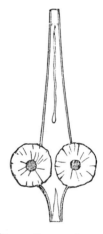

FIG. 105.—PORTABLE AFRICAN BELLOWS.

The bellows described by Dampier in Mindanao and elsewhere in the Malay Archipelago, is evidently borrowed from the Madagascar type ; and into Borneo, Siam, and New Guinea a hollowed trunk takes the place of the bamboos. The sculptures in the Sukuh-temple of Java, attributed to the fifteenth century, represent smiths making Kríses (Creases), the bellows being worked by another man, who holds a piston upright in each hand. Colonel A. Lane Fox is of opinion that the sculptures 'possibly point to a Hindu origin for this particular contrivance.' I agree with him, but I would also trace the Asiatic article back to its old home in Africa—Egypt.

The nature of fuel was determined by the supply of the country. That of Egypt probably consisted of cattle-chips, a material still used by the Fellahs. A later allusion to this article is found in the legend of 'Wieland Smith' : he mixes iron-filings with the meal eaten by his geese, carefully collects the droppings, and out of them forges a blade which cuts a wool-flock or cleaves a man to the belt without turning edge.

I conclude this chapter with the following table,[1] printed by Mr. Day at the end of his 'High Antiquity of Iron and Steel.' It gives at one view the languages, the characters, the phonetic values, the English equivalents, and the oldest known dates of the metals to which he refers. I differ from him in sundry points, and these I have taken the liberty to point out in italics.

---

[1] *Iron*, Jan. 8, 1876.

GENERAL TABLE OF TERMS.

Language		Characters	Phonetic Value	English Equivalent	Oldest known date of
Name	Family				
Egyptian Hieroglyphs.	Hamitic, with Semitic Infusion.		Ba.	Earth, Metal.	2200 to 2300 B.C. (B.C. *4500 ?*)
			Ba.	Iron.	
			Ba'a.	Iron, Earth.	
			Ba'aenpe.	Iron.	
			Bet.	Iron.	
Akkadian.	Semitic.	𒃸	Hurud.	Iron.	Oldest Monuments, at least 2000 B.C. (*B.C. 4000 ?*)
Assyrian.		𒃸	Eru.	Iron.	
Hebrew.		נחושה ברזל ברזל עשות ברזל מוצק	n'ghōshāh barzel barzel yāshūth barzel mūtzāq	Steel. Iron. Bright Iron. Cast Iron.	From 1500 B.C. downwards.
Chinese.[1]	Sporadic or Allophyllian (*Turanian*).	鏤 鐵 金 鐵宦	Low, Lowe. Tie (pronounced Tit). Kin. —	Steel. Iron. Metal. {Iron-masters.	2000 B.C.
Sanskrit.	Aryan.	आर अयस्	Ára. Ayas.	Iron. Iron.	Oldest Sanskrit. Probably B.C. 1500. (*B.C. 400 ?*)
Greek.		χάλυψ σίδηρος κύανος ἀδάμας	Khalyps. Sideros. Cyanos. Adamas.	Steel. Iron. {Blue Metal, prob. tempered Steel. Steel.	Homeric Age. — Hesiod.

[1] I observe that M. Terrien de la Couperie has lately derived the oldest civilisation of China from Chaldæo-Babylonia of the Akkadian Ages, B C. 2400–2300.

CHAPTER VII.

THE SWORD : WHAT IS IT ?

HAVING now reached the early Iron Age, which ends pre-historic annals, it is advisable to answer the question—'What is a Sword?'

The word—a word which, strange to say, has no equivalent in French—is the Scandinavian Svärd (Icel. Sverð); the Danish Sværd ; the Anglo-Saxon Sweord and Suerd ; the Old German Svert, now Schwert, and the Old English and Scotch Swerd. The westward drift of the Egyptian Sf, Sefi, Sayf, Sfet, and Emsetf, gave Europe its generic term for the weapon.[1] The poetical is 'brand' or 'bronde,' from its brightness or burning ; another name is 'laufi,' 'laf,' or 'glaive,' derived through French from the Latin *gladius*. Of especial modern forms there are the Espadon, the Flamberg, Flammberg, or Flamberge,[2] the Stoccado, and the Braquemart ; the Rapier and the Claymore, the Skeyne and Tuck, the small-Sword and the fencing-foil, beside other varieties which will occur in the course of the following pages. 'Sword' includes 'Sabre,' which may also derive from the Egyptian through the Assyrian Sibirru and Akkadian Sibir, also written Sapara ; our 'Sabre' is the Arabic Sayf with the Scandinavian terminative *r* (Sayf-r). Ménage would derive Sabre from the Armoric Sabrenn: Littré has the Spanish Sable, the Italian Sciabola, Sciabla, and in Venice Sabala, from the German Sable or Säbel, which again identifies with other languages, as the Serb Sablja and the Hungarian Száblya. The chief modern varieties of the curved blade are the Broadsword, the Backsword, the Hanger, and the Cutlass, the Scymitar and Düsack, the Yataghan and the Flissa. These several modifications will be considered in the order of their invention. Lastly the Egyptian 'Sfet' originated through Keltic the word Spata or Spatha[3] (Spatarius = a Swordsman) conserved to the present day in the neo-Latin names of the straight foining weapon—espada, espé, espée, épée.

Physically considered, the Sword is a metal blade intended for cutting, thrusting, or cut-and-thrust (*fil et pointe*). It is usually, but not always, composed of two

---

[1] Major Jähns (p. 416) would derive *Schwert* (= *das Sausende, Schwirrende,* i.e. whizzing) from the Sansk. *svar,* noise ; and considers it originally a missile pure and simple. He quotes Isidore, who explains *rhomphæa* by *wafan; Schwert* and *framea* = *asta vel gladius ; ensis* = *hevas, hevassa ; mucro* = *swert, gladius* = *wafan ; culter* = *wafansahs, sahse.*

In the hebraising days *Sword* was derived from Sharat, to scratch, and *Sabre* from Shabar, to shiver.

[2] Of the Flamberge and the 'flamboyant,' or wavy blade, more hereafter.

[3] Muratori (*Antiq.* ii. 487) notes, '*Spatam sive spontonem,* and *sponto, spunto,* i.e. *pugio*' (Adelung). Of *spatha* more to come.

parts. The first and principal is the blade proper (*la lame, la lama, die Klinge*). Its cutting surface is called the edge (*le fil, il filo, die Schärfe*),[1] and its thrusting end is the point (*la pointe, la punta, die Spitze* or *der Ort*, the latter mostly opposed to the *Mund* or sheath-mouth).

The second part, which adapts the weapon for readier use, is the hilt, hilts or heft (*la manche, la manica, die Hilse* or *das Heft*), whose several sections form a complicated and a prodigiously varied whole. The grip is the outer case of the tang, *alias* the tongue (*la soie, la spina*, or *il codolo ; der Stoss, die Angel, die Griffzunge* or *der Dorn*), the thin spike which projects from the shoulders or thickening of the blade (*le talon* or *l'épaulement, il talone, der Ansatz* or *die Schulter*) at the end opposed to the point. Sometimes there are two short teeth or projections from the angles of the shoulders, and these are called 'the ears' in English, in German, and in the neo-Latin tongues.

The tang, which is of many shapes—long and short, straight-lined or curvilinear, plain or pierced for attachment—ends in the pommel or 'little apple' (*le pommeau, il pomolo, der Knauf* or *Knopf*), into which it should be made fast by rivets or screws. The object of this globe, lozenge, or oval of metal is to counterpoise the weight of the blade, to prop the ferient of the hand, and to allow of artistic ornamentation. The grip of wood, bone, horn, ivory, metal, valuable stones, and other materials, covered with skin, cloth, and various substances, whipped round with cord or wire, is protected at the end abutting upon the 'chape '[2] or guard proper (*la garde, la guardia, die Parirstangen, die Leiste* or *die Stichblätter*) by the hilt-piece, which also greatly varies. It may, however, be reduced to two chief types—the guard against the thrust, and the guard against the cut. The former was originally a plate of metal, flat or curved, circular or oval, affixed to the bottom of the hilt, dividing the shoulders from the tang : in fact, it was a shield in miniature (*la coquille, la coccia, das Stichblatt*). We still use the term 'basket-hilt,' and apply 'shell' (*la coque, la coccia, der Korb* or *die Schale*) to the semicircular hilt-guards—mostly of worked, chased, embossed, or pierced steel— which appear to perfection in the Spanish and Italian rapiers of the sixteenth century. This hilt-plate has dwindled in the French fencing-foil to a lunette, a double oval of bars shaped like a pair of spectacles. In the Italian foil, which preserves the plate, the section of the blade between that and the grip is called

---

[1] Or '*die Schneide*,' the older forms being *ekke, egge*; while '*valz*' was the middle section of the two-handed Sword.

[2] 'Chape,' derived from *capa*, and a congener of 'cap' and 'cape,' is differently used by authors. Some apply it to the mouthpiece or ring at the top of the sheath ; others to the metal crampet, bouterolle, or ferule at the scabbard-tip, and others to the guard-plate. In Durfey (*The Marriage-Hater Matched*) we find 'the hilt, the knot, the scabbard, the *chape*, the belt, and the buckles' (of a Sword). Skinner explains it as *vaginæ mucro ferreus*. Mr. Fairholt defines *chape* to be the guard-plate or cross-bar at the junction of grip and hilt. Shakespeare, who knew the Sword, speaks of the '*chape* of his dagger' (*All's Well &c.* iv. 3) and 'an old rusty Sword with a broken hilt and *chapelesse*' (*Taming of the Shrew*, iii. 2). Commentators mostly explain this by 'without a catch to hold it.' Dr. Evans (*Bronze, &c.* chap. viii.) has exhaustively described the bronze chapes (bouterolles) in the British Islands.

the *Ricasso* (*a*); the parallel bar is the *Vette traversale* (*b, b*); and the two are connected by the *archetti d' unione* (joining bows, *c, c*).

The guard against the cut is technically called the cross-guard (*les quillons*,[1] *le vette, die Stichblätter*). This section is composed of one or more bars projecting from the hilt between tang and blade, and receiving the edge of the adversary's weapon should it happen to glance or to glide downwards. The quillons may be either straight (fig. 109)— that is, disposed at right angles—or curved (fig. 107). When the two horns bend down from the handle-base towards the point they are called *à antennes*. Others are turned up towards the hilt, counter-curved or inversed—that is, faced in opposite directions—or fantastically deformed (fig. 110).

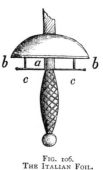

FIG. 106.
THE ITALIAN FOIL.

Opposed to the guard proper is the bow or counter-guard (*la contregarde, l'elsa, la contraguardia, der Bügel*). It is of two chief kinds. In the first the quillons are recurved towards the pommel: the second is a bar or system of bars connecting the pommel with the quillons (fig. 108). The former defends the fingers,

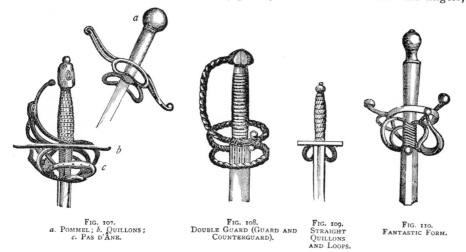

FIG. 107.
a. POMMEL; *b.* QUILLONS;
c. PAS D'ÂNE.

FIG. 108.
DOUBLE GUARD (GUARD AND
COUNTERGUARD).

FIG. 109.
STRAIGHT
QUILLONS
AND LOOPS.

FIG. 110.
FANTASTIC FORM.

the latter serves to protect, especially from the cut, the back of the hand and the outer wrist. This modification, unknown to the ancients of Europe, became a favourite in the sixteenth century, and it is still found in most of our actual hilts. Another product of the early modern age is the *pas d'âne*.[2] At the end of the

---

[1] A congener of our 'quill,' from the Lat. *caulis*, a stalk. Littré is not satisfactory: 'Quillon (*ki-llon*, ll mouillées), s.m. Partie de la monture du sabre ou de l'épée, située du côté opposé aux branches, et dont l'extrémité est arrondie. Dérivé de quille' (cone) 'par assimilation de forme' (in fact, incrementative of) 'quille. Etym. Génev. *quille*; de l'anc. haut-allem. *Kegil*; allem. *Kegel*, objet allongé en forme conique, *quille*.' Burn translates *quillon* 'cross-bar of the hilt of an infantry or light-cavalry Sword.'

[2] This must not be written, as by some English authors, *pas d'ane*. '*Pas d'âne*, instrument avec lequel on maintient ouverte la bouche du cheval pour l'examiner.' Littré has : '*Pas d'âne*, nom donné, dans les épées du xvième siècle, à des pièces

fourteenth century it was composed of two circular or oval-shaped bars, disposed on both sides of, and partly over, the fort of the blade. In the sixteenth century it was generally adopted, and became a complicated and highly-decorated adjunct to the handle. The *pas d'âne* is now almost obsolete : a relic remains in our army-claymore.[1]

We may divide the shapes of blade into two typical forms with their minor varieties :

I. The curved blade (sabre, shable, broadsword, backsword, cutlass, hanger, scymitar,[2] Düsack, Yataghan, Flissa, &c.) is

    a. Edged on both sides (Abyssinian).

    b.   „   concave side (old Greek, Kukkri).

    c.   „   convex (common sabre).

II. The straight blade (Espadon, Flammberg, Stoccado, Braquemart, rapier, claymore, skeyne, tuck, small-sword, &c.) : the varieties are :

    a. The cut-and-thrust, one- or two-handed.

    b. The broad and unpointed (headman's instrument).

    c. The narrow, used only for the point.

It is hardly advisable to make a third type of the half-curved blade, adapted equally for *tac et taille* (cutting and thrusting), which we find in ancient Assyria, in India, and in Japan. It evidently connects both shapes.

The following diagram shows the three forms :[3]

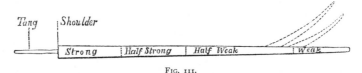

FIG. III.

I have given precedence to the curved blade because cutting is more familiar to man than thrusting. Human nature strikes 'rounders' until severe training teaches it to hit out straight from the shoulder. Again, the sabre-form would naturally be assumed by the sharpened club during the wooden age of imperfect edges ; and the penetrating power would be weak and almost *nil* when the point was merely a fire-hardened stick.

de la garde qui sont en forme d'anneau, et qui vont des quillons à la lame. "Le Seigneur le prit et mit un pied sur la lame . . . alors Collinet s'écria : Venez voir, messieurs, le grand miracle que l'on fait à mon épée ; je l'ai apportée ici avec une simple poignée et sans garde défensive, et voilà maintenant que l'on y met le plus beau pas d'âne du monde." ' *Francion*, vi. p. 237 : ' Pas d'âne, nom vulgaire du tussilage, à cause de la feuille.'

  [1] The Scottish basket-hilt, however, requires improvement, as it does not allow free play to hand or wrist.

  [2] The word is originally the Persian *Shamshír* (شمشير) ; but as the Greeks have no *sh* sound, it made its way into Europe curiously disguised. Jean Chartier (temp. Charles VII.) says, ' *Sauveterres ou cimeterres qui sont manière d'espée à la Turque.*' *Sauveterre* became in Italian *salvaterra* ; and in England *scymitar* was further degraded to *semitarge*. I have no objection to *scimitar*, but *scymitar* is the older form.

  [3] See note at the end of this chapter.

Yet there is no question of superiority between the thrust and the cut. As the diagram[1] shows, A, who delivers point, has an advantage in time and distance over B, who uses edge. Indeed, the man who first 'gave point' made a discovery

FIG. 112.

which more than doubled the capability of his weapon. Vegetius tells us that the Roman victories were owing to the use of the point rather than the cut: 'When cutting, the right arm and flank are exposed, whereas during the thrust the body is guarded, and the adversary is wounded before he perceives it.' Even now it is remarked in hospitals that punctured wounds in the thorax or abdomen generally kill, while the severest incisions often heal. Hence Napoleon Buonaparte, at Aspronne, ordered the cavalry of the Guard to give point. General Lamoricière, a scientific soldier, recommended for cavalry a cylindrical blade, necessarily without edge, and to be used only for the thrust: practical considerations, however, prevented its adoption. Moreover, the history of the 'white arm' tells us that the point led to the guard or parry proper, and this 'defence with the weapon of offence' completed the idea of the Sword as now understood in Europe.

Again, the peoples who fought from chariots and horseback—Egyptians, Assyrians, Indians, Tartars, Mongols, Turks, and their brethren the 'white Turks' (Magyars or Hungarians), Sarmatians, and Slavs – preferred for the best of reasons the curved type. The straight Sword, used only for thrusting, is hard to handle when the horse moves swiftly ; and the broad straight blade loses its value by the length of the plane along which it has to travel. On the other hand, the bent blade collects, like the battle-axe, all the momentum at the 'half-weak,' or centre of percussion, where the curve is greatest. Lastly, the 'drawing-cut' would be easier to the mounted man, and would most injure his enemy.

On the other hand, the peoples of southern latitudes—for instance, those dwelling around the Mediterranean, the focus of early civilisation, where the Sword has ever played its most brilliant and commanding part—are active and agile races of light build and comparatively small muscular power. Consequently they have generally preferred, and still prefer, the pointed weapon, whose deadly

[1] As usual, the diagram is an exaggeration. It directs the thrusting weapon too low, at the anta- gonist's breast, not his eye; nor is it necessary to raise the hand so high in order to deliver the cut.

thrust can be delivered without requiring strength and weight. For the inverse reason the sons of the north would chose the Espadon proper, the long, straight, ponderous, two-edged blade which suited their superior stature and power of momentum.

Such is the geographical and ethnological view of Sword-distribution, but it gives a rule so general that a multitude of exceptions must be expected. As far as we know, the civilised Sword originated in Egypt, but it had many different centres of development. A gradual and continuous progress can be traced in its history till it was superseded by an even older form of attack—the 'ballistic.' Yet some of the earliest blades show the best forms, and the line of advancement at times becomes distorted or even broken. Again, many Southrons, and races that fought on foot, have used the curved weapon, although the converse, the adoption of the straight, pointed Sword by horsemen, is comparatively rare.

I now proceed to consider various points connected with the curved and straight forms of blade. The experience of the Sword-cutter has noticed that the shape of any pattern or model, whether of tool or of weapon, suggests its own and only purpose. This is what we should expect. A swordsman chooses his Sword as a sawyer his saw. Show the mechanic a new chisel, and its form at once explains to him its use: he learns by the general shape, the edge-angle, the temper, the weight, and similar considerations, that it is *not* made to drive nails, nor to bore holes, and that it *is* intended to cut wood or soft substances. Thus, too, the form of the Sword is determined by the duty expected of it.

The Sword has three main uses, cutting, thrusting, and guarding. If these qualifications could be combined, there would be no difficulty in determining the single best shape. But unfortunately—perhaps I should say fortunately—each requisite interferes to a great extent with the other. Hence the various modifications adopted by different peoples, and hence the successive steps of progress.

The simplest and most effective form of trenchant instrument intended for cutting only is the American broad-axe used by squatters in the backwoods. This revival of the proto-historic celt and headman's instrument is a plain, heavy wedge of steel, fixed on a light, tough wooden helve or heft, thus concentrating all the force in the head that strikes the blow. Here there is no uncertainty about the use ; and, were it not necessary in swordsmanship to 'recover guard' and to save self as well as disable the assailant, it would be the best, as it is one of the oldest, weapons derived from the club. But the cutting Sword, which in the short curved form is its congener, has a long blade that allows a choice of cut—a good choice and a bad choice. If the blow be made, for instance, at a tree-branch with the Sword-point (the 'whole-weak'), its sole effect will be to jar wrist and arm unpleasantly. The same result will follow a blow with the 'whole-strong.' In either case the vibration of the blade shows a waste of strength. By the experiment of cutting along the entire length, inch after inch, and by comparing the effect, the swordsman comes at last to a point, about the end of the 'half-weak,' speaking roughly, where there is no jar, and where, consequently, the whole force of the blow becomes effective. But our 'centre of percussion' must not be confounded with the 'centre of gravity.' This balance-position is situated in the middle of the 'whole-strong,' the proper part for guarding, and for guarding only.

The late Mr. Henry Wilkinson, of London, a practical man of science, first proposed a formula for determining the centre of percussion without the tedious process of experimenting with each and every blade. His system was based upon the properties of the pendulum. A light rod, exactly 39·2 inches long, capped with a heavy leaden ball, and swung to and fro upon a fixed centre, vibrates seconds or sixty times per minute in the latitude of London, and the three centres of percussion, of oscillation, and of gravity are concentrated within the ball. If it were a mathematical pendulum—a rod without weight—these three points would lie precisely in the core of the ball, or 39·2 inches from the place of suspension. The blade, to be graduated, is suspended, tight-fastened at the point on which it would turn when making a cut, and is converted by swinging into a pendulum. As

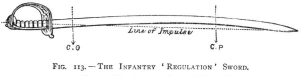

Line of Impulse

c.g.   c.p.

FIG. 113.—THE INFANTRY 'REGULATION' SWORD.
c.g. Centre of Gravity ; c.p. Centre of Percussion.

the length is shorter, so the oscillations are quicker : the blade makes eighty movements to sixty of the pendulum. A simple formula determines the length of such an eighty-vibrations pendulum to be twenty-two inches. This distance, measured from the point at which the blade was suspended, is marked on the back as the centre of percussion, where there is no jar, and where the most effective cut can be delivered.

Again, an examination of the axe shows that the cutting edge lies considerably in advance of the wrist and hand, with the effect of carrying the edge well forward on the 'line of direction,' which, in the Sword, passes directly from pommel to point. If the edge were at the back the tendency of the weapon would be to fall away from the line of cut, and this could be overcome only by a certain amount of wasted force. In nearly all curved Swords, except the Japanese, some contrivance is made to give the feeling which we express by 'the edge leading well forward'; and this point has been carefully studied by nations whose attack is the cut. Usually the line of hilt is thrown forward so as to form an angle with the axis of the blade, and the former is made obtuser or acuter in proportion as the latter is more or less curved. By balancing the weapon upon the pommel the effect becomes evident ; the edge falls forward like that of the axe.

The superiority of the curved blade for cutting purposes is easily proved. In every cut the edge meets its object at some angle, and the penetrating portion

becomes a wedge. But this wedge is not disposed at right angles with the Sword :
the angle is more or less oblique according to the curvature, and consequently it

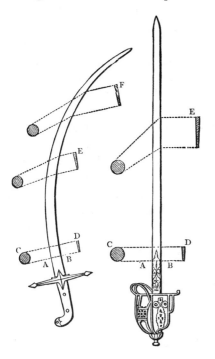

cuts with an acuter edge. The accompanying figures of a 'scymitar' and a claymore, both trenchant blades, prove that,
were the edge to describe a right line (A B)
directed at any object (C), it would act as a
wedge (D), measuring exactly the breadth
of the blade. But the curve throws the
edge more forward, and thus the 'half-
weak' acts like a wedge (E), which is
longer and consequently more acute, the
extreme thickness (that of the back or
base) being a fixed measure. Similarly,
by cutting still nearer the 'weak' or point,
the increased curvature gives a more prolonged and acuter cuneiform (F). Comparing the three sections of the same
blade (D E F), which differ only in the
angle at which the edge is supposed to
meet the obstacle, we see the enormous
gain of cutting power.

The difference between the direct and
the oblique cut is still better shown by the
annexed diagram : 'Let A B C D (fig. 116)

FIG. 114.—SCYMITAR.   FIG. 115.—CLAYMORE.

represent the portion of a Sword-blade, of which A B is the edge and C D the
back, measuring about one-eighth of an inch in thickness. Now, if the object to

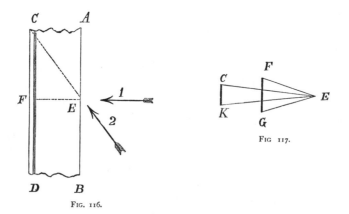

FIG. 116.

FIG 117.

be cut through is presented to the blade at right angles to the edge, as shown
by arrow No. 1, then the section of the blade with which the cut is to be

effected will be as represented in the triangular section F E G (fig. 117). But if the object be presented to the blade obliquely, as shown by arrow No. 2, then the section along the line of the cut will be as represented by the angle C E K. It will readily be seen that in the latter case the acuteness of the angle at E is greatly increased, whilst the substance is the same as in the other case. To effect this it is the custom in many parts of the East to strike with a drawing cut, but the same purpose is secured by bending the blade backwards: the curve itself presents the edge obliquely to the object without entailing the necessity of imparting a drawing motion to the stroke.'[1]

Par parenthèse, it is this drawing motion which, added to the curve of the weapon and its oblique presentation, increases the trenchant power. The 'Talwár,' or half-curved sabre of Hindustan, cuts as though it were four times as broad and only one-fourth the thickness of the straight blade. But the 'drawing-cut' has the additional advantage of deepening the wound and of cutting into the bone. Hence men of inferior strength and stature used their blades in a manner that not a little astonished and disgusted our soldiers in the Sind and Sikh campaigns.

If we consider the sections of cutting weapons, we find them all modifications of that most ancient mechanical contrivance, the wedge, as shown by the following figures:

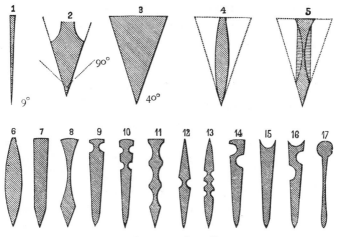

FIG. 118.—SECTIONS OF SWORD-BLADES.

The first form (fig. 118) is the wedge that would be produced by taking for base the dorsal thickness of an ordinary blade, and by continuing it in an even line to the apex of the triangle—the point. The two sides meet at an angle of nine degrees; consequently the edge lacks the thickness, weight, and strength necessary for every cutting tool. For soft substances it should range from ten to twenty

[1] Quoted from Mr. John Latham by Colonel A. Lane Fox, *Anthrop. Coll.* p. 171. Concerning the drawing cut and its reverse, the thrusting cut, I shall have more to say when treating of the 'Damascus' blade in Part II.

degrees, as in the common dinner knife. An angle of twenty-five to thirty-five degrees, being the best for wood-working, is found in the carpenter's plane and chisel. For cutting bone the obtuseness rises to forty degrees, and even to ninety ; the latter being the fittest for shearing metals, and the former for Sword-blades, which must expect to meet with hard substances. But even an angle of forty degrees will be ineffectual upon a thick head, unless the cut be absolutely true. No. 2 illustrates the angle of resistance (forty degrees) and the entering angle (ninety degrees). No. 3 shows that the true wedge of forty degrees is too thick and heavy for use, requiring some contrivance for lightening the blade, while preserving the necessary angle of resistance. The remaining sections display the principal modes of effecting this object. In Nos. 4 and 6 the angle is carried in a curved and bulging line, thus giving the section a bi-convex form. When the back or base is flat this is the Persian and Khorásáni, vulgarly called the 'Damascus blade.' When baseless and two-edged it is the old 'Toledo' rapier—two shallow-crowned arches meeting (3*a*, fig. 124). In both cases the weapon is strong, but some-what overweighted. In the next shapes (Nos. 5 and 7), the two sides are cut away to a flat surface and represent the 'Talwár' of India. When this flat surface is hollowed, as by the black lines of No. 5 (compare No. 8), we have the bi-concave section, as opposed to the bi-convex. This hollowing of the wedge into two broad grooves from the angle of resistance is one of the forms assumed by the English 'regulation' Sword : it was considered the lightest for a given breadth and thick-ness, but it is by no means the strongest, and there are sundry technical objections to it.

The remaining blades in the illustration are grooved in as many different ways. The function of the *cannelure* is to obviate over-flexibility ; it also takes from the weight and adds to the strength. By channelling either side of a thin or 'whippy' blade it becomes stiffer, because any force applied to bend such a blade sideways meets with the greatest amount of resistance that form can supply. Mechanically speaking, it is to crush an arch inwards upon its crown, and the deeper the arch the greater the resistance. Hence the narrow groove is preferable to a broader channel of the same depth. No. 9, hollowed on each side near the base, is a good old form, superior to the 'regulation' (No. 8) : its weak point, the space between the grooves where the metal is thinnest, lies in the best place—near the back, where strength and thickness are least required. No. 10, though somewhat lighter, doubles its weak points. No. 11 is better in this respect : it has three grooves which are far shallower, and consequently the metal between them is thicker. The same remark applies to Nos. 12 and 13, which are sections of claymores, single- and treble-grooved.

No. 14 shows an ingenious method of obviating the weakness caused by deep *cannelures* : it is the section of a blade made at Klingenthal (not 'Klegenthal'), the Sword manufactory established by Napoleon Buonaparte in Elsass-Lothringen. Two very marked grooves are cut in the metal, but not directly opposite each other, and thus the channels can touch and even overlap the axial line. This disposition gives great stiffness, but, as testing shows, the edge is deficient in cutting power, probably from loss of force by vibration.

Nos. 15 and 16 are experimental blades. The former has the groove placed in the base, preserving the wedge-sides intact; but there is great difficulty about grinding this shape, and, the resistance of the arch-crown being wanting, there is a small increase of stiffening—the Sword, in fact, 'springs' almost as readily as the straight form. No. 16 has some good points, but, on the whole, the combination is a failure. Lastly, No. 17, the old 'ramrod-back' regulation blade, is perhaps the

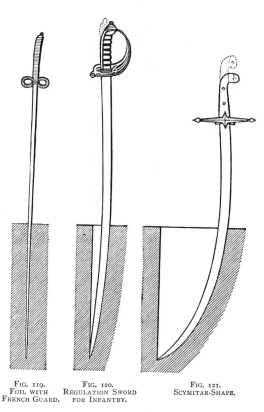

worst of all: the sudden change from the thick round base to the thin sharp edge makes an equal tempering very difficult, and the weapon cleverly undoes its own work, the base acting as check or stop to the cut.

Remains now to consider the Sword as a weapon for point, a use to which, as its various shapes show, it was applied in the earliest ages instinctively, as it were, before Science taught the superiority of the thrust to the cut. We learn from such hand-thrusting instruments — the awl, gimlet, needle, and dinner-fork — that the straight weapon may be considered a very acute wedge with a method of progression mostly oblique. It is easy to prove that the proper shape for a thrusting-blade is pre-eminently the straight. Fig. 119 shows the foil making a hole exactly its own

FIG. 119.
FOIL WITH
FRENCH GUARD.

FIG. 120.
REGULATION SWORD
FOR INFANTRY.

FIG. 121.
SCYMITAR-SHAPE.

size. The 'regulation' Sword (fig. 120), a shallow curve, opens, when moving in a direct line, about double its own width; a figure which the scymitar (fig. 121) increases to five or six times, with a proportionate loss of depth at the same expenditure of force. This augmented resistance to penetration is one, but only one, of the many difficulties in using a curved blade for a straight thrust.

This difficulty probably suggested the 'curved thrust,' a method of pointing which the foil, as opposed to the rapier, has made popular. The point is propelled, not in a straight line, but in the arc of a circle more or less curved to correspond with the blade. The arm makes this cycloidal movement readily enough, but under a disadvantage; as in the cut the space traversed is longer than what is absolutely necessary to reach the object. Moreover, the movement cannot well be applied to the lunge, so as to throw the weight of the body into the attack. Like the 'thrusting-cut,' it is more fitted for horseback than for foot. Although doubtless the best way of pointing with a curvilinear blade, in no case is it better than the straight thrust.

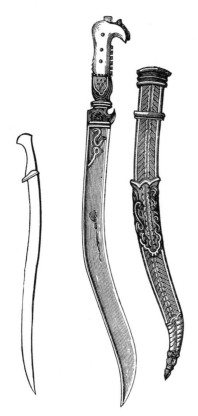

FIG. 122.—YATAGHAN.   FIG. 123.—ORNAMENTAL
                        YATAGHAN AND SHEATH.

The 'curved thrust' so imposed upon Colonel Marey, of the French army, that he proposed in an elaborate work on Swords (Strasburg, 1841) to adopt the Yataghan, whose beautifully curved line of blade coincides accurately with the motion of the wrist in cutting, and which he held to be equally valuable for the point. As a regulation Sword for infantry, it was spoilt by a cheap iron scabbard. As a bayonet it lost all its distinctive excellence: the forward weight, so valuable in cutting with the hand, made it heavy and unmanageable at the end of a musket, and none but the strongest arms could use it, especially when the thrust had to be 'lanced out.' Yet it lasted for a quarter of a century, and only in 1875 it was superseded by the triangular weapon attached to the *fusil Gras*.[1]

Fig. 124 shows sections of the principal forms of thrusting blades. No. 1, whose section, a lozenge, is nearly square, consists of two obtuse-angled wedges joined at the bases, making a strong, stiff, and lasting, but very heavy, Sword. This form dates from the earliest times : we find it in the bronze rapiers of France and England, and it was preserved in many of the Toledan, Bilbao, Zaragosan, Solingen, and Italian rapiers ; it is known to English armourers as the ' Saxon,'

[1] The section of the modern weapon shows that the *baïonnette Gras* is fit only for the thrust ; and, as it stops its own cut, it is useless for the menial and servile offices in which the Yataghan-bayonet, like the old *coupe-choux* Sword, did yeoman's service. I can see no improvement upon the old-fashioned triangular bayonet, which amongst us has been superseded by the short Enfield Sword-bayonet. To the latter I should prefer even the bowie-knife bayonet, of which the Washington Arsenal was once full, and which has been used even lately in the United States. None but practical soldiers realise the fact that the bayonet is meant to be a bayonet, not a Sword, nor a dagger, nor a chopper, nor a saw.

and to workmen as the 'latchen'-blade. Nos. 2 and 3 show two simple methods of lightening it, the former carrying down the axis a fore-and-aft groove instead of the raised mid-rib on either face, which was used in the days of the Trojan war. No. 4 is the so-called 'Biscayan' shape, the *trialamellum* of more ancient days, with three deep grooves and as many blunt edges, by which the parries were made. Theoretically it is good : practically and technically speaking, it is inferior to either of the preceding. There is so much difficulty in making the blade straight and of even temper that many professional men have never seen one which was not either crooked or soft. Yet this is the 'small-Sword' proper, the duelling weapon of the last century, which stood its ground as far as the first quarter of the present century. It had a curious modification—the Colichemarde blade, so called from its inventor, Count Königsmark. This was a trialamellum very wide and heavy in the 'whole-strong' quarter near the hilt, and at about eight inches suddenly passing to a light and slender rapier-section. It was invented about 1680, and became a favourite duelling-blade, the feather-weight at

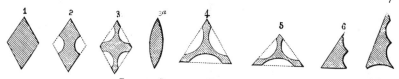

FIG. 124.—SECTIONS OF THRUSTING-SWORDS.

the point making it the best of fencing weapons. It remained in fashion during the reign of Louis XIV. and then suddenly disappeared.[1]

The small-Sword was introduced into England during the eighteenth century, and only after 1789 it ceased to be the almost universal French weapon in affairs of honour. I believe that the change to the *épée de combat* and the foil arose from the popular prejudice that the triangular blade is too dangerous for fair duelling, and that a body-wound with it bleeds inwardly and is almost always fatal. This 'small-Sword,'[2] however, left its descendant in our old bayonet, the grooves being shallower and the ribs raised higher. No. 6, supposed to be an experimental Sword from the Klingenthal manufactory, dated 1810–14, is a curious attempt to add cutting power

[1] Mr. Wareing Faulder (Exhibition of Industrial Art, Manchester, June and July, 1881, *Catalogue*, p. 24) suggests that the Colichemarde 'fell into disuse probably in consequence of its costliness, combined with its inelegant appearance when sheathed.'

[2] Captain George Chapman, in his *Foil Practice, &c.*, a book which will appear in the 'Bibliography' (Part III.), rightly distinguishes between the triangular small-Sword, used only for thrusting, and the biconvex cut-and-thrust 'rapier,' a term applied by the Germans to the *Schläger*, which has no point. In England most people use 'small-Sword' only in opposition to 'broadsword'; but, as the Art of Fencing may be considered a general foundation for swordsmanship, all men-at-arms should understand and preserve the difference. The writer, however, observes (Notes, pp. 4, 5), that, among the various actions which may conveniently be executed with the triangular 'Biscayan,' there are many which cannot be so easily managed with a flat blade, or with the usual weapon of modern combat, however light and handy. Hence 'fencers among military men should be cautioned against *indiscriminately* attempting with the Sword performances usually taught in lessons with the foil.'

to a quadrangular thrusting blade ; but, as the angles are very acute, the blow will
have hardly any effect. No. 7 is an improvement upon the latter, because it has
more trenchant capacity. The defect of both these Swords is that they have a

FIG. 125.—PIERCED   FIG. 126.—PIERCED BLADE   FIG. 127.—FLAMBERGE   FIG. 128.—GERMAN
    BLADE.   AND SHEATH.   MAIN-GAUCHE.

tendency to turn over in the hand, and to 'spring' at the flat side when the point
meets with the least resistance.

    There are other ways of lightening the blade besides grooving. A favourite

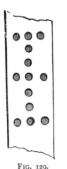

FIG. 129.
PATERNOSTER.

fashion in the fifteenth and sixteenth centuries, the golden age of the
Sword, was to break the continuity by open work, which allowed free
play to the ornamenter's hand. It was also supposed to render the
wound more dangerous by admitting the air. As will afterwards be
shown, certain Eastern and mediæval sabres were hollowed to contain
sections or pennations, which sprang out in small lateral blades
when a spring was touched. A German *main-gauche* in the Musée
d'Artillerie, Paris (No. J. 485), shows three blades expanding by a
spring when a button is pressed in the handle, and forming a guard
of great length and breadth, in which the opponent's Sword might
be caught and snapped. Another rare form was the 'Paternoster
blade,' fitted with round depressions, which enabled the pious to count the number
of his 'vain repetitions,' even in the dark (fig. 129).

It has been shown that the material determines the obtuseness or acuteness of the angle formed by the two planes which meet at the apex to form the edge. There are many varieties of the *fil.* The edge proper V, formed by the angles of resistance (forty degrees) and of entrance (ninety degrees), has already been noticed. Besides this there are the chisel-edge, mostly applied to tools such as the plane ; and lastly bevel-edge, or double-slope, ⌄, which may be called the chopper-edge: the obtuser angle is used for blades intended to cut lead-bars and similar resisting substances.

In the Sword the edge is usually straight. The principal exceptions are the following. The wavy, cutting surface appears in the ' flamberge,' to which flame

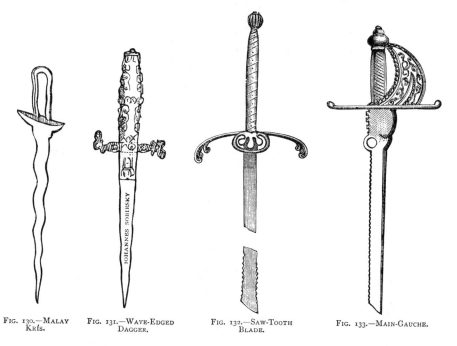

FIG. 130.—MALAY KRÍS. FIG. 131.—WAVE-EDGED DAGGER. FIG. 132.—SAW-TOOTH BLADE. FIG. 133.—MAIN-GAUCHE.

gave a name [1]: it is nowhere better developed than in the beautiful Malay krís (crease). The object seems to be that of increasing the cutting surface. The wave-edged form is well shown in an iron dagger (end of fourteenth or early fifteenth century) of the Nieuwerkerke Collection : similar weapons, taken from the Thames, are found in the British Museum, and they abound in Continental collections. Often the waves are broken into saw-teeth : this apparently silly contrivance is found on a large scale in Indian sabres ; its latter appearance farther west is on the precious saw-bayonet, a theoretical *multum in parvo* equally useless for flesh and

[1] It was also a proper name applied to the Paladin Renaud's Sword. The flamberge of the seventeenth century became a rapier-blade, and no longer ' flamboyant,' and the difference is in the hilt, and especially the guards. The latter were shallower and simpler than the rapier form, and were more easily changed from hand to hand, as was the practice of early fencers.

fuel. Of somewhat similar kind is the toothed edge, which is found in Arab, Indian, and other Eastern weapons. The deepest indentations are in the so-called Sword-breakers (*brise-épées*), mostly of the fifteenth century. It is not easy to explain,

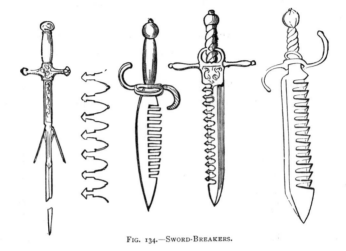

FIG. 134.—SWORD-BREAKERS.

except by individual freak, the meaning of the toothed or broken edge which appears in a dagger of the fourteenth century (fig. 137). Lastly, there is the hooked-edge, spur-edge, or prong-edge, whose projections are generally found in the flammberg (flamberge) proper, or two-handed Sword of wavy contour. The hooks

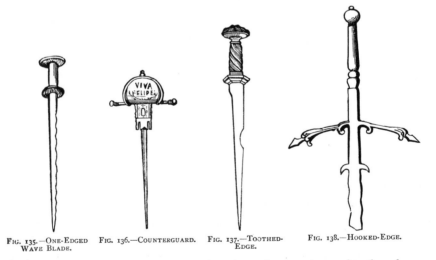

FIG. 135.—ONE-EDGED   FIG. 136.—COUNTERGUARD.   FIG. 137.—TOOTHED-   FIG. 138.—HOOKED-EDGE.
WAVE BLADE.   EDGE.

are either single or double, and the evident intention was to receive the adversary's blade. As a rule the hollow of the half-crescent is towards the point : some project horizontally, but very few are reversed or hollow towards the hilt, as that shape would lead the adversary's blade to the forearm.

The point again differs as much as the edge. The natural point would be the prolongation and gradual convergence of various lines of the solid body, conical, pyramidal, or polygonal, concurring in a common apex. In the Japanese blade the edge-line is bent upwards to meet the back-line. When more strength is wanted the end is bevelled, forming, like the edge, a compound angle between forty and ninety degrees: it is thus fitted to meet hard bodies, and the obtuser the angle the stronger the point.

When edge only is regarded, as in the Schläger and the glaive, the Sword of justice or the Scharfrichter's (headman's) weapon, the point of the very broad thin blade is rounded off. This, as will be seen, is the case with the early Kelto-Scandinavian Swords, miscalled Anglo-Saxon.

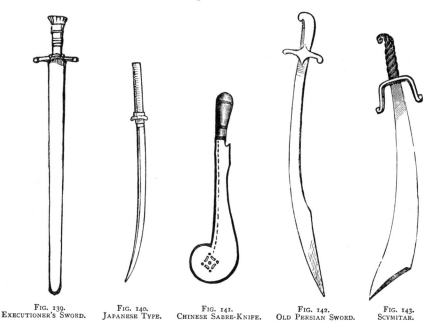

| FIG. 139. | FIG. 140. | FIG. 141. | FIG. 142. | FIG. 143. |
| EXECUTIONER'S SWORD. | JAPANESE TYPE. | CHINESE SABRE-KNIFE. | OLD PERSIAN SWORD. | SCYMITAR. |

There is more variety in the extremities of cutting-blades. The falchion of Ashanti, Dahome, and Benin, the murderous despotisms of western intertropical Africa, terminates in a whorl. This is also the shape of the Chinese sabre-knife, with which criminals were despatched. The old Persian Sword, often called by mistake the Turkish Sword, ends in a point beyond a broadening of the blade. The effect is to add force to the cut; the weapon becomes top-heavy, but that is of little consequence when only a single slash, and no guarding, is required of it. This peculiarity was curiously developed in the true Turkish scymitar, which we see in every picture of the sixteenth century, and which has now become so rare in our museums. The end gradually developed to a monstrous size; the length was cut down for the sake of handiness and the guard was almost abolished, because

parrying was the work of the shield. This exceptional form extended far eastwards and westwards. Some of the Nepaul Swords have a double wave at the
end. It was adopted by the Chinese, who, as usual in their arms, reduced it to
its simplest expression: the pommel is cap-shaped, the handle corded, and the
guard a small oval of metal insufficient to protect the hand (fig. 145). Another good
specimen of the 'Turanian blade' is the formidable Dáo[1] of the Nágá tribe,
south-east of Assam. It is a thick, heavy backsword, eighteen inches long, with
a bevel where the point should be, worn at the waist in a half-scabbard of wood,
and used for digging as well as killing. The Turkish form also extended to Europe
and America, where it became one of the multitudinous varieties of the 'mariner's
cutlass,' from 'curtle-axe'—*curtus* and axe. The 'Turanian blade' is well

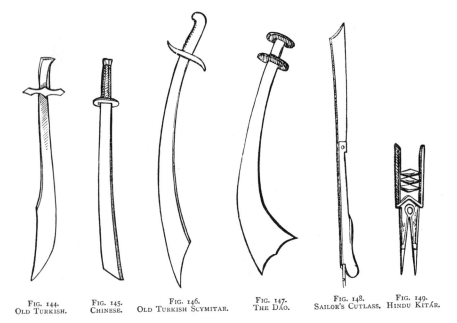

FIG. 144.
OLD TURKISH.　　FIG. 145.
CHINESE.　　FIG. 146.
OLD TURKISH SCYMITAR.　　FIG. 147.
THE DÁO.　　FIG. 148.
SAILOR'S CUTLASS.　　FIG. 149.
HINDU KITÁR.

shown in Eastern scutcheons.[2] Its shape resembles that of a hunter's horn with a
Sword-knot hanging in two ribbons, a survival from remote antiquity. The tincts
are purpure, gules and sable, upon a fasce tenné ('on a fess' or bar) or, vert and
argent. The descriptions are very precise and technical; for instance, Abu

[1] There is another Dáo in the Eastern regions, a
large, square, double-edged blade, with a handle
attached to the centre. The Dah of Burma is originally the same weapon as the Nágá Dáo.

[2] In the *Bulletin de l'Institut Egyptien* (deuxième
série, No. 1, année 1880) there is an admirable
paper on Eastern heraldry, 'Le blason chez les
Princes musulmans,' by E. T. Rogers Bey. He
proves that a heraldic scutcheon is known to the
Arabs as *rank*, plur. *runúk*, and that the word is the
Persian *rang*, colour, from which he would derive
our (man of) 'rank,' a word hitherto unsatisfactorily
explained. As regards the tints, 'azure' is evidently
the Persian *lájawardi*; and 'gules' is better derived
from *gul*, a rose, than from Fr. *gueules* (jaw), which
is L. Lat. *gula*, reddened skin. These three words
suggest that for the origin of heraldry in its present
form we must go back to Persia. Of the Sword in
European heraldry I shall have more to say in
Part II.

el-Mahásin thus notices the Rank (armorial badges) of Anuk, son of Abdullah el-Ashraty : 'The coat was composed of a circle argent cut by a bar vert, upon which was charged a Sword gules. . . . This Rank was very pleasing, and the women of the town had it tattoed upon their wrists.' The Rank was given when a subject was raised to the dignity of Amir.

Before ending the subject of the point I must briefly notice the forked or swallow-tailed blade, a curious subject deserving an exhaustive monograph. The Greeks evidently derived their χελιδὼν or χελιδόνιος ξίφος,[1] and the Latins their *bidens*, from the two-ended chisels so common in Egypt. As will be seen, there was a true forked Sword in Assyria, and the form is commonly found in Indian daggers.

The Chelidonian sabre has two distinct shapes. In one the plates are welded together, and separate at the third or the fourth section near the end. Mr. Latham (Wilkinson's) has a good specimen ; the length of the fork, however, is greater than the united part. In the Prince of Wales Collection (Kensington) there is a two-bladed Sword, the fork only eight inches long, with the additional peculiarity of being saw-edged. In the other form, the Chelidonian proper, the fork is vertical, one prong being above the other. What use it could have supplied in cutting is hard to divine, but the Sword is essentially personal and eccentric. I know only one historical blade of this form, Zú'l-Fikár (Lord of Cleaving), the weapon given by the Archangel Gabriel to Mohammed, and by the latter to his son-in-law Ali bin Ali Tálib, who cleft with it the skull of Marhab, the giant Jew warrior of Khaybar Fort. It appears upon the arms of the Zeydi princes, lords of Sana'á in El-Yemen, Southern Arabia [2] : nearer home it may be seen upon the Turkish standard, some twenty feet long, taken by Don John of Austria from the Turk at Lepanto.[3] The weapon probably owes this honour to having been mentioned amongst the Ahádís, or traditional sayings of the Apostle of El-Islam, ' la Sayfa illa Zú'l-Fikár wa lá Fatá illa Ali ' (there is no Sword to be compared, for doing damage to the foe, with Zú'l-Fikár, and no valiant youth but Ali).

FIG. 150.—GOLD COAST.

Amongst the Chelidonian blades proper I do not include the double blade. A fair specimen of the latter is the Orissa Sword [4] : two slightly oval forms spring from the same hilt, but separate throughout their length. Another shape is found upon the Gold Coast : the blades are disposed like the astronomical sign of Aries, and its only

---

[1] Strange to say, these Sword-names are carefully omitted from Liddell and Scott, 1869.

[2] The information was kindly forwarded to me by Captain F. M. Hunter, Assistant Political Resident, Aden. Along the blade runs the inscription, which will be quoted in Part II., and the characters appear modern. My informant thinks that this Chelidonian does not represent the original Zú'l-Fikár, which was two edged.

[3] This trophy hangs against the staircase wall of the fine armoury belonging to the Museo del Arsenale (Naval Arsenal), Venice. Here, however, it has become a complicated affair with Koranic inscription (ch. xl. vol. i.) ; open-jawed dragons' heads at the hilt, and below the handle a rosette with various complications of ' Yá ' (Allah !).

[4] It is figured in the illustrations following the *Antiquities of Orissa*, by Rajendra Lala Mitra.

use is to slice off noses and ears.[1] The offending member is placed at the commissure, and an upward shear effects the mutilation. I reserve for a future page the 'split Swords,' two blades in one scabbard, which were used in mediæval Europe, and which have been preserved in China.

To conclude this long and technical chapter. The Sword should be tightly mounted and well shouldered-up before and behind, leaving no interval between hilt and blade. The grip must be firm, and the tang secured either by rivets or, better still, by a screw at the pommel: if this be neglected, the weapon will not deliver a true edge. In trials both back and edge should be repeatedly struck with force upon a wooden post. Should the handle show no sign of loosening, and the blade ring with the right sound, it is a sign that the mounting is satisfactory: the reverse is the case if the blow jars or stings the hand: this suggests that the cut will not prove efficient.

NOTE.—The type and model of the straight blade is the form of Rapier which we call the Toledo. It is probably derived from the Spatha or long Sword of the Roman cavalryman; but it assumed its present perfect shape during the reign of Charles Quint (A.D. 1493–1519). The exemplar of the curved blade is the so-called 'Damascus' sabre, dating probably from the early days of El-Islam (seventh century), when Eastern armies were chiefly composed of light Bedawi horsemen. Of these in Part II.

[1] Capt. Cameron and I exhibited a specimen, made for us by good King Blay of Attábo, at a special meeting of the Anthropological Institute of London.

CHAPTER VIII.

THE SWORD IN ANCIENT EGYPT AND IN MODERN AFRICA.

THE present state of our history shows us nothing anterior to Egypt in the civilisation of Language, of Literature, of Science, Art and Arms. We must now modify
and modernise the antiquated and obsolete saying—'ex Oriente lux'—the fancy
that illumination came from India, when the reverse is true. The light of knowledge dawned and dayed not in the East, but in the South, in the Dark Continent,
which is also the High Continent.[1] Nor can we any longer admit that

> Westward the course of empire takes its way.

As Professor Lepsius teaches us, 'In the oldest times within the memory of man,
we know of only *one* advanced culture; of only *one* mode of writing, and of only
one literary development, viz. those of Egypt.' Karl Vogt, a man who has the
courage to say what he thinks, bluntly states: 'Our civilisation came not from
Asia, but from Africa.' For our origin we must return to

> The world's great mistress in the Egyptian vale.

The modern Egyptologist is reforming the false and one-sided theories based
upon the meagre studies of anthropological literature in Greek, Latin, and Hebrew.
Yet in the Nile Valley we are only upon the threshold of exploration—topographical, linguistic, and scientific. Of its proto-Egyptians and its primeval workmanship as yet we know little; and it is truly preposterous to suppose that man began
his artistic life by building pyramids, cutting obelisks, and engraving hieroglyphs.
The 'Cushite School,' based upon the Asiatic Ethiopians of Eusebius the Bishop,[2]
and unfortunately represented by Bunsen, Maspero, Wilkinson, Mariette, Brugsch,
and a host of minor names, has determined that the old Nilotes 'undoubtedly came
from Asia.' The theory utterly lacks proof; and the same may be said of the
popular assertion, based upon Biblical grounds—'The early colonists of Egypt

[1] The Austrian geographer, Dr. Josef Chavanne, estimates the mean altitude of Africa at 2,170 feet (round numbers), or more than double that of Europe (971 feet, M. G. Leipoldt).

[2] He makes his Ethiopians emigrate from India to Egypt—but where? when? how? The 'Asiatic Æthiopians' of Herodotus lie between the Germanii (Persian *Kerman*) and the Indus (iii. 93, &c.). The bas-reliefs of Susiana show negroid types, and Texier found the Lamlam tribe in the marshes round the head of the Persian Gulf to resemble the Bisharin of Upper Egypt. Was *the* Buddha one of these Cushite Ethiopians?

came thither from Mesopotamia.' We seem to be reading fable when told (by William Osburn [1]), 'The skill of these primitive artists of Egypt was a portion of that civilisation which its first settlers brought with them when they located themselves in the Valley of the Nile.'

My conviction is that the ancient Egyptians were Africans, and pure Africans ; that the Nile-dwellers are still negroids whitened by a large infusion of Syrian, Arabian, and other Asiatic blood ; and that Ethiopia is its old racial home. Æschylus had already robed their black limbs in white raiment when Herodotus (ii. 104) made them dark-skinned compared with the Arabs [2] and North Africans. Every traveller finds his description hold good to the present day. Blumenbach declared the old Egyptians to be of Berber origin, the race of Psametik, or the Son of the Sun. Hartmann opined that they were not Asiatics but Africans, and Dr. Morton modified his first opinion, finding the cranium to be negroid. I hope to prove their correctness by making a large collection of mummy skulls.[3] It is certain that the modern Egyptian's hair—that great characteristic of race, according to Pruner Bey—is not silky, as Professor Huxley says, but wiry like that of his forefathers.[4] Moreover, his type, as distinctly shown by the Sphinx, is melanochroic-negroid. Lastly, there are other signs, which need not here be noticed, distinguishing the African—horse as well as human—from the Arabian.

There is a history of ancient Egypt, into which we have not yet penetrated. Herodotus (ii. 142) glances at it when he makes the Ptah-priest at Memphis pretend to an antiquity of 11,340 years,[5] during which reigned 341 generations of kings and pontiffs.[6] Plato does the same when he speaks of hymns 10,000 years old, and Mela[7] when he numbers 330 kings before Amasis, who ruled more than 30,000 years. Mena (Menes), the first man-monarch who founded Memphis (B.C. 4560 ?) some centuries before the Hebrew Creation, was preceded for 13,000 years by the

---

[1] *Monumental History*, &c.

[2] The late Mr. Lane, who was greatly attached to Cairo and its population, insisted upon the Arab origin and kinship of the Egyptian. To those who know both races they appear as different as Englishmen and Greeks. Place an Arab, especially a Bedawi, by the side of a Fellah, and the contrast will strike the least experienced eye.

[3] The first instalment was sent in May 1881 to the Royal College of Surgeons for the benefit of Professor Flower and Dr. C. Carter Blake. I am aware of the difficulty in determining mummy-dates, but the fact of mummification shows a certain antiquity whose later limit is sharply defined. The mummy of King Mer en Rá (Sixth Dynasty), found near the Sakkarah pyramids, had been stripped of its bandages ; but the marks impressed upon the skin showed that the system was that of later years. He can hardly be dated later than B.C. 3000 ; and, reckoning from that period to A.D. 700, when mummifying ceased, we have a population of embalmed bodies of some 730,000,000 in round numbers.

[4] The hair is of intermediate type between negro and Malay. The Nilotes are οὐλότριχοι and ἐριόκομοι, with woolly locks, slightly flat like ribbons, evenly distributed (not in peppercorns) over the scalp. It is also a mistake to make the Nubians λισσότριχοι : none of the Nile Valley races are lank-haired like Hindús, Chinese, and Australians.

[5] The full number of Herodotus is 52,000 years. Mr. Day (p. 59) is scandalised by these dates, which argue for the ' high antiquity theory '; and appears astonished to find ' anything placed centuries previous to the Noahitic Deluge.' Of this more presently.

[6] Each generation contained a ' Piromis, son of a Piromis.' The word, made equivalent to *Kalos k' agathos* (= *galantuomo*), is *Pe-Rome*, the man, opposed to *Pe-Neter*, the god.

[7] Mela has been blamed for repeating Herodotus without understanding him. When he states that the sun twice set at the point where it now rises (' solem bis jam occidisse unde oritur '), he probably means that the greater light left to the west the zodiacal sign which presided at its rising.

'Dynasty of the Gods' (god-kings), suggesting a governmental hierarchy of the fetisheer caste : and this lasted for ages, till the Soldier upset the Priest and raised himself to the rank of Pharaoh [1] and king. Traces of the proto-Egyptian dynasties in which the men of the Pen controlled the men of the Sword long survived ; and in later times the ecclesiastical order again ruled the military. We know nothing of the hierarchical supremacy but its baldest outline. When our modest chronologists allow 6000 years to its incept, they run into the contrary extreme of those who assign to it myriads of centuries. Rodier [2] is more reasonable ; he opines that the cycle of 1,460 years dates in Egypt from B.C. 14,611.

FIG. 151.—1. BRONZE DAGGER ; 2. SWORD (14 inches long).

Again, it will probably be found that ancient Egypt was *not* 'the narrowest strip of land in the world running between a double desert.' The extent of ' Kemi ' [3] has been arbitrarily confined to the Riverine Valley as far as the First Cataract, or seven hundred by seven miles widening out in the Delta-netherland to a base of eighty-one miles. We may fairly suspect that modern Masr is only a slice from the eastern half of the antique Mizraim. The Greeks made the frontier of Asia extend beyond the Suez isthmus and the Nile to the lands of Libya.[4] This Greater Egypt is still suggested by the system of Bahr bilá má, large *Fiumare* now bone-dry, and by the alignment of the oases in the wilderness west of the River Valley with their giant ruins of a proto-historic Past. These may date from the days when the basin of the Bahr el-Ghazal—a lake like the Tanganyika and the Victoria Nyanza—discharged i's annual flood to the North in channels parallel with the ' River Ægyptus.'[5] The lacustrine bed would silt up by the natural process of warping, and the surplus water, no longer able to discharge northwards, would force itself eastwards to the Nile. The easier drainage would presently convert the lake into a river-basin and system, and the lands no longer irrigated would become a waste dotted like a leopard skin with oases or watered valleys.

---

[1] The word at first applied probably to the commander-in-chief. Wilkinson's day derived it from *Phra* (*pa-Ra*), the sun ; now it is explained *Per-áo*, the Great House, in the sense of ' Sublime Porte.'

[2] *Antiquité des Races Humaines.* Paris, 1862.

[3] The ' black land,' opposed to *Tesher*, the ' red land ' (Edom, Idumæa, Erythræa), the wilds of North-Western Arabia. It is also called on the monuments *A'in* (*Æan* in Pliny) and *Ta-mera* (*Mera*, *Tomera*), the 'inundation region.' Another old name, *Aeria*, is from יאר, *Yior*, the Nile. *Kemi* must not be confounded with *Khem*, *Chemmis*, universal nature, the generative and reproductive principle—*Pan*. When Q. Curtius writes that Chemmis '*umbraculo maxime similis est habitus*,' I would change the first word to ' umbilico.' The stepped cone in the Elephanta Caves exactly explains the latter.

[4] Hecatæus and Anaximander divided the globe into Europe (*Ereb*, *Gharb*, the West) and Asia (*Asiyeh*, the East). Their successors added Libya (Africa), a term derived from the Libu or Ribu tribes; and the Father of History a most insufficient fourth— the Nilotic Delta. The latter, however, is ethnologically correct: Egypt is neither Africa nor Asia, but a land *per se*.

[5] In Homer, Ægyptus always applies to the Nile (*Od.* xiv. 268). Manetho makes it the name of a king, Sethos = Seti I. M. Maspero proposes as a derivation of the word, Ha Kahi Ptah (the land of the god Ptah). Hence the Biblical Pathros = Ptah-land (*Ezek.* xxix. 14). Pathyris, the western side of Thebes, and the western Provinces generally, may have named the πάταικοι (Herod. iii. 37), the obscene dwarfs who made Cambyses laugh.

An abundance of popular literature has familiarised the public with the outer aspect of ancient Egypt, but the world is still far from recognising the message she sent to mankind. We must go back to 'the Wonderland on the banks of the mighty Nile' for the origin of all things which most interest us. It is the very cradle-land of language. Her tongue contains all the elements of the so-called 'Aryan,'[1] Semitic, and Allophyllian or Turanian families, and dates long before the days of the present distribution. Bunsen's 'Egypt' first noticed this fact at some length, without, however, dwelling upon its importance. 'All Semitic pronouns and suffixes,' says M. C. Bertin, 'can be traced back to Egyptian, especially the Egyptian of the earliest dynasties'; he might have added much about other mechanical forms. Brugsch tells us (i. 3) that the primitive roots and the essential elements of the Egyptian grammar point to an intimate connection of the Indo-Germanic (!) and Semitic languages.'[2] The Allophyllian or Agglutinative Turanian,[3] a *tertium quid* which is neither 'Aryan' nor 'Semitic,' is also traceable in old Coptic.

What, then, do these facts suggest? Simply that the elements existing in Egyptian travelled from the banks of the Nile and evolved, discreted, and differentiated themselves in many centres. The word-compounding or Iranian scheme found homes in Eastern Europe (Greece, Italy, and the Slavonic or quasi-Asiatic half); in Asia Minor—especially Phrygia—in Mesopotamia, in Persia, and finally in India, where the settlement was comparatively modern. This explains how a philologist would derive Sanskrit from Lithuania. This saves us from the 'Aryan heresy';[4] this abolishes 'Indo-European,' and worse still 'Indo-Germanic'—that model specimen of national modesty. Both are terms which contain a theory and an unproved theory. Again, the word-developing or Arabian scheme, absurdly termed Semitic (from Shem !), increased, multiplied, and perfected itself in Northern Africa and Arabia, while the Turanian, becoming independent and specialised in Akkadian, overspread Tartary and China.

And this one primæval language of Egypt framed for itself an alphabet whence

---

[1] Herodotus (vii. 66) specifies the Arians, a racial name then synonymous with the Medes. This is not the place to enter upon the subject of Aria's enormous development.

[2] As a specimen of the roots—which are most remarkable when they consist of single consonants, whose reduplication made the earliest words—take 'papa' and 'mamma.' The former is from the Egyptian *pa-pa* (root *p*), to produce, the original idea of the begetter; and the latter is *ma-ma* (root *m*), to carry, be pregnant, bear. *Mut* becomes *mátá*, μήτηρ, *mater*, mother: *Mer* (*a-mor*), love; *meran* (*morior*), die, and *more* (*mare*), the sea. In 'Semitic' we have *má*, Heb. and Arab. *má*, water; and a long array of other words (as *ia*, yes, yea ; and *na*, nay) too extensive for notice.

[3] Characterised chiefly by post- instead of prepositions, by additions to the verb which make it causal,

reflective, and so forth, and by the peculiar form of sentences. Examples : the Finn-Ugrian-Magyar and the Turk-Mongol-Tartar, both probably deriving from the ancient *Sakas* = Scythians.

[4] To Aryan I much prefer the older term 'Iranian'; Iran (Persia), which once extended from the Indus to the Mediterranean, being one of the great centres where the 'Aryo'-Egyptian element of language developed itself, and where a typical race is still found. Nor is there much objection to 'Turanian,' Turan being the non-Iranian regions to the east, Tartary and China. But 'Semitic,' which contains a myth and a theory, should be changed into 'Arabian.' Egypto-Arabic attained its purest and highest development in the Peninsula ; Hebrew is a northern and somewhat barbarous dialect ; Syriac is a north-western offspring ; Galla, a western ; and so forth.

are derived all others. This is proved by the fact that each and all begin, as Plutarch tells us old Coptic did, with the letter A. Of its age in Nile-land we may judge from the cartouche containing Khufu's name, left by some workman on an inner block of the Great Pyramid.[1] How many generations of articulate-speaking men must have come and gone before so artificial and artistic a system as the Royal Signature upon the Shield occurred to the human mind!

But Egypt did still more. She was the fountain-head of knowledge which overflowed the world. Eastward the great current set through Babylonia and Chaldæa, Persia and India, Indo-China, China, and Japan, to Australia and Poly-nesia. Westward it flooded Africa and Europe. It may have reached America by two ways. The Oriental line would extend from China and Japan to the Eastern Pacific coast : the Occidental was practicable *viâ* Atlantis, or possibly in the days when Behring's Straits did not exist. It found a new Mediterranean in the great Caribbean Gulf, and new Indies in Mexico and Peru. Indeed, the march of intellect from Egypt is conterminous with the limits of the habitable globe.

The invention of an alphabet would necessarily lead to literature—poetry, his-tory, and criticism. The earliest known manuscript is the Prisse (d'Avennes) Papyrus, a roll dating from the days of Pharaoh Tat-ka-ra, last of the Fifth Dynasty (circ. B.C. 3000). It is a collection of proverbs, maxims, precepts, and command-ments, of which the fifth is, ' Honour thy father and thy mother, that thy life may be long ' : the style is admirable for its humorous vein, and for its graphic descrip-tion of old age—' Senex bis puer.' The earliest epic is the heroic poem of Pentaur, laureate to Ramses II. (B.C. 1333–1300) ; it is the prototype of the cyclic songs which, in Cyprus especially, preceded the *chef-d'œuvre* of the Homerid chief ; and it opens with an ' Arma Virumque cano.' The ' Deadbook ' is the birth of the Drama, and it may date ages before the dialogues of Job. The ' Canticles of Solomon ' are in the evocations of Isis and Nephthys.[2] The *critique* of a young author's production by a purist in style might add a sting to reviewing in the present day.[3] To the Egyptians we must attribute the invention of maps and plans. They first studied heraldry : every nome had its distinctive emblem generally bird or beast ; and each temple and guild its blazon.[4]

Literature would be imperfect without art and science, and accordingly we find their head-quarters and old home in Egypt. These studies humanised the people ; their code suggests the mildness of modern penal law ; and their reverence for letters,

---

[1] For whose erection every ' authority ' gives his or her own date. Mr. Proctor's calculation, based upon the precession of the equinoxes, is B.C. 3350. It appears to me that we also obtain the date from the position of the polar star (α Draconis), which looked down the axis of the great entrance-passage before this long tube was blocked up. We may thus assume between B.C. 3440 and B.C. 3350.

[2] *Records of the Past*, ii. 120 ; and *Trans. Bibl. Soc.* i. ii. 383–85.

[3] Brugsch, vol. ii. chap. xiv.

[4] One nome (*Tanis*) carried a crescent and one star, others had two and three of the latter. The emblem passed over to the Byzantine Empire, and now we see upon the Egyptian flag the crescent and Seb, the five-rayed star. It is thus distinguished from the Turkish, which has seven rays.

for old age, and for the dignity of man, makes them an eternal example to the world. The monuments show their fondness for music and painting. Their knowledge of statuary is proved by a host of works, especially the wooden Shaykh el-Balad (village chief) in the Bulak Museum—a marvel of skill, probably dating from the Fourth Dynasty, B.C. 3700. In architecture they invented the arch, round and pointed ; eight several orders of columns, including the proto-Doric ; Atlantes, Caryatides, and human-shaped consoles. The 'temple of Jízeh' near the sphinx is evidently older than the adjoining pyramids ; it is a model of solidity in which the hardest stone is worked like wood.

In science they especially cultivated geometry, astronomy, astrology, and 'alchemy,' whose name betrays its origin. Their arithmetic taught decimals and duodecimals. Their mathematics arose from measuring fields and calculating the cubes of altars. They knew the precession of the equinoxes : Rodier (p. 31) considers that they learnt it from observing the equinoctial point and the rising of Sothis, the Tuth-star, 'the axle of the skies,' in the same zodiacal sign, and that the studies at Syene date from B.C. 17,932. They knew the motion of the apsides, and the solar and stellar periods ; they invented latitude and longitude ; they denoted by a cross the intersection of the solstices and the equinoxes, and they published annual calendars. In optics they invented the lens. They were not ignorant of the motive power of steam, and possibly the electric fish had taught them the rudiments of electricity.

They were great in the mechanical arts. In medicine they dissected and vivisected : in agriculture they invented the plough, the harrow, the toothed sickle, the flail, and the tribulum ; in carpentry the dove-tail ; in ceramics the potter's wheel, and in hydraulics the water-wheel. In gardening they transplanted full-grown trees. They made glass, porcelain, and counterfeit pearls and precious stones ; and they used emery powder and the lapidary's wheel. They spun silk, and knew the use of mordants for stuffs and dyes for hair. They made 'babies' (dolls) and children's toys of clay, and they moulded masks of papier-mâché. In some points they were strangely modern. For hunting they wore dresses of 'suppressed colour,' not pink nor 'rifleman's green' : we are just beginning to find out our mistakes. They affected falconry, and played at the draughts which led to chess ; and at *morra*, the Roman *micare digitis.* They sat on chairs whose shapes are like ours, not on divans nor on triclinia. In their house furniture they studiously avoided over-regularity ; and Japan is now teaching England and Germany not to weary man's eye by monotony.

And as they were advanced in literature and politics, the religion of earth, so they assiduously cultivated religion, the politics of heaven. The Biblical student has found among the tombs of Nile-land the absolute truth of what Celsus said—namely, that the Hebrews borrowed their tenets and practices from Egypt. Their date of the creation *ex nihilo* (B.C. 4004–4620) was evidently Manetho's period of the succession of Mena, and it is used even in our day. Their genesitic cosmogony, as Philo Judæus shows, and as Origen expressly declares, was an adaptation of Nilotic allegories and mysteries which the vulgar understood factually and literally. Their 'Adam' suggests 'Atum,' whence 'Adima,' the First Man amongst the Hindus. Their App or Apap (Apophis), whose determinative is a snake transfixed with four knife-blades,[1] is the great old serpent, the ophid-giant, Sin, Sathanas. The 'Flood'[2] is the annual Nilotic inundation modified by the Izdubar legends of the Interamnian Plain. Noah, Nuh, Nöe, is suspiciously like Nu or Nuhu,[3] the Sailor of the Waters, the Lord of the Full Nile. Ham suggests Kam, the black race. The ark is the Bahr or Ua (Baris, Argo navis) of Nu, the sacred vessel portrayed in the ruins of Egyptian Elephanta, the boat of Osiris, or Uasur, the man-formed Sun-god ; and the floating cradle of Moses is a mere replica of Osiris' ark. In that complicated idolatry of deceased ancestors, based upon a system of monotheism,[4] or rather the worship of glorified man, which formed the religion of Egypt, the Sun typified human life. He rose as the infant Horus ; he was the Lord Ka of the mid-day ; as Tum he became old and set ; and as Hormakhu (Harmachis) he shone to the under world below the horizon, Night and Death being the forerunners of Light and Life.[5]

The preternatural apparatus of both faiths (original and borrowed) is the same. The four genii of Death—Amset (under Isis), Hapi (Nephthys), Tuamutef (Neith), and Khebsenauf (Sebk)—became the four archangels. Of Urim and Thummim, the latter is the plural of Thmei (Themis), the blind or headless goddess of Truth and Justice.[6] Even such phrases as 'I am that I am'[7] are loans from the hiero-grammat ; Ankh (I am Life) was rendered Yahveh (Jehovah). This 'ineffable name'[8] is borrowed by some, Colenso included, from Semitic heathenism ; but Brugsch shows that Egypt supplied the Mosaic conception of the Creator. There appears, indeed, direct derivation in the unity of the Deity and in the duality of Typhon, Set, Satan, the Evil Spirit. Later ages copied the local Triads of Kemi, in which the third proceeded from the other two. Both ecclesiastical establishments con-

---

[1] See chap. viii.

[2] The popular conception of the Noachian Deluge is a study. There have been millions of local and partial floods ; but wherever and whenever a traveller finds the legend of an inundation he incontinently applies it to 'the Flood.' Dr. Livingstone could not refrain from so doing at the petty Lake Dilolo. And it is to be noted that the Egyptians, accustomed to annual freshets, utterly ignored one general cataclysm as held by the Greeks.

[3] 'Nuhu' is found in the Nahrai tomb, Beni Hasan (Osburn, i. 239) ; other names are Noum, Nouf, and Nef.

[4] Amun Ra (Hephæstus, Vulcan), the veiled Osiris, the 'Hidden One of Thebes,' is thus addressed in a papyrus :—

He is One only, alone sans equal,
Dwelling above in the Holy of Holies.

Another describes him as 'Maker of all things ; whose beginning was the beginning of the world ; whose forms are various and manifold ; the first to exist ; the one only Being, and the Parent of all who live.'

[5] Mr. Froude *metaphysicises* when he tells us that the religion of Egypt is the adoration of physical forces. Mankind do not worship abstractions ; they begin (and mostly end) by adoring man.

[6] Blind because she saw with insight, not physical vision. Her eyes are hidden by blinkers or 'goggles.' Her usual name is Ma, and her ideograph is the ell-measure.

[7] Even 'God save the King' must be referred back to them.

[8] It is an aorist from 'Havah ;' so φύσις from φύω, and *natura* from *nascor*. Mystically, *Ya* is the past, *Ha* the present, and *Vah* the future.

tained Prophets (*Sem*),[1] High Priests,[2] Priests, 'Holy Fathers,' and Scribes. The Decalogue is a *résumé* of the forty-two commandments in the Deadbook (chapter 125). The portable shrines of the great Egyptian gods originated the Tabernacle, which grew to be the Temple; it corresponds with the Σχήνη ἱερὰ or movable tent of the Carthaginians. The African practice of circumcision was probably intended originally as a prophylactic against syphilis, of which traces have been found in prehistoric bones. The peculiar Jewish hatred for pork is reasonless unless we explain it by a superstitious horror of the Typhonian beast. Rationalists tell us that the meat was religiously forbidden because unwholesome in the tropics, a *causa non causa* : it is the favourite food in the Brazil, in China, and in Christian India; even the Maráthás will eat wild hog; nor are the habits of the animal more filthy than the duck's. The truth is that these dietary prohibitions served to make a *differentia*, to disunite man, to pit race against race and to feed the priest.

But while the Hebrews drew largely upon the wisdom (and the unwisdom) of Egypt, they ruthlessly cast out the eminently Nilotic ideas of a Soul, of a Judgment of the Dead, and of a future state of rewards and punishments—three tenets which, in modern days, form the very foundation of all faiths. 'If a man die, shall he live (again)?' asks Job (xiv. 14), in a chapter showing that life once lost is lost for ever.[3] And apparently from the days of Moses this was the peculiarity of 'Semitic' thought; it lived in the Present and had no Future, or rather it spurned the world to come. 'Moses,' says Professor Owen, 'could not admit the after-life, or teach of reward and retribution in a future state, without risk of tainting his monotheism with some trace of the manifold symbolism environing the "divine son of Amen" (Osiris), who after suffering loss of the mortal life, which he had assumed for bettering his kind, became, on resigning his divinity, their judge.' The Hebrews adopted Soul and Judgment, Heaven and Hell, many centuries after Moses from their Assyrian kinsmen,[4] who also supplied them with their present names for the twelve months and sundry astronomical notions. And their modern descendants by universally accepting a Resurrection have done that against which Moses so carefully guarded.

[1] My fellow-traveller, the Rev. W. Robertson Smith, has neglected the derivation of the 'Prophet' grade by Jewry from Egypt; his interesting volume (*The Old Testament, &c.*) wants more Egyptianism. The Prophets of Nile-land had their merits; they foretold that Pharaoh Necho's Suez Canal would be more useful to strangers than to natives.

[2] The High Priest's robe in Jewry had 366 bells, symbolising the days of the Sothic-sidereal year. In the times of the early Pharaohs, the 'Queen of the New Year' appeared in coincidence with the beginning of the solar year. The Sothic æra had been fixed from observations before Thut-mes III. (Eighteenth Dynasty, circ. B.C. 1580).

[3] Yet the end of chap. xix. is distinctly teleological. Were there two Jobs?

[4] Abraham, the legendary forefather of the Hebrews, was a Chaldæan from Ur of the Chaldees. On the east bank of the Euphrates lies Uru-ki, Erech, or Warká, fronted by Ur, Uru, or Mughayr: the Bedawin still call the latter 'Urhha' in memory of 'Ur.' Thus Abraham was a hill-man from the harsh and rugged regions fringing Southern Armenia. Hence the 'Jewish face,' with its strongly marked features and its wealth of hair and beard, appears everywhere in the sculptures of ancient Babylonia and Persia. Hence, too, the superficial observation that the Afghans and hill-tribes west of the Indus are Jews because they have the typical Jewish look. The reason is that all are derived from the same ethnic centre, a great watershed of race.

I need hardly say that the mythologies of Greece, Etruria, and Rome only corrupted Egyptian mysteries and metaphysics. Three instances will suffice : Charon is a degraded Horus ; Minos is Mena, and Rhadamanthus contains the word Amenti, the right side (of Osiris), the west. Nor can we be surprised if Egypt is now giving rise to scientific superstitions. Every reader of 'Pyramid Literature' will note the mysterious influence which Kemi is exercising upon the modern mind.[1]

In the preceding chapters I have noted the development of metallurgy by the ancient Egyptians. They probably began with gold,[2] the easiest of all ores to find and to work ; it was abundant in Upper Egypt, and about B.C. 1600 they found a California in 'Kush' (Æthiopia). They called it Tum, Khetem, and Nb, which is variously pronounced Nebu, Neb, and Nub, whence Nubia. It has two hieroglyphic determinatives ⚊⚊⚊ ⚼, the necklace and the washing-bowl covered with the straining-cloth. The Kemites called silver 'white gold,'[3] showing the movement of invention ; and they could draw silver wire three thousand years ago. Wilkinson (II. chap. viii.) remarks, 'The position of the silver-mines is unknown'; but he wrote before the discovery of Midian, where surface-stones have been picked up containing three ounces per ton. As their pictures prove, they worked iron, although little has outlasted the corrosion of Time. They applied the blow-pipe to the works of the whitesmith. They were well acquainted with soldering by lead or alloys,[4] as is shown by the Shesh or Sistrum of Mr. Burton. I may here remark parenthetically that this *crepitaculum* used in temple-service gave rise to the Maracá or Tammaraka, the sacred rattle, a gourd full of pebbles worshipped by the Brazilian Tupis, who thus acknowledged the mysterious influence of rhythmic sounds.[5] They were skilful in the damascening [6] or inlaying of weapons, an invention claimed

---

[1] In this section of the nineteenth century three popular crazes are producing a literature of vigorous growth. The first is the Shakespearian ; not Shakespeare, but Bacon, or some other Palmerstonian pet, wrote Shakespeare. The second, apparently a byblow of the Book of Mormon, is the descent of John Bull from the 'Lost Tribes,' who were never lost. The third is the Pyramid craze ; and the rough common sense of the public has embodied it in 'the Inspired British Inch' : these Pyramidists mostly forget that *the* Pyramid is one of three greater and some seventy lesser items which form the cemetery of Memphis.

[2] Yet it is remarkable, observes Brugsch (i. 212), that from the earliest ages the curse of the Typhonic gods clings to gold. So Plutarch (*Isis and Osiris*) tells us that the worshippers were directed not to wear the noble metal ; and this still is a general rule in El-Islam.

[3] Silver, the 'next folly of mankind,' says Pliny (*Nat. Hist.* xxxiii. 31), showing his own, and rivalling Horace's 'aurum irrepertum et sic melius situm.' Strange to say, neither old Egypt nor Assyria had a coinage, which Herodotus (i. 94) and a host of other

writers attribute to the Lydians, the forefathers of the Etruscans. Its representative in the Nile Valley was the ring-money, which extended to ancient Britain, and which is still preserved in many parts of Africa. The golden 'manillas' discovered at Dali (Idalium) in Cyprus, where the breaks of the circle are adorned with the heads of animals, lions and asps, show what the now meaningless thickening of these parts originally meant.

[4] 'Lead is also united by the aid of white lead (tin) ; white lead with white lead by the agency of oil' (Pliny, xxxiii. 30).

[5] *The Captivity of Hans Stade*, p. 145.

[6] Properly speaking, to 'damascene' is confined to 'grit' or inlaid iron or steel, the word evidently deriving from Damascus, once so famous for Swords. Johnson (*Dict.*, Longmans, 1805) explains the word 'damask,' 'linen or silk woven in a manner invented at Damascus, by which part, by a various direction of the threads, exhibits flowers or other forms.' Percy (*Metal.* p. 185) inclines towards 'Damascus'; but he suggests that the 'word "damask" applied to steel may have been derived, not from the place of manu-

by those model ' claimants,' the Greeks. Their simple process was to cut out the ground, to hammer in gold and silver, and, finally, to file and polish the surface.[1]

The metallurgic proficiency of Old Egypt would lead to the development of arms and armour, and enable the soldier to win easier victories over the ' vile, impure, and miserable Gentiles '—i.e. all men except themselves. The god Anhar, or Shu, is ' Lord of the Scymitar.' Horus, as a hawk-headed mummied deity, is seated holding two Swords. Amen-Ra, Lord of Hab, is a 'great god Ramenma, " Lord of the Sword." ' The ' wearer of the Pshent or double crown ' (the Pharaoh), the image of Monthu, god of war, was *ex-officio* ' His Holiness' (high-priest) and Commander-in-Chief, who personally led his warriors to ' wash their hearts ' (cool their valours) as the Zulus wash their spears. Like Horus, he is ' valiant with the Sword.'[2] When going to war he was presented with the ' Falchion of Victory,' and thus addressed : ' Take this weapon, and smite with it the heads of the unclean.' In paintings and sculptures he is a large and heroic figure : he draws the bow, he spears or cuts down the foe, and he drives his war-car over the bodies of the slain. His soldiers are divided into Calasiri (Krashr[3] or bowmen) and Hermotybians, the latter unsatisfactorily derived[4] from ἡμιτύβιον, a strong linen (waist- ?) cloth. The two divisions represent the second of the five castes, ranking below the priestly and above the agricultural : they held one of the three portions into which the land was divided. Recruits were taught in the military schools that originated the Pentathlon and the Pancratium, the Palæstra and the Gymnasium. They were carefully trained to gymnastics, as the monumental pictures in the Beni Hasan tombs show ; they used Mogdars or Indian clubs, and they excelled in wrestling, though not in boxing. The royal statues are those of athletes, with their broad shoulders, thin flanks and well-developed muscles. The soldier practised single-stick, the right hand being apparently protected by a basket-guard, and the left fore-arm shielded by a splint or splints of wood, strapped on, and serving for a shield (fig. 152).

The standing army consisted of foot and horse,[5] the latter being mostly in chariots ; and they were divided into corps, regiments, battalions, and companies. The men were officered by Chiliarchs (colonels), Hekatontarchs (captains), and Dekarchs (sergeants), as the Greeks called them. The 'heavies' were armed with a long strong

---

facture but from a fancied resemblance between the markings in question and the damask patterns on textile fabrics.'

[1] This process resembles our niello (nigellum) inlaying. The oldest composition contained most silver and no lead. Percy (*Metallurgy*, p. 23) gives us its history : the first treatise by Theophilus, *alias* Rugerus, a monk of the early eleventh century, was translated by Robert Hendrick (London, 1847).

[2] Plutarch relates (*De Isid.* 2) of Ochus (Thirty-first Dynasty), who, amongst other acts of tyranny, caused the sacred bull Apis to be made roast beef, that he was represented in the Catalogue of Kings by a Sword.

[3] *Krshu, Krasher,* or *Krershra.* The determinative is a squatting archer with bow and arrows. Marvellous to say, Brugsch (i. 51) mentions ' clubs, axes, bows and arrows,' utterly neglecting the Sword.

[4] Egyptian national names give derivation to, but do not derive from, Greek. According to Pollux (vii. 71), however, *Hemitybion* is Egyptian, evidently corrupted.

[5] The horse, apparently unknown to the First Dynasty of Memphis, was familiar to the Second. Mr. Gladstone (*Primer of Homer*, p. 97 : Macmillan, 1878) supposes that the animal came from Libya or Upper Egypt; but the African horse probably originates from Asia. The first illustrations of horses and chariots are found at Eileithyias, *temp.* Aah-mes, Amos, Amosis, B.C. 1500.

FIG. 152.—SINGLE-STICK IN EGYPT.

FIG. 153.—EGYPTIAN SOLDIER AND SHIELD.

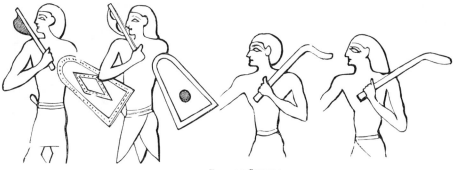

IG. 154.—EGYPTIAN SOLDIERS.

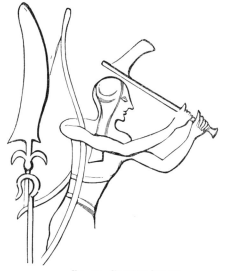

FIG. 155.—EGYPTIAN SOLDIER.

FIG. 156.—1. EGYPTIANS FIGHTING, FROM
PAINTINGS OF THEBES; 2. EGYPTIAN
SOLDIERS, FROM THEBAN BAS-RELIEFS.

spear and an immense shield provided with a sight-hole. Some carried the 'Lisán'-club, the battle-axe, and the mace ; and almost all had for side arms pole-axes,[1] Swords, falchions, and daggers. The 'light bobs' were chiefly archers and slingers, also weaponed with 'Lisáns,' axes, warflails, and Swords. The chariot-corps or cavalry, besides bows and arrows, had clubs and short Swords for close quarters. The battle-axes show clear derivation from the stone celt, which supplied the hiero-glyphs with the word Natr or Netr (Neter, &c.), meaning god, gods, or goddess ( ]).[2] In the Demotic alphabet the axe was K (*Kelebia*).

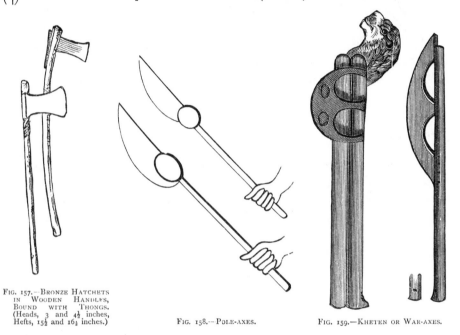

FIG. 157.—BRONZE HATCHETS IN WOODEN HANDLES, BOUND WITH THONGS. (Heads, 3 and 4½ inches, Hefts, 15½ and 16¼ inches.)

FIG. 158.—POLE-AXES.

FIG. 159.—KHETEN OR WAR-AXES.

The action began, at the sound of the trumpet, with an advance of light-infantry, bowmen, slingers, and javelineers. Then came the charge by the ponderous pha-lanx of ten thousand men, one hundred in front by one hundred deep, and flanked by chariots and cavalry. Thus the close combat was not the disorderly system of duels that prevailed in the barbarous Middle Ages of Europe. In storming fortified places they used the pavoise and testudo, the ram, the scaling-ladder, the bulwark or movable tower, and the portable bridge. They were also skilful military miners.

[1] The pole-axe was three feet long, the handle being two; the blade varied from ten to fourteen inches, and below it was a heavy meta ball, some four inches in diameter, requiring a powerful arm. The club in the British Museum, armed with wooden teeth, is not represented on the monuments, and probably belonged to some barbarous tribe.

[2] I have already discussed the Stone Age in Egypt and in Africa (chap. iii.). We must not, however, determine it to be pre-metallic without further study. Herodotus first notices it when he tells us that the Ethiopians in the army of Xerxes used stone-tipped arrows.

The Egyptian phalanx was armed with the large shield, lance, and Sword ; the latter was generally called Seft, ⌐ \, or ⌐ ⎯ ⊹\, or ⌐ ⎯\ ; also inverted to Setf, ⎯\ : it becomes Sifet in Æthiopia, and in Berber Siwuit. The weapon in the hieroglyphs is of four different shapes. The first is the boomerang-Sword ⌐, *m* or *ma*, meaning 'to destroy': this M is the root of the Hebrew and Arabic *Maut* and the Prakrit-Sanskrit, *Mar*. The second is the Knife-Sword ⌐, *At* or *Kat*, the determinative of cutting. These two are joined ⌐ in the root *ma* (cut, mow). The third is the Khopsh, Khepsh, or Khepshi, ⌐, the sickle-Sword, still used in Abyssinia and throughout Africa : with a flattened curve it became the Hindu Kubja, the Greek 'Kopis,' and the Gurkha 'Kukkri.' The second two are combined in the root Smam, ⌐ ⌐ ⌐, 'to smite.' Other names of the Sword are Ta or Nai, ⌐ ⌐, and Nai, Na'ui, or Nakhtui, ⌐ ⌐ ⌐ ⌐.

The falchion (*ensis falcatus*), called Shopsh, Khepsh, or Khopsh,[1] is represented as early as the Sixth Dynasty (after B.C. 3000). Hence, says Meyrick, the Κοπὶς of Argos—Argolis being a very mixed province, where the base was Pelasgian and

[1] I cannot but suspect the word of being a congener of our 'chop.' Mr. Gerald Massey, author of *A Book of the Beginnings*, favoured me with his opinion upon the 'scymitar Khopsh.' He identifies it with the hinder thigh (, *Shepsh*, or , *Khepsh*), of the 'old Genitrix' of the Typhonian type, *Kfa* or *Kefa* (force, power, might); the Goddess of the Great Bear and the place of birth. Hence the (*Ru*) or 'mouth' of the Sword came to be synonymous with the 'edge' of the Sword (Genesis xxxiv. 36). In the Denderah zodiac, the central figure, the 'old Genitrix,' holds the Khopsh-chopper or falchion with the right hand. The 'thigh of Khepsh' is also the Egyptian rudder-oar. The Great Bear Khepsh is one of the earliest measures of the Seasons : the Chinese still say that at nightfall the 'handle of the northern bushel' (tail of Ursa Major) points east in spring, south in summer, west in autumn, and north in winter.

Mr. Gerald Massey's two fine volumes have secured him, and will secure him, much bitter and hostile criticism from the many-headed who are lynx-eyed as to details while they overlook the general scheme. His object has been to show that religion and literature, science and art, originated in Egypt; and here he is undoubtedly right. Relying upon the self-evident fact that the language of the hieroglyphs contains 'Semitic' as well as 'Aryan' roots and derivative forms, he traces these throughout the languages of the world. Whether we judge his work conclusive or not, we cannot but admire and applaud the vast reading and research which he has brought to bear upon the most interesting subject.

And in another way Mr. Massey has done good. He has uttered a lively and emphatic protest against the Sanskritists and their over-weening pretensions. In vol. ii. (p. 56) he shows how shallow is the conclusion that Ophir was in India because the produce brought back by Solomon's fleets had, according to Professor Max Müller, Sanskrit or Dravidian names. '*Koph*' the ape is *Kapi* in Sansk.; but it is pure Egyptian, *Kapi*, whence the Gr. κῆπ-ος or κῆβ-ος. '*Tukkiyim*' (peacocks) resembles the Toki of Tamil and the Togei of Malabar; but the root is evidently the Egyptian *Tekh* or *Tekai*, a symbolical bird. '*Shen habim*' (teeth of elephant = tusks) may derive from the Sansk. *Ibau*, an elephant, but the latter is originally *Ab* in Egyptian. These erroneous views, coming from an authoritative source, are at once accepted, copied into popular books, and find their way round the world, to the confusion of true knowledge. They make it our hapless fate to learn, unlearn, and relearn. See 'ape' in Smith's *Dict. of the Bible*, and, to quote one in dozens, the *Trans. Anthrop. Soc.* p. 435, May 1882,—'the name for ape in "Kings" and in Greek authors, both adopted from Sanskrit.'

Mr. Massey unfortunately has not studied Arabic, hence many views which will hardly find acceptance. In interpreting the hieroglyphics he has wisely preferred the ideographic symbolism and the determinatives which, countless ages ago, preceded the phonetic and alphabetic forms.

the superstructure was Egyptian ; the latter introduced by Danaus, and followed by the Phœnicians, who founded the town Phœnicia. Quintus Curtius (lib. iii.) says : 'Copides vocant gladios leviter curvatos, falcibus similes, quibus appetebant belluarum manus.' Apuleius ('Met.' lib. xi.) also speaks of 'copides et venabula.'[1]

Evidently the Egyptian Sf, Sefi, Seft, or 'Sword' generically,[2] gave rise to the Mesopotamian Sibir, Sibirru, and Sapara ; to the Greek ξίφ-os ; to the Aramæan Saiph, Sipho, and to the Arabic صَيْف (Sayf-un), the second syllables being merely terminative ; while the Latin *spatha* and the German Schwerte, and our Swerde and Sword, are the latest echoes of Sef and Seft. The Germans say rightly, ' Nichts wandert so leicht als Waffen und Waffennamen.'

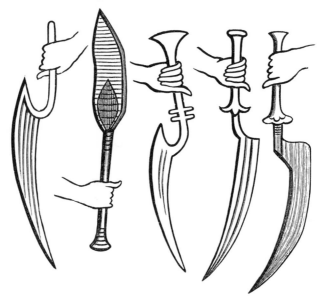

FIG. 160.—DIFFERENT FORMS OF THE EGYPTIAN KHOPSH (KOPIS), WITH EDGES INSIDE AND OUTSIDE.

Another Egyptian name for the sickle-shaped blade is Khrobi,[3] which suggests the Hebrew Hereb (a weapon, a Sword). We are also sure that the words are primitive Egyptian : the proof is that the symbol of 'Má' ('destroy' &c.), the Khopsh or *ensis falcatus*, is the numeral nine ; and the straight flesh-blade (*Kt*) is the pronoun thou, thee : the two together alluded to the oldest religious practice.[4]

The falchion, shaped in the pattern of Ursæ major (?), was thick-backed and weighted with bronze ; the blade, in later days at least,[5] was of iron or steel, as shown by the blue colour. Champollion[6] notices blue Swords with golden hilts in

---

[1] For further notice of the Kopis, see chap. xi.

[2] Also *v.* to decapitate : the Coptic form is *Sebi* or *Sefi*.

[3] Bunsen, v. 758.

[4] Bunsen's *Egypt*, v. 429. According to Castor, the two Swords pointed at the throat of a kneeling man was the priest's stamp denoting pure beasts, fit for sacrifice. He has noted that this survival points distinctly to human sacrifice in older days.

[5] Yet the tombs at Beni Hasan date 900 years before the popular era of the Trojan war.

[6] *Monum.* 262 fol., plates 11, 15.

the tomb of Ramses III., and a 'weapon Kops' with the gold, of which the hilt consists, running up the concave back of the blade. 'The gold was therefore either

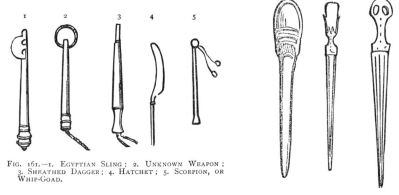

FIG. 161.—1. EGYPTIAN SLING; 2. UNKNOWN WEAPON; 3. SHEATHED DAGGER; 4. HATCHET; 5. SCORPION, OR WHIP-GOAD.

FIG. 162.—EGYPTIAN DAGGERS.

sunk into the iron, or gilded on the back. In other cases the Kops of kings was entirely of gold, or, like other Swords, entirely of brass (copper?). In another

FIG. 163.—EGYPTIAN DAGGER OF BRONZE IN BRITISH MUSEUM.

FIG. 164.—OFFICER OF LIFE-GUARD TO RAMSES II., APPARENTLY ASIATIC.

FIG. 165.—BRONZE SWORD, FOUND AT AL-KANTARAH, EGYPT.

similar weapon, brass (copper?) and iron were blended in the blade.' An iron 'Kops' was found in a tomb at Gurnah.

The Khopsh, a sickle in type, and originally a throwing weapon as well as a cutting arm, was always carried by the Pharaoh, who used it indifferently with the pike (*Taru*), the mace, axe (*Aka, Akhu*), battle-axe, or pole-axe (*Kheten*). Officers and privates, 'lights' as well as 'heavies,' also wielded it in pictures. Those commanding infantry-corps are armed with the simple stick like the Roman centurion and our drill-sergeant of bygone days.

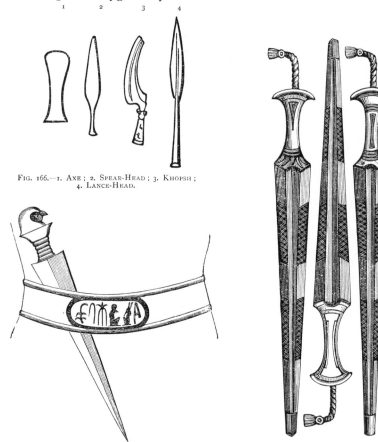

FIG. 166.—1. AXE ; 2. SPEAR-HEAD ; 3. KHOPSH ;
4. LANCE-HEAD.

FIG. 167.—BELT AND DAGGER.

FIG. 168.—EGYPTIAN DAGGERS.

The fourth or long-straight Sword, which does not appear in the hieroglyphs, had a two-edged cut-and-thrust leaf-shaped blade from two and a half to three feet long,[1] with a foining point like that of the Somal.[2] These large weapons seem to have

---

[1] Rosellini shows a long tapering blade with a mid-rib, apparently sunken, and a raised surface on each side. The length is divided into five parts, smooth and hatched (?).

[2] The Somal have retained three other notable peculiarities of ancient Egypt ; the wig (worn by the

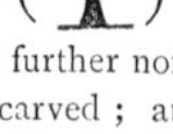

old Nilotes) ; the *Uts* (𓊽) or wooden head-stool acting pillow, which further north was a half-cylinder of alabaster finely carved ; and the ostrich-feather head-gear. The latter was a symbol of Truth among the old Egyptians, because, says Hor Apollo, the wing-

been used by foreign mercenaries. The leaf- also becomes a trowel-form, betraying its origin and derivation, the spear-head. The grip was hollowed away in the centre, gradually thickening at either end, and was sometimes inlaid with metal, stones, and precious woods. The pommel of that worn in the Pharaoh's girdle is surmounted by one or more hawk-heads, this bird being the symbol of Ra [1] (the Sun). The handle is also adorned with small pins and studs of gold, shown through suitable openings in the front part of the sheath. With this weapon the warrior stabs the enemy in the throat, as Mithras strikes the bull behind the shoulder. A modified form was the Sword-dagger, of which two are sometimes represented with the Pharaoh : it was generally carried in the belt. This shape of weapon found its

FIG. 169.—ASSYRIAN DAGGERS, SHEATHS, AND BELTS. (BRITISH MUSEUM.)

way to the Caucasus ; [2] and the Georgian Khanjar, hanging to the girdle in the place of the Sword, is also a survival.

The Egyptian weapon is of various lengths. The bronze blade of Amunoph II., found by Wilkinson at Thebes, measures only five and a quarter inches : others rise to seven and even ten. Mr. Salt's specimen in the British Museum covers eleven and a half inches, including the handle ; and others reach one foot, and even sixteen inches. Many of these blades taper from an inch and a half to two-thirds

feathers are of equal length. The Romans adopted it as a military decoration. 'Your courage has not yet given your helmet wherewithal to shade your face from the burning sun,' say the Kurds, who add to the crest a new feather for every foe slain in fight. The Somal, after victory or murder, stick the white variety in the mop-head. We still use the phrase 'a feather in his cap.' The 'Prince of Wales' feather' is an Egyptian ideograph of Truth. Mr. Gerald Massey seems to think that Wilkinson s '*Thmei*' (II. chap. viii.) is 'only a backward rendering of the Greek "*Themis*"'; that the feathers are '*Shu*' (𝄞𝄞), and

that the goddess is '*Ma*' (▬▬ ▬), or '*Mati.*' But surely the root of *Themis* would be in ' *Ta-Ma,*' *the* Goddess (of Truth) ?

[1] Compare *Ŕaa*, Heb. and Ar., 'he saw'; Gr. ὁράω, and Lat. *Ra-dius.*

[2] Colonel A. Lane Fox remarks that the groove which is constant in these Caucasian blades is a little out of the central line, and does not correspond on each side, an alternation showing that it is derived from the ogee form. I have suggested that the idea arose from the arrow-head 'bellied on a twist,' and have figured the weapon in the next page (fig. 170).

of an inch near the point. Dr. John Evans[1] has a Sword, found at 'Great Kantara' during the construction of the Suez Canal; the blade is leaf-shaped, and measures seventeen inches, and the whole length twenty-two inches and three-eighths (fig. 165). 'Instead of a hilt-plate, it is drawn down to a small tang about three-sixteenths of an inch square. This again expands into an octagonal bar about three-eighths of an inch in diameter, which has been drawn down to a point, and then turned back to form a hook, perhaps the earliest mode of hanging to the belt.' At the base of the blade are two rivet-holes, and the hilt must have been formed of two pieces which clasped the tang. Dr. Evans also mentions a bronze Sword-blade, presumably from Lower Egypt, in the Berlin Museum: it has an engraved line down each

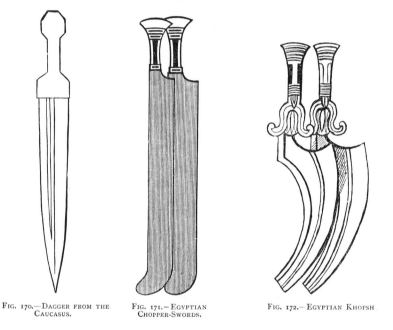

FIG. 170.—DAGGER FROM THE CAUCASUS.　　FIG. 171.—EGYPTIAN CHOPPER-SWORDS.　　FIG. 172.—EGYPTIAN KHOPSH

side of the blade; it is more uniform in width than the Kantara specimen, and the hilt is broken off.

Not a few Egyptian Swords are much thicker at the middle than at the edges, and many are slightly grooved. The bronze is so well tempered, either by hammering, by hydraulic pressure, or by phosphorisation (?), that it has retained spring and pliability after several thousand years, and is still elastic like the steel of our modern days. I have already noticed[2] the Passalacqua and the Harris daggers—both from Thebes. The dagger-handle was generally covered in part with metal like that of the Sword; and the sewing of the leather-sheath again recalls the hide-scabbard of the Somal.[3] The Egyptians, as the hieroglyphs prove, had also single-edged

[1] *Bronze, &c.* p. 298.　　　[2] Chap. v.　　　I sent a small collection of Somali weapons to the
[3] Returning from the exploration of Harar (1853),　　United Service Institution.

cutting-knives shorter than Swords, and apparently of steel; they resemble our flesh-knives,[1] and may correspond with the Greek μάχαιραι (Ang.-Sax. *Meche*), while the daggers proper represent the ἐγχειρίδια and the parazonia.

The long Sword must have been rare or rather barbaric, for it is seldom found in the pictures and bas-reliefs. Yet Rosellini figures one which resembles an Espadon or heavy two-handed weapon of our Middle Ages. An inscription of Ramses takes as booty from the Maxyes (Cyrenians) of Libya one hundred and fifteen Swords of five cubits (seven and a half feet), and one hundred and twenty-four of three cubits long.

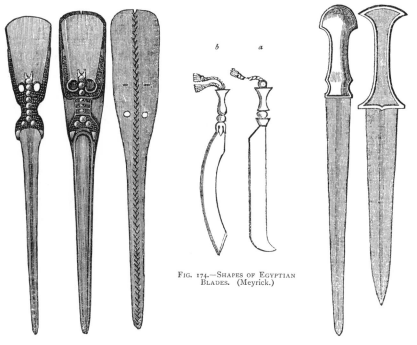

FIG. 174.—SHAPES OF EGYPTIAN BLADES. (Meyrick.)

FIG. 173.—BRONZE DAGGERS AND SHEATH (1 FOOT LONG). (From Theban Tomb, Berlin Museum.)

FIG. 175.—SWORD-DAGGERS.

Meyrick,[2] in his general introduction to the weapons of all nations (vol. i. Pl. 1), gives two forms of Egyptian blades, or rather choppers. One (*a*, fig. 174) is a straight bill-shaped cutting-blade with the tip upturned, and the handle is provided with cords and tassels. This is in fact the old Turkish Scymitar and its offshoots, of which I have already spoken; and thus Egypt led to the chopper-types, which will presently be noticed. The other (*b*) is a curved Scymitar, with a bevelled end and a double cord at the hilt.[3] The former seems to be an imitation of the obsidian flake: the latter is a development of the Khopsh or sickle-Sword.

---

[1] The form is accurately preserved in the formidable Afghan 'Charay' or one-edged knife.

[2] *A Critical Inquiry*, &c.

[3] I have shown that the heraldic Sword in the East preserves this double sword-knot (chap. vii.).

And here I must temporarily abandon the chronological for the geographical order, and briefly treat of the Sword in modern Africa.

In the Dark Continent, as in the New World, the weapon has scant importance. Reviewing the arms of the former 'Quarter,' we must conclude that its favourites are the war-axe (employed in rough work), and the spear [1] (used in fine work); while the Sword proper is confined, as a rule, to Moslem Africa.

We have seen that in olden time the Mashaua (Maxyes) of Libya, bordering upon Egypt, used large Swords. The Adyrmachidæ, or 'first Libyans' of Herodotus (iv. 168), called by Silius Italicus (iii. 219) 'gens accola Nili,' were also armed with curved blades.

Denham and Clapperton inform us that the Knights of Malta exported great numbers of the straight double-edged blades which they affected, to Benghazi, in North Africa, where they were exchanged for bullocks. From the Tripolitan they were borne across the Sahará to Bornu, to Hausa-land, and to Kano, where they were remounted for the use of the negroid Moslem population. Modern travellers note that the trade still continues at Kano, where some fifty thousand blades were annually imported across the Mediterranean—the reason is that these negroids cannot make their own. Hence they are passed on to the Pule (Fulah) and Fulbe tribes, the Hausas, the Bornuese, and others dwelling in the north-western interior. The great Mandenga family, miscalled Mandingos, are also purchasers of European blades, which they mount and sheathe for themselves. Far to the south-east Mr. Henry M. Stanley (*loc. cit.* i. 454) notes that the 'King of Kishakka possesses an Arab scimitar, which is a venerated heirloom of the royal family, and the sword of the founder of that kingdom' (?).

Barth ('Travels') has left us accurate though scanty details concerning the weapons of the North-Western and West-Central Africa. 'Spears and Swords' (say the people) 'are the only manly and becoming weapons.' The blade, mostly made at Solingen,[2] characterises the free and noble Amoshágh or Imoshágh; and all travellers remark that it preserves the old knightly form of crusading days; the low-caste Tawárik carry only the lance and the regular African Telak or arm-knife. The Forawy trust almost wholly to their Swords: the Kel-Owy (Khayl, or people, of the Owi Valley) and the Kel-Geres carry spear, Sword, and dagger. The Imgád, a degraded tribe of the negroid Berbers, are not allowed to use either Sword or spear: similarly the bow is confined to the servile caste among the Somal. The son of the Kazi, near Agades, was armed with an iron spear, Sword, and dagger (vol. i. 395): a Musghu chief had a boomerang-Sword (Front. vol. iii.). Few of the Baghirmi can afford 'Kaskara' (Swords), and they rarely wear the Kinyá or arm-knife: the favourite weapon of these races, as well as the Kamuri or Bornavis,

---

[1] The Baghirmi, according to Denham, adore a long lance of peculiar construction: this spear-worship is also practised by the Marghi and the Musghu. It extended from ancient Rome to certain of the Pacific Isles; while the Fijians worship the war-club. At Baroda in Gujarát superstitious honours are paid to the Gaekhwar's golden cannons with silver wheels.

[2] English and Styrian razors are also largely imported.

is the Njiga or Golîyo, which has been noticed under the name of Danisko.[1] It is a short and double-pointed Egyptian hand-bill, thrown, as well as used for cutting. At Sokoto the traveller found good iron (iv. 180) : at Kano, in Hausaland, he observed a blacksmith making, with the rudest tools, a leaf-shaped dagger, a long-ribbed, highly decorated, and very sharp blade. The Tawárik call the smith 'Enhad'; in Timbukhtu he becomes the Mu'allim or artist.

The Sword-play of North Africa is that of Arabia and India, apparently borrowed from the original Sword-dance.[2] In Tangier it is picturesquely described by a lively Italian writer, Edmondo de Amicis.[3] 'There were three swordsmen, and they used the stick in pairs. It is impossible to do justice to the extravagance and buffoonery (*goffagini*) of that *school*: I call it so because we saw the same style in the other cities of Marocco. There were all the movements of the rope-dance, high leaps without object, contusions, leg-actions, and blows, announced a whole minute before by an immense sweep of the arm. Everything was done with a holy phlegm which would have allowed one of our experts to have distributed, amongst all four, a volley of blows without the least risk of receiving one.'

The old Egyptian Sword-types spread deep into the Dark Continent, and preserve their forms to the present day. The Somal's weapon shows the straight or spear-blade. The Shotel or Abyssinian Sword (fig. 176) is a direct descendant from the Khopsh-falchion. Nothing less handy than this gigantic sickle ; the edge is inside, the grip is too small, and the difficulty of drawing the blade from the scabbard is considerable. The handle, four inches long, is a rude lump of black wood, and the tang is carried to the pommel and there clinched. The coarse and ugly blade has a mid-rib running the whole length, forming a double slope to the edges ; it is one inch broad at the base, and tapers to a point which can hardly be used. The length along the arc is three feet thirty-seven inches ; the curve, measuring from arc to chord, is two inches ; and the projection beyond the directing line is four inches. The rough scabbard of untanned hide is shod with a hollow brass knob, a ferule ruder even than the blade ; and a large iron buckle affixed to the top of the scabbard under the haft, connects with a belt or waist-strap. Such a weapon never belonged to a race of Swordsmen.[4]

The Africo-Arab tribes of the Upper Nile (e.g. the Bisharín) also preserve Egyptian forms derived from the Lisán-stick. The Galla Sword is shorter and simpler than the Egyptian. But the Flissa of Northern Africa, the Yataghan whose type,

---

[1] Chap. viii.

[2] Athenæus (i. 27) speaks of the Thracian dance in arms, 'men jumping up very high with light springs, and using Swords.' At last one of them strikes another, so that it seemed to everyone that the man was wounded.

[3] *Marocco*, page 66 (Milano, Treves, 1876).

[4] Hence the ardent desire of the Abyssinians, when first visited by Europeans, to obtain civilised Swords. Father F. Alvarez (*Hakluyt Soc.* 1881), who lived in Abyssinia between 1520 and 1527, shows the Barnagais (*Bahr-Negush*, or sea-ruler) begging the Portuguese ambassador for his rich Sword and ornaments, 'as the great lords have few Swords' (chap. xxx.). Prester John (the Negush or Emperor) displays 'five bundles of short Swords with silver hilts,' taken from the Moslems (chap. cxiii.). The King of Portugal sends as a present to Prester John 'first a gold Sword with a rich hilt,' and a good fencer, Estevam Pallarte.

by the support of the Duc d'Aumale, supplied France for years with a bad bayonet, if borrowed from the Lisán, has assumed a peculiar curve.   Colonel A. Lane-Fox looks upon this Flissa of the Kabyles (= Kabáil, the tribes) as resembling the 'Kopis-blade straightened, like those represented in the hands of the Greek warrior on the vase in the Museum at Naples.'[1]   Nothing can be better adapted for close fight than the handy stabbing weapon : stuck on the end of a musket, and making the barrel top-heavy, nothing can be worse.   But, as the 'military tailor' in the British army seeks the philosopher's stone in the shape of a suit of uniform that shall be at once warm and cool, heavy and light, airy and impermeable to wet,

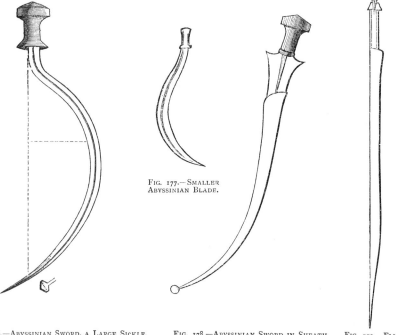

Fig. 177.—Smaller Abyssinian Blade.

Fig. 176.—Abyssinian Sword, a Large Sickle.
(Breadth at hilt, 1 inch ; tapers to point.)

Fig. 178.—Abyssinian Sword in Sheath.
(Scabbard open to allow passage of blade.)

Fig. 179.—Flissa of Kabyles.

handsome and lasting, cheap and good, so the Frenchman would transform the bayonet into a *multum in parvo*, a Sword, a saw, a *coupe-choux*, in fact everything that a bayonet is not and ought not to be.   The absurd Yataghan-bayonet has only lately been banished from the French army, and retains its place in most Continental forces.

The Sword amongst the Dankali tribes, who occupy the south-western shores of the Red Sea, north of the Somal, is evidently of European origin.   The straight, thin blade, with two or more longitudinal grooves, is about four feet long, and broadens towards the point : the handle consists of a pommel, of a grip whipped with wire, and of straight quillons, forming a regular cross-guard.   The modern

[1] *Anthrop. Coll.* p. 184.

weapons are made in Germany—I believe, at Solingen, which seems to supply all Africa north of the Equator.

Our age has at length realised the fact that the heart of Africa is inhabited by a homogeneous race speaking tongues of the same family. It is a large and strong-bodied people, often cannibal, and showing no likeness with the negro of the tobacconist-shops. Scattered amongst these man-eaters, and possibly the aborigines of the country, are comparatively dwarfish tribes, evidently the crane-fighting Pygmies of Homer and Herodotus, now known from their various clans, Aká, Tikitiki, Doko, Wambilikimo (two-cubiters), and so forth. Both the dwarfs and the (comparative) giants, of whom the Mpángwe, or Fans, first became known in Europe, are metal workers, and both work well. They despise arms and tools that chip and snap, and therefore prefer to ours, with ample reason, their charcoal-smelted native produce, and they temper it by many successive heatings and hammerings without water-quenching.[1] According to Major Serpa Pinto (ii. 128) the Barotse temper their iron with ox-grease[2] and salt. He notes, however (ii. 356), that the Ganguellas 'manufacture steel out of wrought iron, tempered by cold water, into which the metal is thrown while hot.'

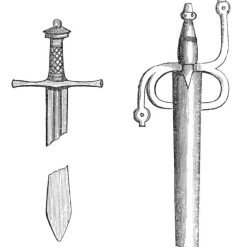

FIG. 180.—DANKALI SWORD.   FIG. 181.—CONGO SWORD.

The Gaboon river also produces the Babanga[3] (?), a leaf-shaped Sword with a square end, made at Batta, and used by the Mpángwe ; a Glaive also leaf-shaped with a long handle, having a point at the butt end, and Swords with triangular blades more or less broadened at the apex.

Upon the glorious Congo river[4] I was shown a Sword belonging to the Mijolos or Mijeres, a tribe inhabiting the upper valley. All declared it to be of native make, and used during the Sword-dance performed in presence of the Prince. But it is an evident copy of some weapon of the fifteenth century ; and the knightly model, like that of the Mpángwe (Fan) cross-bow, had drifted into the African interior. The handle and its pommel were of ivory (in poorer weapons wood is used) : the guard was a thin bar of iron springing from the junction of blade and

---

[1] *Gorilla-land*, p. 227.

[2] Quenching in oil or grease instead of water is a common practice. The workman still 'adds to the water a thin cake of grease, or pours over it hot oil, through which the steel must pass before it enters the water, for by these means it is prevented from acquiring cracks and flaws.' (Beckmann, *loc. cit.* ii. 330.)

[3] Specimens of all these weapons are in the Lane-Fox Collection, Nos. 1088 to 1100.

[4] *The Cataracts of the Congo*, p. 234.

grip ; forming an open oval-shaped *pas d'âne* below, and prolonged upwards and downwards in two quillons or branches, parallel with the hilt and protecting the hand. The blade, which had a tang for hefting, was straight, flexible, and double-edged.

In the Despotism of Unyoro, on the northern shores of the (Victoria) Nyanza Lake, Sir Samuel Baker found a knife of the Egyptian leaf-shape, the *Lingua di Bove* of the Italians. The blade has a high mid-rib, and the handle is whipped round with copper wire. It is evidently used, like the Somal weapon, for stabbing as well as cutting.

The Arabs of Zanzibar preserve the old two-handed weapon of Europe, with a thin, flattish, double-edged blade ending in a bevelled point, and much resembling the executioner's Sword prolonged. They bear the Solingen mark. Zanzibar, however, has two Swords. The shorter weapon (*a*, fig. 183) is three-grooved and single-edged, the blade measuring one foot ten inches ; the handle and sheath are of copper, embossed or engraved, and adorned with fine stones. The second (*b*, fig. 183), which is the usual shape carried by Arab gentlemen, is three feet to three and a half feet long ; the long tang tapers towards the hilt, and is cased in wood and leather ; the pommel is cylindrical, and the grip wants guard and quillons. Demmin (p. 396) finds it 'difficult to understand how this singular weapon could be wielded.' It serves mostly for show, and when wanted is used like a quarterstaff with both hands. But the Zanzibari's Sword is always clumsy, as dangerous to the wielder as the old blade of

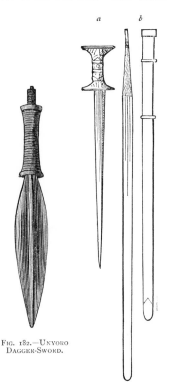

FIG. 182.—UNYORO DAGGER-SWORD.

FIG. 183.—ZANZIBAR SWORDS.

the Gauls and Ancient Britons. Their cousins, the Bedawin living about Maskat, have conserved with a religious respect, many ancient weapons won or bought in older days, and possibly dating from crusading times. These valuable articles travelled far : the Portuguese found amongst the Moors of Malacca 'Swords bearing in Latin the inscription " God help me." '

The Sword is also known to the blood-stained Despotisms that border the West Coast of Africa—Ashanti, Dahome, and Benin. Many of the shapes are borrowed : such are the Maroccan Yataghan, the Turkish or rather Persian Scymitar, and the Malay Krís (crease). Provided with silver hilts and scabbard mountings, they are generally wrapped in cloths, showing only the upper part of the sheath and grip.

Some of the forms have developed till they look almost original, especially the short broad blades pierced with holes like fish-slicers, and ending in circinal curves. They suggest the well-known Indian choppers, and probably in both coun-

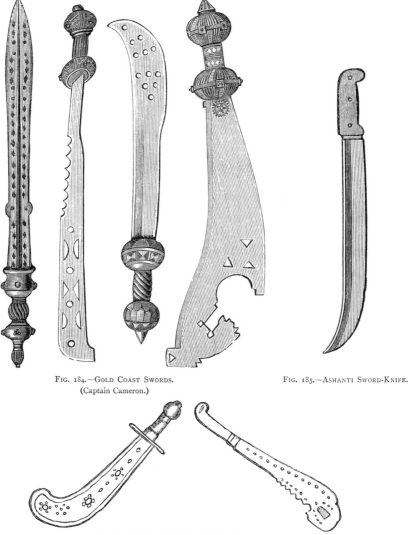

FIG. 184.—GOLD COAST SWORDS.
(Captain Cameron.)

FIG. 185.—ASHANTI SWORD-KNIFE.

FIG. 186.—SWORDS OF KING GELELE OF DAHOME.

tries they derive from Egypt. In Ashanti-land and Dahome they are mostly of iron, some are of brass, and others of gold ;[1] and they are fantastically punched

---

[1] I have noticed that arrant humbug, the cele-brated 'golden axe' which, in 1880–81, caused the last 'Ashantee scare' (*To the Gold Coast for Gold*, ii.). The thing sent to England was certainly not the great fetish which is held to be the national Palladium. An-other memento of the last Ashantee war, 'King Koffee's

into chevrons and pierced with open-work. These 'fish-slicers' are used in sacrifice and in beheading, an operation which they perform very badly. Mr. Henry M. Stanley [1] refers to 'long-handled cleaver-like weapons' amongst the savages of Makongo; and to iron bill-hooks and 'massive cleaver-looking knives with polished blades' in Karagwé.

Gezo,[2] the warrior king of Dahome or Ffon-land, who loved variety in, as well as number of, weapons,

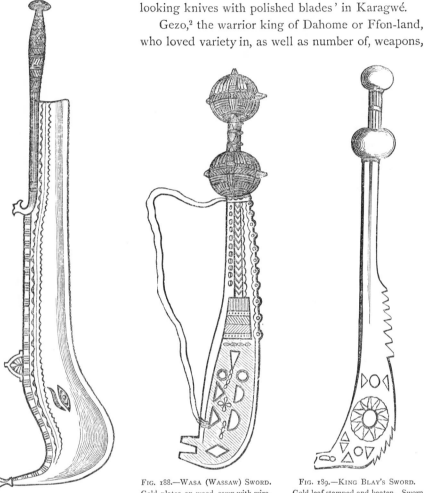

FIG. 188.—WASA (WASSAW) SWORD.
Gold plates on wood, sewn with wire, and then beaten until the stitches can scarcely be seen.

FIG. 189.—KING BLAY'S SWORD.
Gold leaf stamped and beaten. Sworn by before going to war, 'If I come back, cut my head off.'

FIG. 187.—BEHEADING SWORD.
Cutch; also used in Africa.

manufactured Swords with two blades like scissors. He also had *in terrorem* a company of 'Amazons,' called Razor-women, from the 'Nyek-ple-nen-toh' blade. This was simply a European razor on a large scale, with a steel of thirty inches

umbrella, an article of prodigious proportions, and of gaudy material,' only returned to where it was made. The type of the latter may be seen in most Italian market-places, shading the old women's fruits and

vegetables; and Manchester, I believe, had the honour of building it.

[1] *Through the Dark Continent*, i. 21.

[2] Described in my *Mission to Dahome, passim.*

rising from a plain handle of black wood, and kept open by a spring. It was used to decapitate prisoner-kings, and the very look of it made the lieges tremble.

My friend Captain Cameron [1] gives interesting details concerning the Sword in parts of Africa which he first visited, and he has kindly sent me a specimen of the Manyuema (Maniwema) Swordlet drawn to scale. He describes the Wahumla tribe as using double-edged blades of iron shaped like those of the Roman legionary. The chiefs adorn their steel blades with neat open-work in various patterns, and some carry a fringe of bells all along the lower side of the sheath. The belt of twisted hide loops into a rolled fur (often otter-skin), and ends in two bells : it is slung over the left shoulder. The Rehombo chiefs use similar blades with broad and crescent-shaped edges ; the commoners are armed with heavy spears, and short knives, also used when feeding.

The people of the central Copper-lands [2] have only long knives shaped like spear-heads. Stanley (ii. 81) calls them 'short Swords scabbarded with wood, to which are hung small brass and iron bells.' The Swords used by the chiefs under 'King Kasongo' are left unde-scribed : [3] these weapons appear to be like those seen by me on the Congo. These negroes have a kind of sham attack in honour, a custom well known amongst the Bedawin. 'When suffi-ciently bedaubed' (with pipeclay or cin-nabar) 'the chief returned the bag to his boy, and, drawing his Sword, rushed at Kasongo, seemingly intent upon cutting him down ; but just before reaching him, he suddenly fell on his knees, driving the Sword into the ground and rubbing his forehead in the dust.'

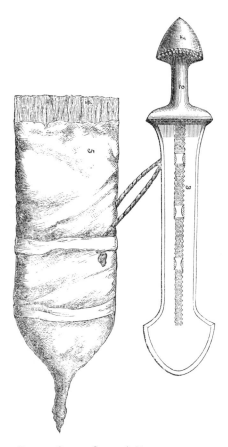

FIG. 190.—CAPTAIN CAMERON'S MANYUEMA SWORDLET, SHEATH, AND BELT. 1. Copper ; 2. Wood ; 3. Steel ; 4. Wood ; 5. Skin.

The Poucue (Pokwé) of the Lunda chiefs is not allowed to the people. This weapon (fig. 191) has also found its way from Egypt into lands far south of the Equator, and may be traced in the dagger-formed knives of the Ovampos. It

[1] *Across Africa*, vol. i. pp. 121, 139 ; vol. ii. 104.

[2] The famous copper mines of the Congo region,

whose yield, says Barbot, was mistaken for gold, are noticed in *The Cataracts of the Congo*, pp. 45, 46.

[3] Captain Cameron has brought home specimens.

is a large two-edged knife, three spans long by four inches broad : the sheath is of leather, and the weapon hangs under the left arm.[1] The Pokwé not a little resembles the short leaf-shaped iron blades from the Gaboon River, West Africa ; and these again suggest the Swords and the spear-heads of the ' Bronze Age.' Stanley (ii. 228) shows the ' Baswa knife ' on the Upper Congo exactly resembling the Pokwé; these weapons ' vary in size from a butcher's cleaver to a lady's dirk ' (?). He also found ' splendid long knives, like Persian Kummars ' (Khanjars ?) and ' bill-hook Swords.'

The Habshi people inhabiting Janjhíra (El Jezírah = the island), off the West Coast of India, south of Bombay, retain a curious relic of their African origin.

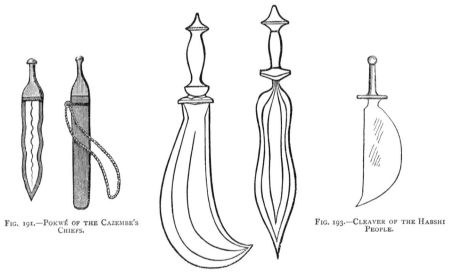

FIG. 191.—POKWÉ OF THE CAZEMBE'S CHIEFS.

FIG. 193.—CLEAVER OF THE HABSHI PEOPLE.

FIG. 192.—GABOON SWORDS, BOTH EVIDENTLY EGYPTIAN.

These negroids, who call themselves Abyssinians, are originally Wásawáhíli from Zanzibar. Their cleaver is a straightened Khopsh wholly of iron, handle, plain cross-guard and pommel (fig. 193). The blade is fifteen inches broad, the back is an inch and a half thick, and the weapon is as heavy as a man can wield. These ex-pirates, under the Habshi Nawwáb, are still feared, on account of their great strength[2] and violent temper, by all their effeminate Indian neighbours. It is well to note that in case of another ' Indian Mutiny,' we can easily raise on the eastern coast of Africa a negroid force sufficient to put it down.

Colonel A. Lane-Fox[3] remarks that one of the most peculiar forms of Sword

---

[1] From *O Muata Cazembe*, which also contains a long and valuable description of the copper mines in South-Eastern Africa, worked by the people since olden time.

[2] According to Marco Polo (lib. iii. cap. 34), the men of Zanghibar (Zanzibar) are ' both tall and stout, but not tall in proportion to their stoutness, for if they were, being so stout and brawny, they would be absolutely like giants; and they are so strong that they will carry for four men and eat for five.'

[3] *Anthrop. Coll.* p. 135.

used in Africa is the corrugated, having an ogee-section. On each face a portion of the blade is sunk on one side only, and on the other face the depression is on the reverse side. Thus the transverse section somewhat resembles the angles of the letter Z. We can understand the use of this device when adapted to the pile of the arrow or the javelin. It would give the weapon a rotatory motion on the principle of the screw-propeller, the action being only reversed instead of the screw propelling itself by acting upon the surrounding medium : in this case the air impinges upon the screw flanges and rotates the arrow, thereby increasing the accuracy of its flight. But the peculiarity has been preserved where it is wholly useless ; and, curious to say, this ogee-form is persistent in all the Swords obtained from the Caucasus, while the iron blades of Saxon and Frankish spears discovered in the graves of England and France have the same distinctive. Both may have derived it from Egypt : the Caucasians through Colchis, and Western Europe by means of the Phœnicians. The illustration is taken from the 'Pagan Saxondom' of Mr. J. Y. Akerman, who was the first to draw attention to the strange resemblance between the Saxon and Hottentot spears.[1]

FIG. 194.—FRANKISH BLADE, WITH MID-GROOVE OUT OF CENTRE.

Thus we see that whilst Egypt originated the three shapes of Sword-blades—straight, curved, and half-curved—the rest of Africa invented positively nothing in hoplology. Negroids and negroes either borrowed their weapons from Egypt or imported them from beyond the sea. Intertropical Africa never imagined an alphabet, a plough, or a Sword.

---

[1] The *Journ. Anthrop. Inst.* (August 1883) has printed an excellent paper 'On the Mechanical Methods of the Ancient Egyptians.' Mr. W. M. Flinders Petrie believes that they cut diorite with lathes and jewel graving-points (diamond ? or corundum abundant in Midian ?) ; and that the diamond was the 'piercing-stone' of early Babylonian Inscriptions.

CHAPTER IX.

THE SWORD IN KHITA-LAND, PALESTINE AND CANAAN; PHŒNICIA AND CARTHAGE; JEWRY, CYPRUS, TROY, AND ETRURIA.

CENTURIES before the Hebrews had left the Delta, a great empire bounded Nile-land on the Asiatic side, reflecting Egypt as the New World reflects the Old; in fact what Kemi was to the West, that Khita-land was to the East. The people were known to the Nile-dwellers as the Khita, Kheta, or Sheta of ⊘ ( ) ᗰᗰ. The Hebrews from the days of Abraham to the age of Nehemiah and the Captivity, called them חתים, Khitím (our Hittites), or the 'children of Heth.'[1] A hunting-inscription of Tiglath-Pileser (Tigulti-pal-Tsira) the First, B.C. 1120–1100, mentions the ⫸⫷ ⫤⫸ ⫷⫸, Kha-at-te (Khatte);[2] he makes them dwell on 'the upper Ocean of the Setting Sun.' The Greeks translated from Hebrew Γῆ Χεττιείμ, and termed the race Χεττιìμ and Χεττεινί. They are the ἑταῖροι Κήτειοι (Keteian or Cetian[3] auxiliaries) of Homer ('Odys.' xi. 520), whose leader Eurypylus, was slain with 'the copper' (Sword), and of whom many perished around him 'on account of gifts to a woman.'

The cradle of this race, which took the lead of Western Asia during the seventeenth and eighteenth centuries B.C., was the rolling prairie between the Orontes and the Euphrates. Joshua represents the Lord saying: 'From the wilderness and this Lebanon even unto the great river, the river Euphrates, all the land of the Hittites, and unto the great sea toward the going down of the sun, shall be your coast' (i. 4). In their palmy days they covered the interval between Egypt and Assyria, extending northwards to Phrygia and Cilicia; eastwards to Mesopotamia and westwards to the Mediterranean. They had walled and fortified cities as 'Tunep or Tunipa (Daphne) in the land Naharayn'[4]—the latter here

---

[1] Gen. xxiii. 18. In 2 Sam. xxiv. 6, 'Aretz tahtim-hodshi' should be read, 'Aretz ha-Hittim Kadesh,' 'the land of the Hittites of (city) Kadesh.'

[2] *Trans. Soc. Bib. Archæology,* vol. v. part 2, p. 354. They were then the paramount nation in Syria, from the Euphrates to the Libanus; and the Assyrians knew the region as Mat-Khatte.

[3] Wild work has been made with this word. Some render it 'large' (i.e. whale-like); the scholiast calls the Cetians a people of Mysia; others confound

them with the Kittaians (Chittim = Cypriots) of Menander in Josephus (*A. J.* ix. 14; Cory's *Frag.,* p. 30; London, Reeves & Turner, 1876); others with the people of Kiti (the circle), the Heb. Galil or Galilee.

[4] 'Two-river' (land) is mostly applied to the great Interamnian plain, Mesopotamia. Here it must mean Syria proper; and Aram Naharayn (Highlands of the Two Streams) admirably describes Palestine, which is composed of a double anticlinal

meaning Upper Palestine—Arathu (Aradus) ; Hamatu (Hamath, the high city) ; Khalbu or Khilibu (Aleppo) ;[1] Kazantana (Gozanitis) ; Nishiba (Nisipis) and Patena, which gave rise to 'Padan-Aram' and to 'Batanæa.' Their northern capital was Carchemish (the Gr. Hierapolis and the modern Yaráblus),[2] on the Euphrates, lately explored : some explain the word as 'Kar' (town of) 'Chemish' the Moab-god) ; others by 'Khem' or 'Chemmis,' the Egyptian Pan. It was captured by Sargon (B.C. 717), and became the head-quarters of an Assyrian Satrapy. Their sacred city was Kadesh (Κάδης, the holy), a synonym of El-Kuds, the Arabic name for Jerusalem ; and even of the City of David it was said (Ezek. xvi. 3), 'her father was an Amorite and her mother a Hittite.' A Hittite tribe extended to the southernmost frontiers of Palestine (Gen. xxiii. *passim*) ; Hebron, one of their settlements, was founded, we are told, seven years before Zoan ('a station for loading animals'), *alias* San or Tanis, the capital of the Egyptian 'Shepherd-Kings.' But the allusion must be to Sesostris-Ramses (II.), who also made San his capital under the name of 'Pi- (city of) Ramessu,' not to the original building by King Pepi of the Sixth Dynasty, who preceded Abraham by a thousand years.

The Hittites were governed by twelve 'kings,' probably satraps, under the Khita-sir or supreme chief. The 'kings of the Hittites' are mentioned as joining the Egyptians (2 Kings iii. 6).[3] Although the Hebrews were ordered utterly to destroy the race, their books prove that the Khita were often in intimate relation with the intruders, as in the case of Uriah the Hittite, one of the thirty of David's body-guard. They worshipped Baal Sutech (Sutekh) the War-god, the 'man of war,' a counterpart of Amun, with his wife (Sakti or active energy), Astartha-Anata, and they also venerated Targatha,

FIG. 195.
CYPRIAN DAGGER.

Derketo or Atargatis—two Syro-Greek words for one and the same person. The Egyptians at times rank the Khita as a 'great people,' and their habitat as a 'great country'; holding them, in fact, almost as their peers : they also speak with reverence of their gods. Like their neighbours of Kemi, the 'Hittites' were a literary nation : the monuments of Nile-land mention a certain Kirab-sar (or sir), 'writer of the books of the Chief of the Khita,' and the determinative is papyrus or parchment. Hebron was also originally called 'Kirjath- (Kariyat) Sepher'—settlement of books.

---

river-valley formed by the Iarunata (Jordan) and the Arunata (Orontes). The whole length and breadth of the country is distributed between the two, with the exception of the small Litani watershed.

[1] The 'Aram wine from Halybon' was produced at Helbún (Halbáun, the inhabitants call it), a gorge-village near Damascus. Being Moslems, they no longer ferment their grape-juice; but the fruit is still famous. The Helbún people speak the broadest

dialect, and are a perpetual laughing-stock to the Damascus citizens. The Aleppites derive their 'Halab' (Aleppo) because Abraham there milked (*halaba*) a cow ; but the place is older than the Genesitic flood, *the* Flood.

[2] This word is corruptly written Jerablus, Jorablus, Jirabis, &c.

[3] In Rawlinson's *Herodotus* (i. 463) we find that the Southern Hittites numbered twelve kings.

The Khita were formidable opponents to Kemi between the seventeenth and the fourteenth centuries B.C. They fought doughtily against Thut-mes III. (*circa* B.C. 1600) during his Syrian campaign, when this 'Alexander the Great of Egyptian history' overthrew the chief of Kadesh, built a fortress on the Lebanon-range and mastered 'Naharayn.' [1] Three centuries later, Kadesh was taken by Osirei or Seti I. (B.C. 1366). A few years afterwards took place the great campaign of his son,[2] Ramses II., or the Great, 'who made Egypt anew,' and who is famous as the Sesostris of Herodotus.[3] He was nearly defeated at the historic battle of 'Kadesh, the wicked';[4] but at last he succeeded in 'throwing the foe one upon another, head over heels into the waters of the Orontes.' Wilkinson (i. 400) shows a city with a double moat, crossed by two bridges: at the outer defence, formed by the river running into a lake, a phalanx of the Khita is drawn up as a reserve corps. 'Wonderfully rich,' says Brugsch, 'is the great picture which represents the fight of the chariots: while the gigantic form of Ramses,[5] in the very midst of the hostile war-cars, performs deeds of derring-do, astonishing friend and foe, his gallant son, Prahiunamif, commander-in-chief of the charioteers, heads the attack upon those of the enemy. The Khita warriors are thrown into the river, and among them is the King of Khilibi (Aleppo), whom the warriors try to revive by holding his legs in the air with his head hanging down.'[6] This was

[1] The decisive action is shown on an Egyptian tomb (Brugsch, i. 291).

[2] Ramses left as memorials of his invasion three hieroglyphic tablets cut upon the rocks on the south side of the embouchure of the Nahr el-Kalb (Dog or Wolf River, the Lycus), a few miles north of the Venerable Bayrut (Berytus, &c.). They mark the ancient road which ascended the rough torrent-gorge to its origin in Cælesyria (El-Buká'a). Even since these pages have been written the coffins and mummies of Ramses II. and his daughter have been found at Dayr el-Bahri in Upper Egypt, and conveyed from Thebes to Bulak by Dr. Emil Brugsch. The same collector has been equally lucky with the remains of Seti I., although Belzoni, who discovered the tomb, sent the sarcophagus to the Sloane Museum.

[3] Sesostris derives from *Ses, Setesu, Sestesu*, or *Sestura*, i.e. 'Sethosis, also called Ramses' (Seti-son?). The Greek Sesostris combines, I have said, the lives of Seti and his son Ramses. According to Brugsch, he is the 'Pharaoh of the Oppression,' and the son of the unnamed Princess (Merris? Thermutis?) who 'found Moses in the bull-rushes.' The Princess Thermutis, says Josephus, named Moshe (Moses) from *mo* (*má* = water) and *uses*, those who are saved out of it (*ses* = to reach land). Possibly it is *Mu-su* = water-son. Josephus was sorely offended by the 'calumnies' of Manetho; this Egyptian priest, who wrote under Ptolemy Philadelphus about the time of the LXX, declared that the Hebrews were a familia of leprous slaves who, when expelled from Egypt, were led by a renegade priest called

Osarsiph (Osiris-Sapi, god of underworld); and that the number was swollen by Palestinian strangers driven out by Amenophis. He gives the number of lepers and unclean at 250,000 (= 50,000 × 5), and the Hyksos, another impure race, number also 250,000. The learned classics accepted this view, duly abusing the 'gens sceleratissima' (Seneca), and the 'odium generis humani' (Tacitus).

[4] The site of Kadesh and the Buhayrat Hums (Tarn of Emessa) or B. Kutaynah, a 'broad' or widening of the Orontes, was first visited by Dr. Thomson of Bayrut in 1846. I rode about the 'lake of the land of the Amorites' in 1870; but found no ruins, or rather ruins of no importance everywhere. It was not then known to me that in A.D. 1200 the geographer Yakut (*Geogr. Dict.* edit. Wüstenfeld) had noticed the water in his day as the 'Bahriyat Kuds' (Tarn of Kadesh). Since that time the Palestine Exploration Fund (July 1881) identified the seat of Atesh or Kadesh with the Tell Nabi Mendeh, a Santon's tomb on the highest part of the hill where the ruins lie. The site is on the left bank of the Orontes, four English miles south of the 'broad.' The city disappears from history after the thirteenth century B.C., but local legend has preserved its memory.

[5] Prof. Ebers, who is familiar with the many portraits of Ramses-Sesostris, declares that he was a handsome man with fine aquiline features, like Napoleon Buonaparte.

[6] This original and instinctive way to revive the

the victory that gave birth to the first of Epic poems, the 'Song of Pentaur the Scribe.'

The war ended by the Egyptian marrying the Hittite's daughter, and making with his father-in-law a highly-civilised extradition treaty engraved upon a silver plate.[1] Another invasion, however, took place (circa B.C. 1200) under Ramses III. This 'Rhampsinitus' of the Greeks, a compound title, Ramessu-pa-Neter (Ramses the god), has left inscriptions concerning his 'Campaign of Vengeance' which cover one side of the temple of Medinah Habu :[2] amongst the conquered foes appears the 'miserable King of Khita as a living prisoner.'

In later times the Khita became well known to Assyrian story.[3] Shalmaneser II. (B.C. 884–852) mentions the 'Hittites and the city of Petra' (Pethor) ; he takes 'eighty-nine cities of the land of the Hamathites,' and Rimonidri of Damascus. Tiglath-pileser II. (B.C. 745–727) speaks of the 'city of Hamatti' (Hamath) and the 'Arumu' (Aramæans).

According to Wilkinson (I. chap. v.) the Khita are represented on the monuments, the Memnonium, Medinah Habu, and elsewhere, as a shaven race with light red skins. Their dress is the long Assyrian robe falling to the ankles : the hair is crisply curled and at times covered with the tall cap of Phrygian type. A characteristic article, which appears in their hieroglyphs, is the pointed and up-turned boot,[4] somewhat like the soleret of the sixteenth century. For armour they had square or oblong shields and quilted coats with bracelets defending their arms. Their weapons were bows, spears, and the short straight Sword, the modern flesh-chopper, then in use among their rival neighbours of the Nile Valley.

These gallant Canaanites[5] were proficients in the art of war. The army was distributed into foot and mounted men. The former consisted of a native nucleus called Tuhir (Táhir ?),[6] the 'chosen ones,' and a host of mercenaries under Hir-pits or captains. Amongst these were the Shardana, Sardones, commonly translated Sardinians ; Brugsch contends that they were Colchians, and derives from them 'Sardonian linen.' They were armed with horned helmets and round shields, spears and long Swords. The Kelau or slingers appear to have been a *corps d'élite* that waited upon the Prince.[7] The tactics included a regular phalanx, a herse or

---

drowned endures to the present day, despite the wrath of the Faculty.

[1] Brugsch (ii. 68) gives the terms of the treaty as translated by Mr. Goodwin (*Records of the Past*, iv. 25) ; and adds instances to prove that it was acted upon. Thus he explains the hitherto mysterious countermarch, the turning back of the Hebrew exodus, at the time when the emigrants were advancing straight upon their objective. His strong point is the identification of 'Baal-Zephon,' about which all the commentators have made such hopeless guesses. He explains it by 'Baal of the North (Typhon, Sutekh or Khepsh), the 'Mount Kasion' of Jupiter

Kasios, a name derived from the Egyptian Hazian or Hazina.

[2] So called from an old Coptic town, long ruined.

[3] Rawlinson's *Herodotus*, vol. i., Essay VII., and reference to Black Obelisk in British Museum. *Synchronous History of Assyria and Judæa*, pp. 1–82, vol. iii. pt. i. ; *Soc. Bibl. Archæology*, 1874.

[4] A Keltic word, *bot* = foot.

[5] In popular Hebrew use, 'Canaanite' meant a trader.

[6] Possibly the 'pure' (Hebr. *Tohar*), in which case the word is 'Semitic.'

[7] Brugsch, ii. chap. xiv. As a rule, slingers were the least esteemed of fighting men.

column of spearsmen like the Egyptian ; and, although the cavalry rode horses their 'strength was in chariots.'

'Hithism'[1] became a study of late years, after the publication of 'Hittite hieroglyphs,' first discovered at Hamah, then at Aleppo, gave it an impulse. Two rock-inscriptions with bas-reliefs were discovered by the Rev. E. Davis (of Alexandria) at Ibriz (Áb-ríz), three hours south of Eregli, the old Cybistra on the great Lycaonian plain.[2] The finds at Carchemish added to the scanty store, and there are said to be Hittite seals in the British Museum. In Dr. Schliemann's 'Troy' (p. 352), I find a Hittite hieroglyph on the stamped terra-cotta ; the middle figure to the right is apparently the fist or fist-shaped glove, the Egyptian symbol of the hand. I shall presently notice the Lycian coin and a gold incision from Cyprus. Three legible characters—the bull's head, the cap, and the bent arm—are traced to the so-called prehistoric statue of Niobe, Mount Sipylus. Evidently Hittite, too, is the bronze tablet in M. Peretié's Museum, Bayrut.[3]

Modern discoveries enable us to characterise Hittite art as a blending of Egyptian with Assyrian, or rather Babylonian, both considerably modified. The former appears in the two sphinxes of Eyub, and in the winged solar disk, which was also borrowed by Mesopotamia from the Nile Valley. The bas-reliefs and gems of Assyria are reflected in the Hittite representations of the human figure ; but the stature is shorter, the limbs are thicker and more rounded, and the muscles are not so prominent. At Boghaz-Keui some of the deities stand upon animals, a posture believed to be early Babylonian.[4] Here, too, the goddesses wear mural crowns, the decoration of the Ephesian Artemis, and Prof. Sayce thence infers its Hittite origin. At Eyub is found the double-headed eagle which is supposed to be the prototype of the old Siljukian and modern European monsters.[5]

The Hittite syllabary has systematic affinities with the Egyptian, as shown by the boot, the glove (or hand), the bent arm, the battle-axe, and the short straight chopper-knife. But before reading these ideographs it was necessary to determine the language, and here difficulties arose. Prof. Sayce denies that the Khita were Semites or spoke a Semitic tongue ;[6] and in this he is followed by Mr. W. St. Chad Boscawen. But the former contended with scant success, that the Cypriote

---

[1] The Rev. William Wright, missionary at Damascus, first suggested that the Hamath inscriptions were Hittite. The study was begun in 1872 by the late Dr. A. D. Mordtmann at Constantinople, where is the original of the silver Hittite dish represented in the British Museum.

[2] *Trans. Soc. Biblical Archæol.* vol. iv. pt. 2, 1876.

[3] Described by M. Clermont-Ganneau in the *Revue Archéologique*, Dec. 1879 ; and figured in the *Palestine Exploration Fund*, July 1881.

[4] In Egypt the king rests his feet upon war-captives ; and making a foot-stool of the enemy is a

Biblical phrase (Psalm cx. 1) which had a literal signification.

[5] For the two-headed eagle in Moslem heraldry (A.D. 1190 and 1217), see p. 108 of Rogers Bey's valuable paper before quoted (chap. vii.).

[6] His chief argument for their Northern origin seems to be founded upon their boots ; he forgets, however, that the Arabs of Mahommed's day wore 'Khuff;' and that legal ablutions were modified to suit them. It is the *cothurnus calceatus* of Pliny (vii. 19) which, as we see on statues and vases, covered the foot and ankle to the calf. The Assyriologist Prof. P. Schrader, followed by Prof. G. Ebers, considers the Khita to be Aramæans.

writing was 'none other than the hieroglyphics of Hamath.'[1]   Mr. Hyde Clarke believes that Khita, Etruscan, and Cypriote are kindred tongues ; and detects their symbols upon the autonomous coins of Spain.   Others have supported the Scythic (Turanian) origin of the Hittites : in our day this was inevitable.   The Rev. Dunbar I. Heath bravely pronounces the language Semitic and made a gallant attempt at interpreting the syllabary.[2]   But nothing final can be done under present conditions : we have not even collected all the characters.[3]

While the Khita were inlanders, the parallel shore-land of the Mediterranean —Syria and Palestine—was occupied by a host of Semitic and congener tribes. The former is a noble word and by no means the 'invention of a Greek geo- grapher' ; Suríyyah denotes the rocky region from Sur or Tsur (זור = rock), a tower (*turris*), Tyre, the Zurai of Tiglath-pileser II., and the Tapau of the hieroglyphs. Thus 'Syria' and 'Tyria' would be synonyms.   Herodotus (vii. 63) fathered a sad confusion when he wrote, 'The people whom the Greeks call Syrians are called Assyrians by the barbarians.'   Assyria is from another root, אשר (Ashur), supposed to signify 'happiness,' and applied, as will be seen, to one of the gods. Syria is the hieroglyphic Khar, Kharu, or Khálu, the 'hinder-land,' that is, behind or north of Osiris (Egypt), and the Akarru or Akharu of the cuneiforms, both from the 'Semitic' root Akhr.   'Palestine' (Syria) is simply the 'land of the Philistines,' the Zahi of the hieroglyphs and mediæval Filistín ; this powerful family, probably connected with the Hyksos, extended eastward from the confines of Egypt, and built Pelusium—'Philistine-town,' not town of πηλὸs or mud.

---

[1] And Carchemish.   'On the Hamathite Inscrip- tions,' *Trans. Soc. Bibl. Archæol.* vol. i. pt. 1, 1876, and vii. 298–443, on Tarrik-timmun.

[2] Mr. Heath kindly explained to me the key of his system published in the *Journ. Anthrop. Instit.* May 1880.   The figures at Ibríz having suggested 'Semit- ism,' he separated root-letters from formatives and found three Aramæan suffixes, *t-na*, *t-kun*, and *t-hun*. These gave an immense probability that he had hit upon the *t*, *n*, *k*, and *h*.   Meanwhile Mr. Boscawen (Pal. Expl. Fund, July 1881) contends that our 'knowledge of Hittite is confined to four syllabic characters and the ideographs.'   The Rev. Mr. Sayce was good enough to explain to me how he had deter- mined eleven values.   A comparison of inscriptions, with the silver boss of Tarkodemos as a *point de départ*, suggested to him that the stirrup-shape ($\widehat{6\,9}$) marks the nom. sing. of proper names, and this in the Egyptian and Assyrian monuments ends in *s*.   He assumes that adjectives agree with their substantives, which they follow by taking the same suffixes.   He was at first disposed to make the broken *k* $\bigcirc$| or |$\bigcirc$), which curiously resembles an old Egyptian sign, signify 'and' (cop. conjunct.) ; but the incised in- scription found by Mr. Ramsey at Bór (old Tyana) proved it the determinative of an individual.   The goat's head seems from the bilingual boss to have the

phonetic value 'tarku,' and is interchanged with $\uparrow$ (*ku*), $\widehat{}$ (*s*), $\underline{\underline{\psi}}$, and $\uparrow \underline{\underline{\psi}}$.   The two spear-heads with the stirrup ($\underline{\underline{\int\int}}$ $\widehat{6\,9}$) appear to represent a patronymic—*Kus*.   The second sign (= *ku*), which seems to be the first pers. sing. of the Aor., can be followed in the same group of characters by $\overline{\overline{777}}$; whence Mr. Sayce inferred the latter to be an adjec- tival participial affix = *u*.   Similarly ·|· = *e*, the acc. plur. ; thus $\overline{\overline{777}}$ ·|· = *ue*.   The bilingual boss also shows |||| or // $\searrow$ = *mi*, the third pers. sing. present tense, and we find indifferently $\underset{6\,9}{||||}$ and $\underset{6\,9}{\overset{||||}{\cdot|\cdot}}$.   The gen. plur. is $\bigcirc$|, but the pronunciation is not deter- mined.   The same is the case with the sock or low boot ($\underline{\underline{\smile\!\!\mathfrak{f}}}$), suggested to be the third pers. plur. of the Aorist.   Lastly, the ideograph of plurality attached to nouns and verbs is) (.

[3] Dr. Guyther, visiting the Merash citadel, has found several new characters in a long inscription on a lion, and fragments of stone with other hieroglyphs have been forwarded from Carchemish to the British Museum.

Beyond the Philistines began the Phœnicians—merchants and traders, travellers, explorers, and colonisers—the 'Englishmen of antiquity.' When Herodotus brings the Phœnicians from the 'Erythrean Sea' he is generally understood to mean the Persian Gulf, where the islands of Tyrus (or Tylos) and Aradus are supposed to be the mother-sites of the homonymous Mediterranean settlements. The popular derivation of 'Phœnicia' is from φοῖνιξ, which again may have been, *more Græco*, a mere translation of the Egyptian Kefeth, Kefthu, Keft, and Kefa, a palm-tree. But the question would be solved if it can be proved that the Phœnicians are the 'Fenekh'[1] of the monuments and the Moslem El-Fenish. Mariette Pasha derived the term Punoi, Pœni, from Pun or Punt, by which he understood Somali-land ; he is easily reconciled with Herodotus by assuming Punt to mean, as most understand it, the opposite Arabian coast.[2] Thus the 'Port of Punt' is the mythical Red Sea (primordial matter?), where red Typhon and the red dragon App or Apáp (Apophis) fought against the white god Horus—the prototype of Baldur the Beautiful.[3]

The Phœnicians left their mark upon the world. For many generations the Mediterranean was a 'Phœnician lake,' and they could boast of a general θαλασσο-κρατία. This enabled their merchants and navigators to diffuse civilisation from Egypt and Assyria to the farthest West. They were the carriers of the world. Their 'round ships' or merchantmen (γαυλοί) and their long war-ships pushed far into the Northern and Southern Atlantic. The topographical lists of Thut-mes III. show a thickly inhabited country (Brugsch, i. 350–51), and, as Mariette Pasha says, a map of Canaan, composed of some hundred and fifteen hieroglyphic names, 'is a synoptical table of the "Promised Land," made two hundred and seventy years before the exodus of Moses.' Among the settlements are Debekhu, now Baalbak, the Baal-city ;[4] Tum-sakhu, the gate or shrine of Tum, the setting sun, now Damascus ; Biarut (*hod.* Bayrut) ; Keriman or Mount Carmel and Iopoo, Joppa, or Jaffa. We find the Jordan in the Egyptian Iarutana, and Shabatuan is the Sabbaticus River of Pliny and Josephus.[5]

The chief cities of Phœnicia, Tyre and Sidon, were of unexampled splendour, depôts of the wealth of the East, as early as B.C. 1500. The arch-Homerid, who curiously enough never mentions Tyre, attributes all the finest works of art either

---

[1] Under Shishonk (Shishak), the contemporary of Solomon, the conquered tribes of Edom and Judah are termed the 'Fenekh and the Aamu (Syro-Aramæans) of a far land.' Brugsch (ii. 210) 'has a presentiment' that these Fenekh are intimately related to the Jews ; and he notes the similarity of Aamu with 'Am,' the well-known Hebrew term.

[2] Some have suspected Punt to be the far later Pándya, or Madura kingdom, in Southern India. Mariette's Punt extended from Bab el-Mandeb to Cape Guardafui ('I was a Guard').

[3] Prof. Rugge of Christiania, however, connects Baldur with Achilles. We can hardly accept his

scheme until the details shall have been better worked out.

[4] 'Bak,' from Beki in Coptic = city, town.

[5] 'In Judæâ rivus Sabbatis omnibus siccatur' (Pliny, xxxi. 18). The idea doubtless arose from the intermittent springs (Siloam, &c.) about Jerusalem. Josephus (*B. J* viii. 5, § 1) makes his Sabbatic R. break the Jewish Sabbath (Saturday) by flowing only on that day and resting during the other six. Hence the fabled Sabbation, whose flood of huge rocks and sand-waves, sixty to two hundred cubits high, issued from the 'Garden of Eden.' It still hems in the ten 'Lost Tribes,' and is believed by the Druzes.

to the Sidonians or to the gods. The eastern coast of the 'Inner Sea' was a centre of civilisation, a school of high culture which added beauty to necessary and useful technical products; and its arts and handicrafts became patterns to the world, even to Egypt, the mother. We have only a few inscriptions to remind us of its literature; but nothing can be more touching or more poetical than the epitaph of Eshmunazar, King of the Sidonians:[1]—'Deprived of my fruit of life, my wise and valiant sons; widowed, the child of solitude, I lie in this tomb, in this grave, in the place which I built,' &c. Phœnicia, too, gave not only her letters but her gods to Greece and Rome. Mulciber, for instance, was evidently Malik Kabir, the 'Great King,' father of the Cabiri, the patron-saints of Palm-land and the Pelasgi; this deity corresponded with the Egyptian Ptah, the Demiurgus-god denoted by the Scarabæus, a symbol as common in Phœnicia as in Nile-land. Melkarth,[2] again, whom Nonnius makes the Babylonian Sun, was the city-god; farther west he became Herakles, the Etruscan Erkle: the latter was an important commercial personage in Phœnicia, for his dog (according to the Greeks) discovered the murex. Melkarth is the Ourshol of Selden ('De Diis Syriis'), who derives the word from 'Ur,' light.[3]

Another Syrian people, often occurring upon the Egyptian monuments, is the Shairetana, whom Layard supposes to be the Sharutinians near modern Antioch. They inhabited a country upon a river and a lake or sea. Their armour was a close-fitting cuirass of imbricated metal plates, worn over a short dress and girt at the waist; the helmet had side horns, and its upper dome was surmounted by a shaft-and-ball crest. Their weapons were javelins, long spears, and pointed Swords. The Tokkari, their neighbours, also carried for offence spears and large pointed knives or straight Swords. The Rebo had bows and long straight Swords with very sharp points. The same is the case with Ru-tennu or Rot-n-n, who often pass in review upon the monuments. They appear to have contained two divisions: the Ru-tennu-hir (upper Ru-tennu) were apparently the peoples of Cœlesyria, while the Ruthens or Luthens are mentioned in conjunction with Neniee (Nineveh), Shinar (Singar), Babel, and other places in Eastern Naharayn (Mesopotamia).

We have no knowledge of the Phœnician Sword except that supplied to us by the legend of the enigmatical Egypto-Argive hero, Perseus. According to Herodotus (ii. 91), his quadrangular fane was at Panopolis-Chemmis in the Theban nome: here his sandal, two cubits long, was shown to devotees; and the land prospered whenever he appeared, as is the case when it sees El-Khizr, the Green Prophet of El-Islam. The Greeks, whom we need not credit, made him the son of Jupiter by the 'Acrisian maid' (Danaë); and the Persians,[4] according to the

---

[1] I quote from *Phœnician Inscriptions*, by the Rev. Dunbar I. Heath, not from the far more poetical version of the Duc de Luynes.

[2] My friend Prof. Socin holds that St. Meklar of Tyre conserves the cultus of Melkarth.

[3] Perhaps from the Egyptian *Ur*, old, ancient, original.

[4] The modern Persians, and, indeed, Persian history and legend, know nothing of this wild legend.

Greeks, declared his son Perses to be the *heros eponymus* of their country, and the ancestor of their Hakhmanish or Achæmenian kings. His chief exploits were two. At Spanish Tartessus or in Libya (Herod. ii. 91) he slew, with the aid of a 'magic mirror' given to him by Neith-Athene, the gorgon Medusa, that old Typhonian head, from whose neck sprang Pegasus and Chrysaor.[1] At Phœnician Joppa (Jaffa)[2] he slaughtered the sea-monster ($\kappa\hat{\eta}\tau o\varsigma$) and saved 'Andromeda,' who is suspiciously like 'Anat.'

In both these feats Perseus used a celestial weapon, the Harpé of Cronos, which Zeus had wielded in his duel with Typhon. The giant or bad-god had torn it from the grip of the good-god, whom he presently imprisoned in a cave; and it was not recovered till the captive was liberated by Thut-Hermes. The Greeks call this Sword "Αρπη (Harpé),[3] and the name is evidently the Phœnician Hereba and the Hebrew Chereb; whilst its description, $\delta\rho\acute{\epsilon}\pi\alpha\nu o\nu\ \acute{o}\xi\grave{\upsilon}$ (*falx acuta*, sharp sickle), identifies it with the Khopsh-blade of Egypt. Perseus performed his two exploits as Hercules slew the Lernæan hydra; and Mercury cut off the head of Argus (*falcato ense*), using the *harpen Cyllenida*.[4]

This legend has greatly 'exercised' commentators. The hero is connected with Io, Belus, and Ægyptus; while he is evidently related to the Cypriot Perseuth and the Phœnician Reseph[5] (flame or thunderbolt). The original fight is the eternal warfare of good, light, warmth, joy, with their contraries. It begins with Osiris-Typhon; it proceeds to Assyria, where Bel the Sun-god attacks the Tiamat or marine monster with the Sapara-Sword or Khopsh. In Persia it becomes Hormuzd (Ahura-mazda) and Ahriman (Angra-manus): in Jewry it is an affair between Bel and the Dragon; in Greece between Apollo and Python. The duello is continued by St. Patrick,[6] who banished for ever snakes from Ireland; and it makes its final appearance as 'Saint George and the Dragon.' This expiring effort of Egyptian mythology is held apocryphal by the Roman Catholic Church, and no wonder.

---

[1] A terra-cotta relief in the British Museum shows Chrysaor (Χρυσάωρ) springing from Medusa's neck.

[2] Joppa, according to tradition (Pliny, v. 14), was built by Kepheus, king of the Æthiopians, and was his capital before 'the Deluge.' The same author tells us that Andromeda's chains were there shown, and that the monster's skeleton (some fish cast ashore upon the harbour reef?) was brought to Rome by the Curule Ædile M. Æmil. Scaurus the younger, who held office in Syria (ix. 4(. The bones were upwards of forty feet long, the backbone one foot and a half thick, and the ribs higher than those of the Indian elephant (a cachelot?). Ajasson declared that the remains should have been sent to those who show in their collections the weapon with which Cain slew Abel. Pausanias (second century) saw the Lydda streamlet red with blood, where Perseus had bathed after killing the 'Ketos.' At Joppa St. Jerome was shown the traditional rock in which holes had been worn by Andromeda's fetters. The spot

is now clean forgotten—at least, all my inquiries failed to find it. The testimony is of the highest character; unfortunately it testifies to impossibilities—all monsters are 'contradictory beings.' The Ketos, whale or shark (*Canis Carcharias*), is evidently the same that swallowed Hercules and Jonah.

[3] Mgr. Bianchini very improperly translates *Harpé* by 'glaive,' and other writers absurdly use 'scymitar.' They could hardly better describe what it was *not*.

[4] The bronze Perseus of Benvenuto Cellini in the Loggie dell' Orgagna of Florence holds a falx-Sword or falchion.

[5] Hence possibly the town Arsúf; and (the Isle of) Seripho, where Perseus was worshipped.

[6] There seem to be three of the name : Palladius, the first missionary to Ireland; Sen Patrick, who studied under St. Germanus and died A.D. 458-61; and Patrick M'Calphurn, also a pupil of St. Germanus, who missionarised about A.D. 440-42.

Dragons do not, and never did, exist, except in memory as prehistoric mon-sters ; moreover, the traveller in Syria is shown three several tombs of 'Már Jiryús' the Cappadocian, a saint who has spread himself from Diospolis-Lydda throughout the world. Under Justinian, the Theseum of Athens was dedicated to 'Saint George of Cappadocia,' and in Cyprus he had as many temples as Venus. The Saxon teacher thus invoked him :

> Invicto mundum qui sanguine temnis,
> Infinita refers, Georgi Sancte, trophæa.

He entered the English calendar when Henry II. married Eleanor, daughter of William of Aquitaine, the Crusader who chose the 'flos Sanctorum' for his patron saint. He is still godfather of the Garter, established by Edward III. in 1350 ; and the most feudal of existing orders wears 'the George' on a gold medallion, and celebrates its festival at Windsor on April 23.

One step in the Saint's progress has been traced by M. Ch. Clermont-Ganneau,[1] an Orientalist whose archæological acumen is unsurpassed even by his industry. A bas-relief group in the Louvre shows the hawk-headed Horus, mounted and in Roman uniform, piercing with his peculiar spear (an *hamatum*, or barb-head), the neck of the crocodile Typhon, Set, Dagon,[2] Python—the Devil. This strongly suggests that Horus and Perseus, Saint Patrick and Saint George, are one and the same person.

The Hereba-blade has not yet been found in Phœnicia, but Wilkinson argues (II. ch. vii.) that the beautiful Swords and daggers, buried with the Ancient Britons and clearly not of Greek or Roman type, are Phœnician work. Carthaginian blades, however, dug up at Cannæ are now in the British Museum.[3] That the nations were congeners we see by the Pœnulus of Plautus, and by such names as Dido (another form of David) and Elissa (El-Isá ,the royal woman) ; by Sichæus, who derives from the same root as Zacchæus ; by Hannibal and Hasdrubal (containing the root Ba'al), and by the 'Suffetes'—magistrates who are the Hebrew Shophetim or Judges.[4] The mercenary armies of Carthage, whose conquests are first alluded to by Herodotus (vii. 165), used Swords of bronze, copper, and tin : Meyrick (i. 7) also mentions brass ; and the highly imaginative General Vallancey compares it with Dowris metal or 'Irish brass.' Dr. Schliemann ('Mycenæ,' p. 76) picked up, at 'Motyë in Sicily,' Carthaginian piles (arrow-heads) of bronze, pyramidal and without barbs (γλωχῖνες or *hami*) ; he found the same style at Mycenæ (p. 123).

---

[1] *Horus et Saint-Georges*, &c. See also a kind of sentimental study æsthetically baptised 'Saint Mark's Rest : the Place of Dragons,' by J. R. Anderson.

[2] From רג (*dag*), a fish, a Ketos, the Phœnician רגון (*Dajun, Dagon*); Dagan is the male, Dalas the female. Simply a fish-god. Sardanapalus was 'he who knows Anu (the god) and Dagon.'

[3] Others found at Cannæ resemble the copper Swords of Ireland, according to the *Encyclopædia Metropolitana*.

[4] The 'tariff of masses,' from the temple of Baal at Marseille, speaks of Chaltzibah the Sufet. Other inscriptions inform us that the Carthaginians had a triad, Baal Hammon (Ammon) ; the Lady Tanith Pen Baal (Tanis or Neith, the πρόσωπον, or face, of Baal), and Iolaus.—*Phœnician Inscriptions*, by the Rev. D. I. Heath.

The Swords of the Lycians probably resembled the Egyptian Khopsh ; and the same was the case with the Cilician falchion. The latter peoples were also armed with the σάρισσα (Sarissa) ; the lance or spear, sixteen to twenty feet long, afterwards used by the people of Epirus and the Macedonian phalanx. It is opposed to the Larissa, the lance of the European Middle Ages, and to the Narissa affected by the Norrenses.

The most remarkable point concerning the Sword amongst the ancient Hebrews is our practical ignorance of its shape and size. Although shekels and similar remains have been discovered in fair quantities, that ' iron race in iron clad,' the Jews of old, has not left us a single specimen of arms or armour. This is the more curious, as we are expressly told that the blade was buried with its wielder.[1] And although we are assured (Gen. iv. 22) that Tubal-Cain, son of Lamech and Zillah, was the first metal-smith, there is no direct mention of iron arms amongst the Jews till after the Exodus. Gesenius proposes to make Tubal-Cain a hybrid word, ' scoriarum faber,' from the Persian ' Tupal ' (iron-slag or scoriæ), and ' Kani (*faber*, a blacksmith). He has been identified with Ptah, Bil-Kan (Assyria), Vulcan, and Mulciber ; and only ignorance of Hinduism prevented mediæval commentators discovering him under the *alias* of Vishvamitra, the artificer of the Hindú gods. Maestro Vizani (A.D. 1588), a famous master of fence, attributes the invention ot the Sword to Tubal-Cain ; we should now place this worthy in the later bronze and early iron age. Unjust claims to discovery are made by all ancient peoples ; and here it would be hardly fair to adduce Bochart's ' Judæi semper mendaces ; in hoc argumento potissimum mentiuntur liberalissime.'

It is, however, amply evident that the Phœnicians and the despised Canaanites were highly-cultivated peoples, whereas the Jews were not. The latter are never alluded to in Egyptian hieroglyphs.[2] Even after they had established their principality upon the bleak and barren uplands of Judæa, they were dependent for their art upon their neighbours. Although gold was so abundant in the days of David that he could collect about one thousand million pounds (one hundred thousand talents of gold and one million of silver) for building the Temple, yet Solomon, the Wise King, was obliged to seek stone-cutters and even carpenters among the Σίδονες πολυδαίδαλοι. Judæa had neither science nor art ; architecture, sculpture, paintings nor mosaics ; comfort nor cookery. The Great Temple that succeeded the Tabernacle of Moses was mainly the work of Hiram of Tyre, the Siromus of Herodotus (v. 104), the Hiromus of Dius, Menander and Josephus (' Apion,' i. 17, &c.), and probably a dynastic name, as ' Haram ' the Sacred.

---

[1] Ezekiel (xxxii. 27). ' And they shall not lie with the mighty that are fallen of the uncircumcised, which are gone down to hell [Sheol = Shuala, the ghost-land of Babylon] with their weapons of war : *and they have laid their Swords under their heads*, but their iniquities shall be upon their bones, though they were the terror of the mighty in the land of the living.'

[2] The Hebrews were probably included under the ' miserable foreigners,' who, at that time, numbered about one-third of the Egyptian people. It was the fashion to find ' Hebrew ' in the 'Aper, 'Apura, 'Aperiu, and 'Apiurui of the monuments ; but Brugsch has shown that these were the original ' Erythræans,' equestrian Arabs of the barrens extending from Heliopolis onward to modern Suez.

Another learned master of arms[1] declares that the first weapon mentioned in Hebrew Holy Writ is the *flammeus gladius* wielded by the Cherubim (Gen. iii. 24), the 'Chereb' which the Septuagint renders 'Ρομφαία.[2] On the Assyrian monuments the Kerubi ('cherub,' which derives, like the Arabic 'Karrúb,' from 'Karb' =propinquity) denotes the colossal figures symbolising the Powers of Good, and guarding the palace-gates. As they prevented the admission of Evil, they found their way to the entrance of the Garden of Eden, whence they warned off sinners and intruders. The 'flaming Sword,' which 'turned every way to keep the way of the tree of life,' was, according to some, the two-pronged blade, the Greek 'chelidonian,' which served as a talisman. Tiglath Pileser I. made one of these forked Swords of copper, inscribed it with his victories, and placed it as a trophy in one of his castles. But the Genesitic Sword is probably the weapon-symbol of Merodach, the Babylonian god and planet Jupiter. This revolving disc represented, like the Aryan 'Vajra,' the lightning or 'thunderbolt' with which our classics armed Zeus-Jovi;[3] and a highly poetical description of it is given in an old Akkadian hymn. Here it is called among other names *littu* (or *litu*), which is, letter for letter, the same as the first of the Hebrew words translated 'flaming Sword' (*lahat ha-Chereb*) : it may also signify the 'Burning of Desolation.' M. F. Lenormant[4] suggests that the true meaning is 'magical prodigy.' But it is safer to stand by the disc-like Sword, which corresponds with the wheels of Ezekiel's vision (chap. x. 9, 10). In the Chaldæan battle of Bel and the Dragon we again find the great flaming Sword, turning all round the circle when wielded by the deity against the 'Drake.' So the Egyptians had long before depicted the solar god with a glory of solar rays, a most appropriate symbol ; and his enemy, Apophis ᚼᚼ ᚼᚼᚼᚼ, the serpent of Genesis, whom he destroys, is a monstrous reptile bristling with a dorsal line of four Sword-blades, like flesh-knives, typifying destruction.

The Hebrews borrowed their metallurgy, like all their early science, from Egypt. M. de Goguet remarked that they were not destitute of technological skill if they could calcine the golden calf and reduce the metal (probably by using natron) to a powder which could be drunk in water—*aurum potabile.*

The Hebrews called the Sword 'Chereb' (חרב, pl. Chereboth), a word that occurs some two hundred and fifty times in the 'Old Testament.' Its root, like the Arabic 'khrb,' means to waste, to be wasted ; and the noun denotes any wasting matter.[5] Mostly it means a Sword (Gen. xvii. 40 ; xxxiv. 25, &c. &c.) ; in other

---

[1] *Trattato di Scherma,* &c. di Alberto Marchionni (Firenze : Bencini, 1547).

[2] This word will be noticed in chapter xi. I cannot wholly agree with Colonel Lane-Fox (*Anthrop. Coll.* p. 99) when he speaks of a 'leaf-shaped Sword-blade attached to the end of the spear, like the Thracian *romphea* and the European *partisan* of mediæval times.'

[3] May not this older form of Jupiter have derived

from the 'Semitic' root יה, Jah (*Yah*), carried westward by the Phœnicians? But this is 'stirring the fire with a Sword,' against which Pythagoras warns us.

[4] 'Les Figures de l'Histoire d'après la Bible,' &c. (the *Athenæum*, Feb. 31, 1880). 'Lahat' (the Germ. *lohe,* our 'low' or 'lowe') is in the singular a 'flame'; in the plural 'spells, enchantments by drugs,' &c.

[5] Mr. Gerald Massey would identify the Jewish Chereb, like the Phœnician Hereba and the Greek

places it is a knife (Josh. v. 2, 3). So we find in Ezekiel (v. 1), 'Take thee a sharp knife [Chereb]; take thee a barber's razor': elsewhere it becomes a chisel (Exod. xx. 25); an axe or pick (Jer. xxxiv. 4; Ez. v. 1, and xxvi. 9), and, finally, violent heat (Job xxx. 30). The Arabic 'Harbah' signifies a dart.

We gather from the Hebrew writings that the Sword was originally of copper: hence the allusion to its brightness and its glittering: this would be followed by bronze, and lastly by iron, ground upon the whetstone (Deut. xxxii. 41). It was not of flint; the 'sharp knives' alluded to in Joshua (v. 2), were mere silex-flakes like the Egyptian. The Sword was used by foot-soldiers and horsemen, the latter adding to the 'light Sword' a 'glittering spear' (Nahum iii. 3). The 'Chereb' was not a large or heavy weapon, and we may safely assume that its forms were those of the Egyptian hieroglyphs. The weight of Goliath's Sword is unfortunately not given (1 Sam. xvii. 45), like that of his spear and his armour; nor are we told anything about the blade which David refused because he had not proved it (*ibid.* 39). But the ease with which the son of Jesse drew out of the sheath thereof and used the Philistine's 'Chereb,' suggests a normal size and weight (*ibid.* 51 and xxi. 9). It was much admired, for the victor said, 'There is none like that' (1 Sam. xxi. 9). From the same chapter and verse we learn that the blade was 'wrapped up in a cloth,' still an Eastern practice, 'behind the ephod' or priest's robe.[1] And the fact of a man falling upon his Sword (1 Sam. xxxi. 4, 5) shows that the blade was stiff, short, and straight, like the Egyptian leaf-blade. Ehud the Benjamite, when about to murder Eglon, King of Moab (Jud. iii. 16), 'made a two-edged Sword-dagger of a cubit length' (or eighteen inches), apparently without a sheath. The frequent mention of the double-edged Sword (or straight cut-and-thrust?) suggests that there were also single-edged blades, back-Swords or, perhaps, falchions. It is hard to understand why Meyrick tells us that the Jews wore the Sword 'suspended in front, in the Asiatic style.' Ehud (*ibid.* 16, 21) girt his weapon under his raiment upon his right thigh, and drew it with his left hand. Again, we read, 'Gird thy sword upon thy thigh' (Ps. xlv. 3); and as Joab proceeded to assassinate Amasa (2 Sam. xx. 8), the 'garment that he had put on was girded unto him, and upon it a girdle with a sword fastened upon his loins in the sheath thereof; and as he went forth it fell out.' The allusions to the oppressing Sword (Jer. xlvi. 16; l. 25) recall the Assyrian emblem of the Sword and the Dove, which are both figured in one image. Perhaps we must so understand the Egyptian Ritual of the Dead: 'I came forth as his child from his Sword.' Apparently the Chereb was worn, as by the civilised Greeks and Romans, only on emergencies and not, like the chivalry of Europe, habitually in peaceful towns.

Harpé, with the Egyptian Kherp, ⊗ ▮ , the sign of majesty typified by an oar or rather paddle— ⊗ ▮ ┃. Thus the Kherp first cut the water like a propeller, then the grain as a sickle, and at last it became a Sword — the reaper of men. This is ingenious, but nothing more : the white arm in Egypt shows no sign of derivation from the oar.

[1] So Jeanne d'Arc's Sword was taken from a church, as will appear in Part II.

The Cultellarii or Sicarii, whom Josephus and Tacitus[1] mention, were mere assassins, like the French Coustilliers and the English Coustrils or Custrils.

That the Hebrews were not first-rate Sword-cutlers, we may infer from the history of Judas the Maccabee.[2] A vision of Jeremiah the Prophet, preceding the victory over Nicanor, had promised him 'a Sword of God, a holy Sword,' not the short Machæra but the large Rhomphæa (2 Mac. xv. 15). After his war with the Samaritans and the Gentiles of Palestine, 'Judas took the Sword of Apollonius (the Syrian general) and fought with it all his life' (2 Mac. iii. 12).

And yet how general was the use of the Sword in Jewry we gather from the fact that it assisted in taking the Census: so David, by one account (2 Sam. xxiv. 9) mustered one million three hundred thousand 'valiant men that drew the Sword.'[3] The expression 'girding on the Sword' (1 Sam. xxv. 13) denoted adults able to serve as soldiers, and also noted the beginning of a campaign (Deut. i. 41). It has been stated that Saul, son of Kish, used the Sword with his left hand, by virtue of being of the tribe of Benjamin. Of the latter, however, we learn (Judg. xx. 16) that many were ambidexters, fighting and slinging with the left as well as with the right. Finally, to be 'slain by the Sword' was evidently as great a misfortune as the 'straw-death' among those muscular Christians, the Scandinavians. The curse of David upon Joab was that there might never be wanting in his house ' one that hath an issue, or is a leper, or that leaneth on a staff, or that falleth on the Sword ' (a suicide). All this makes the fact the more singular that no Jewish Sword-blade has ever been found.

Of the weapons used by the tribes neighbouring the ancient Hebrews we know little. In the famous muster of Xerxes' army,[4] the Assyrians, according to Herodotus (vii. 65), used hand-daggers (ἐγχειρίδια) resembling the Egyptian. The Arabs (vii. 69, 86), like the Indians, were mere savages armed with bows and arrows; and we may note that the former mounted only camels, the horse not having been naturalised amongst all the tribes in the days of the 'Great King' (B.C. 485-465). The Philistine[5] weapons are known to us only by the famous duello between David and Goliath of Gath (1 Sam. xvii.). The account is full of difficulties for the 'reconciler' of contradictory texts; for instance, David is Saul's

---

[1] Tacitus (*Hist.* v. 13) calls them a 'band of murderers.' The ominous word ' Sicarius ' first occurs in Jewish history during Josephus' time (*Bell. Jud.* iv. 7; vii. 11). St. Paul was charged by Lysias with heading four thousand Sicarii, who at great feasts murdered their victims with concealed daggers. Also forty Sicarii bound themselves by the Cherem-oath (the original ' Boycotting ') to slay Paul. The Sica or Sicca will be noticed in another chapter.

[2] The Machabæan epoch is interesting, because during it the idea of a 'resurrection' was established. The word should be written ' Makabi ' if derived from Mi Kamo Ka Baalim Yahveh (Ex. xv. 11).

[3] The number is given in Chronicles (1, xxi. 5) at one million five hundred and seventy thousand without including Levi and Benjamin. Many attempts have been made to reconcile the little difference of two hundred and seventy thousand souls.

[4] I shall notice Assyrian Arms in chap. x.

[5] By a curious feat of etymology, this word, or rather the German ' Philister ' (confounded with *Balestarius* or *Balestæus*, a crossbow-man, the militia of small artisans?) has come to signify in modern parlance one indifferent to ' intellectual interest ' and the ' higher culture.' As applied to the enemy it is simply Prig writ large.

armour-bearer, and yet unknown at Court.[1] Nor is it easy to discover where Gath is. It is popularly identified with Kharbat (ruins of) Gat: this heap of ruins lies west of castled Bayt Jibrín, the 'House of Giants' (tyrants), the Arabic name corresponding with the Hebrew Bethogabra. The field of fight has been found in the Wady El-Samt (Elah of St. Jerome), west of Jerusalem. The people of this part of Palestine, probably descended from the Hyksos or Canaanites, are a fine tall race, bred to fray and foray by the neighbourhood of predatory Bedawin:[2] armed to the teeth, they are adepts in the use of the huge 'nebút' or quarterstaff.

The plain of Philistia, which once supported five princely cities, appears very barren viewed from the sea; but the interior shows well-watered valleys, and the succession of ruins proves that the country belonged to an energetic and industrious race. Gaza ('Azzah), at the southern extremity, was a place of considerable importance, on account of its fine port and its trade with the adjacent Bedawin. It must not be confused with modern Ghazzah.[3]

Goliath, the 'champion of the uncircumcised' (Philistines), and possibly a type of the race, wore armour[4] of 'brass' (copper); unfortunately the materials of his Sword and sheath are not specified.

Leaving Syria, we proceed to Cyprus, which may be considered an outlying part of Palestine. Its size, its position between the east and the west, and its wealth in gold, silver, copper, and iron, made it an important station for the early Pelasgo-Hellenic or Græco-Italic race which passed westwards, using the Hellespont and the Bosphorus for ferry-places, and the Ægean Islands for stepping-stones. Thus Cyprus became the 'cradle of Greek culture, the cauldron in which Asiatic, Egyptian, and Greek ingredients were brewed together.' General Palma

---

[1] *The Old Testament in the Jewish Church*, p. 126, by the Rev. W. Robertson Smith (Blacks, Edinburgh, 1881).

[2] Napoleon Buonaparte was right in attributing the instability of the great empires (Egypt, Babylon, Assyria) bordered by the Bedawin, to the destructive action of the Arab race: 'That most mischievous nation whom it is never desirable to have either for friends or enemies' (Ammian. Marcell. xiv. 4). I have enlarged upon this subject in *Unexplored Syria* (i. 210). The first noted outswarming was of the Hyksos or Shepherd-Kings (B.C. 1480 to 1530?). Another, under the influence of Mohammed the Apostle of Allah, changed the condition of the Old World; and in the present day, Turkish dominion in the regions frontiered by Arabia is being seriously threatened. Hence Ibn Khaldún of Tunis, who in A.D. 1332 began to write philosophical history, assigns to empire in the East three generations (= 120 years) and three several steps. The first, youth, is of growth (campaigning and annexing); the religion being fanaticism and the form of government a limited monarchy of a semi-republican type. The second, manhood, is a period of 'rest and be thankful,' of not 'stirring up things quiet'; of enjoyment, of easy

scepticism, of luxury, of despotism. The third, age, is decline and fall, the triumph of financiers and capitalists; of aversion from war and from 'territorial aggrandisement'; it is distinguished by employing mercenaries, by religious disbelief, by tyrannic rule. (*Ibn Chaldun und seine Culturgeschichte*, Baron A. von Kremer. Wien.)

[3] This has apparently been done by the Rev. Mr. Porter, the author of that unpraiseworthy *Murray's Handbook*. His Strabo had told him that Gaza lay seven stadia or furlongs from the sea; and St. Jerome that a new town had been built. Yet we are led three miles from the shore to modern Ghazzah, and are gravely told of Moslem absurdities concerning the Makám or tomb of Samson. The old port of which the Ancients speak has evidently been buried by the sands which are attacking Bayrút, and the only survivor of the past may be the site of Shaykh Ijlin on the coast, south of the Mínat or present roads. In noticing Askelon, Mr. Porter tells us all about the old story of Ascalonia, Scallion, Shalot: nothing about the Egyptian Ac-qa-li-na. For a third edition the learned author should take the trouble to consult Brugsch Pasha's Egypto-Syrian studies.

[4] See chap. iv.

(di Cesnola) [1] has proved, by his invaluable finds, which have 'added a new and very important chapter to the history of art and archæology,' that early Cypriote art was essentially Egyptian, modified by Phœnician and Assyrian influences, and eventually becoming Greek. Hence, too, with the dawn of Hellenic civilisation, migrated westwards some of the fairest classical myths. Cyprus was the very birthplace of Venus, [2] an anthropomorphism which rendered infinite service to poetry, painting, and sculpture. Idalium (Dali) was the capital of Cinyras, Kinnári the harper, [3] the Crœsus of his day; it was the site of Myrrha's sin and the death-place of her son Adonis. The latter, who corresponds with the Tammuz of Palestine and the Assyrian Du-zi (Son of Life), is made by Ammianus Marcellinus (xxii. 14) an 'emblem of the fruits of the earth cut down in their prime.' Here was the *atelier* of Pygmalion, Fa'am Aliyun (*Malleus Deorum*), the hammer of the gods; [4] and here upon his breathing statue of ivory he begat Paphos, the king. Finally, here flourished the poets who preceded the Homerid chief; and here was born Zeno, the Stoic, the 'Phœnician.'

The history of Cyprus begins soon after the beginning. An inscription of Thutmes III. speaks of the 'false breed of the Kittim'; and the island is everywhere on the monuments called Asibi. In the cuneiforms the word is 'Kittie': we also find 'Atnán': hence, possibly, the Hellenic 'Akamantis.' It is the 'Chittim' of the Hebrews (Joseph. 'A. J.' i. 7), and perhaps their 'Caphtor'; the latter word, however, appears to be the Egyptian 'Kefa' or 'Keft' (a palm or Phœnicia), converted into the son of Javan and grandson of Japhet. 'Kittim' and its congeners survive in the Greek Citium, now Larnaca, from 'larnax,' a mummy-case, a coffin. I have already noticed (chap. iv.) the disputed origin of 'Kypros' and 'Cyprus.'

The Autochthones of Cyprus are supposed upon very slight grounds to have been 'Aryans' from Asia Minor, Phrygians, [5] Lycians, [6] Lydians, or Cilicians.

[1] *Cyprus*, before quoted.

[2] Aphrodite or Venus (Urania and Pandemos, Porné and Hetæra), at once the feminine principle in nature, the original mother and the idea of womanly beauty, was a universal personage. In Egypt she was Athor the Goddess of Pleasure, and Ashtar in Nilotic Mendes. Amongst the Arabs she became Beltis, Baaltis the feminine of Bel or Ba'al, and Alitta (Al-ilat the goddess); among the Sidonians Ashtoreth (1 Kings xi. 33); in Phœnicia, Ishtar and Astarte, which Gesenius takes to be a Semitisation of the Persian Sitáreh, a star (*i.e.* Venus); in Byblos, Dionæa and Dione; in other parts of Syria, Derceto, Atergatis (Ta-ur-t, Thoueris), and Nani, the latter still surviving in the Bibi Nani (Lady Venus) of Afghanistan. In Cyprus she was Anat, Tanat, or Tanith (Ta-neith = Athene?); in Persia and Armenia Mítra (Herod. i. 131), Tanata, and Anaitis = Anahid, the planet Venus; and in Carthage, Tanit Pen Baal.

[3] In Heb. Kinnúr, a lyre of six to nine strings resembling the Nubian article. Hence, probably, κιθάρα, Cithara, Chitarra, Guitar, Zither; but there

is a modification by the Persian Sih-tárah or 'the three-stringed.'

[4] Thus in Jeremiah (xxiii. 29), 'Is not my word like as a fire? saith the Lord; and like a hammer that breaketh the rock in pieces?'

[5] I see with pleasure that Mr. W. P. Palmer proposes to continue his exploration of Phrygia; his lecture before the Hellenic Society (Dec. 14, 1882) promises much. The western half of the great western plateau of Asia Minor, this land of monotonous grandeur, is directly connected with the Ægean Sea by a single line of cleavage which extends from Miletus to Celænæ. Egyptian art and influence found its way to Greece *via* Phrygia as well as through Phœnicia, especially in the early days of the Argonauts and the *Iliads*, when Greece began to be connected with nearer Asia. Hence the wide diffusion of the Midas-myth (B.C. 670): the long-eared king's tomb was discovered in 1800. I have elsewhere noticed how far Phrygia extended to the West, leaving indelible marks in Spain and Portugal.

[6] The Lycian tongue, as far as we know, resem-

There must have been an early 'Semitic' innervation, as we see by such names as Amathus ; this is the Greek form of Hamath, the 'high town,' typically explained by the Hebrew 'Amath,' grandson of Canaan. The Phœnicians settled chiefly in the south of the island and made it an outpost of Tyre and Sidon. Herodotus tells us that there were also, according to their own account, Ethiopians (vii. 90), by which he means Cushito-Asiatic tribes from the head of the Persian Gulf.

The staple of Cyprus, from the heroic ages to the Roman days, was the copper-trade and the manufacture of arms and armour. To the legendary Tyrio-Cyprian king Cinyras was attributed the invention of the hammer, anvil, tongs, and other metallurgic tools. This favourite of Venus was only the *hero eponymus* of the Phœnician Cinyradæ, who ruled the isle till subdued by Ptolemy Lagi (B.C. 312). They were opposed to a Semitico-Cilician family of priests and prophets, the Tamyridæ. Homer ('Il.' xi. 19) describes the breast-plate of worked and dama-scened steel (? κύανος) adorned with gold and tin, which King Cinyras sent to Agamemnon. Alexander the Great highly prized, for its lightness and temper, the blade given to him by the King of Citium ; and we know that he used it in battle, slaying 'with his Cyprian Sword' Rhæsales the Persian. Demetrius Poliorcetes wore a suit of armour from Cyprus, which had been tested by darts shot from an engine distant only twenty paces. In Herodotus (vii. 90) the Cyprian contingent of Xerxes' army was weaponed after the manner of the Greeks.

Cyprus would derive her art from the Phœnicians, whose bronze dishes were found in the Palace-cellars at Nineveh. Gem-engraving, and working in *pietra dura*, were highly cultivated, as is proved by General Palma's works, and by the Lawrence-Cesnola collection, 'Album of Cyprus Antiquities.'[1] Glass- and crystal-cutting were well known at a time when Herodotus (ii. 69) could describe the former only as 'fusible stone '—perhaps, however, alluding to paste gems. But Theophrastus, a century and a half after the historian, mentions glass as reported to be made by melting a certain stone. I have already alluded to the peculiar decency and decorum of the glyptic remains in the Isle of Venus, where the festivals were described as being ultra-Canopic in character.[2]

The 'finds' of Cyprian weapons have little importance ; perhaps due care was not devoted to the subject. Dali (Idalium) produced a fine dagger with an open ring for ornament between handle and blade, together with a hatchet and spear-head in copper. Here also was found the bronze tablet of the Duc de Luynes, the

---

bles Zend ; and the coin with a triquetra (Rawlinson's *Herod.* i. 212) has three characters apparently Hittite. The Lycian confederacy of twenty-three towns (six cities being chief) was strong enough to resist Crœsus (Herodotus). Their relationship was by the 'distaff-side' (*Mutterrecht*), as opposed to the 'Sword-side' ; and we find traces of the same antique and logical practice among the Greeks : ἀδελφὸς is evidently derived from δελφύς.

[1] Major di Cesnola *On Phœnician Art in Cyprus* : the proofs are 'gold and silver ornaments of remarkable beauty and grace,' which are said to resemble the produce of Hissarlik.

[2] The Cyprian Venus was worshipped in the form of an Umbilicus or Meta, according to Servius (ad *Æn.* i. 724). Others compare it with a pyramid.

discoverer of the Cypriote syllabary,[1] which has caused, and still causes, so much discussion. Alambra yielded a number of copper tools, needles, bowls, mirrors, hatchets, spear-heads, and daggers (Cesnola, Pl. V.). Among them is a sickle-shaped implement (*a*), of the shape called a 'razor' by writers on Etruscanism; it may be anything between

FIG. 196.—(Plate V.)
NOVACULA.

a razor, a sickle, and a pruning-hook.[2] A tomb at Amathus supplied copper axes and iron arrow-heads (p. 280), and another an iron dagger (p. 276). There is a charming dagger from the Curium treasure (Pl. XXI. p. 312); and we are told (p. 335) of 'an

FIG. 197.—(Prague Museum.)   FIG. 198.—(Klagenfurth Museum.)   FIG. 199.—SILVER
NOVACULA?   NOVACULA, SICKLE? RAZOR?   DAGGER.

iron dagger with part of its ivory handle.' The straight blade, the flesh-chopper, and the leaf-shaped Egyptian Swords are found on a patera[3] (p. 329), and the broken

[1] *Numismatique et Inscriptions Cypriotes*, Paris, 1832. The Dali inscription is compared with the Lycian at the end of vol. i. pt 1, *Soc. of Bibl. Archæol.* 1872. Discussing the eighty characters, the Duc de Luynes found twenty-seven Egyptian, twelve Lycian, and seven Phœnician. This would suggest that the syllabary is a branch of the picture-writing which grew to be an alphabet proper in the Nile Valley, and which, modified by the Phœnicians, passed into Greece. Others hold it to be an imperfect modification of the Assyrian cuneiforms, introduced about B.C. 700 and lasting till Alexander's day. I have already noticed that the cuneiforms were originally pictures of natural objects; and that the same is evidently the case with the Chinese syllabary. Some of the Cypriot signs show a faint resemblance to the Devanagari alphabet, which we know to be a modern offshoot from South Arabian or Himyaritic. A gold incision from the

Curium treasury (Plate xxxiv. No. 7) consists of two crescents adossed, which may be either Hittite or a simple ornament. Mr. Sayce, indeed, derives the syllabary from Khita-land. Of the crescent and the star I have already spoken; no date can be assigned to it in decorative art.

[2] I have figured a similar but broader blade as the Novacula in *Etruscan Bologna*, p. 66. The Prague Museum has about a dozen of these sickles found near Tepl: one (*b*) with a rivet-hole and a kind of beading. In the collection of Carinthian Klagenfurth I found a sickle (*c*, No. 1711) fifteen and a half cent. long by four broad, with an Etruscan inscription ᴍ◇◁A꓿◁꓿. See Chap. X.

[3] The winged Sphinxes upon this patera with hawks' heads are peculiarly Egyptian. *The* Sphinx, which may be older than the Pyramids, is a man-

statue of a warrior from Golgoi carries a falchion or flesh-chopper slung under the quiver to the left side (p. 155). The tombs containing horsemen in terra-cotta invariably yielded one or two spear-heads seven to ten inches long, whilst the figures of foot-soldiers were accompanied by a battle-axe, knife, or dagger. The decapitation of the Gorgon by Perseus adorns a sarcophagus also found at Golgoi (Pl. X.) ; and the head of Medusa (Pl. XXII.) apparently suggested that of the Hindú Kali, with the tongue lolling out as if gorged with gore. The mediæval finds of arms seem to have been more important than the ancient. There is a tempting notice, but only a notice, of the Venetian weapons taken from the two casements of Famagosta, of old Amta-Khadasta,[1] the Ammochostos of Ptolemy (v. 14, § 3) : especially interesting are the rapiers, whose handles bore the Jerusalem Cross and the owners' crests inlaid with gold.

On the mainland north of Cyprus lies a most remarkable land which, forming a point of junction, a connecting-link between the East and the West, was one of the tracks of primitive emigration from Asia to Europe, and *vice versâ*. This *tête de pont*, commanding the island-bridge and the various stepping-stones of rock, is the famous Troas, occupied of old by a branch of the great Phrygian race. Hence the interest attaching to the excavations of Dr. Henry Schliemann. His works are too well known to require any detailed notice of the five (seven ?) cities 'whose successive layers of ruins, still marked by the fires that passed over them, are piled to the height of fifty (two and a half) feet above the old summit of the Hisárlik hill.'[2] The explorer's labours, according to his editor, have passed through the 'several stages of uncritical acceptance, hypercritical rejection, and discriminating belief' : I can only remark that the question of Troy appears farther from being settled (if possible) than it ever was ; we now know only where it was not. The excavator began by placing his city of Priam in the second stratum from below, at a depth of twenty-three to thirty-three feet under the surface ; and afterwards raised it to the third layer. It is regretable that the learned author did not submit his lively volume 'Troy' to a professed archæologist. We should not have heard so much about the Svasti, a Hittite ornament, nor should we have been told that the Trojans used 'salt-cellars or pepper-boxes' (p. 79) ; that the Ramayana Epic was 'composed at the latest eight hundred years before Christ' (p. 103), and that the 'ivory, peacocks, and apes are *Sanskrit* words with scarcely any

---

headed lion—the 'union of force and intellect.' Later types change the human head to that of an asp, a ram, and a hawk ; and supply the latter with wings. The same is the case with the Sphinx of Troy and Assyria : it is mostly alate. The Grecian Sphinx changed the bearded human head to that of a woman ; the Gyno-Sphinx in Egypt being later than the Andro-Sphinx. We find the female in the doorway of the Xanthus frieze and over the sarcophagus at Amathus (*Cyprus*, pp. 264-267). Those who would understand the peculiar beauty, not only of line but of expression, which

the Egyptians threw into the face of the Sphinx have only to study the statue standing to the proper left of the main entrance to Shepheard's Hotel, Cairo. It came, I believe, from the great Dromos of the Serapeum, the Apis-tombs of the marvellous Memphis cemetery.

[1] Meaning Holy Lady or Great Goddess, the Syria Dea. Preceded by the digamma, the word became Famagosta, and was corrupted to Fama Augusti and to Ammochosti, a sand-heap.

[2] See his diagram, p. 10, *Troy and its Remains.*

alteration.'[1] When, therefore, I speak of 'Troy proper,' and 'Trojan stratum,' I mean only Dr. Schliemann's Troy.

The townlet had preserved, at the time of its destruction, the technological use of stone, which, indeed, was found in the four lower strata, and even in the Acropolis of Athens. It occurs, however, in conjunction with gold and silver, copper, bronze, and traces of iron, but no tin.[2] The people were, like most barbarians, very expert metallurgists; and if Dr. Schliemann's diorite be true diorite,[3] they must have worked with highly-tempered tools. Copper, either pure or slightly alloyed, was the most common metal: we read of a key, a large double-edged axe, a vase-foot, nails, clothes-pins (ἔμβολα), a curious instrument like a horse's bit (p. 261); a bar, a big ring, a chauldron (λέβης), a ridge (φάλος) for the helmet-crest (λόφος), two whole helmets, three crooked knives, and a lance with a mid-rib (p. 279). Upon the so-called 'great Tower of Ilios'[4] was found a large mould of mica-schist for casting twelve different articles, axes and daggers. Thus we learn something about the long copper knives which the Homeric heroes carry besides their Swords and use in sacrifice: also we may now reasonably conclude that the Iliad-poets could not, as has often been asserted, have ignored the fusion and the casting of metals.[5] Near this important mould appeared a fine lance (p. 279), and long thin bars, either with heads or with the ends bent round, determined to be hair- or breast-pins. Iron showed only in a sling-bullet, although Dr. Schliemann often mentions 'loadstone.'[6]

The 'upper Trojan stratum' yielded other moulds for bar-casting and a four-footed crucible, in which some copper was still visible. The gates supposed to be the Scæan or left-handed[7] had two copper bolts (p. 302). The so-called 'Palace

[1] See chapter viii. These assertions are fair specimens of the harm done to philology, in uncritical England, by the one-sided and *ad captandum* views of the 'Sanskritists.' Mr. Gerald Massey hardly exaggerates when he says (i. 135), 'It looks as if the discovery of Sanskrit were doomed to be a fatal find for the philologists of our generation.' The peculiar mixture of philology, in its specialist form, with the science of religion and the tenebræ of metaphysics has, it appears to me, done much harm to all there; but it delighted the half-educated public. It met with scant appreciation in acute France and in critical Germany, where the editing, or rather mutilation, of texts, has been severely chastised. But the Sanskritist, much to the discredit of Oriental studies and of philology in England, has given us an indigestion of Sanskritism; during the last great Oriental Congress in London he almost monopolised time and attention, to the prejudice of Orientalism in general. Apparently a protest is on the point of being raised; but, unhappily, Teutonism is still a scourge in Great Britain, and the typical Solar myth, 'like Hermann's a German.'

[2] Except, of course, in the bronze.

[3] Charles Rau (?), an American, by means of a

bow, and without using metal, bored a hole through an axe of diorite: it occupied him ten hours a day for four months (Jähns, p. 6).

[4] In mediæval Romance 'Ilios,' 'Ilion,' and 'Ilium' were applied to the Palace of Priam.

[5] *Juventus Mundi*, by the Right Hon. W. E. Gladstone, p. 529.

[6] May it not be the black hæmatite used in Cyprus? Compare the goose's head, the sacred basket, and the frog, Egyptian symbol of embryonic man and of Hor-Apollo (Harpocrates), in General Palma (Appendix, p. 364). But is this able writer sure about his 'hæmatite'?

[7] I.e. to one looking north and therefore west. The old Egyptians faced to the south (Hín or Khount), which they called 'upwards' or 'forwards,' in opposition to the North, which was the lower (Khir) or hinder part (Pehu). Thus their right was west (Unim) and their left east (Semah): the right leg of Osiris was the western side of the Delta. So Pliny (ii. 6) makes his observer front southwards. The Assyrian and Semites faced east (Kadam or front, opposed to Akhir or Shalam, the sun's *resting*-place): hence their right (Yemen) was the south, and their left (Sham) was north. They introduced this fashion

of Priam'[1] produced a dozen long thin pins for hair or dress; and one of a bundle of five, fused together by fire, had two separate heads, the upper lentil-shaped, and the lower perfectly round (p. 312). Thick nails, fitted for driving into wood, were rare; the labour of two years produced only two. Finally, there were fragments of a Sword, a lance, and other instruments.

The first article found in the so-called 'Treasury of Priam' was a copper shield (ἀσπὶς ὀμφαλόεσσα), an oval salver measuring in diameter less than twenty inches. The flat field is surrounded by a rim (ἄντυξ) an inch and a half high; the umbo (ὀμφαλός)[2] measured two and one-third by four and one-third across, and this boss was bounded by a furrow (αὖλαξ) two-fifths of an inch across (p. 324). Thus Antyx and Aulax, suited for mounting a guard of hide, recall Ajax's seven-fold shield, made by Tychius[3] ('Il.' vii. 219–223); and Sarpedon's targe, with its round plate of hammered 'Chalcos,' and its hide-covering attached to the inner edge of the rim by gold wires or rivets ('Il.' xii. 294–97). Near the left hand of a Lebes-chauldron, two fragments of a lance and a battle-axe were firmly attached by fusion. There were thirteen copper lances, from nearly seven inches to upwards of a foot long, with one and a half to two and one-third inches of maximum breadth; the shafts had pin-holes for attachment to the handle; the Greeks and Romans inserted the wood into the neck of the metal-head of the lance. There was a common one-edged knife six inches long; and of seven two-edged daggers, the largest measured ten and two-thirds by two inches. The grips averaged two to two and three-quarter inches, and the tang-ends, where the pommels should be, were bent round

FIG. 200.—COPPER SWORD WITH SHARP END, FROM THE 'TREASURY OF PRIAM.'

at a right angle. Doubtless the tang had been encased in a wooden haft; had it been of bone some trace would have remained, and the point, which projected about half an inch, was simply turned to keep the handle in place. This anti-

---

into Ancient India, where, consequently, Dakshina (dextra, the right hand) became the south, and survives in our 'Deccan.' The practice even extended to Ireland where Ɛᵢᵢᵢ or Ɛᵢᵢᵢ (Erin, Ierne) has been derived from the Keltic ᵢᴧᵢ, behind, the west; and ᵢᵢ, an island, the isle lying west of France and Britain.

[1] Travellers who have inspected the excavations deride these pompous terms: the ruins look well in book-illustrations, but the reality is mean in the extreme.

[2] Dr. Schliemann shows the human umbilicus adorned with a cross. The significance of such phrases as 'omphalos of the earth' applied to Delphi and Paphos, is generally misunderstood. Any traveller in India who has seen a Lingait temple would at once

explain it, as well as the illustration in Wilkinson (vol. i. ch. iv. p. 270) showing the Lingam-Yoni, whose worshippers are 'cherubim' (i.e. winged Thmei). Similarly the symbol of Chemosh of Moab and of sundry classical gods was a cone. The Dea Multimamma, Cybele, miscalled 'Artemis' (Diana) of the Ephesians, was a statue, not a cone, but it stood upon an inverted pyramid. The uninitiated as little understand the Crux Ansata or Egyptian Cross, the emblem of life and fecundity, which was adopted by the Coptic Christians. The sacred Tau (Tau of Ezekiel ix. 6) gave rise to the Maltese Cross in Phœnicia, and in Assyria became the emblem of Shamas the sun.

[3] I need hardly remind 'Grecians' that Tychius is supposed to have been a personal friend of the arch-Homerid.

quated contrivance is not yet wholly obsolete, especially when the metal is left naked. The only sign of a Sword (p. 332) was a fragmentary blade five inches and two-thirds long by nearly two inches broad, and with a sharp edge at the chisel-like end. Many golden buttons, not unlike our modern shirt-studs, were found in the 'Treasury'; they had probably served to ornament the belts or straps (τελαμῶνες) of knives, shields, and Swords.[1]

We gather from Dr. Schliemann's labours that his 'Troy,' at the time of its destruction, was a townlet still in the local Stone-age; at the height of the Copper-Bronze Period; and, perhaps, in the earliest dawn of the Iron-epoch. Apparently it had an alphabet, of which the Grecian enemy could not boast;[2] and, comparing its remains with those of Mycenæ, its culture fully equalled, if not excelled, that of contemporary Hellas. It is curious to observe that the deeper the diggings, from twenty-four feet downwards, the greater were the indications of technological skill. According to Herodotus (ii. 118), the Egyptians bore witness to the power of Troy,[3] yet there is an utter absence of Nilotic influence in the remains, and Brugsch denies that there is any allusion to it on the monuments of Egypt. A similar disconnection with Phœnicia and Assyria appears. The resemblance of the terra cottas to those found in Cyprus and in some of the Ægean islands suggests that there was an early relationship between the Phrygian Trojans and the Phrygian Greeks, both being 'Indo-Europeans';[4] and that the eternal Trojan war was, like the later contest between Russia and Poland, Federals and Confederates, nothing but a family feud, a venomous quarrel of rival cousins.

To conclude the ever-interesting subject of Troy. Homer, or the Homerid so called, describes the city according to current legends, as an untravelled Englishman of to-day would describe the Calais of Queen Mary. There is no reason to believe that he saw it, much less that he painted like the photographing of Balzac. Hence it is a daring more than sublime, to find the Scæan Gate and the Palace of Priam. Even the number of superimposed settlements differs. Dr. Schliemann ('Ilios,' &c.) proposes seven, while Dr. Wilhelm Dörpfeld[5] reduces the number to six. These, according to Professor Jebb, are as follows: (1) The Greek Ilium of the latest or Roman age, extending to about six feet below the surface. (2) The Greek Ilium of Macedonian age taken by Fimbria in B.C. 85; it extends over the plateau adjoining Hisárlik. (3) A Greek Ilium of earlier age, taken by Charidemus (B.C. 359); it appears confined to the little mound. (4)

---

[1] Upon this point Dr. Schliemann's *Mycenæ* is more explicit.

[2] It is, I need hardly say, still a disputed point whether the Homeric Greeks could or could not write. See chapter xi.

[3] M. F. Lenormant, the *Academy*, March 21 and 28, 1874.

[4] I must again protest against the use, while compelled by want of another to use the term 'Indo-European,' which, applied to language, contains an unproved theory. India did not supply Europe either with speech or with population. The popular belief appears erroneous as is its appreciation of Darwinism, which did *not* derive man from monkey. The original Egyptian roots developed themselves into a host of dialects which flourished and perished before Pali and Sanskrit, a professor's tongue, like mediæval Latin, never understood of the people, assumed their present shapes.

[5] *North American Review.*

Another unimportant village ; possibly No. 3 in its earliest form, when the Æolic settlers occupied Hisárlik : the evidence of the pottery[1] suggests these to have been the oldest Hellenic remains. (5) Prehistoric city ; and (6) a distinct stratum of ruins also prehistoric. To these Dr. Schliemann adds (7) the earliest prehistoric buildings founded on the floor-rock fifty-two feet below the surface and fifty-nine above the present level of the plain.

Finally, Mr. W. W. Goodwin[2] comes to the 'ultimate conclusion' about Hisárlik, that it shows only two important settlements. The first is the large prehistoric city extending over the hill and plateau. The second is the historic Ilium in its three phases of primitive Æolic occupation of the Acropolis, the Macedonian city, and the Roman Ilium.

The immediate neighbours of Troy were the Lydians, whom history makes the forefathers of the ancient Etruscans.[3] Herodotus (i. 94) tells the tale of Tyrrhenus and his emigration, which, however, differs from the account of Xanthus Lydius preserved by Nicolaus of Damascus. In the 'Iliad' (ii. 864), the Lydians appear only as Mæonians. They were a people of Iranian speech, to judge from such words as *kav* (*canis, kyon, svan*, &c., a dog), and 'Sardis' from 'Sarat' or 'Sard,' in old Persian Thrade and in modern Persian Sál=a year. Apparently their language had affinities with the Etruscan and Latin ; for instance, Myrsilus, son of Myrsus, the Græco-Lydian name of Candaules (Herod. i. 7), has been compared with Larthiali-sa ; and Servilius from Servius, the *l* denoting son (*filius*), shows the same peculiarity. The Lydians were a civilised people who first coined gold (Herod. i. 94) and stamped silver (*ibid.*) ;[4] their name will ever be connected with music. With them twelve was a sacred number ; it formed the perfect Amphictyony of the Ionians, and it survived in the Confederacy of Etruscan cities (Livy, v. 33). Finally, the tomb of Alyattes[5] is apparently a prototype of the Etruscan sepulchres ; and the peculiarity of these 'homes of the dead' suggests direct derivation from Egypt rather than coincidental resemblance.

Until late years it has been accepted as an historic fact that the old colonisers of Tyrrhenia dwelt for years as conquerors in Lower Egypt. The Tuisa, Tursha Toersha, and Turisa of the monuments wear a close-fitting *calotte* with a tall point, whence a long thin tassel falls to the back of the neck, like one of the Cyprus caps and the older style of Moslem Fez.[6] But Brugsch[7] converts the

[1] Professor Jebb quotes M. Dumont, *Céramique de la Grèce Propre.*

[2] The *Academy*, Dec. 9, 1882.

[3] I have treated the question popularly in *Etruscan Bologna* (London : Smith, Elder, & Co., 1876). The study owed its existence to the Rev. Isaac Taylor, who, using the Family Pen once too often, supported the Turanian origin of the Etruscans in a marvellously uncritical and unscholar-like book, *Etruscan Researches* (London: Macmillan & Co., 1874).

The stater of Crœsus was the first gold coin known to the Greeks. Most of the classical authors declare that silver was first coined at Ægina by order of Pheidon (circa B.C. 869).

[5] Hamilton (*Asia Minor*, vol. i. pp. 145–6) has carefully described this most interesting monument.

[6] See the 'colossal male head' in General Palma di Cesnola, *Cyprus*, p. 123.

[7] Preface to *History of Egypt*, p. xvi ; and vol. ii. 124, where a list of racial names is given. Brugsch, it should be noted, is here entirely opposed to his predecessors, De Rougé, Chabas, &c.

monumental Tursha into Taurians : he wholly discredits the existence of a Pelasgo-Italic confederacy in the days of Mene-Ptah I. and of Ramses III. ; and he positively asserts that the Egyptians of the Fourteenth Dynasty knew nothing of Ilium and the Dardanians, Mysians and Lycians, Lydians and Etruscans, Sardinians, Greek Achæans,[1] Siculians, Teucinians, and Oscans.

However that may be, the Etruscans, the *acerrimi Tusci* of Virgil, were a people of high culture, to whose inventive and progressive genius Rome owed her early steps in arts and arms.[2] A flood of light has been thrown upon this page of proto-historic lore by the extensive excavations of late years in the Emilian country about Bologna, the Felsina or Velsina of Tyrrhenia. My late friend, the learned and lamented Prof. G. G. Bianconi, forwarded to me the accompanying sketch (fig. 202) of an exceptional iron blade found in the ruins of Marzabotto.[3] It is described as follows (p. 3) in a work, printed but not published, by the learned archæologist Count Gozzadini of Bologna, ' Di ulteriori scoperte nell' antica necropoli di Marzabotto nel Bolognese ' [4] :—

'Within a cell only thirty centimètres deep, and disposed two mètres distant from one another, lay three skeletons whose heads fronted eastwards. On each was an iron Sword-blade, sixty-two centimètres long by four and a half broad near the tang (*spina*), and fining off to an olive-leaf point ; all have the mid-rib or longitudinal spine. Partly attached by oxidation to one blade is a remnant of the iron scabbard, slightly convex posteriorly and showing in the upper part a rectangular projection, perhaps to carry the hook attached to the balteus. The sheath-front has a mid-rib like the blade, and the wavy mouth is adapted to the Sword-shoulders. On this face only are two buttons (*borchie*) in high relief, connected by a band (*listello*). The tang, twelve centimètres long, shows the length of the hilt, which, being made of more perishable material, has altogether disappeared.'

The long narrow rapier-blade with the mid-rib is first seen in the Egyptian bronzes ;[5] the step was easy to the harder metal. That the iron form was common in Etruria as its bronze congener at Mycenæ, is proved by the discovery of three in a single tomb ; moreover, as has been said, a fourth has been preserved for years in the Marza-

FIG. 201.
THE MARZABOTTO
BLADE.

---

[1] As opposed to the Aqaiuasha or Achæans of the Caucasus (ii. 124).

[2] ' I have seen it affirmed that in those times (early Roman) the youth was instructed in the Etruscan learning, as they are now in the Greek ' (Livy ix. 35).

[3] Described in *Etruscan Bologna*, p. 144. The blade is in Count Aria's collection. The Sword of Misanello, *une longue epée de fer*, also in that museum,

is noticed in p. 359, *Transactions of the Congress of Bologna* in 1871.

[4] One vol. folio large quarto, with 17 Tables. It was preceded by ' Di una necropoli a Marzabotto nel Bolognese,' 1865, large quarto, with 20 Tables. Count Gozzadini is one of the earliest students who followed in the steps of M. Boucher de Perthes.

[5] A fine specimen of a dagger from Thebes with the rapier-blade, and a broad flat hilt of ivory, is in the Berlin Museum.

botto collection. All are similar in form, which is highly civilised. The number of the blades also suggests that they are of native make, not left by the Boians and the Ligaunians, who, according to the late Prof. Conestabile, may have buried in the Marzabotto cemetery. The date of the latter is somewhat uncertain ; but it cannot be much more recent than the burial-ground of Villanova, where Count Gozzadini found an *æs rude*, and which he dates from the days of Numa, B.C. 700. He is followed by Dr. Schliemann ('Troy,' p. 40), and opposed by that learned and practical anthropologist M. Gabrielle de Mortillet ('Le Signe de la Croix,' &c. pp. 88–89), who would assign a far earlier epoch.

Count Gozzadini [1] gives a valuable description of a fifth Etruscan Sword lately discovered at the 'Palazzino' farm, parish of Ceretolo and commune of Casalecchio, some ten kilomètres south-west of 'Etruscan Bologna.' In an isolated tomb, carefully excavated by the proprietor (Marchese Tommaso Boschi), was found a skeleton, the feet fronting southwards. On its left, extending higher than the head, was an iron lance-point,[2] and on the corresponding shoulder a thick armilla of bronze ; other objects, including an Etruscan Oenochoe, two knives wholly iron, and a chisel of the same metal, lay scattered about the grave which was not stone-revetted. Close to the right side was an iron Sword in a sheath of the same metal and wanting the heft : the general belief was that the weapon had been buried with the wielder.

Count Gozzadini (pp. 19, 20) describes the Sword as follows : 'Slightly bi-convex and two-edged, it measures 0·625 mètre from the tang (*codolo*) to the end of the scabbard ; the tang, not including the part forming the grip, was 0·11 mètre. The breadth is 0·47 mètre at the shoulders, narrowing to a point, as is proved by the scabbard diminishing to 0·27 mètre at the end. The handle showed no sign of cross-bars or guard, which would also have been of iron ; and it is evident that the haft was of some destructible substance which has wholly disappeared. The probability is that the grip was shaped like those of the preceding Bronze Age—that is, bulging out behind the blade for easier hold. The sheath was somewhat more bi-convex than the Sword ; an iron-plate about one millimètre thick, had been turned over horizontally to unite the edges, which, near one of the sides, formed a narrow and gradual line of superposition. This scabbard ended in an ovoid crampet or ferule ; and a fragment of plate iron with a short broad hook, like that generally used for attachment to the belt, probably belonged to it.'

Here, then, we have again a perfect rapier. The only question is whether it was Etruscan, or, as supposed by M. G. de Mortillet, Gaulish.[3] Count Gozzadini argues ably to prove the former case.[4] He acknowledges that the invading Boii

---

[1] *Di un antico Sepolcro a Ceretolo nel Bolognese* (Modena : Vincenzi, 1879), p. 9.

[2] This weapon resembled the bronze forms found at Broilo in Tuscany and in the great collection discovered in 1875 and called the 'Fonderia di Bologna.' An account of the latter is found in *Note Archeologiche*, &c. (Bologna : Fava e Garagnani, 1881).

[3] The learned French anthropologist compared these weapons with those found in the Marne graves. (*Les Gaulois de Marzabotto, Revue Archéol.* 1870-71,&c.)

[4] Count Gozzadini replied in M. G. de Mortillet's

held the city and country for two centuries (B.C. 358–566), until the Romans expelled them for ever. But he shows that these peoples did not use such fine Swords. When treating of the Kelts (chapter xiii.), I shall show that the long unmanageable slashing Claidab or Spatha of these peoples had nothing in common with the strong, bi-convex, and thoroughly-civilised rapier of Ceretolo.

Other blades like that of Ceretolo—long, narrow, and pointed—have been found in tombs notably Etruscan. Such, for instance, was that of Cære, now in the Gregorian Museum, Rome. In December 1879 two other blades were produced by a necropolis in Valdichiana, between Chiusi and Arezzo, where a long Etruscan inscription was engraved upon the foot of a tazza. Two similar blades are also portrayed in relief and colour upon the stuccoed wall of a Cære tomb. Des Vergers[1] describes them as follows: ' La frise supérieure est ornée d'Épées longues à deux tranchants, à la lame large et droite avec garde à la poignée, se rapprochant de celle que les Romains désignaient par le nom de *spatha*. Les unes sont nues, les autres dans le fourreau.' Four such Swords were also produced at Pietrabbondante in the district of far-famed Isernia, and are preserved in the National Museum of Naples. Signor Campanari discovered in an Etruscan tomb a Sword-hilt in bronze attached to a blade of iron.[2] Finally, the Benacci property near the Certosa of Bologna also yielded an iron blade and iron chisels like those of Ceretolo.

The late learned Prof. Conestabile truly asserts, ' Des Épées de même forme et de même dimension ont été trouvées dans d'autres localités étrusques, situées dehors la sphère des invasions Gauloises, notamment en Toscane.' It is certain that such blades have been discovered on both sides of the Alps. As the Romans adopted the Iberic or Spanish blade ; so the Gauls may have substituted for their own imperfect arms the weapons taken from the Italians ; in fact, we know from history that they did so. Moreover, the Etruscans extended their commerce, not only over Transalpine regions, but to that vast region extending from Switzerland to Denmark, and from Wallachia to England and Ireland.[3] This has been proved by the investigations of many scholars : in Germany by Lindenschmidt, Von Sacken, Virchow, Kenner, Weihold, Von Conhausen, and Genthe ; by the Swiss Morlot, De Rougemont, Desor, and De Bonstetten ; by the Dane Worsaäe ; by Gray, Dennis, Hamilton, and Wyllie in England ; by the Belgian Schuermans ; and by the Italians Gozzadini, Conestabile, Garrucci, and Gamurrini. Desor, when receiving the drawing of an iron Sword with bronze handle discovered at Sion, and declared by Thioly to resemble exactly those of Hallstadt, declared : ' De pareilles Épées sont évidemment fabriquées à l'étranger et non dans le pays : elles nous conduisent donc vers ce grand commerce Étrusque qui se faisait pendant la

---

Materiaux pour l'Histoire primitive de l'Homme ; and the paper was entitled by the Editor (not by the author), ' L'Élément Étrusque de Marzabotto est sans mélange avec l'élément gaulois ' (Jan. 1873).

[1] *L'Étrurie et les Étrusques*, vol. i. p. 93. Atlas, p. 2, Pl. II. [2] The bronze is in the British Museum; the iron in the possession of Mr. H. S. Cuming (Meyrick). [3] Genthe, *Program*, &c. p. 15.

première époque de fer, époque sur laquelle on s'est trompé si souvent.' Livy,[1] in fact, proves the extent of arms-manufactory in Etruria, when he relates that in B.C. 205, at which time the Boiian occupation of Felsina ended, Arezzo alone could furnish Scipio's fleet in forty-five days with three thousand helmets, as many Scuta and lances of three different kinds.

But the rapier was not the only form of Etruscan Sword. In Hamilton's ' Etruscan Antiquities,'[2] a human figure carries a cutting Sword like a 'hanger,' wearing the belt at the bottom of the thorax. The Ceramique of Etruria supplies copious illustrations of Swords and other weapons ; but the art is somewhat mixed, and our safest information must be derived from actual finds.

We are justified by these finds in concluding that the Etruscans of Italy had from their earliest times a rapier which, for a cut-and-thrust weapon, is well-nigh perfect. The blade is long, but not too long; broad enough to be efficient without overweight, and strengthened to the utmost by the mid-rib which forms a shallow arch. In chapter xi. I shall compare the Etrurian Sword with that of Mycenæ ; the latter is a marvel of its kind, but it is made of a far inferior metal —bronze.

---

[1] XXVIII. cap. 45. [2] Vol. iv. Pl. XXX. ; it is copied by Meyrick.

CHAPTER X.

THE SWORD IN BABYLONIA, ASSYRIA AND PERSIA, AND ANCIENT INDIA

ALTHOUGH Professor Lepsius maintained and proved that the earliest Babylonian civilisation was imported from Egypt, Biblical leanings, and the fatal practice of reading myths and mysteries as literal history, have led many moderns to hold the Plain of Shinar (Babylon) and the ancient head of the Persian Gulf to be the cradle of culture and the origin of 'Semitism.' We still read, 'Babylonia stands prominent as highly civilised and densely populated at a period when Egypt was still in her youthful prime.'[1] Only in Genesis (x. 10), a document treating of later ethnology, we find mention of Erech,[2] Urukh being the oldest traditional king of Babylon. On the other hand, the Egyptians declared Belus and his subjects to have been an Egyptian colony which taught the rude Babylonians astrology and other arts. The monumental Babylonian or pre-Chaldæan Empire begins only in B.C. 2300, many a century—say a score—after Menes. The late Mr. George Smith warns us that some scholars would make the annals 'stretch nearly two thousand years beyond that time'; but he expressly declares no approximate date can be fixed for any king before Kara-Indas (circ. B.C. 1475 ?–1450 ?). Also, 'The great temples of Babylonia were founded by the kings who preceded the conquest by Hammu-rabi, King of the Kassi' Arabs (sixteenth century B.C.).[3]

FIG. 202.

ASSYRIAN SWORD

The Burbur or Accad inscriptions found in Babylonia do not date before

---

[1] The writer of this sentence is, curious to say, the learned Dr. Birch (p. 5, vol. i., *Soc. Bib. Archæology*, 1872). Even Justin (lib. i.) knew better; he makes Sesostris (ii. 3) 1,500 years older than Ninus, 'the most ancient king of Assyria,' whom he places in B.C. 2196—2144 (Wetzel).

[2] In the LXX Orech; the Cuneiform Uru-ki (City of the Land); in Talmud, Urikut, City of the Dead for Babylon (*hod.* Warka); and in Greek Orchóe, whence perhaps 'Orcus.' Urukh became among the Classics of Europe 'pater Orchamus.'

[3] *Assyrian Discoveries* (London : Sampson Low & Co., 1876), p. 447. He gives, as a scheme of Abydenus and Berosus, the Chaldæan :—

	Years.
Alorus and 9 kings before the Babylonian Flood . .	432,000
86 kings after B. Flood to Median conquest (1st dynasty)	34,080 (33,091
8 Median kings (2nd dynasty)	224 (160?)
11 other (3rd dynasty) . .	unknown
49 Chaldæan (4th dynasty) .	458
9 Arabian (5th dynasty) .	245
Semiramis.	
45 kings (7th dynasty) . .	526

Nabonidus, the antiquary king (B.C. 555), according to a Cylinder found at Sipar (Sepharvaim, Sun-city) and studied by Mr. Pinches, assigns a date to the deified Sargina of about B.C. 3,800 years. He unburied,

B.C. 2000. Ninus, the builder of Nineveh (Fish-town) and the founder of the Assyrian dynasties, is usually placed between B.C. 2317 and 2116. An extract, by Alexander Polyhistor from the Armenian [1] Chronicle, gives, by adding the dynasties, an origin-date of 2,317 years. Berosus the priest, declares from official documents, that Babylon (God's Gate) had regal annals 1,000 years before Solomon (B.C. 993–953), in whose reign dynastic Jewish history begins. Diodorus Siculus, quoting Ctesias (B.C. 395) makes the monarchy commence one thousand years before the Siege of Troy, which we may place about B.C. 1200. Æmilius Sura, quoted by Paterculus, proposes the date B.C. 2145, and Eusebius the Armenian 1340 years before the first Olympiad (B.C. 776), or B.C. 2116. The great kingdom of the Khita (Hittites) [2] was succeeded on the rich lowlands of the Tigris-Euphrates system by Babylon, which the Nilotes called ' Har,' and by the Assyrians, whom the Egyptians called Mat or the People, and hieroglyphs notice the 'Great King of the Mat.' But ⯈ ⯑ Assur [3] was little known till the decline of the Pharaohs in the Twenty-first Dynasty (B.C. 1100–966) of the priest Hirhor and his successors : one of the latter —Ramessu or Ramses XVI.—married, when dethroned, a daughter of Pallasharnes, the 'great king of the Assyrians,' whose capital was Nineveh,[4] and thus led to the Assyrian invasions of Egypt.[5] We may, then, safely hold with Lepsius that early Babylonian civilisation was posterior to, if not imported from, Egypt.[6]

In Babylonia a third element, the so-called ' Turanian ' (Chinese), first emerged from Egyptian and began to take its part in the drama of progress. The almost unknown quantity has assumed magnificent proportions in the eyes of certain students, and great things are still expected from Akkadian revelation. Yet the race typified by the Chinese could have had no effect upon the learning of Egypt.

18 cubits below the surface, the Cylinder of Naramsin, son of Sargina (B.C. 3750?), ' which no king had seen for 3,200 years.' Sir Henry C. Rawlinson (the *Athenæum*, Dec. 9, 1882) is disposed to accept the date ' within certain limits.'

[1] The word is Har-Minni, or Mountains of the Minni. The oldest Armenian inscriptions date from the eighth century B.C.

[2] It was in attacking these Khita that Ramses II. (Sesostris) left his three ' columns ' or tablets on the rocks near the Nahr el-Kalb of Bayrut (chap. ix.). Six Assyrian inscriptions were also known there, bearing the names of Assur-ris-ilim, Tiglath-pileser, Assurnazirpal, Shalmanesar, Sennacherib, and Esar-haddon. No epigraphs were found on the north side of the river, where an ancient aqueduct, overgrown with luxuriant verdure, turns a mill. About three years ago, however, the proprietor, when making a new channel, broke away part of the rock, and a fragment bearing cuneiforms attracted the attention of Dr. Hartmann, Chancellor of the German Consulate. No other steps were taken till October 10, 1881, when M. Julius Loyt-ved, Danish Vice-Consul for Bayrut, bared the face of the cliff and discovered five cuneiform inscriptions, one con-taining 45 lines. They seem to have been hastily cut,

as they follow the shape of the rock whose surface has not been dressed. According to Professor Sayce, they are Babylonian, not Assyrian.

[3] Or Asshur, ' the Arbiter of the Gods,' repre-sented by the winged disc of Egypt.

[4] Nineveh, destroyed by the Medes (Manda or Madu) and Persians in B.C. 583, had thus a life of 1,617 years, assuming its origin at the middle term, B.C. 2200.

[5] Brugsch, vol. i. chap. xvi., shows that Seshonk (Shishak) and other Pharaohs of the Twenty-first Dynasty were Assyrians who ruled ' Mat Muz-ur,' the people of Egypt.

[6] The great scholar derives from Egypt the Cunei-form Syllabarium, which was originally pictorial :— drawing everywhere preceded writing. The astro-nomy of Mesopotamia is Egyptian (the unit of measure being the ell of 0·525 mètre); and the architecture, that prime creation of the human mind, shows by temples, temple-towers, tombs, and es-pecially pyramids (e.g. that at Birs Namrud), an imperfect imitation of the Nile Valley. Herodotus attributes to Babylon the discovery of the Pole, the Sun-dial, and the twelve hours of day, all well known to ancient Egypt. The ' Sabbaths ' are Assyrian.

'At the time when the genealogical tables of Genesis were written (chap. x.) those regions were still so unknown and barbarous that the writer excluded them from the civilised world.' [1]

Our factual knowledge of Mesopotamian civilisation is mostly due to the labours of the present century. Professor Grotefend of Bonn, in 1801–1803, discovered the clue to the Persian cuneiform,[2] cuneatic or arrow-headed character. This great step in advance opened the labyrinth to a host of minor explorers— Heeren (1815), Burnouf (1836), Lassen (1836–44), Hincks, who attacked the Assyrian cuneiform, and, to mention no more, Rawlinson, whose 'Reading made Easy' popularised the study in England. Actual exploration of the Mesopotamian ruins was begun by the learned Consul Botta (Dec. 1842) who, after failing at Koyunjik opposite Mosul, worked successfully at Khorsabad, some ten miles to the north-east : four years afterwards (Dec. 1846) the first collection of Assyrian antiquities reached the Louvre. He was followed (Nov. 8, 1845) by Mr. (now Sir) H. A. Layard, who unfortunately was not an Orientalist : his various discoveries of a stamped-clay literature, and his popular publications, introduced to the public Koyunjik and Kal'at Ninawi (Nineveh), Hillah (Babylon), Warká, Sippara (Abu Nabbah) sixteen miles south-west of Baghdad, and a variety of Biblical sites.

This 'recovery' of antiquities buried twenty centuries ago, and a whole literature of bas-reliefs, enables us to compare the Nile Valley, the cradle and mother-country of science and art, with its rival-successor on the Tigris-Euphrates. The original workmanship of Assyria, like that of Egypt, is still unknown ; and, though she borrowed from Nile-land, her art is rather a decadence than a rise. The difference, indeed, is between the porphyries, the granites, and the syenites of Egypt, and the mud-bricks, the coarse black marbles, the rough basalts, and the undurable alabasters (a calcareous carbonate) of Interamnian Assyria. But the industrious valley-men made the best of their poor material. The ruins show the true Egyptian arch ; the so-called Ionic capital, the original volutes being goats' horns ;[3] the Caryatides and Atlantes, or human figures acting columns ; the cornice, corbel, and bracket ; with a host of architectural embellishments to fill up plain fields. Apparently all migrated from Nile-land. Such were the winged circle, the lotus,[4] the fir-cone, and the rosette : the latter, also found by Dr. Schliemann at ' Troy '

---

[1] The *Athenæum*, July 24, 1880.

[2] That the Assyrians had books appears plainly from the inscriptions : ' In the night-time bind round the sick man's head a sentence taken from a good book ' (a soporific!). Parchment was most probably the first material (*Trans. of Soc. Bib. Archæology*, vols. ii. 55, and iii. 432) ; and the language proves that the papyrus-scroll (Duppu-ga-zu) was known.

[3] We find in Assyria the wild goat standing upon a capital, now the arms of Istria. The same appears at Palmyra (Prof. Socin's Collection). The winged bulls probably suggested, like the Egyptian Cherubs, our angels' wings. These motors should now be for-

bidden in statuary by Act of Parliament ; or the artist should be compelled to supply the pinions with the muscles necessary for working them. I need hardly say that the required development would convert the human dorsum to the appearance of the two-humped camel. The late Gustave Doré's admirable illustrations of Dante (*Purgat.* xix. 51) sin greatly in this way.

[4] A goddess in alabaster has in each hand a lotus flower, which she holds against her breasts. This is characteristic of old Egypt, which derived the plant from the Equatorial African Lake-region. The same figure again wears a large Egyptian wig, the hair falling in ringlets upon the shoulders.

(p. 160), became the *rosa mystica* of Byzantine art, and was used by Christians to denote their origin. Again, we have the key-pattern, which is Trojan and Chinese as well as Greek; the honeysuckle, a symbol of the Homa or Assyrian 'Tree of Life';[1] the guilloche-scroll or wave-pattern; and the meander, also miscalled the Tuscan border: the latter is common in Egypt and Cyprus, and possibly derives from the Hittite Svasti, erroneously called Svastika.[2] Assyria equally excelled in literature,[3] in painting, in sculpture, in the minor arts, and in metallurgy. She made transparent glass: a crystal lens[4] found at Nineveh accounts for the diminutive size of some inscriptions. Her sons worked enamel, and thus adorned the humble brick: like their Egyptian teachers, they were skilful in ivory-carving, in cutting cylinders of jasper and *pietra dura*, and in gem-engraving on carnelian, onyx, sardonyx, amethyst, agate, chalcedony, and lapis lazuli.

As regards Assyrian metallurgy, few articles of iron have been found in the river-valley's damp and nitrous soil, but the metal is denoted, as in Egypt, by a blue tint, and the god Ninib is termed the 'lord of the iron coat.' Gold and silver were profusely used as ornaments. Lead was dug in the Montes Gordæi (Kurd Mountains) near Mosul, the original Ararat of 'Noah's ark.' Copper vessels, bright as gold when polished, were found in the palaces of Nimrúd: the ore was brought from the northern highlands heading the Tigris Valley, where the Arghana ma'adan (Diyar-i-Bekr mine) long supplied the Ottoman Empire. The place that exported their tin is disputed.[5] They worked well in bronze: of this alloy many castings have been found: utensils, as pots and cauldrons, cups, forks and spoons, dishes, and plates, plain and ornamented; tools, as picks, nails, and saws; thin plates; the so-called razors;[6] lamps; weapons; an ægis-like object also found in Egypt; lance-heads, shields, and door-sockets each weighing six pounds and three and three-quarter ounces.[7] The bronze gates of Balawat, with plates eight feet long showing the triumphs of

---

[1] The Soma, a weed in India (*Asclepias gigantea*), is a derivation from Homa. The Persea, or Egyptian Tree of Life, was probably the *Balanitis Ægyptiaca*.

[2] The careless confusion of Svastika, the worshipper-sect, with Svasti, the symbol, was made by me in my Commentary on Camoens (chap. iv. 'Geographical'). Burnouf (Emile), in *La Science des Religions*, made the Svasti the feminine principle; and the Pramantha, or perpendicular fire-stick, the male. If used on sacrificial altars to produce the holy fire (*Agni*), the practice was peculiar, and not derived from every-day-life: as Pliny knew (xvi. 77), the savage uses two, never three, fire-sticks. The Svasti is apparently the simplest form of the guilloche. According to Wilkinson (II. chap. ix.), the most complicated form of the guilloche covered an Egyptian ceiling upwards of a thousand years older than the objects found at Nineveh. The Svasti spread far and wide, everywhere assuming some fresh mythological and mysterious significance. In the north of Europe it became the Fylfot or crutched cross.

[3] Assyria, like Egypt, cultivated geometry and algebra, which have been supposed to originate from revenue surveys and altar measurements. She used the Astrolabe and popularised square roots and fractions, with a denominator of 60, the sole representative of the decimal and duodecimal systems. With her fall (B.C. 555) coincides the birth of literature in Greece, where writing became general about B.C. 500. The Assyrians were great in magic and in divination, such as birth-portents, dog-omens, &c. &c.

[4] Again Egyptian. Wilkinson, II. chap. vii.

[5] The nearest site would be the Caucasus, which in early ages yielded a small supply. Layard (p. 191) supposes the tin to have been obtained from Phœnicia; and, 'consequently, that used in the (Assyrian) bronzes of the British Museum may actually have been exported, nearly three thousand years ago, from the British Isles.'

[6] A 'copper instrument from Koyunjik' (Layard, p. 596) is shaped exactly like the so-called Etruscan razors. See chap. ix.

[7] Layard, *Nineveh and Babylon*, p. 163.

Shalmaneser II. (B.C. 884–850), attest high art. Layard supplied the British
Museum with many iron articles from the north-western palace at Nimrúd, and
some had iron cores round which bronze had been cast for economy. Amongst
them were iron chain-armour, two rusty helmets ornamented with bronze ; picks,
hammers, knives, and saws.[1] The approximate date may be assumed at B.C. 880.

In mimic war (hunting) the Assyrians were proficients. Many hundreds of
bas-reliefs, which are more natural because less conventional than those of Egypt,
illustrate the chase of the lion, stag, and jungle-swine; the wild horse, ass, and bull.
They were equally skilled in the art of war, which is shown in all its phases, the
march, the passage of streams, the siege, the battle, the sea-fight, or rather the
river-fight, the pursuit, and the punishment of prisoners by torturing, impaling,

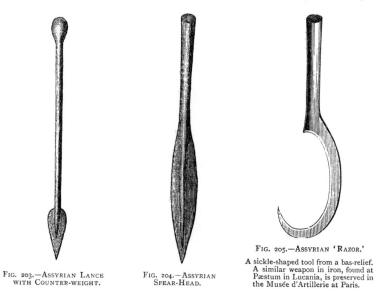

FIG. 205.—ASSYRIAN 'RAZOR.'

A sickle-shaped tool from a bas-relief.
A similar weapon in iron, found at
Pæstum in Lucania, is preserved in
the Musée d'Artillerie at Paris.

FIG. 203.—ASSYRIAN LANCE
WITH COUNTER-WEIGHT.

FIG. 204.—ASSYRIAN
SPEAR-HEAD.

flaying alive, crucifixion, and 'tree-planting' or vivi-interment. The abominable
cruelties of these Asiatics, still practised by the Persian, the Kurd, and the 'unspeakable' Turk, contrast strongly with the mildness of the African Egyptians.
Their walls, single or double, were provided with the fosse and the rampart, and
with machicolations, crenelles, and battlements ; the last two originally shields
like the Egyptian cartouche. The *places fortes* were attacked by the wheeled
tower,[2] the iron-pointed battering ram, the scaling ladder, and the pavoise, or large
shield common throughout Europe in the fifteenth and sixteenth centuries.[3] In
the field pennons are attached to the lances, and the standard-bearers carry eagles.

[1] See chap. vi. He figures one of the latter
(*Discoveries in the Ruins of Nineveh aud Babylon*,
p. 195) : it measured 3 feet 8 inches long by 4⅝ inches
in breadth.

[2] 'Assyrians placing a human-headed bull on a

car,' with levers and ropes (Layard, p. 112), reminds
us of the statue of Ramses II., and shows that the
people could move enormous weights. Both societies
had 'unbounded command of naked human strength.'

[3] Demmin, pp. 293–94.

The action begins with missiles, slings, darts, and arrows ; the mace and spear then play their part, and the Sword is never absent. The warriors—who appear on foot or horseback, with gorgeous caparisons, in chariots or swimming with floats of inflated skins— wear helmets of many shapes, crested, crescented, capped with the *fleur-de-lys* and perfectly plain ; some are close-fitting with ear-flaps, the common skull-cap (*namms*) of Ancient Egypt, and the Indian Kan-top. The head-gear usually ended in a metal point—the *pickelhaube*. The sculptors show imbricated armour or hauberks (mail-coats) of the Norman type, with stockings of iron- (?) rings, gaiters, and boots laced up in front. The shields, either circular or rounded at the top and straight at the bottom, cover the whole body.

The Assyrian Sword, like the Egyptian, is of four principal shapes. One, a

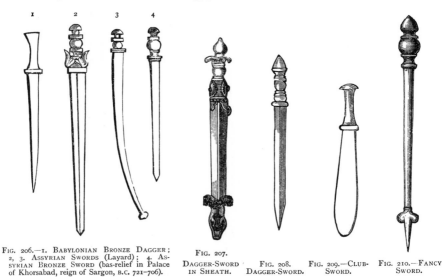

FIG. 206.—1. BABYLONIAN BRONZE DAGGER; 2, 3. ASSYRIAN SWORDS (Layard) ; 4. ASSYRIAN BRONZE SWORD (bas-relief in Palace of Khorsabad, reign of Sargon, B.C. 721–706).

FIG. 207.
DAGGER-SWORD IN SHEATH.

FIG. 208.
DAGGER-SWORD.

FIG. 209.—CLUB-SWORD.

FIG. 210.—FANCY SWORD.

long poniard of Nilotic form, is carried by all classes from king to slinger. The other (*Malmulla*,? fig. 206, 3), by some translated 'falchion,' appears slightly curved, not like the Turkish scymitar, but with the half-bend of the Japanese and the Indian Talwár. The curved blades in the bas-reliefs mostly characterise conquered peoples. The third is the Sa-pa-ra or Khopsh, of which an illustration will be given (p. 208) ; and the fourth is a club-shaped blade thickening at the end, which is almost pointless.[1] In the cuneiforms a ' double Sword ' is often mentioned : it may be of the kind called by the Greeks ' Chelidonian ' (chap. ix. and xi.).[2] Fancy weapons appear in the bas-reliefs—for instance, the Sword from the Nineveh palace of the Sardanapalus-reign, B.C. 1000 (fig. 210).

Mostly the weapons have richly decorated hilts and scabbards. In a royal

[1] We have still to explain ' Kakku ' (weapon ?) and ' Gizzin ' (scymitar ?).

[2] In the Tablets we read of the ' Star of the double Sword ' (Kakab gir-tab) ⁓ᵉ �646ᵉ. ' Hammasti,' also, is the ' blade of the double Sword.'

sculpture the pommel is formed by a mound or hemisphere—a constant ornament—and below it is a ball between two flat discs : the upper jaws of two lions,
placed opposite each other, embrace the blade and the grip where it presses
against the metal sheath-mouth.   Another has a lion's head on the handle.   The
two-lion scabbard is common, and sometimes the beasts are locked in a death
embrace.   In another specimen the royal blade is much broader than usual, and
two lions couchant form the ferrule, embracing the sheath with their paws and re-
trogardant or bending their heads backwards (fig. 212).   The ferrule of another is
enriched with a guilloche.   In the inscriptions of Assur-bani-pal [1] (Sardanapalus) we

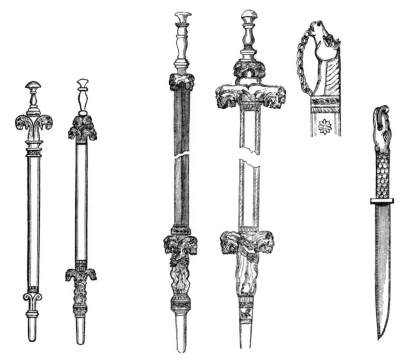

FIG. 211.—ASSYRIAN SWORDS.   FIG. 212.—ASSYRIAN SWORDS.   FIG. 213.—ASSYRIAN DAGGER.

read of a 'steel Sword and its sheath of gold,' and of 'steel Swords of their girdles.'
Another legend runs—'He lifted his great Sword called "Lord of the Storm,"'
proving that the Sword, like the horse, the chariot, the boat, and other favourites,
had names and titles.

The dagger is often decorated with the head of the hippopotamus (a Nilotic, or
rather African, beast) surmounting an imbricated handle (fig. 213).[2]   This poniard is
worn in the girdle, and in some cases it appears under and behind the surcoat.   The

[1] 'Ashur create a Son,' B.C. 673.   *Assyrian Dis-*
coveries, by G. Smith (London : Sampson Low, 1876).
[2] For instance, that in the bas-reliefs of Burs

Nimrúd, B.C. 1000, now in the Louvre.   The hippopotamus is now never found out of Africa.

longer weapon is carried by a narrow bauldric slung over the right shoulder and meeting another cord-shaped band at the breast, in fact suggesting our antiquated cross-belts. The Sword is always worn on the left side.[1] A royal Sword-belt bears several ranges of bosses and globules, which may be pearls : that of the

FIG. 214.—ASSYRIO-BABYLONIAN ARCHER in war coat, leggings, and fillet. Bas-relief, B.C. 700. (Museum of the Louvre.)

FIG. 215.—ASSYRIAN FOOT SOLDIER with the coat, helmet and tall crest, greaves or leggings, target and lance. Bas-reliefs of Nineveh of Sardanapalus V. B.C. 700.

FIG. 216.—ASSYRIAN SOLDIER HUNTING GAME. Bas-relief of Khorsabad, of the reign of Sargon. (British Museum.)

eunuch-attendant has three wide rows, the central broken here and there by round plates. A Magian wears a broad scarf with long hanging fringes cast obliquely over the left shoulder : it is edged with a triple series of small rosettes placed in squares, and it passes over the Sword, to which, perhaps, it acts bauldric. A soldier's bauldric is coloured red, like the wood of the bows and arrows. Another eunuch wears the Sword-belt buckled

FIG. 217.—FOOT SOLDIER OF THE ARMY OF SENNACHERIB (B.C. 712-707). From a bas-relief in the British Museum. The shape of the conical helmet is modern Persian ; the coat and leggings appear to be of mail : the shield is round, large, and very convex.

FIG. 218.—ASSYRIAN WARRIOR, WITH SWORD AND STAFF.

FIG. 219. — ASSYRIAN WARRIORS AT A LION HUNT.

FIG. 220.—ASSYRIAN EUNUCH In mail-coat, with mace, bow, and dagger-Sword.

over the waist-sash, and holds in his right hand a scourge : this was the emblem of official rank, as the Egyptian carried a hide-Kurbáj.[2] Another soldier has, besides the Kamar-band (waist-sash), a red belt, and what seems to be its tassels hanging from the shoulders before and behind.

[1] With cavalry as well as infantry (Layard, p. 55). Upon this, a very complicated subject, I shall have much to say.   [2] Whence the French *cravache*.

The Sword and the Sword-dagger seem to have been universally used in Assyria—none but captives and working men are without them. The vulture-headed ' Nisroch the god ' (of Nebuchadnezzar) carries two long poniards in his breast garment, whereas Ashur in statues shoots his bow. Assur-bani-pal 'destroys the people of Arabia with his Sword.' The king in his car, with his Cidaris (tiara) and fly-flap, has two daggers and a Sword in his girdle, from which hang cords and tassels. Another rests his right hand upon a staff, and his left upon the pommel of his weapon. A third plunges a short straight blade, like the matador's *espada*, between the second and third vertebræ of a wild bull, where the spinal cord is most assailable : this would be done to-day in the spectacula of Spain. Swords are worn by the magi and the eunuchs ;[1] and one of the latter draws his weapon to cut off a head. The body-guard bears by his side a Sword longer than usual, and holds arrows and other weapons for his lord's use. Even the executioner does his work with the Sword.

Happily for students, an ancient Assyrian bronze Sword was bought by Colonel Hanbury from the Bedawin at Nardin.[2] He could not ascertain whence it originally came, but it was probably placed in the hands of a statue, perhaps of Maruduk (Mars, father of Nebo or Mercury[3]) : it certainly resembles those with which the god is represented upon the Cylinders[4] when fighting with the Dragon. The dimensions are :

Length of blade	16 inches
Length of hilt	$5\frac{3}{8}$,,
Total length	$21\frac{3}{8}$,,
Width at hilt	$1\frac{1}{8}$,,
Width at hilt base	$1\frac{7}{8}$,,

The weapon has a richly jewelled hilt inlaid with ivory. It is of the kind known in the Assyrian inscriptions as ⌇⌇⌇ (Sa-pa-ra).[5] It bears the following (cuneiform) inscription in three places : (1) along the whole length of the flat blade, inside edge ; (2) along the back ; and (3) on the outside edge, where it is divided into two lines :—

---

[1] This abomination popularly derives from Semiramis (Sa-am-mu-ra-mat) of Assyria, and extended far and wide. Even in the earlier part of the present century eunuchs were manufactured for Christian and Catholic Rome. The practice is still kept up in Egypt, Turkey, and Persia, although strictly forbidden by the Apostle of Allah.

[2] Col. Hanbury exhibited it at the British Museum. Notes by Mr. W. St. Chad Boscawen, read April 6 : *Trans. Soc. Bib. Archæology*, vol. iv. Part II. 1876.

[3] Nebo, in the inscriptions, holds a golden reed or rod, as the Homeric Hermes is Χρυσόρραπις ; he also leads the ghosts to Hades. The Chaldæan gods were, like the Egyptian, deceased ancestors, and they

were followed by natural objects, *Anu* (sky), *Bel* (earth), *Hea* (sea), personified into a vast and various mythology. Sun, moon, and æther, were the first Triad of Babylon. Thus the Chthonic gods of Greece, Uranus (the Egyptian *Urnas*), Gaia and Thalassa (Assyrian), preceded the Olympic anthropomorphism. Of course they were represented with human shapes. Presently the priest introduced as godheads cosmo-poetic causes and effects, which presently peopled the Pantheon with glorified men. For, I repeat, man worships only one thing—himself.

[4] George Smith. *Chaldæan Genesis*, pp. 62, 95.

[5] *Sibri* or *Sibirru*. I have noted the probable derivation of this word from the Egyptian Sf, Sayf, or Seft ; and its resemblance to our ' sabre.'

E-kal Vul-nirari sar kissati abli Bu-di-il Sar Assuri
Abli Bel-nirari Sar Assuri va—

(The Palace of Vul-nirari, King of Nations, son of Budil,[1] Sar (king) of Assyria, son of Bel-nirari, Sar of Assyria, and—)

And now, proceeding east, we may note that the Persepolis sculptures distinctly show, as we might expect, Assyrian and Babylonian derivation. The Persians are,

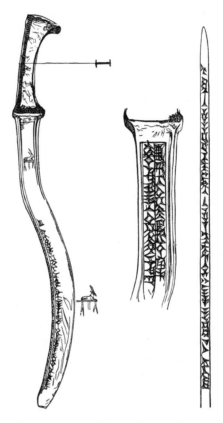

FIG 221 —BRONZE SWORD BEARING THE NAME OF VUL-NIRARI I., FOUND NEAR DIARBEKR

despite their prodigious pretensions, a comparatively modern people,[2] and they were rude enough when armed only with sling, lasso, and knife. The date of Hakhámanish (Achæmenes), the *hero eponymus* of the ruling family, can hardly be made to

---

[1] Budil (says Mr. Boscawen) succeeded his father in B.C. 1350. He defended the north-eastern peoples, the Nari and the Guti, Gutium or Goim ; he also built largely, and his son, Vul-nirari (Vul is my hope), from whose palace the Sword came, was one of the greatest of the early Assyrian kings. The British Museum has a long inscription recording his resto-ration of the causeway leading to the Temple of Ashur.

[2] Layard advocates the theory that the Persians and Hindús separated from a common centre about B.C. 1500. But of what Hindús does he speak? Certainly not of the 'Turanian' tribes, which peopled the peninsula before the Brahmin immigration.

precede B.C. 700. This was about the time (B.C. 721–706) when Sargon II. first mentions the Greeks as the Yaha of Yatnan (Yunan=Ionia), who sent him tribute from Cyprus and beyond. The Medes, before the reign of Cyaxares had conducted the Persians from the Caspian regions into Media Magna, were mere barbarians, like the Iliyát or Iranian nomades of the present day, who number from a quarter to a half of the population. But in starting into life Persia succeeded to a rich inheritance—Babylon. To this conquest (B.C. 538) she was led by her hero king, Cyrus the Great, or rather Kurush[1] the elder, son of Cambyses (Xenophon), not father of Cambyses (Herodotus), and a contemporary of Darius the Mede.[2] Their courage and conduct, their loyalty and simplicity, their wise

FIG. 222.—PERSIAN ARCHER. From a bas-relief of Persepolis, the ancient capital of Persia (B.C. 560). The long coat, probably of leather, descends to the ankle. The head-dress has nothing of the helmet, but nevertheless indicates workmanship in metal.

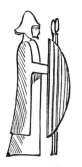

FIG. 223.—PERSIAN WARRIOR. From a bas-relief of Persepolis; a cast is in the British Museum. The shield, high enough to rest on, is almost hemispherical; the helmet, with ear and neck coverings in one single piece, differs from the Assyrian.

FIG. 224.—THE PERSIAN CIDARIS, OR TIARA.

laws, their generosity and their love of truth,[3] now unhappily extinct, raised them in Herodotus' day to the proud position of 'Lords of Asia.'

Between the bas-reliefs of Khorsabad and those of Persepolis there is the same difference as between the early Egyptian sculptures and the degenerate days of what Macrobius calls the 'tyranny' of the Ptolemies.[4] The drawing is less pure,

[1] The Greeks having no *sh* sound, turned Kurush into Kyros.

[2] Media was North-Western Persia, from Armenia to Azerbáiján, south of the Caspian. 'Great Armenia' afterwards included Georgia and Abkhasia. From their racial name Manda or Mada came the Greek Mantiene and Matiene. (See *Bib. Archæology*, Nov. 9, 1882.)

[3] Herod. i. 136, 138, &c. All writers assure us that the ancient Egyptians and Persians, the Chinese and Hindús (Marco Polo), were truth-telling races who abhorred a lie. 'How sweet a thing is truth!' exclaimed a Nile-dweller. In the Carpentras Inscription the Lady Ta-Bai 'spoke no falsehoods against any one.' In the trilingual Behistun Inscription (B.C. 516) Darius the king says, 'Thou who mayest be king hereafter, the man who may be a liar, and who

may be an evil-doer, destroy them with the destruction of the Sword' (col. iv. par. 14). They are now emphatically the reverse. The wild tribes, such as the Bedawin, the Iliyát, and the outcasts of India, still preserve the old characteristic. 'The word of a Korager' is proverbial on the West Coast of the Hindu Peninsula. I cannot but attribute the deterioration to extensive commerce, contact with strangers, and change of faith. The subject, however, is too vast and important even to glance at in these page ; but I may note that the Hindú has deteriorated even in my day. In 1845 the trade-books of a Sahukár (merchant) were received as evidence in our law courts. In 1883 the idea would be scouted.

[4] The conquests of Alexander the Great had given the civilised world a unity of language. The Ptolemies, having asserted Greek mastery in Egypt,

the forms are heavier, the anatomical details are wanting or badly indicated—they are, in fact, clumsy imitations of far higher models.

Herodotus (VII. ch. lx.–lxxxiii.), when reviewing the army of Xerxes (Khshhershe = Ahasuerus [1]) in B.C. 480, numbers forty-five nations, of which only the six (including Colchians and Caspians) wore Swords. The long straight dagger was carried by the Pactyans, by the Paphlagonians, by the Thracians, and by the Sagartians, who spoke Persian, and who were in dress half Persians and half Pactyans (Afghans ?).[2] The Sagartian Nomades (chap. lxxxv.) were armed with a short blade and with lassos of plaited thongs ending in a running noose : this denotes that they were

FIG. 226.
PERSIAN ACINACES.

FIG. 225.—PERSIAN ACINACES.
(Here worn on right side.)

FIG. 227.—SWORD FROM
MITHRAS GROUP.

FIG. 228.—SWORD IN RELIEF,
PERSEPOLIS SCULPTURES.

cattle-breeders.[3]   Chapter liv. again mentions 'the Persian Sword of the kind which they call ἀκινάκης (Akinakes) :' like the Roman *pugio* and the modern *couteau-de-chasse*, it was straight, not curved, as expressly stated by Josephus.[4]   The Persian troops wore only these 'daggers suspended from their girdles along their right

established that perfect toleration which is proved by the Septuagint, Manetho and Berosus.

[1] Famous in the Book of Esther (Amestris), which contains scant traces of the faith of Israel.   This terrible virago (B.C. 474) caused the massacre of 800 men at Shushan, and 7,500 in the provinces.   From the Pehlevi name of Xerxes (Khshhershe), possibly we may derive the modern titles, 'Shah' and 'Shahanshah.'

[2] Hence, perhaps, Pukhtu or Pushtu, the Afghan language, an old and rugged dialect of Persian type.

[3] The South American lasso has been pitted, of course on horseback, against the Sword.   Many a

murder has been committed with it in the Argentine Republic, the victim being 'thugged' unawares and dragged to death.   Needless to say, the lasso was well known in Egypt (Wilk. i. 4), where it was used to catch the gazelle and even the wild ox.   The Pasha or Indian lasso was ten cubits long, with a noose one hand in circumference.   It was composed of very small scales, ornamented with leaden balls ; and was not regarded as a 'noble weapon.'   The Roman gladiators, called 'Laqueatores,' derived their name from the lasso : they must not be confounded with the 'Retiarii.'

[4] *A.J.* xx. 7, sec. 10.

thighs.' Hence Cambyses died of a wound on his right side, and Valerius Flaccus describes a Parthian as—

Insignis manicis, insignis acinace dextro. (*Arg.* vi. 701.)

Julius Pollux explains it as a περσικὸν ξιφίδιον, τῷ μηρῷ προσηρτημένον (a Persian swordlet fastened to the thigh), and Josephus compares it with the Sica or Sicca.[1] The favourite weapon was the bow, although Darius speaks of the Sword as the instrument of punishment.

The Indians, afterwards so celebrated for their Swords, were in B.C. 480 barbarians

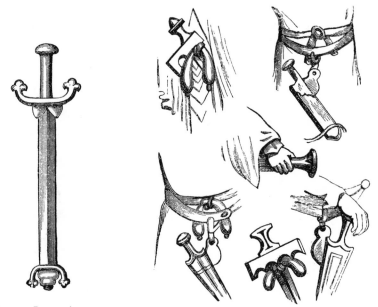

FIG. 229.—PERSIAN ACINACES.
From a bas-relief at Persepolis.

FIG. 230.—DAGGER-FORMS FROM PERSEPOLIS.

dressed in cottons and armed with only cane bows and arrows. Of the twelve peoples who supplied the one thousand two hundred and seven triremes, the Egyptians had long cutlasses, the Cilicians 'Swords closely resembling the cutlass of the Egyptians,' the Lycians[2] daggers and curved falchions, and the Carians daggers and 'enses falcati,' which apparently were not used by the Greeks (chap. xciii.).

Representations of the Persian Acinaces abound in the sculptures of Chehel Munar (the Palace of the Forty Columns) at Persepolis. Apparently there are two kinds. Porter's[3] illustration (Plate 37) shows a handle like the modern weapon sheathed and slung to the right side: Ammianus Marcellinus (xiv. 4) and all

---

[1] To be noticed in a future chapter (xii.).
[2] Chap. ix.
[3] *Travels in Georgia, Persia, &c.* (1817–20), by Sir

Robert Ker Porter. Other illustrators are Le Bruyn, Chardin, Niebuhr, nd Leake (*Athens,* ii. pp. 22–26).

classics insist upon this unswordsmanlike peculiarity.[1]   The other (Plate 41), worn
by a robed Persian, and generally carried in the front-knots of the belt, has a
crutch-handle and wavy blade, like the Malay Krís (crease).   In other places
(Plates 53 and 54) a human figure stabs the roaring monster in the belly with a
common 'Khanjar'-dagger.   The traveller considers the stout little weapon with
broad blade and ferruled sheath apparently tied to the right thigh as the Persian
Sword of that age, which the classics describe as very short.   The lineal descendant
of this weapon, now obsolete in Persia, is the Afghan Charay, a congener of the
Egyptian flesh-knife Sword.

According to Quintus Curtius : 'The Sword-belt of Darius was of gold, and
from it was suspended his scymitar, the scabbard of which was composed of one
entire pearl.'   The practice of inlaying blades and hilts, still popular in Persia,
may explain Herodotus (ix. 80), that amongst the spoils taken at Platæa by the

FIG. 231.—ACINACES OF PERSEPOLIS.   FIG. 232.—ACINACES OF MITHRAS GROUP.

Greeks 'there were acinaces with golden ornaments.'   That of Mardonius was long
kept as a trophy in the temple of Athene-Parthenos in the Athenian Acropolis.
On the other hand, as was elsewhere done, blades of gold were given *honoris causâ*.
Hence in the 'Iliad' (xviii. 597) we see Hephæstus making youths with golden
cutlasses upon Achilles' shield.   According to Xenophon the royal gift of Persia
was a golden scymitar, a Nisæan horse with golden bridle, and other battle-gear.
Herodotus (viii. 120) makes Xerxes present the Abderites with a golden scymitar
and a tiara.   Diana is girt with a golden falchion (Herod. viii. 77).   The golden
blade is not unknown to more modern days.   In the 'Chronicles of Dalboquerque'
(Hakluyt, vol. ii. p. 204) two pages stand behind the King of Cananor, one with a
Sword of gold and the other with a scymitar of gold.   The weapons are distinguished from the 'Swords adorned with gold and silver' (vol. i. 117).   The King
of Siam also sent to Dom Manoel of Portugal 'a crown and Sword of gold'
(vol. iii. 154).   Cuzco supplied a unique gold celt.

The influence of the great Babylonio-Assyrian centre extended Egyptian art

[1] It may, however, have been treated as a dagger, while the Sword was worn on the left.

and science to farthest Asia. From Iran we pass, with the course of civilisation, eastward to India. Here the Hindú proper did not succeed in establishing himself amongst the original Turanian possessors of Hindustan, or the upper country, before the Eighteenth Egyptian Dynasty.[1] The South was and is still essentially Turanian —witness Malabar and its 'nepotism.'

Unfortunately, India preserves no trustworthy Hindú records of the past. Although Herodotus called it the 'most wealthy and populous country in the world,' yet the absence of temples and other ruins suggests barbarism when Egypt and Assyria, Greece and Rome, were flourishing. While Buddhism is made to date from the sixth century B.C., and we have subsequent notices of Buddha's chief worshippers,[2] there was evidently very little civilisation in the days of Alexander (B.C. 327). Nearchus made the Indians 'write letters on cloth smoothed by being well beaten'; and Strabo (xv. 1) doubts whether India knew the use of writing. They derived their art and literature from Græco-Bactria, and they only degraded the former—Art in her highest form never travels far from the Mediterranean. The beautiful human animals and *mauvais sujets* who were the citizens of Olympus became in grotesque India blue-skinned, many-headed and multi-armed monsters —the abortions of imagination.

India's two great epics ('Mahabhárat' and 'Ramáyana') and fifteen Puranas are mere depositories of legendary and imaginative myths, containing few of the golden grains of truth hid in tons of rubbish. All the anthropology we learn from them is that India had a primitive (Turanian?) race, called in contempt Rakshasas or demons. It was mastered by Brahminical attacks, typified in later days by Rama and other heroes, probably during the exodes of Hyksos and Hebrews from Egypt; and long subsequently arose Buddhism, to be followed by the rule of the Moslems and Europeans.[3]

The Dhanurvidya,[4] or Bow-Science, contains the fullest description we possess of the ancient Indian arms and war-implements, but the date of composition is exceedingly doubtful. The Hindú delights in vast numbers. Assuming the population of the earth at one thousand and seventy-five billions, his Aksauhini, or complete army, according to the Nitiprakáshika, an abstract Dhanurvidya by the sage Vaishampáyana, amounts to two thousand one hundred and eighty-seven

---

[1] Wilkinson (*Egyptians*, II. chap. v.) remarks, 'If there is any connection between the religions of Egypt and India, this must be ascribed to the period before the two races left Central Asia'; and Layard, it has been said, would place that period about 1500 B.C. I again protest against the idea that the Egyptian ever came from, or had ever anything to do with, 'Central Asia,' beyond civilising it.

[2] Chandragupta (Sandracottus?) B.C. 316; his son Bindusara, B.C. 291; and his grandson (Dharm) Asoka or Priyadasi, B C. 250–241, whose children divided the empire. The Topes are probably Phallic buildings.

[3] I would explain the fact that India is confounded with East Africa by the classics and by mediæval geographers as a survival of the connection of the continents in the Miocene and, perhaps, in even later ages.

[4] Utilised by Horace Hayman Wilson in his article 'On the Art of War as known to the Hindús.' Dhanu (Sanskr. the bow) came to signify any missile or weapon; and hence, Dhanúrvidya comprised the knowledge of all other arms. The bow was also named; for instance, that of Vishnu was called Shárnga (Oppert, p. 77).

millions of foot, twenty-one thousand eight hundred and seventy millions of horse, two hundred and eighteen thousand seven hundred elephants, and twenty-one thousand eight hundred and seventy chariots. The scale of salaries in gold [1] is equally liberal and absurd.

The Hindú mind—so far justifying the term 'Indo-Germanic'—connects everything with metaphysics, [2] or a something that goes beyond physical phenomena. Hence it ascribes all arms and armour to supernatural causes. Jáyá, a daughter of primæval Daksha (one of the Rishis or sacred sages), became, according to a promise of Brahma, the creator, the mother of all weapons, including missiles. These are divided into four great classes. The Yantramukta (thrown by machines); the Panimukta (hand-thrown); the Muktasandhárita (thrown and drawn back) and the Mantramukta (thrown by spells, and numbering six species), form the Mukta or thrown class of twelve species. This is opposed to the Amukta (unthrown) of twenty species, to the Muktámukta (either thrown or not) of ninety-eight varieties, [3] and to the Báhuyuddha (weapons which the body provides for personal struggles). All are personified—for instance, Dhanu, the bow, has a small face, a broad neck, a slender waist, and a strong back. He is four cubits high and is bent in three places; he has a long tongue, and his mouth has terrible tusks; his colour is of blood, and he ever makes a gurgling noise; he is covered with garlands of entrails, and he licks continually with his tongue the two corners of his mouth. [4]

The Sword (Khadga, [5] As, or Asi) belongs to the second class. According to the sage Vaishampáyana it was a superior weapon, introduced especially and separately by Brahma, who produced 'Asidevatá.' This 'Sword-god' appeared on the summit of the Himálayas shaking earth's foundations and illuminating the sky. Brahma entrusted the arm, then fifty thumbs long and four thumbs broad, to Shiva (Rudra), still its supreme deity, in order to free the world from the Asuras or mighty dæmons. Shiva, after his success, passed it on to Vishnu, the latter to Marici, and he to Indra. The Air-god conferred it upon the guardians of the World-quarters, and these to Manu, the son of the Sun, for use against evil-doers.

---

[1] The Commander-in-Chief drew four thousand Varvas (gold coins) per mensem. Prof. Oppert, with true German *naïveté*, says (p. 8), 'If this scale of salaries is correct, and if the salaries were really paid, one would be inclined to think that an extensive gold currency existed in ancient India.' That the country worked its gold mines is proved by the Wynaad and other diggings, lately reopened, but we may fairly doubt the coinage;—at least, till a coin be found.

[2] I now borrow from Professor Gustav Oppert, *On the Weapons &c. of the Ancient Hindus* (London: Trübner, 1880). Unfortunately the work is unillustrated. Its capital fault is not adducing proofs, or offering highly unsatisfactory proofs, of the antiquity to be attributed to its authorities, the Shukraniti (p. 43); the Naishedha (p. 69), and the various pagodas showing fire-arms (p. 76). The Mánavad-

harmashástra, or Institutes of Menu (Halhed, p. 53), speaks of 'darts blazing with fire,' a well-known missile, but not to be confounded with fire-arms proper. And the Institutes in their actual form are comparatively modern.

[3] Prof. Oppert gives the names of all these subdivisions; and, at the same time, a lesson in Hindú absurdity (p. 11).

[4] Here we have the true Indian imaginativeness. The idea of a Western anthropomorphising a bow after this fashion!

[5] Prof. Oppert says that Book III. of the Nitíprakashika is entirely devoted to the Khadga. In the Shukraniti, as will be seen, the word denotes a two-handed Sword six feet long. The Professor translates it 'broadsword.'

Since that time it has remained in his family. The Khadga has a total of nine names : carried on the left side and handled in thirty-two different ways, the weapon became a universal favourite. Amongst the four arts to be studied besides the Káma-Shastra (*Ars Amoris*), women are. enjoined by the Sage Vatsya (Part I. p. 26)[1] to ' practise with Sword, single-stick, quarter-staff, and bow and arrow.'

The Ili (hand-sword, p. 17) is two cubits long and five fingers broad ; the front part is curved ; there is no hand-guard, and four movements are peculiar to it. The Prasa, or spear, in some works becomes a broadsword. The uterine brother of the Sword is the Pattisha or two-bladed battle-axe. The Asidhenu (dagger), the ' sister of the Sword and worn by kings,' is a three-edged blade, one cubit long, two thumbs broad, without hand-guard, carried in the belt, and used in hand-to-hand conflict. The Maushtika (fist-

FIG. 234.
a. JAVANESE BLADE, SHOWING INDIAN
DERIVATION. *b.* HINDÚ SABRE.
From a bas-relief at Bijanagar.

FIG. 233.— HINDÚ WARRIORS
From memorial stones of Bijanagar, of which the Kensington Museum
possesses photographs. The date of these monuments corresponds
with our Middle Ages.

Sword, stiletto [2]) is only a span long, and thus very handy for all kinds of movements.

The sage Vaishampáyana, a pandit or pedant lecturing on the Art of War, warns us that the ' Efficiency of the weapon is subject to great changes. In different ages and places the quality of an arm is not the same, for the material and mode of construction greatly vary. Moreover, much depends upon the strength and ability of the person using such weapons, in preserving, increasing, or diminishing their efficiency.' It may also be remarked that many of his weapons appear to be the results of a brain quickened by opium or hashísh.

The sage Shukra, or Preceptor of the Dæmons, also discourses learnedly, in his ' Shukraniti,' on armies and weapons, including firearms. The only practical part

---

[1] He lived between the tenth and thirteenth centuries and wrote a notable Ovidian work. A translation is now being printed (not published) by the Hindoo Káma-Shastra Society of London and Benares.

[2] The Italian word is evidently a diminutive of the Latin *stilus*, or rather *stylus* (στῦλος). Dagger (Germ. Dolch) is from the Keltic *dag*, point. Degen, a larger weapon, originally means a warrior ; hence the Anglo-Sax. Thaegn and our Thane.

of chap. v. (Oppert, pp. 82–144) is his description of the lucky and unlucky marks on horses. The Arabs have a similar system, and a horse with inauspicious signs sells, however well bred, for a small sum. And there is wisdom in verse 242 (p. 124) :—

> A non-fighting King and a ne'er-faring Priest (Brahman)
> Earth swallows as Snake the hole-dwelling beast.

As regards the Sword, Shukra says (Lib. iv. sect vii. p. 109, verse 154) :—

> Ishadvaktrashcaikadháro vistáre chaturangulah
> Kshurapránto nábhisamo drahamushtissucandraruk
> Khadgah prasáshchaturhastadandabudhnah ksuránanah.

The Sword is a little curved and one-bladed ; it is four-fingers broad, and sharp-pointed as a razor ; it extends up to the navel, has a strong hilt, and is brilliant as the beautiful moon. The Khadga (two-handed Sword) is four cubits (or six feet) long,[1] broad at the hilt, and at the end-point sharp like a razor.

From neither of these works do we learn anything about an interesting subject

Fig. 235.—Battle-Scene from a Cave in Cuttack, First Century a.d.

—the elephant-Sword. It is mentioned by the Italian traveller Ludovico di Varthema (A.D. 1503–1508), who makes it two fathoms long and attached to the trunk. Athanasius Nikitin calls it a scythe. Knox in his 'Ceylon' also speaks of a sharp iron with a socket of three edges 'placed on the teeth' (tusks ?). It was probably derived from the West. Antigonus, the great elephantarch ; Seleucus, and Pyrrhus armed their beasts with 'sharp points of steel in the tusks'—veritable Swords. In Da Gama's day each animal wore ten blades, five to the tusk.[2]

It must be borne in mind that upper India about the beginning of our æra was mostly Buddhist, and consequently she bred men of peace. Yet the caves and the cave-temples supply in bas-relief specimens of Sword-bearers, and even of free fights. The weapon is mostly the short stout blade, corresponding with the Persian Acinaces, but worn in modern fashion on the left side. Mr. James Fergusson has kindly supplied me with two illustrations. The first (fig. 235) is the battle-scene

---

[1] Strabo (xv. 1, § 66) makes the Indian Sword three cubits (= four feet and a half) in length ; and the Greeks of the Alexandrine day notice two-handed Swords and bow-drawing with the feet.　[2] Roteiro, p. 115.

showing two Swords. A huge chopper or falchion, with a tooth on the back, is wielded in the left hand, the right supporting the shield.[1] The other, straight with one median ridge, is broad at the end instead of being pointed. The second (fig. 236), which Mr. Fergusson calls the 'first Highlander,' is of the same date, and it shows

FIG. 236.—THE FIRST HIGHLANDER.

very distinctly the handle—which might be modern—the sheath, and the mode of wearing. It is more distinct in the photograph than in the woodcut made by the author's artist.

The temple-caves of Elephanta or Gharapuri (cave-town) in the Bay of Bombay, described by Forbes and Heber, Dr. Wilson and Mr. Burgess, show a very different and superior article. This comparatively modern basilica—burrowed out of the rock and dedicated to Shiva or Mahadeva, the third person of the Hindu Triad, and the representative of destructive-reproduction in his Trimurti or triple form —contains a multitude of alt-reliefs from ten to fourteen feet high, and so prominent that they are almost 'under-cut,' joined to the parent-rock only by the back. At the north-east angle stands the figure of the hero Arjuna, the presumed ancestor of the Pandya Princes. This

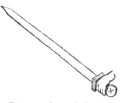

FIG. 237.—ARJUNA'S SWORD.

---

[1] This is evidently inverted. The huge falchion, an exaggeration of the Kukkri, may be seen in the British Museum, one blade inscribed with Pali characters. Most of these huge weapons were used in sacrificing; and the low-caste Mhars still behead with falchions the buffalos offered to Kali.

Brave, an especial favourite in Southern India,[1] holds, in the right hand, perpendicularly and point upwards, a short, straight blade, with a bevelled point like the Roman; there is a small hand-guard; the fist fills the grip, and the large pommel confines the hand, as is still the fashion throughout India.

FIG. 238.—JAVANESE SCULPTURES WITH BENT SWORDS.

The military tactics of the earlier Hindús are familiarly shown by our game of chess.[2] But their pandits and students, writing in the closet, borrowed or devised a whole body of 'strategemata,' making it easy to find amongst them the Phalanx, the Legion, the Wedge, or the Crescent attack.

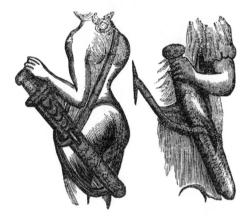

FIG. 239.—PESHÁWAR SCULPTURES.

Professor Oppert informs us[3] that the Arka (*Calatropis gigantea*), the huge swallow-wort with milky and blistering juice, which grows wild all over the peninsula, if 'used with discretion when iron is being forged, contributes greatly to the excellence

---

[1] He constantly appears in the Mahabhárata, especially in Book I.

[2] Some writers are determined to find chess amongst the Romans, and quote the Panegyric of Piso, and the game of Latrunculi. But if so, where are their chessmen? The earliest allusion in any known author is in Anna Comnenas Alexias, when the First Crusade had done some good by mixing the Eastern and the Western worlds.

[3] *Loc. cit.* p. 61.

of the Indian steel.' The simple is well known to the native alchemist, to the doctor, and to the vet., but I was not aware of its being generally applied to iron-working.

I reserve for Part II. details concerning the modern Indian Sword and the blades imitated from it. Lieutenant-Colonel Pollok (Madras Staff Corps)[1] describes, unfortunately without illustration, the Burmese Dalwel ('Dalwey,' vol. ii. p. 18) or fighting-Sword, a 'nasty two-handed weapon with a blade about two feet long, and as sharp as a razor' (i. 51). He also notices the Dha, or Dhaw, a knife six inches long, equally fitted for domestic use and stabbing.

NOTE.—My lamented friend Dr. Burnell, whose loss to Anglo-Oriental philology is so deeply felt, took a notable part in reducing Hindú claims to remote antiquity. Whereas Sir William Jones, a *littérateur* thoroughly well imposed upon, dated the Laws of Menu from A.D. 1280, Burnell boldly assigned them to the fourth century A.D., and partly to a much later period. The Theatre of Kalidása (Sakuntala, Urwasi, &c.) he has attributed to the sixth century instead of the first ; in fact he leaves nothing to B.C. but parts of the Vedas and the earliest Buddhist texts.

We can accept the reform unhesitatingly. The oldest Hindú inscription (Girnár) dates from about B.C. 250 ; the oldest Cave-temple from still later. The alphabet is a lineal descendant from the Egypto-Phœnician. The earliest Hindú buildings were wooden : India had no architecture which could vie with those of Greece or monarchical Rome, much less with the mighty works of Egypt and Mesopotamia. The Hindú's 'iron-built' cities were probably clay-walled settlements. His mythology was Egyptian tempered with Greek : for instance, the four Yugas or periods, in the fourth of which (Kali, the black Yuga) we now are. And considering how early Christianity found its way into the Peninsula, and the highly subjective and receptive nature of the people, I cannot but believe that they borrowed largely from the sacred writings of the stranger. It is easier to hold that Christ originated, or at least influenced, Krishna, than with Volney to hold Krishna the original of Christ. In 1852 Mr. Pocock wrote about 'India in Greece'; in 1883 we want a change of venue to 'Greece in India.' 'Yavana' (Greek) entered India with Alexander, and this gives a *terminus a quo* though not *ad quem.*

---

[1] *Sport in British Burmah* (London : Chapman and Hall, 1879).

CHAPTER XI.

THE SWORD IN ANCIENT GREECE: HOMER; HESIOD AND HERODOTUS: MYCENÆ.

'HOMER and Hesiod,' says Herodotus,[1] 'lived, as I hold, not more than four hundred years before my time.' This would date them between B.C. 880–830. The contemporaneity of the bards, their cousinship, and even their existence, has been copiously doubted: some place Hesiod before, others two hundred or three hundred years after—

Blind Milesigenes thence Homer called ;

and we have come to look upon Homer as one of the Homeridæ, the *heros eponymus* of the bards who produced the 'Iliad' and the 'Odyssey.'

Assuming, with Dr. Schliemann, the date of the Trojan war at about B.C. 1200,[2] Homer, according to the 'Father of History,' would flourish about four centuries and a half after the wars he sang.

'I wish I could have proved Homer to have been an eye-witness of the Trojan war. Alas, I cannot do it! At his time swords were of universal use, and iron was known, whereas they were totally unknown at Troy.[3] Besides, the civilisation he describes is later by centuries than that which I have brought to light in the excavations. Homer gives us the legend of Ilium's tragic fate as it was handed down to him by preceding bards, clothing the traditional facts of the war and destruction of Troy in the garb of his own day.'[4]

Metallurgically speaking, the sacred Bards and Heroes of Hellas, whose works formed the Holy Writ of Greece,[5] lived at the height of the Copper and in the beginning of the Iron Ages. Metal, not yet cast ($\chi\omega\nu\epsilon\upsilon\tau\delta\nu$), would be worked in

---

[1] Lib. ii. cap. 53.

[2] The earliest date of the famous siege is B.C. 1370 (Justin, like the Arundelian marbles, gives B.C. 1184), and the latest is B.C. 724–636. In *Troy and its Remains*, we find (p. 123) that the age proposed for the founding of the city is B.C. 1400; that the war took place after the reigns of six kings (p. 27), say two centuries, or in B.C. 1200; and that Homer lived 200 years after the destruction of the city (p. 91), or in B.C. 1000. Thus Herodotus and Dr. Schliemann do not agree ; but what possible agreement can there be upon such a subject ?

[3] Would it not be more prudent to say 'not hitherto found' ?   [4] Dr. Schliemann, *Ilias.*

[5] The Arab, or rather the Moslem, practice of Koran-reading may explain that of ancient Greece. There are two distinct ways : the vulgar, as though it were a profane book ; and the learned with peculiar intonation (*Kirá'at*), of which there are some seventy systems. The Hindús recite with a similar artful modification. So the Hellenes would either pronounce their scriptures, Homer and Hesiod, according to popular accent, or intone by quantity. That men ever wrote accents without pronouncing them is one of those wild theories which can commend itself only to a savant. Besides, we know that as late as the eleventh century there were Greek authors who wrote indifferently according to accent or quantity.

primitive fashion with the hammer ($\sigma\phi\hat{v}\rho\alpha=\sigma\phi\nu\rho\acute{\eta}\lambda\alpha\tau\sigma\nu$),[1] and there were two manners of hammer-work, the Holosphyraton, in solid mass, and the Sphyraton or plate-work. Casting and soldering were invented (for the Greeks), according to Pausanias[2] and Pliny,[3] shortly after Homer's day by the Samians Rhœcus and Theodorus. The latter, who lived between B.C. 800 and 700, may have introduced core-casting, so well known to Egypt and Assyria. The joints would be united by the normal mechanical means,[4] and the ornamental house-plates would be attached to the walls and floors with nails and studs. The idea of the firmament being a copper dome vault is known to Pindar as well as to the 'Iliad' and the 'Odyssey.'[5] Tartarus, below Hades,[6] had a similar threshold, and Atlas in Euripides had copper shoulders.[7]

Ornamentation ($\delta\alpha\iota\delta\acute{\alpha}\lambda\lambda\varepsilon\iota\nu$) was applied with gravers, burins, and similar instruments ; to domestic implements (cups and goblets, craters or bowls, cauldrons and tripods) ; to sacred vases for the temple ; and to trumpets,[8] arms, and armour. Besides the brazier ($\chi\alpha\lambda\kappa\varepsilon\grave{v}s$) we find the gold caster ($\chi\rho\nu\sigma\sigma\chi\sigma\acute{o}s$) who gilds the bull's horns.[9]

The Homeric bards[10] and Hesiod are well acquainted with iron ($\sigma\acute{\iota}\delta\eta\rho\sigma s$),[11] and with steel in its various forms—Cyanus, Adámas, and Chalyps. The former mentions seven metals, the Haft-Júsh ('seven boilings'), which he, like the Persians, had learned from Egypt. Quenching in water, or tempering, was well known to the 'Odyssey,' as we learn from the sputtering of Polyphemus' eye[12] :—

> And as when armourers temper in the ford
> The keen-edg'd poleaxe, or the shining sword,
> The red-hot metal hisses in the lake, &c.[13]

And he would, doubtless, know that steel is softened by simple exposure to gradual heating. *Síderos* is common wrought iron ; so we find $\sigma\iota\delta\acute{\eta}\rho\varepsilon\sigma\nu$ for the

---

[1] The tools known to the *Iliad* were those of Central Africa, anvil, hammer, and tongs (*Il.* xviii. 477, and *Od.* iii. 434-5).

[2] viii. 14 ; ix. 41. [3] xxxv. 12, 43.

[4] E.g. $\delta\acute{\varepsilon}\sigma\mu\sigma\iota$, bands or ties ; $\mathring{\eta}\lambda\sigma\iota$, studs ; $\pi\varepsilon\rho\acute{o}\nu\alpha\iota$, pins, fibulæ ; and $\kappa\acute{\varepsilon}\nu\tau\rho\alpha$, points (*Il.* xviii. 379 ; xi. 634 ; Pausanias xi. 16). [5] iii. 2.

[6] *Il.* viii. 20. The Assyrian Hadi or Bet Edi, 'House of Eternity,' probably Grecised, by an after-thought, to $\mathring{\alpha}\iota\delta\acute{\eta}s$—invisible. See the earliest 'Miracle-play,' the descent of Ishtar into Hadi ; *Soc. Bib. Archæol.* vol. ii. part i. p. 188.

[7] Eur. *Ion.* I.

[8] From the copper trumpet comes $\chi\alpha\lambda\kappa\varepsilon\acute{o}\phi\omega\nu\sigma s$, ringing-voiced (*Il.* v. 785). The *Iliad* applies the epithet to Stentor (*Il.* v. 785), and Hesiod (*Theog.* 311) to Cerberus.

[9] *Od.* iii. 425.

[10] For instance, Stasinus or Hegesias, author of the *Kypria* or Cyprian *Iliad* (Herod. *Lib.* ii. 117), assigned to the end of the eighth century B.C., when Kypros may have had her 'Homeric School.' It was in nine books, of which the argument has been preserved by Proclus in Photius ; and it forms a kind of introduction to the *Iliad*. See Palma's *Cyprus*, p. 13. 'Homer' is said to mention iron thirty times.

[11] Dr. Evans (*Bronze*, p. 15) quotes Dr. Beck's suggestion that the -eros of Sid-eros is a 'form of the Aryan *ais* (conf. *æs*, *æris*). In another place (*Stone*, p. 5), he alludes to the possible connection of Sideros with $\mathring{\alpha}\sigma\tau\grave{\eta}\rho$ (a meteor), the Latin Sidera, and the English Star.

[12] *Od.* ix. 391.

[13] This is a fair instance of 'elegant translation.' What Homer says is :

> E'en as a blacksmith-wight some weighty hatchet or war-axe
> Dippeth in water cold with a mighty hissing and sputt'ring,
> Quenching to temper, for such is the strength and steeling of iron.

The reply will be that Homer does not say it in this way ; and to this reply I have no rejoinder.

Iron Age[1] and σίδηρος πολιός,[2] which should be translated, not 'hoary,' but iron-grey.' The 'black' (dark-blue) 'Cyanus' (κύανος) mentioned by the 'Iliad,'[3] would be a fusible or artificial steel made to imitate the true blue-stone or lazulite (Theophrastus, 55).[4] The adamas (ἀδάμας) of Hesiod,[5] who specifies the iron of the Cretan Idæi Dactyli, would be a white and tempered metal ; while χάλυψ (steel in general) either named or was named by the well-known Chalybes. That the harder substance was not rare, we see by the injunction,[6] ' Do not, at a festive banquet of the gods, pare from the five-pointed branch (hand) with bright steel, the dry from the fresh ': i.e. don't cut your nails at dinner. So at the Battle of the Ships,[7] Homer studs a great sea-fighting Xyston (pole), twenty-two cubits long, with spikes of iron ; and elsewhere speaks of a 'cyanus-footed table.'[8]

Yet copper was *the* metal for arms and armour. While the shield of Hercules was made of alabaster (not 'gypsum'), ivory, elektron (the mixed metal) and (pure) gold, the hero is armed with a 'short spear tipped with gleaming copper ' ;[9] and he fastens around his shoulders a 'Sword, the averter of destruction,' which the context suggests to be of the same material. The 'fair-haired Danaë's son, equestrian Perseus,'[10] bears a Sword of copper with iron sheath hanging by a felt-thong (μελάνδετον ἄορ).[11] The seven-hide shield of Ajax[12] was χάλκεος, of copper—not 'brass-bound' as Lord Derby has it. The lambs' throats are cut with the 'cruel copper' (χαλκός[13]), and Diomede pursues Venus with the same weapon.[14] Hephaistos makes for Achilles a shield of gold and silver, copper and tin ;[15] and canny Diomede's armour[16] is of copper, which he changes for gold, ' the value of a hundred beeves for the value of nine.'

In the 'Iliad' close-handed combat succeeds to missile-using. As Strabo remarks,[17] Homer makes his warriors begin their duellos by weapon-throwing and then take to their Swords. But the latter is *the* weapon, rivalled only by the hand-spear. Hence the Egyptian-taught Argives are insulted as arrow-throwers ;[18] and Diomede reviles his foe as 'an archer and woman's man.'[19] The taunts are still known to savage tribes of modern day.

The Homeric Sword has five names. The first is *Chalcos* (copper, and perhaps base metal), used like the Latin *ferrum.* The second is *Xiphos,* a word still generic in Romaic poetry and prose ; the diminutive being *Xiphidion.* The third is *Phásganon,* pronounced Pháshganon,[20] and the fourth is *Aor.* Thrace,[21] a famous manufactory of art-works even in early ages, produced the best and largest of these

[1] Hes. *Opera,* 174, sq.   [2] *Ibid.* ix. 366.
[3] xi. 34, 35, &c.
[4] Dr. Schliemann is assuredly singular when translating the Homeric Cyanus by 'bronze' (Preface to *Mycenæ,* p. x.). Millin (*Minéralogie Homérique*) holds it to be tin. The 'Cyanus' of Pliny (xxxvii. 38) is lapis lazuli.   [5] *Opera,* 149 ; *Theog.* 161, and *Scut.* 231.
[6] *Erga,* 742-43.   [7] *Il.* xv. 677.   [8] xi. 629.
[9] *Scut.* Ll. 125-132.   [10] *Scut.* 216-224.
[11] *Ibid.* So early was that detestable invention, the metal scabbard, introduced. Thus we must understand the φάσγανα καλά, μελάνδετα (*Il.* xv. 713).

Compare Eurip. *Phœn.* 1091. There is much more to be said concerning ' Phasganon.'
[12] *Il.* vii. 220.   [13] *Il.* iii. 292.   [14] *Il.* v. 330.
[15] *Il.* xviii. 474 sq.   [16] *Il.* vi. 236.   [17] x. 1.
[18] *Il.* iv. 242, xiv. 479.   [19] *Il.* xi. 385.
[20] The Romaic *gh* is, as far as I know, the only modern European representative of the 'Semitic' *ghayn,* which French writers must transliterate by R : e.g. Razzia for Ghazweh.
[21] Even in the army of Perseus we are told by Livy (xliv. 40), the Thracians marched first brandishing, from time to time, Swords of enormous weight.

blades; we find a Thracian Xiphos, possibly of steel, 'beautiful and long,' in
the hands of the Trojan prince Helenos;[1] and Achilles at the funeral games
offers as a prize a Thracian Phásganon, fair and silver-studded.[2] This hero[3]
was drawing his mighty Xiphos[4] from the sheath (κολεός, *culeus, vagina,*
scabbard) to assault Agamemnon, when at Athene's instance, 'still holding
his heavy hand upon the silver hilt, he thrust back the great Sword into the
scabbard.' The Xiphos with silver studs or bosses occurs in sundry places,[5] and
one, with a gold hilt and a silver scabbard fitted with golden rings, belongs
to Agamemnon. Dr. Schliemann explains the epithet Πάμφαινον[6] by the
line of gold bosses lying near one of the Swords; they were
broader than the blade and covered the whole available space
along the sheath. Thus the Homerid's Helos (ἧλος), usually
rendered 'stud' or 'nail,' was applied to the bosses, or buttons,
that break the mid-rib or that stud the blade near the handle.[7]
Paris slings on a copper silver-studded Xiphos.[8] Menelaus,
with the same weapon, strikes off his enemy's Phalos—the
helmet-ridge bearing the Lóphos-tube which confines the Hip-
pouris or horse-tail crest. Patroclus, when arming himself,[9]
hangs from his shoulders the silver-studded Xiphos of copper
(ξίφον ἀργυρόηλον, χάλκεον); and Achilles has a large-hilted
Xiphos.[10] Peneleos and Lycon,[11] having missed each other
with the spear, ran on with the Xiphos, which is here again
called Phásganon; but Lycon's weapon broke at the hilt
(καυλός = *caulis*), and the Xiphos of Peneleos 'entered, and
only the skin retained it; the head hung down and the limbs
were relaxed.' On the shield of Achilles[12] Hephaistos[13]
figures youths wearing the golden Xiphos slung from silver
belts.

Opposed to the Xiphos, a straight 'rapier blade,' as we shall
presently see, was the φάσγανον or dirk, probably a throwing-
weapon like the Scax and Scramasax. The two are often confounded in the
dictionaries. Phásganon is supposed to be *quasi* Σφάγανον, a euphonic transposi-
tion, like the verb φασγάνειν (to slay with the Sword). The root is evidently
Σφαγ, which appears in σφάγη (slaughter) and in σφάγειν (to slay): there is also
a form φάσλανον for σφάλανον. This is a two-edged leaf-shaped blade (φάσγανον
ἄμφηκες):[14] Thrasymedes gives one to Diomede, and with it Rhesus is
slaughtered in his sleep. The word frequently occurs: black-hilted Phásgana,
with massive handles, are mentioned,[15] and the common Phásganon is found in

---

[1] xiii. 576. [2] xxiii. 307. [3] i. 210, 220.
[4] *Il.* i. 190, it is called a Phásganon.
[5] ii. 45. [6] *Il.* xi. 30.
[7] Studs, flat-headed, like rivets, are still let into
the iron blade by modern Africans.
[8] iii. 334. [9] *Il.* xvi. 130. [10] xx. 475.

[11] *Il.* xvi. 335. [12] xviii. end.
[13] So Aristophanes (*Clouds*, 1065) alludes to the
Sword forged by Hephaistos and presented to Peleus
by the gods, as a prize for resisting the temptations of
Atalanta.
[14] *Il.* x. 256. [15] xv. 712–12.

'Odys.' xi. 48 ; in Pindar (N, 1. 80), and in the Tragedians. In another passage,[1] however, it becomes a large (μέγα) Phásganon.

The fourth term is ἄορ,[2] usually set down, like the English 'brand,' as poetical ; it is not used in Romaic and the Neo-Greek dictionaries ignore it. The Aor seems to mean a broad, stout, strong blade. With the sharp Aor (ἄορ ὀξὺ) drawn from his thigh, Ulysses digs the furrow one cubit wide,[3] and Hector cuts in two the ashen spear of Ajax.[4] Automedon draws a long Aor.[5] This, too, is the weapon of earth-shaking Neptune, the 'dreadful tapering Sword' (τανύηκες ἄορ),[6] 'thunder-bolt-like, wherewith it is not possible to engage in fatal fight, for the fear of it restrains mankind.'[7] Phœbus Apollo has a golden Aor (χρυσάωρ).[8] Here we see the vague meaning of the poetic word, like our 'hanger,' for it now means the god's golden bow and quiver carried on the shoulder.

Homer's fifth is the Μάχαιρα, hung by a single belt close to the Sword-sheath, and used for sacrifices and similar uses. It afterwards became a favourite with the Lacedæmonians ; it was then a curved blade, as opposed to the Xiphos or uncurved. Again, in Plutarch and other writers, the Machæra seems to mean—like Spatha—a long straight blade. Homer does not mention the κοπὶς, but Euripides uses it[9] in conjunction with Machæra.

We must not expect to see the Sword so frequently drawn in the 'Odyssey,' which, *pace* Mr. Sayce, appears later than the 'Iliad.' We note in it more character and less movement ; more unity and less digression, and, finally, less fighting and more amenity and civilisation. But 'Othyssefs,' the 'man with whom many were wroth,' has been a soldier, and he does not forget his old trade. Besides, commerce was still armed barter, and voyaging was enlivened by piracy. Copper, or base metal, continues to be the basis of metallurgy, and the hero owns it in quantities, besides gold, silver, and electrum. Euryalus tells Alcinous that he will appease the guest (Ulysses) with an all-copper brand (ἄορ παγχάλκεον), whose hilt (κώπη) is silver, and whose scabbard is of newly sawn ivory.[10] The suitors would slay Telemachus with the sharp copper.[11] In the final struggle, the catastrophe of the poem, Eurymachus, drawing his sharp Sword of copper, calls upon his friends to do the same, and to shield themselves with the tables against the fast-flying shafts. In the 'Frogs and Mice,' the spear is a good long needle ; the 'all-copper work of Mars.'[12]

Wrought iron is prominent in the 'Odyssey' as in the 'Iliad.' Athene-Mentes[13] sails over the dark sea to Temesa (Temessus) for copper, and also brings

---

[1] *Iliad.* xxiii. 824.

[2] Sanskritists hold it to have been originally ἄσορ, and to derive from असि (asi), a Sword ; whence आरिक (ásik), a swordsman (Fick, *Wörterbuch der indogermanischen Grundsprache*). It is probably connected with ἀείρω, because 'carried' on the shoulder by the bauldric.

[3] *Od.* xi. 24.
[4] *Il.* xvi. 115.
[5] xvi. 473.
[6] *Il.* xiv. 385.

[7] In his illustrations of the *Iliad*, Flaxman rarely arms his warriors with the Sword, even at the Fight for the Body of Patroclus. It is to be hoped that artists in future will kindly take warning.

[8] *Il.* xv. 256 ; also *Hymn to Apollo*, 396.
[9] *El.* 837.
[10] *Odys.* viii. 401–5.
[11] *Odys.* iv. 695.
[12] Line 125.
[13] *Odys.* i. 180.

back shining iron (αἴθωνα σίδηρον). Menelaus does the same.[1] The 'cruel iron' balances the 'cruel copper.'[2] The 'long-pointed iron,' so fatal to the Trojans, is apparently the spear, which began the duels. Prudent Penelope places the bow and the grey iron (πολιόν τε σίδηρον) ready for the suitors;[3] and the Palace contains store of wrought iron (πολύκμητος σίδηρος).[4] The axe (πέλεκυς), sharpened on both sides,[5] is of copper; but the hatchets, through whose rings or handle-holes (στειλειή) the copper-tipped arrows must be shot, are of iron.[6] 'Iron,' we are told, 'of itself draws on a man'[7] (Tacit. 'Hist.' i. 80), a sentiment repeated elsewhere in the same words.[8] And the Sword is alluded to in more than one place without the material being specified.[9]

In the 'Hymn to Hermes,'[10] Mercury the god 'vivisects' the mountain tortoise with a scalpel of grey iron (γλυφάνῳ πολιοῖο σίδηρου). The Glyphanus was a carving-tool, a chisel, or a knife for reed-pens.

The dispute whether the so-called Homeric poems were written or were orally preserved still awaits sentence. We twice find the word γράφειν, but its primary meaning is 'to mark,' 'to cut,' and, lastly, 'to write.' Thus Ajax,[11] when inscribing (ἐπιγράψας) the lot, might simply have scraped upon it 'Ajax his mark.' Yet there is nothing against writing, and there is much in its favour. For instance—

Γράψας ἐν πίνακι πτυκτῷ θυμοφθόρα πολλά (σήματα).[12]

'Having on tablet writ' can mean nothing else. Pliny[13] accepts this writing given to Bellerophon on codicilli or tablets.[14] Horace, who was not only a great poet, but a masterful genius, mentions writing in Homer's day, and makes the early inscriptions laws cut into wood (leges incidere ligno). Herodotus[15] tells us that he himself saw Cadmeian (that is, old Phœnician) characters; and the tradition is that Danaus introduced letters from Egypt, which, I repeat, produced the one alphabet the world knows. Dr. Schliemann ('Troy,' Appendix by the Editor) found at seven and a half mètres (twenty-five feet) below the surface of the so-called Homeric Troy, many short inscriptions in 'ancient Cypriote characters,' and as many Greek epigraphs were discovered at Mycenæ. Evidently the 'Iliad' and the 'Odyssey' might have been cut in rude Phœnician characters upon wooden tablets or scratched on plates of lead. Professor Paley would date the literary Homer from B.C. 400; but that is a different phase of the subject.

Herodotus is the outcome of Homer, or, if you please, of the Homerids and of Æschylus. The work of this prose rhapsodist, besides being a history, a logography, a record of travel, and a study of ethnology and antiquity, is at once an Epic and a Drama. It is epic in the heroic and romantic tone; in the unity of

[1] iv. 83-4.
[2] xi. 520. In Buckley's translation (Bell, 1878), χαλκός is mostly translated 'steel' (pp. 62, 72, 198). Translators are almost as misleading as dictionaries.
[3] xxi. 3. [4] xxi. 10. [5] v. 230.
[6] xxi. 127. [7] xvi. 295. [8] xix. 13.
[9] x. 535, xxi. 34 and 119, xxii. 329 &c.
[10] Line 40. [11] Il. vii. 187.
[12] Il. vi. 169. [13] xiii. 28.
[14] He also mentions writing on leaden plates and on linen cloths as in ancient India; such, probably, were the books of Numa. [15] v. 29.

action, a mighty invasion-campaign ; and in the frequent digressions which aid, if they retard, the one primary object. It is a tragedy in the scenic displays (the review of Xerxes, for instance), in the action of Destiny, the circle of Necessity, the Nemesiac hypothesis, and the jealousy of the gods (*Deus ultor*) ; while the catastrophe is represented in 'Calliope' by the destruction of the Persian host, the home-return of the victors, and the lurid scenes at the close. It ends with an epigram, a kind of *Vos plaudite*: 'The Persians . . . chose rather to dwell in a churlish land and exercise lordship, than to plough the plains and be slaves of other men'—a sentiment which would 'bring down the house' in the Highlands. All is written with a distinct purpose, and the sensible chronology is derived from Egypt. There is something poetical, too, in the enormous numbers. The magnificent-impossible host of five millions two hundred and eighty-three thousand two hundred and twenty men,[1] and the one thousand three hundred and twenty-seven triremes to be defeated and destroyed by a handful of nine thousand Greeks and three hundred and seventy-eight ships, is highly imaginative. The philosophic and sceptical modern mind will hardly be satisfied till the details are confirmed by the contemporary evidence of inscriptions, for instance, the Behistun, which is a running commentary upon 'Thalia.' Hellas ever was, and is, and will be, by virtue of her mighty intellect and her preponderating imagination, 'Græcia mendax.' Eastern history tells us nothing about the marvellous Persian invasion. We may fairly believe that there was a great movement headed by some powerful Satrap,[2] who determined to crush the wasp's nest to the West ; but we can go no farther. It is simply incredible that the Great King, who at the time was Lord Paramount of the civilised world, should lead to so little purpose millions of warriors—men, the flower of Asia, whose portraiture is the most favourable of any we possess, and whom the Father owns to have been not a whit inferior in prowess to the Greeks.[3] And for this view I duly apologise to 'Herodotus and his shade.'

The poet-historian gives an interesting description of the Sword amongst the Scythians whom the Greeks and Persians call Sacæ (Shakas) or Nomades.[4] To judge from Hindú legend—for instance, that of Shak-ari, 'foe to the Shakas,' a title of the historical Vikramáditya (A.D. 79)—the Sacæ were 'Turanians'— Mongols or Tartars. When he makes them worship Ares-Mars, he probably derives the idea from their adoring the emblem of war, an iron dirk (ἀκινάκης σιδήρεος.[5] 'A blade of antique iron,' he tells us, 'is placed on the summit of every such mound (a flat-topped pile of brushwood three furlongs square), and serves as the image of Mars ; yearly sacrifices are made to it.' The victims were cattle, horses, and one per cent. of war-prisoners. 'Libations of wine are first

---

[1] vii. 186.

[2] From *Kshatram* (crown, reign) and —*pá* (defender). These viceroys of Asia Minor, who sometimes held more than one province, received and despatched embassies, levied armies of mercenaries, and even engaged in foreign wars without orders of the Great King (Herod. iv. 165–7 ; Thucyd. i. 115 &c.).

[3] ix. 62.   [4] vii. 64.

[5] Grote, *History of Greece*, iii. 323.

poured upon their heads, after which they are slaughtered over a vase, and the vessel is then carried up to the top of the pile and the blood poured upon the Akinákes.'[1] In the Scythian graves of Russian Cimmeria (the Crimea) and of Tartary, the Swords are mostly bronze. Dr. M'Pherson, however, found one of iron (1839) in the great tomb of Kertch, the old Milesian Panticapæum, so called from its river, Anticapes;[2] it was a short dagger-like thrusting blade, resembling the old Persian, with mid-rib and curved handle. In the days of Attila, a Sword, supposed to be one of the ancient Scythian weapons alluded to by the Greek, was accidentally found, and was made an object of worship.[3] Janghíz (Genghis) Khan when raised to the throne repeated this sacrificial observance, which, however, can scarcely be called a 'Mongolic custom.'[4] It seems common to the Sauromatæ (northern Medes and Slavs), the Alans, the Huns, and the tribes that wandered over the Steppes.

The Scythians also swore by the emblem of Mars. 'Their oaths,' says Herodotus,[5] 'are accompanied by the following ceremonies. Into a large earthen bowl (κύλιξ) pouring wine, they mingle with it blood of the parties to the oath, who wound themselves superficially with a knife or an awl ; then they dip into the bowl an Akinákes, and arrows, and a battle-axe (*sagaris*), and a javelin (*akontion*), all the while repeating manifold prayers. Lastly, the two contracting parties drink each a draught from the bowl, as do also the most worthy of their followers.'[6] In the 'Anabasis,'[7] the Greeks swear by dipping a Sword, and the barbarians a lance, into the victim's blood.

So far these ancient authors : we must now see how they are confirmed by modern authorities. Dr. Schliemann's investigations at Mycenæ[8] are the more interesting, as the finds are supposed by him to be synchronous with those of Burnt Troy ; and they enable us to compare the former in her prosperity with the latter in her exhaustion. The energetic explorer doughtily supports the use of copper for arms and utensils ; and, with whole truth, makes it the staple metal of the heroic ages. As he found no tin at Mycenæ or in the great layer of copper scoriæ at Hisárlik (Troy), while 'Kassiteros' is repeatedly mentioned by Homer, he contends that the bronze of the Greek city was imported, and therefore rare and

---

[1] This word is erroneously translated 'Scymitar,' a weapon which, in its present shape, dates from about the rise of El-Islam.

[2] Rawlinson's *Herodotus*, 60. The learned commentator quotes Müller, *Hist. Græc.* (iv. 429), Amm. Marcellinus (xxxi. 2), Jornandes (*De Reb. Geticis*, cap. xxxv.), Niebuhr's *Scythia* (p. 46, E. Tr.), &c. In vol. iii. 60, he gives a ground-plan of the tomb, whose chief place also yielded a gold shield, a whip, a bow, a bow-case, five statuettes, and an iron Sword. The space by the side contained a woman's bones, with a diadem and ornaments in gold and electrum. Other barrows in Russia and Tartary showed bodies resting upon sheets of pure gold weighing forty pounds, with bronze weapons and ornaments set with rubies

and emeralds. Herodotus' description of the scalping (ἀποσκυθίζειν, iv. 64) would apply to the North American 'Indians' of our day ; and the sending a messenger to Zalmoxis, god of the Getæ (iv. 94), is the practice of modern Dahome and Benin.

[3] Rawlinson, iii. 54.

[4] 'Mongol' denotes an especial race ; the word is much abused by non-Orientalists.

[5] iv. 70.

[6] This process of 'mixing bloods,' as a token of brotherhood, is familiar to all travellers in pagan Africa.   [7] ii. 2.

[8] *Mycenæ, &c.* (London : Murray, 1878). It is regretable that this handsome and expensive volume should be printed upon blotting paper.

expensive. Unfortunately he did not analyse the thin copper wire which carried the necklace-beads.

It is a new sensation to descend with Dr. Schliemann into the old Mycenian tombs where sixteen or seventeen corpses had been simultaneously interred (?). Sepulchre No. 1, attributed to Agamemnon and his two heralds,[1] produced a variety of interesting articles, especially the golden shoulder-belt (τελαμών) that decorated the mummy.[2] My photograph shows it attached to a fragmentary two-edged Sword. Between the middle and the southern body lay a heap of broken bronze blades, which may have represented sixty whole Swords: some bore traces of gilding, and several had gold pins at the handle. Two blades lay to the right of the body, and their ornamentation strikingly resembled the description in the 'Iliad.'[3] The handle of the larger Sword (No. 460) is of bronze, thickly plated with intaglio'd gold; and a broad plate of the same metal, similarly worked, passes round the shoulders of the Sword. The wooden scabbard must have been adorned with golden studs and a long broad plate (fig. 244), shaped some-what like a man, with a ring issuing from the neck. The other Sword in a similar style of art seems to have been even richer. Dr. Schlie-mann[4] considers No. 463 (fig. 245) a remarkable battle-axe, of which four-teen were found in the 'Trojan treasure.'[5] It is evidently a Sword-

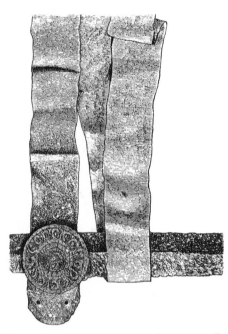

FIG. 241.—GOLD SHOULDER-BELT, WITH FRAGMENT OF TWO-EDGED BRONZE RAPIER. (Sepulchre I.)

blade, and the same may be said of Nos. 464, 465 (fig. 244).

At the distance of hardly more than one foot to the right of the mummy-body were found eleven bronze Swords; two were tolerably preserved, and both were of unusual size—two feet ten inches and three feet two inches. The golden plate of the wooden Sword-handle is given in p. 305. These weapons, also, had gold plates attached to the pommels by twelve pins of the same metal with large globular heads. The body at the south end of Sepulchre I. was provided with fifteen bronze Swords, of which ten had been placed at its feet. As a rule, the wooden sheaths had mouldered away, but the gold studs or bosses, which adorned them like the

---

[1] *Il.* i. 320.   [2] These illustrations are from photographs bought at Athens.
[3] ix. 29-31.   [4] P. 307.   [5] *Troy*, 330-31.

binding of a book, lay along the remains of the warriors who had wielded them The whetstone (Sepulchre I.) was of very fine sandstone.

The fourth Sepulchre was almost as interesting in its supply of Swords. Excavating from east to west, the explorer came upon a heap of more than twenty bronze blades, most of them with remnants of wooden scabbards and handles. The flat, round pieces of wood, and the small shield-like or button-like, disks of gold with intaglio-work, seemed to have been glued in unbroken series along both sides of the sheath ; and, the largest being at the broad end with a gradual diminishing in size,

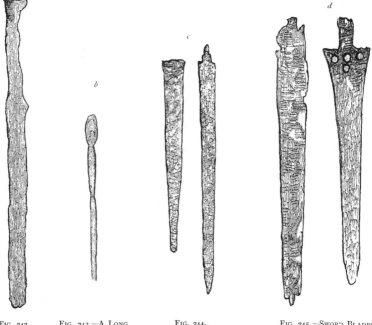

FIG. 242. FIG. 243.—A LONG FIG. 244. FIG. 245.—SWORD BLADES.
(Sepulchre I. Mycenæ.) GOLD PLATE. NOT BATTLE-AXES. (Sepulchre I. Mycenæ.)

they determined the width. The wooden hilts bore similar plates of intaglio'd gold ; the remaining space had been studded with gold pins, and gold nails were fixed in the large pommels of wood or alabaster. The quantity of fine gold-dust left no doubt that the handles and scabbards had been gilt. The smith evidently did not possess the knowledge of gilding silver: he first plated the metal with copper and then the copper with gold. The golden cylinder (No. 366), adorned at both ends with a broad border of wave-lines, and the field filled with interwoven spirals, all intaglio-work, probably belonged to a heft of wood. Along the middle runs a row of pin-holes ; there are four flat pin-heads, and in the centre is the head of a larger stud by which it is attached.

Sepulchre IV. also yielded forty-six bronze Swords, more or less fragmentary. Of these ten were short and single-edged : their solid metal measured when entire from two to two feet three inches in length.   The handles are too thick for mounting in wood, and the tangs end in rings for suspension to the 'Telamon' or to the girdle (ζώνη, ζωστήρ).   The chopper-shaped blade(fig. 246), evidently of Egyptian derivation, is broken at the point, which may incline either way, probably inwards. The other (fig. 246) is the normal leaf-shape.   Dr. Schliemann believes [1] that they explain the Homeric φάσγανον, which he makes 'perfectly synonymous with

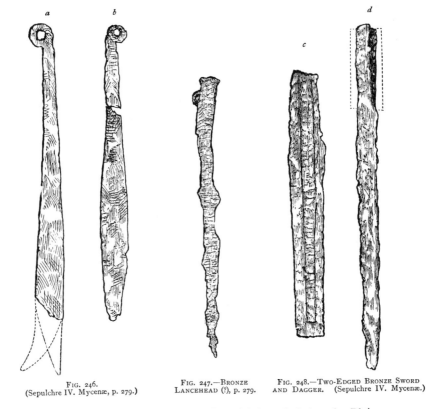

FIG. 246.
(Sepulchre IV. Mycenæ, p. 279.)

FIG. 247.—BRONZE
LANCEHEAD (?), p. 279.

FIG. 248.—TWO-EDGED BRONZE SWORD
AND DAGGER.   (Sepulchre IV. Mycenæ.)

Xiphos and Aor.'   Here I venture to differ with him, holding the Phásganon probably to have been the short Egyptian Sword, used like the boomerang-blade for throwing as well as cutting.

The double-edged weapon with the long narrow tube (αὐλός) was judged to be a dagger-knife, the hollow being intended to save weight ; to me it appears a lancehead, and the attached ring seems to prove its use (fig. 247). The fragmentary two-edged blade of bronze (a fig. 249) shows a mid-rib broken by serrations intended either for ornament or for jagging the wound : the same toothings appear in another weapon (b fig. 249), which is supposed to be a dagger.   No. 446 is a short two-edged

[1] P. 279.

blade showing at the shoulders, on either side, four large flat head-pins of gold. A gold plate extends all along the middle part of the blade on both sides, and fragments of the wooden sheath are visible in the middle as well as at the end.

We now come to the most startling part of the collection. It proves indubitably, if Dr. Schliemann's conclusions be correct, and if the blades [1] do not belong, as they may do, to a later date, that the highest form of Sword, which became the fashion during our sixteenth century, was known in B.C. 1200. It is a curious comment upon the fact, how soon perfection was reached in the 'White Arm,' compared with the slow progress of fire-arms, which had to await the invention of the self-igniting cartridge. Plate No. 445 (p. 281) gives a two-edged blade with a midrib, in fact the rapier, which can be used only for the point. It measures two feet seven inches (*a* fig. 250), and at the top are attached remnants of its wooden scabbard. The lower end of its neighbour (*b* fig. 250) is adorned with three flat golden pin-heads on either face. No. 448, measuring two feet ten inches long, is very well preserved ; by its side lies its alabaster pommel (fig. 249). No. 449 has retained part of its heft, which is gold-plated and attached by gold pins. Vertical lines of intaglio work run along the blade and give it a truly beautiful aspect.

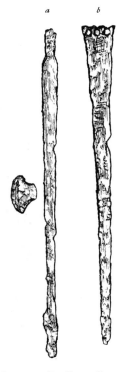

FIG. 249. — TWO-EDGED BRONZE SWORDS AND ALABASTER KNOB. (Sepulchre IV. Mycenæ.)

Dr. Schliemann (p. 283) notices the length, in some cases exceeding three feet, compared with the narrowness of these grand blades. He adds, 'So far as I know, Swords of this shape have never been found before.' I would refer him to the Villanova (Etruscan) blade described in chapter viii.

The fourth Sepulchre also yielded three shoulder-belts of gold. No. 354 measures four feet one and a half inch long by one and seven-eighths inch in width (fig. 241). On either side of the band is a narrow edging made by turning down the gold plate : the field is occupied by a row of rosettes, six oval petals surrounding a central disk and the whole encircled by dots or points. At one end are two apertures in the shape of hour-glasses ; these served to attach the clasp to the other extremity, as is shown by the small hole and two cuts (p. 308). The second 'Telamon,' a plain band four feet six inches long by two to two and one-third

[1] Jähns (pp. 91, 92) cannot but suspect that many of the weapons which show a marked Oriental cast are not Atreidan but Carian. This tribe about the thirteenth century B.C. spread itself, under the mythical king Minos, over the Ægean Archipelago, and colonised even the seaboard of Greece. Such words as Hymettos, Lykabettos, &c. are supposed to be Carian. The symbol of their gods was the double-axe, so common in Mycenæ ; and, as Thucydides said, their practice was to bury weapons with the dead, which was not customary in Greece.

inches broad, was, the discoverer suggests, possibly made for the funeral : it is too
thin and fragile for general wear.   To some blades were still attached particles of

b   *a*
FIG. 250.—RAPIER-BLADES OF MYCENÆ.

well-woven linen, which the discoverer considers to have been sheaths (p. 283).
The natives of India and of other hot-damp regions retain, I have said, the custom

FIG. 251.—WARRIOR
WITH SWORD.

of bandaging their blades with greased rags.   We are also
shown (p. 304) a gold tassel probably suspended to a belt of
embroidered work.

The first of the tomb-stones found in the Acropolis above
the sepulchres (p. 52) shows (very imperfectly) a hunter standing
in a one-horse chariot : he grips in his right a long broad-sword.
The second tomb-stone (p. 81) has a naked warrior, who holds
the horse's head with his right, and raises in his left a double-
edged blade (fig. 251) : Dr. Schliemann finds the figure 'full of
anguish ' (p. 84) ; the head is in profile, and the body almost fronts the spectator.   The

huntsman-charioteer holds in his left a sheathed Sword of the long dagger type, ending in a large globular pommel. Many such articles were found in the tombs, and the author (p. 225) draws attention to the size of the 'knob' upon the signet ring. Mostly they were of wood or alabaster (p. 281) with golden nails, and frequently plated with precious metal. I would suggest that the perforated ball of polished rock-crystal (No. 307) found in Sepulchre III., and the large-mouthed article (No. 308) coloured red and white inside, were also Sword-pommels.

The Treasury supplied 'five unornamental blades of copper or bronze,' with rings of the same metal. The large Cyclopean house, which the energetic discoverer would identify with the Palace of the Atreidæ, yielded a straight, two-edged, thrusting-blade of bronze : the shoulders were pierced with four holes, and there are as many in the tang for attaching the handle (fig. 252). The heft was of various substances, wood, bone, and ivory, amber, rock-crystal, and alabaster, and it was often plated with metals, especially the most precious. Of the latter, six specimens are given (pp. 270-71), all highly decorated with intaglio work of circles and spirals, rope-bands, and shell-like quaquaversal flutings.

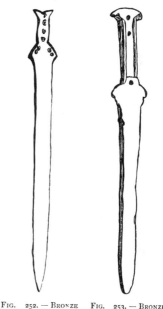

The general opinion that Homer ignored soldering[1] gives unusual interest to a large bronze dagger found in No. III. Sepulchre, six mètres and a half below the surface (p. 164). Two blades are well soldered together in the middle (fig. 253). The same art appears (p. 280) in the attachment of two long narrow plates of thick bronze. Crickets (*cicadæ*) and other ornaments were also found of gold worked in *repoussé* and composed of two halves soldered together.

FIG. 252. — BRONZE SWORD FOUND IN THE PALACE (p. 144).   FIG. 253. — BRONZE DAGGER. TWO BLADES SOLDERED.

The goldsmiths of Mycenæ were true artists. They had work in plenty ; Dr. Schliemann estimates the metallic value of his finds at five thousand pounds. An admirable bit of work (p. 251) is the goat standing, like that of Assyria and Istria, with gathered legs upon the top of a pin.[2] Another (No. 365) is the lion-cub, apparently cut and tooled. As in modern India, the circles, spirals, and wave-lines are excellently executed, and so is the gold-plating upon buttons of wood (pp. 258–59). The old Greek city, too, had a peculiar treatment of the whorl, which, combining two and even three—either *dextrorsum* or *sinistrorsum*—about a common centre, and making the lines of at

[1] Yet soldering iron was known to Egypt in the Eighteenth Dynasty.

[2] The position may be seen in life all over India, where the jugglers teach goats to stand and be hoisted in that position.

least two continuous, deserves to be called the 'Mycenæ spiral.' This ornament passes from the gold trinkets and the tomb-stones of the Acropolis to the 'Treasuries' of much later date.

An intaglio of gold is especially interesting, because it represents a Mono-machía or duel. He to the proper right, a tall beardless or shaven warrior, without helmet, and clad only in 'tights' and 'shorts,' bears the whole weight of his body upon his left leg, extending the right, as in a lunge, and is about to plunge his straight and pointed dagger-blade into the throat of his bearded foe (p. 174). A signet-ring displays a gigantic warrior who has felled one opponent, put to flight a second, and is stabbing a third with a short broad straight blade. The vanquished man attempts to defend himself with a long Xiphos (p. 225). Perhaps the subject may be Theseus clearing out the thieves. A gold button shows a square formed by four sacrificial chopper-knives of Egyptian shape (p. 263, No. 397).

The characteristics of the Sepulchres are the orientation of the remains, the heads lying to the East, and their imperfect cremation. The latter is familiar in Hindú-land, although the people hold the fire-funeral to be a fire-birth, when the vital principle called 'soul' or 'spirit' has been purged of its earthly dross. The regular layers of pebbles, which by ventilating the floor would give draught to the flames, have also been noticed in ancient Etruria.[1] The only *viaticum* or provisions for the dead were unopened oysters : the rest was probably burnt. The utensils are jugs and vases of terra cotta (plain and painted), copper tripods and cauldrons, urns and kettles, and cups and goblets, the latter one- and two-handed. The ornaments, of gold and electrum, are foil-work and plates upon wood, beads of glass and agate, studs and buttons, crosses and breast-covers, lentoid gems and masks, crowns and diadems. The weapons, all of bronze,[2] are axes and arrows, lances, knives, daggers, and Sword-blades ; while gold and alloys are abundant. We may fairly say that iron is absent from the Acropolis of Mycenæ as well as from the Burnt City of the Troad. And there is a remarkable similarity in the pattern and construction of sundry articles, especially the gold tubes with attached spirals.

Dr. Schliemann's discoveries have been subjected to much adverse criticism.[3] As far as they go, they prove that the warriors of Mycenæ used three varieties of Swords—the Xiphos, the Phásganon, and the Kopis.

---

[1] The Etruscans, however, like the Jews, disposed the feet of the corpse eastward, as told in *Etruscan Bologna* (p. 22). Although the author should not say so, the public has not done wisely to neglect this book ; its most valuable part, the osteological details of the Etruscan, deserved a better fate and, perhaps, secured a failure. Yet it had the prime advantage of angry abuse by a certain critical journal, whose predilection for the commonplace (*quâ* commonplace) is expressed by vituperation of all that is not commonplace. In my case I may say of it with Diderot : 'Perhaps they do me more credit than I deserve ; I should feel humiliated if those who speak ill of so many clever and worthy people took it into their heads to speak well of me.'

[2] See 'Analysis of Mycenæan Metals' (pp. 367–376, *Mycenæ*. But the book is almost as self-contradictory as *Troy*.

[3] For instance, by Mr. W. J. Stillman, a traveller and a scholar. In the New York *Nation* (August 18) he writes on 'The True Age of the Mykenæ Finds' ; and, after a fresh examination, he declares the objects post-classical, 'probably representing the burial-place of a colony of Celts between the fifth and the second century B.C.' What chiefly militates against this theory is the cremation of the human remains.

The ξίφοs of Mycenæ is the long, straight, rapier-shaped, cut-and-thrust (*cæsim et punctim*) blade ; its only guard is a cross-bar, which, like the scabbard, is beautifully ornamented. The word Xiphos is still applied in Romaic to a straight Sword opposed to Spati (Σπάτι),[1] the sabre, the broadsword.

The φάσγανον or dirk which Meyrick (Pl. IV. fig. 16), and sometimes perhaps the Ancients, confound with the Xiphos, is a straight blade, mostly leaf-shaped and showing its descent from the spear. It is rarely longer than twenty inches. In Romaic poetry the word is still applied to knives and Sword-daggers like the Yataghan. My idea that the Phásganon was used for throwing does not derive from the classics, but from the similarity of the blade to the Seax and the Scramasax.

The Κοπίs, which Meyrick makes an Argive weapon, and which English

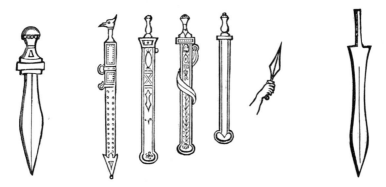

FIG. 254.—PHÁSGANON. FIG. 255.—GREEK PHÁSGANA. FIG. 256.—SHORT SWORD (PHÁSGANON) OF BRONZE, FOUND IN A CRANNOG AT PESCHIARA, AND PROBABLY GREEK.

translators render simply by 'Sword,' has been derived by me from the Egyptian Khopsh, whose 'inside cutting curve' it imitates, merely flattening the bend. Writers on hoplology have mostly ignored its origin. They follow Xenophon, who speaks of it as being used by the Persians and Barbarians ; and Polybius, who assigns its use to the Persians before the Greeks—apparently an anachronism. They remark that on vases it is the weapon of the Giants, not of the

---

[1] Dictionaries derive this word from σπάω (to draw). I find it in the Egyptian 'Sft.' It is evidently a congener of Σπάθη (dim. σπάθιον, also Romaic, and verb σπαθάω = I wield (the weapon). Spáthe means primarily a broad blade of wood or metal ; secondarily a weaver's spatel or spaddle, a spatula (Latin *tela*) ; an oar-blade, a scraper (for horse-currying), and a broadsword. Scotchmen still apply 'spathe' to the weaver's lath (*The Past in the Present*, p. 11), which preceded the 'pecten.' It is also used for Carnifex in Tertullian (*De Cult. Fem.* cap. xiii.), and in botany for a shoot of fruct fication. In Anglo-Saxon it became *Spad* ; Icelandic *Spadi*, our spade. The Latins (Tacit. *Ann.* xii. 35 ; Veget. *De Re Mil.* ii. 15) converted it to *spatha* ; and hence the neo-Latin *espée* and *épée*, *espada* and *spada*, from which we derive our (suit of) 'spades.' See the play of words upon ' Metal de Espadas ' in Camoens' ' Rejected Stanzas ' (canto iv. vol. ii. p. 437 of my translation). It has been subjected to other corruptions ; and in Chaucer (*Knightes T.* 1662) ' Sparth ' is a battle-axe :—

' He hath a sparth of twenti pound of wighte.'
Even the learned Major Jähns derives ' Spatha ' from ' Spatel.'

Gods, and that the Amazons wield it against Hercules. Hence Señor Soromenho [1] would assign its origin to the Arabs, and Colonel A. Lane-Fox to the Roman legionaries. The latter authority, indeed, contends that its form is 'obviously derived from the straight, leaf-shaped, bronze sword, of which it is simply a curved variety.' Here, I think, he reverses the process. Specimens of the Kopis are rare ; one was found in a tomb, said to be Roman, between Madrid and Toledo, and another of the same find is in the British Museum.

The peculiarity of the Kopis is, I have said, its cutting with the inner, not the outer curve, and thus suggesting the use of the point and the 'drawing cut' instead of the sheer cut. This peculiarity was inherited from Egypt, and long appeared in Greek blades. It is well shown in the fragment of a bronze Kopis-like broadsword from the collection of Don Giovanni Bolmarcich, the Arciprete of Cherso :

FIG. 257.   FIG. 258.—KOPIS   FIG. 259.—KOPIS   FIG. 260.—KUKKRI BLADE
                      WITH POMMEL.   WITH HOOK.   OF GURKHAS.

the relic was found in the Island of Ossero with an immense variety of bronzes, Greek, [2] Roman, and prehistoric or protohistoric. General Pitt-Rivers has a bronze Sword-blade from Corinth—a very fine specimen. The handle has an H section, the pommel measuring two and a quarter inches across, and the grip three and a half inches in length. There is no tang ; the blade springs from the shoulders, which are prominent ; the length is twenty-seven inches, and the section that of the Toledo rapier. It is, however, slightly leaf-shaped. In the Armeria Real of Turin (section Beaumont to north-west), two Greek blades are shown in a glass case. One is especially interesting. The total length, all being in one piece, is three feet and a half ; the blade has a mid-rib ; there is a straight simple cross-bar at the shoulders, and the hilt ends in a crutch, like the Hindú antelope-horns and the scroll-hilt of the Danish Swords.

[1] Quoted by Colonel A. Lane-Fox, *Anthrop. Coll.* p. 174.

[2] I have described it in *Scoperte Antropologiche*

in Ossero (Trieste, 1877). The point is evidently broken off.

The inside edge has been preserved from days immemorial by the Abyssinian Sword;[1] an exaggerated sickle or diminutive scythe. It reappears in various parts of Africa, as shown by Barth's Travels (chap. ii. 37 &c.). His 'Danísko,' which he translates 'hand-bill,' is used by the people of a highly interesting province—'Adamáwa.' The general weapon in the neighbourhood is the 'goliyo' or bill-hook of the Marghi, and the Njiga of the Baghirmi. It is a heavy and clumsy 'Khopsh' of the boomerang type.[2]

FIG. 261.
THE DANÍSKO.

The inside edge characterises, to a certain extent, the Albanian yataghan, and the Flissa of the Kabáil (Kabyles); and it is thoroughly well developed in the formidable Korá or Kukkri of the Gurkha or Nepaulese mountaineers, whose edge swells out to a half-moon.

The Mycenæ finds do not enlighten us upon the subject of the Ἄορ and other forms of the Greek Sword. We know nothing of the Thracian Ῥομφαία, the Rumpia of Gellius (x. 25), which the A.V.[3] translates 'Sword.' Most writers hold it to be a Thracian lance, like the European 'partisan;' and Smith's 'Dictionary of Antiquities' describes it as a long spear resembling the Sarissa, with a Sword-like blade. This comes from Livy (xxxi. 39), who tells us that in woodlands the Macedonian phalanx was ineffectual on account of its *prælongæ hastæ*, and that the Rhomphæa of the Thracians was a hindrance for the same reason. But in modern Romaic usage it denotes the flammberg (*flamberge*), or that form of the wavy blade which the Church places in the hands of the angelic host. It is always carried by 'Monseigneur Saint Michel, the Archangel, the first knight who in the quarrel of God battled with the Dragon, the old enemy of mankind, and drove him out of heaven.'[4] Mycenæ supplied no specimen of the χελιδών (*gladius Chelidonius*), the broad blade with a bifurcated swallow-tailed point. It is mentioned by Isidore (xviii.) and by Origen (chap. vi.); and I have alluded to it in Chapter VII. We are unable to specify the shape of the Athenian Κνήστεις (*Knesteis*) or the Lacedæmonian ξυίναι (*Xyinæ*), which Xenophon calls ξυήλαι (*Xuelæ*). They may have been, to judge from their use, thick cut-and-thrust daggers, in fact *Coupe-Choux*. Nor do we know what kind of blade was carried by the Xystophori (ξυστοφόροι) in addition to the *Xyston*: the latter was either the footman's spear (δόρυ) or the horseman's lance; in the 'Iliad,' as has been seen, it is a long pole studded with iron nails.

According to history, the Greek infantry Sword was a straight two-edged blade, rather broad, and of equal width from hilt to point, which was of bevelled shape. For cavalry they preferred the sabre or cutting weapon.[5] Iphicrates (B.C. 400), when improving arms and armour, must have found spear and Sword too short, for he 'doubled the length of the spear and made the Swords also longer'

---

[1] See chap. viii.

[2] See chap. iii. The Danísko is the hatchet-yataghan of Demmin, p. 397.

[3] Gen. iii. 24; Zech. xiii. 7; Apocalyp. i.

[4] Here we find St. Michael a heavenly archetype of St. George. In the vault of the Superga, Turin, Monseigneur carries a rapier instead of a flamberge.

[5] Xenophon, *De Re Eq.* xii. 11.

(Diod. Sic. xv. 144 ; Corn. Nepos, xi.). Plutarch (in 'Lycurg.') tells us that a man in the presence of Agesilaus jeered at the Spartan blade, which measured

only fourteen to fifteen inches long, saying that a juggler would think nothing of swallowing it';[1] whereto the great commander replied, 'Yet our short Swords can pierce our foes.' And when a bad workman complained of his tool, the Spartan suggested with dry heroism, 'You have only to advance a pace.'

Dodwell[2] relates that an iron blade found in a tomb at Athens was two feet five inches long, including its handle of the same metal. Most of our museum specimens, both of bronze and iron, are of fair average dimensions. That of Mayence measures nineteen and a half inches (a fig. 265), and that of the

FIG. 262.- GREEK XIPHOS (Jähns).

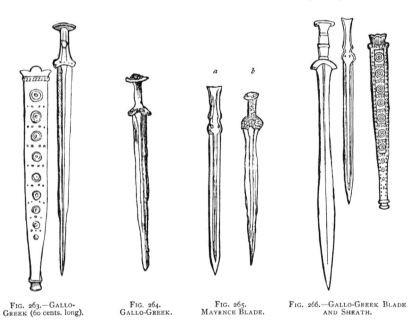

FIG. 263.—GALLO-GREEK (60 cents. long).

FIG. 264. GALLO-GREEK.

FIG. 265. MAYENCE BLADE.

FIG. 266.—GALLO-GREEK BLADE AND SHEATH.

Museum of Artillery thirty-two. The Pella blade in the K. Antiquarium, Berlin, is only twenty-one centimètres, including four for the heft.

The Swords called Gallo-Greek,[3] with bronze blades and sheaths (figs. 263, etc.),

[1] A world-wide juggling trick, which seems to have originated in Egypt. In Apuleius (*Golden Ass*, lib. i.) a *circulator* or itinerant juggler swallows a very sharp two-edged cavalry broadsword and buries in his entrails a horseman's spear. This 'Thracian Magic' is still practised by the well-known Raf'ai Dervishes.

[2] He figures the blade in his Tour (i. p. 443).

[3] Galatians, Keltic Gauls, who established themselves in Western Asia Minor after the destruction of their leader Brennus at Delphi (B.C. 279). Florus (ii. 10) calls the Gallo-Græcians 'adulterated relics of Gauls' : Strabo also alludes to the Phrygians and the three Galatian peoples (iv. 1). As Ammian. Marcell. tells us (xv. cap. ix.), ' Galatæ is the Greek trans-

are of moderate length—twenty-five inches. Pausanias[1] alludes to perhaps a shorter weapon (ταῖς μαχαίραις τῶν Γαλατῶν). And we are told that when Manlius invaded Galatia he found the Swords were *prælongi gladii.*[2]

The Greek fashion of carrying the Sword apparently varied with the times, and, perhaps, with the length of the weapon ; it is easy to draw a dagger from the right, but awkward to unsheathe a full-sized blade. Some writers make the Greeks carry the weapon on the right, and others on the left : Homer seems purposely to leave his description vague, e.g. :—

Ἡ ὅγε φάσγανον ὀξὺ ἐρυσσάμενος (or *σπασσάμενος*) *παρὰ μηροῦ.*

Drawing the grided dirk fro' the sheath which hung by his thigh-side.[3]

The words *parà merou* are similarly used elsewhere,[4] but which thigh is not specified. Hector's sharp Sword hangs below his loins both huge and strong, and brandishing it he rushes to his death by Achilles' spear.[5] The Trojan, too, strikes Ajax,[6] who carried his weapon after Assyrian fashion, 'where the two belts cross upon his breast, both that of the shield and that of the silver-studded Sword.' The ' Parazonium ' dagger, with its metal scabbard, was usually attached to the Sword-belt[7] on the other side. Shaped like an ox-tongue ('Anelace,' or *Langue-de-bœuf*), and measuring twelve to sixteen inches long, it was common to Greece and Rome ; I have shown its origin in Egypt.

FIG. 267.—BRONZE PARA-ZONIUM (16¾ inches long).

The part played by the Hellenes upon the great stage of the world's history was their development of civil life— of citizenship. As a nation, they wanted the life-long practice of arms and training for warfare, brought to absolute perfection by the Romans. Their annual games, as shown by the Pindaric Odes, were mostly trials of speed and agility. They had the Bibasis or gymnastic dance, and, to mention no other, the Pyrrhic or Sword-dance, like all ancient and many modern peoples ; but these mimicries soon became in the cities mere women's work. They wore side-arms at home only during the Panathenaic fêtes, where orchestral actions and attitudes were displayed ; and they had not those military colonies like the Romans, where every man was a soldier and every soldier was a veteran. Their *gymnasia* and *palæstræ* were schools for calisthenics, which the sturdier Italians held in

lation of the Roman term Galli.' They consisted of three tribes, each with its capital : the Tolistobogii (= Tolosa + Boii) at Pessinus ; the Tectosages (of Aquitaine) at Ancyra, now Angora, famous for wool and cats ; and the Trocmi, with Tavium for principal city, lay to the east bordering on Pontus. This people, like the Gauls, their kinsmen, was 'admodum dedita religionibus ' (Cæs. *B. G.* vi. 16).

[1] x. 32.   [2] Livy, xxxviii. c. 17.

[3] *Il.* i. 190.   [4] *Il.* xvi. 437.
[5] *Il.* xxii. 310-60.   [6] *Il.* xiv. 405.
[7] In the *Iliad* (iv. 185) we find the ζωστήρ and the ζῶμα different. Menelaus wears the former outside, the Sword below it, and a μίτρα or metal plate on the breast. The ζωστήρ was probably a broad girdle strengthened with metal, and considered part of the ὅπλα : thus ζώννυσθαι, to 'gird one's loins,' is to prepare for battle.

contempt. They were, like the gymnastic-grounds of the Spartan girls, mere hot-beds for growing beauty and good breeders; for attaining the perfection of form duly to be transmitted. This process, indeed, began with the bride, who furnished her nuptial chamber with the finest possible models in painting and statuary. Hence every well-bred citizen at Athens, every 'gentleman,' was expected to be handsome. The Beautiful, the Good, and the Holy grew to be almost synonymous. Physical man was raised to his highest expression, till he became the mythological, ideal god-man. This anthropomorphism found its final stage in Phidias; the Parthenon was its expression, and Olympus its culmination.[1] Since the ancient man-breeding and man-shaping system was abandoned, and the race became intimately mixed with foreign blood, chiefly Slav and Hebrew, the reverse has become noticeable: a Greek of the classical type is now rarely seen.

FIG. 268.—'HOPLITES' (HEAVY ARMED).[2]   FIG. 269.—GREEK COMBATANTS WITH SWORD AND LANCE.

Then came the intellectual age of Greece. Already in B.C. 450 Protagoras the Sophist, of the Cyrenaic school, had made 'man the measure of all things.' The individual becomes a duality; as Aristotle expresses it, the animal life is one of sensation, the divine life of intelligence. And this change of view gradually extinguished the holy fire of art.

The Hellenes, even in their best times, did not pay that attention to the use of arms which was a daily practice with the more practical Romans. They had no gladiatorial shows, the finest *salles d'armes* in the world. The ὁπλοδιδακταὶ (ὁπλοδιδασκολοὶ) or army *maîtres d'armes*, and professors of the noble arts of offence and defence, were not required by law in Lacedæmon. They practised the Sword, as we learn from Demosthenes; he compared the Athenians 'with rustics in a fencing school, who after a blow always guard the hit part and not before.'[3] Yet they preferred the pentathlum, the pancration, and military dancing; the fencing-room was a secondary consideration. Indeed, Plato objected to the useless art of Sword-exercise, because neither masters nor disciples ever became great soldiers—a stupendous Platonic fallacy![4]

[1] Doubtless Pythagoras and Socrates were mono-theists after the fashion of the Egyptian priests; but the Olympus of the many-headed was peopled by a charming bevy of *coquins* and *coquines*.

[2] From the treatise of M. Rodios, ΕΠΙ ΠΟΛΕ-ΜΙΚΗΣ ΤΕΧΝΗΣ (Athens, 1868); the soldier wears an Etruscan helmet, and the pelta shield resembles an ivy leaf.   [3] *Philip*. i.

[4] To name merely the *sommités* : Alexander the Great, Eumenes, and Ptolemy; Hannibal; Sulla,

Nor did Hellas greatly prize herself upon mere arms. The soldier at Athens and amongst all the Ionian and kindred races occupied, it is true, an honourable position ; in the four castes [1] he followed the priestly, and he preceded the peasants and the mechanics. But the Hellene was essentially a citizen—a politician. He chose his magistrates and pontiffs, and he could aspire to become one himself. He spent his life in the Agora, canvassing laws and constitutions, treaties and alliances. His minor delight was gossip, euphuistically expressed by ' hearing new things.' Hellas soon learned that her *forte* lay in literature, poetry, oratory, and philosophy, in engineering, and in the fine arts. She excelled the world in the exquisite rules of proportion ; in the breadth of idea, and in the clearness and perfection of the literary form : these arts she bequeathed as a heritage to mankind, who have nowhere and never surpassed her. While the grand old Kemites built for eternity, and subjected even size [2] to solidity, Hellas elaborated the principle of Beauty and carried it to its very acme. Her spoilt children were avid of novelty : they constructed every possible system of cosmogony, of astronomy, of geology (except the right one) ; and they ' paraded their knowledge,' as Bacon says, ' with fifes and drums.' Hence their teachers of the Nile Valley told them ' they were ever children' ; and hence they excelled their teachers.

This is not the place to discuss Greek tactics, nor is there anything new to say about them : authors are contented with borrowing from the treatises of Ælian and Arrian, who lived in the days of Hadrian. I will only remind the reader that even during the ' Iliad '-ages the Greek army had its scheme of battle. Nestor advises his warriors to keep their ranks in action after the wont of their forbears ; and in two places [3] we have allusions to a rude phalanx or oblong rectangle of civilised Egypt and Khita-land. Xenophon [4] tells us that the army of Agesilaus appeared all bronze ($\chi\alpha\lambda\kappa\dot{o}\nu$) and red ($\phi o\acute{\iota}\nu\iota\kappa\alpha$) ; the latter survives in our most inappropriate British scarlet. For the heavy-armed Hoplite-swordsmen and the light Peltasts, who had apparently no Swords, the student will consult any ' Dictionary of Antiquities.'

Another unpleasant feature in Greek warfare was its indifference to human life, so much regarded by the Romans. The former preserved their old barbarous practice of putting to death their war-prisoners ; whilst even during the first Punic War the latter had a system of exchange combined with a money-payment for any number in excess on either side.

Fabius, Marius, Sertorius, Cato, Brutus, Julius Cæsar, Mark Antony, Pompey, Metellus, Marcellus, Trajan, and Hadrian. All these commanders were famous swordsmen, concerning whose personal feats with the weapon we have ample notices.

[1] The Albanians still preserve the four castes which do not intermarry. These are : Soldiers (or Landowners), Tradesmen, Shepherds, and Artisans.

[2] Some of the Greek statues were larger than any Egyptian. Olympian Jove stood 60 feet, Apollo 45 (Pausanias), and the Image of the Sun (commonly called the Colossus of Rhodes) 105 feet, exceeding everything in the Nile Valley. I need not refer to Mount Athos and the Charonion of Antioch. The oldest known Greek statue is a portrait produced at Miletus in B.C. 550, and inscribed : ' I am Chares, son of Kleisis, ruler of Teichiousa, an offering to Apollo.' The style of this and other archaic works (vases, &c.), which are rare, connects it with Assyrianism, about the age of Assurnazirpal (B.C. 880).

[3] *Iliad,* ii. 362 and iv. 297 sq.

[4] *De Ages.*

Greece rarely appears in arms except in defensive warfare (as against the Persians), in civil wars between citizens and citizens, and in semi-civil wars, as between the Athenians and the Spartans, the Dorians, Ionians, and Æolians. A glance at any of their campaigns—the 'Anabasis,' for instance—gives us their measure as soldiers ; and what else can we expect from a race whose typical men were Themistocles and Alcibiades ? They were too clever by half ; too vain, too restless, too impulsive (ever 'shedding tears'), too self-assertive to become disciplined men-machines. They were always ready for a revolt, for a change of officers ; and it must have been a serious thing to command them. In this point, perhaps, they are rivalled by the Frenchman, one of the best soldiers in Europe, and also one of the most difficult to manage. Great captains—Turenne and Napoleon Buonaparte, for instance—shot their recalcitrants by the dozen till the survivors learned to 'tremble and obey.'[1] Like the French, too, and the Irish, the Greeks had more dash than firmness. They gained victories by the vigour and gallantry of their attack, but they did not distinguish themselves in a losing game. Here England excels, and hence Marshal Bugeaud said, ' She has the best infantry in the world ; happily they are not many.' We must make them so.

Hellas owed her successes in foreign wars mainly to the barbarous condition of her neighbours. The Romans and all the peoples of Asia Minor, save her own colonies,[2] were far behind her when, after the fashion of the equestrian races of Northern Asia, she had exchanged the chariot for the charger ;[3] and when she borrowed from Egypt the arts of warfare by land and sea, the paraphernalia of the siege, the best of arms and armour, and even the redoubtable phalanx. But she lost pre-eminence, physical and moral, when the rival races rose to be her equals, and even her superiors, in weapons, organisation, and discipline. She began with beating, and she ended with being thoroughly beaten by, the Romans.

Greek literature does not abound, like Roman and Hebrew, in perpetual allusions to the Sword : it refers more frequently to the spear and bow. Yet Athenæus ennobles the end of his curious *olla podrida* (the ' Deipnosophists ') with some charming lines alluding to the Queen of Weapons. The first passage begins with : —

---

[1] But who is to do this under a Republic ? And here we foresee troubles for our neighbours in the next Prusso-Gallic War.

[2] For instance, the ' Holy City' of Miletus, with its 300 dependent towns. When we speak of ancient Greece we must remember that it extended from Asia Minor to Sicily, Italy, and even Southern France ; and from Egypt to Albania. Modern Greece is a mere mutilated trunk.

[3] Demmin (p. 106, &c.) tells us that ' the Greeks had not even a term to denote the action of riding on horseback '; and that ' even in French a proper verb does not exist, as the expression *chevaucher* means rather to stroll (*flâner*) on horseback.' As his English translator remarks, the assertion is hardly admissible in the face of such words as ἱππεύειν (*equitare*), *cavalcare*, to ride the horse ; ἱππεία (riding), ἱππεύς and ἱππότης (a rider, a knight), and ἐπιβεβηκώς, mounted (*scil.* on horseback). His interpretation of *chevaucher* is equally erroneous. *Chevaucher*, a fine old word, now only too rare, exactly expresses our ' to ride ' : *Il chevaucha aux parties a'occident*, is quoted from a French MS. (early fourteenth century) by Colonel Yule in his preface to Marco Polo ; and the word occurs twice in the same sentence with the same sense.

> I 'll wreathe my sword in myrtle bough,
> The sword that laid the tyrant low,
> When Patriots burning to be free
> To Athens gave equality.[1]

The second is the song of Hybrias the Cretan :—

> My wealth is here, the sword, the spear, the breast-defending shield,
> With this I plough, with this I sow, with this I reap the field ;
> With this I rape the luscious grape and drink the blood-red wine,
> And slaves at hand in order stand, and all are counted mine ![2]

And here arises a curious question.   Do races, as is generally assumed, decline and fall like nations and empires ?   Does the body politic obey the law of the body corporal ?   Do peoples grow old and feeble and barren after their most brilliant periods of gestation ?   Or rather do they not cease to be great, and to bear great men, because their neighbours have grown to be greater, and because genius is repressed by unfavourable media?   I cannot see that Time has greatly changed the peasant of the Romagna, the mountaineer of the Peloponnesus, the Persian become a Parsi in Bombay, or the modern soldier of the Nile Valley, who, under Ibrahim Pasha, defeated the Turks in every pitched battle.   But the conditions of Italy, Greece, Persia, and Egypt, are now fundamentally altered : they are no longer superior to their surroundings ; they are environed by races stronger than themselves.   Hence, perhaps, what is popularly called their degeneracy.

---

[1] Lord Denman's translation.   [2] D. K. Sandford.

CHAPTER XII.

THE SWORD IN ANCIENT ROME ; THE LEGION AND THE GLADIATOR.

THE *rôle* played by pagan Rome on the stage of history was twofold—that of conqueror and that of regulator. In obeying man's acquisitive instinct she was compelled to perfect her executive instrument, the fighter. To her we owe the words 'arms' and 'army,' 'armour' and 'armoury.'[1] As *pugna* derives from *pugnus*, the fist, so *arma* and its congeners derive from *armus*, the arm : 'antiqui humeros cum brachiis armos vocabant,' says Festus. Well knowing that the 'God of Battles' favours superiority of weapons as much as, and in select cases more than, 'big battalions,' she ever chose the implements and instruments she found the best ; and, following her own proverb, she never disdained to take a lesson in arms even from the conquered.

But Rome soon learnt that to make good soldiers she must begin by making good citizens. She insisted upon the civilising maxim 'Cedant arma togæ,' without, however, the invidious precedence which Sallust calls 'those most offensive words of Cicero'

—— Concedat laurea linguæ.

She subordinated the Captain to the Magistrate, and she proclaimed to both the absolute Reign of Law. The idea presented itself to the Greek mind in the shape of Fate, Anagké, Nemesis : Rome brought it down from the vague to the realistic, from the abstract to the concrete, from heaven to earth. Thus, while Greece taught mankind the novel lessons of ordered liberty, free thought, intellectual culture, and patriotic citizenship, Rome, by her reverence for Law, in whose sight all men were equal, preached the brotherhood of mankind. Hence Christendom ever has been, and is still, governed by a heathen code, by that Roman jurisprudence which flowed from the Twelve Tables, like the laws of Jewry from the Ten Commandments. Indeed the 'Fecial College,' which pronounced upon the obliga-

---

[1] 'Armour' is from the Lat. *armatura*, through O. French *armeure* and *armure* ; *armoire* is *armarium*, originally a place for keeping Arms, and *armamentarium* is our arsenal. It is not a little curious that 'finds' of Roman weapons are so rare, bearing no proportion to the wide extension of the rule. We must also beware of the monuments which are apt to idealise and archaicise : this is notable in the shape of the helmet, the pilum, and the Sword. Jähns specifies as the best place for study the Romano-German Central Museum at 'Mainz,' under Professor Dr. Lindenschmit (p. 192).

tions of international war and peace, is an institution which might profitably be revived in the modern world.[1]

Rome was single-minded in her objective, conquest ; and unlike the Greeks, from whom she borrowed, she was not diverted by art or literature. All her poets for a thousand years fit into one volume. Her art, indeed, can hardly be said to exist ; history is silent concerning any save a few exceptional Roman architects. Varro laughs at the puppets and effigies of the gods. The triumph of Metellus (B.C. 146) introduced Art, but the Helleno-Roman artist contented himself with copies and with portrait-statues of the great. In the days of their highest luxury and refinement, the toga'd people were connoisseurs and purchasers who diffused instead of adding to knowledge. Others, as Virgil said, might give movement to marble and breath to bronze : the Art of the Roman was to rule the nations, to spare the subjected, and to debase the proud. 'Fortia agere Romanum est.'

For the constitution of the Roman army we must consult the estimable Polybius,[2] its early historian, Livy, and the latest of the great authorities, Vegetius, in the days of Valentinian II. (A.D. 375–92) ; not forgetting Varro,[3] who treats of weapon changings.

Whilst the militia consisted of three bodies, the citizens, the allies, who were sworn, and the auxiliaries or mercenaries ; the characteristic of Roman organisation was the Legion—that is, *legere* (they chose). Emerging by slow degrees from the Phalanx or close column,[4] it learnt to prefer for battle the *acies instructa*, haye or line, and the *acies sinuata*, with wings ; and it reserved for especial purposes the *agmen pilatum* or close array, and the *agmen quadratum* or hollow square.

The reason of the change is manifest. The Phalanx or oblong herse was irresistible during the compact advance. The wise Egyptian inventors made it perfect for the Nile Valley. But it lost virtue in woodlands and highlands ; it was liable to be broken when changing front, and the long unwieldy spears which it required caused confusion on broken ground.

The Legion consisted, strictly speaking, of heavy-armed infantry—of Milites, from *Mil-es*, because reckoned by their thousands. They were preceded by the Velites, Ferentarii, or Rorarii, 'light infantry,' *éclaireurs*, who cleared the way for action ; in the first century they were reinforced by the Accensi Velati.[5] Whilst the Auxiliaries fought with bows and arrows, and some, like the Etruscans, with the 'funda' or sling, the Veles carried two to seven light throw-spears (*hastæ*

---

[1] In our day the only 'Fecialists' are the Moslem States.

[2] *Polybii Historiarum quæ supersunt.* The voluminous and luminous writer, a contemporary of Scipio Africanus, and a captain who witnessed the destruction of Carthage, was born A.U.C. 552 (B.C. 204), nearly three centuries after the Latin conquest of Etruria. He was called 'Auctor bonus in primis,' and Scipio said of him, 'Nemo fuit in requirendis temporibus diligentior' (Cicero, *De Off.* iii. 12, and *De Rep.* ii. 14).

[3] *De Linguâ Lat.* iv. 6.

[4] Livy, viii. 8.

[5] Also called Adscriptii, Supernumerarii, and Velati, because wearing only the *sagum* or soldier's cloak, opposed to the officer's *paludamentum*. Properly speaking, they were rear-troops, ranged in battle order behind the Triarii. During certain epochs the Rorarii stood next to the Triarii, and the Accensi, less trustworthy than either, formed the extreme rear.

velitariæ) about three feet long in the shaft, with a nine-inch lozenge-shaped head of iron.[1] For close quarters he wore on his right side a Parazonium-dagger, and on the right a broad cut-and-thrust blade of moderate size. His defences were an apron of leather strips, studded with metal ; and a Parma,[2] the small round shield, like the Cetra, some three feet in diameter.[3]

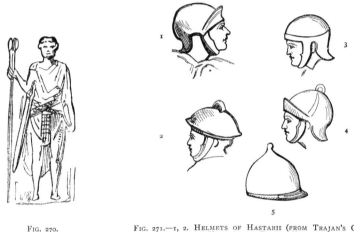

FIG. 270.

FIG. 271.—1, 2. HELMETS OF HASTARII (FROM TRAJAN'S COLUMN);
3, 4. HELMETS OF HASTARII ; 5. BRONZE HELMET (FROM CANNÆ).

The Legion proper was a line or rather a triple line of Hastarii[4] or legionary spearmen. Livy[5] briefly describes the Acies, when it emerged from the Phalanx, as 'drawn up into distinct companies, divided into centuries. Each company contained sixty soldiers,[6] two centurions, and one ensign or standard-bearer.[7] First in line stood the Hastati in fifteen companies with twenty Velites.[8]

[1] The weapon is well shown in a monumental tablet on the Court wall of the Aquileja Museum.

[2] The Clypeus, or Clipeus, of favourite Greek use, was also round, but larger than the Parma. Our 'buckler' (*buccularius clypeus*) takes its name from having on it an open mouth (*bucca*, *buccula*), in Chinese fashion, instead of the *umbo*.

[3] In Livy's Phalanx (A.U.C. 415) the Velites were light-armed men, carrying only a spear and short iron pila (viii. 7).

[4] A congener of the Keltic *Ast* = branch ; whence the Fr. *arme d'hast*. It was the Greek κοντός, *contus*, or lance, an unbarbed spear, a royal sceptre : under the Republic it collected the hundreds (*hastam centumviralem agere*) ; it noted auctions (*jus hastæ*), it was the weapon of the light infantry-man (*hasta velitaris*), and it served to part the bride's hair (Ovid, *Fast.* ii. 560). *Hastarius* and *hastatus*, *hasta* and *quiris* are synonyms ; the *gæsum* was a heavier weapon and barbed, and the *jaculum*, with its diminutives, *spiculum*, *vericulum*, or *verutum*, was a lighter javelin. Virgil uses *hastile* poetically. [5] *Loc. cit.*

[6] The number of men greatly varied ; the extremes of the Legion are 6,800 including cavalry under Scipio, and 1,500 under Constantine. In Livy's Legion there were 5,000 infantry and 300 horse (viii. 8). Perhaps we may assume an average of 4,000 foot— a full Austrian regiment. Each line of the three numbered 10 cohorts, and each cohort three maniples. The latter were named from manipulus, a handful (of grass, &c., *Georg.* i. 400), because this rustic article at the end of a pole was the standard of Romulus.

[7] The Signa, ensigns, or standards, were different in the legions. The Vexillum, or colours of cavalry, was a square of cloth, also called Pannus (πῆνος). The word is a congener of the Gothic *Fana* and *Fan* ; the Ang. Sax. *Pan* ; the Germ. *Fahne* ; the French *bannière* and our *banner*. Hence, too, *Gonfanon* = *Gundfano*. When the Eagle became imperial, and the Vexillum a Labarum with a cross, this standard was splendidly decorated, and led to the French oriflamme. The latter was made of the fine red (silk ?) stuff called *cendalum*, cendal, or sendel.

[8] These 'light bobs' were re-organised and regu-

Behind them were the Principes with heavy shields and complete armour, also numbering fifteen companies. These thirty companies were called Antepilani, because there were fifteen others placed behind them with the standards ; each of the latter consisted of three divisions, and the first division of each they called a Pilus. The first ensign was at the head of the third line proper, the Triarii. Behind them stood the Rorarii, whose ability was less by reason of their youth and inexperience ; and, lastly, in the rear, came the Accensi, a body in which little confidence was reposed. The Hastati began the fight, and if unable to gain the day, passed to the rear through the ranks of the Principes. The latter now marched forwards to action, the Hastati following. Meanwhile the Triarii continued kneeling behind the Ensigns ; the left legs extended to the front, the shields resting on the shoulders ; the spear-points erect with butts firmly fixed in the ground, so that the line bristled as if inclosed by a rampart. If the Principes failed, "res ad Triarios rediit." The Triarii, after receiving the Principes and Has-tati into their intervals, closed files and fell upon the enemy in a compact body.[1] This was the most formidable attack, when the enemy, having pursued the vanquished, sud-denly beheld a new line starting up.'

Thus far Livy. I am tempted by the subject of the Roman legionaries, those ' mas-sive hammers of the whole earth,' to add, despite its triteness, a few details.

The Hastatus or spearman, a young light-armed soldier, preceded the colours ; hence

FIG. 272.—HASTATUS (FROM TRAJAN'S COLUMN).

he was called Antesignanus. He wore for defence a plain or crested helmet which varied with his legion.[2] He had a bronze breast-plate thirty-two inches long, or a cuirass of thin metal plates defending the chest and forming shoulder-pieces. A kilt[3] of the same material protected his lower body ; greaves or leggings (*ocreæ*) his legs, and the Scutum or shield his flank. This article ($\sigma\kappa\hat{v}\tau o\varsigma$, leather, dog-skin ?), a curved rectangular oblong, larger than the Parma, measured about four feet by two and a half feet ; the framework was of wood, and the covering had a strong boss and metal platings. As his name denotes, the Hastatus was armed with the full-sized spear, and with a long or short 'gladius' or 'ensis.' The latter was carried on the right, as a rule ; as will be seen, it greatly varied in size and shape. The soldier, when excited in battle, threw away his spear and drew

larly established in A.U.C. 541, after the battle ot Cannæ.

[1] In fact, it formed phalanx, a word originally meaning a block or a cylinder.

[2] The officer's was adorned by way of honour-able decoration with three (ostrich ?) feathers black and scarlet.

[3] The original kilt was the waist-cloth, man's primitive dress in the Tropics and the lower Tempe-rates. It became an article of defence under the Greeks and Romans ; and thence it spread over most of Europe. The Maltese long preserved it, and the *Fustanella* is still worn in Greece and Albania. In Ireland it was ancient, as it is modern in Scotland.

his Sword ; the Etruscans did the same.[1]   The shield-umbo was also used in close combat to bear down the opponent.

The second line, which like the third followed the standards, was composed of the Principes or Proci, soldiers of mature age.   The name seems to denote that originally they formed the front line, as the Greek Promachoi and our Grenadiers.[2] Lastly came the Triarii (third line men), a reserve, so called from their position— veterans of tried valour who were expected to retrieve the fortunes of the day.   At first they were the only Pilani[3] (javelineers), as opposed to the two first lines (Antepilani).   Their redoubtable weapon, which conquered so much of the old world, and which descended by inheritance to the Franks, was about six feet and three-quarters long, composed of an iron (two feet) with oval or pyramidal head, set by a broad tang in a wooden socketed shaft treble its length.   The latter was round at the heel and squared about the shoulders, as we learn from Livy,[4] when describing the Phalarica or fire-missile.   Both Principes and Triarii also carried Swords, the former at the right hip, the latter above it : as has before been noticed this is a most complicated snbject.   The bandsmen wore, like the Signa-bearers, a peculiar helmet ; they consisted of tubicines (using the *tuba*, a long Etruscan trumpet), of cornicines (the *cornu* being a writhed horn), and of buccinatores, blowing a short simple instrument.   The Roman officers were armed like the men.

FIG. 273.—CENTURION'S CUIRASS, WITH PHALERÆ OR DECORATIONS.

Under the term *utraque militia* was included the legionary cavalry whose number varied little in proportion to the infantry.   In Polybius' day the ratio was two hundred to four thousand.   This arm was clad in a complete suit of bronze less heavy than the Greeks and the Gallo-Greeks ;[5] the buckler of ox-hide was round, oval, or polygonal.   The horseman's weapons were a Spear (*contus*), often accompanied by a javelin, a waist-dagger, and a Sword worn on the right ; the latter, unlike ours, preserved the form of the infantry weapon.   The Greek cavalry in the Roman service at the siege of Jerusalem, as we learn from Josephus, carried long Swords suspended to the right flank.

Lastly, the Legion was followed by its massive *tormenta* (artillery) : catapults

---

[1] Livy, ix. 35.   [2] Livy, viii. 8.

[3] *Pilum*, like our 'pile,' a congener of the Teutonic *Pfeil*, is not a Roman invention, and was probably borrowed from the Samnites (Sallust. *Cat.* 51, 38).   The *pilum murale*, used for piercing walls (Cæsar, *B. G.* v. 40), was a round or quadrangular shaft of three cubits, with an iron of the same length (Polybius, vi. 23, 9).   The *pilum* was perpetually changing size and proportions ; moreover, there were two kinds, the heavy and the light.   The

figures in the text are those of the Mayence *pilum* (Jähns, p. 201).

[4] Livy, xxi. 8.

[5] Under Trajan and Septimius Severus the cavalry adopted the iron or bronze *Hamata*, hooked metal chains, forming a kind of mail-coat, and the *Squamata*, scales sewn on to linen or leather. Demmin (p. 121) erroneously makes the latter 'chain-armour,' and yet his illustration shows the scales.

(for darts) and *balistæ* (for stones), escorted by the *vexillarii* or oldest soldiers, under their own *vexillum*, and worked by the Sappers or *fabri* (*lignarii*, &c.). The camp-followers (*calones*, *lixæ*) and the baggage (*impedimenta*) brought up the rear.

The Roman infantry was carefully drilled. Vegetius tells us that recruits were exercised with osier-bucklers and stakes double the weight of the normal Swords. There were also regular *champs de Mars*, 'sham-fights' with wooden Swords and with javelins whose points were sheathed in balls.

In the effeminate days of the Empire, shortly after Constantine, military discipline was relaxed, and the decay of the Legion became complete. Instead of shouldering their packs the men carried them in carts. The Hasta was given up, and the helmet and the cuirass were dispensed with as too heavy. Vegetius[1] had reason to ascribe the defeat of the Legion by the Goths to the want of its old defensive armour.

It was not only when campaigning that the Romans studied the use of arms. In the Campus Martius and the other seven 'parks' of the Capital, crowds of young men practised riding, swording, and athletics. Another mighty *Salle d'Armes* was the Amphitheatre. To a purely military nation, gladiatorism had great merits. 'C'estoit, à la verité,' says Montaigne,[2] 'un merveilleux exemple, et de tresgrand fruict pour l'institution du peuple, de veoir touts les jours en sa presence cent, deux cents, voire mille couples d'hommes, armez les uns contre les aultres, se hacher en pieces, avecques une si extreme fermeté de courage, qu'on ne leur veit lascher une parole de foiblesse ou commiseration, jamais tourner le dos, ny faire seulement un mouvement lasche pour gauchir au coup de leur adversaire, ains tendre le col à son espee, et se presenter au coup.'

It appears to me that the nineteenth century wastes much fine sentiment upon the 'detestable savagery of the Lanista,'[3] and upon the wretches

> Butchered to make a Roman holiday.

The *ludus gladiatorius*[4] began as a humane institution amongst the Etruscans, who, instead of slaughtering, upon the funeral pyre, slaves and war-captives, like Achilles and Pyrrhus, allowed them to fight for their lives. The *munus* at Rome, moreover, was originally confined to public funerals, and it was an abuse which allowed it at private interments, at entertainments, and at holiday festivals in general.

According to Livy[5] 'when Scipio exhibited gladiators at Carthage' (B.C. 546) 'they were not slaves or men who sold their blood, the usual stuff of the Lanista's school.'[6] The service was voluntary and gratuitous. Combatants were often sent by petty princes to show the courage of their people; others came for-

---

[1] *De Re Mil.* i. 16.

[2] *Essais de Montaigne*, l. ii., chap. 24 (Paris: Garnier Frères, 1874).

[3] Or *maître d'armes*, a word borrowed by Rome from Etruria. The legionary teachers were termed *armi loctores* and *campidoctores*.

[4] Athenæus (iv. 41) relates from Hermippus and Ephorus that the Mantineans were the inventors of Gladiatorism proper (μονομαχοῦντες), suggested by one of their citizens, Demus or Demonax, and that the Cyreneans followed suit. [5] Livy, xxviii. 21.

[6] In early Roman days the Gladiator was infamous; even Petronius Arbiter (*Satyr.* cap. 1) uses 'you obscene gladiator' as an insult.

ward in compliment to the General, and some decided their disputes by the Sword. Amongst persons of distinction were Corbis and Orsua, cousins-german, who determined to fight out their claims to the city called Ibes, and they 'exhibited to the army a most interesting spectacle,' the elder swordsman easily mastering the artless attacks of the younger.

Even when the gladiators at Rome were condemned criminals and captives whose lives were forfeited by the old laws of war, some humanity remained. Although the malefactors doomed *ad gladium* were to be slain within the year, those sent only *ad ludum* might obtain their discharge within three years. And under the Empire to join the shows became 'fashionable:' Severus was compelled to forbid freeborn citizens, knights, senators, and even women from entering the arena.

The life of the gladiator was one to make the 'honest poor' curse their lot. He was trained in the best climates, and fed with the most succulent food (*sagina gladiatoria*): hence Cicero[1] calls rude health and good condition 'gladiatoria totius corporis firmitas.' He became one of a *familia* or brotherhood after taking the oath, which Montaigne gives from Petronius (117):—'Nous jurons de nous laisser enchainer, brusler, battre et tuer de glaive, et de souffrir tout ce que les gladiateurs légitimes souffrent de leur maîtres, engageant très-religieusement le corps et l'âme à son service.' In other words, he had plenty of society and he was disciplined. Under the Lanista he practised daily at the schools, and the *ludus matutinus* near the Cœliolus or little Cœlian Hill was frequented by all classes.[2] Here he 'fought the air' (ἀέρα δέρειν), a Σκιαμαχία like our fighting the sack; he contended with the *rudis* (rod or wooden Sword); he cut at the Palus, the 'post-practice' of German universities and modern regiments, and he strengthened back and shoulders with the Halteres (dumb-bells, *dombelles*), and with other artifices. Thus a wound, fatal to a man out of training, would only disable one in such splendid condition.[3] Pliny,[4] indeed, makes light of his danger. Speaking of C. Curio's two pivot-theatres, which during representations could be wheeled inwards or outwards, this model grumbler declares : 'The safety of the gladiators was almost less compromised than that of the Roman people, which allowed itself to be thus whirled round from side to side.'

If worsted in combat and sentenced to receive the Sword (*ferrum recipere*), the gladiator, prepared for his fate, met it with manly firmness. When the down-turned thumbs granted mercy, the vanquished got his *missio* or discharge for the day. Augustus humanely abolished the barbarity of shows *sine missione*, where no quarter was given. The victor was presented with palms, whence *plurimarum palmarum gladiator*; and with cash, which doubtless commended him to the other sex. We read of old gladiators, showing that the career was not necessarily fatal.

---

[1] *Philip.* ii. 25.

[2] Marius and Pompey the Great both 'kept up' their swordsmanship in these schools and in the Champ de Mars, the latter till the age of fifty-eight.

[3] Hence his simple medication when *hors de combat*, 'refreshing himself with a drink of lye of ashes.' Can they mean the antiseptic charcoal, whose use has been revived of late years?

[4] *Nat. Hist.* xxxvi. 24.

These veterans, and sometimes novices who had fought only in a few *munera*, were, at the request of the people, discharged the service by the Editor or Exhibitor of the games. They were then presented with a Rudis (*rude donati*), and, as Rudiarii lived happily ever afterwards.

We have also notices of distinguished gladiators. Diogenes Laertius[1] does not disdain to mention as the fourth Epicurus, 'lastly, a gladiator.' Spartacus, Crixus, and Œnomaus broke out of Lentulus' fencing-school, escaped from Capua, and made a camp at Vesuvius; they used the Swords made out of iron plundered in the slave-houses to such effect that Athenæus declares, 'If Spartacus had not died in battle, he would have caused no ordinary trouble to our countrymen, as Eunus did in Sicily.'[2]

Gladiatorial shows were first exhibited (B.C. 246) in the Forum Boarium by Marcus and D. Brutus at their father's funeral, during the Saturnalia (our Christmas) and the Minerva feasts.[3] They were abolished by Constantine ' the Great' (A.D. 306–33), but the edict seemed to give them fresh life; Frank prisoners were slaughtered by the hundred in the arena of Trèves. They were finally suppressed (A.D. 404) by Honorius, who made a martyr of the monk Telemachus. I need hardly relate how this meddling ecclesiastic rushed into the amphitheatre to separate the combatants, and was incontinently stoned by ' the house.'

But the time had come for abolishing these glorious *spectacula*; as mostly happens, long custom and familiarity had merged the use into the abuse, and caused Lactantius to exclaim ' tollenda est nobis!' The misuse had begun under Divus Cæsar, who collected so many gladiators for the fights that his enemies became alarmed, and restricted the number. Caligula, the ' Bootling,' was devoted to the sport, and made some gladiators captains of his German guards. He deprived the ' Mirmillones'[4] of certain weapons. One Columbus coming off victorious in a fight, but slightly hurt, he caused the wound to be infused with poison, which got the name of Columbinum. The nervous Claudius (' Caldius ') assisted at the *spectacula* ' muffled up in a pallium, a new fashion!' Having spared, at the intercession of his four sons, a conquered prize-fighter, he sent a billet round the house reminding the spectators how much it behoved them to get children, since these could procure favour and security for a gladiator. In later years he became savage. If a combatant chanced to fall, especially one of the Retiarii, he ordered him to be butchered that he might enjoy the look of the face in the agonies of death. Two combatants happening to kill each other, he ordered some little knives to be made of their Swords. He also delighted in seeing Bestiarii, and he made the sport most brutal and sanguinary. Nero, during his ' golden quinquennium,' ordered that no gladiators, even condemned criminals, should be

---

[1] *Sub v.* Epicurus.

[2] *Deipn.* vi. 105. Eunus was the slave-leader in the Servile War, which began B.C. 130

[3] The first Roman artist who painted gladiators was Terentius Lucanus (Pliny, *N. H.* xxxv. 34).

[4] The Mirmillo, *alias* Gallus, is supposed to be derived from a Keltic word, meaning a fish.

slain ; and he persuaded four hundred senators and six hundred knights, some of unbroken fortunes and unblemished fame, to fight in the arena. He espoused the cause of the Thraces or Parmularians, and often joined in the popular demonstrations in favour of the Prasine or 'green faction,' without, however, compromising his dignity or doing injustice. In his later and crueller days,[1] hearing the master of a family of gladiators say that a Thrax was a match for a Mirmillo, but not so for the exhibitor of the games, he had him dragged from the benches into the arena and exposed to the dogs, with this label, 'A Parmularian guilty of speaking blasphemy.' And, as 'Mero' scandalised the world by his passion for singing and harping, so Commodus degraded himself by amateur gladiatorship. He was cunning of fence, but in the most cowardly way. A powerful man and a practised gymnast, he wore impenetrable armour and fought with a heavy Sword, whereas his antagonists were allowed only blades of tin and lead. Even the humane Trajan[2] exhibited after his victories some ten thousand Dacian 'monomachists.' The militarism of the Romans, however, made them familiar with butchery. Thus Tacitus[3] says: 'The Germans gratified us with the spectacle of a battle in which above sixty thousand men were slain.' This 'gladiatorial show' took place near the canal of Drusus, where the Roman guard on the Rhine commanded a view of the other shore.

The gladiators used both forms of Swords, the straight two-edged blade and the curved.[4] The Dimacheri carried, as the name denotes, two weapons : these may have been either two Swords of the same size, as carried by the Japanese,[5] or possibly Sword and dagger, a practice long preserved on the shores of the Mediterranean. The same may be said of the *duos gladios* borne by the Gaul whom Torquatus slew. The Hoplomachi, armed *cap-a-pie*, must also have been Swordsmen. The Mirmillo[6] was weaponed with a curved blade, cutting inside ('gladio incurvo et falcato') : in Montfaucon, he carries a long convex shield and a Sica or short-Sword.[7] Opposed to the Mirmillo was the Retiarius, armed with net and trident : Cortez found net-soldiers in Mexico, as was natural to fishermen. Winckelmann shows a fight between the two : Retiarius has netted his fish and

---

[1] If Nero was the monster represented by the commentaries and the contemporary Christians, we must wonder how this anti-Christ was loved in life by Acte, the 'sweet and pure-minded Christian'; and why the citizens of Rome sorrowed for his death. And there is much suggestion in the fact that the greatest persecutors of the earliest Christians were the best of the Cæsars, for instance, Vespasian, Titus, Diocletian and Julian.

[2] See the character given to him by Eutropius, viii. 4.

[3] *De Morib. Germ.* xxxiii.

[4] Mariette, *Recueil*, No. 92.

[5] The learned Mr. Tylor is notably in error when he informs Mr. Herbert Spencer (*Ceremonial Institutions*, pp. 174–75) that the Japanese two-sworded

man (Samurai) wore sword and dagger. The blades used to be of equal length. Of the Japanese sword I shall treat in Part II.

[6] Copied by Smith (*Dict. of Ant.* p. 456) from Winckelmann (*Monumenta Inedita*, Pl. 197) : the latter, by the by, was murdered at Trieste.

[7] The word seems to be a congener of *Sahs, Sax,* or *Seax,* the weapon supposed to have named the Saxons. It was either straight or curved, the main object being to fit it closely to the body or under the armpits. Hence it was a favourite with the Sicarius (Ital. *sicario*), the Assassin. Gregory of Tours has (ix. 19) 'Caput sicharii siccâ dividit.' A fanciful derivation of Sicily is from *sica*, because Cronos threw one away at Drepanum. From the diminutive form *Sicula* and *Silicicula* comes the English 'sickle.'

proceeds to use the *fuscina* or *tridens*, while a toga'd Lanista, rod in hand, stands behind him and points out where to strike.

The Samnites were distinguished by the oblong tribal *scutum* [1] and the leaf-shaped Greek Sword : so says the Comte de Caylus ; but on the monument erected by Caracalla to Bato, the weapon is straight up and down. The Thræces or Threces (Thracians proper) [2] had round shields, and instead of the huge Swords noted by Livy, the short knife called by Juvenal *falx supina*.[3] The Thracian's Sword closely resembles that used in the Isle of Cos. Winckelmann [4] gives a combat between two Thracians, each backed up by his Lanista. We find also a naked Gladiator, with Sword and shield, fighting another in breast-belt, apron (*subligaculum*), and boots, with a shield and a three-thonged *flagellum* or scourge.

The Gladiators were an order distinct from the Bestiarii (θηριομάχοι), who fought against wild beasts ; these were exhibited in the Forum, those in the Circus. Again, Bestiarii, who can boast that St. Paul once belonged to them, must not be confounded with the criminals thrown *ad leones*, without means of defence, like Mentor, Androclus, and early Christian communists.[5] The beast-fighters had their *scholæ bestiarum* or *bestiariorum* where they practised weapons, and they received *auctoramentum* or pay. The arms were various : mostly they are shown with a Sword in one hand, a veil in the other, and the left leg pro-tected by greaves. Under Divus Cæsar criminals for the first time encountered wild beasts with silver weapons. The modern survival is the Spanish bull-fight. Gladiatorism lasted in England after a fashion till the days of Addison ; amongst professional Swordsmen, the highest surviving name is that of

> —— the great Figg, by the prize-fighting swains
> The monarch acknowledged of Mary'bone plains.[6]

To conclude this discursus on gladiatorism. Most popular sports are cruel, but we must not confound, as is often done, cruelty with brutality. The former may accompany greatness of intellect, the latter is the characteristic of debasement. Every nation is disposed to 'fie-fie' its neighbour's favourite diversion. The English fox-hunter and pigeon-shooter [7] are severe upon bull-fighting and cock-

[1] This hide-shield, which supplanted the *clypeus* or *clipeus*, the large round article of osier-work, was also Sabine.

[2] Petronius Arbiter, chap. i. 7.

[3] *Falx* is properly a large pruning knife, plain or toothed, with a coulter or bill projecting from the back of the curved head. Besides this, there are many forms ; one is a simple curve ; another is a leaf-shaped blade with an inner hook, while a third bears, besides the spike, a crescent on the back. 'Falx' is the origin of our 'falchion,' an Italian augmentative form, or perhaps the Spanish *facon*. Cæsar (*Comm.* iii. 14) speaks of *falces præacutæ*.

[4] *Loc. cit.*, copied by Smith.

[5] Mentor is mentioned by Pliny (viii. 21). The tale of Androclus is well known ; he was pardoned, and presented with his friend the lion, whom he used to lead about Rome, doubtless collecting many coppers.

[6] He is called by Captain Godfrey 'the Atlas of the sword,' and Hogarth immortalised this valiant 'rough' in the *Rake's Progress* and *Southwark Fair*.

[7] It is regretable to see this unmanly and ignoble 'sport' spreading abroad : there was pigeon-shooting at Venice during the Geographical Carnival, *alias* Congress, of September 1881. All honour to the English Princes who are discountenancing the butchery at home. Fox-hunting is another thing ; the chief good done by it seems to be the circulation of about a million of money per annum.

fighting—the classical and Oriental pastime preserved in Spain and in Spanish South America.[1] The boxer, who imitates, at a humble distance, the Cestus-play of the Greeks and Romans, looks scandalised at *la boxe Française*, with its garnishing of *savate*; and at the Brazilian *capoeira*, who butts with his woolly head. And so *vice versâ*. Absence or presence of fair play should, methinks, condemn or justify all the various forms of sport which are not mere or pure barbarities. And, applying this test, we shall not harsh judge the gladiatorial games of Rome.

I now proceed to describe the Sword amongst the Romans, a simpler subject than in Greece.

As the so-termed founding of Rome took place during the early Iron Age of Southern Europe, it is probable that the citizens, like their predecessors the Etruscans, originally made their blades of copper and bronze, the leaf-shape being borrowed from the Greeks, as we see it retained by the gladiators. The material would last into the Age of Steel, but even in her early years Rome must have preferred the harder metal. Pliny expressly tells us that Porsena, after his short-lived conquest, prohibited the future masters of the world from using iron except in agriculture; it was hardly safe to handle a stylus. Polybius notes that in his day bronze was entirely restricted to defensive armour—helmets, breast-plates, and greaves. All offensive weapons, swords and spears, were either made of, or tipped with, steel. To this superiority of material we may attribute the Roman successes in the second Punic war (B.C. 218–201), and their conquest of the gallant Gauls, when their foes could oppose nothing better than bronze. They had reason to call a Sword *ferrum*.[2]

The Romans called the Sword Ensis, Gladius, and Spatha. The two former are used as synonyms by Quinctilian,[3] but the first presently became poetical. The derivations are eminently unsatisfactory. Voss would find Ensis in ἔγχος, *hasta*; Sanskritists in *Asi*, a Sword, the Zend *Anh*. Gladius is popularly drawn *a clade ferenda, quasi cladius* (Varro and Littleton); Voss prefers κλάδον (*ramus*), a young branch, the earliest Sword: to others it appears a congener of the Keltic *Clad*, the destroyer. Of the derivation of 'Spatha' I have already treated: Suetonius[4] makes it equivalent to Machaira; but this word and its diminutive Machærium are loosely used.

The Roman Sword was, like their other weapons, longer and larger, heavier and more formidable than that of the Greeks.[5] The earliest form, the 'hero's arm' of Virgil and Livy, was a short single-edged cutting weapon of bronze, also called the 'Gallic Sword,' because long preserved by that people. It is shown in the arm of

---

[1] I have described cockfighting in the Canary Islands (*To the Gold Coast for Gold*, i., chap. 9). The celebrated story of Themistocles and the game-cocks made the pastime classical. Alexander the Great is said to have crucified a tax-gatherer at Alexandria who killed and ate a famous fighting-cock. Verdict, S. H. R.

[2] So Μελίη and the O. Germ. *Ask* (an ash-tree)

signify a bow: there are many instances of such nomenclature.

[3] Quinctilian, *Inst. Orat.* xii. 11. Marchionni (p. 123) makes the Gladius short and broad for infantry, and the Ensis long and broad for cavalry, in fact, synonymous with Spatha. This view is not unusual.

[4] In *Claud.* cap. 15.

[5] Florus, ii. 17.

the Roman Auxiliary (fig. 276).   Another very early, if not the earliest, shape was
the leaf, which varied in length from nineteen inches (the blade found at Mayence)
to twenty-six inches (the Bingen find).   The latter is peculiar ; the hilt is ornamented with bronze, and it has a cross-guard.   Upon another blade (fig. 277), of
which a cast is in the Artillery Museum, Paris, appears the armourer's mark,
Sabini (opus).

The third form, which is most generally identified with the Roman soldier,
greatly resembles that which was introduced into the French army by, not without
financial benefit to, Marshal Soult.   The average length may be assumed at
twenty-two inches, with a grip of six inches and a cross-bar (not always present)

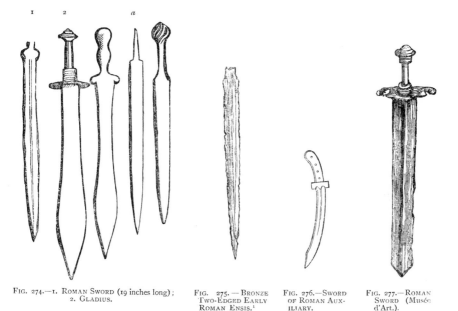

FIG. 274.—1. ROMAN SWORD (19 inches long) ;   FIG. 275. — BRONZE   FIG. 276.—SWORD   FIG. 277.—ROMAN
        2. GLADIUS.   TWO-EDGED EARLY   OF ROMAN AUX-   SWORD (Musée
                                             ROMAN ENSIS.[1]   ILIARY.   d'Art.).

four inches and a half long and four lines thick.   Some specimens show a distinct
hilt-plate (fig. 274, 2).   A mid-rib ran along the blade, which was either straight or
slightly narrowing, and it ended in the bevelled point (*langue de carpe*).[2]   This thick
heavy blade, used *cæsim et punctim*, was most efficient for hand-to-hand work, and
the Roman soon mastered the truth, unknown to most Orientals, that the cut wounds
and the thrust kills.'[3]   Accordingly they soon learned to despise the old Sword,

[1] This blade greatly resembles one found in Ostir-
botten, Finland, except that the latter preserves the
tang.   *Trans. Congress of Bologna of* 1871, p. 428.

The point was called *cuspis*, which never
applies to the *mucro, acies,* or edge.   ' Differt a
mucrone quæ est acies gladii,' says Facciolati.

[3] See chap. vii.   In Hugues de Bançoi's *Battle
of Benevento* we read : ' Le Roy Charles ' (brother of

St. Louis, and then fighting to take Sicily from
Manfred) . . .   'crioit de sa bouche Royale à ses
Chevaliers de serrer les ennemis, leur disant, *Frappez
de la pointe, Frappez de la pointe, soldats de Jésus
Christ.*   Et il ne faut pas s'en étonner, car ce Prince
habile avait lu dans le Livre de l'Art Militaire
que les nobles Romains n'avoient pas imaginé de
meilleure manière de combattre que de percer les
ennemis avec la pointe de l'épée.'

short and crooked. The national weapon must have been used by Æmilius at the Battle of Telamon (B.C. 225), for Polybius notes that the Roman blade could not only deliver thrust but give the cut with good effect.

Shortly after that fight the Romans, during their earliest invasions of the Spanish Peninsula (B.C. 219), intended to subvert Carthaginian rule, adopted the Gladius Hispanus, including the *pugio* (fig. 280); and the change from bronze to steel became universal after the battle of Cannæ. The superior material aided them not a little in conquering their obstinate rivals. The Roman Proconsul M. Fulvius captured (B.C. 192) Toledo (Τώλητον), Toletum, 'a small city, but strong in position;[1] and the superior temper of the steel, attributed with truth, I believe, to the Tagus-water, recommended it to the conquerors. A later conquest of the Regnum Noricum[2] (Styria, B.C. 16) gave them mines of equal excellence. From Pliny and Diodorus Siculus[3] we know perfectly how the Celtiberians pre-

FIG. 278.—SWORD AND VAGINA (SHEATH).　　　FIG. 279.—DITTO.　　　FIG. 280.—THE PUGIO.

pared their iron ores. Of this material was made the Spatha or Iberian blade, a name adopted under the Empire, especially under Hadrian (A.D. 117–138). Long, two-edged, and heavier than the short Xiphos-Gladius, it added fresh force to the *impetus gladiorum.*

In Cicero's time the Sword must have been of full length to explain the joke against his son-in-law; and Macrobius expressly tells us that Lentulus was wearing a blade which justified the 'chaff.' During the days of Theodosius (A.D. 378–394), the straight and strong weapon of Hadrian's time again shortened till it was

[1] Livy, xxxv. 12. According to Spanish tradition, Toletum (probably a Carthaginian-Punic word) was founded B.C. 540 by Hebrews, who called it Toledoth, in Arab. Tawallud, the 'mother of cities.'

[2] Properly the South-Danube country from the Wienerwald to the Inn. The great seat of the iron works was at Lauriacum (Lorch, near Enns). After B.C. 16 the province was ruled by a Procurator.

[3] See chap. vi.

[4] In Tonini's *Rimini avanti l' era volgare* (p. 31) we read that the Spatha-blade 'Come ognuno sa, presso i Greci quanto presso i Latini, *est genus gladii latioris*; onde Isidoro nelle *Origini* (xviii. cap. 6) ha che alcuni *spatham latine autumant, eo quod spatiosa sit, id est lata et ampla.*' But this is a dictionary derivation. In chap. viii. I have traced it back to the Egyptian *Sfet,* and in chap. xiii. I shall show that it is the straight broadsword as used by the Kelts.

not twice the size of the hilt; in fact it became a 'Parazonium.' The General's Sword (says Meyrick) was called Cinctorium, because carried at the girdle that surrounded the lorica, just above the hips; 'it greatly resembled the Lacedæmonian Sword.'

The Parazonium, *pugio*[1] or dagger, accompanied the Gladius under the later Empire, and was carried in the same, or in another, belt, generally on the opposite flank. It is the Greek ἐγχειρίδιον, and we have seen its origin in Egypt. The metal was successively pure copper, bronze and steel. The shape of this two-edged stiletto is either lanceolate (fig. 280 *b*),[2] showing its descent from the spear, or the straight lines converge to a point (*ibid. a*). It has a notable resemblance to the daggers found in Egyptian tombs (*ibid. c*), and the weapon with the Z-section, still used in the Caucasus and in Persia.[3] The tang is usually fitted to receive a wooden plate on either side: a favourite substance was the heart of the Syrian *terebinth* (the 'oak' of Mamre).

FIG. 281.—TWO-EDGED ROMAN STILETTOS.

The bronze hilt of the Gladius was retained long after the blade was made of steel. The common grip was of wood set with metal knobs or rivets; the richer sorts were of bone and ivory, amber and alabaster, silver and gold. The heft ended in a *capulus*; this metal pommel[4] was, in its simplest state, a plain mound or a stepped pyramid. But presently the 'little apple' became the seat of decoration;[5] Pliny moans over it, and Claudian speaks of *capulis radiantibus enses*. This fashion lasted deep into the Middle Ages. The haft was often capped with the head of some animal after Assyrian fashion, and that of the eagle recurved was a favourite in Rome. In the Armeria Reale (Turin)[6] there is a fine Roman chopper-blade with a peculiar handle, and a ram's head for hilt. The handle was usually without guard-plate, and at most it had only a simple cross-bar or a small oval.[7]

The original *vagina* (sheath) was of leather or wood, ending in a *fibula* or half-moon-shaped ferule of metal. Some scabbards on the monuments, where the Sword, like the helmet and the *pilum*, is conventionally treated, show the scabbard with three opposing rings on either side; and, as the belt had only one or two, it is not easy to explain the use of the other five.[8] In the luxurious days of the Empire, the sheath, like the heft, the pommel, and the ferule, was made of gold

[1] Parazonium = παρά + ζώνη. *Pugio*, our 'poniard,' is from *pugnus* (πύξ), the fist; others take it from *pungere* to prick.

[2] Smith (*Dict. of Ant.* p. 809) borrows figs. *a* and *b* from Beger (*Thes. Brand.* v., iii. p. 398, 419).

[3] See end of chap. viii.

[4] Smith (*loc. cit.* p. 195) renders *capulus* by 'hilt.' Pommel, however, best explains Ovid's legend of Theseus (*Met.* vii. 423), who, appearing for the first time before his father Ægeus, was known by the carving on his ivory *capulus*, and thus escaped Medea's aconite. Moreover, a 'golden hilt set with beryls' would have been very awkward to handle.

[5] Virg. *Æn.* xii. 942.

[6] Section Beaumont. The grip has four hollows to fit the fingers. This indentation-system has been revived of late years, as shown by the swords of Victor Emmanuel and General Lamarmora in the Municipal Museum, Turin.

[7] Guard plates, accompanying cross-bars, have been found in Gaul.

[8] These rings appear on the scabbard of Tiberius.

and silver reliefs, *repoussée*-work, and incrustations of precious stones disposed upon every part, made it a *chef-d'œuvre* of art. Such is the 'Sword,' or rather 'Parazonium, of Tiberius' dug up at Mayence in 1848, and now in the British Museum. The scabbard, the mouth, the rings on either side, and the ferule are strengthened and beautified by reliefs in gold and silver, and the central field bears the portrait

of the beautiful 'Biberius.' Another Parazonium (Anglo-Rom. Coll.) has an iron blade and a bronze scabbard.

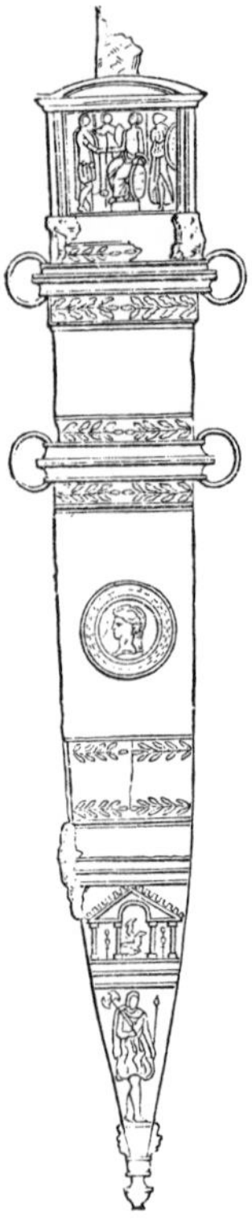

A reform of this over-luxury ensued under Constantius II. (A.D. 350), and under the noble and glorious Julian[1] 'the Apostate.' The latter took a lesson from the Eastern Persian, Parthian, and Sarmatian (Slav ?); moreover, he adopted the iron face-guard known at Nineveh, and the mail-coat found upon the Trajan column. These revivals and improvements extended deep into the Age of Chivalry.

The Sword was carried in the *balteus*, an Etruscan word applied indifferently, it would appear, to the bauldric ($\tau \epsilon \lambda \alpha \mu \acute{\omega} \nu$), or to the waist-'belt' ($\zeta \acute{\omega} \nu \eta$ or $\zeta \omega \sigma \tau \acute{\eta} \rho$, *cingulum*). Both were of cloth or leather, either plain or decorated with embroidery, with metal plates, splendid and elaborate rings and fibulæ, and buckles and brooches of the most precious material. It is generally said that the Gladius, and its successor the long cut-and-thrust Spatha, were worn belted to the right, as amongst the Persians. The old Ensis, on the other hand, was slung to the left, like the Egyptians, Assyrians, Hindús, and other 'barbarians.'[2] The latter fashion enabled the Swordsman to draw his weapon safely by passing hand and forearm across his body under the shield. He would also in this way grip the hilt with the thumb at the black of the blade, where it should ever be held, especially when delivering the cut. I believe, however, that the Sword was

Fig. 282. — SWORD OF TIBERIUS. worn by the Romans, as amongst the Greeks, on either flank.[3]

We have no knowledge, except from books, of Roman fancy-Swords. Such, for example, was the *Cluden* or juggler's 'shutting'-Sword, which ran up into the hilt. 'So great is your fear of steel,' says Apuleius in his defence, 'that you are afraid to dance with the "close-Sword."'

Roman blades of iron are not often found, and yet they must have been made by the million. Captain Grose[4] figures a leaf-shaped blade, like that of the

[1] Here I rely upon Ammian. Marcell. (xxiv. 4 ; xxv. 3, 4, and *passim*). So great a reformer could not escape detraction in its most venomous form. His last words (attributed) *Vicisti, Nazarene*, must, I think, have been pronounced in Syriac-Arabic, *Nasart' yá Nasráni*.

[2] Jähns, p. 198. He gives an illustration (Pl. xvii. 14) of the 'Annæus' monument at Bingen ;

there is a double balteus worn round the waist for the Spatha, or long Sword, to the right, and the Pugio to the left, both being carried perpendicularly. The Roman Parazonium is also rare in collections.

[3] In this matter we must be careful how we trust to engravings, especially from vases, &c. The careless artist often reverses the figure.

[4] *Military Antiq.*, vol. ii. ; Pl. xli.

modern Somal, taken from the Severn near Gloucester. Meyrick tells us[1] that Woodchester produced an iron Sword-blade resembling a large and broad knife (the oldest form of Gladius ?) and a dagger (*pugio*), nearly one foot long, and much resembling the modern French bayonet. He mentions another iron Gladius nineteen and a half inches long, with a fibula of brass. Rev. T. Douglas, in his 'Nænia Britannica'[2] shows the find in a Kentish barrow. The Sword measures thirty-five and a quarter inches from pommel to point ; the iron blade, thirty inches by two inches broad, is flat and two-edged. The wooden grip had decayed ; the scabbard was of wood covered with leather and the weapon hung by a leather strap to the left side. Excavations at South Shields produced, says the Rev. J. Collingwood Bruce,[3] five Roman Swords, two to three feet long, with wooden scabbards and bronze crampets or ferules.

If Greece produced the golden youth of European civilisation, Rome bore the men of antiquity. She taught by example and precept the eternal lesson of individual and national dignity, of law and justice, and of absolute toleration in religious matters. She had no fear of growing great, and scruples about 'territorial aggrandisement' were absolutely unknown to her. The *quondam* Masters of the World effected their marvels of conquest and colonisation with these arts, urged by a forceful will, a will so single-viewed and so persistent that it levelled every obstacle. A similar gift of determination and perseverance made the Turks and Turcomans of a former generation, mere barbarians on horseback, bear down all opposition : hence the Arab still says: 'Mount your blood mare and the Osmanli shall catch you on his lame ass!' In virtue of an equal obstinacy, the Kelto-Scandinavian (I will not call him an 'Anglo-Saxon'), the modern Englishman, has trod worthily in the footsteps of the old Italian, and from his 'angle of the world,' his scrap of bleak inclement island, has extended his sway far beyond the orb known to his Cæsars. May he only remember the word 'Forwards!' and take to heart the fact that to stand still is to fall back.

The Roman of the Republic was incomparably the first soldier of his age ; and he equalled the best of the moderns in discipline, in loyalty to his leaders, and in enduring privations, hardship, and fatigue. But a glance at any of his campaigns—the famous 'Commentaries' suffice—shows how completely dependent he was upon the quality of his commander. Handled by second- and third-rate men, such as generals mostly have been, are, and will be, he was ignobly defeated, in his most glorious days, by the barbarous Gauls of Brennus ; by the half-servile hordes of Hannibal ; by the degenerate Greeks of Pyrrhus with their 'huge earth-shaking beasts,' and by the armed mob which the Cheruscan Arminius (Ormin or Hermann) led against the incompetent Varus. His campaigns, invariably successful in the end, were marked by many reverses ; and in cases of sudden and sinister emer-

---

[1] Quoting Lyson's *Woodchester Antiquities* (Pl. xxxv.).

[2] Pl. i. fig. 10. Quoted in *The British Army*, &c.,

by Sir Sibbald David Scott, a well-studied work containing a considerable amount of information.

[3] *Soc. of Antiq.*, June 29, 1876.

gencies he was too often scared and put to flight. In fact, he could not fight a 'soldier's battle'; nor has any race done this effectively in modern days except the English and the Slavs.

But when following military genius, the Roman soldier performed prodigies of gallantry and valour. A Julius Cæsar, a conqueror in fifty pitched battles, whose practice was to order *venite* not *ite!* whose military instinct could cry at the spur of the moment in the Pharsalian fight, *faciem feri, miles!* and who could reduce mutineers to reason by one word, *Quirites!* never failed to point the way to victory. We learn from the Great Epileptic [1] himself the secret of his unexampled success; the care with which he cultivated the individual. 'He instructed the soldiers (when exposed to a new mode of attack), not like the general of a veteran army which had been victorious in so many battles, but like a Lanista training his gladiators. He taught them with what foot they must advance or retire; when they were to oppose and make good their ground; when to counterfeit an attack; at what place and in what manner to launch their javelins.' [2]

His very arrogance was effective in making him a ruler of men, as when on receiving bad tidings he struck his Sword-hilt, saying, 'This will give me my rights!' And of his 'politiké' (as the Greeks call it) we may judge by what Polyænus [3] tells us of him. 'The Romans had been taught by their commanders that a soldier should not be decorated with gold or silver, but place his confidence in his Sword,' says Livy.[4] But Divus Cæsar encouraged his men to decorate their weapons with all manner of valuables for a truly soldier-like reason, that they might be the less ready to part with their property in flight. And though he plundered freely and rifled even the fanes of the gods, according to Suetonius, he was careful, like a certain modern Condottiere, to see that his men were well fed and regularly paid by means of the 'loot.'

The Roman soldier had another valuable gift, which has not wholly left the Latin race. He knew the 'magic of patience,' and was aware that 'le monde est

---

[1] During the critical action at Thapsus, Cæsar, according to Plutarch, was *hors de combat* with a fit of epilepsy, the *comitialis morbus* (Afric. War, chap. 14). I have noticed in my Commentaries on Camoens (i. 40) the strange fact that some of the greatest men of antiquity were subject to this 'falling sickness.' The Egyptians held it to be a manifestation of the power of Typhon; hence the 'divine disease' of Apuleius (Defence), and the strange fancies of dæmoniac possession which prevailed in the earliest ages, and which have not yet died out. The learned Canon Farrar (*Life, &c. of Saint Paul*, Appendix, vol. i.) holds that this perhaps was the 'thorn in the flesh' (2 Cor. xii. 7) alluded to by the great Apostle. He quotes from Hausrath the 'trances' of Sokrates, the fits of Mohammed, and the faintings and ecstasies of Saints Bernard, Francis, and Catherine of Sienna; and to these he adds George Fox, Jacob Böhme, and Swedenborg.

[2] This is an illustration of genius taking pains

and a lesson to the leader of troops; but how many of the moderns have practised it, or have been capable of practising it? Suvóroff (Suwarroff), it is true, taught his men bayonet-exercise, with his coat off and his sleeves tucked up: Mediocrity shudders at the idea. The Russian had, by the way, curious ideas concerning the use of the weapon. 'Brothers! never gaze into the enemy's eyes; fix your sight on his breast, and prod your bayonet there.' The first rule for the General is to be ever looking after his men, to live, as it were, in the saddle, and to lead the attack when requisite. What were the habits of poor Lord Raglan and of his successor General (Jimmy) Simpson? No wonder that we had the mortification of the Redan affair.

[3] *Strategemata*, viii. 28. The 'Macedonian' flourished about the middle of the second century (Christian era).

[4] ix. 40.

la maison du plus fort.' So in the Napoleonic days the Spaniards believed chiefly in General ' No Importa' (no matter), and made little of defeat, hoping it might lead to victory. Nor did the Roman soldier degenerate till the citizen set him the example. Velleius Paterculus dated the decline of Roman virtue after the destruction of Carthage, when civil disputes were decided by the Sword ; others to the invasion of luxury with Lucullus. Yet Pliny could boast of his fellow-countrymen : ' They have doubtless surpassed every other nation in the display of valour.'

But the Roman soldier generally prevailed against races whom he excelled in size, weight, and muscular strength. His superiority in arms, like that of the Greek, was not conspicuous when he came into contact with the ' barbarians,'[1] especially with the northern barbarians, after they had learned the moral training and confidence of discipline and the practical art of war, as well as, if not better than, himself. For the man of the higher European latitudes has ever surpassed the Southron in strength of constitution, in stature, in weight, in muscular power, and in the mysterious something called vitality. Hence it is a rule in anthropology that the North beats the South ; in the Southern hemisphere the reverse being the case, as we see in the wars of the Hispano-American republics, Chili *versus* Peru. In Europe I need only point out that the Northmen of Scandinavia conquered Normandy and that Norman-French conquered England. The only exceptions are easily explained. The genius of Divus Cæsar made his Romans overcome, overrun, and subjugate Gaul. Napoleon the Great found the road *à Berlin* open and easy. But intellectual monsters like these two are the rare produce of Time ; and human nature requires a long period of rest before repeating such portents.

Those who read history without prepossessions and prejudices are compelled to conclude that the life and career of a nation are mainly determined by its physical size and its muscular strength. We have only to learn how many foot-pounds a race can raise and we can forecast its so-called ' destinies.'[2]

---

[1] This word has a universal history of its own, and contains a lecture on anthropology.

Its form is onomatopoetic, the earliest form of expression, as the Egyptian *miao*, for a cat ; and it admirably conveys the idea of muttering or stuttering. Again, it is a reduplication of sounds ; another absolutely primitive construction, and the effect is emphasis.

' Berber-ta ' (Berber-land) was applied by the ancient Egyptians (Catalogue of Thut-mes III.), whence our modern term Barbary.

The word in Hebr. ' wild beast feeding in waste ' migrated to India, and was there corrupted to वर्वर (Varvara), a barbarous land, one who speaks unintelligibly.

' Berber ' passed over to Greece from Egypt, and became βάρβαρος, meaning a foreigner whose language was not Hellenic, and who, therefore, was little better than a beast. (N.B. Shakespeare would have been a barbarian in Persia and Hafiz in England.)

' Barbaros ' broadened its meaning in Rome, where it was applied to all peoples who could not speak or who mispronounced Greek and Latin. See Strabo, xiv. 2, on ' Barbaros' and to ' barbarise '; thus unhappy Ovid could wail :

' Barbarus hic ego sum quia non intelligor illis.'

Lastly, the ' proto-Aryan ' term ' Barbarian ' has now grown to full size, and is applied generally to the rude, the fierce, the uncivilised, and those who contumaciously ignore the ' higher culture.'

[2] This is materialism pure and simple ; but all the teaching of modern science points to the material. The mysterious ' life ' is no longer ' vital power '; it simply represents the sum total of the energies and protoplasm. ' Life is a property of protoplasm or bioplasm, and is the latest product of thought and research.' And I may add that Consciousness, like Will, is a property of life in certain of its forms ; a state and condition of cerebral and other atoms ; the mere consequence of hitherto unappreciated antecedents.

CHAPTER XIII.

THE SWORD AMONGST THE BARBARIANS (EARLY ROMAN EMPIRE).

MOST works on Arms and Armour, when treating of Rome, describe the weapons of her European neighbours 'upon whom she sharpened the sword of her valour as on a whetstone.'[1] The extent of the subject will here confine me to a general glance, beginning with the Dacians on the east and ending with the British Islands. I must reserve details concerning the Kelts, the Scandinavians, the Slavs, and other northern peoples for Part II., to which they chronologically belong.

The Dacians, especially of Dacia Trajana, Hungary, and Transylvania, Moldavia, and Wallachia, are known to us chiefly by the bas-reliefs on the Trajan Column. It was built by that emperor, who, like Hadrian, followed in the footsteps of Divus Cæsar, to commemorate the conquests of A.D. 103–104 ; and it dates three years before his death in A.D. 114. The Dacian Sword was somewhat sickle-shaped, with an inner edge, like the oldest Greek and its model, the Egyptian Khopsh. A Dacian Sword on the trophy belonging to Dr. Gregorutti, of Papiriano, is a curved sabre without a cross-bar.

I have elsewhere noticed the Thracian Sword. Dr. Evans[2] mentions the fragment of a remarkable bronze blade from Grecian Thera ; it has a series of small broad-edged axes of gold, in shape like conventional battle-axes, inlaid along the middle between two slightly projecting ribs. The same author, speaking of the beautiful bronze Sword in the Berlin Museum, reported to have been found at Pella in Macedonia, mentions the suspicion that it may belong to the Rhine Valley.[3]

Ancient Illyria has transmitted the Roman Gladius to comparatively modern ages. Bosnian tombs of Slavs, Moslem, and Christian, show the short straight thrusting Sword, with simple cross-bar and round pommel. It looks as if it had been copied from some classical coin.

The ancient cemetery at Hallstadt in the Salzkammergut, occupied by the Danubian-Keltic Alanni or Norican Taurisci, is especially interesting for two reasons. It shows the Bronze Sword synchronous with the Iron, and it proves that the change of metal involved little of alteration in the form and character of the weapon. This, however, was to be expected, as both were adapted for the same purpose—the thrust, not the cut. Of the twenty-eight long Swords, six were

---

[1] Florus, ii. 3.

[2] *Bronze*, &c. p. 297. From *Aarbög. f. Nord. Oldk.* 1879, pl. i.

[3] *Bronze*, &c., p. 298. From Bastian and A. Voss, *Die Bronze-Schwerter des K. Mus. zu Berlin,* 1878, p. 56.

of bronze, nineteen of iron, and three with bronze hefts and iron blades ; there were also forty-five short Swords, iron blades with bronze or ivory handles. The blade, about one mètre long, is leaf-shaped, two-edged, and bevel-pointed. The small and guardless grip of 2·5 centimètres, when made of bronze, meets the blade in a hollow crescent, like the British Sword in the Tower, and is fastened with metal rivets. The pommel is either a cone of metal or a crutch with a whorl ending either arm.

Dr. Evans[1] mentions that in one instance the hilt and pommel of an iron Sword are in bronze, in another the pommel alone ; the hilt-plate of iron being flat and rivetted like the bronzes. In others the pommel is wanting. He has a broken iron Sword from this cemetery, the blade showing a central rounded rib, with a small bead on either side. Also a ' beautiful bronze Sword from the same locality, on the blade of which are two small raised beads on either side of the central rib, and in the spaces between them a three-fold wavy line punched in or engraved. In this instance a tang has passed through the hilt, and was formed of alternate blocks of bronze and of some substance that has perished, possibly ivory. A magnificent iron Sword from

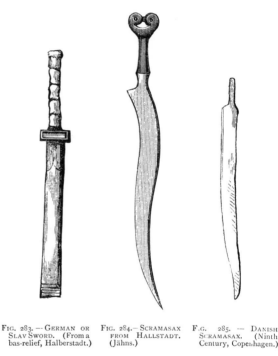

Fig. 283. — German or Slav Sword. (From a bas-relief, Halberstadt.)   Fig. 284.— Scramasax from Hallstadt. (Jähns.)   F.g. 285. — Danish Scramasax. (Ninth Century, Copenhagen.)

Hallstadt, now in the Vienna Museum, has the hilt and pommel of ivory inlaid with amber.' Other grips were of bronze, wood, or bone. The sheaths were mostly of wood, which seemed to have been covered with leather. Most of the blades were buried without scabbards, and the bronze had been purposely broken.

The forty-five short Swords represent the Ensis Noricus (μάχαιρα Κέλτικα), and were in use till the Roman days. The iron-blades are either leaf-shaped or formed like the peculiarly English anelace or anlas, more or less conical and sharp-pointed ; and the grip of bronze or ivory ended in a simple crutch. Amongst them is a distinct Scramasax which may be compared with the late Danish weapon.

---

[1] *Bronze*, &c., p. 299, from Von Sacken and Lindeschmit's *Alterthümer*. The first finds by Herr Namsauer in 1846–64 were 6,000 articles from 993 graves.

Bronze blades are comparatively rare in Italy, although the use was long retained and the weapon is often mentioned by Latin writers in verse and prose.[1] This seems to decide the question against the Roman origin of the North-European Sword: of course it is possible that, like the Runic alphabet, they might have been copied from coins; but there are other points which militate against this view. Dr. John Evans[2] notes a peculiarity which he has often pointed out by word of mouth, but which has not as yet been noticed in print. 'It is, that there is generally, though not universally, a proportion between the length of the blade and the length of the hilt-plate; long sword blades having, as a rule, long hilt-plates, and short sword blades short hilt-plates. So closely is this rule of proportion preserved, that the outline of a large sword on the scale of one-sixth would in some cases absolutely correspond with that of one which was two-thirds of its length if drawn on the scale of one-fourth.' This suggests derivation, as if an original *modulus* of the weapon had appeared in a certain racial centre and thence had radiated in all directions. Nor have we any difficulty in determining that this centre was the Nile Valley.

The bronze Swords of Italy present varieties not found in Britain.[3] The blade-sides are more nearly parallel, and many have a slender tang at the hilt, sometimes with one central rivet-hole, sometimes with two rivet-holes forming loops at either side of the 'spine.' In others the blade slightly narrows for the tang, and each side has two semicircular rivet-notches. In many Italian and French Swords the blade is drawn out to a long tapering point, so that its edges present a sub-ogival curve. On an Italian *quincussis* or oblong bronze coin, six inches and five-eighths by three inches and a half, and weighing about three pounds and a half, is the representation of a leaf-shaped Sword with a raised rib along the centre of the blade.[4] Upon the reverse appears the figure of a scabbard with parallel sides and a nearly circular chape. Another coin of the same type, engraved by Carelli,[5] has an almost similar scabbard on the reverse, but the Sword on the obverse is either sheathed or is not leaf-shaped, the sides being parallel: the hilt is also curved, and there is a cross-guard. In fact upon the one coin the weapon has the appearance of a Roman Sword of iron, and on the other that of a leaf-shaped Sword of bronze. These pieces, says Dr. Evans, were no doubt cast in

---

[1] I have already noticed the copper Ensis and coppered shield attributed by Virgil (*Æn.* viii. 74) to the people of Abella, an Italian district under Turnus.

[2] *Bronze*, &c., p. 277. The author also notices the small handles of bronze Swords, 'a fact which seems to prove that the men who used these swords were but of moderate stature' (*Prehistoric Times*, p. 22). He denies their being very small, and he justly believes that the expanding part of the hilt was intended to be within the grasp of the hand. I have already explained that the hand was purposely confined in order to give more momentum to the cut.

[3] *Bronze*, &c., p. 297; taken from Gastaldi, Pellegrini and Gozzadini. The author remarks (p. 287) that some of the bronze daggers from Italy seem also to have had their hilts cast upon the blades in which the rivets were already fixed. This is not unfrequent with the Sword, and the object seems mere imitation; like the Hauranic stone-doors, panelled as if to pass for wood.

[4] *Bronze*, &c., p. 283, we find that the British Museum contains a specimen. *Catalog. Italy*, p. 28

[5] *Bronze*, &c., ibid., quoting from *Numm. Vet. Ital. Descript.*, pl. xii.

Umbria, probably in the third century B.C., but their attribution to Ariminum is at best doubtful. From the two varieties of Sword appearing on coins of the same type, the inference may be drawn, either that bronze blades were then being super-seded in Umbria by iron, or that the original type was some sacred weapon, sub-sequently conventionalised to represent the article in ordinary use.

The iron Swords of the Italian tribes are rarely mentioned, and then cursorily. Diodorus Siculus, for instance, tells us (v. 33) that the Ligures had blades of ordinary size. They probably adopted the Roman shape, which had proved itself so serviceable in the field.

Proceeding further westward we find Diodorus Siculus (v. cap. 33) dwelling upon the Celtiberian weapons.[1] 'They had two-edged Swords of well-tempered steel; besides their daggers, a span long, to be used at close quarters. They make weapons and iron in an admirable manner, for they bury their plates so long under-ground as is necessary to eat away the weaker part; and, there-fore, they use only that which is firm and strong. Swords and other weapons are made of this prepared steel; and these are so powerful in cutting, that neither shield nor helm nor bone can withstand them.' Plutarch[2] repeats this description, which embodies the still prevalent idea concerning the Damascus (Persian) scymitar and the Toledo rapier. Swedenborg[3] intro-duces burial among the different methods of making steel; and Beckmann, following Thunberg, declares that the process is still used in Japan.

FIG. 286. — BLADE AND HANDLE OF BRONZE WITH PART OF EAGLE (Kessel).

General A. Pitt-Rivers' collection has two Swords from Spain. The first is a bronze, sub-leaf-shaped, with a thin protracted point. The length is twenty-one inches; the breadth at the swell two inches, thinning near the handle to one inch and a quarter; the tang is broken, and there are two rivet-holes at the shoulder, which is two inches wide. The other, which the owner calls a 'Kopis,' also twenty-one inches long, and two inches and a half in width, has a broad back and a wedge-section. The cutting part is inside, and the whole contour remarkably resembles the Kukkri or Korah of Nepaul, and, in a less degree, the Albanian Yataghan and the Kabyle 'Flissa.' The Kopis, however, has a hook-handle as if for suspension; and there is a swelling in the inside of the grip.

'As the Celtiberians,' continues Diodorus, 'are furnished with two Swords, (probably *espada y daga*), 'the horsemen, when they have routed their opponents, dismount, and, joining the foot, fight as its auxiliaries.' The Lusitanians, most valiant of the race, inhabited a mountain-land peculiarly rich in minerals. Justin[4] speaks of the gold, copper, lead, and vermilion, which last named the 'Minho'

---

[1] See chap. vi.   [2] *De Garrul.*   [4] Lib. xliv. 3. Martial also alludes (i. 49; iii. 12,
[3] *De Ferro*, i. 195.   &c.) to the metallic wealth of his native province.

river. Of the iron he says : ' It is of an extraordinary quality, but their water is more powerful than the iron itself ; for the metal being tempered in it becomes keener ; nor is any weapon held in esteem among them that has not been dipt in the Bilbilis or the Chalybs.' [1]   Strabo [2] represents Iberia as abounding in metal, and arms the Lusitanians with poniard and dagger, probably meaning dirk and knife.

The Northern neighbours of the Celtiberians—the warlike old Keltic [3] Gauls —were essentially swordsmen : they relied mainly upon the Claidab.[4] When they

entered Europe they had already left behind them the Age of Stone ; and they made their blades of copper, bronze, and iron. The latter, as we learn from history, entered into use during the fourth or fifth century B.C., the later Celtic Period, as it is called by Mr. Franks. The material appears to have been, according to all authorities, very poor and mean. The blade was mostly two-edged, about one mètre long, thin, straight, and without point (*sine mucrone*) ; it had a tang for the attachment of the grip, but no guard or defence for the hand.

Yet their gallantry enabled the Gauls to do good work with these bad tools. F. Camillus, the dictator,[5] seeing that his enemy cut mostly at head and shoulders, made his Romans wear light helmets, whereby the Machairæ-blades were bent, blunted, or broken. Also, the Roman shield being of wood, he ' directed it for the same reason to be bordered with a thin plate of brass '

FIG. 287. — GALLIC SWORD OF BRONZE (Jähns).

(copper, bronze ?). He also taught his men to handle long pikes, which they could thrust under the enemy's weapons. Dionysius Halicarnassus introduces him saying, while he compares Roman and Gaulish arms, that these Kelts assail the foe only with long lances and large knives (μάχαιρας κοπίδες) [6]

---

[1] Pliny (xxxi. 4, 41) also notices the Salo or River Bilbilis (Xalon) ; and the Celtiberian town of the same name, now Bombola, the birthplace of the poet Martial, is near Calatayud (Kala'at el-Yahúd = Jew's Fort), or Job's Castle. Of the Chalybes I have already spoken.

[2] *Roman Archæology*, by Angelo Maio.

[3] The words Κέλται, Γαλάται, Γάλλο (meaning Armati, pugnaces, Kämpfer, fighters), evidently derive not from Coille, a word, but from the old word Gal (battle), or Gala (arms). The name suited their natures : they were never at peace, and their bravery was proverbial : the Greeks called it Κελτικὸν θράσος = Keltic daring.

[4] Cladibas or Cladias = *gladius*. I have noticed the shape when speaking of the Hallstadt finds.

[5] Polyænus, *Strategemata* ; Dion. Halicar. xiv. chap. 13.

[6] Plutarch (*De Cam.* cap. xxvii.) also arms the Gauls, when attacking the Capitol, with the Kopis. ' The first to oppose them was Manlius. . . . .

Meeting two enemies together, he parried the cut of one who raised a Kopis (κοπίδα) by hacking off his right hand with a Gladius' (ξίφος). I presume that ' Kopis ' is here used for the *pugio*, dirk, or shorter sword. Borghesi *Œuvres Complètes*, vol. ii. pp. 337-387, says : ' In use and form, in grip and in breadth of blade, the Kopis much resembles our *Sciabla*, (Sabre).' But its comparison with the falx and pruning hook and a medal of Pub. Carisius suggest a substantial difference : while the broadsword is edged on the convex side, the Kopis had a sharpened concave. Count Gozzadini, like General A. Pitt-Rivers, compares the Kopis with the Khanjar or Yataghan, and quotes Xenophon (*Cyrop.* ii. 1, 9 ; vi. 2, 10) to prove that it was peculiar to Orientals. I have traced the word to the Egyptian Khopsh or Khepsh, and repeat my belief that it is the old Nilotic sickle-blade with a flattened curve. But, as might be expected in the case of so old a word, the weapon to which it was applied may have greatly varied in size and shape.

of sabre shape (?). This was shortly before his defeating and destroying Brennus and the Senonian[1] Gauls, who had worsted the Romans (B.C. 390) on the fatal *dies Alliensis*,[2] and who had captured all the capital save the Capitol.

The Gauls of Cæsar's day[3] had large iron mines which they worked by tunnelling ; their ship-bolts were of the same material, and they made even chain-cables of iron. They had by no means, however, abandoned the use of bronze arms. Pausanias[4] also speaks of ταῖς μαχαίραις τῶν Γαλατῶν. Diodorus[5] notes that the Kelts wore ' instead of short straight Swords (ξίφους), long broad blades (μάκρας σπάθας[6]), which they bore obliquely at the right side hung by iron and copper chains. . . . Their Swords are not smaller than the Saunions (σαυνίων[7]) of other nations, and the points of their Saunions are bigger than those of their Swords.' Strabo[8] also makes the Gauls wear their long Swords hanging to the right. Procopius,[9] on the other hand, notices that the Gallic auxiliaries of Rome wore the Sword on the left.[10] According to Poseidonius,[11] the Gauls also carried a dagger which served the purpose of a knife, and this may have caused some confusion in the descriptions.

Q. Claudius Quadrigarius in Aulus Gellius,[12] noticing the ' monomachy ' of Manlius Torquatus with the Gaul, declares that the latter was armed with two gladii. Livy describes the same duel in his best style. The Roman, of middling stature and unostentatious bearing, takes a footman's shield and girds on a Spanish Spatha—arms fit for ready use rather than show. The big Gaul, another Goliah, glittering in a vest of many colours, and in armour stained and inlaid with gold, shows barbarous exultation, and thrusts out his tongue in childish mockery. The friends retire and leave the two in the middle space, ' more after the manner of a theatrical show than according to the law of combat.' The enormous Northerner, like a huge mass threatening to crush what was beneath it, stretched forth his shield with his left hand and planted an ineffectual cut of the Sword with loud noise upon the armour of the advancing foe. The Southron, raising his

[1] Brennus is evidently a congener of the Welsh *brenhin* (the king). The Senones have left their name in Illyrian Segna, once a nest of pirates and corsairs, south of Fiume the Beautiful. I shall notice them in a future page.

[2] Livy, xxii. 46.

[3] *Bell. Gall.* iii. 13 ; vii. 22.

[4] Lib. x. cap. 32.

[5] Lib. v. cap. 30.

[6] See chapters viii. and xii. Here the word is evidently applied generically to a straight two-edged broadsword, about 1 mètre long. In the Middle Ages the weapon gave rise to many curious varieties, as the *Spatha pennata* and the *Spatha in fuste*.

[7] According to Vegetius (ii. 15) the Saunion was the light javelin of the Samnites, with a shaft 3½ feet long, and an iron head measuring 5 inches. Thus it would resemble the Roman *pilum*. But Diodorus evidently means another and a heavier weapon which

could hardly be thrown. Meyrick and Jähns (p. 390) do not solve the difficulty.

[8] Lib. iv. 4, § 3.

[9] *De Bell. Pers.*

[10] The Northumberland Stone in Montfaucon (vol. iv. part 1, p. 37) shows a Gaul wearing sword and dagger on either side.

[11] In Athenæus, lib. xiv., the celebrated philosopher called the Apamæan or the Rhodian, a contemporary of Pompey and Cicero, left, amongst other works, one called Τέχνη τακτική (*de Acie instruenda*).

[12] Lib. vii. cap. 10. It is evident that the Duello did not, as many authors suppose, arise with the Kelts. All we can say is that they may have originated in Europe the sentiment called *pundonor* and the practice of defending it with the armed hand. The idea was unknown to the classics ; and, with the exception, perhaps, of the Arabs, it is still ignored

Sword-point, after pushing aside the lower part of the enemy's shield with his own, closed in, insinuating his whole body between the trunk and arms of his adversary, and by two thrusts, delivered almost simultaneously at belly and groin, threw his opponent, who when prostrate covered a vast extent of ground. The gallant victor offered no indignity to the corpse beyond despoiling it of the *torques*, which, though smeared with blood, he cast around his neck.

Polybius,[1] recounting the battle at Pisæ, where Aneroestes, king of the Gæsatæ,[2] aided by the Boii, the Insubres, and the Taurisci (Noricans, Styrians), was defeated by C. Atilius (A.U.C. 529 = B.C. 225), shows the superiority of the Roman weapons. He describes the Machairæ of the Gauls 'as merely cutting blades . . . altogether pointless, and fit only to slash from a distance downwards: these weapons by their construction soon wax blunt, and are bent and bowed; so that a second blow cannot be delivered until they are straightened by the foot.' The same excellent author,[3] when describing the battle of Cannæ (B.C. 216), tells us that Hannibal and his Africans were armed like Romans, with the spoils of the preceding actions; while the Spanish and Gaulish auxiliaries had the same kind of shield, but their Swords were wholly unequal and dissimilar. While the Spanish Xiphos was excellent both for cutting and thrusting, the long and pointless Gallic Machæra could only slash from afar. Livy[4] also notices the want of point and the bending of the soft and ill-tempered Keltic blades.

When Lucius Manlius attacked the Gauls, B.C. 181, the latter carried long flat shields, too narrow to protect the body.[5] They were soon left without other weapons but their Swords, and these they had no opportunity of using, as the enemy did not come to close quarters. Phrensied with the smart of missiles raining upon their large persons, the wounds appearing the more terrible from the black blood contrasting with the white skin; and furious with shame at being put *hors de combat* by hurts apparently so small, they lost many by the Swords of the Velites. These 'light bobs' in those days were well armed; they had shields three feet long, *pila* for skirmishing, and the *Gladius Hispanus*, which they drew after shifting the javelins to the left hand. With these handy blades they rushed in and wounded faces and breasts, whilst the Gallic Swords could not be wielded without space.

Passing from books to monuments, we see on an Urban medal of Rimini, dating from the domination of the Senones, a long-haired and moustachio'd Gaul, and on the reverse a broad Spatha, with scabbard and chain. This is repeated on another coin of the same series, where a naked Gaul, protected by an oblong shield, assails

---

by the civilised Orientals of our day, especially by the Moslems.

[1] Lib. ii. caps. 28, 30, and 33.

[2] Simply meaning Spearmen. Gaisate = *hastatus* from Gaisa (*gæsum*), the Irish *gai*, any spear. Isidore (*Gloss.*) translates 'Gessum' by 'hasta vel jaculum Gallicè, βολίς.' The word survives in the French *guisarme, gisarme*, &c. The Gæsum probably had a kind of handle and a defence for the hand.

[3] Lib. xxii. cap. 46.

[4] Lib. xxxviii. 21.

[5] The naked bodies and narrow shields are well shown in the battle-scene on the Triumphal Arch of Orange (Jähns, Plate 29).

with the same kind of Sword. A third shows the Gaul with two *gladii*, one shorter than the other.[1] The scabbards and chains were of bronze or iron.

According to Diodorus,[2] the Gauls advanced to battle in war-chariots (*carpentum*, *covinus*, *essedum*). They also had cavalry;[3] but during their invasions of Italy they mostly fought on foot. They had various kinds of missiles, javelins, and the Cateia or Caia (boomerang, or throwing-club), slings, and bows and arrows, poisoned as well as unpoisoned. They then rushed to the attack with unhelm'd heads, and their long locks knotted on the head-top. In many fights they stripped themselves, probably for bravado, preserving only the waistcloth and ornaments, torques, leglets, and armlets. They cut off the heads of the fallen foes ; slung them to their shields or saddlebows, and kept them at home as trophies, still the practice of the Dark Continent. Their girls and women fought as bravely as the men ; especially with the *contus* or wooden pike, sharpened and fire-hardened. The waggons ranged in the rear formed a highly efficient 'lager.' The large Keltic stature, their terrible war-cries, and their long Swords wielded by doughty arms and backed by stout hearts, enabled them more than once to triumph over civilised armies.

Divus Cæsar, who is severe upon Gallic *nobilitas*, *levitas*, and *infirmitas animi*, employed nine years in subduing Gaul (B.C. 59-50). Before a century elapsed, the people had given up their old barbarous habits and costume, their fur-coats, like the Slav and Afghan *postín*, with sleeves opening in front ; their saga-cloaks or tartan-plaids [4] which were probably imitations of the primeval tattoo ;[5] their copper torques and their rude chains and armlets. Gallia Comata shore her limed and flowing locks, and Gallia Bracchata (Provincia, Provence) doffed the '*truis*' (trews or trowsers) which were strapped at the waist and tied in at the ankles.[6] Their women adopted Roman fashions, and forgot all that Ammianus Marcellinus had said of them : 'A whole troop of foreigners could not withstand a single Gaul, if he called to aid his wife, who is usually very strong and blue-eyed, especially when, swelling her neck, gnashing her teeth, and whirling her sallow arms of enormous bulk, she begins to strike blows, mingled with kicks, as if they were so many missiles sent from the string of a catapult.' Of their old and rugged virtue we may judge by the tale of Ortiagon's gallant wife and the caitiff centurion.[7] Thus Gaul was thoroughly subdued by

---

[1] Borghesi (Tonini's *Rimini*, &c., p. 28 and Tables A 3 and B 6) makes one of these gladii a 'Kopis.'

[2] Lib. v. cap. 30.

[3] The cavalry was organised in the Trimarkisia (three marka, or horses) composed of the 'honestior' (afterwards the knight), and the clients (squires). The host that attacked Hellas, under Brennus, had 20,400 horsemen to 752,000 foot.

[4] The pattern is almost universal. Moorcroft found it in the Himalayas, and I bought 'shepherd's plaid' in Unyamwezi, Central Africa.

[5] The first use of tattooing was to harden the skin, a defence against weather. The second (and this we still find throughout Africa) was to distinguish nations, tribes, and families.

[6] 'Galli bracchas deposuerunt et latum clavum sumpserunt.' Diodorus Sic. (v. 30) has βρáκας ; in Romaic βράχι ; in Italian *braghe*, Germ. *Brüche*. Our word 'breech-es' or 'Breek-s' is a double plural ; 'breek' being the plur. of the A. S. *broc*, a brogue. Aldus and other old writers mistranslate the *bracchæ* by plaid, or upper garment. Jähns more justly renders *sagum* by plaid (p. 431).

[7] Livy, xxxviii. 24.

Roman civilisation and the Latin tongue ; she contributed to literature her quotum of poets and rhetoricians ; her cities established schools of philosophy, and she saw nothing to envy in Gallia Togata—Upper Italy.[1]

The Alemanni or Germans (Germani) east of the Rhine inhabited, at the time of the Roman conquests, a dismal land of swamps and *silvæ* : even in the present day a run from Hamburg to Berlin explains the ancient exodus of tribes bent upon conquering the 'promised lands' of the south, and the modern wholesale emigration to America. These 'warmen' were formerly surpassed by the Gauls in bravery,[2] but they had none of the Keltic levity or instability. The national characteristic was and is the steadfast purpose. Till lately the German Empire was a shadowy tradition ; yet the Germans managed to occupy every throne in Europe save two. They never yet made a colony, yet cuckoo-like they hold the best of those made by others ; and their sound physical constitution, strengthened by gymnastics, enables them to resist tropical and extreme climates better than any European people save the Slavs and the Jews. In the great cities of the world they occupy the first commercial place, the result of an education carefully adapted to its end and object ; and their progress in late years seems to promise 'Germanism' an immense future based upon the ruins of the neo-Latin races.

FIG. 288.—FOUND AT AUGSBURG (66 centimètres long. In Sigmaringen Museum).

We have the authority of Tacitus for the fact that the Germans of his day did not (like the Kelts)[3] affect the short straight sword : 'rari . . . gladiis utuntur.'[4] The national weapon was the spear[5] of a peculiar kind ; 'hastas vel ipsorum vocabulo frameas gerunt angusto et brevi ferro.' The derivation of the word and the nature of the weapon are still undetermined.[6] Modern authorities hold the oldest *framée* to have been a long spear, with a head of stone, copper, bronze, or iron, shaped like a Palstab or an expanding 'Celt ;' and Demmin[7] shows the same broad shovel-shaped base in the Abyssinian lance. It was either thrown or thrust, and the weapon must not be confounded with the enormous *hastæ* of

---

[1] Italy has declared herself *Una*. But without considering a multitude of origins, one for almost every province, she is peopled in our modern day by two races, contrasting greatly with each other. The Po is the frontier, dividing the Græco-Latin Italians to the south from the Gallic and Frankish Italians (Milanese, Piedmontese, &c.) to the north. The latter, originally Barbari, are the backbone of the modern kingdom : the Southerners are the weak point.

[2] *Bell. Gall.* vi. 24.

[3] Jähns (in his Plates 27–30) unites ' Kelten und Germanien, Germanien und Kelten.'

[4] *De Mor. Germ.*, cap. 6.

[5] So we find the god Tyr or Tuisco (regent of

Tuesday), the Monthu or Mars of the North, figured in the Runes as a barbed spear ↑ (resembling the planetary emblem of Mars. He afterwards became the Sword-god. From the Tyr-rune is derived ᚛ᛁ᚜ Er (=hêru, the sword), or Aer, which resembles the Greek ἄορ, and which Jacob Grimm connects with ῎Αρης, *æs* and *Eisen* (Jähns, p. 14).

[6] The older derivation is from *ferrea*. Jähns (p. 407) gives a host of others—*Bram* (thorn, bramble) ; *Pfriem* (punch, awl) ; *Brame* (a border, edging) ; *ramen* (to aim, strike), &c., &c.

[7] *Arms*, &c., p. 419.

Tacitus,[1] in whose day the Roman spear was fourteen feet long. It was a formidable weapon; those who knew it spoke with awe of 'illam cruentam victricemque frameam'; and the Germans long preserved the saying 'one spear is worth two Swords.' Yet, strange to say, it is rarely found in graves, where the throwing-axe of stone and bronze, pierced or unpierced, one-edged or two-headed (πέλεκυς ἀμφιστόμος, bipennis), is so common.

In time the word *framea* was apparently applied to wholly different weapons. Thus Augustinus makes it an equivalent of *spatha* or *rhomphaia*; and Johannes de Janua ('Glossary') explains it as 'glaive aigu d'une part, et d'autre espée.'

Iron, according to Tacitus,[2] was known to the Germans, but was not common. His statement is supported by 'finds' in the old tumuli and stone rings, known as Riesenmauer, Hünnen-ringe,[3] Teufelsgraben, Burgwälle, and others. The myths of giants, dwarfs, and serpents suggest an Eastern origin for the metal. Bronze blades, on the other hand, are common. A typical specimen from the Elbe valley in the Klemm collection is thus described by Jähns.[4] The whole weapon is 23·25 centimètres long, the blade being 18·5, with a maximum breadth of 1·625. The shape is conical, tapering to the point; a high and rounded midrib is subtended on either side by a deepened line which runs to the end. Between shoulders and blade the front view shows on either side a crescent-shaped notch. The grip is narrower at the middle, where there is a long oval slit for making fast the handle; and there are two rivet holes on either side of the shoulders, whence the midrib springs. It shows no pommel, the place being taken by a shallow crutch.

Iron Swords are rare: even in the second century B.C., when the Romans had given up the softer metal, the Gauls and Germans preserved it. This is especially noticed when Germanicus marched against Arminius, B.C. 15;[5] and as late as the days of Tacitus, Germany could not work the raw metal.[6] Remains of iron *Spathæ* have mostly been found in very bad condition; the material also is poor and badly made. The Held or champion used two kinds of blades; and the mètre-long two-edged German Sword is not to be distinguished from that of the Kelts. The Spatha was especially affected by three tribes: the Suardones (Sworders?), the Saxones (Daggermen)[7] and the Cherusci; in process of time it reached the Goths,[8]

FIG. 289.—BRONZE.

75 centimètres long; Pommels of bronze and bone. From Hallstadt Diggings.

---

[1] *Annals*, ii. cap. 14.   [2] *De Mor. G.* cap. 6.

[3] The *steendysser* of Denmark, dolmens of France, and cromlechs of England.

[4] P. 416, Pl. xxviii. 4. In p. 417 he gives a list of many bronze-finds.

[5] Tacit. *Annals*, ii. 14.

[6] Cap. 42 and 6.

[7] So the Longobards may be Long-halberts, and the Franks Francisca-men.

[8] Vegetius (ii. 15) makes them use 'gladii majores quas Spathas vocant,' and Isidore (68, 6) says that the *gladii* were 'utraque parte acuti.'

and at last *wafan* (weapon) applied only to the Sword. The blade (*blat, blan*, in Mid. Germ. *valz*), with its two edges (*ecke, egge*), was often leaf-shaped, as if copied

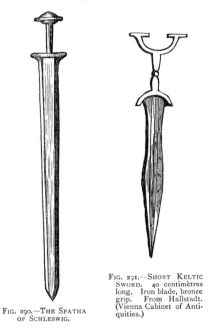

FIG. 291.—SHORT KELTIC SWORD. 40 centimètres long. Iron blade, bronze grip. From Hallstadt. (Vienna Cabinet of Antiquities.)

FIG. 290.—THE SPATHA OF SCHLESWIG.

directly from the bronze Sword. Others were smaller in the middle than at heft or point, for facility of unsheathing. The tang reached the pommel end, and the grip or hilt [1] was lined with wood (birch or beech), bone, and other material, covered with leather, fishskin, and cloth. There was no cross-bar, but the crescent extending over the shoulders, and serving to contain the rivets, was sometimes supplied with a guard-plate (*die Leiste*).[2] The weapon had a solid scabbard, often of iron, even when the blade was bronze, and was hung by riems or leathern straps to the warrior's left.

The other German blade was single-edged and curved : it was a semi-Spatha, half the size of the Spatha, and it hung to the warrior's right side. This weapon was probably the Sahs,[3] Seax, Sax, the favourite of the Saxons ; also called Breitsachs and Knief (knife), and at later times, *scramasaxus*, Scramasax.[4] A large iron knife, with a yataghan curve, it was used

---

[1] In Scandinavian, the noblest of the Germanic tongues, *hjalt* ; in O. Germ. *helza* ; Ang. S. *helt, hielt*, and in Mid. Germ. *helze, gehilze* (Jähns, p. 419).

[2] Jähns (p. 419) has three kinds of hilts. The oldest is the crescent, noticed above (fig. 293) ; it is adorned with spirals and various figures. The second, which seems to be more general in the Sahs, or short weapon, has in the place of pommel a crutch or crescent, with the horns more or less curved, and either disunited or joined by a cross-bar. Here again spirals were disposed upon the planes : we shall see them highly developed in the Scandinavian weapons of a later date. The third hilt was a kind of tang, continuing the blade, and fitted with rounded edges for making fast wood, horn, or bone : it had generally a bulge in mid-handle. The pommel proper is little developed in these Swords.

[3] 'Sahs' seems to have an alliance with the Latin 'saxum' (Jähns, p. 8, quoting Grimm). 'Hamar' (hammer) had the same meaning. From 'sax' we may probably derive the Zacco-sword of the Emperor Leo (*Chronicle*) : 'Item fratrem nostrum Ligonem cum zaccone vulneravit.' The Laws of the Visigoths mention both weapons, long and short : 'plerosque

verò scutis, spatis, scramis' (battle-axes ?) '. . . . instructos habuerit.' 'Nimith euere saxes' (take to your knife-swords), said Hengist, and the oaths 'Meiner Six !' (by my dirk), and 'Dunner-Saxen' (thunder sword) in Lower Saxony, are not forgotten.

[4] I have spoken of the Scramasax in chap. v. Demmin (p. 152) and others deduce 'scrama' (broadsword) from 'scamata,' the line traced on the ground between two Greek combatants (!). Hence, too, he would derive 'scherma' and 'escrime'—fencing. Others prefer 'scaran' (to shear), which gave rise to the German 'schere' (scissors), and our 'shears' and 'shear-steel.' The word, however, is evidently a congener of the Germ. 'schirmen,' to protect, defend. Jähns (p. 418) observes that the Sahs varied greatly in size. Some authorities make it a Mihhili Mezzir (muchel knife), a large *cultellus*. But the Frisian Asega-buch shows it to be a murderous weapon, forbidden to be worn in peace. The finds yield at times a dirk, and at times a broadsword ; such, for instance, are the Copenhagen Scramsahs, 90 centimètres long, and that of Fronstetten, which, though imperfect, weighed 4·5 lbs. The British Museum contains a fine specimen of the Scramasax with engraved Runes.

either as a dirk or a missile. Some of these throw-Swords had a hook by way of pommel for better securing the hilt. The Schwertstab (Sword-staff) or Prachtaxt is described and figured by Jähns [1] as a kind of *dolch* [2] or dagger, attached to a long hollow metal haft, like that of a Persian war-axe. It is a rare article, and its rarity leads him to believe it was symbolic of the Saxnot (Sword-god) Zio, Tui, or Tuisco. Dr. Evans [3] considers the weapon 'a kind of halberd or battle-axe;' others, a commander's staff or *bâton* of honour; but the article is too widely used to be so explained. A fine specimen of the Schwertstab with handle and blade of bronze, was found at Årup in Scania, and an analogous form is shown in a Chinese blade.

History, even written by their enemies, shows that the Ancient Germans were an eminently military and martial people. The bridal present consisted of a caparisoned horse, a shield, a spear, and a Sword. At their festivals, youths danced naked before the Sword-god, amidst drawn blades and couched spears. Their lives were spent in hunting and warfare. Despite their barbarism, a thorough topographical knowledge of their bogs and bushes, mountains and forests, enabled them to inflict more than one crushing defeat upon the civilised Romans.

The highly-developed Teutonic brain also invented a form of attack which suited them thoroughly. It was theirs, as the Phalanx, borrowed from the Egyptians, became Greek, and its legitimate outcome, the Legion, was Roman; and, subsequently, the Crescent, adopted by the Kafirs, was Moslem. 'Acies,' says Tacitus,[4] 'per cuneos componitur.' The Keil or Wedge was not unknown to the Greeks and Romans; [5] but they used it subordinately, whilst with the Germans the 'Schweinskopf,' the 'Svinfylking' of the Scandinavians, was national: they attributed its invention to Odin, the country god. The apex was composed of a single file,[6] and the numbers doubled in each line to the base; while families and tribesmen, ranged side by side, added moral cohesion to the tactical formation.[7] It lasted a thousand years; and it played a conspicuous part in the Battle of Hastings, where the Normans attacked in wedge, and finally at Swiss Sempach. During its long life it underwent sundry modifications, especially the furnishing of the flanks with skirmishers; evidently the Wedge was admirable for the general advance against line or even column; but it was equally ill-calculated for a retreat.

---

[1] P. 421. Pl. xxviii. 15.

[2] The word is the Ang. Sax. *dolc*, a wound, which thus gave a name to the weapon that wounded.

[3] *Bronze*, pp. 261-63. Figs. 329 and 330.

[4] *Germ.* 6.

[5] Jähns (p. 439) quotes Asclepiodotus (vii. 3) and Ælian (xviii. 4), who describe the *cuneus* as Scythian and Thracian, *i.e.* barbarous. Unfortunately Jähns also cites the 'Boar's head' of the Laws of Menu (Houghton's *Manava-Dharma Shastra*, vii. 187), *in the eighth century* B.C.; Menu being centuries after Tacitus. I have noticed that the disposal of

our chessmen shows the Hindú form of attack, the infantry in front, the horse and elephants (castles) on either wing, and the Rajah or Commander-in-chief in the centre and not in front.

[6] In its purest form the Standard-bearer stood alone at the apex, as Ingo in King Odo's battle at Mons Panchei (Montpensier), A.D. 892.

[7] 'Quodque præcipuum fortitudinis incitamentum est, non casus, nec fortuita conglobatio turmam aut cuneum facit, sed familiæ et propinquitates' (Tacit. *Germ.* 7).

Most writers now consider the Cimbri a Keltic people, and possibly congeners of the Cymry or Welsh. Yet in the second century B.C. we find them uniting, as Pliny tells us,[1] with the German Teutones or Teutoni (Thiudiskô, Teutsh, Deutsch). The 'Kimpers' of Italian Recoaro, the supposed descendants of the invaders who escaped the Sword of Marius (B.C. 102), undoubtedly spoke German.

Plutarch[2] describes the Cimbrian Sword as a large heavy knife-blade (μεγάλαις ἐχρῶντο καὶ βαρείαις μαχαίραις), They had also battle-axes, and sharp, bright

degans or daggers: the latter were highly prized, and their cuneiform shape caused them to be considered symbols of the deity.[3] As usual amongst barbarians, the weapons of the chiefs had terrible names, so as to strike even the hearer with fear.[4] Their defensive weapons were iron helmets, mail coats, and white glittering shields. Eccart holds that these arms and armour must have been taken from the foe : their barrows, in Holstein and elsewhere, having produced only stone-celts and spear-heads with a few copper Sword-blades, but no iron.

The Scandinavian Goths (Getæ) and Vandals were held by the ancients to have been originally one and the same people.[5] Their Bronze Age is supposed to have begun about B.C. 1000, and to have ended in Sweden at the opening of the Christian era. They used short Sword-blades, which made them, unlike the Kelts, formidable in close combat, and the Goths claimed to have introduced the spear[6] to cavalry-men. Identical weapons were used by the Lemovii of Pomerania and their kinsmen the Rugii. The latter lived on the southern shores of the Baltic about Rugenwald, and this place,

FIG. 292.—DANISH SWORD.

(Bronze ; 85 centimètres long. Copenhagen.)

one of the focuses of the Stone Age,[7] preserves, like the Isle of Rugen, the old barbaric name. The Danes mostly affected the long-handed *securis Danica (hasche Danoise)*. The Fenni (Finns) of Tacitus had neither Swords nor iron: they used only bows and stone-tipped arrows.[8] The bronze Sword from Finland 'with flanged hilt-plate and eight rivet-holes,'[9] must have found its way there.[10]

We now proceed to the Keltic population of the ' Home Islands of Great

[1] *Nat. Hist.*, iv. 14.
[2] *In Mario*, 23.
[3] In later times they were carefully cleaned for another object, to show their Runic inscriptions.
[4] Malet's *Introduction to the History of Denmark.*
[5] Pliny, iv. 14. Procop. *Bell. Vand.* i. 1.
[6] In O. Germ. Sper = hasta, lancea; Sperilîn = lanceola, sagitta ; Ang. Sax. Sper, Engl. spear ; Germ. Speer. The word seems to be a congener of Sparre, spar. Less commonly used is Spiess = hasta, cuspis ; Scand. Spjot ; O. Germ. Speoz, Spioz ; Ang. Sax. spietu ; Fr. espié, espiel, espiet, espieu ; Ital.

spiedo ; Engl. spit. It seems to ally with the Lat. spina, and the Germ. Spitze (Jähns, p. 413).

[7] The peculiar celts, chisels, spear-points, &c., extended over all the peninsula of Jutland, and as far south as Mark Brandenburg (Jähns, p. 6).

[8] Neither Cæsar nor Tacitus mentions the use of the bow amongst the ancient Gauls and Germans, although the graves yield arrow-heads of stone, bone, and iron.

[9] Dr. Evans, *Bronze*, &c., p. 299.
[10] I reserve Scandinavian weapons for Part II.

Britain,' and find there evident offshoots of the Gauls. We have no metal remains of the pre-Keltic 'aborigines' (Iberians? Basques? Finns?) except their palæoliths; and the history of our finds commences with the two distinct Keltic immigrations advocated by Professor Rhys, the Goidels (Gauls) who named Calyddon or Caledonia (*Gael doine* or *Gael dun* = forest district) and the Brythons.

The authentic annals of England, says Mr. Elton,[1] begin with the days of Alexander the Great, that is, in the fourth century B.C.; the next historical station being the invasion of the Anglo-Saxons[2] in the middle of the fifth century A.D. He does not trace any continuity of race in Kelt or Saxon with the palæolithic men of the Quaternary Age, or with the short dark-skinned neolithics who succeeded them. The two were followed by a big-boned, round-headed, fair-haired family which brought with them a knowledge of bronze and with it the Sword.

Colonel A. Lane-Fox has summarised the four principal theories[3] concerning the source of bronze in Great Britain. Dr. Evans[4] prudently finds 'a certain amount of truth embodied in each of those opinions'; but he also concludes that No. 4 must commend itself to all archæologists. I quite agree with this view, provided that the common centre be Egypt, and that Western Asia be held only a line of transit. We have full proof of the immense antiquity of bronze in the Nile region, whence the art would radiate through the world. But the almost identical proportions of the alloy (nine copper to one tin) and the persistent forms suggest that a wandering race of metal-workers, somewhat like the Gypsies of a later age, are the originators of the *Stations*, the *Fonderies*, and the *Trésors*. The first step from Egypt would be to Khita-land and Phœnicia; and these 'Englishmen of Antiquity' would carry the art far and wide. Sir J. Lubbock opines that the Phœnicians were acquainted with the mineral fields of Cornwall between B.C. 1500–1200; somewhat niggard measure, for the Bronze Age in Switzerland is dated from B.C. 3000. On the other hand, Professor Rhys absolutely denies that there are any traces of Phœnician art in England.

Dr. Evans[5] assumes the total duration of the Bronze Period in Britain at between eight and ten centuries. He would divide this sum into three several stages,[6] and

---

[1] *Origins of English History* (London: Quaritch, 1852).

[2] The Sword amongst the Anglo-Saxons and the Franks will be described at full length in Part II.

[3] These are:

No. 1. That Bronze-casting spread from a common centre by conquest or migration.

No. 2. That each region discovered the art independently, and made its own implements.

No. 3. That the art was discovered and implements were made in one spot, whence commerce disseminated them.

No. 4. That the art was diffused from a common centre, but that the implements were constructed in the countries where they were found.

[4] *Bronze*, &c., p. 475.

[5] *Bronze*, p. 473. I would notice that upon the subject of 'Celts' the learned author joins issue with the peculiar views of M. de Mortillet, before noticed. *Bronze*, &c., p. 456.

[6] The three divisions are:

No. 1. Characterised by flat or slight flanged celts and knife-daggers, found in barrows with stone implements.

No. 2. Age of heavy dagger-blades, flanged celts and tanged spear-heads, such as those from Arreton Down. In these two the Sword is unknown.

No. 3. Palstaves, socketed celts (introduced from abroad); true socketed spear-heads, Swords, and the variety of tools and weapons found in the hoards of the old bronze-founders.

to the last, which produced the bronze Sword, he assigns a minimum duration of four hundred to five hundred years. This was followed by the Early Iron Age, or later Keltic Period. The metal may have been used in southern Britain, peopled long before Cæsar's time by immigrant Belgii, not later than the fourth or fifth century B.C., the approximate date of the earliest iron Swords in Gaul.[1] Lastly, by the second or third century B.C. the exclusive use of bronze for cutting implements had practically ceased in Belgic Britain ; the Roman historians do not lead us to suppose that the weapons, even of the northern Britons, were anything but iron.

It has been suggested that the bronze Swords found in Britain were either Roman, or at all events of Roman date. The discussion began as early as 1751,[2] on the occasion of some bronze blades, a spear-head, and other objects being discovered near Gannat, in the Bourbonnais. It opened with greater vigour between the German and Scandinavian antiquaries in 1860, and the late Thomas Wright was an ardent advocate of the ' Italian view.'[3] Dr. Evans, who has carefully considered the question, concludes :[4] ' The whole weight of the argument is in favour of a pre-Roman origin for these swords in western and northern Europe.' And he notices, apparently with scant respect, the three provinces to which the bronze antiques of Europe have been assigned. These are the Mediterranean with Græco-Italic and Helveto-Gallic subdivisions ; the Danubian, including Hungary, Scandinavia, Germany, and Britain ; and the Uralian, comprising the Russian, Siberian, and Finn regions. Finally he quotes the bronze socketed sickle, the tanged razor, the two forms of Sword, the shield with numerous concentric rings, with sundry other articles specially British, to show that Britain was one of the great centres of the bronze industry.

Lead-bronze, well known in ancient Egypt, is found extensively in Ireland, where some specimens of ' Dowris metal' have as much as 9·11 parts in 99·32.[5] The Phœnicians would certainly teach the use of an article which takes a fine golden lustre. Dr. Evans[6] notes the remarkable prevalence of lead in the small (votive) socketed celts supplied by Brittany. Professor Pelligot found some of them containing 28·50 per cent. and even 32·50 per cent. of lead, with only 1·5 per cent., or a smaller proportion, of tin. In others, with a large percentage of tin there was from eight to sixteen per cent. of lead. Some of the bronze ornaments of the opening Iron Period also contain a considerable proportion of lead ; in the early Roman *As* and its parts the figures are from twenty to thirty per cent. A socketed celt from Yorkshire gives, copper 81·15, tin 12·30, and lead 2·63 per

---

And a great peculiarity in Britain is the absence of nearly all traces of the Later Bronze Period in graves and barrows.

[1] Dr. Evans, *Bronze*, &c., p. 300, quoting M. Alexandre Bertrand. For the condition of the Ancient Britons during the Bronze Period, see *ibid.* p. 487.

[2] In the Académie des Inscriptions et Belles Lettres of Paris. (Dr. Evans, *Bronze*, &c., p. 20).

[3] ' On the True Assignation of the Bronze Weapons,' *Trans. Ethn. Soc.* N. Ser. iv. p. 7).

[4] *Bronze*, &c., p. 274. See also Introductory Chapter, p. 20.

[5] See chap. v.

[6] *Bronze*, &c., p. 417.

cent. In this case, Mr. J. A. Phillips expresses an opinion that 'the lead is, no doubt, an intentional ingredient.'[1]

Apparently the Roman invaders unduly depreciated the ancient Britons. Strabo[2] declares them to be cannibals; yet he includes amongst their produce gold, silver, iron, and corn. Cæsar[3] makes them use the ring money of Egypt, but Dr. Evans[4] has proved that England had a gold coinage in the first century B.C. It is an old remark that a people can hardly be savages when they employ the *currus falcatus* or scythe war-car, the ꞩꞃꞇoꞇ cꭤꞃbꭤꝺ or 'Carbad scarrda' of the Irish, the Welsh *kerbyd*, borrowed from the Gallic Kelts.[5] Pomponius Mela also assures us that they had cavalry, besides *bigæ* and *currus*.[6] Their works in glass, ivory, and jet, and their incense cups suggest extensive intercourse, commercial and social, with the Continent. During the ninety years which separated Julius Cæsar and Claudius, the Britons had made progress in letters, and had built important towns. The amount of Latin blood introduced into England has, perhaps, been undervalued by our writers; but the discovery of Roman ruins, which rapidly proceeds and succeeds, will draw the attention of the statistician, and that 'new man, the anthropologist,' to a highly interesting subject.[7]

The bronze Swords of the ancient Britons are of two kinds: the leaf-blade and the Rapier, both well cast. The total length of the former is about two feet, the extremes being sixteen inches to thirty, and in rare cases more. The blades are uniformly rounded, but with the part next the edge slightly drawn down so as to form a shallow fluting. The breadth appears greatest at the third near the point, and this would add to the facility of unsheathing. In almost all cases they are strengthened by a rounded mid-rib more or less bold; or they show ridges, with and without beading, or parallel lines that run along the whole blade or the greater part near the edges. Some combine mid-rib and ridges. The shoulders are either

---

[1] *Bronze*, &c., p. 421. The list of analyses shows lead chiefly in the Irish finds.

[2] *Geog.* vii. 2.

[3] *Bell. Gall.* v. 12.

[4] Evans's *Coins of the Ancient Britons*. I have not yet read the work.

[5] Cæsar (iv. 33): 'Genus hoc est eis essedis pugnæ;' and he speaks again (v. 15) of *essedarii*. The scythe-car was known to Assyria, Jewry (the *Faldat* of Nahum ii. 3), and Persia, where Xenophon and Plutarch attribute to it the highest importance; even the pole ended in a lance. It became a favourite with all Keltic peoples. At Sentinum (B.C. 296) the Gauls almost defeated the Romans by suddenly throwing on a force of one thousand 'esseda currusque.' The Tectosages, when engaged with Antiochus Soter in Phrygia (B.C.), ranged in front of their attack 240 scythe-cars, some with two and others with four horses. Antiochus the Great armed his chariots not only with two scythe blades, but also with lances ten cubits long (?), laterally projecting (Livy, xxxvii. 41). The historian also notices the Arab dromedary-riders, 'archers who carried their swords four cubits (= 6 feet) long, that they might be able to reach the enemy from so great a height.' When the Gæsatæ crossed the Alps (B.C. 228) they were accompanied by a vast number of war-cars (Polybius, ii. 4, 5 says 20,000 ἁρμαμάξας καὶ συνωρίδας) which did good service at the battle of Telamon. Ossian's *Fingal* offers a long description of the war-car and its uses. Many remains of these two-wheeled vehicles have been found in Keltic Europe (Jähns, pp. 394–96).

[6] *Geog.* iii. 6.

[7] I cannot but attribute to Italian blood the high and aquiline features which distinguish the Briton from the Northern German; the latter has been intimately mixed with the Slav race, as a glance at the Berlinese suffices to show. Portraits of the Cavalier period explain my meaning. In the Hanoverian times the 'Roundhead' again came to the fore, and hence the popular 'John Bull' portrayed in the pages of Mr. *Punch*. He is a good working type, but he has not the face to command or to impose.

plain, notched, or flanged. In rare instances the outer part of the hilt is of bronze: Dr. Evans engraves [1] a specimen of this kind. The total length of the weapon is twenty-one inches, of which the globular pommel and the grip, made for a large hand, occupy five. The hilt has the appearance of being cast upon the blade: it seems to have been formed of bronze of the same character, and there are no rivets by which the two castings could be attached. The shallow crescent, whose hollow faces the mid-rib (fig. 293), is a characteristic feature, and endures for ages in the northern bronzes.

The handle of the leaf-blade usually consisted of plates of horn, bone, or wood, riveted on either side of the hilt plate. The latter differs considerably in form,

FIG. 293.— BRITISH SWORD, BRONZE. (Tower.)

and in the number and arrangement of the rivets, by which the covering material was attached. Some have as many as thirteen piercings; they seldom, however, exceed seven. The apertures are either round holes or longitudinal slots of greater or lesser extent. There is a pronounced swelling in the grip when the tang is of full length. At the end it expands, evidently for the purpose of receiving a pommel formed by the material of the hilt. This tang end is a fish-tail more or less pronounced. One illustrated by Dr. Evans [2] has two spirals attached to the base of the hilt, a rare form in England, but common in Scandinavia. Another [3] pommel-end has a distinct casting, 'and is very remarkable on account of the two curved horns extending from it, which are somewhat trumpet-mouthed, with a projecting cone in the centre of each.' This manilla-end appears to me Irish.

We have seen the rapier in Mycenæ and Etruria.[4] It reappears in northern Europe, England, and France, perfectly shaped; and, though of rare occurrence in hoards, it seems to belong to the period when socketed celts were in use. There is no difficulty in tracing the intermediate steps between the leaf-shaped dagger and the rapier. The latter measures from twenty to twenty-three and a half, and even thirty and a quarter inches, with a breadth of five-eighths inch, widening at the base to two and three-eighths to two and nine-sixteenths inches. The largest have a strong projecting mid-rib, while their weight is diminished by flutings along either side. Another form of blade is more like a bayonet, showing a section nearly square; while a third has a flat surface where the mid-rib would be, a form not yet obsolete. Few are tanged;[5] mostly we find the base or shoulders

[1] Bronze, &c., pp. 286-87. It was found in the river Cherwell and it is now in the Museum at Oxford. The first notice was in the Journ. Anthrop. Inst., vol. iii. 204.

[2] Ibid. p. 287. The author suggests that it may be foreign.

[3] Ibid. p. 288.

[4] I have already referred to the bronze dagger from Thebes, now in the British Museum, with its narrow rapier-like blade and broad flat hilt of ivory.

[5] Dr. Thurnam considered the tanged dagger more modern than that which was attached by rivets in the base of the blade, and his classification is followed by Dr. Evans, Bronze, &c., p. 222.

of the blade provided with drill-holes or with notches, to admit the nails ; and in some the wings are broadened for this purpose.[1]

During the Late Celtic Period the Britons, like the Gauls, were armed with *gladii sine mucrone*, which Tacitus[2] calls *ingentes* and *enormes*. These Spathæ must have grown out of the bronze rapier. A monument found in London and preserved at Oxford shows the blade to have been between three and four feet long.[3]

All history declares the Ancient Britons to have been of right warlike race ; and Solinus[4] relates of them a characteristic trait. 'When a woman is delivered of a male child, she places its first food upon the father's Sword, and gently puts it to the little one's mouth, praying to her country gods that its death may be, in like manner, amidst arms.'

The ancient Irish seem to have been rather savages than barbarians, amongst whom the wild non-Celts long prevailed over the Goidels or Gaels. Ptolemy calls the former *Ivernii*, and it has been lately suggested[5] that this may have been the racial name throughout the British Islands. The same savage element, which is still persistent, was noticed by Tasso, when speaking of the Hibernian crusaders :[6]

> Questi dall' alte selve irsuti manda
> La divisa del mondo ultima Irlanda.[6]

The modern Irish, who in historical falsification certainly rival, if they do not excel, the Hindús, claim for their ancestry an exalted grade of culture. They found their pretensions upon illuminated manuscripts and similar works of high art ; but it is far easier to account for these triumphs as the exceptional labours of students who wandered to the classic regions about the Mediterranean. If ancient Ireland ever was anything but savage, where, let us ask, are the ruins that show any sign of civilisation ? A people of artists does not pig in wooden shanties, surrounded by a rude vallum of earth-work.

Ireland, like modern Central Africa, would receive all her civilised weapons from her neighbours. The Picts of Scotland would transmit a knowledge of iron-working and of the Sword to the Scotti or Picts of the north-east of Hibernia.[7] This is made evident by the names of the articles. Ⳑᴧ⅃ᴼᵉᴧⱮ or cᴧⳑᴼⱮ, the Welsh *kledyv*, is simply *gladius* ; and ⱲⱮⱼᴧ is ' tuck,' or a clerk's Sword. So ⱡᴧⱮⱮ, the

---

[1] The most perfect form of the bronze rapier is found in Ireland ; of this and of the moulds I shall treat in Part II.

[2] In *Agric.* cap. 36.

[3] Montfaucon, *Suppl.* iv., p. 16 ; Smith, *s. v.* ' Gladius.'

[4] ' Pliny's Ape.'

[5] Prof. Rhys, of Oxford.

[6] ' These men from horrid woods, a hairy band,
Sends far from earth divided Irish-land.'

[7] The word ' Pict,' says Prof. Rhys, is first applied by a writer of the third century to the people beyond the Northern Wall and on the Solway. It evidently arose from their tattooing. He opines that ' Scotti ' is of Brythonic origin having the same sig_nification. This is better than the old ЅᴄⱼᴼⱮ (Scjot), the dart which named the Scythæ and the Scoti The Picts, both of Alban and Ireland, called them-selves Cruithing—' which an Irish Shanachie has rightly explained to mean a people who painted the forms (Crotha, Ir. ᴧ ᴘ ᴧ) of beasts, birds, and fishes on their faces, and not on their faces only, but on the whole of the body.' Again we find ourselves in
—' infinita, arcana Africa orrenda.'

lance head, derives from the Gaulish spear (*lanskei*) which Diodorus Siculus terms λαγκία, a congener of the Greek λόγχη and of the low Latin *lancea* or *lanscea*, meaning either spear (*hasta*) or Sword.

CONCLUSION.

WE have now assisted at the birth of the Sword in the shape of a bit of wood, charred and sharpened. We have seen its several stages of youth and growth to bone and stone, to copper and bronze, to iron and steel. When it had sufficiently developed itself Egypt gave it a name, SFET ; and this name, at least fifty centuries old, still clings to it and will cling to it. In the hands of the old Nilotes the Sword spread culture and civilisation throughout adjoining Africa and Western Asia. The Phœnicians carried it wide and side over the world then known to man. The Greeks won with it their liberty and developed with it their citizenship. Wielded by the Romans, it enthroned the Reign of Law, and laid the foundation for the Brotherhood of Mankind. Thus, though it soaked earth with the blood of her sons, the Sword has ever been true to its mission—the Progress of Society.

In Part II. we shall see the Sword attain the prime of life, when no genius, no work of art was too precious to adorn it ; and when, from a weapon of offence, it developed exceptional defensive powers. Here begins the Romance of the Sword.

INDEX.